PATRIOTISM, POLITICS, and POPULAR LIBERALISM in NINETEENTH-CENTURY MEXICO

PATRIOTISM, POLITICS, and POPULAR LIBERALISM in NINETEENTH-CENTURY MEXICO

Juan Francisco Lucas and the Puebla Sierra

Guy P. C. Thomson
with
David G. LaFrance

A Scholarly Resources Inc. Imprint
Wilmington, Delaware

Scholarly Resources Inc.
104 Greenhill Avenue
Wilmington, DE 19805-1897

Library of Congress Cataloging-in-Publication Data

Thomson, Guy P. C., 1949–
    Patriotism, politics, and popular liberalism in nineteenth-century
Mexico : Juan Francisco Lucas and the Puebla sierra / Guy P. C.
Thomson, with David G. LaFrance.
      p. cm. — (Latin American silhouettes)
    Includes bibliographical references and index.
    ISBN 0-8420-2683-5 (alk. paper)
    1. Lucas, Juan Francisco. 2. Lucas, Juan Francisco—Military
leadership. 3. Puebla (Mexico : State)—Politics and government.
4. Mexico—History—19th century. 5. Political leadership—Mexico—
Puebla (State)—History—19th century. 6. Violence—Mexico—Puebla
(State)—History—19th century. 7. Nationalism—Mexico—Puebla
(State)—History—19th century. I. LaFrance, David G. (David
Gerald), 1948– . II. Title. III. Series.
F1326.L83T5   1998
972' .48—DC21   97–37865
                                                              CIP

To the memory of my father, John Patrick Laing Thomson
(8 April 1920–22 October 1996)

Acknowledgments

I have incurred many debts of gratitude over the long period since this book's inception. Warwick University's generous study leave policy was fundamental for encouraging the time-intensive research that went into this project. Also crucial was a grant from the Economic and Social Research Council, which funded the bulk of the research. Further smaller grants from the Twenty-Seven Foundation, the British Academy, and the Warwick University Research and Teaching Innovations Fund enabled me to return on successive occasions to the Mexican archives.

I am also grateful to the staff of numerous archives and libraries: in Britain, the British Library, the Institute of Historical Research, and the University of Warwick; in Mexico, the Archivo General de la Nación, the Archivo Histórico Militar de México, the Hemeroteca Nacional, the Centro de Estudios de Historia de México (CONDUMEX), the Universidad Iberoamericana, the Biblioteca Nacional, the Biblioteca Lagragua of the Universidad Autónoma de Puebla, Puebla State's notarial archive, and the municipal archives of Tetela de Ocampo, Cuetzalan del Progreso, Zacapoaxtla, and Chignahuapan; in the United States, the University of Texas's Nettie Lee Benson Collection. The notes accompanying David LaFrance's chapter on the Revolution of 1910–1917 acknowledge his debts to an even wider range of libraries and archives. Apart from these public sources, David and I benefited from the hospitality and generosity of the Ayala and Manzano families, the granddaughters of Juan Francisco Lucas, who gave us unrestricted access to family papers and photographs in Puebla de Zaragoza.

In bringing the work to fruition, I received encouragement from Alistair Hennessy, David Brading, Josefina Vázquez, Charles Hale, Jesús Ferrer y Gamboa, Antonio Annino, Raymond Buve, Mary Kay Vaughan, Florencia Mallon, Antonio Escobar Ohmstede, Eric Van Young, Marco Antonio Velázquez, and Keith Brewster, several of whom read parts of the work. Bill Beezley was particularly important in confirming my belief in the project, as he was tireless in helping me refine the manuscript for publication. Richard Hopper at Scholarly Resources was also constant in his support, while his staff, particularly Michelle Slavin, labored patiently in overcoming an unforeseen obstacle that delayed publication by almost a year.

Research far from home requires more than just the support of archivists and librarians. In Mexico City, I appreciated the friendship and hospitality of Ricardo and Tati Yocelevsky and their circle, Luis Medina and Blanca Torres, Josefina Vázquez, Pedro and Gloria Hiriart, the Portilla-Livingstone family, and Ricardo Rendón. In Puebla, David LaFrance, Carlos Contreras, Mary Kay Vaughan, Marco and Gloria Velázquez, Marco Vivanco, Blanca Lara, Juan Carlos and Clara Grosso, and the Villa-Woodcock family all contributed to making 1984–85 an unforgettable study leave. In Tetela de Ocampo, Germán Romero and numerous other Tetelenses introduced me to the mysteries and magic of the Sierra.

Support was also abundant on the home front: from my family, from my "compadres" Anthony McFarlane, Christopher Abel, and Jenny Burns; and, above all, from Louise, whose love and patience ensured that paternal absence inflicted no visible damage on Joseph and Peter.

Guy P. C. Thomson

Contents

Introduction

This book has its origins in two incidents that occurred twenty-five years ago during doctoral research in Mexico. The first was a visit in December 1971 to Cuetzalan, a coffee town in the center of the Puebla Sierra. I was struck by the contrast between the thousands of Nahua Indians who, dressed in their brilliant white cotton *mantas*, colorfully embroidered blouses, and formidable headdresses, were converging from outlying villages upon Cuetzalan's Sunday market, and the monumental backdrop of Belle Epoque public buildings, Gothic churches, and coffee warehouses of this remote town seemingly constructed at the end of the last century. Cuetzalan del Progreso appeared to be from another world than Puebla de Zaragoza (formerly de los Angeles), the provincial capital whose history I was investigating. How, I asked, have these Nahua Cuetzaltecos succeeded in maintaining such demographic and cultural mastery of this lush swath of the Sierra Madre in the face of the modernizing influences that normally accompany the transition from subsistence agriculture to commercial coffee production?

The second incident was the Independence Day parade on 16 September 1972 in Mexico City when I beheld a company of short Indian-looking men who moved at a fast trot. The troop was armed with machetes and dressed in cotton pantaloons tied beneath the knee, brown woolen *jorongos* (ponchos), heavy-duty sandals, and enormous floppy beehive hats. The rear of the company was brought up by two small pieces of mountain artillery. I was informed by someone in the crowd that these were the Zacapoaxtlas, descendants of men who had defeated the French expeditionary force at Puebla on 5 May 1862. Why would the ancestors of mountain Nahuas fight so bravely for such an abstract entity as the Mexico of 1862, so far from their homes? And why would they continue to be honored a century later in the nation's capital?

The Nahuas of Cuetzalan del Progreso and the patriotic Zacapoaxtlas remained a mystery during twelve busy years of academic apprenticeship, until imminent sabbatical leave in 1983 obliged me to draft a hasty research project. Suitably broad and relevant to attract Social Science Research Council (SSRC) funding, "Coffee and Politics in the Puebla Sierra, 1850–1900" would permit me to explore this enigmatic region, which had preserved Nahua coffee growers and produced patriotic peasants. At this initial stage of the research, I was interested in exploring the intersection between Liberal politics and the development of coffee as a cash crop, a relationship that was evident throughout much of Central America. However, I soon found that the rise of Liberal politics preceded the onset of coffee as the central Sierra's main crop by almost forty years. Indeed, Liberal politics and the development of coffee at first proved quite incompatible. From the 1850s to the 1880s the Liberal Party in the Sierra districts of Zacapoaxtla and Tetela nurtured popular support among the peasant communities of the southern Sierra, which contributed significantly to the defeat of the Conservatives in the Three Years' War (1858–1861), to the defeat of Maximilian's empire (1864–1867), and to Porfirio Díaz's rise to national power in 1876. Liberal leaders in the Puebla Sierra sought not only to control regional and state politics but also to open up the Sierra to economic development through common land privatization, transport improvements, and the expansion of tropical commodities, particularly sugar, tobacco, and coffee.

While Liberal military leaders developed clientele in peasant communities throughout the Sierra during the 1850s and 1860s, merchants moved up from the tropical lowlands of Veracruz and down from the cold district capitals of the highlands to plant coffee as well as to expand sugar, aguardiente, and cattle production. In Cuetzalan, Liberal politics and economics collided. Behind Francisco Agustín Dieguillo (Palagustín), a Nahua National Guard captain who had fought the French at the battle of 5 May 1862, Cuetzaltecos violently resisted, on repeated occasions between 1868 and 1894, the encroachment of white coffee planters on the town's commons. The municipality's transition to commercial coffee production was postponed for thirty years. When it finally went ahead, Nahua farmers grew the coffee on land secured through the *desamortización* (privatization of village commons decreed in 1856), and most non-Indians were confined to processing and marketing.[1] Cuetzalan's unusual cultural landscape was a consequence of this hard-won compromise.

The postponement of the coffee revolution in Cuetzalan left me with the option either of moving into the twentieth century to study Cuetzalan's golden age, or of choosing a new research project. A study of the rise of the Liberal Party in the Sierra during the third quarter of the nineteenth century would shift away from a sociocultural and economic focus to a more political and biographical approach. After reading Lawrence Stone's "Revival of the Narrative" and Jesús Ferrer Gamboa's *Los tres Juanes de la Sierra de Puebla*, and sensing the vitality of a local oral tradition relating to the Puebla Sierra's Liberal patriotic past, I was convinced to take the leap.[2]

The lives of the *tres Juanes*—Juan Crisóstomo Bonilla, Juan Nepomuceno Méndez, and Juan Francisco Lucas, the leaders of the Sierra's Liberal Party, so tantalizingly broached by Ferrer Gamboa—begged closer scrutiny. In the career of Palagustín, leader of Cuetzalan's Nahuats, there seemed to be a link between the less acculturated Indian communities of the interior and north of the Sierra and the martial peasant patriots of the baili-wick of the *tres Juanes* in the south of the Sierra adjoining the altiplano.[3] Throughout his thirty-year campaign, Palagustín could count on logistical support from Xochiapulco, a military colony on the southern edge of the Sierra, established on confiscated haciendas by the leaders of Puebla's Liberal Party. Guiding Xochiapulco throughout this period was Juan Francisco Lucas, a Nahua who had fought alongside Palagustín at the battle of 5 May 1862.[4] Their friendship, which was consummated when the Cuetzalteco leader pro-vided sanctuary for Lucas during the early part of the French Intervention, en-dured for over thirty years. This pact between two Nahua leaders, and the command over men and supplies that it ensured along a strategic axis running down the middle of the Puebla Sierra, provided regional leaders, such as Juan N. Méndez and Juan Crisóstomo Bonilla, with the key for controlling the wider politics of the Puebla Sierra. In turn, the *cacicazgo* of the *tres Juanes* attracted the attention of national leaders of all political complexions, alert to the strategic importance of the Puebla Sierra from the revolution of Ayutla in 1854 until long after Porfirio Díaz's victory in 1876. Here, then, was an op-portunity to explore the roots of midnineteenth-century Mexican liberalism through an examination of its key local actors.

Nineteenth-Century Mexican Liberalism

In the summer of 1867 the Liberal Party, led by Benito Juárez, won a dou-ble victory. The defeat of Napoleon III's Hapsburg puppet, Maximilian, also condemned the Conservative Party, deeply implicated in this ill-fated European imperial adventure, to political extinction. The result of this tri-umphal "Second War of Independence" was a fusion of a radical, secializ-ing constitutional Liberalism with a heroic, martial patriotism, bound together through the annual celebration of patriotic birthdays (such as the battle of 5 May 1862) and explained to citizens through patriotic school texts. Constitutional Liberalism and martial patriotism now became the twin foundations of the Mexican nation-state and its most visible political consensus. The triumph of patriotic Liberalism also marked the arrival of a new generation of leaders, recruited as often from the provinces as from the capital, of whom several of the most prominent—Benito Juárez, Porfirio Díaz, Ignacio Altamirano, Ignacio Ramírez, Juan N. Méndez—were mesti-zos and Indians who entered a political club previously monopolized by Creoles. Popular patriotic heroes, radical secularizing ideas, and a leader-ship of plebeian origin all set apart Mexico's Reform from its Latin American counterparts in the thoroughness of the break with the ancien régime, with the exception perhaps of the Colombia of the radical constitu-tion of Rio Negro between 1861 and 1886.[5]

Inspired by the French Revolution, the Mexican Reform nevertheless fell short of its Jacobin mentor in the degree to which the ideals of political liberty and equality before the law were embraced and implemented within the country at large. For D. A. Brading, the Reform, because of its failure to accommodate or supplant the centrality of Catholicism in the lives of most Mexicans, is "best viewed not as an essay in 'nation-building,' but rather as an exercise in 'state-building.'"[6] This view is shared by Richard Sinkin, who concluded that the Reform achieved only the first stage of nation-building by concentrating power around a strong secular state. The realization of the egalitarian and democratic ideals of the constitution of 1857 had to await the aftermath of the revolution for even partial fulfillment.[7] François-Xavier Guerra, applying a broader modernization model that embraced social and cultural as well as political life, reaches similar conclusions. In spite of a modern ideology, a democratic political language ("Ciudadano" replacing "Don" or "Excelencia" even when addressing the president), and plebeian leaders in office, nineteenth-century Liberalism and Liberal elites were remote from the mass of Mexicans. The exercise of political power continued to rest upon patrimonial and paternalistic relations among people locked within "traditional collectivities," that is, haciendas and Indian communities. "Modern sociabilities" and Liberal-republican forms of association were confined to isolated, disenfranchised pockets, disconnected from the regional and national structures of power. Guerra agreed with contemporary Mexican critics, such as Justo Sierra and Emilio Rabasa, that Mexican politics after 1857 inhabited a "constitutional fiction." The bluff was eventually called by the victorious democratic movement led by Francisco Madero in 1910.[8]

The gulf between the democratic ideals of the 1857 constitution and day-to-day undemocratic electoral practices was demonstrated in great empirical depth by Laurens Ballard Perry and Daniel Cosío Villegas, although Cosío Villegas qualified the view of the Restored Republic and the early Porfiriato as unrelenting executive dictatorships by acknowledging the period as a golden age of press freedom.[9] Brian Hamnett's recent study of Juárez further confirms this early hardening of democratic arteries. Initially in the radical camp, Juárez, after 1864, increasingly used emergency powers (constitutionally unchecked centralized executive power) to discipline the states and ensure congressional majorities.[10] By Díaz's accession to power in 1877, so effective was the central command over the electoral system through state governors and jefes políticos that emergency powers and armed federal interventions in state politics were no longer necessary for achieving stability. Charles Hale charts how swiftly a younger generation of "conservative liberal" intellectuals, who appealed to the positivist maxim of "Order and Progress," displaced the Jacobin ideologues who had helped Díaz to power.[11]

The creeping executive centralism of Reform Liberals once in power, from the hapless Comonfort through Juárez and Lerdo to Díaz, was not, of course, the only story. Nineteenth-century Mexican Liberalism sprang from many sources and followed several channels. Two broad and competing strands of Liberalism—moderate and radical ("puro")—stand out. Both forms came together at times between 1854 and 1867 but continued to divide the Liberal Party long after the defeat of the European Intervention. Moderate Liberalism, associated with the provincial elites who created the First Federal Republic in 1824, was a continuation of eighteenth-century Bourbon administrative rationalization, secularization, and state developmentalism combined with economic liberalization. For moderates, Liberal reforms were designed to subject the Church to the state (though not necessarily to separate the two), curtail corporate privileges and special legal jurisdictions, and remove administrative barriers to economic activity.[12] Although this reform mission presumed a degree of centralization of power over the entire territory, the moderates opted for a federal system of sovereign states that would guarantee political control by propertied creole elites and ensure greater provincial autonomy from the former viceregal capital.[13]

Radical Liberalism derived from the receptiveness of a small but influential number of intellectuals, and of villages and municipalities, to the ideas of individual liberty, social contract, popular sovereignty, and municipal autonomy following the collapse of the Spanish monarchy in 1808.[14] The constitution of Cádiz was vague about provincial, especially American, representation but specific about the rights of municipalities (defined as any settlement numbering over five hundred souls) to be represented by elected councils that would exercise political and judicial authority over the municipal territory. Well before Independence in 1821, in spite of the suspension of the Cádiz constitution between 1814 and 1820, a spontaneous process of municipal foundation was well under way, especially in the Indian districts of the Mexican southeast, where communal assertiveness had long been evident. From the 1820s, village elders of Indian communities in the southern part of the immense state of Mexico (now Guerrero) asserted the right to appoint their own justices of the peace and establish new autonomous municipalities independent of mestizo-controlled headtowns. These villages provided critical support to regional caciques, such as Juan Alvarez and Gordiano Guzmán, who spearheaded the revival of federalism from the late 1830s that culminated in the Liberal triumph in the revolution of Ayutla in 1854. Similar receptivity to federalist overtures could be found in southern Michoacán throughout the peripheries of Jalisco and in the Puebla Sierra.[15]

Once the ancien régime had been officially laid to rest with the promulgation of the 1857 constitution, Liberal divisions reappeared over the form of the new secular state. Moderates, and even some radicals, favored a more centralized and presidentialist system. Most provincial radicals, however, preferred strong legislative checks upon the federal executive power. The radicals won most of the constitutional debates, leaving their imprint

upon America's most progressive constitution. However, moderates succeeded in holding onto the presidency throughout the next two decades.
Hence, the Liberal-Conservative struggle in the Three Years' War and the
patriotic fight against the French Intervention disguised a continuing battle
between moderates and radicals.[16]

Although the relationships between the executive and the legislature
and between the states and the federation remained a volatile issue, with
the triumph of Liberalism in 1867, a less audible but no less explosive tension involved municipal sovereignty and local-level political representation.[17] During the Restored Republic the idea of the "free municipality,"
although enshrined in state and federal constitutions, was buried in practice. The consequence of this official neglect was that Porfirio Díaz drew
support from confederations of municipalities, embodied in local National
Guard battalions, during the revolts of La Noria and Tuxtepec, a constituency that he subsequently ignored.[18]

The military triumph of the Liberals against the Conservatives in 1861
and the Europeans in 1867 was only a qualified success when it came to
the realization of the democratic ideals of the constitution of 1857. Yet,
after the restoration of the republic in 1867, no government, least of all that
of the patriotic hero Porfirio Díaz, was prepared to reform the "democratic
fiction" to bring it more in line with the authoritarian, day-to-day reality of
Mexican politics due to the symbolic status of this document. The constitution and the secular pantheon of patriotic heroes—most prominently Benito
Juárez—that encircled it were paraded as symbols of legitimacy by successive regimes, even by erstwhile enemies.[19] But equally, this tantalizing
menu of constitutional rights served as an inspiration and justification for
opponents to governments perceived as unlawful.

Notable additions have been made to our understanding of the practice
of constitutional Liberalism, in particular the question of popular participation. Alicia Hernández has described the Liberal and democratic movement
of 1845–1880 as "a period of expanding citizenship when political representation achieved its strongest popular content. . . . The strength of the Liberal
revolution was sustained by this new spirit of collaboration between the people and the elite."[20] Like Daniel Cosío Villegas, Hernández favors a consensus view of the Liberal family throughout the Reform, the Restored
Republic, and the early Porfiriato. This pact of coexistence between political
elites and pueblos broke down during the Porfiriato as former revolutionaries
manipulated the electoral system to ensure their continuity in power. This
study of the rise and fall of a provincial Liberal Party, the Montaña of the
Puebla Sierra, demonstrates that this coexistence was real, but that it was a
much more conflictual process than Hernández maintains. However, her approach is refreshing because it presents the Reform as a much more inclusive
process in which political leaders were obliged to take account of the struggle by citizens, individually and collectively, to assert their rights. By treating

the electoral process as more than simply a rubber stamp wielded by those already in power, exploring how villages made use of new Liberal institutions such as the National Guard, and observing the extent of popular mobilization behind provincial rebellions, Hernández moves beyond simple models of clientelism and caciquismo to explain why people chose to rebel or to obey.[21]

Where Hernández sees a single, albeit quarrelsome, Liberal family starting to knit together a young nation by sharing a new democratic vocabulary and participating in democratic institutions, Florencia Mallon, in her path-breaking book, observes a fragmented polity containing a multiplicity of competing and mutually irreconcilable liberalisms and nationalisms.[22] Her principal subjects are not the national or regional leaders, or even the local caciques, but the communities themselves. By applying detailed ethnographic knowledge, derived from recent anthropological studies, to the politics of the Puebla Sierra between 1854 and 1876, Mallon discerns patterns in the response of peasant communities to great regional, national, and even international events. Her basic premise is that through a process of negotiation, confrontation, and conditional cooperation with regional and national leaders, peasant communities in the central and southern Puebla Sierra, with the help of local intellectuals (often bilingual schoolteachers), succeeded in gaining concessions from the Liberal state and in modifying the application of the Liberal reform program to accord with local needs.

This grass-roots movement was seen most clearly in the democratically controlled village companies of the National Guard and in local communal control of the process of land privatization. By analyzing the discourse of correspondence between villages and higher authorities, Mallon demonstrates how communities incorporated modern Liberal republican ideas into an older language that invoked immemorial communal rights and the paternal responsibility of higher authorities to protect obedient and patriotic subjects. This democratic and locally contrived "communitarian liberalism" was sometimes effective at pressing claims of entitlement to land, tax exemptions, pensions, or freedom from military service.[23]

Mallon draws upon many of the primary and secondary sources used in the research for this book. While we often reach similar conclusions, our perspectives and methodologies are different. Mallon zooms in on the communal assemblies of nineteenth-century Sierra villages from a world system and comparative perspective. This work will travel out from the biography of a single Sierra Nahua leader, Juan Francisco Lucas, who is central to both studies, to chart his relationship with the villages and higher authorities. While this study will construct the politics of the region by mapping the personal ties and communications between leaders, Mallon fathoms the internal political dynamics of communities in order to make sense of their external relations. Mallon is more concerned with deciphering and analyzing the content of the communications than with the particular identity of the messengers and interlocutors. Perhaps the greatest difference lies in the structure of the two books. This work is a chronologically arranged political narrative that emphasizes the importance of contingency in determining political allegiances. Mallon selects three exemplary periods of conflict within Liberalism for detailed narrative analysis and intersperses them with thematic sections dealing with communal politics, peasant nationalism, and local history. Readers will be able to continue stories started by Mallon in this narrative. While these two studies complement each other, at times there are notable differences of interpretation that will be pointed to throughout this book.

The historian of nineteenth-century Puebla is obliged to look to local archives, in the absence of an archive of the state executive (sold during the 1930s to a paper factory for pulp).[24] Zacapoaxtla and Tetela possess excellent municipal archives that contain the records of the former political districts that once extended over much of the central and southern Sierra. The local perspective is tempered by the abundance of material on this war-torn region in national archives and contemporary memoirs and chronicles. The descendants of Juan Francisco Lucas in Puebla have retained much of his official and private correspondence, to which the authors were generously allowed unrestricted access. There was less success in the search for the papers of other prominent Liberal leaders, such as Juan Crisóstomo Bonilla, Juan Nepomuceno Méndez, and Ramón Márquez Galindo. However, it soon became clear that Lucas was the key to the success of Puebla's Liberal Party due to his unique capacity for harnessing the region's military potential and for responding to the needs of the Indian communities of the Puebla Sierra.

Juan Francisco Lucas was a Nahua soldier from Comaltepec (Zacapoaxtla) who entered the Liberal army during the revolution of Tuxtepec in 1854 and remained in command of the Brigada Serrana until his death in 1917.[25] This volume takes the form of a narrative that explores the interaction of the political and military careers of Lucas and the regional and local leaders closest to him. Lucas led an eventful and colorful life, spanning both Liberal revolutions, encompassing the Indian and non-Indian worlds, and linking Mexico's villages with the district, state, and national capitals.

1

Regional Leader

"When I became the first president of the village (in the year 1936) I went to meet General Francisco Lucas. . . . We had no secretary then and, at times, not even a schoolmaster. We needed funds to buy paper, ink, and pencils, but all the money was sent to Tzicuilan. Because of this we thought it best to become independent."[1] Twenty years after his death, the authority of General Juan Francisco Lucas was still invoked by Don Gabriel Taytzin, a Nahua village official intent upon establishing the autonomy of the barrio of Zacatipan from Tzicuilan (Cuetzalan), its headtown. The memory of Lucas is still present throughout much of the Puebla Sierra: eighty or so inhabitants of Xochiapulco (the town he founded) claim direct descent from him; the mestizo peasants of the barrios around Tetela de Ocampo horde anecdotes about the man's bravery and cunning; Anacleto Juárez of Tlaxpanaloya (sixty miles to the north of Tetela), and many others, are convinced that Lucas was capable of converting himself at will into a jaguar, a parrot, or any other creature; and most Poblanos learn of Lucas from oral accounts or patriotic school texts, viewing him as a benign, bearded *tata*.[2]

Although Lucas is highly esteemed among the people of the Puebla Sierra, historians have tended to lump such local and regional leaders under generic headings such as "caudillos," "caciques," "*serranos*," or "*hombres líquidos*." Alan Knight placed Lucas squarely among his "*serrano*" category of popular leader: "*serrano* protest was remote and inarticulate . . . (and) captained by traditional caciques of conservative mien."[3] While this term accounts for Lucas's preference for maintaining a distance from powers at the state and national levels, it overlooks his modernity and the consistency of his Liberal convictions. The term "*hombre líquido*" that Enrique Márquez uses to describe the rise of Gonzalo N. Santos, cacique of the Huasteca Potosina, suggests a relationship between Lucas and external powers that is too comfortable and opportunistic.[4] The title "Patriarch of the Sierra" that Lucas had earned by the 1880s, his habitual use of Nahuatl, and his preference for simple cotton drill and sandals imply that he embodied principally traditional and indigenous cultural elements. Yet he was also very much a man of his times: a Liberal and free thinker, an anti-Catholic

friend of the Methodist Church, a believer in progress, a patriot, a beneficiary of the *desamortización*, and a free-booting entrepreneur. Lucas can
only really satisfactorily be understood by breaking up his seventy-year
career into manageable chronological segments, portraying him against the
contemporary political landscape. Consistent patterns can then be discerned and changes detected.

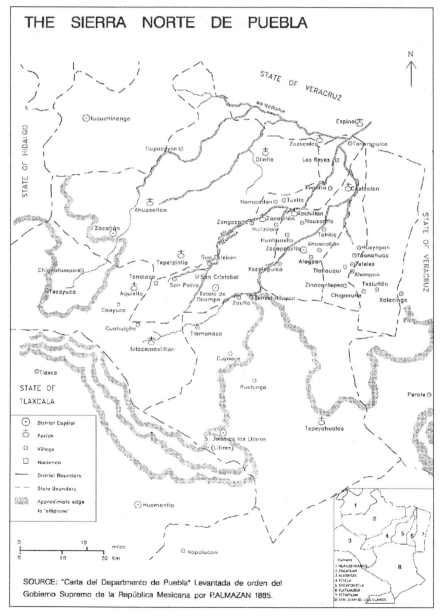

THE SIERRA NORTE DE PUEBLA

SOURCE: "Carta del Departmento de Puebla" Levantada de orden del
Gobierno Supremo de la República Mexicana por P.ALMAZAN 1885.

Record of Service[5]

Lucas formed part of a generation of regional National Guard commanders who achieved prominence during the protracted period of civil and foreign conflicts between the American War and the revolution of Tuxtepec.[6] Commanding informal militia of Nahua peasants recruited from the Cuatecomaco ridge to the southwest of Zacapoaxtla, Lucas first went into battle in support of the Liberal revolution of Ayutla in 1854–55. These irregular troops then helped secure the state of Puebla for the Liberals during the Three Years' War (1858–1861). Two years later, now regularized into companies of National Guard, Lucas's forces successfully resisted French and Austrian attempts to pacify the Sierra and went on to participate in the Austrian defeat at Puebla in April 1867. During the Restored Republic (1867–1876), Lucas was the principal organizing hand behind two major regional rebellions against the state and federal governments. He then organized forces in the Puebla Sierra in support of Díaz's abortive revolt of La Noria in 1871–72 and his successful revolution of Tuxtepec in 1876–77.

Once his *patrón* achieved national power, Lucas provided critical support to the gubernatorial ambitions of his fellow Tetelense Liberal leaders Juan Crisóstomo Bonilla (Puebla state governor, 1877–1880) and Juan Nepomuceno Méndez (Puebla state governor, 1880–1885). Surviving the eclipse of his *serrano* patrons after 1885, Lucas maintained an intense correspondence with Díaz throughout his thirty-year presidency and lent qualified support to Governors Rosendo Márquez (1885–1892) and Mucío Martínez (1892–1911) while ensuring that his influence continued to be felt in the Sierra. He was one of the last regional caciques to abandon Díaz in the face of the rebellion led by Francisco Madero in the winter of 1910–11. During the armed phase of the revolution, Lucas, as commander in chief of the Brigada Serrana, retained his hold over the Puebla Sierra and established close relations with such national leaders as Madero, Victoriano Huerta, and Venustiano Carranza while flirting with leaders from other parties such as Emiliano Zapata of Morelos and Domingo Arenas of Tlaxcala.

Perceptions of Lucas

Lucas's endurance as a regional leader derived from his ability to appeal to three main constituencies: the Indian communities of the Puebla Sierra, the region's expanding mestizo population, and various state and national level leaders. The history and storytelling traditions of the Sierra's Indian population have attracted the attention of anthropologists and ethno-historians over the past two decades. Lucas has been portrayed as a "man-god": a natural leader who succeeded in preserving the continuity of the "systems of politico-religious leadership" that have served as forces of ethnic cohesion and resistance in the Nahua and Totonac communitites of the Sierra since the Conquest.[7] Florencia Mallon depicts Lucas as a local Liberal intellectual who, by attempting to ensure that the rights and obligations of the Liberal state were introduced in accord with established norms of justice, succeeded in appealing to Indian villagers' expectations of the "good father," which earned him the title of "Patriarch of the Sierra" in his later life.[8] Antonio Rimada Oviedo and Carlos Bravo Marentes recorded oral accounts about Lucas principally from the mestizo communities of southern Tetela (but some from Totonac communities as far as Huauchinango in the northern Sierra). Both anthropologists favor magic, especially *tonalismo* (belief in kindred animal spirits) and *nagualismo* (witchcraft), as the key to understanding Lucas's appeal. Evidence for Lucas's supernatural powers is found in tales of his ability to be in two places at once, his love for cats (he was reputed to travel between his home in Tetela and ranch at Taxcantla accompanied by at least eight of them), his reputation for sudden disappearances from the battlefield and reemergence on another front, and his mastery of disguise (scrutinizing enemy lines dressed as a full-skirted woman and taking refuge from the enemy by hiding in the carcass of a dead mule).[9]

These interpretations are persuasive but hard to document from contemporary written records, which are the basis for this study. Explicit references to the moral obligations of the "good father" suffuse much of the correspondence between villages and district authorities. But no evidence was found of Lucas posing as a religious leader or of being seen as endowed with supernatural powers. Rather, abundant rational reasons for his influence emerge from the documentation, such as his ability to enforce constitutional guarantees, to protect and enhance village autonomy, to mediate in disputes between villages, and to represent communities to higher authorities. However, this is not to deny that many contemporaries would have ascribed supernatural powers to such a leader.

If Lucas had merely confined his appeal to an exclusively Indian constituency, he would not have risen much higher than village politics. The key to his political ascent and longevity lay in his appeal to the expanding and restless non-Indian population, which was intent upon increasing its presence in, and control over, Indian communities. In his research on Tetela de Ocampo, Rimada Oviedo found that stories of Lucas's daring and mysterious exploits help to resolve Tetela mestizos' cultural ambivalence, by creating a common body of myths relating to a "good" and heroic Indian. By extolling Lucas's achievements and his contribution to national Liberal and patriotic struggles, Tetela's mestizos are able to demonstrate their egalitarianism and cultural inclusiveness, in contrast to the elitism, racism, and conservatism that they attribute to their neighbors in Zacapoaxtla (Tetela's great rival for the mantle of *serrano* patriotic-Liberalism). In Tetela and Zacapoaxtla, the pride of mestizos in the region's Indian heritage is manifested in regional literature, local histories, festivals, and ceremonials.[10]

Lucas is central to this pan-ethnic and *indigenista* regional identity that first was expressed by Liberal military commanders such as Méndez during the patriotic resistance to the Empire.

Lucas mythology is also used in local territorial rivalries. Towns assert their historic and Liberal patriotic credentials and accuse their neighbors of treachery and betrayal. The most vitriolic of these rivalries exists between Zacapoaxtla and Tetela. Both towns argue over who provided the National Guard battalion that contributed so heroically to the defeat of the French expeditionary force at Puebla on 5 May 1862. Lucas was born near Zacapoaxtla, lived much of his life in Tetela, and died on his farm half way between the two. The soldiers he recruited to defend Puebla in 1862 came from both towns and from a constellation of villages running along the southern boundaries of both districts. The matter is further complicated by numerous changes to the municipal and district boundaries made between 1854 and the 1880s. The recent publication of the Intervention memoirs of Lauro Luna (a Tetelense) will add tinder to this debate. Luna claims that in April 1862, General Méndez doubted the loyalty of Tetela companies and resolved not to lead them to Puebla in May. Indeed, Méndez trusted more in Lucas's forces from Xochiapulco than in his own troops from Tetela.[11]

Very soon after his recruitment into the Liberal army, Lucas's reputation as an effective commander, recruiter of men, organizer of supplies, and skillful mediator spread far beyond the Puebla Sierra. Liberal generals such as Ignacio Alatorre and Porfirio Díaz saw Lucas and his Tetelense mestizo mentors, Méndez and Bonilla, as exemplars of republican virtue and democratic values, seen in their concern for the plight of the Indian, their enthusiasm for spreading literacy and education, and their eagerness to take up the sword whenever the Republic or the constitution was threatened.[12] In purely military terms, Lucas's contribution to Díaz's rise to power and to the consolidation of his regime was vital, at times even critical. Lucas's *cacicazgo* represented to Díaz the ideal compromise between the emphasis of the constitution of 1857 upon individual rights and guarantees, the Liberal commitment to economic growth and progress, and respect for the customs and sensibilities of the Indian population (from among whom Díaz himself had emerged).[13]

Puebla's state government possessed a less ideological and more pragmatic evaluation of Lucas. While Lucas repeatedly proved his worth by curbing and channeling Indian rebelliousness into Liberal patriotic and insurrectionary struggles (even if on occasion these were directed at the state government), he also provided a bridge into potentially autonomous *cacicazgos* of the Sierra. In addition, Lucas's well-disciplined soldiers, particularly those of Xochiapulco, provided successive state governments after 1876 with a palace guard that they could rely upon for maintaining order, not only in the Sierra but also in the capital and elsewhere in the state.

Caciquismo in the Puebla Sierra

The simplest definition of Lucas is that he was a cacique.[14] The Puebla Sierra, much like highland Chiapas, has been renowned in the twentieth century for its caciquismo (political dominance exercised by a hierarchy of local strongmen who controlled access to public appointments and elected positions). In both regions, caciquismo derived from the ability of local leaders to exploit the cultural and institutional gulf between villages still governed internally along colonial precepts—with supreme authority exercised by a council of elders (*pasados*), a civil-religious administrative hierarchy, and a cult of ethnic distinctiveness—and the wider constitutional system and mestizo national culture. The means that caciques have used for controlling villages range from traditional forms of patronage, such as co-parenthood and the sponsorship of community festivals, to appointments to the posts of village secretary and schoolteacher, the manipulation of federal and state agencies and finances, the oversight of trade and transport and the monopolization of aguardiente distribution, and violence and intimidation.[15]

Although the roots to caciquismo in the Puebla Sierra have been detected in colonial and even pre-Conquest times, the phenomenon developed more during the later nineteenth century as a consequence of two overlapping revolutions.[16] The first was a commercial revolution in the *tierra caliente* of the Sierra, with the development of sugar, aguardiente, coffee, and cattle production for the highland market, which was hastened by the sale of common lands. The second was the Liberal revolution, to which mestizos in the Sierra enthusiastically adhered in order to consolidate their hold over the local and district administration. Both the boom in demand for tropical commodities and the revolution in government invited a proliferation of political intermediaries.

Three tiers of caciquismo can be observed in the Puebla Sierra during the later nineteenth century: the village (barrio), the municipality, and the district. At the base of the pyramid was the barrio cacique, often the village secretary who doubled as a schoolmaster and store operator and offered credit and aguardiente on the side. Generally outsiders appointed to villages through the jefe político's patronage, these men wheedled their way into villagers' favor by becoming self-appointed legal advisers, who claimed to represent the indigenous village council to the higher authorities on such matters as the validation of land titles, the modification of tax contributions, the quest for permits to hold constitutionally proscribed religious festivals, and even to achieve political secession for a barrio from an oppressive municipal cabecera.[17]

Until the mid-nineteenth century, these village shysters faced little competition and went undisturbed in their control of a village's external relations. After the revolution of Ayutla, with widening Liberal-Conservative ideological polarization and intensified warfare, competition for these offices grew. Indian communities also began to break with the custom of leaving external relations to appointed *gente de razón* by putting forward their own leaders. The proliferation of elected civil and military posts that accompanied the Liberal reform—mayors of the new *juntas municipales*, local justices of the peace, National Guard captains—combined with rapidly increasing literacy to provide opportunities for career mobility for Indians beyond the civil-religious hierarchy of their communities. A new brand of cacique emerged: leaders who were elected (rather than appointed from above) and expected to represent the community in the face of the multiplying demands of the Liberal state.

Lucas began his political career as a barrio cacique, inheriting his father's following of *indios cuatecomacos* after José Manuel's assassination in 1858. Since many barrio caciques (Lucas included) were captains of the National Guard, it would appear that the Mexican system resembled its Brazilian equivalent of *coronelismo*. While there are similarities, the Mexican system was microcosmic and socially and politically more fluid than in Brazil, where a single *coronel* might exercise absolute control over his estate often extending to hundreds of square miles. Caciquismo in the Puebla Sierra had little to do with land ownership, the basis of *coronelismo*. Rather, it was based either upon literacy and bilingualism, commerce, or, during the wars, upon military command.[18] This network of village strongmen provided the sinews of Lucas's *cacicazgo* from the 1860s until the demobilization of the National Guard during the late 1880s.[19]

A second tier of caciquismo operated within the often extensive territory of the municipality. The key to political power here was the president of the council, who aspired to control all political life under his jurisdiction including: the drafting of censuses and electoral registers; the organization of municipal, state, and federal elections; the control of the municipal board of school inspection; the organization of the National Guard; and the nomination of military commanders, mayors, justices of the peace, and secretaries for the various barrios. In areas of the Sierra with a significant non-Indian population, the presidency and most posts within the municipal cabecera would have been held by *gente de razón*, while outlying, more indigenous barrios would have had Indian alcaldes but usually mestizo secretaries. In the more indigenous parts of the Sierra, such as the predominantly Totonac *tierra caliente* of Tetela, municipal cabeceras such as Tuzamapa or Jonotla possessed double administrations, with Indians occupying the post of *gobernador* (a colonial vestige) and even sometimes the municipal presidency. However, a degree of external control from the district capital was ensured through the appointment of non-Indian secretaries. The route to power at the municipal level was through the control of the commercialization of tropical commodities, particularly sugar loaf, aguardiente, and, increasingly from the 1850s, coffee.[20]

The control of commerce, credit, and taxation contributed far more to sustaining these municipal caciques in the interior of the Sierra than the ownership of land. However, along the southern edge of the Sierra, where land ownership was more concentrated, a more familiar pattern of landed wealth translating directly into political power was evident. The following landowning families were associated with the political control of municipalities: Bonilla-Castilla of Aquixtla, owners of the hacienda of Coayuca; Domínguez and Márquez, landowners of Chignahuapan; Molina-Alcántara of Zacapoaxtla, owners of the haciendas of Mazapa and El Molino; Bernal of Zautla, owners of the hacienda of Almajac; and Antonio Rodríguez Bocardo, great landowner of Cuyoaco.

The different tiers of caciquismo were closely integrated, offering opportunities for promotion to higher levels. With the intensification of warfare in the Sierra from the 1850s, such opportunities multiplied, especially for successful National Guard commanders. After the revolution of Tuxtepec, Nahua captains from outlying barrios were elected to the presidencies of Zautla and Cuetzalan in a spectacular reversal of the established ethnic hierarchy in these two municipalities. Apart the prospect of career mobility, the administrative hierarchy itself was never rigid. Since time immemorial, a village unhappy with its lot would attempt political secession to join another less oppressive municipality, or even to become independent as a separate municipality. A discontented municipality might also seek annexation to a more benign district, as Xochiapulco did in June 1870. Secessions contributed to a cacique's prestige, and Lucas was a master of this art of administrative gerrymandering.

A third tier of caciquismo occupied roughly the same political sphere as the jefe político, the agent of the state executive on the district level.[21] These district caciques graduated from the control of a particular municipality, extending their regional control through the district organization of the National Guard. They were nearly always *gente de razón* who derived a livelihood from commerce, aguardiente distilling, and cattle dealing, with commercial interests and properties spanning extensive swaths of highland and lowland. Lucas was exceptional in this sense. His election to the leadership of Tetela in 1879 caused a storm of controversy in a town accustomed to centuries of creole political supremacy.[22] An inquiry into an attempt on his life later in the year revealed a widespread conspiracy among Tetela's *gente decente*.[23]

By the end of the French Intervention, Lucas was securely established as the most powerful leader in the southern and central Sierra. He was distinguished from other regional leaders by his consistently maintained Nahua identity and by his refusal of any higher political office that might have involved his leaving the Sierra for prolonged periods. Lucas knew that the key to his influence was his intimate knowledge of the Sierra, his accessability, and his ability to act quickly and directly in local disputes. Promotion to any higher office in Puebla or Mexico City would have immediately neutralized these advantages.[24]

Lucas and Liberalism

As a Liberal cacique of a predominantly Indian area, who presented himself as the protector of the Indian population, Lucas stands rather on his own in central Mexico during the later nineteenth century. Liberalism and Indian communities are not supposed to be comfortable bedfellows, and it is often claimed that peasant communities are by nature conservative and averse to major administrative and institutional changes.[25] Liberal leaders such as Benito Juárez and Ignacio Altamirano, both of Indian descent, were intolerant of the hermeticism of Indian communities.[26] Conservatives have been seen as the more natural patrons of Indian communities restructured during the colonial period under clerical supervision.[27] Indeed, the Liberal blueprint for a strong secular state and a regime of individual private property posed a direct threat to four central elements of Indian community life: patriarchal government by elders, the system of compulsory offices and community services, the exuberant external celebration of the cult under the patronage of the clergy and confraternities, and communal control of land.[28] How did Lucas reconcile his Liberal convictions with the claim to be the protector of the Indian communities of the Puebla Sierra?

The Reform coincided with (or provoked, Conservatives argued) a period of great political instability and almost continual warfare, experienced with particular intensity in the mountainous regions of southeastern Mexico, where Liberal leaders took refuge throughout the Three Years' War and the French Intervention. For their part, the Conservatives, backed after 1862 by the French and Austrians, ineffectually strove to reassert control over the sierras from the state capitals. Hence, it was the remoter, more autonomous Indian communities in the sierras, rather than the more acculturated towns and villages of the altiplano, which first received direct exposure to the Reform program. These communities also experienced the increased military and fiscal demands accompanying civil and patriotic warfare. On this seemingly unpromising terrain, Liberals succeeded in gaining an upper hand over the Conservatives in the competition for popular support.[29] The party did so by ensuring that Liberal reforms, if not always palatable, at least were not so objectionable as to provoke the kind of rebellious response that these regions had habitually reserved for confronting the injustices of Church and state during the eighteenth and early nineteenth centuries.[30] Lucas was a key influence in curbing village rebelliousness and accustoming Indian communities to selected elements of the Reform program.

The Mexican Reform was an extraordinarily ambitious legislative project that sought to sweep away centuries of corporate privileges, ethnically discriminatory practices, and fiscal inequalities and replace them with a single constitutional charter that outlined in detail the rights and obligations of equal citizens. The Liberal reforms and guarantees with the most radical implications for how communities in the Sierra organized themselves were: 1) the formation of the National Guard, involving, for the first time, the widespread arming of civilians and the election of Indians to positions of military command; 2) the abolition of the Indian head tax (the *capitación* revived by Conservative administrations during the late 1830s), which the Liberals replaced by the universal *pensión de rebajados* (a mustering-out tax); 3) the abolition of the *Dominica*, a tax paid by Indians to the Church to fund education in Christian doctrine, and its replacement by the *Chicontepec*, a municipal tax to fund compulsory public and secular education; 4) the forced sale of Church, confraternity, and municipal property; 5) the subdivision and privatization of village commons; 6) the abolition of unremunerated and compulsory labor services (known as *faenas* or *topiles*); 7) the ending of compulsory payment for religious services and sacraments; 8) the ending of imprisonment for debt, corporal punishment, and the death penalty; 9) the prohibition of religious dress, vows, excessive bell-ringing, and religious festivals and processions beyond church compounds; and 10) the establishment of a civil registry of births, deaths, and marriages applying to all citizens.

Four areas of Liberal reform that particularly involved Lucas include: taxation, festivals, and *faenas*; the National Guard; the *desamortización*; and secular schooling.

Taxation, Festivals, and Faenas

The abolition of the racially discriminatory *capitación* and its replacement by a universal mustering-out tax (*pensión de rebajados*) to be paid by all citizens not serving in the National Guard, regardless of race, had especially far-reaching implications for Indian communities. Originally conceived as a short-term measure to fund the costs of patriotic defense, the *rebajado* tax quickly became the bedrock of state government finances. As a Liberal military commander commented in 1860: "The *rebajado* tax was introduced into the Departments which recognize the Constitutional Government as a kind of head tax, which, from the information I have received, the Indians and other day laborers satisfy without great repugnance. This tax consists of a contribution of two *reales* a month from all who are not in active military service; it is easy to collect, for once the censuses are drafted, the villages are in charge of gathering it and this they appear to do regularly and punctually."[31]

Apart from its fiscal effectiveness, the *rebajado* tax also grew to be seen by Indians as a charter of Liberal citizenship and equality before the law. For the first time, Indian municipal authorities were entitled to tax non-Indians residing within the municipal boundary. Under wartime conditions, this arrangement appears to have been acceptable to both ethnic groups. If it was Indians who were joining in the National Guard, then *gente de razón* were prepared to pay their tax in order to be left alone, and vice versa. During the quarter century of civil and patriotic wars, this tax succeeded in balancing the rights and obligations of citizenship within a context of ethnic diversity. However, in more peaceful times the collection of the *rebajado* (or the "personal tax" as it came to be known after 1877) could be a potent source of conflict. Each ethnic group would compete for control of the municipal government and then raise the tax in a discriminatory or punitive manner.

Another new tax with widespread political and social repercussions was the *pensión de Chicontepec*, which was set up to fund compulsory public and secular education, replacing the *Dominica*, the tax paid by Indians to the Church to fund education. This tax further strengthened the secular power by removing a key aspect of village life from clerical control. Clerical influence was further weakened by the abolition of *faenas*, which the clergy in the Sierra had customarily received from widows and orphans in Indian communities, and the ending of the compulsory payment of parish dues. The primacy of the clergy on the village level was yet further undermined by the abolition of clerical patronage of religious confraternities, combined with the forced sale of their properties. Finally, the clerical monopoly over village ritual, ceremony, and the life cycles was challenged by the prohibition of religious dress, limitations upon bell-ringing, processions and religious festivals beyond the church compound, and the establishment of a civil registry of births, deaths, and marriages applying to all citizens.[32]

In their response to requests from villages for relaxation of the applications of laws against religious processions and fiestas, Liberal district authorities had to balance considerations of political security (the threat to civil authority if the clergy were to regain its control over ceremonial life) against the dangers of provoking disorders within communities still strongly attached to Catholic ritual.[33] Lucas took these fiscal and external aspects of the Reform seriously. When serving as popularly elected jefe político in 1879–80, he faced a conspiracy organized by Tetela's priest and Conservative families in alliance with villages that had been petitioning for greater religious freedom, particularly the right to organize festivals.[34]

In district capitals such as Tetela and Zacapoaxtla, the clergy was able to count upon powerful allies to ensure that the Liberal zealots in the *juntas patrióticas* (local bodies established to organize patriotic festivals) did not entirely exclude the Church from all external manifestations of the cult or use of public space. In Tetela, the parish priest was banished on at least three occasions (1855, 1880, and 1903), each involving a matter of ceremonial precedence, veiling deeper political divisions (Méndez ordered the first expulsion, Lucas the subsequent two).[35] By contrast, in Zacapoaxtla, apart from brief expulsions of priests following Liberal and Republican victories

during the Three Years' War and French Intervention, the clergy never lost
its influence among the town's most powerful families and continued to
enjoy comparatively unrestricted access to the use of public space in the
district capital as well as to exercise its influence more widely throughout
the district's numerous Indian communities.

A constitutional stipulation that had an even greater impact upon how
the people of the Sierra responded to the Reform (and one which occupied
much of Lucas's time as an organizer, conciliator, and mediator) was
Article 12, which guaranteed that no person could be obliged to provide
personal services without fair compensation and full consent.[36] Following
the promulgation of the Puebla's version of the constitution in 1861, the
state congress had prohibited any person, including public officials, from
demanding forced services or employing anyone without remuneration. It
had also abolished the category of *topil* (village bailiff used for organizing
faenas) and the services of "ministers of the rod, couriers and postmen,
sacristans and bell ringers," although it permitted the continuation of
"nightly rounds and guardians of roads and paths, and those services which
vecinos required for their common benefit and security."[37] This last clause
would allow district, municipal, and barrio authorities to retain the system
of *faenas* for maintaining roads and constructing public buildings. But the
faena system was to be voluntary, *faeneros* were to be paid, and, most notably, "the class called 'de razón' would also be expected to provide *faena*
service, or a financial contribution."[38] This law affected the clergy, long-
established creole families, and the civil government of districts and municipalities who could no longer count upon the time-hallowed custom that
Indian men, women, and children would provide household and courier
services, as well as compulsory labor for the building of churches, roads,
and other public works. Subject barrios and individual Indians responded
enthusiastically to this law since it promised to emancipate them from centuries of enforced servility.

Documentation abounds on Indians asserting their constitutional right
to freedom of employment. In 1862 two Xochiapulquense fathers, José
Palomino and Juan José Nepomuceno, exercised their daughters' right to
leave service in the household of Don Nicolás Bonilla of Yautetelco.[39] In
the same year Zacapoaxtla's *juzgado* (civil court) forbade the priest,
Manuel González Herrera, from demanding weekly *faenas* from the barrio
of Xalacapan for the construction of a corral (and reminded him in the
same communication that the woodland around the Guadalupe chapel belonged to the Indians, not to the Church).[40] In March 1869, Cuetzalan's
judge complained to the jefe político that the couriers he could normally
depend upon to carry messages between outlying villages, the municipal
seat, and the district capital were no longer prepared to work for him.
Moreover, he had no funds to pay them. What annoyed Ignacio Arrieta was
the willingness of these same *topiles* to continue serving the "justice of the

peace of the Indians of the cabecera."[41] The reply eventually arrived from the state government that councils should budget for rewarding such services, which had been so abused in the past.[42]

A curious case arose in neighboring Xochitlán later in the year that illustrates the political complexity of the issue of labor services. The municipal president of Xochitlán asked to be allowed to continue nominating José Vicente as minister of the rod (one of the constitutionally proscribed offices) even though the council had no funds to pay him, on the grounds that ever since he had been granted the post, he had been quiet and obedient, whereas before he had been very querulous.[43] Both the Cuetzalan and Xochitlán cases indicate the ethnically glutinizing function of these largely honorary posts and the potentially destabilizing effect of the abolition of personal services upon the relations between Indians and *gente de razón*.[44]

While the Xochitlán case suggests that certain services were not unpopular with Indians, the weight of evidence confirms that *faenas* for road and bridge building and the construction of public buildings in the municipal and district cabeceras were universally unpopular, especially when the work was far from home. One of the attractions of serving in the National Guard, or joining a village band, was to escape such services (although this immunity was often not respected).[45] But not every male could chose one of these alternatives, particularly once the age of warfare passed into the age of progress. Hence, long after the abolition of compulsory services, villagers were expected to contribute to the upkeep of roads and paths and the construction of works of public utility, such as bridges, schools, pavements, and council buildings. This obligation placed great powers of discretion in the hands of the authorities. During the 1870s these powers were increasingly abused. Lucas was caught between the higher authorities (including railway companies), who asked him to use his influence in the villages to mobilize labor for public works projects, and villagers, who invoked their constitutional right to freedom from compulsory services.[46]

During the 1860s and 1870s the demand for *faena* labor grew as expanded district and municipal governments sought to house themselves in more decorous buildings, district capitals competed with each other to achieve securer and speedier access to their subject municipalities, and sugar, *panela*, and aguardiente producers and coffee merchants pressured for improved communications. In the districts of Tetela and Zacapoaxtla, projects for road improvements, bridge construction, and school and town hall buildings multiplied.

In Tetela one objective was to improve communications between the district capital in the *tierra fría*, the expanding sugar and aguardiente producing towns of San Esteban Cuatempan and Huitzilan in the *tierra cálida*, and Zapotitlán in the *tierra caliente*. The principal obstacle was crossing the Zempoala River that links highland Tetela with lowland Jonotla. In March 1867, while the district's National Guard battalion marched upon the Austrian garrison holding the state capital, Zapotitlán's alcalde, Manuel Luiz, pleaded desperately to the jefe político for help in persuading subject barrios to provide men for building the bridge across the Zempoala. It was vital to have sufficient men since work was about to start on the main arch. One month later (after Puebla had fallen to the Republicans), Manuel Luiz had to report that the main arch had collapsed due to heavy rains.[47] This bridge was completed finally in August 1870.[48]

During the revolution of Tuxtepec in 1876, labor problems associated with bridge building clashed again with the demands of military campaigning. In October 1876, two weeks before the battle of Tecoac, Bartolomé Ayance, Indian military commander of Huitzilan, was criminally charged for fining more than sixty Huitziltecos for not performing their *faenas* in the construction of the Tepeapa bridge. Ayance had imprisoned and fined many of these men. He then spent their fines in Rafael Luna's store on aguardiente which he sold back to the prisoners, further indebting them. While he claimed that the fines were to pay for the completion of the bridge, Ayance used the money for acquiring land titles. Although the court absolved Ayance from criminal responsibility "taking into consideration his status and the condition in which the pure race of Mexicans finds itself, as well as his services over four months in directing work on the bridge," it severely reprehended him.[49]

The attempts by the clergy, district, and municipal authorities to reimpose *faenas* against the will of the communities contributed to the popular support for the revolution of Tuxtepec in the Puebla Sierra. After Díaz's victory, Indian soldiers from Zacapoaxtla and Cuetzalan attempted to hold their leaders to their promises of the restoration of constitutional freedoms.[50] The mood had not changed in the following year when Lucas unsuccessfully attempted to persuade the authorities of Xochitlán to provide labor for the construction of the bridge at Falcosama. Xochitlán's municipal president, Ignacio Castañeda, convoked an open meeting of the council, but uncertainty over jurisdiction and opposition to *faenas* obliged Lucas to leave Xochitlán empty-handed.[51]

The National Guard

The continuation of the system of *faenas* for works of public utility was not the only duty expected of the Sierra's villagers by the Liberal state. During the civil and patriotic wars and subsequent rebellions, the emphasis of constitutional government shifted from rights to duties. Civil authorities were temporarily suspended, alcaldes and aldermen were ordered to hand over their staffs of office to military commanders (generally local men); schools were closed to become barracks; and villages were mobilized, not only to provide fighting men but also cash and prodigious quantities of *totopo* (tortillas), coffee, *panela*, and *chilpotle* for the armies at the front.[52] Lucas's authority (and personal solvency) were key factors in persuading villages to contribute in all of these areas, which allowed *serrano* commanders to sustain campaigns for months on end, while expeditionary forces from the altiplano were generally obliged to withdraw after a few days.

Personal wealth and business acumen were a necessary but not a sufficient basis for a cacique in the Puebla Sierra during the nineteenth century. Lucas's influence within the National Guard is essential to understanding his popularity among the Indian population as well as his utility to fellow *serrano* Liberal leaders and higher authorities. Throughout his zone of influence, he attempted to ensure that the age of the arbitrary and hated *leva* (draft) was replaced by a more ordered and voluntary system of military recruitment. Lucas divided the central Sierra into two zones: one was used for active military recruitment, the other was used for supply. The land-hungry Nahua barrios on the southern margins of the Sierra, adjoining the hacienda districts of the altiplano, provided the majority of National Guard recruits in exchange for exemption from all taxes, regular pay, the promise of land, enhanced municipal status for outlying barrios, and guarantees against the *leva* and military service beyond the region. Further into the Sierra, adjoining the coastal plains, Indian communities were exempted from military service in return for paying the *rebajado* and for supplying campaigns.[53]

The effective organization of the National Guard in the Sierra required linguistic, diplomatic, and administrative skills, which few non-Indian leaders possessed. Having grown up in a peasant family with Nahua as his mother tongue, Lucas had these gifts. By the end of the French Intervention, within a decade of becoming a soldier, Lucas had developed strong ties of friendship, cemented through co-parenthood, with a network of National Guard commanders and village authorities throughout the Sierra. His skills as an artilleryman and an infantry leader and his mastery of the ambush (the Aztec tactic of *coapechar*, meaning to entice the enemy into dense woodland, cutting off paths of retreat)[54] forged personal ties that made him indispensable to the Liberal leadership at the state and federal levels.

The Desamortización *in the Puebla Sierra*

Although the abolition of compulsory personal services, voluntary military service, and the *rebajado* tax were broadly popular among Indian communities, the *desamortización* was greeted by many with fear and suspicion. The celebrated Ley Lerdo of 25 June 1856 decreed the sale of all property held by Church and by civil corporations beyond that required for their immediate administrative needs. This law revealed the gulf between the Liberal leadership wedded to the ideals of a modern, secular society of proprietary citizens, and the reality of a rural society composed in large part of village communities, strongly committed to the communal ownership of land and fervently attached to rituals and festivities organized by religious corporations, principally, confraternities. The challenge that Liberal leaders in the Puebla Sierra faced was how to apply the *desamortización* without antagonizing the villages.

The *desamortización* was applied to the Puebla Sierra haphazardly, over a thirty-five-year period, obeying the short-term financial exigencies of state and municipal governments continually faced with extraordinary wartime costs. For the Sierra's Liberal mestizos, the *desamortización* provided an opportunity to extend their landholdings while simultaneously undermining the clerical control over ceremonial life. If the district capital of Tetela is representative, municipal governments in the Sierra owned few *propios* (properties), and what little they owned they resisted selling until obliged to do so by the escalating costs of patriotic resistance toward the end of the French Intervention. Lucas profited directly from this by marrying the daughter of the principal beneficiary of the sale of Tetela's municipal estates. However, his own conviction that those privileged with the possession of private property should also contribute to the public good, through such causes as education, ensured continuity with the past (income from Tetela's *propios* had been largely spent on primary education).[55]

The 25 June 1856 law had more radical implications when applied to Church property. Although the Church in Tetela had little property, confraternities possessed substantial capital funds, numerous agricultural plots, and sizeable herds of cattle, all of which local entrepreneurs eyed covetously. Several of Tetela's most prominent Liberal leaders—Bonilla, Méndez, Rivera, and Luna—acquired land and livestock which confraternities under direct patronage of the parish priest were obliged to sell (the funds of *mayordomías* and brotherhoods, organized independently of the parish priest, were unaffected at first).[56]

During the Three Years' War, state governor Miguel Cástulo Alatriste and the Huauchinango general, Manuel Andrade Parraga, conducted a systematic campaign of clerical *desamortización* throughout the Sierra. Intended to release funds to pay for the Liberal war effort, the campaign greatly reduced the capacity of peasant communities to finance their ceremonial lives. However, no evidence was found of appreciable opposition from Indian communities to ecclesiastical disentailment. Perhaps the psychic loss in a diminished ceremonial life was compensated by the material benefit that accrued from the ending of compulsory parish fees and with reduced festival expenses. Perhaps folk religion and the veneration of the saints were affected little by the destruction of the confraternities.

Municipal authorities were also willing to disguise corporate survival on the barrio level. When in August 1864 Tetela's military commander ordered the liquidation of the funds and properties of *mayordomías* and brotherhoods, which hitherto had been exempted from the Ley Lerdo, village authorities throughout the district insisted that, since Parraga and Alatriste's campaign of confiscation in 1860, no such bodies had existed. They confirmed, however, that although major festivals for the saints were no longer held, every week or fortnight a saint was taken out to help with the collection of alms ("eggs, maize kernels and other little things"), but only for the sake of funding a particular Mass and not for the living of the priest.[57] After the European Intervention, requests from villages for permission to hold religious festivals reveal that voluntary collections for paying for Masses and processions were still being made, but with the funds no longer lodged with *mayordomos* or their treasurers.[58]

The sale of municipal and ecclesiastical property was only a minor part of the Liberal program of *desamortización*. After the defeat of the European Intervention in 1867, with the clergy and the Conservatives vanquished, the main thrust of the Ley Lerdo was now directed at village commons. Although access to common land was controlled by village councils, the commons actually belonged to the *común de naturales del pueblo* (the villagers as a collective unit). The Ley Lerdo, with its exclusive recognition of private and individual ownership, rendered village councils and the "común de naturales" redundant as owners of land.

Communal response to the application of the law privatizing commons varied greatly from one village to another. Two broad patterns of response can be discerned, approximately corresponding to the southern and the center-north Sierra. Throughout the southern Sierra, where Indian communities had lost much of their land and political autonomy to haciendas and creole-controlled headtowns during the colonial period, the Liberal Reform offered a prospect for villages to upgrade their political status and regain their lands. Once separate municipal status had been established, villages could claim a *fundo legal* (a 600-yard limit that villages could claim as their minimum territorial base) for constructing the municipal cabecera, as well as receive ejidos for grazing livestock and for firewood. Nothing in the Ley Lerdo prevented this time-honored strategy.[59] Indeed, the political circumstances of the times favored the practice. Following the revolution of Tuxtepec, several barrios that had served in the patriotic and Liberal armies were rewarded with municipal status and generous boundaries at the expense of neighboring haciendas and their former cabeceras.[60]

Apart from these officially sponsored measures to encourage new municipalities of smallholders, in the southern Sierra, several absentee large landowners, in the face of pressure from assertive barrios or from resident *peones* and uncertain about the precise boundaries of their estates, chose to sell the less commercially viable parts of their haciendas in lots. Thus, political factors favoring the revival of villages were complemented by market factors that tended to favor the fragmentation of large estates into smaller units. Besides, in this cold zone of sheep grazing and sedentary cereal agriculture, villagers and estate owners were less voracious in their demand for land than their counterparts at lower altitudes, where communities and planters sought large reserves for future milpas and the expansion of plantations. Hence, the *desamortización* in the southern Sierra did not provoke significant opposition, as long as municipal authorities ensured that villagers were given precedence in the allocation of lots. Conflict did erupt over which faction of a village should receive land rather than over the principle of the passage from communal to individual ownership.

In the central and northern Sierra, where Indian communities retained a much greater sense of territoriality and recent non-Indian immigrants were beginning to establish çoffee estates or fence cattle-raising enclosures, the *desamortización* rang more alarm bells. Privatization of commons threatened to legalize and render permanent the presence of *gente de razón* on Indian community land to which, hitherto, they had enjoyed only customary access as tenants. Once *gente de razón* became property owners, it was feared that they would take control of municipal government. Moreover, because of the fluidity and mobility of the population of the Sierra, whether it was Nahua corn-planters on their seasonal trek to the *tierra caliente* or mestizo entrepreneurs moving down to plant corn, coffee, or sugarcane on the piedmont, the *desamortización* had geo-political implications for relations between neighboring municipalities and adjoining districts.

Thus, in the central and northern Sierra, the *desamortización* was more problematic, provoking one major rebellion in Cuetzalan between 1868 and 1870 and numerous smaller uprisings. Lucas's moderating influence was critical in the successful containment of these movements, sometimes by peaceful mediation but also by negotiating locally acceptable privatization arrangements (generally involving the exclusion of outsiders from participating in the property booty) in exchange for support from these communities in regional insurrections against Juárez and Lerdo governments. Lucas's intervention in these disputes reassured not only aggrieved Indian communities but also anxious *gente de razón*, who lived in fear of a caste war.[61]

Secular Schooling

The application of the laws on compulsory services and the *desamortización* reveal the willingness of Liberal leaders to compromise in order not to antagonize either Indian communities, concerned about the loss of local control over land, or district and municipal governments, anxious to introduce improvements in services and communications. Sierra Liberals were also obliged to trim the agenda of a more evangelical side to the Liberal Reform: the pledge of the constitution of 1857 to introduce free, compulsory, and secular primary education throughout Mexico.[62] Educational reform was dearer to hearts of Sierra Liberals than either the abolition of *faenas* or common land privatization, reforms which they recognized as alien to the customs and needs of Sierra communities. Education, by contrast, offered the tantalizing prospect of at once transforming Indian communities into a Liberal citizenry and overcoming the alienation that mestizos felt about the world of magic and ethnic distinctiveness that surrounded them.

It was no accident that the three principal Liberal leaders of the southern Sierra—Juan Francisco Lucas, Juan Nepomuceno Méndez, and Juan Crisóstomo Bonilla—began their careers as village schoolteachers (Lucas as an unpaid literacy teacher in Cuatecomaco and Comaltepec at the age of 17, Méndez before joining the National Guard in 1847, and Bonilla as director of La Cañada's school at the age of 14). From the 1850s, primary education in the Sierra was set to become a battleground between the clergy and a rising group of Liberals. For three centuries, the Roman Catholic Church alone had provided rudimentary education to Indians in Christian doctrine in their native languages. Liberals resented the Church's monopoly over Indian education and favored bilingual (preferably Spanish) education controlled by municipalities.[63]

Soon after the revolution of Ayutla, Tetela's sub-prefect, Juan Nepomuceno Méndez, dispatched a commissioner to the *tierra caliente* of Tetela to review the collecting of the head tax and the state of education.[64] The commissioner's reports expressed indignation at the parlous state of education in the Totonac villages of northern Tetela: "There are no other schools in these villages than those for teaching youth the Christian Doctrine in their own language." Most communities contained no literate adults to occupy elected local offices or secretaryships, exposing Indians to the whims of the clergy and outsiders. Moreover, villages could not afford to establish schools because their inhabitants, "burdened by having to pay parochial dues," were too poor to pay local taxes. Meanwhile the clergy, whose *Dominica* tax was intended to fund education, made only half-hearted efforts to persuade parents to send their children to school.[65] The commissioner's reports in 1855 revealed much more to Méndez than educational shortcomings. His findings also touched on a range of issues that would facilitate the Liberals' control over the district during the subsequent decades: the fiscal potential of these *panela*-rich municipalities; the possibility of displacing almost defunct Church schools and finances with a network of secular village schools controlled from the district capital; the potential for filling the administrative vacuum on the local level with a newly trained local clientele of literate village secretaries; and the political benefit that would derive from responding energetically to local grievances over boundary incursions by tax collectors and land-grabbers from the neighboring jurisdictions of Zacapoaxtla and Teziutlán.

Between the 1850s and 1870s, secular schooling became the key to extending the Liberal Party's political control at the village level.[66] The district of Tetela became a nursery for the expansion of secular primary education for boys, girls, and adults, with the municipalities of Tetela and Xochiapulco achieving the highest levels of literacy outside of the state capital.[67] However, the receptivity of villages to such novel institutions usually directed by outsiders varied enormously between communities. As with the *desamortización*, receptivity to the educational policies of the Montaña (the Liberal Party of the Sierra) was greatest in the southern Sierra where a tradition of municipal schooling was already well established in many communities before the Reform. In San Francisco Ixtacamaxtitlán, the schoolmaster in 1870 was Angel Cabrera, nephew of the Liberal priest José María Cabrera. True to this municipality's proud Liberal and patriotic antecedents (going back to the Insurgency), the Cabrera family had established one of the most successful schools in the state, serving as a model for schools in Ixtacamaxtitlán's subject barrios.[68] For a salary of twenty-five pesos a month, Angel Cabrera taught according to the Lancastrian system of "mutual teaching," accompanied by simultaneous "material action," avoiding "pure abstraction," and the Hollendorf system, which recommended a minimum of rules so as not to burden the memory with "sterile facts." Apart from reading, writing, and arithmetic, the school taught "Elementary Notions" of Sacred History, Profane, Ancient, and Modern History, the History of Mexico, Geography, Geometry, Castillian Grammar and Spelling, the "Rights and Obligations of the Mexican Citizen," and, finally, Christian Doctrine.[69]

A few miles to the northeast, in Xochiapulco, a more radical anticlerical pedagogy took root: Nicolás Pizarro's "constitutional" catechism replaced the Catholic catechism of Ripalda, and schoolteachers took over as cultural intermediaries from the priest. Both Bonilla and Lucas served for short periods as directors of Xochiapulco's main school, and Lucas even donated land for the construction and upkeep of schools in three of Xochiapulco's dependent barrios.[70] However, schooling in Xochiapulco progressed far beyond the patronage requirements of these Liberal leaders or the practical needs of a community of smallholding peasants.[71] The municipality attracted a series of anticlerical Masonic school directors, who were disciples of an austere, primitive evangelical Christianity and viewed themselves at the vanguard of an educational revolution that would emancipate the oppressed Indian population and result in the dawning of a new age of Christian Socialism.[72]

A passage from a speech given by Rafaela Bandala, a Xochiapulco schoolmistress, on the occasion of the funeral of Miguel Méndez (son of General Juan N. Méndez, the principal Liberal caudillo of the Sierra) in 1888, is much in the anticlerical style:

> For three centuries, the education of the popular masses was maliciously neglected by the clergy; the friars were like giants and the indigenous race, the most ignorant, because the conquistadors, priests, and encomenderos had obliterated their civilization. The indigenous race, I

repeat, constituted the eternal seam of gold which these lubricious priests devoured in gold pieces by the million. But then came Independence, the beneficent ideas of the French Revolution echoed throughout the country, and like a sun illuminating the darkness, the Liberal party rose up against the friars. The Liberal party, for whom in our state Juan Francisco Lucas is the Father, Juan N. Méndez the Son, and the late Juan C. Bonilla was the Holy Spirit, has freed Mexico from the poisonous snake that imprisoned it, by giving the Nation its Independence, the Mexican people its humanitarian constitution, and our Patria the immortal glories of the fifth of May, and the proletarian class its numerous schools from which to imbibe education.[73]

The aim of teachers, such as Colonel Indalecio Sánchez and Manuel Pozos, who together directed Xochiapulco's schools for almost forty years, was to drill boys, girls, and adults in the knowledge of their rights and obligations as citizens, instill a reverence for a secular and republican pantheon of heroes (Cuauhtémoc, Xochitl, Hidalgo, Washington, Juárez, Lincoln, Garibaldi), encourage patriotism and self-sacrifice, inculcate a fascination for universal history and a reverence for scientific inventions, in short, to civilize and de-fanaticize communities which they saw as inhabiting a world of magic.[74] A further example of Liberal zeal occurred in the festivities that Manuel Pozos, the schoolmaster, organized in Xochiapulco to consecrate Juárez's birthday in March 1901. Pozos inaugurated the nine days of festivities with the biblical slogan, "If you are not for freedom, you are its enemy." Each day, between seven and ten at night, after long days in the field, every resident in the municipality was expected to illuminate the front of his or her house with candles and the national flag with the motto, "Peace is respect for the rights of others." Each head of the family was obliged to give an hour's reading daily from Nicolás Pizarro's *Catecismo Constitucional*, the anticlerical law of 14 December 1874, the constitutional reforms of 24 September 1873, and a passage from "The Life of Juárez," a biography of the man who was considered the supreme Liberal. For the benefit of children who had been asleep, the same program was applied daily in each of the municipality's eight public schools, while civic speeches were given in the streets and squares.[75]

Few, if any, village schoolteachers of the more indigenous central and northern Sierra would have attempted a cycle of festivities as ambitious as those devised by Pozos. Among the Totonac communities of the *tierra caliente* of Tetela, where there was no tradition of secular schooling and where illiteracy was universal in outlying barrios until the middle of the century, the obstacles facing municipal authorities attempting to improve and expand primary education were immense. Apart from the difficulty of recruiting and retaining qualified teachers for remote monolingual villages, municipal and district authorities received reports of drunken teachers using school buildings for selling aguardiente and for cockfights;

widowed mothers having to take their sons out of school to avoid hunger; violent opposition to Liberal teachers from Catholic villagers; and opposition to the school from local employers.[76]

In general, more progress was made in cabeceras such as Jonotla, where inspectors reported the boys and girls of a mixed school to be bright, clean, and full of enthusiasm at a prize-giving ceremony in December 1868. The prize-giving committee, comprised of the parish priest and two aldermen, then traveled to inspect the schools in the outlying villages of San Francisco Zoquiapan and Santiago Ecatlán. The committee noted that Zoquiapan's school was in a state of "complete abandon" with the children hardly started on "reading, doctrine, and writing." By contrast, the children of Ecatlán "were found in a very good state, comparatively, given that they are Indians and 'Totonaquitos cerrados' (dull Totonacs) . . . we greatly admired the quickness and the ease in which they answered the questions we put to them. Two girls in particular gave us hopes for the future."[77] Traveling through the same region in 1927, Moisés Saenz, sub-secretary of public education, found the same unevenness in educational provision and standards between communities. Moving up to the southern Sierra, he lamented the deteriorated state of schools in Tetela de Ocampo, once the center for progressive pedagogy for the entire state. But he was full of praise for Xochiapulco's continued dedication to the progressive educational ideals and responsiveness to the new federal programs.[78]

Lucas placed an enormous importance upon schools and literacy. His success in becoming the "Patriarch of the Sierra"—the personification of the Puebla Sierra's unique blend of patriotism and radicalism—was as closely related to his participation in Bonilla's creation of a statewide network of secular schools as it was to the successful command of the National Guard during the civil and patriotic wars. It was the new generation of schoolteachers who spread the language of constitutional rights, of patriotic duty and reward; selected and organized the veneration of the secular pantheon of Aztec warriors, European and American radicals and nation-builders, and Mexican liberal-patriotic heroes; and led their children into the streets and plazas on national holidays and in prize-giving ceremonies.

Conclusion

Two critical factors influenced Lucas's rise to regional preeminence: the hierarchy of political patronage that held the nineteenth-century Mexican state together; and the extraordinary capacity of the Reform to put down popular roots in even the most remote and least modern of locations. Caciquismo in the Puebla Sierra built upon enduring colonial precedents of ethnic separateness and hierarchy. From the mid-nineteenth century, caciquismo became more intrusive, competitive, and politically contingent.

However, to be effective in the longer term, the authority of local and regional caciques still needed to be founded upon recognized codes of reciprocity. Likewise, the demands of the new Liberal state, if they were to draw a positive response from the culturally complex terrain of the Puebla Sierra, could not simply be doctrinaire, top-down prescriptions but rather had to be accepted locally. Consequently, applied Liberalisms varied from one Sierra community to another just as the region's caciquismo presented a kaleidoscope of locally competitive ideological and personal rivalries. Lucas's success lay in his ability to scout a path through this jungle of political uncertainty by responding to demands from leaders at higher levels and assuaging local anxieties about the Liberal Reform, while gathering loyal clientele.

2

Tetela in the Puebla Sierra

In 1944, Captain Martín Rivera Torres, Lucas's nephew, described his uncle's region of influence to be "the Sierra de Zacatlán; a part of that of Chignahuapan; Tetela de Ocampo; Zacapoaxtla; a part of Tlatlauqui and of Teziutlán; parts of Jalacingo, Altotonga, and Papantla, in the state of Veracruz; as well as some parts of Libres in this state."[1] This territory comprised a belt of the Sierra Madre Oriental, whose southern boundary touches the altiplano and faces the principal communications axis running between the port of Veracruz and the national capital. Lucas's influence was at its strongest in the Nahua communities along this southern boundary of the Puebla Sierra, where the resources of villages were at their most fragile and most exposed to external pressures for land, labor, taxes, and military recruitment. His enduring influence in these communities derived from his ability to moderate, at times even to neutralize, these external pressures, in accord with the Liberal guarantees embodied within the constitution of 1857. Achieving this task depended upon access to a defensible zone of retreat in politically friendly territory. The district of Tetela provided this sanctuary. Lucas's rise to regional political prominence was closely associated with the emergence of a group of Liberal leaders from Tetela de Ocampo who used the town's command over the resources of the district to mount repeated challenges upon the state and federal powers from the late 1850s until their political eclipse in 1885.

Demography and Ethnicity

In 1792 the Sierra Norte contained 138,773 (27 percent) of the Intendancy of Puebla's overall population of 506,654, of whom 26,768 (17 percent) were listed as Spaniards and *castas*, the remaining 112,005 (83 percent) listed as Indians. Between 1792 and 1869 the population of the Sierra grew at an average annual rate of 0.4 percent, almost double the rate of the province/state (0.23 percent). The rate of population growth increased markedly after the mid-century, with the population of the Sierra growing at almost 2 percent per annum between 1869 and 1878. Comparisons

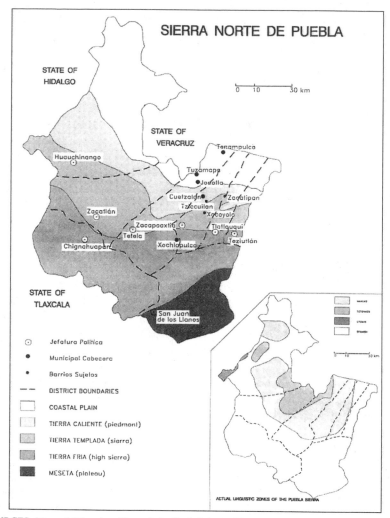

SOURCES: *Mapa del Estado y Plano de la Ciudad de Puebla,* Guia Roji, Mexico, 1982; Pierre Beaucage, "Anthropologie économique des communautés indigènes de la Sierra Norte de Puebla (Mexique) 2. Les villages de basse montagne," *Canadian Review of Anthropology* 10, no. 2: 119.

between districts are misleading because of frequent boundary changes. Nevertheless, from Table 2–1, it is evident that Tetela's population growth rate of 0.8 percent per annum between 1792 and 1869 led the region. Until the mid-nineteenth century, over two-thirds of the population of the *partido* resided in the temperate municipality of Tetela. Thereafter, the hot country municipalities of Jonotla, Zapotitlán, and Tuzamapa took the lead, although the municipality of Tetela's population remained dynamic during the war-torn decades of the 1860s and 1870s. This was due as much to immigration from other districts as to natural increase (*see* Table 2–2).

Table 2–1.　Population of the Puebla Sierra by District: 1792, 1869, 1878, and 1910[2]

	1792	1869	1878	1910
Llanos (including Libres, Zacapoaxtla, Tlatlauqui)	41,928			
Libres		17,919	24,754	
Tlatlauqui		14,749	15,046	23,646
Zacapoaxtla		23,376	24,800	37,749
Teziutlán	9,940	19,630	23,550	37,498
Tetela	9,346	24,995	27,047	37,598
Zacatlán	41,625	35,131	50,129	72,501
Alatriste		25,783	31,493	32,927
(formerly parts of Libres, Tetela, and Zacatlán)				
Huauchinango	35,934	39,887	44,812	92,105
Total Sierra Pop.	*138,773*	*201,470*	*241,631*	
(percentage of total)	(27%)	(29%)	(31%)	
Total Pop. of State	*506,654*	*697,788*	*784,466*	

Table 2–2.　Population of Partido/Sub-Prefecture/District of Tetela, and Municipality of Tetela, 1792–1910[3]

	Partido/District	*Municipality*
1792	9,346	
1849	17,437	
1860		12,699
1868	24,995	
1871	26,142	15,617
1878	27,047	16,285
1910	37,598	

At the height of its territorial development in 1871 (just after annexing Xochiapulco), Tetela contained nearly 27,000 inhabitants, grouped in six municipalities and four parishes, residing in some forty-eight scattered villages. Non-Indians were concentrated in the municipality of Tetela, in the cold highland south of the district, while Totonac, Nahua, and Otomi Indians formed the majority in the other five municipalities located at lower altitudes in the *tierra caliente*. In 1792, non-Indians (1,604 Spaniards and 442 *castas*) had comprised 28 percent of the population, with 7,300 Indians making up the other 72 percent.[4] As late as 1848 the sub-prefect of Tetela could still describe his *partido* as comprising a constellation of twenty-four villages, each characterized by a distinctive linguistic orientation, and with Indian languages—Nahuatl or Totonac—predominating in all but the cabecera, Tetela de Ocampo, a few outlying *rancherías*, and in the municipality of Tenampulco in the *tierra caliente* (*see* Table 2–3).

By 1910 the linguistic picture had been transformed. Indians now made up only 18 percent of the population of 37,598, with non-Indians comprising the remaining 82 percent. In purely linguistic terms, acculturation in the district of Tetela was an overwhelming process during the nine-

Table 2–3.   Linguistic Orientation of Tetela's Villages in 1848 as reported to Zacatlán[5]

Town/Village	Ethnic Groups and Languages Spoken
Pueblos of the Municipality of Tetela	
Tetela de Oro	Creoles and Indians who speak Castillian and Mexican
San Pedro	pure Indians who speak Mexican
San Cristobal	pure Indians who speak Mexican
San Estévan	pure Indians who speak Mexican
Rancherías of the Municipality of Tetela	
Xonocuautla, Rancho Viejo, Tilapan, Tececuilco	Creoles who speak Castillian
Xilititla and Zitlalcuautla	Creoles and Indians who speak Castillian and Mexican
Taxco and Xochitlán	pure Indians who speak Mexican
Pueblos of the Municipality of Jonotla	
Jonotla	pure Indians who speak Totonac
Ecatlán	pure Indians who speak Totonac
Zoquiapan	pure Indians who speak Mexican
Pueblos of the Municipality of Tuzamapa	
Tuzamapa	pure Indians who speak Totonac
Tetetilla	pure Indians who speak Totonac
Santos Reyes	pure Indians who speak Totonac
Tenampulco	pure Indians who speak Totonac, with some Creoles who speak Castillian
Pueblos of the Municipality of Zapotitlán	
Zapotitlán	pure Indians who speak Totonac
Zongozotla	pure Indians who speak Totonac
Nanacatlán	pure Indians who speak Totonac
Tuxtla	pure Indians who speak Totonac
Huitzilan	pure Indians who speak Mexican

teenth century, the most telling consequence of the commitment to universal primary education in Castillian. The scale of the decline in Tetela of Indian spoken as a first language, between 1792 and 1910, was far greater than in neighboring Zacatlán or Huauchinango, which had comparable ethnic balances to Tetela in 1792.[6]

Climate and Topography

Tetela's leaders would not have achieved the influence they attained during the war-torn period between 1847 and 1876 without mountains. No district on the plateau was able to sustain a political project during this time. Even holding the state capital, with its commanding fortress of Guadalupe and Loreto, was more a tactical liability than an advantage for successive governors and military commanders from the Three Years' War until the revolution of Tuxtepec.

The principal districts of the Puebla Sierra—Teziutlán, Tlatlauqui, Zacapoaxtla, Tetela, and Zacatlán—extend north from the edge of the altiplano in the *tierra fría* through a belt of pine-clad peaks, down to a band of temperate ledges and valleys where the district capitals are located, down again more precipitously through the humid *tierra cálida* of the principal declivity to the piedmont and the rolling and partly forested plains of the *tierra caliente* until reaching their boundaries with the state of Veracruz. Given this tangled precipitous topography and marked changes in altitude, each Sierra district (apart from highland Alatriste and lowland Huauchinango) contains a wide range of climactic and ecological conditions arranged in altitudinal layers. (*See* map, p. 26.)

Amid this natural diversity, the Puebla Sierra exhibits two areas of uniformity. First, the geology of this entire swath of the Sierra Madre Oriental, from the Cofre de Perote in Veracruz in the southeast, sloping northwest to the piedmont of Pahuatlán on the border with Hidalgo, is formed from a fold of Jurassic limestone, pitted and wrinkled in places by mineral-bearing volcanic plugs and lava flows. Second, the Puebla Sierra is exposed throughout the year to prevailing northerly winds. Excessively humid in summer, these winds bank up thick curtains of mist, reducing mean temperatures for these altitudes by ten to fifteen degrees and reducing visibility to a few yards. Heavy rainstorms, often accompanied by thunder and lightning, have been known to last for a week. Combined with the impenetrable mists, these downpours often exercised a decisive effect upon military affairs. As late as April, cold northerlies can bring frosts (temperatures well below five degrees are registered in Zautla, Chignahuapan, Zacatlán, Aquixtla, Tetela, and San Juan de los Llanos) thereby destroying harvests.[7]

A consequence of this limestone geology and heavy rainfall is the deep scarring of the landscape into a multiplicity of gorges converging upon four tributaries of the Tecolutla River, which empties into the Gulf of Mexico south of Tuxpan. Of these tributaries—Necaxa, Lazazalpan, Zempoala, and Apulco—the latter two exercised a decisive impact upon the political geography of the Sierra during the nineteenth century, particularly that of Tetela. The Zempoala tributary links Tetela's highlands with its lowlands, historically endowing this central polity in the Sierra with a physical unity, and potential economic and administrative reciprocity, unmatched by other Sierra districts. The Apulco, which bounds Tetela to the south and east, carries the heaviest current of any of the Tecolutla's tributaries through the steepest part of the Sierra, causing correspondingly deeper scarring. Gorges with perpendicular precipices of up to eighty meters provided an incomparable natural defense against forces from the altiplano and rival districts to the east, particularly Zacapoaxtla.[8] Thus, Tetela, on its southern boundaries, resembles a natural fortress, possessing the additional advantage of escape routes to the north along the Zempoala and Apulco tributaries to zones of refuge in the *tierra caliente*.

An additional strategic advantage (although one which in the longer term proved to be an economic handicap) is the remoteness and inaccessibility of the district capital of Tetela de Ocampo from the altiplano. The other highland district capitals—Teziutlán, Tlatlauqui, Zacapoaxtla, Chignahuapan, and Zacatlán—can all be reached within a few hours' march from the altiplano. Indeed, these towns had acquired a dominance over their districts precisely because of their proximity to the altiplano and their positions on the main routes into the Sierra. Tetela was peculiar in this respect, being uniquely enclosed by the dense "Sierra Alta." Any force from beyond the district seeking to take Tetela risked isolation and encirclement, which explains why occupying forces generally abandoned the town within a few days, if not hours.

If Tetela possessed a route of retreat via the Zempoala to the northeast, its defensive potential was also enhanced by the vast pine-clad and canyoned region to the south, within the districts of Tetela, Alatriste, and Libres. At the time of the Conquest, this extraordinarily tangled mountain mass was included within the ancient *señorios* (pre-Conquest feudal domains) of Ixtacamaxtitlán and Zautla, which, like the *señorio* of Tetela itself, had maintained their autonomy over the post-classic period, although they acknowledged the suzerainty of Mexico-Tenochtitlán. Zautla and Ixtacamaxtitlán provided cover for Hernán Cortés's advance upon the Aztec imperial capital and it is said that it was this region which inspired Cortés's choice of the crumpled handkerchief for describing Mexico to Charles V.[9] Throughout the nineteenth century, beginning with the Insurgency when the Osorno clan took refuge here, this area offered sanctuary for rebel forces facing pursuit.[10] However, Ixtacamaxtitlán's Liberal reputation was rooted in an older animosity toward the wealthier and politically dominant altiplano cabeceras of Chignahuapan and San Juan de los Llanos, which were founded by the Spaniards.[11] In Ixtacamaxtitlán and Zautla, Tetela's Liberal leaders found some of their most loyal allies among the National Guard of their remoter Nahua barrios. Mountainous Ixtacamaxtitlán and neighboring Zautla and Xochiapulco also offered cover for forces awaiting the start of campaigns on the altiplano.[12]

If access to Tetela from the south was difficult (although this route was taken by the French and Austrians in 1864 and by General Alatorre in 1872), the two principal routes of communication between Tetela and the altiplano were hardly much easier. To reach Tetela from the pulque- and cereal-producing zones of Tlaxco on the northern altiplano of Tlaxcala, the traveler (or military commander) had to cross the high range of the Sierra de Tlaxco into the valley of Chignahuapan. From there, the mule track to Tetela ascends another range of mountains before entering a long, narrow valley bounded by steep slopes and cut across by the dramatic gorge of the Zempoala, before it broadens into the pocket of maize fields and temperate fruit orchards. Tetela de Ocampo stands here with its still-fortified church and atrium built on a volcanic plug. When an enemy force reached this far into the Sierra, it was in grave danger first of ambush, then, upon arrival, of finding its supply lines cut.

Access to Tetela from Zacapoaxtla and Zautla to the east and southeast was even more hazardous. The choice was between a seemingly interminable, steep-sided valley carrying the Zitlacuautla tributary of the Apulco, passing though the villages of Huahuaxtla and Ometepec, where Conservative, Austrian, and Federal forces suffered some of their most spectacular defeats, and an alternative route across the teaming Apulco and then over some of the highest peaks in the Puebla Sierra (the southeastern flanks of which are skirted by the extensive Taxcantla ranch, in the possession of Lucas from 1868). Even today, only the roughest (and frequently impassable) road connects Tetela with Zacapoaxtla.

Because of the narrow and vertiginous quality of these valleys (in effect, ravines and canyons), neither the Apulco nor the Zempoala served as an easy route of transport and communication. Although, at the time of the Conquest, the upper Apulco valley provided a vital route linking the eastern Sierra with the altiplano (and on to the valley of Mexico), this route was increasingly neglected in favor of cart routes over the plateau and several northwest and southeast routes, following the principal mountain ridges, which linked the lowlands with the highlands. Over time, this pattern of communications tended to favor the commercial development of Teziutlán and Huauchinango, towns at the opposite extremes of the great declivity of the Puebla Sierra, which falls from the southeast to the northwest, at the expense of Tetela and Zacatlán.[13] Today the visitor to Tetela or Zacatlán steps back into the nineteenth century, while Huauchinango and Teziutlán are noisy modern towns reflecting their greater commercial hinterlands.

Teziutlán stands on the simplest and shortest route between the eastern Puebla altiplano and the tropical lowlands (including Tetela's extensive *tierra caliente* municipality of Tenampulco where Teziutecos established important cattle estates during the later nineteenth century). Huauchinango is similarly favorably placed as a lowland entrepôt, serving its own sierra, the sierra of Zacatlán, and the immense Huasteca and lowlands of Veracruz, and funneling goods to Mexico City through the Sierra de Tulancingo. Teziutlán and Huauchinango's greater accessibility to the exterior explains why both towns were repeatedly used by external political forces, from 1854 to 1876, in variations of a pincer movement directed at containing and confronting rebels occupying the core districts of the Sierra.[14]

If Teziutlán and Huauchinango possessed an advantage in their ease of access to external commercial circuits and the rich tropical lowlands, Zacapoaxtla was the most favorably placed district capital for gaining access to the central Sierra, including the municipalities of Jonotla and Tuzamapa in the *tierra caliente* of Tetela. As a consequence, Zacapoaxtla attracted a greater number of substantial merchants than Tetela, Zacatlán, or Tlatlauqui. During the eighteenth century, Zacapoaxtla was also favored by the clergy as the center for ecclesiastical administration, the training of priests, and tithe collection. After the revolution of Ayutla, the town became a center for the coordination of resistance to the Liberal Reform.[15] Liberals in Tetela and Zacatlán, where the Church was weaker, saw Zacapoaxtla as a frontline of the Conservatives with their clerical and, between 1862 and 1867, European allies.

A Conservative, pro-clerical disposition was also associated with Zacapoaxtla's eastern neighbor, Tlatlauqui, the main center for the Franciscan evangelization of the central Sierra during the sixteenth century. Tlatlauqui possessed the slightest commerce of all the highland district capitals and the weakest command over its *tierra caliente*. Tlatlauquenses attempted to overcome this disadvantage by attracting state and federal backing for transport improvements and European colonization.[16] Tetela's physical isolation discouraged any such illusion of becoming a destination on any commercial artery linking the altiplano with the coast. Thus, while well located strategically, Tetela was not favorably placed as a commercial center, either in relation to the lowlands of its own district, where it faced intense competition both from Teziutlán and Zacapoaxtla, or in relation to the altiplano.

Tetela's distance from the principal commercial circuits was not a major obstacle for the district's principal commerciable commodities: silver from the mines around the district capital, and *panela* and aguardiente from the *tierra caliente*. Silver and *panela*, as low-volume, high-value goods, were easily transported over a network of long-distance mule tracks. The high tax yield from silver and aguardiente also helped sustain the costs of district administration. Moreover, the metallurgical and smelting skills of Tetela's *real de minas* (silver-mining settlement) were also turned to good effect in periods of rebellion and warfare, from the Three Years' War until the Tuxtepec Revolution, when an arsenal was established near Tetela.

Although advantaged by possession of silver mines and an active trade in sugar loaf and aguardiente, Tetela was poorly placed to exploit cattle. Beef cattle were bred in the lowlands of Teziutlán and Tetela's remotest northern municipality of Tenampulco, fattened in *potreros* (cattle pastures) in the Sierra, and marketed in the highlands through dealers in Zacapoaxtla and, especially, Teziutlán, where many families prospered from this lucrative trade.[17] However, cattle breeding and fattening on a large scale, especially in this period of common land privatization, was a potentially disruptive process among the largely arable and maize-farming peasantry, as the Cuetzalan rebellion of 1868–1870 revealed. Indeed, the Indian communities of Cuetzalan, as well as those of Tetela's lowland municipalities of Tuzumapa and Jonotla, looked to Tetela's district leadership to protect their commons from encroachment by land-grabbing cattle ranchers. This service the Tetela leadership did its best to provide since so many Tetelenses derived their livelihood from the *panela* trade and the sale of aguardiente to the same villages. It was partly upon this basis of reciprocity that Tetela's leadership constructed its political hold over its territory, gaining an edge over its more divided neighbors.

Territoriality

Tetela's nineteenth-century political and territorial aspirations built upon colonial, even pre-Conquest, precedents. From long before the Conquest, the rulers of Tetela claimed jurisdiction over a large swath of the highlands as well as suzerainty over an extensive region of the lowlands. The caciques of Tetela who met Cortés at Tzaóctlan in August 1519 were descended from Nahua military colonists who had settled in what, until the twelfth century, had been a Totonac region. Together with the neighboring *señorios* of Tlatlauquitepec, Ixtacamaxtitlán, and Zacatlán, Tetela served as a client of the Mexica against the Totonacs to the north and independent Tlaxcaltecos to the south. Totonacs still occupy some highland communities close to Tetela (Ahuacatlán, Eloxochititlán, and Totutla), but, for the most part, they had been pushed back to the lowlands (from where they emerged originally in the early ninth century, after the fall of Teotihuacán).[18] Throughout the colonial period, highland Tetela was politically, although not territorially, attached to lowland Jonotla in a single *corregimiento* (colonial district).[19]

Hence, the reciprocity between highland Tetela and lowland Jonotla rested initially upon the pre-Conquest expansion of Nahua groups into the territory of Totonacapan. During the colonial period, Nahuas and Totonacs intermittently clashed in Jonotla. The cabecera in Tetela endeavored to resolve these tensions.[20] Helping to sustain this straggling polity was the *real de minas* near Tetela, which attracted non-Indian migrants from the altipano to settle the temperate valleys around Tetela, near the principal silver mines at La Cañada and Tonalapa. By the late eighteenth century these colonists formed the densest belt of non-Indian migrants to be found in any Sierra jurisdiction.[21] They worked small proprietary farms or rented land from Indian communities where they became increasingly dominant. However, the hostility of Tetela's *república de indios* was directed not at these non-Indian settlers but channeled instead into legal suits in the defense of community lands along Tetela's southern boundaries, which had been illegally expropriated by large landowners from Tlaxcala and San Juan de los Llanos during the later sixteenth century.[22] Tetela's ancient sense of territoriality is also seen in the deliberate construction of houses and barrios along its western boundary with Zacatlán, a process which was repeated during civil wars in the mid-nineteenth century under Lucas's supervision.[23]

This continuing assertiveness of the *república de indios* of Tetela masked a process of displacement of Indians by creole and mestizo settlers in the highland valleys around Tetela by the end of the colonial period. In the tropical lowlands of Jonotla, by contrast, Indian communities remained more assertive, a consequence of population recovery, immigration of highland Nahua corn planters, and new village foundations by Negros and Mulattos, who were initially brought to the region for the sugar industry.[24] Population growth sparked a process of new cabecera foundations: Zapotitlán in 1673, Tuzamapa in 1694, Zongozotla in 1709, Nanacatlán in 1714, and Tenampulco in 1777. One by one, the cabeceras that eventually would form Tetela's six municipalities gained their autonomy.[25] All of these secessions and village foundations were achieved as a consequence of local initiative provoking a pragmatic response from the cabecera of the *corregimiento* in Tetela, which was concerned with maintaining the flow of tribute.

Tetela-Jonotla as a viable political entity was reconfirmed in 1787 when it became a *sub-delegación*, along with Huauchinango, Zacatlán, and Teziutlán (Zacapoaxtla and Tlatlauqui remained under San Juan de los Llanos). With the first Federal Republic in 1824, Tetela-Jonotla emerged as a separate *partido*, with Zacapoaxtla also gaining separate *partido* status in the following year (Tlatlauqui had to wait until 1849).[26] These *partidos*, in turn, were grouped into *departamentos* (of which there were seven in the state) with Tetela and Huauchinango belonging to Zacatlán between 1826 and 1861. The *partidos* of Zacapoaxtla, Tlatlauqui, and Teziutlán belonged to the department of San Juan de los Llanos. Hence, the Puebla Sierra was divided into two larger administrative-judicial blocs, with the frontier between them running along the eastern boundary of Tetela.

By the mid-nineteenth century, this boundary had come under increasing pressure from Zacapoaxtla, which in 1849 attempted unsuccessfully to annex Tetela's tropical dependencies of Zapotitlán, Zongozotla, Nanacatlán, and Tuxtla.[27] These territorial ambitions in Tetela were rooted in growing Zacapoaxteco commercial interests, particularly in Jonotla, which Zacapoaxtla again attempted to annex in 1870 (in exchange for ceding Xochiapulco to Tetela).[28]

At mid-century, Tetela also faced pressure much closer to the cabecera, from neighboring Aquixtla, with the uprooting of boundary stones and the violent intimidation of barrio dwellers on the southwestern flank of the district.[29] This boundary with Aquixtla remained a flashpoint throughout the subsequent quarter century of armed conflict. Lucas was personally responsible for settling soldier-peasants along this flank, who, in cooperation with his allies (the Márquez clan in the Zacatlán barrio of Otlatlán), succeeded in keeping their Conservative adversaries in Aquixtla and Chignahuapan at bay.

In spite of the threat to the integrity of its tropical dependencies from Zacapoaxtla, the district of Tetela emerged territorially strengthened from the revolution of Ayutla in 1854. Indeed, the widespread support in the Sierra for the revolution had much to do with the desire of the future district capitals, such as Tetela, Zacapoaxtla, Tlatlauqui, and Teziutlán, to emancipate themselves from their former colonial cabeceras. Resentment of the latter three *partidos* toward San Juan de los Llanos was expressed with particular virulence.[30]

The *partido* and sub-prefecture of Tetela enjoyed a more comfortable relationship with its cabecera in Zacatlán. Indeed, long after being separated administratively, throughout the civil and patriotic wars, the Zacatecos and Tetelenses cooperated to great effect. The eastern boundary of Tetela, marked by the precipitous Apulco gorge, served as the battle line of Liberal *serranos* throughout the second half of the nineteenth century. Only after the revolutionary convention of Aguascalientes in 1915, with the decision of the Márquez of Otlatlán to ally with the Conventionists and the choice of the Tetelenses under Lucas to opt for the Constitutionalists, did the Tetela-Zacatlán alliance fragment. However, after the massacre of the Márquez family in 1920, Lucas's successor, Gabriel Barrios, rebuilt the alliance, which served as the basis of his *cacicazgo* until Plutarco Elías Calles removed him from the Sierra in 1929.

The departments (renamed "prefectures" during Santa Anna's centralized regime) were finally abolished in 1861 when the new state constitution declared Tetela free from the tutelage of Zacatlán, placing Aquixtla under its jurisdiction.[31] However, Tetela still lacked judicial autonomy, being obliged to take all civil and criminal cases either to San Juan de los Llanos or Zacatlán for adjudication. After the European Intervention (during which the French had unsuccessfully attempted to establish a new state with its capital at Zacatlán), Tetela's judicial dependency devolved upon Zacapoaxtla. Finally, after much petitioning from the Tetelense deputy, General Juan Crisóstomo Bonilla (who had furnished the dubious proof that Tetela possessed more than 30,000 inhabitants) and in the face of a threat of revolt, Tetela was granted its own Juzgado de Primera Instancia (court of first appeal) and was formally constituted as a judicial district, composed of the municipalities of Aquixtla, Tetela, Tuzamapa, Jonotla, and Zapotitlán.[32]

With the annexation of Xochiapulco in June 1870, balanced by the unlamented loss of troublesome Aquixtla to the new district of Alatriste, Tetela reached the peak of its territorial development. In 1871 the district comprised six constitutional municipalities—Tetela de Ocampo, Zapotitlán, Huitzilan, Jonotla, Tuzamapa, and Xochiapulco—each with one alcalde, five *regidores,* and one *síndico.* Tetela de Ocampo and Xochiapulco both possessed *villa* status, meriting two alcaldes each. Under the jurisdiction of the six full ayuntamientos were a further twelve *juntas municipales* (each comprised of a single alcalde, *regidor,* and *síndico*) who represented villages subject to the municipal cabeceras.[33]

Tetela de Ocampo also served as the seat of the jefe político.[34] Although the position was at first envisaged as simply an agent of the executive on the district level, the introduction of the elective principle in 1861, and his greatly enhanced executive role, transformed the jefe político from a mere rubber stamp of the governor to the fount of an extensive network of patronage and the symbol of district sovereignty. By the early 1870s, the jefe político exercised patronage over three hundred posts.[35] (*See* Table 2–4.)

Table 2–4. Public Servants in the District of Tetela in 1874[36]	
Group	*Number*
Jefe político, his secretary and scribe	3
Post Office	3
Administration of Sealed Paper	1
Revenues (administrator, scribe, two collectors, two guards)	6
Civil Registry	9
Six ayuntamientos and twelve *juntas municipales*	101
Schoolteachers (in 1879)	42
Judicial functionaries in Tetela de Ocampo	15
Judicial functionaries in the district	87
National Guard commanders, officers, and non-commissioned officers (in 1869)	72
Total	*339*

With the restoration of the direct popular elections for the jefes políticos following the revolution of Tuxtepec, the district of Tetela had become a veritable city-state, controlling its own revenues, National Guard, and justice, with its southern boundaries defended by loyal military colonies of landholding peasants. With one Tetelense in the interim presidency (Méndez), another as the Governor of the Federal District and future Puebla state governor (Bonilla), and another soon to be elected jefe político of Tetela (Lucas), the twenty years of privation and armed struggle must have seemed worthwhile. However, this moment proved to be the zenith of the Tetelenses in state and national politics. By the mid-1880s, Tetela's political assertiveness had been successfully curbed through a process of conciliation and armed repression by the federal and state governments.

Aguardiente and Economic Reciprocity

From the early nineteenth century, the commercialization of *panela* and the production and sale of aguardiente grew to exercise a pervasive impact upon politics and inter-ethnic relations throughout the Sierra. By mid-century, the production, commerce, and consumption of aguardiente had become so widespread that it is easy to overlook its political significance. Oblique references are made to aguardiente in notarial contracts (e.g., that a buyer of land should not set up a still because the seller has the local monopoly); in reports on preparations of community festivals (e.g., that aguardiente should not be sold for the duration of festivities), in explanations for why porters and muleteers had delivered goods late or why soldiers had reported for duty in a dishevelled state (because of heavy drinking on the way). But there are no tidy statistics for the production, sale, or taxation of the commodity that probably contributed more to the personal wealth of village notables, and to their ability to influence the rest of the population, than any other product.[37]

Apart from its obvious commercial and fiscal importance, aguardiente played a vital political role around elections, National Guard musters, and troop mobilizations. Aguardiente was also important in ritual. Swigs served as necessary pledges in business dealings. Village secretaries would occasionally accompany their correspondence to the jefe político with jars of cane syrup.[38] Aguardiente consumption also eased relations between the Indian officeholders and non-Indian village secretaries. Indeed, the local aguardiente producer-cum-village secretary and tax collector (often doubling as the village schoolmaster) was the key to the wider patronage network of the district.[39]

In the district capital of Tetela, most of the prominent families—Méndez, Luna, Rivera, Bonilla, Cabrera, Palacios, López, Manzano, Zamítez, and Posadas, including three prominent Liberal military commanders (Pilar Rivera, Juan N. Méndez, and Lauro Luna)—either owned aguardiente distilleries or dealt in the liquor.[40] Aguardiente distilling in the highland valleys around Tetela linked these families (mostly merchants who also dabbled in agriculture, milling, baking, lard making, mining, and investments) directly with the *panela* dealers in the *tierra cálida* and with the *panela* producers in the *tierra caliente*, where the cane was grown and refined on small, primitive *trapiches* (sugar presses).

The principal centers of cane and *panela* production were Huitzilan and Zapotitlán, which occupied a precipitous swath of territory between Cuautempan and the *tierra caliente* of Jonotla. Commercial interests in Zacapoaxtla, Tetela, and Zacatlán had jostled for control over this area ever since its native ruler, Actatzintecuhtli (meaning "lord of canes. . . . who took this name because of the abundance of sugar cane") had submitted to the Cortes soon after the Conquest.[41] During the nineteenth century, particularly in times of war, the authorities in Tetela monitored this zone closely, since village authorities and their opponents were tempted to ally with forces from beyond the district, threatening Tetela's principal source of revenue and challenging its control over the north of the district.[42]

Wills left by *panela* dealers in Huitzilan and Zapotitlán from the 1840s to the 1880s reveal a small guild of men who kept general stores in the cabeceras, lived in substantial tile-roofed dwellings in the main squares, and owned a good number of small ranches with *trapiches*. These dealers succeeded in dividing up the longer-distance market for *panela* between them, through the control of credit to *panela* and cane producers.[43] In both municipalities, the principal *panela*- and aguardiente-producing families enjoyed a virtual monopoly of senior municipal offices throughout the second half of the nineteenth century. These families were closely tied to the

principal commercial and aguardiente-distilling families in Tetela de
Ocampo through trade, credit, and compadrazgo. They were also vital to
the overall administration of the district in peacetime and in war.[44]

Strategies of Authority and Obedience

Commerce and credit can help to explain the strength of political ties between leading *gente de razón* in the highland district capital and their
counterparts in municipal cabeceras far away in the *tierra caliente*. But
why did Indian authorities in subject villages continue to obey their municipal and district cabeceras, particularly when demands upon them increased so markedly during the quarter century of civil and patriotic
warfare following the revolution of Ayutla? On a visit to the Sierra in
1927, Moisés Saenz, secretary of public education, noticed an ambiguity
in Indian community politics. Non-Indian village secretaries seemed to
command a Pavlovian obedience and deference from villagers, yet
democratically elected Indian village officeholders and elders continued
to possess an unrivaled and unquestioning authority.[45] In his research on
Huitzilan, James Taggart confirmed this ambivalence in mestizo-Indian
relations, observing a seemingly contradictory oscillation between violent hostility and reverential deference to dominant non-Indian entrepreneurs (namely, the coffee and aguardiente merchants and cattle
dealers who controlled Huitzilan). Taggart gives the example of the funeral of a prominent non-Indian landowner, murdered in a gunfight by
his brother, attended not only by his own estate dependents and debtors
but also by the entire community. The funeral procession was led by one
hundred Nahua insurgents, who were then engaged in a struggle to wrest
land from the small but powerful non-Indian landed group of whom the
deceased had been the most prominent member.[46] Why such a unanimous expression of collective grief should be shown over the death of
one who had exercised such a dominant and exploitative hold over the
municipality was not clear. Taggart surmised that the intensive network
of compadrazgo, credit, and commercial ties between this powerful entrepreneur and many members of the community was behind this demonstration of unity.

During the nineteenth century, non-Indians were far less dominant in
Huitzilan (and in Tetela's other municipalities in the *tierra cálida* and
tierra caliente) than when Taggart worked in Huitzilan during the 1960s
and 1970s. However, in relative terms, the intrusion of non-Indian commercial farmers, village secretaries, and schoolmasters that accompanied a
prolonged period of warfare and the application of a hefty bundle of
Liberal reforms represented a major change in the internal organization and
external relations of Indian communities. Frank Schenk's study of the im-

pact of these changes in an inaccessible district of the state of Mexico demonstrates how distance from the seat of state government facilitated non-compliance with outside directives.[47] However, when the source of administrative initiative was as much the district as the state capital, and when district authorities, such as those in Tetela, were determined to tighten their hold over the district, the option of "obedezco pero no cumplo" (I obey but I do not carry out) was not available. District government then became a matter of negotiation. Subject authorities adopted positions ranging from pledges of filial obedience to intimations of the danger of rebellion in their communications with the jefe político, who frequently was referred to in correspondence as "Father of the District."[48]

The language of village-jefe político communications reveals some of the shared assumptions about what constituted good government. The analogy between the jefe político as the father and the subject community as his children identifies an ideal, patriarchal basis for power relationships inherited from colonial times.[49] The ideal of patriarchal authority was that power should be exercised fairly in accordance with natural justice. Nahua families were patrilocal, patriarchal, and patrilineal, with the senior male responsible not only for the welfare of the domestic group but also for organizing work groups from among neighboring families for planting distant maize plots in the *tierra caliente*.[50] In turn, village government in the Sierra deferred to councils of elders (*pasados*—past officeholders) who, because of the unusual longevity in the region, could be very old and very numerous.[51] Indian communities were notoriously intolerant of men who failed to live up to what was expected of the good father of the family. Nahua folk tales are redolent with examples of the fate awaiting the idle or negligent male.[52]

In contrast to the village and the municipality, the district-level government possessed no such natural, built-in checks upon improper behavior. Traditions of paternal responsibility and filial obedience therefore had to be formally invoked in correspondence. The direct popular election of jefes políticos introduced in 1861 was an attempt to make them more accountable. But, ultimately, the quality of district government depended upon the whims of gubernatorial patronage. The legitimacy of regional caciques, such as Lucas, rested upon their ability to resist poor or arbitrary district government. Lucas could appear as the good father—the "Patriarch of the Sierra"—who strove to restore the moral equilibrium of districts brought to the point of rebellion by oppressive jefes políticos and the rapacious private interests which they were failing to keep in check. During the Liberal era, such a counterpoise was doubly necessary for, once the new lines of jurisdiction were set, villages found less easy recourse to the option of secession and the search for a less oppressive cabecera, the time-hallowed local strategy which was the antidote to arbitrary authority throughout the colonial period.[53]

Conclusion

This chapter has shown how certain natural strategic advantages, historical precedents in the control of an extensive territory, and economic factors associated with the growth of the *panela* and aguardiente business bolstered the political aspirations of Tetela's Liberal leadership during the second half of the nineteenth century. Tetela's political ascendancy was constructed hesitantly, almost accidentally. Without the challenge of Conservative Zacapoaxtla, its politically assertive and economically more dynamic neighbor, Tetela most probably would have remained a sleepy *serrano* backwater, content with maintaining its traditional tributary relationship over its five municipalities. The fact that forgotten "Tetela de Oro," briefly renowned for its short silver boom during the later eighteenth century when it acquired its own mint, had become a century later "Tetela de Ocampo," the birthplace of Puebla's Liberal revolution, owed much to chance.

3

Rebellion and Revolution

Juan Francisco Lucas was born to María Francisca and José Manuel Lucas on 24 June 1834, in Zacapoaxtla's adjacent barrio of Comaltepec.[1] His father made a living by grazing sheep on the municipal commons and on land rented from the neighboring hacienda of Xochiapulco and Manzanilla, where he also worked for a time as the administrator.[2] He also carded and dealt in wool, a common occupation among the residents of the land-hungry barrios of the cold, southern Sierra adjoining the cereal-producing hacienda districts of the plateau. Between 1837 and 1847, Juan Francisco attended Zacapoaxtla primary school, completing his formal education at the age of fourteen whereupon he was sent to Altotonga, in the Sierra de Veracruz, to work for his father's wool business.[3] Although Juan Francisco was proficient in carding and weaving, in Altotonga he was engaged principally in selling his father's wool to handloom weavers.[4] Clearly, the Lucases were a comfortably off Indian family, with commercial and agricultural activities spanning a large swath of the southern Sierra and with aspirations to respectability and political influence that would accrue from Juan Francisco's literacy.

In Altotonga, Juan Francisco acquired a taste for business which he retained for the rest of his life. However, in 1850, his commercial apprenticeship was cut short when, as he later recalled, "I was summoned by my father to settle the problem that had arisen between the inhabitants of Comaltepec and the hacienda of Manzanilla." At the age of sixteen, Juan Francisco returned to the *ranchería* of Cuatecomaco (near Comaltepec, and where the family had just moved) to act as his father's secretary in pressing home a legal suit over customary access to the hacienda of Xochiapulco and Manzanilla. This dispute had gone on for almost a century.[5]

The Cuatecomaco Ridge

The Cuatecomaco ridge was populated by three squatter barrios—Cuatecomaco, Texococo, and Cuacualaxtla—which were settled by Nahua Indians whose livelihood depended upon access, as renters, to the hacienda of Xochiapulco and Manzanilla, an arable and cattle-fattening estate belonging to the Salgado family since the end of the eighteenth century. The irregular status of the *indios cuatecomacos* lends some credence to a story recorded by Manuel Pozos, a local schoolteacher, that these Indians were the beleaguered last remnants of the Teteltipan, a tribe never vanquished by Spanish domination. Pozos claimed that this tribe had originally inhabited the land later occupied by the hacienda. They had paid the price for clinging to their freedom by seeing their best maize and grazing lands denounced by Spaniards as *baldíos* (vacant lands). He also claimed that José Manuel Lucas was chosen to represent the *indios cuatecomacos* because of his descent from a noble Aztec warrior.[6]

However doubtful this claim may be, given the decline of the Aztec nobility and the unimportance of the hereditary principal among the Nahua, by the 1840s, José Manuel nevertheless was acknowledged as the leader of the three squatter barrios located along the Cuatecomaco ridge, to the southeast of Zacapoaxtla. On two occasions, he took the dispute with the hacienda to the state capital. On another, he organized a mass invasion of the estate, transporting the Salgado family along with its goods, servants, and animals to Zacapoaxtla, where they were deposited at the edge of the main square.[7]

The Xochiapulco conflict had its origins in the appropriation of lands left vacant after epidemics, especially the devastating pandemic of *matlazahuatl* (smallpox) of 1737. With demographic recovery during the second half of the eighteenth century, Indians sought to reoccupy land that they claimed originally had been theirs. In 1755, Captain Antonio González de Herrera, the owner of the hacienda of Xochiapulco, disarmed Indian farmers who had settled on the eastern margins of the estate, along the Cuatecomaco ridge (by removing their machetes and axes). He then ordered the squatters to leave his land and reported them to the authorities.[8] By dint of the owner's influence with the Real Audiencia, the case was resolved in his favor, on the condition that he return the tools to the Indians and give them preference over others in rental agreements. This remained the position for the *indios cuatecomacos* until the recrudescence of tensions with the owner during the 1840s.

Throughout the 1830s and 1840s, the Salgado family failed to make any profits from the hacienda of Xochiapulco and Manzanilla.[9] This fact conforms to John Tutino's concept of "agrarian decompression": that throughout much of the first two-thirds of the nineteenth century, highland haciendas were failing to compete with a resurgence of Indian community agriculture and the proliferation of small farms.[10] Mallon asserts the contrary: that the agrarian tensions around the hacienda of Xochiapulco arose from the intensification of sugarcane production in the area, displacing Indian grazing and corn farming. This causation is impossible given that sugarcane is not grown at this altitude due to the frequency of late frosts.[11]

The Cuatecomaco ridge was not the only agrarian trouble spot in the vicinity of Zacapoaxtla. The area to the west of Zacapoaxtla possesses some of the finest land for growing maize in the southern Sierra. With Indian population recovery, competition over access to this land increased. A community which became particularly assertive in reclaiming lost commons during the early 1840s was San Miguel de Huahuaxtla. Because of its strategic position on the only easily traversable route between Zacapoaxtla and the neighboring district capital of Tetela, and also on the road between highland Zacapoaxtla and the municipality of Xochitlán in the *tierra calida*, Huahuaxtla became an important focus of political and military conflict throughout the subsequent thirty years. In 1840 this Nahua village renewed litigation against the neighboring mestizo barrio of San Esteban de Tetela, in an attempt to regain its legal boundaries, which were last agreed upon in 1709.[12] The Huahuaxtecos, many of whom were obliged to migrate for much of the year to the *tierra caliente* to plant maize, claimed that "during the insurgency, the inhabitants of Tetela burnt the houses of Huahuaxtla, killed the alcalde, and stole the papers." They now had no land for planting maize, since San Esteban's encroachments had reached the walls of the church.[13]

The Cuatecomaco dispute and Huahuaxtla's attempts to regain its despoiled commons were linked. The southern boundary of Huahuaxtla's commons in 1709, which its inhabitants aspired to recover, was marked by the Cuatecomaco ridge. Moreover, the village's legal action in 1840 was brought by "all the past and present justices of the peace of the village," among whom was Juan Lucas, José Manuel's brother and Juan Francisco's uncle and godfather. During the 1860s, Juan Francisco became the unofficial spokesman for Huahuaxtla whose maize farmers were by then occupying land within the boundaries of another private estate, the Rancho de Apulco, situated at one of the few easily traversable river crossings, linking Zacapoaxtla with the *tierra caliente* of its district, a place of great strategic importance.[14]

Between them, Cuatecomaco and Huahuaxtla effectively hemmed in Zacapoaxtla from the northwest, west, and southwest. The battle line between two mutually hostile axes of villages—a crescent of rebellious villages to Zacapoaxtla's west and a constellation of client villages to the east—was already being drawn during the 1840s.

Agrarianism and Liberal Politics

By the early 1850s, relieved of one-half of its territory in the war with the United States and beset by seemingly unresolvable political and ideological divisions, Mexico had reached the brink of national disintegration. In 1853, in desperation, officers of the regular army invited the patriotic yet

politically inept and discredited General Antonio López de Santa Anna to return from exile to assume the presidency. His ultra-Conservative, over-
centralized, and visibly corrupt regime clashed with the mood of wounded
national pride, enlightened introspection, and revived federalism within the
Liberal Party that had appeared after Mexico's humiliating defeat in 1848.
Uncoordinated and localized federalist skirmishes broadened into a national
movement led by the moderate Poblano Liberal, Ignacio Comonfort, and the
old insurgent and federalist, Juan Alvarez, from the coast of Guerrero. The
political significance of localized agrarian disputes, such as the conflicts in
Cuatecomaco and Huahuaxtla, was suddenly enhanced, as federalist leaders
offered help with their resolution in exchange for military support.[15]

In Puebla after the American War, armed peasants throughout the
mountainous peripheries of the state intensified their pressure for resolution
of land conflicts, taking advantage of the power vacuum in state and
national politics. Between May and December 1851 the Indian leader Juan
Clara, with a following of over one thousand Pitzotzin Indians, led a rebellion in the southern district of Chiautla. Between June and November 1852,
Juan Climaco Rebolledo's rebellion in the sierra of central Veracruz spread
across into much of eastern Puebla, its suppression incurring crippling military expenditure for Puebla's governor, Juan Mujica y Osorio. On the
plateau, banditry became more flagrant during 1853, while in the state capital itself, clerical conspiracies, military coups, and barrio riots increasingly
took the place of the formal administration of city and state.[16]

In the early 1850s, José Manuel broadened his petitioning on behalf of
the barrio of Cuatecomaco, from matters of customary rights and rental
terms upon the hacienda of Xochiapulco, to the question of ownership. He
now claimed to speak not only for the squatter barrios but also for the
peones residing within the boundaries of the hacienda.[17] Rather than seek
annexation to the municipality of Zacapoaxtla, José Manuel chose to petition for separate municipal status for the Cuatecomaco barrios.[18] Since the
seventeenth century, this had been normal practice for population centers of
more than one thousand souls that lacked formal political status and sufficient land for their subsistence.[19]

José Manuel chose a politically sensitive though ultimately propitious
moment for pressing this solution to the agrarian problem. The owners of
the hacienda of Xochiapulco and Manzanilla, the brothers Domingo and
Francisco Salgado, were facing a critical problem of indebtedness, prompting the sale of some smaller properties and leaving them at least open to
the idea of expropriation with compensation.[20] In 1852, José Manuel
decided to bypass the cabecera at Zacapoaxtla and go directly to San Juan
de los Llanos to press Cuatecomaco's claims.

In San Juan de los Llanos, former seat of the *alcalde mayor* (colonial
district administration), situated in the center of a region of large cereal estates, the authorities were unlikely to be sympathetic to agrarian claims.

Indeed, the *juzgado* promptly imprisoned José Manuel. After three months, he was transferred to Zacapoaxtla, where at the end of September 1852 men from the barrios of Cuatecomaco, Texococo, Cuacualaxtla, and Yautetelco stormed the jail, releasing him and the other prisoners. The armed conflict with Zacapoaxtla that would rage well into the 1870s had begun.[21]

Undeterred by his incarceration, early in 1853 José Manuel decided to appeal directly to Santa Anna. He traveled by foot to Mexico City accompanied by his son, possibly Juan Francisco's only visit to the national capital. They were at first encouraged by the president's positive response but dismayed later in the year when Santa Anna decreed that no settlement upon private land could constitute itself as a formal political entity without the owner's consent. Santa Anna, on the advice of his Conservative minister, Lucas Alamán, placed a moratorium on the formation of new municipalities and restricted municipal councils to departmental and prefectural capitals.[22] Santa Anna's last measures included the re-introduction of an Indian head tax and the tightening of secular enforcement of the payment of parish fees. These measures were designed to restore the Indian population to its separate corporate status and to stall the avalanche of local initiatives directed at village formation and hacienda repartition, which had been building up since the early 1840s.[23]

Compounding the tensions between the assertive villages along the Cuatecomaco ridge and their cabecera was a conflict between the parish priest of Zacapoaxtla and his parishioners in the villages of Comaltepec, Atagpan, and Cuacualaxtla over the payment of parish fees and tithes. These barrios chose José Manuel to represent them.[24] The conflict with the Church, combined with Santa Anna's legal barriers to village formation, convinced José Manuel to approach the Liberal Party in 1854, at the beginning of the revolution of Ayutla.

Lucas's Adhesion to the Liberal Party

The struggle between Zacapoaxtla and the *indios cuatecomacos* led by José Manuel would almost certainly have remained a local and containable "Indian problem," had not the political conflicts following the revolution of Ayutla converged upon Zacapoaxtla. Throughout the 1850s and 1860s, Zacapoaxtla repeatedly served as a springboard for Conservative attempts at political resurgence in state politics. To act as a counterpoise, Liberal administrations encouraged disobedience among Zacapoaxtla's dependent Indian barrios, promising satisfaction of their political and agrarian aspirations.[25] Under such circumstances, José Manuel's small yet well-organized agrarian movement could exploit its bargaining position to break out from the vicious circle of enforced obedience to the cabecera in Zacapoaxtla, punctuated by occasional disobedience, imprisonments, and jailbreaks.

Several factors contributed to the drift from petitioning and litigation to outright warfare. The first was the enthusiastic response of the neighboring sub-prefecture of Tetela to the Ayutla movement.[26] By mid-August 1855, Tetela de Oro and most of its subject municipalities had embraced the Plan de Ayutla.[27] The response from Zacapoaxtla was belated. Zacapoaxtla's council only adhered to the Plan de Ayutla on 14 November 1855, disavowing it a month later.[28] While there is no evidence of Tetela Liberals actively encouraging the Cuatecomacos before the outbreak of the Three Years' War in 1858 (indeed, Tetela cooperated with Zacapoaxtla in the pursuit of prisoners freed by José Manuel on 5 October 1855), the existence of a zone of retreat in this Liberal district weakened the authority of Zacapoaxtla over its already discontented western barrios.[29]

If Liberals locally proved guarded in their attitude toward Indians entering politics and pursuing agrarian claims, no such reserve was shown by Juan Alvarez during his brief, two-month presidency between October and December 1855. Aware of José Manuel's influence in the region, Alvarez sent him arms, ammunition, and instructions to organize military forces in the Zacapoaxtla area. José Manuel chose the barrio of Cuatecomaco as the headquarters for this force.[30] One of his first actions under this novel presidential patronage was to lead, at daybreak on 5 October 1855, "a considerable force of Indians" in storming the Zacapoaxtla jail, releasing all the prisoners and taking twenty rifles. Several of those released figured prominently in subsequent conflicts as National Guard commanders and community leaders in the new municipality of Xochiapulco. Most of the escaped prisoners took flight to the districts of Tetela and Zacatlán.[31]

While the storming of the jail was a common occurrence, the theft of rifles by Indians caused a considerable stir throughout the Sierra. Even Liberal district administrations, such as that of Ramón Márquez in Zacatlán, spoke of the imminence of a caste war.[32] The events in Zacapoaxtla sparked troubles elsewhere in the districts of Zacapoaxtla and Tetela. In Huahuaxtla, Huitzilan, and Zapotitlán, Indian leaders "Luis," Pablo Lázaro, and José Diego, all prominent dealers in *panela*, demanded repayment of the now abolished head tax and attempted to topple the municipal governments.[33] Although none of these conflicts came to much, they revealed the potential for alliances between rebels in the highlands and caciques in the lowlands, along the sugar route, the line of supply upon which Lucas later would depend for replenishing the front line with rations.[34]

In any case, José Manuel was far more concerned with achieving municipal status for Xochiapulco than organizing a regional inter-ethnic conflagration. The struggle of the Cuatecomaco Indians was not against the *gente de razón* of the Sierra, but against the town that had successfully denied municipal status to any of the thirty-two settlements (four haciendas, sixteen *rancherías*, and twelve ranchos) that depended upon the only cabecera in the southern part of the district, La Villa de Zacapoaxtla.[35] Locally, prospects for upgrading scattered *rancherías* and ranchos into a municipality had never been better (Cuatecomaco was listed as a *ranchería*).

If the future of the hacienda of Xochiapulco and Manzanilla as a viable enterprise was uncertain due to Salgado's indebtedness, the fate of the hacienda of Mazapa, the only other large estate in the jurisdiction, was also now in question. In July 1855, Mazapa's owner, Rafael Molina Alcántara, died intestate, leaving a widow and ten children to argue about the division of the estate and numerous other ranches and urban properties.[36] These properties, many adjacent to the landless barrios organized by José Manuel, offered an additional opportunity for the satisfaction of their agrarian aspirations.[37]

If partible inheritance and inter-elite economic rivalry weakened the territorial hold of Zacapoaxtla over the settlements under its jurisdiction, there was nevertheless political unanimity among the Zacapoaxteco elite that something should be done to counteract the mischievous external forces that had been stirring up "their Indians." The prefect of Zacapoaxtla, Mariano Martínez, decided that a preemptive strike on the Cuatecomaco ridge by the full force of Zacapoaxtla's National Guard, in three columns, each of one hundred men, would quell the disorders once and for all.

Given that José Manuel's activity so far had been confined exclusively to bloodless jailbreaks, the vindictive attack by the Zacapoaxtecos upon the *ranchería* of Cuatecomaco and the rancho of Cuacualaxtla on 30 November 1855 was unjustified and imprudent.[38] The Zacapoaxtecos fell into the same trap that would ensnare successive forces (Conservatives in 1857–1860, Austrians in 1864–1866, Federals in 1869–70 and 1871–72) during the subsequent quarter century. Led by José Manuel, Francisco Dinorín, and José María Ascensión, armed principally with machetes and wooden spears, the *indios cuatecomacos* inflicted a humiliating and historic defeat upon the forces from the cabecera in a gully between the Tepechichil and Minillas peaks. Many of the Zacapoaxtecos were killed in flight by the women accompanying José Manuel's force.[39] Relations between Xochiapulco and Zacapoaxtla never recovered from this first major reverse in the balance of ethnic power in the southern Sierra since the Conquest.

Isolation and Dispersal

However spectacular the victory over Zacapoaxtla, José Manuel was acutely aware of the vulnerability and political isolation of his forces in a region where even Liberal district authorities regarded such insolence by Indians as profoundly threatening to the social order.[40] Henceforth, the pursuit of his goals would require greater attention to be paid to developing alliances beyond the district. The immediate consequence of the defeat of the Zacapoaxtecos was that Salgado abandoned his estates and moved his family to Tlatlauqui. José Manuel promptly moved his forces onto the hacienda, sending a vanguard across the district boundary into Tetela.[41]

Before leaving for Mexico City, José Manuel gave instructions to his chiefs to establish a village on the estate. Alvarez congratulated José Manuel on his triumph and approved the foundation of the village, promising that it would be granted the category of municipality once the constitutional order had been re-established. He also provided José Manuel with more arms, encouraging him to continue his heroic defense of the Liberal cause.[42]

News of the victory at Minillas spread quickly throughout the Sierra. If the jailbreak of early October provoked fears of a caste war, the bloody battle of 30 November surely offered proof that the caste war had broken out. Far from recognizing José Manuel's victory as a triumph, authorities in the neighboring Liberal districts of Zacatlán and Tetela regarded the Xochiapulco movement with apprehension.[43] Encircled by hostile authorities, without a zone of retreat, José Manuel's force was violently dispersed on 7 December, with many rebels losing their lives or suffering arrest.[44] The pursuit continued into 1856, with Tetela's authorities arresting suspects as late as October under the vagrancy laws.[45]

One of the first to be arrested in Tetela on 7 December was Juan Francisco, who had set off in pursuit of his father after the dispersal of his force.[46] Taken first to Tetela de Oro, from where he was sent to Zacapoaxtla, then on to Libres, Juan Francisco ended his journey in the Puebla state penitentiary early in January 1856. There, he might have served out an ignominious sentence had not dramatic events in mid-January brought his release in exchange for service in the artillery.

The Rebellion of Guitián and the Plan de Zacapoaxtla

On 11 December 1855 a popular uprising broke out in barrios of the state capital, encouraged by priests and led by the Conservative cavalry officer, Francisco Guitián, proclaiming for "religión y fueros" and against the Plan de Ayutla.[47] The moderate Liberal state governor, Francisco Ibarra y Ramos, succeeded in swiftly suppressing the movement, but the Conservative revolt passed to the Sierra where the initiative was taken by Zacapoaxtla's parish priest, Francisco Ortega.[48]

After the promulgation of the Ley Juárez in November that abolished the special *fueros* of the clergy and the army, Ortega had begun to organize an uprising in the Sierra to coincide with a popular movement in the state capital. On 12 December 1855, the day after Guitián's *pronunciamiento* in Puebla (and Comonfort's takeover of the presidency from Alvarez), Francisco Ortega and Zacapoaxtla's military commander, Colonel Lorenzo Bulnes, issued the Plan de Zacapoaxtla, declaring the

Puebla Sierra to be in revolt and claiming to speak on behalf of the entire district.[49] Driven from the state capital, Guitián's forces joined up with discontented Conservative military officers from throughout the republic and converged upon the Sierra.

The Conservative insurrection in Puebla soon acquired a leader of national renown. Early in January 1856 the Poblano Conservative (later monarchist) statesman, Antonio Haro y Tamariz, escaped from custody on his journey into exile and took charge of the rebellion.[50] Following the defection to the rebel camp of a Liberal force sent to suppress the rebellion, Haro y Tamariz was able to advance swiftly upon the central valley of Puebla, laying siege to the state capital on 17 January and taking it six days later. The fall of Mexico's second city to the Conservatives posed a particularly severe threat to the Liberal regime, given the city's strategic location on the route to Veracruz, its important bishopric and still influential Church bodies. The victorious Ayutlan National Guards, which had begun to be disbanded, were hastily reassembled and sent to Puebla to defend the Liberal republic.[51]

By late February, Comonfort had amassed 12,000 troops that he led personally to retake Puebla. The Liberal army met Haro y Tamariz's much smaller force of 3,500 at Ocotlán on 8 March. After several hours of bloody fighting, causing almost 800 losses on the rebel side (119 dead, 98 wounded, 180 fallen prisoner, and over 400 dispersed), Haro y Tamariz withdrew to Puebla, which he defended for fourteen days until submitting to Comonfort's superior force on 22 March 1856.[52]

During this intense fighting, Juan Francisco Lucas served his military apprenticeship as an artilleryman during the battle of Ocotlán and the siege of Puebla. It is uncertain which army Lucas, drafted along with many others from the penitentiary, was fighting in.[53] Whether as part of a Liberal or Conservative unit, Lucas nevertheless took to arms naturally, particularly to light artillery. In the subsequent thirty years, Lucas's reputation as a military commander rested upon his ability to combine effective guerrilla warfare with daring attacks upon Sierra towns with the help of artillery. He remained a soldier on the active list until his death in 1917.

The defeat of Haro y Tamariz and the proven complicity of the Puebla clergy in the Conservative uprising had two important consequences in Puebla.[54] The first was Comonfort's decision to hurry through the intervention of Church wealth in Puebla in order to undermine Conservative political ambitions. The second was the decision to strengthen the Liberal state administration by transferring the governorship from the moderate civilian, Ibarra y Ramos, to General Juan Bautista Traconis, a ruthless commander from beyond the state, bringing to an end forty years of locals occupying the state executive.[55] The selection of the state of Puebla as a test case for the forceful and exemplary implementation of the Liberal reform program was a political decision with fateful consequences. From September 1856, commencing with an abortive Conservative barracks revolt in Puebla, followed by General Juan Calderón's uprising on the central plateau, the political order throughout the state steadily disintegrated.[56]

The Liberal state government managed to hold onto the state capital for another year. However, in December 1857 the city's garrison pronounced behind General Miguel María Echeagaray, seconding General Zuloaga's Plan de Tacubaya in Mexico City. When in early January 1858, Comonfort resigned the presidency, Puebla's Liberal state government fled to the Sierra Norte, where it remained for the rest of the decade. The Three Years' War had begun.

Xochiapulco's Alliance with Tetela

Throughout 1856 and 1857 the Liberal state government was too heavily occupied in the central and southern parts of the state to exert much influence in the Sierra. Moreover, Sierra Liberals remained largely parochial, concerned with maintaining order in their own districts. Yet the Comonfort government was eager to control this region of strategic importance under threat from the Conservatives, especially from Zacapoaxtla's paroled troops. After the submission of Conservative rebel forces in Puebla in March 1856, the principal leaders were sentenced to fight "los indios bárbaros, el enemigo común" in the north of Mexico. However, Zacapoaxtla's officers and troops were returned to their home district, where the Conservatives continued to exercise authority.[57]

To preempt an anticipated renewal of the Conservative offensive in the Puebla Sierra, in early April, Comonfort dispatched three of his most able generals to Zacapoaxtla: Tomás Moreno (Alvarez's old insurgent companion), Ignacio de la Llave, and José María Arteaga.[58] Moreno pushed the rebel leaders into the district of Papantla, where they were caught and sent to Veracruz. He then proceeded to appoint Liberal authorities, including José Manuel and Juan Lucas and José Antonio Atahuit, the principal leaders from Xochiapulco and Huahuaxtla, as councillors in the district capital.[59]

Unaccustomed to being governed by Indians, the Zacapoaxtecos removed these men from office soon after the withdrawal of the Liberal generals. The war of attrition between Xochiapulco and Zacapoaxtla resumed. However, the Plan de Zacapoaxtla had broadened the conflict beyond the immediate vicinity of the cabecera.[60] Becoming particularly attenuated early in 1856 were the relations between Zacapoaxtla and its geographically isolated and hitherto unassertive neighbor to the west, Tetela de Oro.

After the battle of Minillas on 30 November 1855, the prefect of Zacatlán, Ramón Márquez, had ordered Francisco Pérez, sub-prefect of Tetela, to form two columns of infantry to help Zacapoaxtla in the pursuit of José Manuel and his rebel troops. One column, under Manuel Arroyo, reached Zacapoaxtla on 1 December, coinciding with Ortega's promulgation of the Plan de Zacapoaxtla. The other, under Pérez, failed to reach Zacapoaxtla. Without Pérez's authorization, Arroyo was unable to second the Plan.[61] The Tetela sub-prefect's absence was probably deliberate since he had his own reasons for choosing not to pursue the Cuatecomaco rebels with any energy.

Apart from acting as sub-prefect of the district of Tetela, Francisco Pérez was a prominent farmer and tenant of the Rancho de Taxcantla, the district's largest arable and grazing estate, and of several other ranches belonging to the municipality of Tetela. Following the law of 26 June 1856, instructing municipalities to sell off their properties, Pérez had acquired private title to these estates.[62] Taxcantla lay on the western boundary of the hacienda of Xochiapulco and Manzanilla. Pérez had also recently acquired land to the east and south of Salgado's estates: a farm close to Zacapoaxtla in Jilotepec (later to form part of Xochiapulco) and a house and a small farm in Huahuaxtla.[63] He soon became an important producer of maize and dealt in aguardiente, accounting for the purchase of a house on the road between Huahuaxtla and Xochitlán, the route used by Indians bringing sugar loaf from the *tierra caliente*.[64] As one of the few large landowners in this part of the Sierra, Pérez was a rival of the Salgados of Xochiapulco and Manzanilla. The challenge posed by José Manuel Lucas against this estate was unlikely to damage Pérez's business and might even benefit him.

As a result, Pérez avoided any military engagement with José Manuel's following. Indeed, his sympathy for their plight is suggested by the case of Miguel Sánchez of Ometepec (a barrio adjoining the Rancho de Taxcantla, many of whose inhabitants grazed their animals on his estate) who, in December 1855, was accused of "having a pact with the *indígenas* of Zacapoaxtla." Pérez paid the bail and testified to Sánchez's innocence.[65]

Tetela paid dearly for its prevarication in coming to Zacapoaxtla's aid in the suppression of the Cuatecomaco rebels. On 1 January 1856 a force from Zacapoaxtla arrived in Tetela to demand a loan of 1,000 pesos. Juan N. Méndez (by now the sub-prefect but masquerading as an alderman charged with the administration of justice) reluctantly complied, instructing all contributions to be paid to his brother, Mariano Méndez, who would pass on the amount to the Zacapoaxteco commander.[66] Méndez thereby avoided any official complicity with Zacapoaxtla's Conservative rebels. Nevertheless, this tributary status was clearly unsatisfactory for Tetela and its cabecera Zacatlán, both towns that had declared their Ayutlan allegiances.

It was a Conservative rebellion in the sierras of Tulancingo and Zacatlán in November 1856, behind General José Ignacio Gutiérrez, that finally obliged Tetelenses, in the interests of political survival, to adopt a less passive stance and to explore the possibility of a closer association with José Manuel.[67] By August 1856, José Manuel had regrouped his forces, now numbering six hundred, to stage a daring raid on Zacapoaxtla. Although the attack was successfully repulsed (with the death of six of the assailants), three months later, Agustín Roldán, Zacapoaxtla's Conservative commander, asked for three hundred reinforcements or, at the very least, three hundred rifles for arming the locals.[68] To preempt the formation of a Conservative axis linking the sierras of Tulancingo and Puebla, President Comonfort dispatched to Zacatlán General Manuel Soto, who promptly deployed a force in Tetela under General O'Horán. Given this external support, Tetela's lethargic Liberal sympathizers could now hardly remain inactive in the face of the buildup of Conservative power in Zacapoaxtla.

With the help of Cuatecomaco Indians entrenched upon the heights of Ometepec above Tetela, which prevented any westward movement of Zacapoaxteco forces, O'Horán succeeded in holding the Conservatives at bay. However, he advised his superior officer that the Liberal position in the Sierra was weak, with only José Manuel preventing a complete rout.[69] Only with the defeat of General Orihuela's Conservative insurrection in the central valley of Puebla early in December 1856 was the Liberal state government able to regain control of the Sierra.

Twelve months of comparative peace followed. Throughout 1857, José Manuel regrouped his supporters, keeping up the pressure on the Zacapoaxtla authorities.[70] The revolution of Tacubaya on 17 December 1857, followed by the suspension of the Liberal constitution, brought this period of tranquility to a close. Encouraged by events in the national capital, the commander of the Puebla garrison, General Echeagaray, pronounced, compelling Liberal governor Alatriste's flight to the Sierra, where Puebla Liberals would lead a peripatetic existence for the next decade.

Early in 1858, at Zautla, a town on the southern margin of the Sierra (next to Xochiapulco), a Zacapoaxteco force attempted to assassinate Juan Francisco, seriously wounding him. A few days later the same band murdered José Manuel. Command of the Cuatecomacos passed immediately to his wounded son, Juan Francisco, now twenty-four years of age.[71]

Conclusion

From 1852 to 1858 the local struggle between the landless Nahua barrios along the Cuatecomaco ridge, behind their leader, José Manuel Lucas, and the municipal authorities in Zacapoaxtla became ever more directly embroiled with the wider issues that divided Mexicans between the aftermath of the war with the United States and the outbreak of the Three Years' War. The racial intensity of this conflict, the constitutional issues it raised regarding municipal autonomy and equality before the law, the attraction to both Liberals and Conservatives of the strategic location of the southern Puebla Sierra, and their search for allies combined to upgrade the importance of an essentially local movement of maize farmers in search of greater security of tenure and enhanced political autonomy.

By the onset of the Three Years' War in January 1858, a new political geography had taken shape in the Sierra, forged by conflict between competing Liberal and Conservative axes. José Manuel and his followers found themselves on the boundary between Conservative Zacapoaxtla and Liberal Zacatlán, and nestled against a wavering Tetela. This position enhanced their bargaining power while obliging the Tetelenses to decide upon their political priorities and ideological affinities. After the battle of Minillas, Tetela served as a zone of tactical retreat for the Cuatecomacos, leaving it vulnerable to punitive raids and fiscal exactions mounted by Zacapoaxtecos. By 1858, Tetelenses were faced with assertive Conservatives to the west (Tulancingo, Chignahuapan, and Aquixtla) and east (Zacapoaxtla, Tlatlauqui, and Cuetzalan). However ambivalent the Tetelenses may have remained about which side they backed, with the arrival of General O'Horán they were no longer permitted the luxury of choosing.

Little in the behavior of Tetela leaders between 1854 and 1858 suggested that this district would eventually take the lead of the Liberal revolution in the state of Puebla. However, by the onset of the Three Years' War, pressure from Conservatives in Zacapoaxtla and the availability of four companies or more of now-seasoned *indios cuatecomacos* persuaded Tetela's leaders that more could be gained from joining the Liberal side in the mounting conflicts than from performing police duties for the benefit of neighboring authorities in Zacapoaxtla.

4

The Three Years' War

On 22 December 1857 the state government, headed by Miguel Cástulo Alatriste, a young lawyer from the city of Puebla, arrived in Zacatlán de las Manzanas, a Liberal haven since the Insurgency.[1] Soon most of the state, except for pockets in the Sierra, was controlled by the Conservatives under General Echeagaray.[2] Never during the Three Years' War could Liberals retake the state capital, which remained in Conservative hands until 5 January 1861, a full fortnight after the decisive Liberal victory at Calpulalpam (Hidalgo) that ended the war. Throughout the war, Puebla's Liberals commanded more popular support and fielded many more men than their adversaries, yet they suffered a crippling handicap. Enforced peripateticism, far from promoting cooperation, encouraged damaging inter-personal rivalries, often reaching outright conflict. As if these internal divisions were not enough, Liberal commanders—Alatriste, Méndez, Márquez Galindo, Carbajal—refused to cooperate with leaders from neighboring states or acknowledge the authority of military commanders such as Pascual Miranda and Pedro Ampudia, whom Benito Juárez had appointed to bring some order to the front in Puebla.

Part of the problem lay with the structure of the Liberal army in Puebla, which was an amalgam of regular state forces commanded by Cástulo Alatriste (from the center of the state); National Guard infantry and artillery behind Méndez, Márquez Galindo, and Rafael Cravioto (from Tetela, Zacatlán, and Huauchinango, respectively); semi-private squadrons of cavalry commanded by leaders such as Carbajal (from Tlaxcala); and numerous small guerrilla bands led by local caciques. At the beginning of the war, the *indios cuatecomacos* fell within this last category. Three years later, they had become a vital auxiliary force within the Liberal National Guard.

The Rise of the *Indios Cuatecomacos*

During March and April 1858, General Echeagaray and his successor, General Manuel Noriega, took the Tacubaya Conservative counter-revolution to the Sierra. By late March the towns of Chignahuapan, Zacatlán,

Tlacuilo, Pahuatlán, and Jicotepec in the western and northern Sierra had adhered to the Plan de Tacubaya. By mid-April, the towns of Hueytlalpan, Huitzilan, and Zapotitlán in the interior of the Sierra (in the prefectures of Zacatlán and Tetela) had rejected the constitution. By early May, Teziutlán and Tlatlauqui, strategic district capitals in the southern Sierra, had adhered to the Plan de Tacubaya.[3] Zacapoaxtla finally proclaimed for "religión y fueros" on 22 July.[4] Alatriste and Méndez were forced to take sanctuary across the state border in Veracruz, thus leaving Liberals holding out only in Huauchinango and Ahuacatlán.

Early in May 1858, Alatriste and Méndez returned to the Sierra with a small force of National Guard under orders from Juárez to reestablish the constitutional administration in the Puebla Sierra. Reeling from a succession of defeats at the hands of General Echeagaray in Veracruz, Puebla's Liberal military commanders must have doubted their ability to achieve this task. Colonel Méndez briefly took Zacatlán on 5 July, defeating Generals Oronoz and Ignacio Gutiérrez, only to be ejected a few days later. Meanwhile, Governor Alatriste descended to the Gulf plains to help in the successful recapture of the port of Tuxpan from the Conservatives. While awaiting Alatriste's return, Méndez assembled a force of around three hundred men on the Mecapalco hacienda near Teziutlán.[5] From here, Méndez made his first contact with the *indios cuatecomacos*, now led by Juan Francisco Lucas still recovering from his wounds.[6] Desperate for support, Méndez promoted Lucas to the rank of captain, promising arms and ammunition for his men.[7] This was the start of a close partnership between the Tetela caudillo and the Xochiapulco cacique, which would endure until well into the 1880s. The partnership brought an immediate dramatic return for Méndez and the Liberal cause in the Sierra.

Two days after recruiting Lucas's force, Méndez surprised the enemy at the Ranchería de las Filipinas on the border between Puebla and Veracruz. Méndez had less than 500 men facing an enemy numbering 800 backed by four pieces of artillery and 200 Indian sappers (men expert in cutting tracks through woodland and in building and repairing fortifications). In an inspired bluff, Colonel Dimas López, from Zacatlán, blew a cavalry charge on his bugle (Méndez commanded no cavalry at this time), prompting the flight of the enemy at the height of battle. Méndez scored an unexpected but resounding victory.[8] Due to the mountainous terrain, the booty from such victories in the Sierra tended to be large. The Conservative force suffered 139 losses (78 prisoners, 20 wounded, and 41 dead) and abandoned most of its equipment. Much of this was passed directly to Captain Lucas to properly equip his troops.[9]

The battle of Las Filipinas made an important psychological contribution to the rise of the Sierra Liberals. For the first time, Liberal military commanders observed the martial potential of the Indian foot soldier fighting on his own terrain. The perception of the Indian soldier as a reluctant conscript and likely deserter changed to one of aggressive defender of his home, under the authority of a trustworthy local commander of the same race. As a result of the victory, Juárez's forces in the area gained the confidence that they could now take on a fully equipped regular army. Méndez began to look at the Sierra not simply as a refuge for the Liberals but also as a platform for projecting the Liberals to victory on the plateau.[10]

The victory at Las Filipinas also intensified the rivalry between Méndez and Alatriste for the leadership of the state. The battle marked the beginning of the schism that divided Puebla's Liberal Party between Montaña and Llanura factions throughout much of the rest of the century. After the victory, Alatriste and Méndez fought together to recapture the strategic town of Teziutlán. However, the Conservative hold over Zacapoaxtla proved more solid, delaying Alatriste's anticipated advance upon the central plateau and state capital.[11]

Agustín Roldán and the Counter-Reform in Zacapoaxtla

From the Plan de Zacapoaxtla (December 1855), General Roldán had been energetically countering José Manuel's mobilization of Indian villages. Roldán established his own agents in villages to encourage Indians to disobey the reform laws, resist Liberal military recruitment, and organize defense forces to protect the district from Liberal assaults. An incident in November 1856 reveals how Conservative leaders sought to influence Indian villages. While leading a force from Zacapoaxtla to take Tetela de Oro, Conservative agent Fernando López was surprised and captured near Ometepec (Tetela) by José Manuel, captain of the Cuatecomacos. López was handed over to Colonel Manuel Soto, commander of Zacatlán's National Guard, for interrogation. Found on him was a diary of the route that López had taken through the Sierra since General Orihuela's *pronunciamiento* in Puebla on 20 October 1856. The diary, which amounts to a political geography of the Conservative Sierra, describes meetings with parish priests and Conservative leaders throughout the central Sierra. Also found on López were numerous pieces of white paper engraved with the words "Pilita de San Cayetano No. 13," which Soto supposed to be a watchword. Apart from this stamp, Soto also found on López a collection of little stones, each engraved with a viper and inscribed "Teutli" ("Our Lord" in Nahuatl).

In 1862, José María Maldonado, the Liberal military commander of the Sierra, commented that the possession of such stamps and *piedrecitas* was common in the Sierra. A leader would make such donations in the expectation that one day the gifts would be reciprocated, usually through the holding of a party involving the copious consumption of aguardiente. The use of such objects in these troubled times was possibly a consequence of the need felt by Conservative lay and religious leaders to counter Masonic influences among the Indian population. Masonry was reported to be particularly prevalent among the Liberal barrios of Xochiapulco. José María Maldonado believed that the compadrazgo ceremony was being debased because of its excessive use for short-term political advantage. Indians were attracted to Masonry because of its exclusiveness (ceremonies were held in Nahuatl), its secrecy (ensured by the initiation ceremony), and its independence from the clergy, the traditional figures of authority.[12]

The complaints of the *vecinos* of San Esteban and Huahuaxtla against Conservative agents suggest that General Roldán had difficulty in gaining the active support of villagers in the area to the west of Zacapoaxtla where Liberals from Tetela were beginning to have more success. The oppressive involvement of his agents—José María Gómez in Huahuaxtla and Fernando López in the Tetela barrio of San Esteban—provoked serious disorders in these villages. *Vecinos* in San Esteban and Huahuaxtla were angry with López and Gómez for betraying their trust and misappropriating village funds for personal and political gain. Huahuaxtla's grievances came to a head at the end of the Three Years' War. One hundred fifty *vecinos* (mostly Indian, judging from the absence of surnames) complained that Gómez had embezzled the community's funds for three years. Gómez claimed that he was securing Huahuaxtla's land titles from Mexico City when he was using the money to buy arms for Roldán.[13] In San Esteban, using the services of a bilingual resident, López had pressured the *vecinos* to oppose the *desamortización* of village commons, to disobey, and, eventually, to rebel against the authorities in Tetela.[14]

In 1858, however, the most immediate and pressing concern to General Roldán was not Huahuaxtla or San Esteban but the mounting challenge from the *indios cuatecomacos*. These forces had not been deterred by the defeat in November 1856 or by the murder of their leader in January 1858. On the eve of the victory of Las Filipinas in July 1858, Roldán reported rebels assembling in the Xochiapulco area in groups of two hundred.[15] The victory increased the daring and frequency of these attacks upon the cabecera. Roldán charged that the *indios cuatecomacos* were continually being egged on by the Constitutionalists. He asserted that for several years they had been able to buy gunpowder and other military supplies from a commercial house in Tetela belonging to Leocadio Méndez (Juan N. Méndez's uncle), found sanctuary in Tetela when pursued by the Zacapoaxtla authorities, and now were equipped with rifles and "fine ammunition" (presumably the booty from Las Filipinas). Small groups of armed Indians attacked and robbed the ranches and haciendas of peaceful citizens daily, and a force numbering more than two hundred constantly threatened the cabecera. Moreover, Roldán observed, a new leader had emerged alongside José Manuel in Xochiapulco: José María Ascención, one of the twenty-four Indians who had escaped from the Zacapoaxtla jail in October 1855. Roldán accused Ascención of continually inculcating the Indians with the idea of there being "no other government than that emanating from Don Juan Alvarez, with whom they have been in continual relations since he offered them the possession of various haciendas and ranches and promised them self-government."[16]

Hoping to disabuse the Cuatecomacos of this appetite for autonomy, and in the face of approaching Liberal forces under Méndez and Alatriste, Roldán decided to stage a preemptive strike against Xochiapulco. Backed by two hundred Indians and forty-one *gente de razón*, Roldán attacked the rebels encamped at the Rancho de las Lomas on 27 July 1858. After two hours of fighting, the Cuatecomacos fled, leaving four dead and twenty-six wounded. Roldán's force (which suffered no losses) went in pursuit to the *rancherías* of Tetela.[17]

A stalemate had been reached with Roldán firmly established in Zacapoaxtla, and able to count on loyal Indian auxiliaries. The Cuatecomacos could harass but not challenge the cabecera. Roldán possessed the advantage of clerical support and backing from the Conservative state government in Puebla. By contrast, the Tetelenses seemed timid in their support of the Cuatecomacos. Moreover, Alatriste's peripatetic Liberal leadership was still unaccustomed to the Sierra terrain, unsure of its support, and distrustful of local Liberal leaders.

The Alliance Between the Tetelenses and the Cuatecomacos

After the Las Filipinas victory, rather than placing his infantry at risk on the plateau, Méndez moved into the northwestern Sierra and joined Antonio Téllez Vaquier's newly formed Liberal force, based at Pahuatlán and Jicotepec, near Huauchinango. With the help of the cavalry from the plateau under Tlaxcalteco commander Antonio Carbajal, Méndez and Téllez Vaquier succeeded in recapturing Zacatlán and Chignahuapan from the Conservatives in late August 1858.[18] Méndez then assumed the prefecture of Zacatlán, placing his fellow Tetelense National Guard commander, Pilar Rivera, in charge of the sub-prefecture of Tetela on 3 September 1858.[19] Méndez now had a much stronger base from which to organize the assault upon Roldán's stronghold in Zacapoaxtla; however, despite several efforts, Méndez and later Alatriste failed to take the town. As a result, Liberal offensives on the central plateau had to proceed with the Conservatives still in control of the principal town of the Sierra.[20]

In mid-November 1858, Méndez and Téllez Vaquier occupied the southern Sierra towns of Tlaxco and Ixtacamaxtitlán, from where they prepared rearguard support for Alatriste's forces on the plateau. By 13 December 1858, Alatriste and Liberal forces from Oaxaca and Veracruz had succeeded in encircling the state capital, but were neither strong enough, nor sufficiently united, to undertake a prolonged siege. Moreover, Puebla's Liberals were still exposed on their eastern flank from the Conservative garrison at the fortress of Perote (the key stronghold on the Mexico-Veracruz road). On 20 December 1858, General Echeagaray, commander of the Perote garrison, impatient with the hesitancy of his superiors, pronounced against the state and federal executives (Francisco Pérez and Felix Zuloaga) in the Plan de Navidad. Although Echeagaray failed to attract Miguel Miramón to head the rebel Conservative movement, he did succeed in propelling the Conservatives onto the offensive.[21] The Liberal offensive against Puebla was promptly called off, with most forces withdrawing to the Sierra.

In January 1859, Méndez renewed the campaign upon Zacapoaxtla, this time leading forces from Zacatlán and Papantla himself. Anticipating an offensive of altogether grander proportions, General Roldán recalled the one hundred Zacapoaxtecos who had been garrisoning the Perote fortress under Echeagaray. Suggesting that the soldiers should return to Zacapoaxtla to sow maize, Roldán neglected to inform them that they were returning to defend the district against a Liberal army.[22] On 4 February 1859 forces under Méndez and Téllez Vaquier took up positions in Huahuaxtla and Apulco. However, the first attack did not come from the Liberal army encamped on the heights of Apulco but, as Roldán had predicted, from within the ring of defense forces that he had established around the cabecera. A force of four hundred Cuatecomacos attacked Zacapoaxtla on 5 February but was easily repulsed by Zacapoaxtla's militia leaders, Rafael Molina Islas and Ignacio Betancurt. This victory, however, was Pyrrhic.

Conservative Zacapoaxtla was now defended by only three hundred men, less than half the size of the force that had successfully repelled Alatriste in November 1858.[23] Meanwhile, Méndez had gathered the National Guard from Tetela, Zacatlán, Huauchinango, and "Los Defensores Xicotencatl de Tlaxcala" numbering five hundred and twenty men. Méndez's forces were joined by one hundred Cuatecomacos commanded by Captains Juan Francisco Lucas and José Gabriel. After several skirmishes, the Liberals occupied the village of Huahuaxtla. Indian sappers constructed a wooden bridge over the Apulco that enabled Méndez to use artillery to a devastating effect.[24] After a further battle at Apulco and the burning of houses in Las Lomas, the Conservatives took flight. Accompanied by a bedraggled following of fifty men and a few officers, Roldán reported to General Miguel Negrete at the fortress of Perote on 19 February.[25] After five years of resistance to the Reform, Conservative Zacapoaxtla had fallen. Its streets of patrician houses were now patrolled by the *indios cuatecomacos* who formerly had populated the town's jail.

The Méndez-Alatriste Leadership Struggle

Roldán's failure to secure Zacapoaxtla should not detract from his achievement in fostering a network of political allegiances that would survive the subsequent decades of civil strife. Roldán and his patrician Zacapoaxteco allies, Molina Islas and Betancurt, discovered that Indians, particularly from communities bordering the clerical stronghold of Tlatlauqui, could be mobilized, armed, and made into effective fighters. The state's Conservative leadership had failed to appreciate Zacapoaxtla's symbolic importance, deploying forces raised by Roldán on guard duty at the fortress of Perote while failing to provide an adequate regular force to back these village defense units.

For their part, the Liberals rejoiced at the defeat of the "fanatical and arrogant" forces of Zacapoaxtla at the hands of "soldiers of the people." Upon entering the town, as though to advertise that the new Liberal order had commenced, Méndez ordered the imprisonment of the parish priest, Trinidad Mayorga.[26] The fall of Zacapoaxtla to the Liberals had immediate implications for the town's conflict with its rebellious western barrios as well as for the rivalry with Tetela. The victory also provided the Liberal cause throughout the Mexican southeast with the possibility of an important strategic advance. The fortress of Perote was now cut off from Zacapoaxtla, its principal supplier of food and manpower, bringing into question the ability of the Conservatives to hold the eastern plateau region of the state.[27] Finally, the apparent collapse of the Conservative axis in the eastern Sierra permitted Liberal forces to redeploy against Conservative strongholds at Chignahuapan and Tulancingo in the western Sierra and the Sierra de Tulancingo.[28]

However, in terms of the effective prosecution of the Liberal war effort on the state and national level, Méndez's victory raised as many problems as it solved. Méndez now became an obvious contender for leadership of the Liberal forces in Puebla while Alatriste's claim to overall political and military command of the state looked correspondingly weaker. The rise of Méndez in the Sierra threatened to upset an unwritten convention followed since Independence: state governors should come from the central valley of the state or from Puebla City (with the exception of the first state governor, Carlos Avila y García, who was born in Cuetzalan). The rise of a rustic National Guard commander also offended another convention dear to Mexico's Liberals: leaders should be civilians, with the benefit of a higher education, preferably in law.

As a lawyer from the state capital, Alatriste considered himself to be a natural successor to the state government in the age of Liberal Reform. Like Méndez, Alatriste's humble background required him to leave school at the age of twelve to work in his father's tailor shop. However, at seventeen, Alatriste returned to school at Puebla's Caroline College, where he earned a law degree within only three years (the norm for law was five). At twenty-three, he had been appointed to a full teaching post at the college of San Juan Letrán in Mexico City where, on the eve of the war with the United States, he formed part of a young literary circle (he founded an

Academía de Literatura in 1846).[29] Even during the height of resistance to the Conservatives in the Sierra, Alatriste favored the sanctuary of the mountain redoubt of Ixtacamaxtitlán and the intellectual company of its learned Liberal priest, José María Cabrera, in preference to working out a common military strategy with Méndez in neighboring Tetela.[30]

If higher education and intellectual interests set Alatriste apart from Méndez, patriotic service as officers in the National Guard during the war of 1846–47 had brought the two men together. However, the localized organization and recruitment of the National Guard—Méndez had belonged to the Zacatlán battalion and Alatriste to Puebla City's Hidalgo battalion in 1846–47—tended to encourage further fragmentation and rivalry within Puebla's Liberal Party. The struggle between lawyers from the central valley and military men from the Sierra would divide Puebla's Liberal Party into Llanura and Montaña factions until the mid-1880s. The origin of this division lay in the estrangement between Alatriste and Méndez following the fall of Zacapoaxtla in January 1859.

Alatriste saw himself primarily as a civilian leader, intent on establishing a new, radical Liberal order in the city of Puebla. He felt uncomfortable in the Sierra and frequently removed the provisional seats of the state government, established first in Teziutlán and then in Zacapoaxtla, in premature attempts to shift the struggle to the central region of the state. By contrast, Méndez placed the construction of a strong military and political base in the central Sierra above all other objectives. From the perspective of the Liberal leadership in Veracruz, concerned with hastening the success of the Liberal struggle on the state and national levels, neither Poblano was ideal for state leadership.

By September 1859 relations between Méndez and Alatriste had reached the breaking point, with a series of denunciations of Alatriste's leadership from Sierra towns culminating in his recall to Veracruz and the appointment of Méndez to the supreme command of Puebla's forces.[31] The seeds of mutual distrust between the two leaders were sown in May 1859, when Melchor Ocampo (the Minister of War) informed Alatriste that he had sent one thousand rifles to Méndez in Zacapoaxtla with instructions to form two battalions of National Guard.[32] Méndez withdrew with these arms to resume his prefecture in Zacatlán, the town having been recaptured from the Conservatives by Antonio Carbajal on 21 February 1859. Alatriste remained in Zacapoaxtla, now a *villa* and established as the provisional capital of the state since 15 June 1859.

Once located in Zacatlán, where he had nurtured close ties with prominent National Guard officers since his participation in the Zacatlán battalion during the American War, Méndez set about strengthening his forces.[33] With the Zacatlán battalion receiving 375 new rifles, Rafael Cravioto in Huauchinango was bitter that his large force received only 125.[34] Alatriste was incensed that neither the state forces under his command nor the

National Guard of Zacapoaxtla had received any new rifles. Moreover, strategically vital districts such as Teziutlán, where Alatriste was attempting to establish his influence, were also left out of the spoils.[35] By contrast, the Cuatecomacos, who had already been rewarded with an abundance of weapons after the Las Filipinas victory, received 60 new repeating rifles. Overall, Méndez's division of weapons made it clear that he sought to consolidate his influence in the western Sierra of Tetela and Zacatlán. He left Zacapoaxtla, Teziutlán, Tlatlauqui, and Huauchinango out in the cold.

Zacatlán, however, like Zacapoaxtla, was a difficult town to defend, overlooked by peaks with lines of retreat complicated by vertiginous gorges. Méndez's decision to fortify Zacatlán coincided with its selection by Conservative President Miguel Miramón as the capital of a new department. On 14 June 1859 the one-thousand-strong Liberal force was ousted from Zacatlán by a Conservative force of a similar size raised from the Sierra of Tulancingo and Chignahuapan (the preferred Conservative recruiting ground since 1855) under Ignacio Gutiérrez (known by his Liberal opponents as "nacho el loco"). Three days of sacking the houses and businesses of prominent Zacatlán Liberals followed—hardly a propitious beginning for the Conservative plan to make Zacatlán the capital of a viable department. Gutiérrez soon withdrew from the desolate and largely depopulated town that Méndez fleetingly reoccupied in July 1859, only to see it retaken by General Oronoz, sent from Puebla to take up the military governorship of the new department. Liberal forces in the western Sierra reconcentrated at the more easily defendable town of Ahuacatlán.[36] In July the Conservatives' offensive moved to Huauchinango, and on 5 August a *pronunciamiento* from his own garrison obliged Alatriste to abandon Zacapoaxtla.[37]

Conservatives occupied Zacapoaxtla on 18 August and Tetela two days later. Upon taking Tetela, Zacapoaxteco troops, eager to avenge Tetela's encouragement of the Cuatecomacos, proceeded to imprison members of the Méndez family, including Leocadio, the chief Liberal arms supplier. To gain their release, the National Guard company of Tetela agreed to hand over their arms.[38] With this booty, the Zacapoaxtecos withdrew to prepare for the inevitable Liberal counterattack. Méndez was incensed at Alatriste's recklessness in losing Zacapoaxtla, at the indignities suffered by his family during the attack upon Tetela, and by the pusillanimity of Tetela's National Guard in handing over their weapons. After this incident, Méndez and the Cuatecomacos tightened their association, and on 30 August 1859, Lucas, leading Tetela and Cuatecomaco forces, succeeded in retaking Zacapoaxtla for Alatriste.

Recrimination over Alatriste's withdrawal from Zacapoaxtla (the governor claimed to have been tricked by an invitation to attend the festival of Xochitlán's patron saint) brought the conflict between Alatriste and Méndez to a head.[39] Uncertain of his position in Zacapoaxtla now that the provisional state capital was occupied by Cuatecomaco forces loyal to Méndez, Alatriste withdrew and established his headquarters some distance away at Ixtacamaxtitlán. From this mountainous redoubt, but in easy access to the *llanos* of Tlaxco, Huamantla, and San Juan, Alatriste hoped to be able to prevent the regrouping of Conservatives under General Echeagaray on the plateau. However, his forces were too poorly equipped and his cavalry under Carbajal too indisciplined to permit any major engagement with the enemy or lay siege to the state capital.[40]

Late in September 1859, Méndez and leading officers of the National Guard of Zacatlán drew up a list of complaints relating to Alatriste's leadership. The officers claimed that abusive treatment of civilians and military incompetence were contributing to demoralization and desertions. They requested that the National Guard of Zacatlán be permitted to take the lead of the Liberal war effort in the Sierra. This *pronunciamiento* against Alatriste, seconded by Rafael Cravioto, Pilar Rivera and the officers of the Battalion of National Guard of Tetela de Oro, and the Ayuntamiento of Teziutlán (prompted by Tetela occupying forces under Rivera), convinced Melchor Ocampo to recall Alatriste to Veracruz and confer emergency powers on Méndez on 10 October. Juárez confirmed Ocampo's decision and instructed Alatriste to hand over the archives and governorship of Puebla to Méndez.[41] Alatriste ignored the orders from both the military commander and president. Soon, Alatriste and Méndez were at war.

Although Alatriste could not match the extent of support Méndez enjoyed in the Sierra, he could count on Carbajal and his formidable Tlaxcalteco cavalry.[42] Throughout October and November 1859, troops loyal to Méndez (Galindo, Cravioto, Rivera, and Lucas and the Cuatecomacos) clashed on several occasions with forces commanded by Alatriste. Carbajal's forces—"Los Carbajales"—consolidated their reputation for rapine and abuse of the Indian population, and left a path of destruction in their wake.[43] Fearful of prompting desertions from his Indian infantry, Méndez persisted in his strategy of holding territory within the Sierra by consolidating alliances with the Indian population and avoiding sorties on the plateau. Zacapoaxtla and Zacatlán changed hands on several occasions, with Lucas and the Cuatecomacos contributing vitally on each one to the recapture of these symbolically important but untenable district capitals.[44] Apart from Carbajal's near monopoly of the cavalry, which enabled Alatriste effectively to encircle the Sierra, an additional factor hampering Méndez's attempt to assert his control over the state government was the refusal of Alatriste's state secretary, Joaquín Martínez, to hand over the archives or submit to Méndez's authority.[45]

The conflict between Méndez and Alatriste grew more acute during the first half of 1860. Alatriste failed to make much impression upon the southern Sierra where Méndez's control remained firm, through Lucas and the Cuatecomacos.[46] However, with the help of Carbajal, Alatriste pressed on with his plan to isolate and encircle the Méndez *cacicazgo*. The theft and rape inflicted by Carbajal's indisciplined troops upon villages within the southern parts of the districts of Tlatlauqui and Teziutlán in April spread fear and alarm throughout the central Sierra, which only served to consolidate popular support for Méndez in this area. Lucas began to emerge as the protector of the Indian population.[47]

Juan Francisco Lucas, c. 1862, age c. 28

In mid-April, deploying only slightly less brute force, Carbajal succeeded in overthrowing *mendecista* officials in Zacatlán, placing its National Guard under the control of Agustín Cravioto. Méndez paid the penalty of keeping Rafael Cravioto short of weapons when the National Guard of Huauchinango went over to Alatriste in late April.[48] By the summer of 1860, in spite of his official backing from Juárez and Ocampo, Méndez's authority as military governor was confined to the districts of Tetela and Zacapoaxtla, hemmed in from all sides by hostile Liberal or Conservative forces.

The Liberal leadership in Veracruz watched Poblano infighting with mounting impatience. Finally, on 1 May 1860, Ocampo dispatched General Pedro Ampudía to take control of Liberal forces in the state and to install General Pascual Miranda as governor. Alatriste accepted Miranda's authority as supreme military commander of the state, although he added, rather ambiguously, that he would dedicate himself to the civil administration. Méndez was at first guarded. He declined an invitation from Ignacio de la Llave (the Minister of the Interior, responsible for carrying out the federal intervention) to meet in Teziutlán, claiming that his father's illness prevented him from leaving Tetela. Instead, he invited the minister to Tetela. On the following day, Méndez acknowledged Miranda's authority. A similar reluctance was evident in Zacatlán, the other half of the Méndez *cacicazgo*. Ignacio Soza (the National Guard commander recently ousted by Agustín Cravioto and resident in Ahuacatlán) declined an invitation to meet the minister in Zacatlán, claiming to be unable to ride horseback because of an injury. Ramón Márquez Galindo, faced with the minister's imminent arrival, recognized Miranda's authority without ado.[49] From Ampudía's arrival in Teziutlán until the end of the war, the Liberal war effort in the state of Puebla remained under direct federal control, with the authority of both Méndez and Alatriste placed in abeyance. The problem of Carbajal's undisciplined and rapacious forces, which was so damaging to the image of the Constitutionalist cause within Indian villages and to Liberal morale more generally, was addressed by placing all Tlaxcalteco forces under a separate commander: General José de la Luz Moreno.[50]

The new federally imposed state government established itself in Teziutlán and set about organizing the state's finances and military resources under the supervision of De la Llave. On 10 May, Ignacio Romero Vargas, a lawyer from Acatzingo and future state governor (1870–1876), was appointed to direct the state's finances. He was charged with the liquidation of the capital funds of Church bodies and religious confraternities, supervising the salarying of the priesthood, and coordinating the *rebajado* tax for funding the National Guard.[51] His spell in Teziutlán gave him firsthand experience in the Sierra, demonstrated the strengths and weaknesses of the region's military leadership, and, above all, revealed the prodigious yield that could be expected from the *rebajado* tax if well managed.[52]

After traveling throughout the Sierra, De la Llave and Romero Vargas reported on the state of Liberal forces. They conceded that both the financing and the recruitment of the National Guard had proved successful. The problems lay not in finance but in the rudimentary training, indiscipline, fragmentation of command, and their ineffectiveness in any offensive capacity.[53] They doubted whether the National Guard on its own could effectively sustain the Constitutionalist cause in Puebla. To contribute to the victory, the Guard needed to be led by at least two battalions of regular troops with "a rigorous daily military education."

One such battalion was already being formed in Teziutlán. The aim was to establish regular forces of 1,600 infantry, 300 cavalry, and, "in the shadow of these," a National Guard of 1,500 to 2,000 men, ready for service when called upon. Once organized, regular companies would be sent to all the towns in the Sierra at present garrisoned by the National Guard. The existing National Guard would be reduced or entirely demobilized. The resulting military presence in the Sierra would be: 60 men in

Teziutlán (a new regular force); 100 men in Zacapoaxtla (National Guard); 50 men in Tetela (National Guard); 100 men in Zacatlán (a new regular force); and 100 men in Huauchinango (National Guard).[54]

To the federally imposed Miranda government, this project must have seemed rational. It offered a means for reasserting control over the strategic Puebla Sierra and of directing Liberal forces at the single objective of bringing down the Conservatives and recovering the state capital. However, the project ignored the political realities of the Sierra, particularly the extent to which the National Guard had grown to embody local power. The project remained a dead letter.

The 440 well-armed men who formed the Zacapoaxtla Section, Brigade of the State of Puebla, commanded by Márquez Galindo, Pedro Contreras, and Lucas in May 1860 were not, as De la Llave speculated, "national guards who, torn away from their daily occupations, are obliged to lend active military service, for which they are untrained and toward which they feel a natural repugnance." They were men who had joined the National Guard voluntarily. While they were attracted by the fiscal immunity accompanying the service, they were appreciative above all of the political advantages that being armed and organized gave them in their dispute with the cabecera over the hacienda of Xochiapulco and Manzanilla. The muster list for this force testifies to the numerical importance of the Cuatecomacos and to the presence of troops from Zautla, Tetela, and Zacatlán, the towns that over the following three decades would provide the military underpinnings and territorial basis of the Montaña *cacicazgo*.

Table 4–1. National Guard, Brigade of the State of Puebla: Zacapoaxtla Section on Active Duty in May 1860	
Unit	*Number of Men*
Officers	23
Artillery	13
1st Tetela Company	37
2nd Tetela Company	50
1st Cuatecomaco Company	70
2nd Cuatecomaco Company	103
3rd Cuatecomaco Company	40
Tececuilco Company	15
Zautla Company	33
Zacapoaxtla Company	37
Zacatlán Company	9
Cavalry	10
Total	*440*

Armament: 225 percussion rifles, 87 flintlock rifles, 149 bayonets[55]

In any case, the Liberal government was in too fragile a position in Teziutlán to risk a major military reorganization in the Sierra. The ruthless *desamortización* applied by Romero Vargas to the great estates of San Juan de los Llanos and the arbitrary levies and rapine of Carbajal's forces soon provoked the last Conservative offensive in the Sierra of the Three Years' War. The fortress of Perote still remained in Conservative hands. Conservative forces were also active in neighboring Veracruz. The assault upon Liberal forces in the southern Sierra came first, however, from within the region, presaging a pattern of Conservative mobilization of Indian communities in this area that would continue into the 1880s.

In August 1859, at the head of three hundred Cuatecomaco infantry, Lucas left Zacapoaxtla to confront a rabble of five hundred poorly armed villagers commanded by Baltazar Telles Girón (alias "The Bandit"). The attackers came from villages in southern Zacapoaxtla, Tlatlauqui, and Teziutlán that had borne the brunt of Carbajal's rapine and foraging in this area. Lucas dispersed the rebels and sent them home to their mountains and barrios.[56] Elsewhere in the Sierra, the federal intervention had effectively quelled the armed conflict between the Méndez and Alatriste factions. However, Teziutlán, the seat of the Liberal state government, remained a target for Conservative incursions from Perote and Veracruz. In September 1860 an attack led by General Ignacio Alatorre was repulsed with the entire Conservative force, numbering three hundred infantry and sixty cavalry, with archives, ammunition, and animals falling into Liberal hands in a repeat of the Las Filipinas victory.[57]

On 22 October 1860 a more successful assault occurred on the Liberal state government in Teziutlán by four hundred cavalry led by General Felipe Chacón (Conservative military commander and state governor). However, this offensive left the Conservative flank in the central valley dangerously exposed to Alatriste's forces that were massing at Huamantla for an assault on the plateau. Upon learning of a conspiracy in the capital among the propertied families, who were tired of six years of extraordinary taxes, Chacón beat a retreat to Puebla City. The Liberal victory at Calpulalpam on 23 December and the fall of the Miramón government in Mexico City on 5 January 1861 forced Chacón to hand over the city to Fernando María Ortega who, two days later, conferred the state governorship upon Alatriste.[58]

Conclusion

The great violence and intensified ideological polarization that distinguished Mexico's Three Years' War left a deep imprint on the political geography of the Puebla Sierra. As a result of a novel and disturbing pattern of political assassinations, atrocities, and retaliatory plunderings, traditional enmities and rivalries between neighboring towns were deepened. The defense of "religión y fueros" or the constitution, which served to legitimize these vendettas, required people in each town to consider their ideological allegiances. Violence perpetrated by neighbors became benchmarks in Liberal-patriotic or Conservative histories. The first vengeful attack by Zacapoaxtecos upon Xochiapulco on 30 November 1855, the repeated sacking of Liberal Zacatlán by forces from Conservative Chignahuapan and Tulancingo in June and July 1859, the return plundering of Chignahuapan by troops from Zacatlán, Méndez's long-awaited capture and purge of Zacapoaxtla in February 1859, and Zacapoaxtla's retaliatory sacking of Tetela and the properties of the Méndez family in August 1859 were unprecedentedly violent episodes in a hitherto peaceful Sierra.

The racial element in determining political affiliations became more explicit. People in Chignahuapan and Zacapoaxtla, who were mostly Creoles or mestizos, stressed their Hispanic pedigrees and regarded the inhabitants of Tetela, Xochiapulco, and Zacatlán as *nacos* (Nahuas).[59] Any involvement with the Indian population that broke with the traditional forms of patronage or treated Indian forces as equal partners, such as the Tetela Liberals' incorporation of the Cuatecomacos into the National Guard under their own commanders, was regarded as fomenting a caste war.

Not only did these conflicts confirm in people's minds that their neighbor was their enemy, but they also discouraged unity within towns and villages, which divided increasingly into factions. People of similar ideological persuasion or party affiliation sought alliances with subject villages in order to prosecute their causes more effectively by raising military recruits and supplies. For example, Zacapoaxtla was not uniformly a Conservative town. Its hinterland of mainly Nahuat villages came under pressure both from Liberal and Conservative military commanders as well as from the clergy. Tetela also contained a substantial Conservative element, but its inaccessibility left Conservatives there without the external support available to their counterparts in Chignahuapan or Zacapoaxtla.

By the end of the Three Years' War, in addition to these internal divisions, each larger town had come to acquire an identifiable ideological predisposition toward one or the other party. The district capitals and cabeceras of the *tierra fría* close to the cereal estates of the altiplano—Zacapoaxtla, Zautla, Tlatlauqui, San Juan de los Llanos, Chignahuapan, and Tulancingo across the state boundary in Hidalgo—tended more toward the Conservative Party and would later collaborate with the Intervention. The district capitals and cabeceras farther into the Sierra—Tetela, Ixtacamaxtitlán, Zacatlán, Ahuacatlán, Huauchinango, Zapotitlán, and Pahuatlán—where there existed little concentration of land ownership at this stage, and whose bourgeoisie depended more upon employment in the district bureaucracy and in trade, looked to the Liberal Party. Warfare reinforced these dispositions, diminished the tolerance that had characterized these towns in more peaceful times, and tied them more closely with, or pitted them against, their dependent villages.

The intrusion of forces beyond the Sierra also contributed significantly to the ideological coloring of political geography. No a priori reason explained why the Cuatecomacos should have become, by 1861, almost a model Liberal military colony. In 1855 chance brought together a local agrarian conflict with a Liberal, federalist revolution commanded by the agrarian-inclined Alvarez. In 1857 chance again brought together the beleaguered rump of the Liberal state government with local Nahua forces, who were already armed, experienced in the art of mountain warfare, and commanded by a captain who had received his military training in the artillery. Once established, these alliances, of necessity, tended to become firm associations, strengthened by personal friendship, kinship, and compadrazgo.

Liberals by no means possessed a monopoly of political initiative, although this quality tended to be their trump card. National Conservative leaders such as Haro y Tamariz and Miramón and their regional and local counterparts, Gutiérrez, Telles Girón, Roldán, Betancurt, and Molina, labored hard at building up a Sierra clientele in more remote towns such as Cuetzalan, and among those families who supported the clergy in the district capitals and in surrounding barrios. The Conservatives were helped in their construction of reliable village defense forces by the brutal foraging and recruiting tactics of Liberal commanders such as Carbajal and Márquez Galindo. The military's relation with villages and the issue of military recruitment were two areas where Lucas began to demonstrate his worth to the Liberal cause. Eschewing conscription, Lucas succeeded in persuading villagers to provide men and supplies voluntarily in exchange for guarantees.

The final pattern that emerged during the Three Years' War was the conflict and rivalry within the Liberal camp, witnessed by the debilitating rivalry between Méndez and Alatriste. This was in part a reflection of the personalized and localized nature of the political structure in the Sierra, which was made up of a constellation of semi-autonomous National Guard caciques: Méndez in Tetela, Márquez Galindo in Zacatlán, Soza in Ahuacatlán, Rafael Cravioto in Huauchinango, and Lucas in Zacapoaxtla. It also reflected the competing military and civilian visions of Liberalism, the former, by necessity, more popular, and the latter, more elitist, anticipating that an educated lawyer, rather than a rustic militia commander, would naturally inherit the reins of power in the state capital, once the unpleasant business of the war had ended. The leadership squabble between Méndez and Alatriste also resulted from broader regional rivalries.[61] Sierra leaders, confident of being on their home ground, began to sense their greater strength in wartime, while Liberals from the plateau, insecure on the uncertain terrain of the Sierra, yearned for peace and the resumption of civilian control from the state capital. Although Méndez had impressed the Liberal leadership by his dedication and tactical skills throughout much of the war, by the autumn of 1860, Alatriste once more seemed the more likely contender for the governorship.[60]

Méndez failed to sustain the momentum that initially had earned him federal support and had isolated Alatriste. In order to consolidate his leadership of the Constitutionalist movement and secure the governorship after the fall of Puebla in December 1860, Méndez should have achieved: firm control over the National Guard of the Sierra; full control over the state from the federal interventors based in Teziutlán; and loyal friendships on the plateau and in the state of Tlaxcala, to enable the Tetela caudillo to press home the attack upon Puebla.

As it happened, the unity of the Sierra National Guard dissolved once the Cravioto family, who controlled the important northern flank, moved behind Alatriste. The federally supervised state government in Teziutlán collapsed during the last months of the war in the face of Conservative assaults from the fortress of Perote. Méndez, who failed to fill the vacuum, handed Alatriste's peripatetic "civilian" state administration based at Ixtacamaxtitlán a decided advantage. Finally, the conflict between Méndez and Carbajal prevented the Tetela caudillo from using the territory and forces of Tlaxcala in any movement on the state capital in December 1860. This strategic advantage redounded to Alatriste. In January 1861, Alatriste took over the administration of the state while Méndez had to satisfy himself with a seat in the state legislature and the command of the Tetela National Guard.

In contrast to the mobile Carbajal and peripatetic Alatriste, Méndez and Lucas were tied to their territory, having forever to be on guard against the possibility of a vindictive attack from the Zacapoaxtecos, who had refused to acknowledge the independence of Xochiapulco. Méndez's ally in Zacatlán, Márquez Galindo, was also challenged on two fronts, from Cravioto in Huauchinango and from the Conservatives in Chignahuapan. Hence, by necessity, the core of Méndez's *cacicazgo* was defensive, based upon the alliance between the Tetela and Zacatlán National Guards and the Cuatecomacos.

5

From Reform to Patriotic Resistance, 1860–1863

The Liberal victory over the Conservatives and the capture of Mexico City in December 1860 did not bring peace, least of all to the state of Puebla. The Liberal state government resumed the task of implementing the Reform Laws that the Three Years' War had interrupted. The Conservatives still regarded Puebla as the key to the return to the old order. They hatched conspiracies, invaded the state, and presented a constant challenge throughout 1861 and 1862 to Liberal civil governors Alatriste (14 January–3 September 1861) and Ibarra y Ramos (5 September 1861–6 January 1862) and, once a state of emergency had been declared, to a succession of military governors (Generals José María González de Mendoza, Santiago Tapia, and Ignacio Mejía). In particular, Conservative guerrillas in southern Puebla, backed from Guerrero and Oaxaca, threatened the new Liberal order.

Méndez, the Sierra, and the Constitutionalist Order in Puebla

In the northern Sierra, maintaining the new Liberal order proved less difficult than in the south of the state. Liberal forces, in control for most of the Three Years' War, had already applied much of the Reform before the formal promulgation of the Reform Laws on 1 January 1861. With the exceptions of a minor rebellion in the villages of Tlatlauqui and eastern Zacapoaxtla and an abortive invasion by Ignacio Gutiérrez from Tulancingo, the north of the state enjoyed the quietest year since the outbreak of the revolution of Ayutla.[1]

On the face of it, Méndez had lost the contest with Alatriste that had so handicapped the Liberal war effort in the Sierra. As the reward for his services to the Constitutionalist cause during the Three Years' War, the Tetela caudillo received the command of the district's National Guard battalion and a seat in the state legislature.[2] Of the two, Méndez considered his presence in the Sierra of more importance. Abandoning the Sierra would have left the

Tetela National Guard and the Cuatecomacos vulnerable both from Huauchinango and Zacapoaxtla.

Soon after the Liberal victory, Lucas and the Cuatecomacos succeeded in their struggle for municipal status and land. In January 1861 the district of Zacapoaxtla elected Pablo Urrutia to be their jefe político.[3] The wealthy Papantla merchant immediately proposed independent municipal status to the Cuatecomacos in exchange for handing in their arms. The new municipality, to be called Xochiapulco, would comprise the barrios of Las Lomas, Yautetelco, Jilotepec, Atzala, and Eloxochitlan, with the cabecera formed at the Rancho de Cuacualaxtla.[4] Lucas wanted to keep fifty men armed to deter attacks from the reactionaries, but Urrutia appeased the cacique by inviting him to select thirteen men for the jefe político's personal guard as well as to send twenty-five men to the cabecera to be armed and equipped.[5] He also assured Lucas that the Cuatecamacos, though disarmed, would remain the trusted reserve force upon whom Urrutia could call when needed. With the jefe político of Zacapoaxtla in control of the armory, it must have been obvious to Lucas that the Cuatecomacos would no longer be an independent military force.[6]

Although the partial disarming of the Cuatecomacos weakened Méndez's position, an opportunity soon appeared for the Tetela caudillo to reassert his influence. Since early April, a group of deputies led by Méndez had been attempting to impeach Alatriste for his conduct during the Three Years' War. In August 1861, when Alatriste decided to lead a force against a Conservative rebellion in Tecali, the legislature forced him to resign the governorship, naming Ibarra y Ramos as interim governor and convoking a new gubernatorial election.[7]

Méndez used his influence within the National Guard to promote the candidature of Ibarra y Ramos, a moderate Liberal industrialist from the state capital. Accompanied by Márquez Galindo, his fellow Zacatlán deputy, Méndez toured the northern districts. In Zacapoaxtla, José María Maldonado later recalled in his memoir that Méndez mobilized an estimated four hundred armed Indians (presumably the Cuatecomacos) "by offering their leaders music to take back to their villages as well as other gifts that those Indians like." The political use of martial music and wind-instrument bands became a particular stock in trade of Méndez in the Puebla Sierra.[8] The Indians were instructed to march to Puebla City to intimidate the followers of Ortega, thereby ensuring Ibarra y Ramos's election in the state capital.[9] Governor Ibarra y Ramos, in his first important appointment, named Méndez Secretary of Government and Militia as a reward for his services.[10]

The European Intervention

While factions within Puebla's Liberal Party jostled over the fruits of their victory, prominent Conservative exiles engineered Europe's last monarchist adventure in the New World. Throughout 1861, the Juárez government faced mounting pressure from a Triple Alliance (France, Spain, and Great Britain) of debt collectors that culminated in the blockade of the port of Veracruz and the invasion by French troops in December 1861.

Although France did not declare war upon Mexico until April 1862, the Juárez regime considered itself at war from the moment the Europeans landed on Mexican soil. As early as October 1861, anticipating the invasion, Juárez had sent General Miguel Negrete (a Poblano from Tepeaca who had recently deserted the Conservative cause) to Huauchinango to organize a brigade of volunteers for the Army of the East.[11] Upon news of the French landing in December, these forces were summoned to Puebla. Tetela's battalion—now named the Sixth Battalion of the National Guard of Puebla—was composed of six companies: four from Tetela, one from Zacapoaxtla, and one from Xochiapulco. They were the first to arrive in the state capital, to be greeted by their *paisano*, General Méndez.[12]

With the declaration of a state of emergency on 4 January 1862, Puebla's governorship passed from the civilian Ibarra y Ramos to General González de Mendoza. Puebla Liberals now faced a war on two fronts. As the three thousand French troops disembarked at Veracruz, Conservative forces mounted a challenge from the south of the state. This attack tied up regular forces and the National Guard throughout the first four months of 1862 (and ultimately claimed the life of Alatriste in the heroic defense of Izucar de Matamoros on 11 April 1862).[13] Once more, Puebla's Liberal leadership pinned its hopes on the northern Sierra for recruitment, supply, and, ultimately, sanctuary.

Recruitment in the Sierra and the Victory of 5 May 1862

The French invasion in December 1861 obliged Urrutia to reverse his policy of demobilizing the Cuatecomacos. The jefe político of Zacapoaxtla called upon Lucas to recruit from Xochiapulco and instructed Captain José Relvas to organize the forces of the district capital. Throughout the first four months of 1862, Urrutia and Eduardo Santín (who was given the military command of Zacapoaxtla on 9 February and Tlatlauqui on 10 June) attempted, mostly unsuccessfully, to grapple with the problem of recruitment. Most of the district's Indian population proved averse to National Guard service, and even the Cuatecomacos would only provide replacements for the battalion for short periods of service under their own commanders.[14]

The Nahua and Totonac settlements in the north of the district proved the hardest to mobilize. The excuses of village authorities ranged from Evaristo Castañeda of Xochitlán's feeble "I lack a bugle" for summoning the National Guard to parade, to reports from villages in Cuetzalan and Nauzontla that all the men were planting crops in the coastal lowlands or had fled to the hills to avoid enlistment. The trickle of "patriotic" recruits was mostly from forcibly enlisted inmates of village jails, vagabonds, adulterers, and troublemakers whom village authorities happily dispatched to the district capital. Obedient young men of fighting age had become suspiciously scarce throughout the district of Zacapoaxtla.[15]

While Urrutia and Santín's recruitment drive was met by evasive village authorities and a disobedient and unpatriotic citizenry in Zacapoaxtla's northern municipalities, they faced a more serious problem in the southern part of Zacapoaxtla, and in neighboring Tetela and Tlatlauqui. Since the Three Years' War, it had become evident that most villages in this area (apart from those in Xochiapulco) resented military service either because of its implied support for the Liberal cause (which, if we are to believe Maldonado, they were instructed by their priests to oppose) or because of the experience of rapine, theft, and *leva* under the dreaded Carbajal in 1860. It had also become evident that many influential families in the three districts saw the French as potential allies against the advance of Liberalism.[16]

Prompted by their Conservative allies, the French quickly learned to take advantage of these anti-Liberal popular sentiments in the Sierra. In mid-April 1862, Lucas warned Urrutia of an imminent uprising—the so-called Galindo conspiracy—led by prominent Zacapoaxtla National Guard officers in league with village mayors. Their intent was to prevent the dispatch of barrio contingents and to murder Liberal commanders and officers of the district's National Guard.[17] In desperation, Urrutia turned for aid to Lucas, who provided one hundred men for suppressing the uprising but regretted that he could spare no more since Xochiapulco (which Zacapoaxtla still had not recognized as a municipality) had also to be defended.[18]

As the French army advanced upon the altiplano in April 1862, the Sierra National Guard was numerically depleted and ideologically divided. Far from the image presented by history textbooks of the patriotic and indomitable Zacapoaxtlas, the response from the district of Zacapoaxtla to the call to arms was disappointing (with the notable exception of the new municipality of Xochiapulco). In early April 1862, Xochiapulco forces had reached a full complement of around four hundred men. But Nauzontla, Xochitlán, and Cuetzalan could muster only sixty-three men between these municipalities.[19]

Zacapoaxtla was not alone in facing difficulties with recruitment. The unity and enthusiasm that Captain Lauro Luna observed among Tetela's National Guard battalion when it arrived in Puebla in December 1861 had dissipated by April 1862. During the first four months of the year, Puebla's Sixth Battalion of National Guard (principally Tetelenses) was deployed, almost continually, in the south of the state to counter the Conservatives, and in Veracruz to deter any French movement inland. Luna reported that demoralization set in after Alatriste's defeat at Atlixco on 11 April 1862 with several companies finding it impossible to secure replacements.[20] By the first battle with the French at Acultzingo on 28 April, the Sixth Battalion numbered a mere 196 officers and men.

In desperation, Colonel Méndez returned to the Sierra in mid-April to replenish the ranks but could muster only 107 men from Tetela.[21] Morale in Tetela was further diminished by the efforts of Rafael Cravioto to undermine Méndez's authority over the battalion. Luna, Méndez's adjutant, stated in his memoir that half the battalion "rose in rebellion" when ordered to march to Puebla to confront the French in early May. Méndez finally arrived in the state capital on 3 May leading a mere eighty men, mostly from Xochiapulco and Cuetzalan under Captains Lucas and José María Huidobro. None of the men was from Méndez's home district, Tetela.[22] Moreover, even some of this small contingent had been recruited by force.[23]

Without the Cuatecomacos from Xochiapulco, reinforced by a small company of Nahuas from Cuetzalan under Francisco Agustín, the central-southern Sierra would not have succeeded in dispatching a contingent for the defense of the state capital, and Mexico would not have had its legendary Zacapoaxtlas. With the arrival of six thousand French troops under General Lorencez on the Mexican tableland in April 1862, General Negrete's division moved to engage the enemy at Acultzingo on the Puebla-Veracruz border. After a lengthy skirmish on 28 April, Negrete's forces, made up largely of artisan National Guards from the cities of Querétaro and Puebla, fell back to the state capital, where on 5 May the Sixth Battalion fought with conspicuous bravery and effect in the successful defense of the city against the French army.

So firmly embedded in the Mexican victory is the myth of the indomitable Zacapoaxtlas that it is difficult to evaluate the actual contribution of the Sixth Battalion. Several contemporary reports testify to its energetic crossfire, which discouraged and distracted the French during the first attack upon the fortresses of Guadalupe and Loreto, and to a later charge that prompted the flight of a section of the French forces.[24] General Negrete in his report to Ignacio Zaragoza, the Commander in Chief, makes generous claims for the Sixth Battalion.[25] The serious wounds to Méndez (putting him out of action for almost three years) and to two other officers confirm the battalion's involvement in heavy fighting. Yet the Sixth Battalion on 5 May 1862 had only 150 men (6 commanders, 18 officers, and 126 soldiers) among a defending force of over 6,000. Their value resided principally in the accuracy of their firing, which had been developed through previous experience in mountain combat. The appearance of the Xochiapulco guardsman, with his beehive hat, short brown woolen poncho, short *manta* trousers, sandals, and long-bladed machete, might also have contributed to the shock and confusion observed among the French units of North African Zouaves.[26]

Whatever the contribution of Puebla's Sixth Battalion of National Guards to the victory on 5 May, by mid-July 1862 it had become a dispirited unit. Soon after the battle, the Sixth Battalion suffered in a surprise encounter with the enemy, resulting in the desertion of several guardsmen. Zaragoza eventually released the battalion from service, having failed to receive from Zacapoaxtla the reinforcements and supplies necessary for sustaining it.[27] Only a bedraggled force of less than thirty returned to Zacapoaxtla. Thus, the heroic contribution of Zacapoaxtlas to the early patriotic struggle was confined to the battle of 5 May, after which these troops had served only as a worrying liability to the high command. Low morale due to overlengthy stays of service throughout the first five months of 1862, the lack of financial and moral support from Zacapoaxtla and Tetela, the rivalry between Méndez and Cravioto (with the Huauchinango commander succeeding in preventing the dispatch of half the battalion on the eve of the French attack on Puebla), and the loss of their leader, Méndez, who had retired to Tetela after the battle to recover from a serious wound, all contributed to the disintegration of the force that had been at full strength in December 1861.

The Struggle for Zacapoaxtla

Only in desperation had Urrutia turned to Lucas for help with recruitment in January 1862. The jefe político feared that a fully armed and mobilized Xochiapulco would threaten the balance of power in the district. Urrutia's distrust of Xochiapulco was confirmed after the battle of 5 May, when he resumed disarming the municipality. Colonel Santín, the military commander of the district, opted for the opposite course: that of disarming the National Guard of the cabecera and re-arming the Cuatecomacos. Their differences culminated in an armed confrontation between Urrutía and Santín—the district's civil and military authorities—on 11 July 1862. This division within the Liberal leadership brought into the open the conflict between Liberal and Conservative Zacapoaxtla that had smouldered since the Liberal victory in the Three Years' War.

Conflict came to a head in July 1862 when Santín convened a military tribunal in Zacapoaxtla to investigate the "Galindo conspiracy" of mid-April. Mariano Ochoa, the attorney of the Sixth Battalion of the National Guard, chaired the court with the rest of the bench comprising one colonel and six captains from Zacapoaxtla's battalion, which included the Cuautecomaco commanders, José Gábriel Valencia and Lucas. The latter asked to be excused, claiming not to possess the requisite skills (an example of his tactical use of humility).[28] The court brought festering local rivalries to a head.

Since his appointment in February 1862, Santín had suspected the loyalty of Zacapoaxtla's National Guard to the Liberal and patriotic cause.[29] The tribunal gave Santín a chance to tackle the problem through military justice. Convinced by the evidence of sedition brought before the court,

Santín decided to disarm the National Guards of the cabecera, and passed their weapons on to Lucas.[30] Urrutia was incensed, and decided to bring the tribunal to a close by arming the forty young musicians of Zacapoaxtla's recently formed wind band. This *pronunciamiento* called for the removal of Santín.[31] To legalize this action, Urrutia convoked a junta of the alcaldes and justices of the peace from all the district's barrios, urging them to attend a meeting in Zacapoaxtla's Plaza de Armas.[32] Santín moved quickly with a force of Cuatecomacos and troops from neighboring Tlatlauqui to suppress the movement and restore order. Urrutia disclaimed involvement in this uprising and refused to relinquish control of the district. With Urrutia still officially in command of the district, Santín was left no option but to return to Puebla.[33]

The precipitant of these events was the imminent return to Zacapoaxtla of the last ragged contingent of the Sixth Battalion led by Pilar Rivera.[34] A fellow Tetelense, close friend, and comrade in arms of Méndez during the Three Years' War, Rivera and his depleted battalion remained the core of the Méndez machine.[35] Faced with the arrival of an unruly band of guardsmen, and fearing the loss of control over Lucas's Cuatecomacos, Urrutia decided to act.[36] In the short term, his uprising achieved its objectives. The military tribunal was abandoned, Santín left Zacapoaxtla for Puebla, and Urrutia remained at his post as jefe político.

Patriotic Recruitment and the Rise of Cenobio Cantero

Concerned by these divisions in the Sierra, Governor Mejía sent Colonel José María Maldonado to bring order to the strategically critical district of Zacapoaxtla. Maldonado's arrival coincided with the increase in French troop arrivals at Veracruz and the recognition that a full-scale war with France was imminent.[37] Given the weakened state of the Sixth Battalion, Governor Mejía commissioned Márquez Galindo to establish a new battalion of "patriotic volunteers," called the Batallón Mixto de la Sierra, to be raised from the entire Sierra. The districts of Zacapoaxtla and Tetela were excused since their National Guards would be reorganized under Urrutía for the defense of Papantla.

On 29 July 1862, Urrutia instructed all the cabeceras in the district to raise *contingentes de sangre* for the defense of his hometown, Papantla.[38] The response to Urrutia's call to arms was disappointing. The jefe político reported to Márquez Galindo that of the 270 men sought, only 70 (60 of whom were Cuatecomacos) had presented themselves by mid-August.[39] Lucas, who was the key to any successful revival of the district's National Guard, maintained a deafening silence in Xochiapulco.[40] In a final bid to reassert his authority and to counter "the discouragement and lack of patriotism that exists in this district," Urrutia ordered twelve handpicked

National Guard officers to visit all the municipalities of the district to encourage enlistment.[41] Four officers deserted by the end of the month and
Captain Ireneo Reyes (soon to become Xochiapulco's principal commander
after Lucas) ignored Urrutia's orders.[42]

Urrutia blamed Lucas for the lack of cooperation. In his report to
Márquez Galindo, Urrutia regretted that this officer had ignored his letters
and failed to encourage enlistment.[43] Lucas finally replied to Urrutia's letters
on 19 August. He asserted that he had complied with the request for sixty
men a fortnight earlier and had sent them directly to Márquez Galindo
(neatly bypassing the authority of Urrutia). He added that he was sending
Urrutia another twenty-four men, who were fully armed and ready for war.
These men arrived in Zacapoaxtla on 20 August but, to Urrutia's surprise and
chagrin, were unarmed.[44] By sending men without rifles, Lucas combined
prudence with parsimony. After all, he had recently returned the weapons
that Urrutia had lent to him. Urrutia could now use these arms to equip the
Xochiapulco contingent upon its arrival in Zacapoaxtla. Lucas surely
intended this as a symbolic gesture of reciprocity between the citizens of two
free municipalities.

Ramón Márquez Galindo, Commander of the Zacatlán National Guard, c. 1863

While Urrutia's experience with rebuilding the National Guard battalion in Zacapoaxtla was disappointing, Márquez Galindo's attempts to raise
the Batallón Mixto in neighboring Tlatlauqui proved little short of
catastrophic. In targeting this district as the least likely to resist recruitment

of the two hundred men still needed to make up the new battalion, Márquez Galindo seriously underestimated the strength of the anti-Liberal and anti-patriotic sentiment in Tlatlauqui and nearly incited a mass Indian uprising in the southern Sierra as a result.

The Zacatlán commander arrived in Tlatlauqui in late July at the head of a mule train carrying two hundred new Enfield rifles. He wanted to take advantage of the Sunday market and National Guard muster to announce publicly the contribution that the sons of the district would soon be making to the defense of the fatherland (not before posting guards at each corner of the square). He then had three hundred Tlatlauqueños rounded up, confined to barracks, and informed that shortly they would be marching to the plateau to fight the French expeditionary force.[45] The night of 4 August, Tlatlauqui was occupied by a small army of Indians from villages located along the boundary between the districts of Zacapoaxtla and Tlatlauqui, led by the Atagpan National Guard captain, Cenobio Cantero. Crying "Long Live Religion and Death to the Government," the rebels stormed the barracks and the jail, released the conscripts and prisoners, and appropriated more than two hundred rifles and munitions. Márquez Galindo and his officers took flight. Unwittingly, they had succeeded in catalyzing a popular Conservative front in the southern Sierra to match Lucas's Liberal front in Xochiapulco.

Over the subsequent decade (until his death at the hands of six men from Tzinacantepec in 1873) the political life of Cenobio Cantero ran parallel to that of Lucas.[46] Both of these Nahua Indians could count on loyal support from the villages of the southern Sierra. Cantero was more than simply "every priest's war horse for whatever they want," as Maldonado contemptuously described him.[47] Like Lucas, Cantero became a popular leader because he embodied the desire of Indian barrios to resist outside abuse and encroachments upon their autonomy.

Spurned by the Tlatlauqueños, Márquez Galindo returned to Zacapoaxtla to find several villages poised to rebel behind Cantero to resist recruitment. Disregarding orders forbidding recruitment for the Batallón Mixto in Tetela, Márquez Galindo marched west to find a district on the verge of rebellion behind Francisco Zamítez (a continuation of the movement observed by Luna in April and May 1862).[48] Only the arrival of Maldonado, who convinced Márquez Galindo to withdraw from the district (without a single recruit), prevented a conflagration.

Defeated in the Sierra, Márquez Galindo took his search for recruits to the plateau. He chose the community of Ocotepec (in the district of Libres), whose men agreed to serve in the Batallón Mixto in exchange for land to be expropriated from the hacienda of Buenavista.[49] Leading almost two hundred men from Ocotepec, Márquez Galindo returned to Zacapoaxtla, hoping to intensify recruitment. Instead, he met an armed confederation of villages. In the first skirmish, he lost a hundred rifles, and many of the fresh recruits from Ocotepec deserted. Again, the unfortunate Zacatlán commander had to beat a humiliating retreat. On 20 August, still with a pitifully small force, composed mainly of the remaining *peones* recruited from Ocotepec and motley village dissidents and adulterers, Márquez Galindo led the Batallón Mixto de la Sierra into battle.[50]

Márquez Galindo's recruitment drive in July and August 1862 revealed that the military administration of the southern Sierra was a shambles and the Constitutionalist order was precarious at best. Voluntary recruitment, in exchange for promises of political and material advantage, and forced enlistment of a traditional kind, had both exacerbated deep-seated inter-ethnic and inter-community conflicts that would echo throughout the subsequent decades. Much of Tlatlauqui was in open rebellion behind Cantero. Tetela under Zamítez (while Méndez convalesced from his wound) was seemingly oblivious to its patriotic responsibilities and languished in a state of officially tolerated revolt against the republican authorities. Teziutlán had become a contrabandist's paradise with the civil and military administration entirely in the clutches of a tight *camarilla* of merchants. Meanwhile, the political order in Zacapoaxtla remained precarious with some villages making common cause with Cantero while others, such as Xochiapulco, reluctantly lending support to Márquez Galindo but refusing to offer anything more than lip service to the unpopular Urrutia. It fell to the republican inspector, Maldonado, to sweep this Augean stable clean.[51]

José María Maldonado and Republican Resistance in the Sierra

Maldonado, a Liberal *hacendado* from Totimehuacan, had organized a National Guard unit from among his estate tenants during the American War. Early in 1862 he had formed the Seventh Battalion of Puebla's National Guard, taking part in the battle of 5 May, thereby acquiring patriotic credentials rivaling those of Sierra leaders such as Méndez, Lucas, and Márquez Galindo. However, having no special loyalties in the Sierra, Maldonado was especially valuable to the Liberal leadership.[52] For three years he commanded the Republican cause in the Sierra during which he single-mindedly pursued the aim of resisting and defeating the European Intervention. He organized a voluntary system of military recruitment (using Lucas's influence) and created a centralized fiscal administration to displace the Conservative *camarillas* that controlled towns such as Zacapoaxtla and Teziutlán.

Maldonado possessed a strong personal motive for pursuing the fiscal improprieties of the *camarillas*. In September 1862 he handed over his hacienda and ranchos in Totimehuacan, with all their livestock and grain, for the support of the Army of the East, in exchange for the exclusive right to collect the debts of the customhouses of Zacapoaxtla, Tlatlauqui, and

Teziutlán. This deal accounts for why Maldonado's memoirs are so well informed about the venality of the district political machines he aspired to bring under more direct control.[53]

Apart from the Conservative *camarillas*, the most conspicuous obstacle Maldonado faced in the Sierra was the Atagpan cacique, Cantero, now leading a well-armed reactionary movement. After resolving the conflict in Tetela between Zamítez and Méndez, Maldonado led a large force of five hundred Cuatecomacos, commanded by Lucas, to Tlatlauqui. He succeeded temporarily in pacifying Cantero with the promise of the cessation of forced recruitment, while allowing the Indian leader to retain a small force of militia.[54] In return, Cantero agreed to give back the 150 rifles taken on 4 August from Márquez Galindo, within two months, on pain of a fine of 2,000 pesos.

The next obstacle in the way of Maldonado's reorganization of patriotic forces in the Puebla Sierra was Pablo Urrutia, who clung obstinately to the leadership of this strategic district. Throughout the second half of 1862, the French with their Conservative Mexican allies massed forces in the foothills of the Sierra Madre of Veracruz and eastern Puebla, delaying the advance onto the tableland until they had established adequate supply lines and acquired sufficient draft animals. Agents scoured the Mexican southeast for mules and wagons.[55] The commercial opportunities for provisioning an army approaching 30,000 proved too great for many merchants in the southern Sierra to resist. In Liberal Teziutlán, merchants disguised their commercial undertakings with the enemy. By contrast, in Conservative Zacapoaxtla, where economic interest coincided with ideological empathy, merchants openly traded with the French.

The French soon learned that Zacapoaxtla offered a cornucopia of military supplies and eager anti-Republican recruits. Urrutia claimed to stand above the conflicts dividing the district. He pretended to maintain a distance from the Zacapoaxtecos who were dealing directly with the French. However, Maldonado observed that most of the district's top administrators had close ties to the French or to the Conservative landowning families of San Juan de los Llanos. These officials practiced systematic and deliberate mismanagement of the censuses to raise the National Guard tax. Maldonado also identified intimate ties between Urrutia and these Conservative families, and close kinship links to the clergy whose influence throughout much of the district was pervasive. Moreover, these families received large payments from the Bishop of Puebla to ensure their support for the Intervention. Maldonado concluded that Zacapoaxtla under Urrutia was a strategic liability.[56]

Maldonado probably ordered Lucas to lead the armed movement that on 1 October 1862 toppled Urrutia. The state governor ordered Maldonado to take military command of the district, but, wise to the entrenched position of Conservatives in the district administration, the Republican commander declined the appointment.[57] For a short time, Lucas occupied the supreme command of the district, although Pascual Bonilla, the jefe político's secretary, was the effective power.[58] Having declined Zacapoaxtla, in mid-October, Maldonado was put in command of Libres, the vital breadbasket which the state government was determined to deny to the enemy. Zacapoaxtla went (on Maldonado's advice) to Julio González, hitherto in charge of war supplies in Teziutlán.

In late October, the Conservative threat grew in Zacapoaxtla and Tlatlauqui. González had swiftly become the instrument of Zacapoaxtla's clerical party, while Cantero had taken control of Tlatlauqui, harassing Maldonado's position on the plateau. Posing as followers of Lucas, Cantero's forces even occupied the district capital of Altotonga in Veracruz. Although Lucas disclaimed any involvement of his men with Cantero's forces, Maldonado asserted that Márquez Galindo's return to the southern Sierra, where he was pursuing an even more ruthless conscription than in July and August, brought Lucas and Cantero together for a short time in a common front against the *leva*.[59] To meet this threat from enraged villagers, Maldonado was appointed in early November to command Tlatlauqui, while Zacapoaxtla was passed from Julio González to his brother, Rafael, whom Maldonado considered more patriotic and less dishonest.[60] Again, using the good offices of Lucas, Maldonado succeeded in placating Cantero. On assurances that there would be no further forced recruitment or food levies for the Republican army, Cantero agreed to hand over seventy rifles, half of which went to Lucas and the other half to the formation of a battalion of National Guard in Tlatlauqui.[61]

Up to this moment, there is no evidence that Cantero had any direct contact with the enemy. However, in early December, agents of the French army entered the Sierra offering Indians freedom from all taxation in exchange for their support for the Intervention. The threat to the Republican base in the Sierra became immediate, and Lucas warned the commander of Tetela's battalion of National Guard that many villagers in his area had expressed an interest in this offer.[62] Moreover, an old champion of the old order loomed again on the edge of the Sierra, ready to lead these villages into battle against the Republicans.

By mid-December, Ignacio Gutiérrez had sided with the Empire, reviving the Conservative Tulancingo-Chignahuapan axis in the western Sierra. In Mexico City, it was feared that Gutiérrez would re-establish his contacts with the Indian population of Zacapoaxtla, in an attempt to re-establish the east-west axis that he had struggled to sustain during the Three Years' War.[63] Meanwhile, a French force occupied the fortress of Perote with instructions to gather mules and supplies for the main expeditionary force still immobilized in Veracruz.[64] By the end of 1862, the survival of the Republican cause in Puebla demanded that the Zacapoaxtla problem be resolved.

Governor Mejía made an imprudent attempt to impose Ignacio López, a Tetelense, upon the government of Zacapoaxtla, which prompted a further revolt. Like Márquez Galindo, López had earned the contempt of the Indian population of Zacapoaxtla and Tlatlauqui by his harsh recruitment drives during the Three Years' War. Maldonado arrived in Zacapoaxtla on 27 December 1862 to take over the direction of the district, whose leading families were on the point of rebellion.[65] To preempt this event, timed to coincide with the approach of the French army, Maldonado summoned Tetela's battalion (renamed the Cazadores de la Montaña and controlled by Bonilla, Rivera, and Luna, all intimate friends of Méndez and loyal to Maldonado). He then ordered the Cuatecomacos to separate from the Zacapoaxtla battalion.[66]

Maldonado proceeded swiftly to commission a fresh National Guard census throughout the district, realizing that this would be the key to obtain military and fiscal control. Simultaneously, he began the reorganization of Zacapoaxtla's battalion, separating it from the new Xochiapulco battalion. In close consultation with Lucas, he relieved it of untrustworthy officers and enlisted men (among whom were many suspected followers of Cantero).[67] The creation of a separate Xochiapulco battalion had several long-term consequences. Until now, as Maldonado observed, the Cuatecomacos "were not organized into companies but were a confused rabble [Maldonado had initially favored the term "force" but replaced it with "rabble"] of men lacking military training and discipline."[68] Military secession from Zacapoaxtla and subjection to National Guard ordinances represented the second step (after the granting of independent municipal status in 1861) in Xochiapulco's political emancipation from its former cabecera. This process culminated in Xochiapulco's secession from the district of Zacapoaxtla and annexation to Tetela in June 1870.

Early in January 1863, Santín returned to Zacapoaxtla to assume direct responsibility for the organization of the Xochiapulco battalion and the Batallón Mixto (now to be raised exclusively from Libres, Zacapoaxtla, and Teziutlán). These units would form a new brigade of the National Guard under General Antonio Osorio, Commander in Chief of the Army of the East, with its headquarters in Zacapoaxtla.[69] To ensure his control of local forces, Maldonado appointed Lucas as his second in command on 13 January 1863.[70] On the following day, he ordered Lucas to lead as many men as possible to Teziutlán to prevent a French column from taking the town.[71]

Leading two hundred infantry, and backed by a squad of Tlaxcalteco cavalry under Doroteo León, Lucas prevented the French force from seizing the town. By forcing their withdrawal, Lucas denied the enemy the large quantity of Republican war supplies that had been assembled there by Julio González.[72] Santín ordered one thousand porters and all available mules to go to Teziutlán to carry these supplies farther back into the Sierra. Maldonado was delighted by the victory, which confirmed his infantry's mastery of mountain warfare and reinforced the myth of the invincibility of the *serrano* infantry that originated in the victory over the French on 5 May 1862.[73]

Just as Maldonado was feeling more confident about the security of the Republican front in the southern Sierra, he was abruptly recalled by González Ortega to Tlaxcala. Maldonado was dumbfounded by the order. All his work over the previous six months was now threatened. Apart from Lucas, there was no one in Zacapoaxtla to whom he could confidently entrust his command.[74] Maldonado insisted that he be allowed to remain in Zacapoaxtla rather than hand over the town to the French, who were marshaling in Perote. The danger was particularly acute now that Santín had marched to the capital with five hundred men in the Batallón Mixto. Only four hundred National Guards commanded by Lucas in the Xochiapulco battalion remained to guard Zacapoaxtla.[75]

Ignoring González Ortega's order, Maldonado proceeded with strengthening Zacapoaxtla's fortifications. Cantero's villages along the border between Zacapoaxtla and Tlatlauqui displayed mounting opposition to the instructions to send five hundred beams for needed fortifications. Opposition also came from Ehuiloco, close to Zacapoaxtla, whose mayor refused to send the fifty men requested for the construction work. Protests also came from Cuetzalan.[76]

By early March 1863, most of the French expeditionary force (28,000 men) had arrived on the Puebla tableland, and the second battle for the city of Puebla commenced. On 17 May the French claimed victory, with the complete surrender of González Ortega's force. The defending army of 14,000 was dissolved and the Republican commander and his officers taken to General Forey as prisoners of war. After the defeat, more than 6,000 Republican soldiers volunteered for the collaborationist Mexican force under General Leonardo Márquez. The only bright spot was that many of the most talented officers managed to escape within days of imprisonment to resume resistance to the Intervention.[77]

The French army entered Mexico City on 10 June 1863 with scarcely a skirmish. Within a month, an "Assembly of Notables" had resolved upon the adoption of an imperial form of government with the crown to be offered to Maximilian von Hapsburg, Archduke of Austria.[78] Throughout July, most of the towns of the Puebla tableland, and many within the Sierra, submitted to the Empire.[79] The Republican state government withdrew to the Sierra to organize resistance.

Conclusion

The first eighteen months of the Intervention in the Sierra were more a continuation of the wars of the Reform than a patriotic struggle against the European invaders. The chief problem facing the Liberal leadership in the southern Sierra was the Counter-Reform, a broadly based Conservative reaction. This movement embraced a mixture of sentiments and loosely coordinated actions including: the opposition of Indian villages to forced military recruitment, forced loans, and labor levies; the resistance of local and district authorities to the imposition of leaders from beyond their districts; the opposition of district National Guards to the imposition of outside commanders; and the determination of local patrician families and the clergy to maintain their ancestral control of local and district politics.

Apart from its opposition to Liberalism and to external interference, the Counter-Reform also reacted to the threat posed by Xochiapulco to a social order rooted in three and one-half centuries of creole dominance and Indian submission. Xochiapulco demonstrated how much a persistent Indian leader such as Lucas could achieve by rallying the support of marginal peasants, organizing them in militias, and contracting them out conditionally to a national patriotic struggle. But even more disturbing than the rise of Lucas, who always kept carefully within the bounds of legality and respected the sanctity of private property, were Liberal leaders such as Márquez Galindo, who were prepared to trade the landed estates of their Conservative opponents for military support from Indian communities and hacienda *peones.*

The strength of the Counter-Reform in the central and southeastern Sierra and the attractions of this area as a source of recruits and supplies both to the Liberals and to the French multiplied the pressures on Lucas from the Xochiapulquenses, who were attempting to consolidate their newly won municipal autonomy; from Urrutia and the Conservatives in Zacapoaxtla; from the Republican authorities; and from the villages who supported the Conservative Indian leader, Cantero. A wrong move against any one of these groups might negate all the gains of the previous six years. Hence, Lucas was obliged to steer a prudent course between outright submission to Urrutia, whose attachment to the Constitutionalist and patriotic cause was always secondary to his loyalty to Zacapoaxtla's Conservatives, and too conspicuous an assertion of autonomy under the external patronage of the Constitutionalist leaders Santín and Maldonado, which might have invited retaliation from Zacapoaxtla against its upstart neighbor, Xochiapulco.

Conservative Zacapoaxtecos badly timed their challenge to the Liberal military authorities in the "Galindo conspiracy" of April 1862, less than a month before the distinguished participation of the Sixth Battalion in the victory over the French on 5 May 1862. Soon after, Urrutia failed to coordinate his challenge to Santín and Maldonado's tightening grip over the district with the widespread popular repudiation of Liberal recruitment policies led by Cantero. By demanding only partial disarmament and by promising exemption from forced recruitment, Lucas offered Cantero's forces the same guarantees that the Xochiapulquenses had come to expect.

Lucas's growing stature in the eyes of his friends and enemies within and beyond the Sierra was due to more than simply his skill as a mediator and conciliator. His unquestioned command over six hundred hardened mountain infantry and his effective deployment of them against the Conservatives and the French were now the basis of his prestige.

6

The Battle for the Sierra, 1863–1866

After the fall of Puebla in May 1863, the Sierra once again resumed the key strategic role that it had played during the Three Years' War: as a provider of supplies and men for both Republican and Imperialist forces and as a sanctuary for the Constitutionalist authorities. Mexican officers who escaped imprisonment after the fall of Puebla—Generals Jesús González Ortega, Miguel Negrete, and Fernando María Ortega—together with Maldonado and Rafael Cravioto (who had remained in the Sierra during the siege of the capital) alternated in the peripatetic Puebla governorship until finally capitulating to the Empire in 1866.[1]

By the beginning of June 1863, Negrete was already in Huauchinango reorganizing patriotic forces after he had been granted the right to use 50 percent of the yield from Tuxpan's customs.[2] He declared the state's National Guard law to be in force, which instructed all able-bodied men between fifteen and sixty years of age in Puebla and Tlaxcala to take up arms. All those unable to enlist due to illness or disability were expected to provide a gun or a horse. Military commanders of all settlements were instructed to draw up censuses to facilitate recruitment and taxation.[3]

Negrete promoted Lucas to the rank of Lieutenant Colonel on 10 June in recognition of the importance of the Xochiapulco forces in securing the Republican front in the districts of Zacapoaxtla and Tlatlauqui during May and June 1863 when Cantero, in collusion with Conservative elements in Zautla and Zacapoaxtla, again had rebelled.[4] The alliance between Cantero and Vicente de Nochebuena, a *contraguerrilla* leader from Quimixtlán, was particularly threatening. Quimixtlán was close to San Andrés Chalchicomula, a Conservative plateau district of large cereal estates. The Republican hold upon the plateau was fragile, with most large landowners prepared not only to deal with the Europeans but also to welcome them.[5] Using Lucas's forces, Maldonado succeeded in defeating the rebels. However, Cantero and Nochebuena rose again in September and took control of Tlatlauqui, which became the first district capital of the Sierra to proclaim for the Empire.[6]

The French Offensive in the Sierra

Early in July 1863, in response to the Imperialist threat in the southern
Sierra, Negrete marched southeast from Huauchinango to impose his authority and secure the southern Sierra against the long-anticipated French
offensive. Upon arrival in Zacapoaxtla, Negrete relieved Maldonado of the
interim governorship conferred upon him in June by González Ortega, promoting him to Brigadier General in the regular army in mid-August. Lucas
received a further promotion to the rank of Colonel on 30 July when he was
given the command of the Zacapoaxtla battalion of National Guard.[7]
Backed by forces from Xochiapulco, Negrete proceeded to Jalapa where he
imposed General Luciano Prieto as governor of Veracruz. He returned via
Teziutlán where he appointed commanders and officials loyal to himself,
and conferred promotions upon all and sundry. Negrete then returned to
Tetela where he elevated the still-convalescent Méndez to the rank of
Brigadier General and Bonilla to that of Colonel.[8]

*General Miguel Negrete, Commander of Republican forces
in the Puebla Sierra, 1863–64.* Archivo Fotográfico, Centro
de Estudios de Historia de México (CONDUMEX)

In mid-August, the general French offensive commenced in the Sierra,
across a line stretching from Huauchinango to Teziutlán. Lucas was escort-
ing a convoy of mules and porters with supplies for Zacatlán, where the

new Republican headquarters were being established, when he received instructions to mobilize all the men he could for the defense of Teziutlán against a French attack.[9] On his return from Zacatlán, Lucas briefly took Chignahuapan, whose leaders had been organizing opposition to Republican authorities in villages throughout the districts of Zacatlán, Tetela, and Zacapoaxtla. The Chignahuapan forces regrouped, attacking the Xochiapulquenses near Aquixtla on 24 August. Although Lucas succeeded in holding the line against the Conservatives at the barrio of Tonalapa (on the Tetela-Zacatlán boundary) over the next eighteen months, this counterattack demonstrated the strength of Conservative forces in the western Sierra and underlined the pressing need to establish reliable allies in the villages in this area.[10]

Negrete instructed Lucas, in conjunction with the jefe político of Tetela, to make "expeditions to the surrounding rebel barrios and villages, either to destroy them, or to provide recruits for the army."[11] Lucas resisted such drastic measures but chose instead to consolidate the National Guard units in villages opposed to their cabeceras. The potential for such alliances was evident in the jurisdictions of Zautla, Ixtacamaxtitlán, and Tetela, along the southern margins of the Sierra, where long-standing tensions had existed between communities since colonial times.[12] But Lucas also established important alliances with newly formed National Guard companies in villages farther into the Sierra, along Tetela's western boundary with Zacatlán. By the end of 1864, Lucas could count on two hundred fifty armed men in the villages of Cuautempan, Ixtolco, Hueytentan, Tonalapa, and Xaltatempa along this boundary, willing to defend Tetela against the enemy in Zacatlán's barrios of Santa Catarina, San Baltazar, Cuacuila, and San Miguel Tenango.[13]

The consequence of this defensive recruitment was that the social base of Lucas's sphere of influence shifted westward. This change of strategic emphasis from Zacapoaxtla to Tetela was doubly necessary now that Tlatlauqui was firmly aligned with the Empire. Many of Tlatlauqui's barrios, and those of neighboring Zacapoaxtla, mobilized forces to serve the French army. In late August and early September 1863 the French advanced into the Sierra following two lines of entry from their bases in San Juan de los Llanos and Tulancingo (Hidalgo). To the west, Colonel Baron Alphonse Edouard Aymard moved from Tulancingo to attack Negrete, who had withdrawn the Republican headquarters from Huauchinango to Necaxa.[14] To the east, Colonel Jesús Lalanne occupied Tlatlauqui and entered Zacapoaxtla at the head of 807 Zouaves, 500 Mexican cavalry (commanded by Antonio Rodríguez Bocardo), and 600 "auxiliaries" (recruited from villages in Tlatlauqui and Zacapoaxtla) on 13 September. Rather than face certain defeat, Maldonado had already withdrawn his forces on 7 September to a stronger position. The patriotic "war of guerrillas" had begun.[15]

Prompting Maldonado's withdrawal was his suspicion that the barrios adjacent to Zacapoaxtla would join the enemy at the first opportunity. During the building of the town's fortifications between December and January, Maldonado had noted the "unpatriotic, fanatical, and reactionary" sentiments of Jilotepec, Las Lomas, Yautetelco, Comaltepec, Jaitic, Ehuiloco, Ahuacatlán, Tatoxcac, and Actopan, villages that had shirked on their labor levies and which he suspected of being firmly in the thrall of the priests and Conservative families of Zacapoaxtla.[16] Surrounded by so many hostile neighbors, Maldonado appreciated the impossibility of defending Zacapoaxtla.

The site of Zacapoaxtla also posed tactical dilemmas. The qualities that made Zacapoaxtla suitable as a ceremonial and commercial center presented only hazards for its military defendability. Situated at the end of a narrow bluff, with precipitous slopes on all three sides, high ridges overlook the town to the south, west, and east. The town's position on this raised mesa, highly visible from all the surrounding hills, was ideal for the purpose of symbolic and ceremonial domination of the surrounding landscape and villages, which accounts for the occupation of the site since before the Conquest. However, the location was a military liability in the age of artillery. Without sufficient troops and artillery to station in the redoubts constructed on the hills, Zacapoaxtla was an easy target. Any siege force need only occupy and mount artillery upon any one of them to be able to hold the town to ransom.

Hence, the time-honored convention for defense forces was to withdraw to the much more easily defendable escarpment to the north, the summits of Apulco. Holding Apulco also blocked the invader's access to the *tierra caliente*, whose wealth in revenues and supplies was always a principal motive for entering the Sierra. The tactic of withdrawal from the cabecera had an additional advantage: the attacking force had its expectations raised by the ease in taking the town and the apparent pusillanimity of its defenders, leaving them unprepared for the real battle that would often occur a few days later. This tactical sequence was repeated on several occasions throughout the 1860s.

The final consideration that prompted Maldonado's retreat was that his forces were greatly outnumbered. Since early June, his troops had been depleted by Negrete's thirst for men and supplies. With a defending force of only three hundred, withdrawal was his only option. On this occasion, Maldonado was unable to withdraw to the heights of Apulco because they were already occupied by "traitorous forces" which had moved up from Cuetzalan and Xochitlán. Instead, Maldonado occupied the Gran Poder de Dios, the highest hilltop in the area, with two pieces of mountain artillery. After a day and a half of fighting, Maldonado spiked his cannon and withdrew to Xochiapulco, leaving perfidious Zacapoaxtla to the enemy. The French and Conservative Mexican forces entered the town on 13 September, to be received "with bellringing, flag waving and serenades while Commander Lalanne was almost dragged by the priest and the *vecinos* to the church where a Te Deum was sung."[17]

Following the occupation of the town, the French commander pro-posed an armistice. Although uncertain about his authority to represent the Republican cause in Negrete's absence (Negrete had been pushed back from Huauchinango across the border into San Luis Potosí), Maldonado accepted the invitation to meet with Lalanne in Zacapoaxtla. Leaving Lucas in charge of the main force in Xochiapulco, Maldonado, "accompa-nied by only one officer, Porfirio Saavedra, and six others, all Indians, especially selected and typical of the race," walked to Zacapoaxtla. Mal-donado described this bizarre meeting with Lalanne, Rodríguez Bocardo, and Miguel Molina Alcántara that concluded with a banquet and the hospi-tality of a bed for the night. Maldonado declined Lalanne's offer of a large cash payment in exchange for demobilizing the forces of Xochiapulco. The French commander, in turn, politely refused Maldonado's condition that the French evacuate Zacapoaxtla and the whole Sierra between Teziutlán and Huauchinango.[18] Both belligerents did agree to an eight-day suspension of hostilities.

The truce gave Maldonado time to assess the state of Republican forces in the southern Sierra. He considered following Negrete to San Luis Potosí, but Xochiapulco's principal commanders (Lucas, Luis Antonio Díaz, Ireneo Reyes, and others) persuaded him to remain in charge, offer-ing their personal possessions to sustain the campaign against the French.[19] On 25 September 1863, Maldonado convened all of his forces, assembling more than five hundred men from Xochiapulco (Zacapoaxtla), Contla and Tlamanaca (Zautla), Tuligtic and Cuahuigtic (Ixtacamastitlán), and Ometepec (Tetela). He coaxed the commanders of these villages (all of them *tierra fría*, land-hungry mountain communities situated on the edge of the Sierra close to the tableland) to resolve to march against the com-mercial centers of Xochitlán and Cuetzalan in order to deny the enemy the resources of the *tierra caliente*. It was never hard to persuade soldiers from highland settlements to invade the wealthier communities of the *tierra caliente*. These were routes which they traveled seasonally in search of land for planting corn, and the process of highland attrition of the lowlands had been going on since long before the Spanish Conquest.[20]

The campaign began on 30 September 1863, with the taking of Xochitlán without a single shot fired. The garrison of 150 men surrendered to Reyes and two hundred Xochiapulquenses, who claimed a booty of twenty cases of am-munition and 150 rifles, which they sent to the Republican headquarters at Huahuaxtla. Five days later, Lalanne and Rodríguez Bocardo counterattacked with 600 men, surprising the Republican force defending the strategic bridge across the Río Apulco. Unfamiliar with the terrain and the powerful current of the Apulco river, the French force, under intense fire, discovered that they were caught between the uncrossable river and an enemy protected by a thick cover of woodland. The attackers panicked and fled. Between 4 A.M. and noon, Lalanne lost at least 300 men to the enemy with many others carried off by the torrent. The Republican force captured 500 rifles and fifty boxes of ammunition. In his report, Maldonado attributed the great victory to Lucas. If Maldonado's estimates are to be believed, less than three hundred largely Indian (and formally untrained) infantry had inflicted damage comparable to French losses at the battle of 5 May 1862.[21] After putting the enemy to flight, Lucas occupied the heights of Apulco.[22]

In spite of the impressive victory at Apulco on 4 October 1863, Maldonado needed ten days to retake Zacapoaxtla partly because the captured ammunition had to be reworked to fit the different bore of the Mexican rifles. The principal delay, however, resulted from the advance by Imperialist forces from Chignahuapan and Aquixtla upon Tetela de Oro. Lucas's infantry was promptly re-deployed to defend Tetela's western flank against the forces of Chignahuapan and Tulancingo.[23]

The towns, villages, and *rancherías* along the western and southwestern flanks of the Sierra, from Chignahuapan and Aquixtla, south to Tlaxco in Tlaxcala, and sweeping west through Ixtacamaxtitlán to Libres, had been mobilized by the Conservatives since the Three Years' War. By late 1863, the greatest threat to Republican positions in this area came from Lieutenant Colonel Antonio Domínguez and his renowned Chignahuapan cavalry squadron. To confront this threat, Lucas developed a close alliance with Dionisio Leal, the National Guard commander of Cuahuigtic, a village in a dominant position on Tetela's southern flank. Lucas exploited the village's ancient conflict with the hacienda of Coayuca and promoted the secession of Cuahuigtic from its cabecera, Aquixtla, where the Conservative (now Imperialist) owner of the Coayuca hacienda, and priest, José Ignacio Castilla, resided.[24]

Late in October, Domínguez, leading the Chignahuapan squadron and 350 infantry (only 150 of whom were armed, the other 200 waving clubs) from Otlatlán, captained by the Márquez brothers (future allies of Lucas), captured Zacatlán.[25] Leading a daring counterattack with 600 Tetelenses and Xochiapulquenses, Lucas quickly recaptured Zacatlán. But a month later, Conservative troops returned to storm and occupy the Republican mountain stronghold of Ahuacatlán.[26] Soon, however, a series of startling Republican gains in the central and southern Sierra temporarily relieved the pressure on Zacatlán and the western front.

Republican Consolidation in the Central and Southern Sierra

Maldonado and Lucas eventually drove the French from Zacapoaxtla on 15 October 1863. Lucas went on to retake Tlatlauqui in the face of stout re-

sistance from Cantero, who retreated to Xocoyolo, a village commanding the road to Cuetzalan, Zacapoaxtla's lifeline with the *tierra
caliente*.[27] By the end of September, after driving the enemy from the
tierra fría and occupying Xochitlán, Maldonado judged the time right
for taking Cuetzalan, the refuge (Maldonado believed) of all the
Conservative elements in the district. In two skillful maneuvers, which
involved the cutting of new paths through dense woodland, Lucas defeated Cantero's forces at Xocoyolo and then dispersed the main
Conservative Zacapoaxteco force at an aguardiente factory belonging to
the Luque family. Lucas entered Cuetzalan on the evening of 22 October,
and withdrew within hours to Zacapoaxtla with a considerable booty of
ammunition.[28]

Driven from the *tierra cálida*, the French and their Mexican allies re-
grouped along the southern margins of the Sierra for a renewed offensive.
Cantero led the way with a successful attack on Tlatlauqui. Maldonado and
Lucas responded with one thousand men, retaking the town on 24 October.
Meanwhile, defense forces organized by Lucas in the Zautla barrios of
Contla and Tlamanaca (like Cuahuigtic, they became loyal allies to Lucas
in future struggles) held a French force at bay until Lucas and Maldonado
returned from Tlatlauqui to defeat the French at the hacienda of Mazapa,
just south of Zacapoaxtla.

In spite of these setbacks, Zacapoaxtla's Conservatives and their Indian
allies were able to regroup by early November under the command of
Rafael Molina. They re-claimed Xocoyolo and Cuetzalan and harassed the
Republican northern flank. On 24 November, Maldonado and Lucas, with
thirteen hundred men and one piece of artillery, marched again upon
Cuetzalan, now occupied by nine hundred "traitors." The precision firing of
the artillery, under the direction of Lucas, ignited the enemy's ammunition
store. Under a torrential thunderstorm, the Conservatives were routed from
their trenches by Xochiapulquenses wielding machetes. The Conservatives
abandoned Cuetzalan in panic. During the plundering that followed,
Urrutia, former jefe político of Zacapoaxtla, was discovered taking refuge
under a shop counter in an advanced state of inebriation. Lucas intervened
to save his life.[29]

By December 1863, Maldonado's Republican front had reached its
apogee in the Sierra. The Republicans held all district capitals. The
enemy had suffered a series of major defeats and been driven from the
southern Sierra and from the *tierra cálida*. Maldonado commanded three
thousand hardened, voluntarily recruited soldiers from a compact constellation of villages between Zacapoaxtla and Zacatlán, which Lucas
counted at 2,625 (*see* chart on page 96). Provided that these men were allowed to serve under their own commanders close to home and offered
sufficient financial inducements, they would follow Lucas and
Maldonado in the defense of their fatherland.

Table 6–1. **Estimated Strength of Lucas and Maldonado's Forces in December 1863**

Battalion	Commander	Number of Men
Zacapoaxtla	Maldonado	500
Xochiapulco, Contla, Tlamanaca, and Ometepec	Lucas	800
Tulictic and Cuahuigtic	Dionisio Leal	300
Zacatlán	Dimas López	500
Tetela de Oro	Francisco Zamítez	500
Tlatlauqui	Miguel León	25
Total		2,625[30]

Badly bruised by this series of defeats, the French refrained from further campaigns in the southern Sierra for the rest of 1863, choosing instead to control the plateau. Only after the arrival of an Austrian army in mid-1864 would the Europeans risk reentering the Puebla Sierra to confront the now infamous Republican stronghold.

The First Republican Offensive against San Juan de los Llanos

With the relaxation of the external threat, rivalries within Republican ranks resurfaced. Teziutlán, with its wealthy landowners and merchants, valuable customhouse on the trade route between the altiplano and the coast, and strategic location close to the fortress of Perote and the route to Veracruz, was repeatedly taken and retaken throughout 1864 by different Republican factions, Conservatives, and even by Governor Hernández y Hernández of Veracruz, who coveted its customs revenue.[31]

Lucas, apart from retaking Teziutlán for Maldonado on three occasions, consolidated Republican control in a swath of the southern Sierra extending from Tlatlauqui through Zacapoaxtla, Zautla, and Ixtacamaxtitlán to the border with Tlaxcala. Maldonado also began to deploy Lucas's forces on the plateau, in preparation for a possible advance upon the central valley.[32] In mid-June 1864, Maldonado ordered Lucas to take San Juan de los Llanos, the capital of the northern cereal zone, in order to confront the Austrian expeditionary force that had landed in May. Lucas led two companies of National Guard from Xochiapulco, numbering 500 men, a force of 300 cavalry (the *plateados* commanded by Antonio Pérez), and a motley bunch of officers (the best known were Baltazar Girón from Cuyoaco, Abraham Plata and Ignacio Cuellar from Tlaxcala, and Paulino Noriega from the Sierra de Hidalgo).[33] These troops put to flight a French force occupying the hacienda of Xicalahuata. Girón then released his cavalry upon the neighboring hacienda of Potzingo, and instructed his troops to carry off anything they wanted to Zacapoaxtla.

Lucas was appalled. First, he attempted unsuccessfully to quell the disorders. Then, realizing that the element of surprise necessary for capturing San Juan de los Llanos had been lost, he ordered a hasty retreat to Zacapoaxtla. Maldonado agreed with Lucas that, in spite of Llanos landowners' refusal to pay Republican taxes and their known Imperialist sympathies, Republican forces had no right to plunder their goods. The 330 mule loads of booty from the haciendas of Potzingo and Xicalahuata were ordered to be returned (with the exception of the weapons).[34]

Apart from the uncomfortable relationship between the Republican infantry and cavalry, this incident reveals an important element of Lucas's strategy. Once Lucas began to extend his influence southward, close to the cereal and pastoral haciendas of the plateau, it became less realistic to base his appeal upon the Xochiapulco formula of confrontation between landless barrios and neighboring haciendas. The settlements along the edge of the altiplano depended on employment upon or rental access to the land of the haciendas.[35] Laying waste to these haciendas would harm villagers and alienate hard-won sympathy and support.

Lucas extended his influence by appealing to villagers with guarantees against forced enlistment, arbitrary taxation, and external intervention in their affairs. By 1864 he had consolidated his hold in areas that hitherto had been militantly opposed, or at best indifferent, to the Reform. The correspondent of *El Eco Patriótico* in Teziutlán estimated in June 1864 that Lucas had at least eight hundred men with four hundred rifles on a war footing in the southern Sierra. Much of this armament had been brought by "forces from the plateau" that had abandoned Roldán and Francisco Balderrábano, the Conservative leaders in this area during the Three Years' War. Of the five hundred armed villagers once commanded by these Conservative leaders only twenty now remained. The rest had gone over to Lucas.[36]

Throughout 1864, Maldonado successfully extended his control of the Sierra, from Teziutlán to Zacatlán. However, Republican military capability remained essentially defensive, based upon village companies under elected local commanders. Cavalry was available to accompany Republican infantry, but only on terms dictated by autonomous cavalry commanders whose depredations frequently alienated the inhabitants of areas in which they operated. Military paralysis often resulted from disagreements between cavalry and infantry commanders. Just such a disagreement between Republican infantry and cavalry officers resulted in the storming and sacking of Zacatlán by the enemy in June 1864.[37]

The Failure of Republican Offensives in the Western Sierra

During the second half of 1864, the western Sierra front, from Tlaxco north to Huauchinango, became increasingly active. Adopting the strategy followed during the Three Years' War, Imperial commanders chose Tulancingo as the base of operations for confronting Republican forces in the Sierra de Hidalgo, the Huasteca, the Sierra de Puebla, and the plains of Apam and Tlaxco. Crushing Republican resistance in the Puebla Sierra was crucial to Emperor Maximilian, not only because this region threatened the Mexico City-Veracruz lifeline but also to prevent Juárez's army in the north from joining Díaz's forces in the south.

Although Maximilian possessed able and energetic Mexican commanders—Francisco Pérez and Francisco Pavón—in the Puebla region, this was an immense front to cover. Domínguez's Chignahuapan squadron, upon which Pavón depended for keeping the Republicans at bay in the Puebla Sierra, proved to be a formidable offensive force, but it lacked sufficient backing from garrisons on the plateau to be able to sustain an occupation of Zacatlán or Tetela for more than a few days. Consequently, this area suffered a vengeful succession of attacks and counterattacks between the towns of Chignahuapan and Zacatlán, with a similar conflict, albeit somewhat milder, between Aquixtla and Tetela. For much of 1864 a stalemate existed in the Puebla Sierra with villages on the peripheries supporting the Imperialists, and those farther into the Sierra backing the Republicans. However, rivalry between Republican commanders neutralized any advantage that patriotic control of this strategic region offered to Juárez and Díaz in their struggle against the Empire.

Throughout the second half of 1864, Lucas continued to defend the western Sierra against attacks from Chignahuapan and the Sierra de Tulancingo with forces from Xochiapulco, Tetela, and Libres.[38] The vital contribution of these forces was acknowledged when Díaz conferred military command of the state upon Fernando María Ortega late in 1864. One of Ortega's first acts, upon arriving in the Sierra, was to promote Xochiapulco to the status of *villa*, giving the municipality the same status as its neighbor and rival, Zacapoaxtla. Ortega honored it further with the title of "La Villa del Cinco de Mayo." The decree also ordered the land of the haciendas of Manzanilla, Xochiapulco, and Jilotepec to be distributed among the Xochiapulquenses who had fought at the battle of 5 May 1862 according to rank, with the state compensating the owners.[39]

By rewarding them for their patriotic services, Ortega hoped that the Xochiapulquenses would spearhead the first major Republican offensive beyond the Sierra. Unwisely, he chose to assemble his small army at Zacatlán (numbering fifteen hundred men of whom Xochiapulco contributed six hundred).[40] Anywhere else in the southern or western Sierra would have been better than Zacatlán, overlooked by hills and enclosed on two sides by a precipitous canyon. But Ortega was not a *serrano* and, like Alatriste before him, felt uncomfortable in this region. Also, like Alatriste, he specialized in premature offensives.

On the night of 8 December the Chignahuapan cavalry battalion surprised the Republican forces assembling at Zacatlán. A heated battle raged until Ortega ordered a withdrawal, leaving Zacatlán's streets littered with thirty-seven Republican dead, a multitude of wounded, nineteen prisoners, three hundred rifles, thirty-nine cases of ammunition, one piece of artillery, and sixty saddled horses. Republican offensive capability in the western Sierra was destroyed for several months. Although the Republicans reoccupied Zacatlán within days, the idea of an offensive was abandoned. Ortega now occupied Ahuacatlán as a more tenable stronghold.[41]

The defeat at Zacatlán was not the only casualty of Juárez's new appointment in the Sierra. Ortega arrived in December 1864, just as José María Maldonado and Rafael Cravioto, in close coordination with General Gerónimo Treviño, commander of four hundred men from the Legión del Norte (mainly from Nuevo León), were poised to launch simultaneous attacks on the fortress of Perote and the district capitals of San Juan de los Llanos, Jalacingo, and Altotonga. These attacks were to be in preparation for a major offensive on the plateau. This more promising maneuver was abandoned in favor of Ortega's offensive on the western front with its unfortunate results.[42]

The Austrian Offensive in the Southern Sierra

Imperialist forces had been wary of taking the initiative in the southern Sierra since the disastrous defeats suffered by Franco-Mexican forces in 1863. However, by February 1865, Count Franz Thun-Hohenstein, the Austrian supreme commander of the Puebla region, felt sufficiently confident about the state of his forces and the prospect of receiving local support to order the renewal of the campaign in the Puebla Sierra. He sent Major Alphon Freiherr von Kodolitch to attack Teziutlán, which was garrisoned by 1,290 troops (principally from Oaxaca) under Ortega. With the help of 100 Mexican cavalry from San Andrés Chalchicomula under Hermenegildo Carrillo and 100 Nahua infantry from Altotonga under Miguel Melgarejo, Kodolitch caught the garrison off guard and occupied the town early on the morning of 5 February. After three hours of resistance, the Republican force fled leaving sixty dead, many more wounded, thirty prisoners, eighty horses, sixty rifles, ammunition, the regimental banner of Treviño's northern legion, and the regimental brass band.[43] Predictably, Tlatlauqui immediately adhered again to the Empire.

To prevent any further dissolution of the southern front, Maldonado gathered five hundred men, who left Zacapoaxtla on 6 February under Lucas with orders to recapture Teziutlán. Lucas attacked the town on 7 February. However, the arrival of Conservative cavalry commanded by Rodríguez Bocardo, the news that Tlatlauqui had been occupied by French troops, and word that Kodolitch was marching directly upon Zacapoaxtla persuaded Lucas to beat a hasty retreat via Chignautla in order to reach

Zacapoaxtla before the enemy. Disgusted at the disorganization within Republican ranks in the Puebla Sierra, Treviño withdrew to Papantla, leaving Zacapoaxtla exposed to the Austrians, who entered the town on 17 February 1865.[44]

Undeterred by two major defeats in such rapid succession, Ortega proceeded with his plan for a general offensive in the western Sierra to coincide with a Republican offensive in the Sierra de Hidalgo. From late January 1865, Republican cavalry under Generals Cacho and Cuellar from Oaxaca had been gathering in the western Sierra and meeting up with Antonio Pérez's *plateados*, regularized bandits recruited from Tlaxcala's Malinche region.[45] Rather than wait for his forces to reach full strength, Antonio Pérez impatiently and unwisely attacked Chignahuapan on 17 February. The Imperial garrison not only successfully repelled the attack but also swiftly moved into a vigorous counterattack.

Backed by eight hundred infantry recruited from Chignahuapan, Tlaxco, Aquixtla, and the *"rancherías* of Ixtacamaxtitlán," on 18 February Domínguez's cavalry squadron finally broke Tetela's front line of defense at the barrio of Tonalapa. On the following day, Tetela de Ocampo, defended only by one hundred infantry and a small force of cavalry under General Ortega (who was passing through on his way to the western front), fell to the Imperialists. The luckless Ortega lost twenty-three men, much of his armament, and all of his baggage. A complete rout was avoided when Méndez (recently promoted by Ortega to Brigadier General and Chief of the Tetela and Xochiapulco line) finally stirred from his convalescence to escape into the surrounding mountains with one hundred Tetela National Guard and thirty cavalry, with the battalion's armament intact.[46] The Imperialists proceeded to sack the houses of many of Tetela's most prominent Liberals, including that of Gregorio Zamítez (containing a gunpowder factory), Francisco Pérez (soon to become Lucas's father-in-law), Juan Rosales, Juan N. Méndez, and Leocadio Méndez (for almost a decade, the principal supplier and financial backer of the Xochiapulco battalion).[47]

The occupation by Imperial forces of the district capitals caused the three principal Republican leaders—Maldonado, Cravioto, and Ortega—to abandon plans for an offensive on the plateau. However, all was not lost. As the French had learned in 1863, capturing the district capitals was a far cry from the pacification of the districts themselves. In February 1865, with Ortega's larger Republican force now in tatters, the southern Sierra returned to guerrilla warfare.

"La Guerra de Guerrillas"

Zacapoaxtla, once more under Imperial control, was returned to the kind of government that its Conservative families preferred. The young Conservative Zacapoaxteco, Pascual Bonilla, was appointed Imperial prefect of the district.[48] Before withdrawing from Zacapoaxtla, Ortega promoted Lucas to the rank of Brigadier General, with command over Republican forces in the district of Zacapoaxtla.[49] The Xochiapulco battalion was placed under Juan Crisóstomo Bonilla, close friend and compadre of Lucas.[50] This left Maldonado without a civil or military post. Having gathered his family, who had taken refuge in the hills before the fall of Zacapoaxtla, Maldonado left the Sierra to continue his dogged service to the patriotic cause from the south of the state.[51]

Under their new commander (for the first time not a member of the Lucas family), the Xochiapulquenses returned to the earlier tactic of harassing the cabecera with surprise attacks. The first occurred on 23 February when Lucas, Bonilla, and Luis Antonio Díaz confused the Austrian garrison in Zacapoaxtla by attacking the town from three different points. Count Thun narrowly escaped capture by taking refuge in the church tower.[52] The Xochiapulquenses, led by Lucas, attacked again on 26 February and 3 March, on the last occasion wounding several Austrians.[53] Incensed, Thun personally led a counterattack upon Xochiapulco's cabecera, which so far had escaped any direct action during the European Intervention.

Backed by Tlatlauqui forces under Cantero, the Austrians invaded Xochiapulco on 14 March 1865, occupied the plaza, and set fire to the still unfinished public buildings. Having taken refuge in the surrounding hills and angered by this injustice, the Xochiapulquenses returned the attack, surrounded the Austrians, closed off their lines of escape, and engaged them in "deadly fire." The Imperial force eventually broke out of the encirclement and retreated to Zacapoaxtla in complete disarray. They left behind 32 dead and 154 prisoners. The Austrian defeat owed much to the blocking of routes of escape with branches and logs. Bonilla later reported that the attack on Xochiapulco had been inspired and financed by the Vargas family of Tlatlauqui and that no Zacapoaxtecos, wise to the wily tactics of their neighbors, had participated.[54]

This action was the first major defeat suffered by Austrian forces in Mexico. But the bad news was tempered by reports that Rafael Cravioto in Huauchinango had adhered to the Empire in exchange for a large cash indemnity.[55] His example was followed by a rash of further adhesions by communities in the Sierra de Hidalgo and the Huasteca.[56] For the first time since the Intervention began, the southern front of the Sierra was seriously exposed on its northern flank, the region upon which it depended for supplies of food, revenue, and sanctuary.

Stung by the defeat of 14 March 1864, Count Thun (probably advised by Pascual Bonilla) wrote to Lucas and Luis Antonio Díaz offering a resolution of the "land question," hinting that the owners of the hacienda of Xochiapulco and Manzanilla were prepared to give up their claim. In return for settling the question of lands, Thun urged Lucas and Díaz to lay down their arms and to recognize the Austrian objective of conciliation, not conquest.[57] Lucas declined Thun's request for submission on the grounds that the Empire, a creation of Mexico's discredited Conservative Party, lacked any legitimacy. He stated his intention to continue leading his men in resistance.

Lucas stated that resistance among the Xochiapulquenses had become a way of life. He acknowledged Thun's reference to the "gentlemanly" conduct of forces, but regretted that this had not been reciprocated by Imperial forces in recent fighting in Zacapoaxtla when Xochiapulquense prisoners had been viciously murdered. He assured Thun that the thirty Austrian prisoners were being attended to before his own soldiers. These prisoners were returned on 6 April when hostilities resumed.[58]

During the second half of March, Pascual Bonilla, believing a purely military solution to be impossible given the difficulty of pursuing rebels in mountain terrain, made a further attempt at conciliating Xochiapulco by satisfying agrarian demands. He hinted that the Xochiapulquenses might be allowed to retain their arms, in order to allay their fear of "an invasion from the Zacapoaxtecos." He considered Lucas, "wise like all Indians," to be concerned above all with his own interests and with avoiding disorders. Further, he considered him trustworthy and open to negotiation.[59] By early April, however, Bonilla still had received no reply from Lucas to his proposal.

Count Thun never seriously considered an alternative to a strictly military solution to Republican resistance in the Sierra. The Austrian commander received conflicting advice from his Mexican allies, who differed over the strategy necessary for pacifying the Sierra. Conservatives in Zacapoaxtla favored strong garrisons of Austrian troops along an axis stretching northwest from Zacapoaxtla through Tetela to Hueytlalpan (in the *tierra caliente* of Zacatlán), combined with the suppression and, presumably, the annihilation of the Republican strongholds at Xochiapulco and Huahuaxtla. This would provide a barrier against the Republican strongholds of Huauchinango, Zacatlán, and Tetela in the western Sierra, enabling the Imperialists to consolidate their hold in the central and eastern Sierra. There was even talk of desirability of Austrian colonies.[60]

By contrast, the Imperial Prefect in Puebla, Fernando Pardo, recommended the occupation by Austrian garrisons of the central Sierra towns of Tetela, Cuetzalan, Xochitlán, and Nauzontla. Apart from their accessibility from Zacapoaxtla, which all parties agreed should be the bulwark against the Republican menace, there was the additional advantage that the inhabitants of these towns were strongly opposed to the new breed of Indian warrior characterized by the Xochiapulquenses. They preferred the more pacific Indians of their own jurisdictions. The occupation of these towns would also cut off the Xochiapulquenses from their sources of supply and deny them avenues of retreat. Besides, not to occupy these towns would be to allow the Xochiapulquenses to move into the interior of the Sierra from where they would be able to resist indefinitely. This would expose the Imperial forces to the danger of surprise attack and, as had already happened on several occasions, of being trapped with no line of retreat. Pardo's final advice was that Roldán be relieved as commander of the Mexican forces in Zacapoaxtla, since he saw him as the major obstacle to peace in the district. There was "loathing and vengeance" felt toward Roldán locally, his legacy from the Three Years' War and also from his more recent fighting.[61]

No movement on any front could be made before the return of the thirty Austrian prisoners, which took place on 6 April. Count Thun then immediately announced the start of the Sierra campaign. Four and one-half companies of light infantry, numbering 730 men and 25 cavalry under Captain Bernhard, were dispatched from Puebla and arrived in Zacapoaxtla to a rapturous welcome of bells, rockets, and wind bands.[62] Thun proposed to start the campaign on 12 April, timed to coincide with an attack upon Tetela from the west by the Twelfth Company of Zacatlán, which was backed by local forces from Chignahuapan, Aquixtla, and Ixtacamaxtitlán and supported by Hungarian (Uhlanian) cavalry from San Juan de los Llanos.[63]

Aware of an imminent attack, Republican forces in Xochiapulco moved in a preemptive strike. On 12 April, a small force of Xochiapulquenses established itself above the road between Zacapoaxtla and Tlatlauqui, with the intent to capture a battery of artillery on its way to Zacapoaxtla. Two companies of local forces, commanded by Cantero, succeeded in dislodging them and inflicting heavy losses. On the following day, three columns of Austrian and Mexican troops attacked Xochiapulco from the north, east, and south. Again the population withdrew to the surrounding hills from where they engaged the enemy in intense fire, obliging the Austrian force to withdraw (without suffering any losses). This "ephemeral" victory (in the words of Pascual Bonilla) nevertheless persuaded the Austrians to delay their offensive.[64] Republican forces, occupying Huahuaxtla, still controlled the road to Cuetzalan, effectively blocking Zacapoaxtla's access to the north of the district. Following the battle, Lucas forbade the commander of Cuetzalan (the wealthiest town in the *tierra caliente*) to send any supplies to Zacapoaxtla.[65]

Thun faced other problems in his Sierra offensive. He was counting on a significant contribution from local forces. For this purpose, he had instructed Miguel Melgarejo, cacique of Altotonga, who had helped in the capture of Teziutlán in January, to organize forces in his area and in neighboring Teziutlán. At first, Melgarejo proved uncooperative by expressing a preference for retirement. He insisted that he had no need for the four hundred rifles that Thun had sent him, and that the armament that he already possessed was quite sufficient for maintaining order. General Carrillo insisted that Melgarejo raise the force. The cacique of Altotonga reluctantly complied, but, rather than recruit in his own area, he moved to Teziutlán where he carried out a forced recruitment that brought the district to the verge of rebellion against the Imperial authorities. By late April, Melgarejo had managed to recruit only fifty of the one hundred fifty men he was expected to contribute to the offensive upon Xochiapulco.[66] Unable to delay the offensive any longer, Thun handed over the command of Zacapoaxtla forces to Captain Bernhard and ordered hostilities to commence on 25 April 1865.

Mediation, Armistice, and Republican Surrender

The resumption of hostilities coincided with the arrival in Zacapoaxtla of Francisco Villanueva, the Imperial inspector. Villanueva immediately wrote to Lucas and expressed regret at the recent events and invited him with the Republican Generals Méndez and Ortega to a conference. Méndez agreed to attend, but only on the condition that hostilities and all troop movements cease along the line between Zacatlán and Zacapoaxtla. This was agreed on 27 April 1865. A conference was then held at Xochitlán on 3 May and an armistice signed by Villanueva, Ortega, Méndez, Juan Ramírez, Márquez Galindo, and Bonilla (representing Lucas, who was not present). The terms of the armistice confirm the strength of the Republican position at this time.

The first condition was that Comaltepec, a barrio on the northern edge of the town of Zacapoaxtla (and Lucas's birthplace), should remain neutral and that the water course between Comaltepec and Zacapoaxtla should not be obstructed (clearly a matter which had been troubling the cabecera). The Republican authorities of the district would continue to occupy Huahuaxtla, control the bridge over the Apulco, and charge *alcabalas* upon goods crossing their line. The Republican positions at Tetela and Ahuacatlán were also recognized. Ortega, Ramírez, and Márquez Galindo were permitted to travel to Puebla to arrange a fuller agreement. Here, Count Thun agreed to a full armistice on 17 May with the terms of peace to be renegotiated every twenty days. On returning to Xochitlán in June, the same leaders, this time with Lucas present, declared their determination to continue adhering to the principles of the 1857 constitution and not to recognize the Empire, without actually declaring the renewal of hostilities.[67] Peace would last for less than a month.

On 13 July 1865, Lucas informed the Austrian commander that hostilities would resume on 15 July, in accordance with the terms of the armistice signed in Puebla on 17 May.[68] The Austrians, numbering two thousand men including troops from Zacapoaxtla, Llanos, and Chalchicomula, moved quickly. On 16 July they attacked and dislodged the Xochiapulco force from the heights of Apulco. Lucas and Bonilla ordered a retreat to Tetela, which was already under attack by two thousand men led by Captain Tancredo Della Salla. Eight hundred of Della Salla's small army had been recruited from the *rancherías* of Tlaxco, Chignahuapan, Zacatlán, and Ixtacamaxtitlán, which demonstrated Austria's success with recruitment in the Sierra. Four hundred Republican National Guards defended Tetela backed by two hundred men from Cuahuigtic under Colonel Dionisio Leal. After intense fighting, Méndez ordered the Republican forces to withdraw north to the *tierra caliente*.[69]

For the first time since the beginning of the Intervention, Republican forces (except the Xochiapulquenses) abandoned the southern and western Sierra. Austrian forces with their Mexican allies swept into the *tierra caliente*. They occupied Hueytlalpan and Olintla and pushed the Republicans onto the plains of Papantla. Austrian garrisons occupied Xochitlán and Cuetzalan, as Fernando Pardo had advised, although Roldán continued to command Mexican forces in the district. The Xochiapulquenses, for their part, chose not to migrate to the *tierra caliente* but to continue the resistance in the southern Sierra. Xochiapulco remained abandoned with its population living in the hills and canyons.[70]

The rapid sweep of Imperial forces through the southern Sierra into the *tierra caliente* in mid-July by no means shattered Republican resistance. Towns might be occupied but, throughout much of the Sierra, organized resistance continued as rebel leaders waited to recover their lost positions. In Xochiapulco, resistance became a matter of survival, now that policy had unequivocally slipped from the velvet glove to the iron fist. In late July, an incident in Las Lomas, a much-contested village on the border between Xochiapulco and Zacapoaxtla, illustrates this shift in policy of Zacapoaxtla's Austrian garrison toward its troublesome neighbor. Count Thun reported that on 19 July inhabitants of Las Lomas had cruelly killed and disfigured a Mexican ally of the Austrians. To punish this crime, Thun led two columns to the village. After a short exchange, the armed villagers took flight. Thun ordered the Austrian and Mexican force to raze the village and all of the surrounding milpas.[71]

The consequences of this action resounded throughout the next decades. Who should resettle Las Lomas and to whom would it owe allegiance, became the apple of discord between Zacapoaxtla and Xochiapulco. The inhabitants evicted by the Austrian force were resettled on the Xochitonal peak to form the barrio of Ixehuaco, where they remained armed as National Guards (recruited originally by José Manuel Lucas in 1857) until the 1890s.[72]

Fearful that Xochiapulco would be next in line, Lucas and Bonilla, accompanied by the commanders Antonio Díaz, Reyes, and Francisco Dinorín and two hundred infantry, reoccupied Xochiapulco on 4 August in an attempt to preempt its occupation. Roldán approached with a superior force from the north, backed by troops from Cuetzalan. Lucas decided to abandon the cabecera, but, before departing, he instructed his soldiers to torch their houses, having at first set an example by burning his own home.[73] Roldán briefly occupied Xochiapulco, gleefully completing the immolation of the town which

Zacapoaxtecos regarded as the source of all the district's suffering over the previous decade. Before returning to Zacapoaxtla, Roldán's forces destroyed more fields planted with maize to further discourage the Xochiapulquenses' return.[74] This tactic backfired and further intensified local contempt for Roldán, since much of Xochiapulco's land was at this time being planted by residents of Zacapoaxtla's barrios, who filed large claims for compensation to the Austrian military authorities. Lucas seized the opportunity to attack, driving Roldán's force back within Zacapoaxtla's defenses.

The result of these two skirmishes, and the crop and house burning which accompanied them, was that the occupation of Xochiapulco no longer possessed any tactical advantages for Lucas. He therefore moved his men west to join Méndez in an attack upon the Austrian garrison in Tetela de Ocampo on 17 August. After three hours of fighting, the Austrian cavalry sent from Chignahuapan and led by Lieutenant Eduardo de Mastrek scattered the Republican force.[75] Méndez sought refuge again in the *tierra caliente*. Lucas, in desperation, turned to the fir-clad mountains between Tetela and Zacapoaxtla in search of a base for his forces.

Here, on the boundary between the two districts, stood the hacienda of Taxcantla, which occupied a commanding position along a precipitous limestone escarpment overlooking the torrential Apulco River from the west. It was occupied by a force of enemy infantry from Aquixtla and Ixtacamaxtitlán under the Aquixtla commander, José María Bonilla. On 23–24 August, Lucas ousted this force. Throughout the rest of the Intervention, and long afterward, Taxcantla provided a sanctuary for Xochiapulquense forces.

Taxcantla's remoteness and defendability could not compensate for the loss of the strategic advantages and fecund maize fields of Xochiapulco. By early September, the Austrian garrison in Zacapoaxtla felt sufficiently confident about its control over the southern Sierra to mount an offensive against Papantla, the key to the Barlovento coast. The Austrian and Mexican force of around two thousand met a smaller Republican force commanded by Méndez and a local Veracruzano, General Lara, at El Paso de los Naranjos. Although the Republicans lost many men in this battle, they prevented the Imperial forces from reaching Papantla and compelled them to return to Zacapoaxtla.[76] Méndez, with his fellow Republicans Fernando María Ortega and Ramón Márquez Galindo, remained in a desperate attempt to recruit forces in the *tierra caliente* of Teziutlán.[77]

With Republican forces surviving only precariously in the *tierra caliente*, and with Juan Crisóstomo Bonilla seriously ill with dysentery, Lucas now was the sole remaining senior Republican commander in the southern Sierra. His most pressing problem was how to feed his men, now accompanied by women and children, having lost their subsistence base in Xochiapulco. To this end, Lucas at first attempted to establish a foothold on the plateau (where food was more plentiful) by occupying and fortifying the town of Chilchotla (San Andrés Chalchicomula) with three hundred men commanded by Reyes. But immobile infantry behind fortifications was vulnerable even in the Sierra. On the plateau, such a position was even less tenable. On 11 October, General Hermenegildo Carrillo dispersed Lucas's force.[78]

Returning to the Sierra, Lucas convened a meeting of the dispersed population of Xochiapulco and of neighboring sympathetic villages on the night of 19 October in the barrio of Chilapa (Zautla).[79] The junta, composed of "the elderly, soldiers, and women" resolved not to move to the *tierra caliente* for fear of disease and even greater privation. Instead, Xochiapulco's women and children retreated to the hills while the soldiers fortified their positions at Taxcantla and Ometepec, guarding the two main routes between Tetela and Zacapoaxtla.[80]

The decision to return to Taxcantla caught the enemy off guard and gave Lucas an unexpected triumph. On 20 October 1865, leading a weary and bedraggled force of six hundred, Lucas and Bonilla (who had just recovered from his illness) surprised a column of over one thousand Austrian and Mexican troops headed for Zacapoaxtla, at the barrio of Santecomapa. Trapped in a ravine, the Imperial troops turned and fled, leaving many dead (estimates range from thirty to eight hundred!), a larger number of prisoners, arms, ammunition, and, most welcome of all to Lucas's forces, food. Bonilla later recalled to Luna that on the night of the battle, his troops feasted on bread, ham, and wine, after months of eating only "toasted maize and grass."[81] The Mexican auxiliaries dispersed to their villages and only twenty men of the original force of five hundred returned to Puebla. Mortality among the Austrian troops, who had stood their ground, was particularly high, with only three Austrian soldiers remaining after the battle (over twenty were killed while the others either deserted or fell prisoner). The Austrian commander blamed the Zacapoaxtla garrison, which had failed to come to their aid, for the disaster.[82]

Although this spectacular victory further enhanced Lucas's reputation, the triumph at Santecomapa posed more problems than it solved. Large numbers of prisoners presented an additional burden for his forces, while his mountain redoubt became the target for revenge. Playing for time, on 31 October 1865, Lucas agreed to an armistice to last for a fortnight. The Austrian force would retire to Tetela and Lucas to Xochiapulco, until General Méndez arrived from his headquarters in El Espinal (Papantla) to negotiate a permanent cease-fire.[83]

Austrian desire for revenge proved stronger than the search for peace. On 8 November a force of eight hundred men left Tetela with instructions to wrest Xochiapulco from Luis Antonio Díaz, whom Lucas had left in charge of the small garrison that had reoccupied the abandoned town on 31 October. Again, the Imperialist force was ambushed near Ometepec and, again, was forced to retreat to Tetela. Both sides now realized that a stalemate had been reached. After renewed talks between Lucas and Della Salla in Ometepec, and Bonilla and Zacha in Teziutlán, an armistice was agreed on, to last for a month.[84]

The Austrians used the armistice in the southern Sierra to renew their offensive in the north, with the aim of taking Papantla, the last Republican stronghold in the *tierra caliente*. At first, the Austrians had some success at Tlapacoyan.[85] Then, on 28 November 1865, a Republican force numbering less than five hundred led by Méndez defeated an Austrian force of twenty-five hundred at El Espinal.[86] Failing for the second time to take Papantla, the Austrians withdrew again to the relative safety of Zacapoaxtla. However, Republican leaders in the *tierra caliente* were isolated, knowing that only from the highlands could they hope to challenge the Europeans. Cut off from their villages, Republican forces served as little more than decoys (albeit debilitating ones) to the Austrians.

Two thousand Austrian and Mexican troops again left Zacapoaxtla in early January 1866 for Papantla. They met Méndez at El Espinal on 11 January. Commanding a mere 540 men, Méndez nearly defeated the Austrians. After initial successes, his Republican force was defeated and dispersed by the Imperial rear guard.[87] Méndez now had no option but to sue for peace. He signed a full capitulation at Papantla on 15 January. The Republican government of Puebla was dissolved and its forces disbanded. Republican forces were not obliged to pledge loyalty to the Empire nor to renounce their Republican convictions. They were free to return to their homes. Méndez was to be paid 2,500 pesos to cover his debts in Tetela, and he and Márquez Galindo were given safe passage to the exterior. The Austrian commander, Schonowsky, ordered the Mexican Imperial forces back to their garrisons in the Sierra and on the plateau.[88] Two columns of Indian troops recruited by the Imperialists from Zacapoaxtla and Tetela were also given leave and ordered to return to their homes.[89]

In an annotation on the margin of Major Schonowsky's report on the armistice, Major Zach (on behalf of the Chief of Staff in Mexico City) wrote that he had learned from a separate communication that Lucas had agreed to the conditions of the Papantla armistice. With Lucas's submission, Major Zach concluded that the pacification of the northern Sierra and the coast was completed.[90] In fact, Lucas, ever cautious, waited a fortnight before responding to the new state of affairs. This, after all, was the first time since 1855 that the Xochiapulquenses had faced defeat and, presumably, disarmament.

After lengthy deliberations in Taxcantla, Lucas and his officers decided in early February to send a commission to Papantla to negotiate submission to the Empire. Returning to Xochiapulco on 13 February, Lucas convened a junta of all local officials. After a prolonged discussion, they agreed that Republican forces belonging to the municipalities of Xochiapulco and Zautla, and certain barrios of Ixtacamaxtitlán and Tetela, would submit to the Empire on the basis of the principles agreed on 6 February in Papantla with José María Galicia y Arostegui, the Imperial Inspector of the Sierra.

The agreement stated that all Republican forces would be discharged and disarmed, and their journeys home paid by the Austrian army. Officers would be allowed to keep their weapons, and those who chose not to adhere to the Empire were free to settle wherever they pleased. The Empire would assume responsibility for all debts incurred by Republican forces in the area. Lucas himself was offered an indemnity of 8,000 pesos by the Austrian administration to cover debts incurred in sustaining the Republican cause in Xochiapulco.[91]

The Imperial Inspector, on 21 February 1866, reported from Zacapoaxtla that he expected Lucas to hand in all the arms of his supporters on the following day. With this obstacle to pacification out of the way, he felt sure that the Sierra would finally be obedient to the Empire.[92] However, Galicia failed to distinguish between the official (and, in the case of Xochiapulco, largely tactical) declarations of loyalty to the Empire and the underlying strength of patriotic sentiment. Moreover, considering the force of Lucas's renewed offensive later in the year, it is unlikely that all Republican arms were handed in. In July 1866, Tetela's authorities were still apologizing for not sending surplus arms to the authorities in Puebla because of rumors of a local uprising.[93] To achieve this goal, the Imperial authorities needed the cooperation of local councils over a wide and inaccessible territory. Since the act of submission contained a guarantee confirming all existing officeholders in their positions, full compliance seems most unlikely.

Conclusion

What accounts for the dogged persistence of Republican resistance in the Puebla Sierra between the declaration of the Empire in July 1863 and the final capitulation of the Xochiapulquenses in February 1866? First, both the Republican and the Imperial high commands placed great strategic importance upon the Puebla Sierra and were determined to control it. So determined were the contending forces to secure the Sierra that numerous tactical and strategic errors were made by both sides, resulting in substantial loss of life and equipment and outcomes that were far removed from the initial intentions. The Sierra became the most fought-over zone of Mexico during the Intervention. Imperial pacification bred patriotic insurrection. Patriotic mobilization also provoked local armed reaction. The already acute ideological, ethnic, territorial, and personal rivalries inherited from earlier conflicts multiplied in proportion to this increased external intervention.

It would be wrong, however, to see this two-and-one-half-year period as one of unrelenting conflict and upheaval. There were two periods of intense fighting: the first accompanied the French campaign in the Sierra between September and December 1863, and the second occurred during the longer Austrian campaign of January and July 1865, with 1864 as a year of relative calm (particularly in the central and southern Sierra, less so in the west) during which lines between the contending forces remained fairly stable.

Juárez and Díaz sought to secure a bridgehead in the Sierra between Republican resistance in the north and south of the country, and they saw the Sierra as a strategic reserve available to spearhead campaigns against the Empire at its center. Under Maldonado's tutelage during 1863 and 1864, the rivalries that had so divided and weakened Liberal command of the Sierra during the Three Years' War were moderated. Maldonado respected the spheres of influence of local potentates (such as Cravioto, Márquez Galindo, Méndez, and Bonilla) but was determined to prevent these caudillos from political aggrandizement at their neighbors' expense. Lucas, as Maldonado's closest aide, provided him with the independence of maneuver and mobility along a front from Zacatlán to Teziutlán, which was necessary for defending the Sierra against Imperialist attacks as well as for moderating these rivalries within the Republican camp.

Even the Xochiapulco-Zacapoaxtla conflict was partly mollified by early 1864, as Lucas tailored his appeal to the Conservative villages that had spearheaded the Counter-Reform during the Three Years' War and the earlier part of the Intervention. Under Maldonado's patronage, Lucas extended his core clientele beyond Xochiapulco and the surrounding villages to include communities in Teziutlán, Tlatlauqui, Libres, Tetela, and those in the central Sierra, such as Cuetzalan.

In the winter of 1864, two events conspired to upset the political equilibrium and relative tranquility that Maldonado and Lucas had achieved in the Puebla Sierra. Díaz appointed Ortega as supreme commander of Puebla forces with instructions to pursue a more aggressive policy toward the Empire. Apart from sidelining Maldonado and shelving his careful preparations for the Perote offensive, Ortega's zest for troop mobilization and half-baked offensives created unacceptable demands upon manpower and resources, and antagonized those wavering villages that Lucas had worked so hard to seduce. The second event was the invasion of the southern Sierra by Austrian forces and their Mexican allies in February 1865.

Throughout the second half of 1864, Lucas had succeeded in holding Imperial forces in the western Sierra at bay with a line of military colonies along Tetela's western and southern boundaries. This line proved impossible to hold once the Austrians occupied Zacapoaxtla and Xochiapulco's very existence came under threat. Tetela's western defenses swiftly crumbled under the pressure of local forces recruited by the Austrians on the promise of tax exemptions and the division of Republican spoils. This left Cravioto isolated in the northwestern Sierra. Cravioto adhered to the Empire in April 1865 when he realized that without Lucas and the forces from Xochiapulco, the western front was unsustainable.

Why did forces from Tetela, Xochiapulco, and Zacatlán continue to resist the formidable Austro-Mexican campaign for a further ten months? Luna's memoir presents the patriotic self-sacrifice of the people of Xochiapulco and Tetela as the natural instinct of all good Mexicans. However, his memoir also reveals how local feuds, rancors, and rivalries were important causes for local and regional leaders to take to arms. Méndez, Bonilla, and Márquez Galindo, who were driven from their homes by forces from neighboring jurisdictions, continued the patriotic struggle in the *tierra caliente* because it offered the only prospect of political survival. For Lucas and the Xochiapulquenses, the alternative to fighting the Austrians was even more bleak. Patriotic struggle offered them the opportunity to recover their houses, schools, and maize fields and to preserve the hard-earned status as an autonomous municipality.

The capitulation of Republican forces in the Puebla Sierra in January and February 1866 resulted from three factors: Austrian determination to confront resistance energetically and forcefully (in marked contrast to the timidity of the French in 1863); Austrian success in attracting widespread and active support from villages within the Sierra; and, finally, the exhaustion and territorial isolation of Republican forces once Lucas and his troops were expelled from Xochiapulco, and Méndez and the Tetela battalion were pushed into the *tierra caliente*. As long as the Republicans had been able to encircle Zacapoaxtla by holding Xochiapulco, Huahuaxtla, and the heights of Apulco, French and Austrian attempts at pacification of the Sierra remained ephemeral. Driving Lucas back across the Apulco to Taxcantla, burning Xochiapulco's maize fields and houses, and repopulating villages such as Las Lomas with people who were prepared to aid the Imperial cause broke the back of the patriotic resistance and laid the basis for the Republican capitulation.

7

The Defeat of the Empire

If Maximilian had succeeded in consolidating his Empire diplomatically and in suppressing Republican resistance in the north of Mexico, it is doubtful whether there would have been any serious recrudescence of martial republicanism in the Puebla Sierra, given the generous terms of the armistices. However, the pacification of the Sierra and most of central and southeastern Mexico coincided with a deterioration of the international context for the Franco-Austrian Empire in Mexico. In the face of growing tension between Prussia and the Franco-Austrian alliance that culminated in the Franco-Prussian War, the resolve of Napoleon III to sustain the Mexican adventure faded rapidly, inviting the renewal of Republican resistance.

The revival of Republican fortunes was aided by the ending of the Civil War in the United States. No longer neutral, the American government brought pressure upon the Europeans to withdraw and greatly increased material backing for Republican resistance in Mexico. The deterioration in the Empire's external context was compounded by a crisis within the Imperial Mexican forces. This army had become a baroque amalgam of French, Belgian, Austrian, and Mexican forces without unified command. Marshal Bazaine, the principal French military commander, and Emperor Maximilian scarcely communicated. Austrian forces never accepted the authority of the French commander-in-chief. The army was pathetically underfunded and Napoleon flatly refused to spend any more on Mexico (colonies were intended to yield, not consume, revenues). Financial penury and the steady withdrawal of French troops from Mexico hampered Bazaine's attempt to form Franco-Mexican battalions of *guardias moviles* (mounted guard) to occupy recently pacified areas. Mexican finances from customhouses also diminished following Bazaine's decision in late 1865 to abandon northern Mexico.[1]

Republican forces in the north gathered strength. On 16 June 1866 they defeated Tomás Mejía, Maximilian's best Mexican general, at Matamoros. The concession of the Republican commander that Mejía and his army could go free and unmolested made a deep and lasting impression upon the "traitors" throughout the rest of the country. The trickle of desertions from the Imperial forces soon became a torrent. Meanwhile, dissension among Belgian, French, and Mexican officers grew. Count Thun's Austrian volunteer forces in Puebla also seethed with discontent over irregular pay and conditions of service.[2]

Renewed Republican Resistance in the Puebla Sierra

Maximilian's position further deteriorated in July 1866 with the outbreak of the Austro-Prussian War and the renewal of the Republican offensive in northern and southeastern Mexico. Imperial finances reached the point of collapse, and the army went unpaid. The fragmentation of the Empire was brought into particularly sharp relief in Puebla in August 1866 by Count Thun's resignation, followed by the departure of most of his Austrian officers.[3] Loyalty among Mexican Imperial forces in the Puebla-Veracruz region now began to crumble as many of the officers went over to the Republican side. Communities which had supported the Empire previously were now reembracing the constitution.

The internal collapse of the Imperial army prompted a renewal of Republican resistance in the southern and western Puebla Sierra, the Huasteca, and throughout Veracruz. Republican military resistance in the Sierra had continued on the level of guerrilla warfare since the surrender at Papantla in January 1866. Under the command of Fernando María Ortega and Simon and Francisco Cravioto (whose father, Rafael, remained imprisoned in Puebla until December 1866), Republican forces made little headway until the fall of Huejutla, a strategic point in the Huasteca. This Republican victory in May 1866 prompted the withdrawal of Austrian garrisons from the Huasteca and from much of the Sierras of Hidalgo and Puebla.[4] The *guardias moviles* created to police this vast zone lacked the funds necessary for buying local support and served as vulnerable targets for the resurgent Republican forces.[5] By June 1866 only three European garrisons of two hundred men each at Teziutlán, Zacapoaxtla, and Tulancingo remained in the Sierras of Puebla and Hidalgo. Most other towns were occupied by either wavering Mexican Imperial or Republican forces.

Lucas's movements after the peace in January 1866 are uncertain, but it is likely that he kept his forces prepared for the resumption of the patriotic struggle. On 5 August 1866 he led a daring assault upon Zacapoaxtla, with the help of National Guards from Xochitlán and Nauzontla. The small European garrison took flight, opening the way for the reestablishment of the state's Republican civil administration in Zacapoaxtla in early September.

Meanwhile, Lucas prepared for an attack upon the Imperial garrison at Teziutlán. He planned to link up with the recent successful Republican advances in Veracruz, thus blocking the European line of retreat. Responding to Lucas's initiative, Tetela pronounced for the Republic on 12 August. On the following day, leading some one hundred fifty Xochiapulquenses backed by troops hurriedly recruited in Tetela, Lucas marched to Teziutlán, gathering forces from the villages on the way.[6] He made an unsuccessful attack on Teziutlán on 15 August and was wounded in the attempt. Returning on 21 August, now in command of a greatly strengthened force of two thousand men, Lucas captured and occupied Teziutlán. The Imperial garrison retreated to Perote.[7] In a message to his troops after the battle, Lucas applauded their patriotism and urged them to continue the struggle with the same enthusiasm, until the Mexican flag was reestablished "on the palace of the Moctezumas." He concluded with the exhortation: "Long Live our Independence! Long Live the Republic! Long Live the Sovereign People! Long Live the Citizens who form this Division! Long Live our First Chief, the eminent patriot J. N. Méndez! Death to the tyrannical foreigners!"[8]

Resumption of hostilities in early August was accompanied by measures designed to legitimize action against the Imperial army and to lay the foundations for Juan Nepomuceno Méndez's bid for the state governorship. On 12 August 1866, Méndez invited all the authorities and "principal inhabitants" of the municipality of Tetela to the schoolroom to discuss the resumption of the patriotic struggle of Tetela and Xochiapulco against the Empire. This junta approved a proclamation that received eighty-six signatures (including those of the most notable Tetelense Republican commanders). The proclamation declared that "Our motto will be a Free and Independent Republic." The authority of the Empire, and any orders emanating from it, was declared null and void. All existing authorities were ordered to recognize the Republican government (the act added that all public officials could continue to exercise their functions but in accord with the state constitution of 1861). The decree gave general pardon "to all those who voluntarily or involuntarily lent their material or moral support to the government of the Empire." Finally, copies of this act were sent to Porfirio Díaz, "General in Chief of the Republican Forces of the East" (currently considering his choice for the command of the state) and to all the villages in Tetela and the neighboring districts.[9]

This *pronunciamiento* was an inspired political move by Méndez. After his defeat and capitulation at Papantla, he had been left in too weak a position to resume any leading role in the Republican movement. Many other Puebla Republicans, such as Maldonado, had not submitted to the Empire. Méndez needed to rebuild his claim for leadership, and he chose his own district as the base for achieving this. Familiar with the ambivalence of many of Tetela's leading citizens toward Liberal Republicanism and to the Méndez family, Méndez pitched his appeal in the most conservative terms possible. His act called for no practical changes in the existing government of the cabecera and its dependent barrios. Even officials who "morally and materially" had cast their lot with the Empire were to be pardoned and left undisturbed during the renewed patriotic campaign.

Méndez did not leave the initiative to Tetela de Ocampo, a town that had scarcely distinguished itself in the struggle against the Intervention and where, apart from the batch of leaders close to him (Rivera, Bonilla, and Luna), resided several prominent enemies. Rather, municipalities in Tetela's *tierra caliente* (Huitzilan, Zapotitlán, Jonotla, and Tenampulco), the district's tax base, and in neighboring districts (Hueytlalpan in Zacatlán and Cuetzalan in Zacapoaxtla) were invited to second the *pronunciamiento*. Here, in spite of almost a decade of heavy demands for revenues, supplies, and manpower, support for Méndez remained remarkably solid. Indeed, a popular junta in Huitzilan had disavowed the Empire and pledged loyalty to the constitution and to Méndez, on 10 August 1866, two days before Tetela's *pronunciamiento*. After the *pronunciamiento*, a ripple of confirmations came from throughout the district.[10]

Military success would be necessary for the movement to be sustained. Since 1857, military success for Méndez had been delivered by his compadre, Lucas. Returning to Zacapoaxtla on 24 August, after taking Teziutlán, Lucas convened a junta that named Méndez as "Interim Chief of the State of Puebla," and himself as second in command. In a letter to José Daniel Posadas in Tetela, Lucas wrote of Méndez, "The honor and proven patriotism of this Citizen is the best guarantee for the villages, in such a way that his election fulfills, in my opinion, their aspirations."[11] Two days later, Tetela, not to be upstaged, convened a second junta in the municipal schoolroom. Military and civilian authorities from throughout the district nominated Méndez as interim governor of the state and sent copies of the act to Juárez, Díaz, and Lucas.

In spite of what appeared as a unanimous vote of confidence from Sierra Republicans for Méndez as governor of the state, at this stage of the campaign, Méndez was of greater value to Díaz as a mobile military commander than a sedentary state governor. On the same day that Tetelenses chose their native son as governor, Porfirio Díaz appointed Méndez "Political Chief of the Line of Teziutlán, Tlatlauqui, San Juan de los Llanos, Zacapoaxtla, Tetela, Zacatlán, Huauchinango, and Pahuatlán," with authority to organize forces and name military commanders and jefes políticos throughout this zone. Díaz's "rules of conduct" issued at Tehuitzingo on 26 August gave Méndez draconian powers to reimpose Puebla's National Guard law, order all revenues to be directed to military expenditure, instruct anyone in possession of arms or horses to make them available or have them removed forcibly, confiscate the property of traitors and Frenchmen (provided that inventories were drawn up by an honorable citizen), and order the apprehension, trial, and execution within two hours of civilian and military traitors who fought for the enemy.[12] This commission amounted to carte blanche for the reconstruction of the Méndez *cacicazgo* in northern Puebla. Díaz's "rules of conduct" contrasted vividly with the conciliatory tones of Méndez's 12 August *pronunciamiento.*

Two weeks after conferring command of the Northern Line upon Méndez, Díaz (on Juárez's advice) appointed Rafael J. García as Puebla's state governor based in the temporary capital, Zacapoaxtla.[13] Méndez's swift recognition of this appointment relieved widespread indignation in the Sierra that the governorship should be offered to a leader from the plateau.[14] García (like Alatriste before him) was a lawyer from Puebla, who had no record of active resistance to the Empire (apart from his position as editor of the moderate Liberal newspaper *La Idea Liberal,* which now became the official state newspaper). However, there was no repeat of the leadership tussle that had so hampered the Liberal war effort during the Three Years' War. Indeed, García's relations with Méndez remained harmonious over the subsequent months of resistance to the Empire. He proved to be an efficient administrator, willing to acknowledge, even honor, the leafier patriotic laurels of the military commander of the Northern Line.[15] However, Méndez did disapprove of García's decision to retain Pascual Bonilla, a prominent Conservative and close collaborator with the Intervention, in his post as jefe político.[16] García found the services of this wily and influential traitor too valuable to resist when attempting to confront the complexities of local politics in the Sierra.

Having secured Republican control of the principal district capitals of the southern Sierra, and backed by acts of disavowal from the sugar-rich municipalities of the *tierra caliente,* Méndez and Lucas, backed by Generals Macario González and Ramón Márquez Galindo, turned their attention to the western Sierra, where the Austrians had built up a network of active support in a swath of villages stretching through Tlaxco, Ixtacamaxtitlán, Chignahuapan, Aquixtla, and Zacatlán. Their opportunity came on 9 September, when Vicente Márquez, commander of Imperialist forces in Zacatlán, and the officers of the "Squadron of Chignahuapan" (hitherto the scourge of the Republicans) disavowed the Empire and embraced the patriotic cause.[17] However, the towns of Chignahuapan and Aquixtla remained loyal to the Empire. Méndez realized that Lucas, who had influence in the villages of this area, would be essential for bringing together the leaders from these hardened Conservative strongholds with their reviled Liberal opponents from neighboring Tetela and Zacatlán.[18]

At first, Lucas hesitated to become involved in the western Sierra, where, only a short time before, his forces had suffered severe losses. He needed considerable cajoling from Méndez and the gift of a horse from Márquez Galindo before agreeing to send men and make direct representations to the Aquixtla and Chignahuapan leaders.[19] Lucas secured an armistice after protracted negotiations with José María Bonilla, Antonio Domínguez, and Antonio Herrera, the leaders who had organized Imperialist forces in Aquixtla, Chignahuapan, Ixtacamaxtitlán, and Tlaxco since the Three Years' War. Between 19 and 21 September these jurisdictions disavowed the Empire and recognized the authority of Méndez and Lucas.[20]

From somewhat further afield but within the same theater of operations, more news arrived of Republican advances. Colonel Antonio Pérez, the *plateado* cavalry commander, defeated an Austro-Mexican force on the plains of Apam on 18 September and another Imperialist force near Tulancingo on the following day. These victories on the plateau, where Republican forces previously had had little success, caused widespread Mexican desertions from Imperialist ranks and prompted the decision of Mariano Piz, an important cavalry commander from this strategic region (near the national capital), to change sides.[21] At the same time, the Republican rear guard was further secured when the Imperial force holding Tuxpan capitulated to Rosalino Farfán, commander of Papantla's Republican forces.[22]

With the western and northern flanks of the Sierra secured, Méndez began the long-awaited offensive on the plateau. First, Méndez occupied Llanos on 28 September, putting the Imperial garrison to flight without loss of blood. On the same day, Antonio Rodríguez Bocardo (who had recently joined the Republicans) and seventy cavalry defeated a force of ninety Austrian cavalry near the village of Los Virreyes. He captured large numbers of Imperial infantry and then repelled a counterattack by the Hungarian (Uhlanian) cavalry. Méndez called for Lucas to dispatch reinforcements upon news of the imminent approach of the *contraguerrilla* Dupin, with seven hundred well-mounted and well-equipped men from Nopalucan.[23]

At this time, Lucas was experiencing difficulties with recruitment. Many of the villages that had supported him before the armistice in February had been disarmed. Other villages, particularly those in Tlatlauqui, which had supported the Austrians, had retained their arms and were opposed to the Republican cause. Rafael García, in cooperation with Lucas, dispatched José Ferrer, a Teziutlán merchant, to New York to buy arms.[24] These were to be distributed to villages chosen by Lucas. Unpatriotic villages were ordered to hand in their arms and to pay three months of advanced *rebajado* tax in lieu of military service.[25]

Republican recruitment in the southern Sierra continued to meet considerable resistance. In mid-October, Pilar Rivera reported that he was having great difficulty in recruiting four of the eight companies he had been instructed to send to the headquarters at Libres.[26] On the same day, Méndez reported to Lucas that "the permanent company has risen up, leaving the garrison with all its weapons and marching who knows where." Méndez suspected that Cenobio Cantero may have had something to do with the disorder. He urged Lucas to come immediately with as many men as possible.[27] Later in the day, Bonilla observed to Lucas that the "rebels" were heading toward Xochiapulco "to complain to you about not being paid."[28]

As Méndez wrestled with recruitment problems in the southern Sierra, the Imperialists mounted a renewed offensive in the northern Sierra, which culminated in the sacking of Pahuatlán and Huauchinango. Zacatlán was also threatened, further delaying any advance on the plateau. Republican gains in neighboring Veracruz eventually broke the deadlock.[29] In early July 1866, General Juan Calderón, who had controlled central Veracruz for the Imperialists since October 1865, was defeated at the port of Alvarado.[30] Retreating to the Sierra, Calderón attempted to hold the strategic artery between Jalapa on the plateau and the port of Veracruz. He presumed that his fellow cavalry officers from the cereal districts of the plateau would support him. But Calderón's allies on the plateau abandoned him, one by one: Rodríguez Bocardo (Cuyoaco) and Rafael Cuellar (Tlaxcala) in September, then Carrillo (Tlacolula) and Melgarejo (Altotonga) in late October. On 23 October, Perote proclaimed for the Republic, leaving the Austrian garrison bottled up in the fortress.[31] This enabled infantry forces mobilized by Lucas and Bonilla from the southern Sierra to move unopposed into the Sierra of Veracruz and to occupy Perote.

In late October 1866 the garrison of nine hundred Austrian and Mexican troops at Jalapa under Major Harmens and General Calderón was surrounded by Republican forces commanded by General Ignacio Alatorre and backed by more than six hundred infantry commanded by Lucas, Bonilla, Francisco Javier Arriaga, and Juan Francisco Molina Alcántara, recruited from Zacapoaxtla, Tlatlauqui, Teziutlán, and Libres.[32] On 31 October, news arrived of the surrender of Imperial forces in Oaxaca.[33] Ten days later the entire garrison at Jalapa surrendered, and the Mexican forces joined the Republican army.[34]

The surrender of the Imperial army in Oaxaca and the Republican victory at Jalapa left the way open for a coordinated offensive upon the central plateau. As the leaders from the hacienda districts abandoned the Imperial cause, a broad patriotic front, incorporating old enemies and directed at the tottering Empire, took shape. A further breakthrough came in early November, when cavalry commanded by Rodríguez Bocardo, Cuellar, and Miguel Vega, backed by infantry from Aquixtla and Ixtacamaxtitlán under José María Bonilla, Miguel Bonilla, and Antonio Herrera, all former Imperialists, routed a large French force and captured the city of Tlaxcala.[35]

By early December, Tlaxcala had disavowed the Empire and recognized Benito Juárez.[36] Having overcome a challenge to his authority from Antonio Carbajal, Méndez was given overall command of all Republican forces in Puebla and Tlaxcala by Díaz on 14 December.[37] At this time, Méndez made vociferous protestations of loyalty to Juárez, and condemnations of Jesús González Ortega's bid for the presidency. After all, the Tetela caudillo was grooming himself for the governorship.[38]

While the Republican caudillos gradually consolidated their hold on the tableland, Lucas was kept busy with villagers' grievances in the southern Sierra as once again, they came under intense pressure from military recruitment, taxation, and demands for supplies in support of the Republican offensive. Since his capture of Teziutlán on 21 August 1866, in spite of his high military office, Lucas had insisted upon residing in Xochiapulco. His distrust of Zacapoaxtla had not lessened since it had become the state capital. Old Conservatives and recent Imperialists—such as jefe político Pascual Bonilla—remained in control of the town, whose priest, Miguel Alva, felt sufficiently confident in October 1866 to preach a sermon in favor of the Empire and against the Reform Laws.[39]

Throughout October and November, Lucas delegated day-to-day command of the Northern Line to Lieutenant General Joaquín Casarín. With the start of the campaign on the plateau in early December, Lucas relinquished command to Márquez Galindo. Juan Crisóstomo Bonilla also received a promotion over Lucas, taking overall command of the Sierra offensive between January and April 1867.[40] Evidently, Méndez considered Lucas to be more useful to the Republican cause in the Sierra than leading forces on the plateau. On 5 December 1866, Méndez urged Lucas and Bonilla to ensure that every village and garrison on the Northern Line file their proclamations for Juárez "in triplicate" and to robustly oppose any dissenting voices.[41] Three days later, the Tetela caudillo ordered a general mobilization of Sierra infantry. By late December, Méndez had assembled fifteen hundred men in Tlaxcala, clearly intending an early assault on the state capital.[42] However, it was not until March 1867 that Díaz finally gave the orders to forces from the Puebla Sierra to advance to the state capital to preempt the arrival of Imperial reinforcements under General Leonardo Márquez.

Maintaining an army (albeit a small one) in a region distant from where it had been recruited presented severe supply and discipline problems. Méndez instituted fortnightly rotation of these contingents to uphold morale, discourage desertion, and retain active support from the Sierra villages that provided recruits with cash and supplies. Villages that had offered steadfast patriotic support earlier in the Intervention grew to resent the continual drain of resources. Ometepec, a Nahua barrio situated on the heights overlooking Tetela de Ocampo, was one such village, which had been loyally and actively Republican throughout the Intervention, but whose patriotic fervor cooled perceptibly between December 1866 and January 1867.

Ometepec's Fading Patriotism

Ometepec's involvement in the wars of the Reform and the Intervention resulted more from its location (it guarded the route between Tetela and

Zacapoaxtla) than from any taste for Liberalism or Republicanism. The male population of this poor village, which lacked adequate land for subsistence, was attracted by the tax exemptions accompanying National Guard service. Until 1866, serving the Liberal and patriotic cause had brought many hardships but also some benefits, including access as rentiers and sharecroppers to the surrounding small estates acquired by Tetela's Liberal leaders through the privatization of municipal lands. Francisco Pérez, Lucas, Méndez, and Bonilla all owned land in or close to Ometepec.[43]

Throughout the Intervention, Isidro Segura, a close companion of Lucas, organized Ometepec's National Guard company. Ometepecanos frequently fought alongside the forces of Xochiapulco, with whom they shared common ethnicity, precarious means of subsistence, and a trustworthy leader and sponsor. However, by late 1866, Ometepec's patriotism had faded. In December, Ometepecanos figured prominently among deserters from Rivera's Tetela battalion stationed in Tlaxco.[44]

The barrio had evidently had enough of military service. Segura wrote to Lucas announcing that his company had decided, by a large majority, to hand in their arms and pay the *rebajado*.[45] Rivera ignored their decision, ordering Segura to move his company to Tlaxco. Disobeying their captain, part of the company marched instead to Xochiapulco to talk with Lucas.[46] On arrival, they claimed that Segura had treated them cruelly. Segura rejected the accusation and blamed instead the high-handed behavior of the two non-Indian officers sent by Rivera to gather Ometepec's contingent.[47]

Some indication of the Ometepecanos' dismay with military service is found in a letter from two soldiers, José Eleuterio and José Dionisio, to Lucas: "We are before you in Xochiapulco to show you our exasperation . . . we have fled from San Agustín Tlaxco because we have not been paid a fair wage. We only received 5 reales for each soldier for the twenty days we were there and this treatment left us dying from hunger, and this is why we have come here and now we wish to be under your command (*bajo su dominio*). The Tetela officers do not regard us as their sons, but are blind to our needs and think only ill of us. We beseech you to replace our captain with one of our own, for we know that you see us as your sons."

From this letter, it is evident that the Ometepecanos objected to the terms of service, rather than military service per se.[48] This is confirmed by the arrival of a force of "muchachos de Ometepec" at the camp of Juan Crisóstomo Bonilla in Libres on 18 January, armed with a letter from Lucas explaining their redeployment from Rivera's force at Tlaxco. With Bonilla, they would be serving with troops from Xochiapulco, and under Indian commanders. Bonilla placed Ometepecanos in the First Company of the Second Battalion of Xochiapulco.[49] Ometepecanos were still serving in the Xochiapulco battalion on 5 May 1867, when Luis Antonio Díaz ordered the alcalde of Ometepec to send forty replacements for their contingent.[50]

Throughout the first five months of 1867, in spite of the Ometepecanos serving with the Xochiapulco battalion until well after the victory against the Austrians, this barrio and its neighbor, Tachico, were regarded by the authorities in Tetela de Ocampo as being in rebellion against their municipal cabecera. Apart from their insistence upon acceptable terms of military service, the Ometepecanos and Tachiqueños were also concerned about the privatization of Tetela's commons. As a concession, in March 1867, Tetela's alcalde ordered the adjudication and sale of the Rancho de Mexalititlán (upon which the barrio of Tachico was situated) to be suspended until all the inhabitants of this barrio had returned from the campaign.[51]

Tlatlauqui's authorities reported similar dissidence in December and January, prompting the migration of hundreds of villagers to the sanctuary of Xochiapulco to evade military service and payment of the *rebajado*.[52] With the collapse of the Empire, ideological differences now became secondary to the issues of local autonomy and the constitutional right to resist arbitrary authority. The villages of Tlatlauqui, which for so long had been organized by Conservatives to combat ascendant Liberalism in Xochiapulco, now sought sanctuary in the barrios along the Cuatecomaco ridge. This matter complicated an already entangled political geography and stored up conflicts for the future.

The Fall of the Empire

Republican military prospects, regionally and nationally, grew more promising with Mariano Escobedo's defeat of General Miramón at Zacatecas on 1 February 1867 and with Maximilian's decision to abandon Mexico City on 13 February to join the Imperial forces at Querétaro. The Imperial garrison of less than twenty-five hundred men in Puebla was isolated and faced the much larger Republican Army of the East, commanded by General Porfirio Díaz.[53] Yet, even with a small garrison, Puebla, with its numerous monumental churches and convents each serving as a small fortress, could withstand a prolonged siege. Thus, Méndez's strategy remained to mobilize a steady supply of recruits from the Sierra to man, in fortnightly rotation, the principal garrison towns of the plateau (Tlaxco, Huamantla, and Libres), in preparation for the final assault upon the state capital.[54] Republican cavalry policed the intervening areas.

Méndez was dismayed by the disappointing performance of the southern Sierra, where the response to the call to arms included excessive slowness in assembling contingents, high levels of desertion, and outright disobedience and rebellion. He turned to the formerly less militarily active and largely Totonac northern Sierra, and dispatched Captain Juan Guerrero to the *tierra caliente* to recruit an additional two hundred National Guardsmen to join Márquez Galindo in the state of Mexico.[55] Guerrero's

General Porfirio Díaz, Commander in Chief of the Republican Army of the East, 1867.
Archivo Fotográfico, Centro de Estudios de Historia de México (CONDUMEX)

energetic, at times brutal, efforts to gather forces in this area failed. He was instructed to raise thirty men from each settlement that he passed through on his march across the entire district from Tenampulco to Tetela, in spite of these villages being entirely unarmed and regularly contributing to the *rebajado* (and thereby legally exempt from Guard service). By late March, only forty-nine National Guardsmen from Zoquiapan, Jonotla, Tetetilla, Tenampulco, and Los Reyes were ready to march. Most of these men deserted before reaching the plateau.[56] In any case, the services of the Sierra's Totonacs would not be needed, because the last units of the French army departed from Veracruz on 12 March. This departure left open the road to the state capital.[57]

The appropriate moment came in late March when an Imperial force under General Leonardo Márquez moved into Puebla in order to strengthen the small garrison there. To check this advance, Díaz ordered those remaining units of the Army of the East that had not advanced to the valley of Mexico, most notably Bonilla's Second Division, to attack Puebla (Méndez, Lauro Luna, and Márquez Galindo were already laying siege to Querétaro).[58] After heavy hand-to-hand fighting, in which Bonilla and Lucas personally led their troops with conspicuous bravery, the city fell to the Republicans on 2 April. After Bonilla was wounded, Díaz gave Lucas full command of the Second Division of the Army of the East.[59] Two days after the Republican victory, Puebla's Imperial commander, General Noriega, capitulated. Díaz then advanced to the valley of Mexico, bypassing Mexico City, to join the siege of Querétaro, where Maximilian had established the Imperial government. Upon arrival, he instructed Méndez to return to Puebla to take over the governorship from Rafael Garcia on 25 April. Evidently, Díaz preferred to leave this strategically vital state in the hands of a trusted companion at arms rather than with García, who, as a civilian lawyer, was more naturally aligned with Juárez.[60]

Querétaro fell on 15–16 May, resulting in the capture of Maximilian and the surrender of much of the Imperial army. On 19 June, after a court-martial, Maximilian was executed. Two days later, Republican forces entered Mexico City. Mexico's Second Empire had ended and the Liberal Republic, led by the peripatetic Benito Juárez since 1858, was restored.

Conclusion

Five years of armed resistance against French and Austrian attempts to pacify the Puebla Sierra transformed the political geography not only of the Sierra but also of the entire Mexican southeast. At the Republican victory in May 1867, judging from the widespread opposition to recruitment, high levels of desertion, and mounting village rebelliousness, most *serranos* would surely have favored a return to the calmer times preceding the revolution of Ayutla. However, the Liberal Reform (or "la Revolución," as it had become to be known in the Sierra), in which much of the Sierra had served as a test case, the widespread arming of civilians (particularly Indians), and the rise of a caste of hardened military leaders combined to ensure that there would be no return to the old order. Even if the principal Liberal-patriotic caudillos—Méndez, Márquez Galindo, Bonilla, Cravioto, and Lucas—had requested no more of the nation than its gratitude for their patriotic sacrifices and permission to return peacefully to their homes, such inactivity would not have been allowed by regional and national leaders such as Díaz and Juárez, for whom the Puebla Sierra was now central to their strategic thinking. As the towns and villages of the Sierra counted their dead over the summer of 1867, to secure pensions for their widows and orphans, they were not to know that the price of thirteen years of struggle would be ten more years of warfare.[61]

By 1867, Lucas and the Cuatecomacos had become a cause of national celebrity. In spite of the propensity of *serrano* infantry to desert once they were led beyond the Sierra, the martial qualities of the Nahua communities of the southern and central Puebla Sierra, when fighting on their own turf, had attracted leaders of all parties—Conservatives and Liberals, Imperialists and Republicans. Alvarez and Comonfort valued the Puebla Sierra as a strategic outpost of the revolution of Ayutla. Haro y Tamariz and the Puebla clergy attempted to use the Sierra as a bulwark of the Counter-Reform.[62] Thun staked his military career upon subduing the Sierra, a task which, in the short term, due to Austrian success in mobilizing *serrano* infantry, he managed to achieve. Republican forces from the Puebla Sierra contributed an important chapter to Mexico's Liberal-patriotic history with their heroic participation as "the Zacapoaxtlas" in the battle of 5 May 1862, their spectacular victories over French and Austrian forces sent to subdue them between 1863 and 1865, and their leadership of the liberation of Puebla on 2 April 1867. Lucas, by successfully recruiting fighting men from the Nahua villages, was central to all of these episodes.

The image of Lucas as Liberal-patriotic hero, a Nahua warrior, and a modern Cuauhtémoc was belied, however, by a self-effacing modesty, an apparent lack of political ambition, and an often expressed desire to return to private life. His instinct, like those of the village forces he led, was defensive. Yet, in an age of accelerating economic change, as a more centralized and authoritarian secular state was beginning to take shape, the defense of local autonomy would require ever greater vigilance, mounting political assertiveness, and, on several occasions, renewed armed rebellion. This vigilance could follow no simple formula of coordinating peasant stubbornness along some fixed line of Liberal-patriotic defense. As was evident during the last months of the Intervention, this line had already begun to dissolve. Ten years of warfare had left a legacy of fear, hatred, and acute political factionalism throughout the southern and central Sierra, which the contending parties would seek ruthlessly to exploit.

Since 1855, Lucas had created a line of military colonics between Teziutlán and Zacatlán, and north into the Sierra as far as Cuetzalan. The existence of these "free" communities (the six barrios of Xochiapulco being only the most renowned) upset long-established patterns of authority, deference, and obedience throughout the Sierra. Just as Lucas's patrons—Méndez, Bonilla, and Márquez Galindo—would see the warrior peasants of these communities as ready-made Montaña electoral constituencies, so the enemies of the Montaña, within and beyond the Sierra, would cajole or court these same villages. In May 1867, although Lucas's patriotic career had now ended, his political career had barely begun.

8

The First Montaña Rebellion

Far from hailing a period of peace, the triumph of the Republic heralded a decade of regional insurrections throughout Mexico. Puebla was the first state after the restoration of the Republic to undergo a serious political crisis, which broadened into two years of armed rebellion focusing chiefly upon the Sierra. This unrest began on 14 August 1867 with the protest of Governor Méndez, backed by Guanajuato's León Guzmán, at the terms of proposed constitutional amendments accompanying the Juárez presidential election *convocatoria*.[1]

Juárez had hoped to combine his reelection in October with the concentration of presidential authority. Four of the amendments involved the centralization of executive power at the expense of the legislature: the creation of an upper legislative chamber, a presidential veto over legislative bills, the freeing of ministers from having to answer verbally to Congress, and limiting the power of the permanent commission of Congress to convene special sessions. The states were to introduce the same amendments to their constitutions. Juárez's intention to allow the clergy to vote and serve as deputies also provoked dissent. Many Poblano Liberals believed that militant clerical opposition to the constitution from the Plan de Zacapoaxtla onward, as well as the Church's complicity in the establishment of the Empire, disqualified the clergy from exercising full rights of citizenship. Méndez therefore refused to publish the full *convocatoria* (he omitted the four offending articles), prompting the first political crisis of the Restored Republic.[2]

Méndez would have better served his own political career by keeping quiet. However, along with many of his generation, he favored a strong and independent legislature that would keep the potentially arbitrary executive authority in check. Juárez responded swiftly and forcefully to this defiance, demonstrating the centralism that would mark his presidency. On 19 September, he ordered Méndez to vacate the governorship and nominated Rafael García to replace him. At first, Méndez declined to hand over command of the state (for fear, he explained, of provoking public disorder). Then, on 26 September, Méndez turned over the governorship to García, warning prophetically that he could not be held responsible for any disorders that might ensue.[3]

This reference to the risks of unrest reflected a realistic appraisal of the machine that Méndez, with the active support of Díaz, commander of the Army of the East (now based at Tehuacán, in southeast Puebla), had been putting in place since well before the fall of the Empire. During his short governorship, Méndez had extended his influence beyond the Sierra to embrace the entire state by appointing his friends as jefes políticos.[4] Juárez, aware of the close friendship between Díaz and Méndez, and recent witness to the Tetela caudillo's independence of mind as revealed in his opposition to the *convocatoria*, decided that to allow the Puebla governorship to fall into the hands of such a powerful potential opponent posed too great a risk to the success of his own imminent reelection.

Juan Nepomuceno Méndez, Governor of the State of Puebla, April–September 1867. Archivo Fotográfico, Centro de Estudios de Historia de México (CONDUMEX)

Twice (the second time on Rafael García's advice), Juárez refused to accept Méndez's resignation from his regular army commission. He preferred the Tetela caudillo to be out of electoral politics (disqualified by virtue of his military command) until the presidential election was decided.[5] It was probably at this juncture that Méndez, encouraged by Díaz, began considering the option of rebellion against the state government as evidenced by the generous cache of arms and ammunition that he took with him when he left the state capital. With Díaz commanding the Army of the East based at Tehuacán, a military victory for Méndez must have seemed a foregone conclusion.[6]

The Campaigns for the State Governorship

One of García's first acts on assuming the governorship was to release the Xochiapulco battalion from its garrison duty in the capital and to pay for its return to the Sierra. Returning this force to the Sierra was as fraught with risks as keeping it in the state capital.[7] Ominously, at the same time, Méndez received a shipment of over three thousand modern repeating rifles from the United States (the ones ordered during the struggle against the Empire) that he distributed among friendly communities in the Sierra, especially Xochiapulco.[8] Méndez withdrew to Huamantla in northern Tlaxcala. He explained to Díaz the tactical advantage of remaining close to the center of "our political theater," yet at only a pace from the Sierra, in position to prevent, "with arms if necessary," the displacement of jefes políticos belonging to the "Sindicada" (Méndez's *camarilla*) with the "creatures of García."[9]

Aware of this insurrectionary strategy, Juárez turned his attention to Lucas, the key to Méndez's ability to mobilize the National Guard as a political weapon in the Puebla Sierra. Lucas had retired from active service after the victory at Puebla on 2 April 1867 to live in Xochiapulco.[10] Yet his forces remained on active duty. Indeed, the Second Battalion was probably the most disciplined and effective military force in the state. From the unregulated "rabble" which Maldonado and Santín had organized into regular companies of National Guard under elected officers in 1862, the battalion now comprised seven companies numbering 368 men.[11]

Juárez's decision to establish direct contact with Lucas came on the advice of Antonio Carbajal, who, while acting as agent of the federal executive in Puebla during the electoral period of September and October 1867, had warned that an alliance between Méndez and Antonio Rodríguez Bocardo (cacique of the northern *llanos* of Atzompa) was imminent.[12] Rodríguez Bocardo commanded the cavalry company of the district of San Juan de los Llanos. His decision in September 1866 to join the Republicans had been a turning point in the campaign against the Empire by enabling Méndez to come out of the Sierra and establish a foothold on the plateau.

The renewal of this alliance would give Méndez full control over the north of the state, confining García to the central valley. As it turned out, although the town of Libres disavowed the García government in April 1868, the district did not join the rebellion mounted from the Sierra. However, in October 1867, given Méndez's prestige, Díaz's proximity, and García's military weakness (he complained to Juárez that all the active state forces were away serving in Veracruz), Méndez looked to be the best horse to back.

In a hectic cycle of correspondence, Juárez and García sought desperately to wean Lucas away from Méndez with offers of weapons and reassurances about the *convocatoria*. In reply, Lucas pledged his support for García, stressing that Xochiapulco had suffered more than any other settlement during the Intervention and sought only peace.[13] Encouraged by this profession of loyalty, García proceeded to encroach even more boldly upon the Méndez *cacicazgo*. He purged *mendecistas* from district governments throughout the center and south of the state (Tecamachalco, San Andrés Chalchicomula, Tehuacán, Tepeji, Izucar, and Acatlán), even encroaching upon Méndez's own turf in the north (Teziutlán, Zacatlán, and Huauchinango). García appointed Ignacio Romero Vargas to Teziutlán, removed Ramón Márquez Galindo from Izucar de Matamoros, and appointed Rafael Cravioto to the command of the Northern Line. These moves left Méndez without a single ally in a senior position.[14] To complete his isolation, García urged Juárez to annul Méndez's commission in the army.[15]

García's zeal to eliminate Méndez was not matched by the force necessary for nullifying his influence in the state. When Juan Crisóstomo Bonilla refused to give up Zacatlán, García could do little about it. Elsewhere in the Sierra, deposed *mendecista* jefes políticos continued their electoral work, despite their removal from office. These circumstances enhanced Lucas's value to Juárez and García as a mediator and peacemaker. In early October, Juárez offered supreme authority to Lucas in maintaining order in the southern Sierra. Juárez urged that he work in combination with Rafael Cravioto of Huauchinango and repeated the offer of five hundred rifles. Lucas gratefully accepted this commission.[16] Although García had feared that Lucas would be jealous of Cravioto's appointment to the command of the Northern Line, Lucas and Cravioto soon reached an agreement about spheres of influence in the Sierra. Although Lucas was prepared to pledge loyalty to Juárez, he delayed his replies to García's letters.[17]

The results of the primary elections for the presidency from Puebla's districts showed García's suspicions to have been correct. In the north of the state, support for Méndez and Díaz in the Sierra remained solid. Of the 321 electoral college votes from Teziutlán, Zacatlán, Libres, and Zacapoaxtla (including Tetela), 263 went to Díaz and only 58 to Juárez. The Zacapoaxtla results demonstrate clearly that Lucas had favored Díaz for the presidency and Justo Benítez for the presidency of the Supreme Court.[18] Only in Cravioto's bailiwick of Huauchinango did the *juaristas* win comfortably. Juárez had considered this town of sufficient importance to merit the dispatch of his son-in-law, Pedro Santacilia, as electoral agent (soon to be elected as Huauchinango's congressman) and to sacrifice 20,000 pesos of Tuxpan's customs revenues to help ensure the election.[19]

Elsewhere in the state, the results of the presidential election demonstrate the extent of external meddling in the electoral process. To ensure a *juarista* victory in the state capital, José María Maldonado was sent to supervise the elections. Like Carbajal, Maldonado had developed a hostility toward Méndez during his term as commander of Republican forces in the Sierra, and both men felt aggrieved that they had received so little recognition for their contribution to patriotic resistance. Maldonado and Carbajal's bribes, street demonstrations, and propaganda in Puebla discouraged the city from voting for Díaz, although he was said to be the more popular candidate.

By October 1867 politics in Puebla had become polarized between a largely *juarista* central plateau and the south of the state, home of the party of the Llanura, and a largely *porfirista* north of the state, home of the party of the Montaña.[20] These loose party groupings served as flexible molds for state politics until the national consolidation of the Díaz dictatorship during the late 1880s.[21] Juárez and García saw Lucas as a potential bridge into the uncertain, if not openly hostile, political terrain of the Sierra. Lucas, they hoped, would persuade villagers of the wisdom of voting for official candidates and warn them of the dangers of a return to the disorders of the Reform Wars and European Intervention. If Lucas's peaceful entreaties failed, then García was quite prepared to use more forceful means of persuading Indians to vote for official candidates.[22] From late 1867 until the final rupture with Lucas on 22 June 1868, Juárez continued to encourage Cravioto to establish close relations with the cacique, as well as to deal with Lucas and his commanders directly. The president regarded Xochiapulco as the key to neutralizing Díaz's hold on the Sierra, and he offered to support the town's forces with rifles and credits.[23]

The elections for governor on 30 October 1867 confirmed the extent of Méndez's influence. The Tetela caudillo gained a clear majority with 56 percent of the vote (64,204), with the closest opponents—García and Ignacio Romero Vargas—receiving just over 20,000 votes each. The election caused a storm in the state legislature. Apart from the electoral irregularities reported from around the state, uncertainty still surrounded the question of Méndez's army commission and his constitutional right to participate in the elections.[24] His continuing exile in Huamantla and his absence from Puebla after the first (favorable) results were published suggest that Méndez was becoming accustomed to the life of a semi-outlaw. He preferred (like Díaz) the security of the army camp over the uncertainties of electoral contests and constitutional disputes.[25] However, an opportunity soon appeared for an alliance with the congressional followers of the third horse in the race, Ignacio Romero Vargas, which raised Méndez's hopes for achieving a peaceful route to power.

Sensing that time was on his side, late in November 1867, Méndez instructed his deputies to vote with the *romerista* deputies to annul the results of the October elections on the grounds that García had illegally inspected the electoral lists before the results of the election had been validated.[26] The legislature then voted to remove García from the governorship and to appoint Juan Gómez (whom Méndez trusted) as interim governor, pending new elections to be held on 19 January 1868. With the confirmation of the results of the elections of jefes políticos, which brought many *mendecistas* back into the command of Puebla's districts, Méndez came out of this electoral period in a much stronger position.

Released finally from his military commission, backed by friendly jefes políticos, and aided by a revised electoral law that endowed municipalities with the exclusive authority over the supervision of elections, Méndez could now reasonably expect to reaffirm his majority in the gubernatorial elections of January 1868.[27] However, in spite of receiving over 60,000 votes (almost three times the votes given to his closest rivals García and Romero Vargas), Méndez narrowly missed the absolute majority needed for a clear victory. However, such was the scale of Méndez's lead that a majority on the congressional electoral commission declared him to be the winner.[28] But this majority decision was opposed by a vociferous minority, who required that the election be ratified by the full state congress, where the balance of forces was less favorable for Méndez than it had been in November 1867.[29]

When the congress met in February 1868 to resolve the deadlock, *mendecista* deputies found themselves isolated, no longer able to count on support from the *romerista* deputies who had helped remove García three months earlier.[30] Soon after the elections in January, Romero Vargas withdrew his candidature for the governorship, thereby regaining the right to vote as a deputy. A *mendecista* motion to annul the electoral results from Tehuacán, which would have enabled their leader to demonstrate a clear majority, was defeated. The *romerista-rafaelista* alliance then went on to win a motion (by nine votes against two) that proposed García for the governorship. Facing certain defeat, the six other *mendecistas* had absented themselves from the chamber in disgust.[31]

The state of Puebla was now led by a man who had received a mere 18 percent of the popular vote and who had not taken up arms against the Empire until the last months. Seemingly condemned to oblivion was Puebla's senior veteran of the Reform Wars and Mexico's second war of independence, whose share of the vote in January 1868 had been in excess of 45 percent.[32] Throughout February and March, acts protesting the illegality and injustice of García's election poured in to the state congress from Puebla's enraged municipalities.[33] By April, "symptoms of rebellion" were observed in the districts of Zacatlán, Acatlán, Matamoros, Tecamachalco, and Tehuacán. By the end of May, fifteen of the state's twenty districts had raised petitions requesting that the legislature review its decision on the governorship election.

García, who at first disclaimed knowledge of these petitions (many of which were published in Puebla in the *mendecista* newspaper, *La Montaña*), invoked the state's electoral law that forbade any revision or nullification of an election for governorship once it had been ratified by the congress.[34] With their right to appeal recognized but with García not conceding an inch, several districts invoked their constitutional right to disobey illegally constituted authority.

The Breakdown of Order in the Puebla Sierra

The first armed movement in the Sierra since the fall of the Empire occurred in the north of Zacapoaxtla district. Indians in Cuetzalan, who were opposed to the enclosure of their common land by non-Indians, rebelled.[35] This uprising was the most persistent and serious of a rash of rebellions against municipal authorities in the *tierra cálida* of Tetela, Zacapoaxtla, Tlatlauqui, and Teziutlán during the three years following the application of the Ley Lerdo to village commons in December 1867. The grievances of Indian communities now extended beyond forced recruitment and unjust taxation to concern about the sale of commons to non-Indians who previously had only rented community land. The revolt increased demands upon Lucas as a mediator and a tribune.

Until now, Lucas had operated principally in the Indian communities in the southern Sierra that bordered the plateau. The communities of the center and north of the Sierra were less familiar territory to Lucas. Nevertheless, he was accustomed to raising taxes, war supplies, and occasionally soldiers from farther into the Sierra. Lucas knew Francisco Agustín (Palagustín), the leader of the Cuetzalan rebellion, very well. At the battle of 5 May 1862, Francisco Agustín had served under Lucas's command in the Sixth Battalion. Later on, during the Intervention (possibly following the surrender), Francisco Agustín and his wife offered Lucas sanctuary against pursuit by Zacapoaxtla's authorities at the Rancho de la Providencia, near Cuetzalan. Later, Francisco Agustín, leading a full company from Cuetzalan, served under Lucas's command at the victory over the Imperial forces at Puebla on 2 April 1867. Lucas's influence with Francisco Agustín explains the jefe político of Zacapoaxtla's decision to appoint Lucas to preside over the commission established to mediate in the Cuetzalan dispute. State and district authorities used this opportunity to test Lucas's loyalty to the new order.

As the Cuetzalan conflict received closer attention from Lucas, indignation in the Sierra about the imposition of García as governor reached the boiling point.[36] Rafael Cravioto, acting as Juárez and García's confidant and ally in the Puebla Sierra, reported the events in Zacatlán on 25 February 1868 that prompted the first armed Federal intervention in Puebla state politics since the fall of the Empire: "On 25 February, four hundred rifles proceeding from Tetela arrived in Zacatlán. A great multitude of townspeople, including all the civil and military authorities and the town band, came out to meet them. Rockets were set off, church bells rung, and 'vivas' lavished upon citizens Juan Méndez and Vicente Márquez while 'mueras' were heaped upon governor Rafael J. García and the jefe político Dimás López. This scandal concluded with the tearing down and burning of the decrees which had been posted in public places."[37] For the moment, this danger in the western Sierra seemed more threatening to Juárez and García than a land dispute in some remote municipality. Lucas and Cravioto received instructions to suppress the movement in Zacatlán and prevent it from spreading to the southern Sierra.[38] Three Federal generals were also ordered to Apam to confront the rebels in Zacatlán.[39]

This sizable Federal intervention, which was ordered before the state congress, in session, had a chance to discuss the implications of events in Zacatlán, demonstrates Juárez's extreme concern with events in Puebla. After Díaz's retirement from the army, the most obvious threat to the Juárez government became Miguel Negrete. This hero of the battle of 5 May 1862 had been appointed Minister of War by Juárez in March 1864. Later he lost Juárez's trust when he backed Jesús González Ortega in the presidential contest in 1865. With the restoration of the Republic in 1867, Negrete was given the military command of the state of Veracruz, a post he considered unworthy of a man of his patriotic achievements. He would figure in almost every conspiracy in central and southern Mexico during the Restored Republic and afterward.[40]

Apart from Negrete as a potential protagonist, Puebla's rebels also had friends in Mexico City. A significant bloc in the Federal congress and the influential radical Liberal newspaper, *El Monitor Republicano*, complained vigorously about the electoral irregularities and Federal intervention in the state. The suppression of the movement in Zacatlán, the cradle of the Independence struggles and home of every patriotic and Liberal struggle since 1847, went down badly, and the congressional motion to have the Federal force removed was only narrowly defeated.[41]

Military action by the Federal force this time was avoided. When General Toro arrived in Zacatlán on 5 March 1868, the full ayuntamiento came out to meet him, insisting that the town and the district were at peace. They explained that Zacatlán was merely exercising its right to petition, nothing more. Accepting this explanation, General Toro withdrew to Huamantla.[42] As quickly as the Federal force retreated, the rebels took control again of Zacatlán. Dimás López, the jefe político imposed by García (who had replaced the *mendecista* Juan Crisóstomo Bonilla), was obliged to emigrate to Huauchinango along with many other Zacatecos opposed to the rebel authorities. At the end of March, the rebels still held Zacatlán.[43] By now, García was alarmed that the revolt was spreading, with rebel movements also evident in the center and south of the state at Tecamachalco and Acatlán (behind Albino Zertuche).[44]

The anger of Puebla's electors, in the form of petitions and military rumblings, continued into April. Lucas, who in February had disobeyed García's order to suppress the Zacatlán movement, at last declared his own colors. On 23 April he announced that the Northern Line was about to disavow his authority since the state congress had ignored all petitions from the villages. He had done everything he could to keep the peace, but this had proved no longer possible, "and now I must go with the villages." Lucas warned García that while the governor might be able to count upon the loyalty of the jefes políticos of Teziutlán and Tlatlauqui, he could no longer expect the obedience of the citizens of these districts.[45]

If García interpreted Lucas's warning of disorder as an intention to revolt (particularly since García had learned that Juan Crisóstomo Bonilla in league with Miguel Negrete had planned an uprising to coincide symbolically with the sixth anniversary of the victory of May 1862 against the French), Juárez doubted that Lucas would join an open rebellion. The president warned García to deal with the dissenting villages with great care, observing that Indians were by nature opposed to the disruption that accompanied rebellions.[46] In his defense, García claimed that he had received no petitions from the Sierra concerning electoral irregularities. He accused Ramón Márquez Galindo, the leading *mendecista* deputy, of deliberately withdrawing the petitions, which proved that neither the deputy nor Méndez was seeking peace. Juárez urged García to receive the petitions from Sierra districts so he could learn the nature of their grievances.[47] While García falsely accused Márquez Galindo of deliberately withdrawing the petitions in order to justify the revolt (the petitions were received by the Congress, but no deputy was prepared to act as protagonist), the governor was truthful when he informed Juárez that he had not officially received or read them. For Márquez Galindo, after having failed to convince Congress to debate the petitions, to have gone on then to present them directly to García (the constitutionally correct procedure) would have been to have acknowledged the legitimacy of a governor whom he and the petitioners considered illegal.[48]

Deaf to Juárez's entreaties on the petitions, García instead chose to respond to the crisis in the Sierra by extending his circle of allies and by easing his friends into positions of authority. García established close relations with two powerful opponents of Méndez in Zacapoaxtla: Pascual Bonilla, arch-Conservative and close collaborator with the Empire, and Colonel Miguel Arriaga, commander of Zacapoaxtla's National Guard. Both men had been determined to reassert control over Xochiapulco's forces since

Maldonado and Lucas had secured their autonomy from the Zacapoaxtla National Guard in 1863.[49] The governor's encouragement of a former traitor and a rival for the military control of the southern Sierra could only have increased the exasperation of Méndez's supporters in this strategically critical area.

Violence finally erupted in the southern Sierra on 26 April 1868. Manuel Bandala, a National Guard commander from Teziutlán who had been supplying the Cuetzalan rebels with arms, toppled Mariano Saborido, the jefe político of Tlatlauqui, with the help of Nahua soldiers from Cuetzalan.[50] Lucas, on García's instructions, led one hundred fifty men to Tlatlauqui to restore order. He removed Bandala and substituted Antonio Martínez in his place. Three days later Martínez proclaimed for Méndez.[51] Throughout May, Méndez received pledges of support from Albino Zertuche in Acatlán and Jesús García in Chiautla and from other leading figures in Tetela, Zacatlán, and Huauchinango. He also received sympathetic messages from as far away as the Mixteca of Oaxaca. There were even suspicions about the loyalty of Rafael Cravioto in Huauchinango, without whose support García's control of the Sierra would surely be lost.[52]

The "Sufragio Libre" Rebellion

The southern Sierra moved from disobedience to rebellion in late May. On 27 May, leading a force of five hundred men, Lucas ousted the jefe político of Teziutlán and installed Mariano Murrieta, a *mendecista*, in the name of restoring legitimacy and order. Lucas assured the Perote garrison that he intended no disturbance to the peace.[53] The trickle of disavowals of García's authority now became a flood, making it clear that a rebellion was under way in the Puebla Sierra. The municipalities that withdrew their support from the government and nominated Lucas as the chief of the Northern Line, with powers to convoke a state congress, included Tetela (1 June), Zapotitlán and Zacapoaxtla (5 June), Jonotla (6 June), Zoquiapan (6 June), Huitzilan (7 June), Hueytlalpan and Xochitlán (8 June), Cuetzalan and Tlatlauqui (9 June), Huahuaxtla (10 June), Xochiapulco (10 June), and Libres (13 June).[54] On 10 June, Lucas issued general regulations for the military government of the Sierra, now in a state of war.[55]

Open warfare first flared up in the western Sierra between rebels Negrete and Vicente Márquez, who held Zacatlán and Chignahuapan, and government forces under Rafael Cravioto and Eraclio Soza in Huauchinango and Ahuacatlán. García called on Cravioto and Rodríguez Bocardo to engage the rebels from their positions to the north and south of the Sierra. Both hesitated.[56] The Federal offensive in the southern Sierra also stalled as Juárez himself made a last-minute plea to Lucas not to rebel. The President explained to Lucas that the troublemakers, by pretending that the movement was concerned with the gubernatorial election, were concealing their real objective, which was to "conspire against the freely elected national government." Lucas insisted in reply that the rebellion was directed only at the state government, but he agreed to convey Juárez's warnings to the villages about the grave consequences of rebellion.[57] Meanwhile, Federal forces advanced into the Sierra, approaching Teziutlán and Perote from the south and closing in from the north.[58]

By now the conflict was too advanced for a peaceful solution. Márquez and Cravioto's forces clashed periodically in the western Sierra over strategic Ahuacatlán.[59] In the southern Sierra, the Federal advance was delayed, waiting for Rodríguez Bocardo to declare his colors. This indecision and Cravioto's isolation brought a high cost. On 11 July, Lucas, leading 1,000 men, dispersed Cravioto's force of 300 defending Ahuacatlán. Cravioto blamed General Ignacio Alatorre for delaying the Federal offensive but also suspected treachery among his own following.[60]

Alatorre (on Juárez's advice and backed now by García) was opposed to any immediate military engagement with Lucas's forces while there still remained a chance of a negotiated settlement. Although Juárez was concerned about the threat posed by Negrete, he did not consider the Sierra rebellion to be a substantial challenge to his authority. Apart from the firm alliance with Cravioto, Juárez and García had reliable evidence that their forces could count on an additional ally in the heart of the Sierra. Late in June, Colonel Miguel Arriaga, commander of Zacapoaxtla's battalion of National Guard, had offered to join Alatorre's Federal force when it entered the district.[61]

The *mendecista* order was also fragile in Teziutlán where, after the fall of the district capital to a force of six hundred Xochiapulquenses under Benito Marín on 3 July, the state government began to organize guerrillas from the same villages that the Conservatives, and later the Imperialists, had once cultivated. In early July, Xiutetelco, Atempan, and Chignautla declared in favor of the state government.[62] García promised to re-arm villagers in exchange for support against the rebels in Xochiapulco.[63]

On 7 July, Juan Francisco Molina, jefe político and military commander of the district of Zacapoaxtla, convened a general meeting in the council building to decide what position he should adopt toward the approaching Federal force. Protesting the illegal imposition of García as governor, the injustice of the Federal campaign against the district, and invoking Zacapoaxtla's patriotic services during the "Second War of Independence," the junta decided that the First Battalion of the National Guard, with its arms and munitions, should evacuate the town. Alatorre would be allowed to occupy Zacapoaxtla, whereupon he would be met by the town council, whose members would resign their posts after airing their grievances. Meanwhile, Zacapoaxtla's First Battalion would be stationed on the heights of Apulco, where, considering itself in complete obedience to the Federation, it would not engage Federal troops in battle.[64]

Encouraged by this apparent submission, Alatorre now exhorted Lucas to end hostilities in the four districts he represented.[65] In reply, Lucas begged Alatorre to end his campaign to crush a movement whose only purpose was to protect "the right of the people to elect their governor."[66] Lucas agreed to cooperate with the federal government in the apprehension of Negrete and ordered his arrest (Negrete had already fled to the Sierra de Tulancingo).[67]

On 17 July, Lucas and Alatorre met in Zacapoaxtla. Lucas agreed to a cessation of hostilities and to the proposal that all rebel arms be handed in within eight days, subject to the approval of the villages. On receiving news of the meeting, García expressed his delight to Juárez, announcing that the "Sierra problem," which he considered to have been the work of no more than a few troublemakers (including Lucas), was now concluded.[68]

Lucas then called together all the rebel leaders to consider the terms of the armistice.[69] In his account to Alatorre of the proceedings of this meeting, Lucas explained why Pilar Rivera and Lauro Luna, the commanders of Tetela's National Guard, had found it impossible to accept the conditions, particularly the handing in of arms:

> With the deepest emotion they consider that this condition (disarmament) would strip them, in front of the nation and the entire world, of the laurels which they acquired on the memorable day of 5 May 1862, in the sieges of Querétaro, Puebla, and México. With these arms they have been prepared always to defend republican institutions. Now, as a reward for lending such honorable services, the chief of the nation is imposing such humiliation . . . they consider it their duty to protect their honor, their glory, their dignity as citizen-militiamen, the general interests of the District and the private interests of each individual, and finally, their rights as free men, out of respect for their fallen countrymen sacrificed defending republican institutions, it is their declared will to keep possession of their arms.[70]

With this response from Tetela, the core of the Méndez *cacicazgo*, Lucas resolved to continue the rebellion. Disarmament was simply not an option, even if Zacapoaxtla (his own district) had shown a willingness to hand in its weapons.

In contrast to Lucas, Molina Alcántara, the rebel jefe político of Zacapoaxtla, was prepared to hand over arms belonging to Zacapoaxtla's battalion of National Guard. But he insisted that the forces under Lucas's direct command, the Xochiapulquenses, should be the first to surrender their weapons, with the National Guard battalion of the cabecera complying only after this had occurred.[71] This arrangement had obvious risks. Disarmament of Xochiapulco before Zacapoaxtla threatened to swing back the pendulum of power in favor of the cabecera. If Lucas complied with Molina's advice, he would risk a return to the political situation preceding the revolution of Ayutla, when the unarmed Cuatecomaco Indians faced an armed and politically dominant cabecera.

Pilar Rivera and Tetela's National Guard commanders decided not to await the conclusion of the eight-day truce. They advanced to join Molina Alcántara and the Zacapoaxtla battalion positioned on the heights of Apulco. On reaching Tececuilco on 25 July, Rivera received news that a mutiny had occurred among Molina's troops at Apulco. Rivera contacted Lucas, who urged him to advance to defend Apulco at all costs. Arriving at Huahuaxtla, Rivera met Luis Antonio Díaz, the commander of Xochiapulco's forces, who informed him that the enemy had successfully taken Apulco, without facing resistance, adding that "finally Alcántara jumped on the bandwagon."[72]

In spite of Molina's surrender, 350 of his 400 troops had refused to hand over their weapons and fled.[73] These mutinous soldiers took two of their captains ("Chino" Ramírez and Carlos Cantero, brother of Cenobio) with them as hostages. They temporarily detained Captain Francisco Agustín, who had come up from Cuetzalan with 100 Nahua troops intending to arm them at Xochiapulco. Two rebel movements, Cuetzalan's Nahua *comuneros* and the National Guard of Zacapoaxtla and Tetela, had merged quite accidently. They shared at least one common cause: to resist disarmament by the Federal army.[74]

Following these events at Apulco, Lucas finally declared the formal opening of hostilities against the Federal army. The mass desertion of Zacapoaxtla's National Guards, against the advice of their officers, had clearly demonstrated to him that the villages under his command had rejected the humiliating conditions imposed by Alatorre. Lucas warned Molina of their willingness to fight to the death for their principles: "The villages of the line are resolved to confront anything, even death, because they believe that they have committed no crime, but on the contrary, they have made heroic sacrifices in defense of National Independence and liberal principles, and that having their arms taken away, which for the most part were wrested from the foreign enemy or from traitors, will leave them unworthy even of calling themselves citizens."[75]

Lucas ordered Rivera to hold Apulco while reinforcements were brought from Xochitlán and Cuetzalan, stressing that every effort should be made to bring Molina back into the fold.[76] Finally, Lucas informed Alatorre that a state of war now existed between his forces and the Second Division of the Federal army. He explained that "the terrible condition of disarmament" had been the principal cause for the renewed hostilities.[77] Alatorre received Lucas's communication with great bitterness. He saw the news as a betrayal of the agreement reached in the fruitful discussions of 17 July.[78] As the arms question moved to the center of the conflict, the issue of the contested election for the governorship, which had originally sparked the rebellion, receded into the background.

In spite of the surrender of Zacapoaxtla's First Battalion, Alatorre still faced a hostile Xochiapulco and the fully mobilized National Guard battalion of Tetela, reinforced by fifty men of Aquixtla's National Guard company. This force camped at Huahuaxtla and blocked Zacapoaxtla's access to Xochitlán, Cuetzalan, and Nauzontla.[79] Moreover, having received arms and promises of support from Xochiapulco, Francisco Agustín's movement was reported once more to be threatening the *gente de razón* in Cuetzalan.

General Alatorre and the Defeat of the Rebellion

The *comunero* movement in Cuetzalan continued, on and off, until the 1890s. By contrast, the first general Sierra rebellion of the Restored Republic was shortly to be defeated. At first, Alatorre hoped to take advantage of local rivalries rather than deploy the Federal force directly against the rebels. Before his arrival in Zacapoaxtla, he had been assured that Miguel Arriaga, commander of its First Battalion of National Guard, which comprised some six hundred men in seven companies, was prepared to work with the Federal force against the *mendecista* forces of Xochiapulco and Tetela. But Molina's retreat to Apulco, his surrender, and the mass desertions of the soldiery escaping disarmament had temporarily interrupted this strategy. As a gesture of reconciliation, two days after his surrender on 28 July, Alatorre re-appointed Molina Alcántara as supreme commander of the district of Zacapoaxtla. The Federal commander hoped that this action would bring the mutinous troops back into the fold and that Molina would be able to persuade Lucas and Rivera to end hostilities.

This delicate process of negotiation was interrupted by an attack upon Tetela from the west by state and Federal forces under a separate command, leaving Alatorre no alternative but to press ahead with the campaign. On 30 July a Federal column ousted Tetela's National Guard from its position at Huahuaxtla.[80] Two other columns, approaching from Zautla to the south and from the hacienda of Mazapa to the east, completed the encirclement of Xochiapulco.[81] With such massive deployment of Federal forces, the end must have seemed close for the Montaña. However, two complications delayed the completion of the Federal offensive. First, Cravioto's pacification of the western Sierra and the Federal advance upon Tetela from the west were delayed by an insurrection in the Sierra de Tulancingo. Rebels led by Antonio and Paulino Noriega and Baltazar Telles Girón tied down Federal forces in this area and threatened to invade Huauchinango and Chignahuapan.[82] Second, the *comunero* movement in Cuetzalan against *desamortización* had suddenly become more assertive. Cuetzalan's *gente de razón* now described the rebellion as a caste war that was encouraged, in the opinion of one village authority, by no less than Lucas himself.[83]

The western zone remained a problem for Federal troops even after the fall of Zacatlán on 31 July. The pacification of the Sierra de Tulancingo absorbed Federal forces under General Juan Cortina until mid-August.[84] Following the defeat of the Noriega brothers, Cortina and his cavalry, joined at Chignahuapan by reinforcements from Mexico, entered the district of Tetela.[85] They took the villages of Loma Alta and San Miguel, which forced Negrete back to Tetela de Ocampo. On 17 August the force of one hundred rebel National Guardsmen under José María Bonilla of Aquixtla and a similar force under Rafael Herrera of Ixtacamaxtitlán switched sides to join the Federal force (an established pattern of conduct of these towns when faced with a powerful external threat). Together, this formidable force marched upon Tetela to engage eight hundred rebels commanded by Méndez on the Cerro de Moraxco on 18 August. The battle raged for four hours before the rebels broke and fled into the mountains. Méndez, with no more than fifty men, retreated through Ometepec. General Cortina's victory at the Cerro de Moraxco owed much to men from the Sierra de Hidalgo, especially the Batallón Movíl de Jacala commanded by Lieutenant Colonel Pablo Chávez, whose troops were well practiced in mountain warfare. Cortina also benefited from good knowledge, aided by modern maps, of the topography of the Puebla Sierra.[86]

News of the defeat of the main rebel force at Tetela encouraged the two Federal columns encircling Xochiapulco to press their attack. Realizing that resistance would be futile, Lucas offered his submission, using the good offices of General José María Maldonado, his old companion in the struggle against the French. His forces handed over their arms to General Francisco Carrión on 21 August 1868. General Juan Crisóstomo Bonilla surrendered on the following day.[87] Juárez granted a pardon to Lucas and the leaders under his command, the death penalty for rebellion being commuted to four years of imprisonment. General Carrión marched to Tetela immediately after the agreement and arrested several prominent leaders of the revolt, including Vicente Márquez (whose movement in Zacatlán in February 1868 had initiated the rebellion) and two prominent public employees (Gregorio Zamítez and Vicente Bonilla y Hernández).[88] Lucas's soldiers were given safe-conduct passes to return to their homes. Only Negrete, charged with treachery aginst the *patria*, would face the full force of the law.[89] Alatorre ordered Lucas to remain in Xochiapulco until further notice.[90]

With the Sierra pacified, at the cost of little loss of life, Alatorre could justly claim credit for a masterly use of the Federal velvet glove. He was helped in this task by the instructions he had received in late July from Ignacio Mejía, Minister of War, who had suggested that villages should be permitted to retain such arms as were necessary for ensuring their own security, with the remainder to be handed in to the Federal army. Alatorre instructed Molina, just reappointed as military commander of the district, to pass on this order to Xochiapulco.[91]

Alatorre had been so occupied with the broader strategy of containing and defeating the Sierra rebellion that he had failed even to notice the disturbances in Cuetzalan. Nevertheless, the troubles in Cuetzalan continued in spite of Lucas's submission.[92] Francisco Agustín remained in rebellion for two reasons: because its underlying cause—local opposition to the sale of common lands—had still not been addressed; and because Méndez saw this movement as a way of keeping alive his own challenge to the state government.

On 23 August, twenty Indian rebels from Tzicuilan and Tzinacantepec assembled at Zacatipan (Cuetzalan) where they were joined by forty-five men from Xochiapulco under one of Lucas's captains. They were reported to be well armed and were raising funds by taxing non-Indian ranchers in the districts of Zacapoaxtla and Tlatlauqui. The entire force was commanded by Juan Ignacio Guerrero, whom Méndez had used for organizing patriotic forces in the *tierra caliente* in 1866–67. His objective was to make contact with Andrés Mirón, a *mendecista* National Guard commander in Tlatlauqui, who would bring rifles and ammunition from Teziutlán to be paid for from the funds raised at Zacatipan. Mirón, who commanded two hundred men, had been in Tlatlauqui invoking Lucas's authority to extort cash and supplies from the Nahua community of Yaonahuac.[93]

Here then is evidence of a broader, "fall-back" strategy in Méndez's pursuit of the state governorship. The front line in the southern Sierra, from Teziutlán to Tetela, had always shown itself to be vulnerable to a well-equipped and sustained attack from the plateau, particularly when the attack chose several entries, as in the current Federal campaign. The district capitals were hard to defend in the face of enemy artillery, while villages in the southern Sierra, particularly in Ixtacamaxtitlán, Aquixtla, Zacapoaxtla, and Tlatlauqui, had always proved fickle and willing to work with the enemy. Therefore, for any sustained armed movement against the state or central government, support had to be harnessed from communities farther into the Sierra.

During the last years of the Intervention, Méndez had learned that the traditionally unmilitarized communities in the *tierra cálida* and *tierra caliente* could also be mobilized to defend against outsiders. Since the end of the Empire, tensions in this zone had grown as a result of conflicts over the sale of common lands, especially to the attempt by non-Indians to gain title to land they had formerly rented from Indian communities. The Cuetzalan rebellion revealed how Indians, in an area that traditionally had shown great aversion to military service, were now seeking arms and preparing to collaborate with rebel forces engaged in wider political movements.[94]

On this occasion, force would not be necessary since the possibility of a peaceful (albeit only temporary) solution to the Cuetzalan problem unexpectedly presented itself. In late August, Juan Ignacio Guerrero, the *mendecista* who had recently taken command of the rebels at Zacatipan, proposed a meeting between the jefe político and the principal rebel leaders to be presided over by Lucas without any of Cuetzalan's *gente de razón* present. As a conciliatory gesture, Guerrero offered to return the arms borrowed from Manuel Bandala (the National Guard commander from Teziutlán whose invasion of Tlatlauqui in April had sparked the Sierra rebellion).[95] The meeting must have been a success; shortly before General Alatorre left Zacapoaxtla for Jalapa, he reported the Indians of Cuetzalan to be in obedience to their authorities (explaining that they had not handed over their arms to the district authorities because these had been borrowed from Teziutlán, to where they now would be returned).[96]

An Uneasy Peace

The state of siege in the district of Zacapoaxtla was lifted on 7 September 1868. However, Rafael García and Benito Juárez (now the Puebla state governor's father-in-law) felt uneasy about the peace that had been made. Both Mejía at the Ministry of War, and Alatorre in the Sierra, had been persuaded by Lucas that good patriots, even if they had rebelled, should be permitted to retain their arms. García observed that very few weapons had been gathered up. Most of the rebel leaders were free to travel where they liked or to return undisturbed to their homes, allowing them to be ready to take up arms at any moment.[97] Some former rebels, such as Juan Crisóstomo Bonilla, clamored for political respectability and sought the nomination for the federal congress. García emphatically advised Juárez to oppose this.[98] To make matters worse, García also faced a challenge to his leadership from the well-connected Ignacio Romero Vargas.

Seeking to reassure his political protégé, Juárez ordered Alatorre to remain in the Sierra for another three months with orders to gather up arms from those still considering revolution.[99] On 28 December, Colonel Alonso (whom Alatorre had sent to the Sierra to review the state of public order) reported that the Sierra was "everywhere in perfect peace and submission to the authorities."[100] Apparently these Federal officers were blind to the conflicts that continued to afflict the Sierra.

The Cuetzalan conflict once more flared up in November with the widespread destruction of the properties of the *gente de razón*.[101] With peace still threatened in the northern part of the district, it became doubly important to ensure the pacification of the more militarized and more aggressive communities of the *tierra fria*. On 29 December the federal government ordered the state of Puebla to proceed with the division of the hacienda of Xochiapulco and Manzanilla among the recently rebellious National Guardsmen of the municipality in accord with the decree of Governor Fernando María Ortega of 5 December 1864.[102]

This may have appeared to be an ideal moment for a conciliatory gesture to encourage these hardened fighters to turn their weapons into ploughshares. The Sierra was only precariously at peace. Guaranteeing the political and material status of Xochiapulco would provide the firmest guarantee for this peace. Besides, García badly needed some goodwill from the Sierra in his rivalry with Romero Vargas over the governorship. Also propitious was the recent decision of Lucas to move his home from Xochiapulco to the district of Tetela. This left the federal and state governments freer to renegotiate their relationship with the troublesome military colony. Moreover, Lucas, through his marriage to Ascensión Pérez Contreras in March 1868, had become son-in-law to Francisco Pérez, the principal landowner and one of the wealthiest citizens of the district of Tetela. This alliance put Lucas in a much stronger economic position to assist with the cost of transforming Xochiapulco from what was still a series of squatter barrios on an abandoned hacienda into a municipality of small property holders.[103]

Upon Pérez's death in September 1868, Lucas found himself as the executor of his estate. Lucas was therefore able to invoke the private demands of business to disguise those of political expediency when he asked Juárez to be allowed to move his home from Xochiapulco (which Alatorre had designated as his place of exile) to Taxcantla, just within the boundaries of the district of Tetela.

In spite of the distractions of private life and the conciliatory mood of the federal and state governments, Lucas and the Puebla Sierra would not have peace for another eight years. Alatorre had shown great skill in responding to several of the underlying causes of *serrano* rebelliousness: fear of disarmament, uncertainty about Xochiapulco's territorial claims, and opposition to the sale of Cuetzalan's commons. However, the ostensible cause of the revolt was the widespread belief that General Juan Nepomuceno Méndez had been denied his legitimate right to the state governorship. The peace accords of September 1868 had done nothing to address this problem.

Conclusion

Earlier rebel movements in the Sierra, from the revolution of Ayutla until the defeat of the Austrians, resulted from external intervention in the region and formed part of much broader regional or national movements. The Liberals—Alvarez, Melchor Ocampo, Juárez, Negrete, and Díaz—all sought clientele in the Sierra with varying success. They provided local leaders with ready-made plans, strategies, and military promotions, which *serranos* in turn, particularly leaders such as Lucas who were in touch with the villages, refashioned into projects of their own. The Conservatives—Haro y Tamariz, Padre Miranda, Ignacio Gutiérrez, and Hermenegildo Carrillo—the French, and the Austrians also sought and found allies in the Sierra in the struggle to revitalize this region as a base for combating liberal republicanism.

The rebellion of June–December 1868 departed from this pattern of external mobilization. Although the maverick General Miguel Negrete hovered around its fringes with a wider national purpose that he never clearly articulated, the "free suffrage" rebellion was home-grown. Few of its complex causes were satisfactorily addressed in the peace settlement. The driving force behind the rebellion was the Montaña—Lucas of Zacapoaxtla, Méndez and Bonilla of Tetela, and Márquez Galindo of Zacatlán—a loose regional party, comprised of National Guard commanders, from neighboring towns, who had fought together in the civil and patriotic struggles over the previous decade and formed strong ties of friendship, compadrazgo, and political loyalty.

The rebellion was provoked by the federal exclusion of the Montaña from a share of the political spoils of the Republican victory of July 1867. Because Juárez had played such a decisive role in nominating, imposing, and sustaining Rafael García in the Puebla governorship, the rebellion appeared as a direct attack upon the President and the federal government. But the rebellion was more than a dispute over spoils. The major sticking point in the peace negotiations concerned the right to bear arms. National Guard veterans regarded this right as the key to securing recognition of a broader set of individual rights and guarantees, which they considered they had earned by their sacrifices during the Three Years' War and the war against the Empire. What gave the issue of hard-earned rights, protected by arms, additional urgency was the decision of the state legislature to press on with the sale of village commons. The Cuetzalan rebellion revealed the overlap between issues of patronage, constitutional rights, and the division of communal property. The failure of the federal government to fulfill its promise of 29 December 1868 to divide the lands of the Xochiapulco hacienda among the municipality's war veterans increased their distrust of Governor García and President Juárez and strengthened their determination to retain their weapons to ensure that their rulers kept their promises.[104]

9

The Arriaga Rebellion and the Xochiapulco Revolt

The Sierra was reported officially to be "tranquil" between January and November 1869. García's renunciation in March and Romero Vargas's election to the governorship in September occurred without the usual electoral disturbances.[1] Yet, beneath the surface, the Sierra remained troubled. In January 1869, Tlatlauqui villages rebelled over the division of common lands, calling for help from Xochiapulco (and for the return of Antonio López de Santa Anna!).[2] Rafael Cravioto reported from Huauchinango in the same month that virtually the entire district was in rebellion against the application of the 1863 law for the adjudication of unoccupied lands that villages claimed to be theirs.[3] In February, after issuing a revolutionary plan in the state capital, Negrete took flight to Teziutlán from where he unsuccessfully attempted to resurrect the Sierra rebellion against the state government.[4] In May, the Cuetzalan conflict over the division of the commons flared up again. Nevertheless, compared with 1868, from the perspective of the state government, peace reigned in the Sierra until the elections in November.

The close succession of direct elections for the governorship, the state congress, and for jefes políticos, all within the space of a month, and the unprecedented degree of executive intervention in the electoral process left many electors unhappy with the results. Although voting had been relatively orderly, in mid-November a series of small revolts in the district of Zacapoaxtla broadened into a rebellion commanded by Francisco Javier Arriaga, colonel of Zacapoaxtla's National Guard, against the state and federal governments. The rebellion's directorate was more Conservative and its territorial base at first more narrow (confined mainly to the district of Zacapoaxtla) than the "free suffrage" rebellion of 1868. Yet, these details mattered little to the state and federal governments, who from the start considered the rebellion to be the inspiration of Méndez, and therefore (and in spite of strong evidence to the contrary) engineered by Lucas and Xochiapulco.

The Elections of August–October 1869

García's resignation as governor in March 1869 had surprised no one. He had submitted it previously on several occasions, but each time the state congress had rejected it or Juárez had persuaded him to remain.[5] García was ill suited for the office of governor, particularly during this difficult period of transition from a decade of civil and patriotic struggle to the era of peaceful electoral politics. His dealings with the Sierra were clumsy and provocative. Nevertheless, García was useful to Juárez. The President could use the defense of García's governorship to justify federal intervention in Puebla. Juárez expected General Alatorre to police not only the Puebla Sierra but also the entire southeast. By March 1869, with the Sierra at peace and Negrete's rebellion contained in Guerrero, García's resignation went unopposed.[6] The Acatzingo lawyer, Ignacio Romero Vargas, served as interim governor until elections could name a successor in August.

With no candidate from the Sierra standing, Fernando María Ortega emerged as the Montaña candidate, with Romero Vargas as the candidate of the Llanura. Romero Vargas was a far more formidable opponent to the Montaña than García. He knew the Sierra well, having been in charge of finances (specifically with ecclesiastical disentailment) when the Liberal state government was based in Teziutlán during the last months of the Three Years' War. He profited personally from the properties which he was charged with administering, by accumulating urban real estate which he then used as collateral for acquiring indebted haciendas near his hometown of Acatzingo.[7] After the fall of the Empire, Romero Vargas established a strong congressional group and created a far-flung network of political agents throughout the state. These interests served him well in the election. By contrast, Ortega, a cavalry officer from Puebla, with no personal influence beyond the electorate of the state capital, and lacking Méndez's power base among the National Guard, stood little chance of winning.[8]

Romero Vargas received 48 percent of the vote (58,337) narrowly missing an overall majority, but with a decisive lead over Ortega's 34 percent (42,192). Congressional scrutiny of the electoral results revealed extensive fraud in the state capital and surrounding villages, where an *orteguista* majority was reversed in favor of Romero Vargas. In the Sierra district of Libres, a certain *orteguista* victory was reversed when the alcalde (a *romerista* agent) took the ballot boxes home with him after the election.[9] Montaña deputies Juan Crisóstomo Bonilla and Ramón Márquez Galindo reminded the congress that Méndez's 1867 victory had been nullified following similar denunciations. They also claimed that Romero Vargas had enjoyed an unfair (and unconstitutional) advantage by occupying the interim governorship during the elections. But the Montaña deputies failed to persuade the congress to nullify the election when their opponents produced a constitutional clause stating that charges of electoral irregularities had to be made before the electoral scrutinizing committee had met, after which any electoral results, however irregular, were considered to be valid.[10]

The generalized fraud by both sides during the gubernatorial elections and the orderly (that is, constitutionally proper) congressional deliberations that followed removed, on this occasion, any legitimate grounds for a Montaña rebellion. The Montaña candidate had lost and no one could dispute that Romero Vargas had gained a plurality of the votes. The prospects for a successful armed challenge were therefore much less favorable than in 1868, when electors were exasperated that Méndez had been denied his victory twice and that their petitions were being ignored.

Apart from electing their governor, Puebla's citizens voted for state deputies and jefes políticos. The deputies elected from the Sierra were *romeristas* or *juaristas* (none was a *serrano* and one, Pedro Santacilia, deputy for Huauchinango, was not even from the state).[11] In the popular elections for jefes políticos, the Montaña did a shade less badly.[12] Bonilla, having been blocked from standing for the federal legislature on the un proven allegation that he had been involved in the 1868 rebellion, was elected jefe político of Tetela, although with no absolute majority.[13] But Teziutlán went easily to Benito Marín, nephew of Romero Vargas. Huauchinango went to Francisco Cravioto, Zacatlán to Dimás López, Tlatlauqui to Mariano Saborido, all proven clients of Juárez or García and, now, of Romero Vargas. Juan Francisco Molina, leader of the 1868 revolt, but a turncoat and trusted by no one, was reelected in Zacapoaxtla. Libres went to the *romerista* Toribio Ortiz, although he failed to achieve a majority over the Montaña candidate, Francisco González.[14]

With no deputies and just one jefe político, the Montaña party looked to be a spent force. Romero Vargas had succeeded in getting his friends into most of the elected positions in the state. In the wake of its military defeat, the Montaña was unable to make any impression upon the popular vote. For two months following the elections, apart from the continuing conflict in Cuetzalan over the division of the commons, the Sierra remained quiet.[15] However, the elections of September had left several issues unresolved. In certain districts, notably Zacatlán and Chignahuapan, the fraud had been so flagrant that new elections were convened. In many other districts, no clear majority had been reached. Consequently, new elections were convoked in November, which soon became much stormier than the first.[16]

Initially it seemed that the Montaña would accept the results of the election in Zacapoaxtla.[17] A general amnesty granted to all opponents of the regime, passed by the federal congress on 12 November 1869, encouraged many Zacapoaxtecos to bury their differences with the Juárez regime. However, others resented the leniency with which the rebels had been treated. The reelection of Molina Alcántara as jefe político, and the flagrant imposition of an outside candidate as deputy, were also unpopular among Zacapoaxtecos who sought a less conciliatory policy toward Xochiapulco. On 9 November, rumors reached Puebla of a conspiracy against the jefe político, led by the Conservatives Pascual Bonilla and Miguel Arriaga, who had sent Cenobio Cantero fifty rifles in a bid for his support.[18] The district authorities dismissed these rumors, assuring the state government that peace would continue to reign in their patriotic district.[19]

The Arriaga Rebellion

The rumors proved accurate. Armed movements on 18, 19, and 20 November challenged the authorities of Xochitlán, Cuetzalan, and Zacapoaxtla. The first in Xochitlán was reported as an Indian movement led by a Miguel Dolores, opposed to the privatization of common lands.[20] While this movement was successfully repulsed, on the following day, Vicente Becerra, accompanied by other *gente de razón*, seized all the available arms and ammunition, and were heard to be using the cry "¡Viva la constitución de 1857 y mueren Juárez y Lerdo!" They attacked the Xochitlán council building and the house of the alcalde, Manuel Castañeda, who fled with his family to Cuetzalan. The rebels boasted of support from Xochiapulco, but Castañeda found no evidence to support this.[21] Indeed, Becerra appears to have lacked any popular support, with most of Xochitlán's Indian population reported to have fled to the hills.[22]

In Cuetzalan on the following night, Francisco Javier Arriaga (Miguel's brother) called a conspiratorial meeting. Several prominent Cuetzalan *gente de razón* were present at the meeting in which Arriaga proclaimed himself to be the commander of the "Northern Line of the Army of Restoration." Neither civil nor military authorities attempted to resist, while Nahua village leaders from the subject barrio of Yancuitlalpan pledged their support. Arriaga professed to have a "project" which, with the victory of the movement, he promised would become law. (Arriaga later presented to the federal congress an ambitious plan of transport improvements for the district.)[23] A witness later claimed that Arriaga had invited the *comunero* leader, Francisco Agustín, to join the rebellion, and that Agustín, who had recently returned from Xochiapulco with arms, had accepted. However, as with the events in Xochitlán on the previous day, Xochiapulco was not directly involved in the Cuetzalan conspiracy. Far from seeing Lucas and Xochiapulco behind the movement, the alcalde of Cuetzalan requested thirty or forty soldiers to be sent from Xochiapulco to help reassert control over the municipality.[24]

Early on 20 November, Colonel Arriaga and his following, estimated at between 150 to 300 men, moved south to occupy the district capital where they planned to topple the authorities, declare the district in rebellion, commandeer all available arms, ammunition, lead, and gunpowder, and raise a loan. The rebels entered Zacapoaxtla at daybreak facing token resistance. They imprisoned the judge, equipped themselves properly with arms and ammunition, but could raise only a few hundred pesos in loans. The rebels left Zacapoaxtla at nightfall, having failed to attract more than a few members of the First Company of National Guard to their cause, or to unseat Molina Alcántara, who took refuge with Cenobio Cantero in Atagpan. The failure of the rebels to come away from Zacapoaxtla with more can be explained both by the ideological ambiguity and the tactical hesitancy of the movement.

The rebels claimed to be promoting the Montaña and to form part of the general movement of disavowing state and federal authority throughout the Sierra from Zacatlán to Teziutlán. However, the initial conspiracies were confined only to a section of the Zacapoaxtla National Guard, and the movement went ahead without prior consultation with the principal Montaña leaders (Lucas, Méndez, Bonilla, and Márquez Galindo). Arriaga's first meeting with Méndez and Bonilla, and then separately with Lucas, came on his retreat into the district of Tetela, after abandoning Zacapoaxtla.

The federal military tribunal set up to investigate the rebellion detected a confusion of motives behind the movement. Witnesses to the occupation of Zacapoaxtla on 20 December overheard quite contradictory cries. Some soldiers shouted: "¡Viva la Montaña!," "¡Viva Porfirio Díaz!," "¡Viva la Constitución de 1857!," "¡Muera Juárez y muera su ministerio!"; while others shouted "¡Viva la Religión, Muera el mal Gobierno!," and "¡Religión y fueros!" The title that the rebel army had taken, El Ejército Restaurador, suggests a Liberal and *porfirista* movement (Díaz commanded an Ejército Restaurador de la Libertad in the revolts of La Noria and Tuxtepec). But a more Conservative strand was also audible. Several witnesses asserted that Arriaga was not the only leader but that a certain Juan Sayago, who commanded the First Company of National Guard of Zacapoaxtla, had been attempting to rally members of the battalion behind him, with orders "from above" to organize a "religión y fueros" movement. He had also been instructed to make contact with the Indian leader, Cenobio Cantero (former ally of the Conservatives and the Europeans) of Atagpan.[25]

Another National Guard commander, Rafael Carcamo, who had also been approached by Sayago, explained that he was attempting a "religión y fueros" movement aimed at imprisoning all the public officials of the district, abolishing the constitution of 1857, and reinstating the centralist "Bases Orgánicas" of 1837. Asked who was leading the movement, Carcamo replied "that Sayago had told him that (the leader) was coming from the Monte de las Cruces where he had conferred with General Vicario Gutiérrez (possibly an amalgam of the Conservative generals of the Three Years' War, Juan Vicario and Ignacio Gutiérrez) and with the chiefs Miguel Miramón and Tomás Mejía (who had collaborated with the Europeans and had been executed at Querétaro in June 1867), that in Puebla there was another general who, once he had given the call, would rise up there and put himself at the head of the uprising here." Carcamo's statement suggests that National Guard commanders, perhaps in conjunction with the clergy (another witness claimed that Zacapoaxtla's priest, Abran López, was in league with the rebels), were manipulating Conservative imagery (the names of generals who evoked memories of past struggles against the Liberals) to mobilize support in the traditionally Conservative villages lying between Zacapoaxtla and Tlatlauqui. Several witnesses also commented on the fraternal relations that Pascual Bonilla, former Imperial prefect and prominent Conservative, seemed to enjoy with the rebels.

The weight of the evidence gathered by the tribunal suggested a movement led by National Guard officers, but backed by prominent Zacapoaxteco Conservatives. The movement aimed to recover Conservative control over the district; limit external electoral meddling; shut out corrosive Liberal reforms, such as the *desamortización*, that were alarming the Indian population; and isolate, and hopefully extinguish for good, the subversive municipality of Xochiapulco (upon whom blame for the uprising could be squarely placed if it were to fail).

From Rebellion to Insurrection: The Attack on Xochiapulco

After evacuating Zacapoaxtla on the evening of 20 November, Arriaga took up position on the heights of Apulco to await developments elsewhere in the Sierra. Here he met with Lucas and they spoke at length. A witness remarked that the meeting was held "without the two leaders, who were hidden by an 'ilite' tree, being visible to the troops." This suggests that Lucas was reluctant to be associated with the rebels.[26] Combined with Luis Antonio Díaz's protestations of loyalty in letters to the jefe político, this suggests strongly that Lucas and Xochiapulco were most anxious not to be seen to be directly involved in the rebellion.

Xochiapulco's circumspection is not hard to explain. A committee of the state congress was meeting at this very time to resolve the outstanding differences between Xochiapulco and Zacapoaxtla, the conflict which Romero Vargas considered to be at the root of public order problems of the district, indeed of the entire Sierra.[27] In anticipation of a favorable resolution, Xochiapulco and its outlying barrios had already begun to subdivide the municipality's common land, to popular acclaim. This hardly fitted the anti-*desamortización* sentiments of many of Arriaga's followers. Unfortunately, neither the district authorities nor General Alatorre (the Federal commander dispatched to crush the Arriaga rebellion) believed that Lucas and Xochiapulco could be anything other than deeply involved in the movement. Alatorre's Second Division would pay dearly for its failure to distinguish between friend and foe.

From his position on the heights commanding the main crossing over the Apulco River, Arriaga attempted to consolidate support for the movement in the central Sierra. His proclamation, issued from Apulco on 27 November, expressed *serrano* resentment at affronted liberties, unrewarded patriotic services, and broken promises of reforms that had not yet been delivered. The document explicitly attacked the federal government (in contrast to the 1868 insurrection that had always stressed loyalty to the Federation).[28]

Requests for revenues, food supplies, and reinforcements were sent to municipal cabeceras throughout the districts of Zacapoaxtla, Tetela, and Zacatlán, but they were met with little enthusiasm.[29] Hostile responses from villages confirm that Lucas had not yet given the rebellion his blessing. Moreover, Arriaga's agents were reported to be heavy-handed in their search for recruits and supplies. For example, on 30 November, a force of twenty-five rebels arrived in Jonotla to encourage support for the uprising. The rebel captain imprisoned the alcalde and his secretary, demanding that they hand over all the funds in the municipal treasury and provide one hundred *arrobas* of *totopo* (maize tortillas) to boot.[30] This was not at all Lucas's style of dealing with subject authorities during a rebellion.

If Tetela's municipalities rejected Arriaga's appeals, the responses from authorities in his own district of Zacapoaxtla were hardly more favorable.[31] The villages closest to Zacapoaxtla—Taictic, Ahuacatlán, Ehuiloco, and Atagpan—remained steadfastly loyal to the *jefatura*.[32] Farther north in Cuetzalan, the key to the wealth of the north of the district, parties remained too deeply split over the issue of the division of the commons to be of any value to the rebels. In early December 1869, Francisco Agustín and his band, whom Arriaga had courted on 19 November, were dispersed by defense forces organized by Cuetzalan's *gente de razón*.[33]

If Arriaga had only patchy support from behind the lines, matters on the front went badly from the start. The 20 November attack on Zacapoaxtla had been timed to coincide with an uprising in Libres by the Spanish cavalry officer, Colonel Román Ros. On 25 November, Rodríguez Bocardo routed Ros's force at Cuyoaco.[34] On 28 and 29 November the Federal Sixth Battalion of Light Infantry dispatched from Puebla ousted two rebel bands from their positions just to the south and east of Zacapoaxtla. Only the rebels at Apulco stood in the way of complete pacification of the district.[35]

On 30 November two loyal companies of Zacapoaxtla's National Guard commanded by José de la Luz Molina, backed by the Sixth Battalion, attacked Arriaga's force at Apulco.[36] After a lengthy skirmish, the rebels were dispersed, leaving behind their artillery, many "useless" rifles, the ensign of the rebellion, one dead (the commander of artillery), and eleven prisoners. Some rebels regrouped in new positions at Tecuicuilco and Iztapolapan, on the boundary with Tetela, but most fled to their villages.

At this point, pacification of the southern Sierra could have been achieved quite simply had the state government and Federal commander responded prudently to the state of affairs. The rebels were divided, uncertain about their objectives, eclectic in their ideological reference points, and, above all, isolated. Colonel Arriaga had attempted to harness mutually antagonistic groups (as in Cuetzalan, where Indian *comuneros* soon fell out with disappointed non-Indian office seekers). He also lacked support beyond the district of Zacapoaxtla. Had the rebellion not been defeated militarily, it would probably have fizzled out on its own. Why, then, given the good prospects for peace, did General Alatorre make the fatal decision to send the Sixth Battalion of Light Infantry to Xochiapulco on 2 December, with the unhappy consequence of prolonging and intensifying the rebellion for a further six months?

General Ignacio Alatorre, Federal Commander during the 1868–1870 Sierra Revolts.
Archivo Fotográfico, Centro de Estudios de Historia de México (CONDUMEX)

The Federal Invasion of Xochiapulco

Although federal, state, and district authorities had grown accustomed to imagining Xochiapulco to be behind any unrest in the Puebla Sierra, there is strong evidence to suggest that Xochiapulco was not initially involved in the Arriaga rebellion. However, the military tribunal commissioned by Alatorre was determined to find connections between the rebellion, originated in Xochitlán and Cuetzalan, and Xochiapulco. Witnesses and participants in the events were repeatedly asked whether Lucas was involved in the conspiracy and the uprising. Witnesses included one who had heard Arriaga's horse galloping through Zacapoaxtla in the middle of the night in the direction of Xochiapulco, another who remembered seeing Lucas's signature on documents in Arriaga's possession, and another who reported a full-scale troop mobilization in Xochiapulco on 20 November, reaching the edge of Zacapoaxtla.

These reports shared a common vagueness and an imaginative, almost fantastic, quality. The only hard evidence assembled by the military tribunal was the correspondence between the alcalde of Xochiapulco, Luis Antonio Díaz, and the jefe político as well as between Luis Antonio Díaz and Cenobio Cantero. These letters show that Xochiapulco tried to distance itself from the movement and to maintain peaceful relations with the *jefatura*. On 18 November 1869 (the day of the uprising in Xochitlán, the day before the Cuetzalan conspiracy, and two days before the storming of Zacapoaxtla), Luis Antonio assured the jefe político of Xochiapulco's tranquility, stating that he would migrate to another location rather than become the instrument or the victim of an uprising. But he did report to Molina that an unknown person was spreading alarm through the district. He had heard of nocturnal reunions, and many in Xochiapulco suspected that Cantero planned to invade the municipality to arrest some people who were wanted for trial in Puebla. The followers of Francisco Agustín of Cuetzalan were cited as Cantero's intended victims. Luis Antonio considered this fear to be unfounded after he had received a letter from Cantero (which he sent on to Molina), in which the Atagpan leader stated that he had no intention of putting his men at the disposal of anyone.[37] On the day of the insurrection, Molina had appealed urgently to Luis Antonio for help. Xochiapulco's alcalde had replied that he would do all in his power to support the *jefatura* but regretted that, without arms or ammunition, there was little that he could do, apart from preserving the peace within its own jurisdiction.[38]

Molina should not have been surprised by this response. He personally had disarmed Xochiapulco during the previous twelve months. Had Xochiapulco remained armed, the municipality would have been an obvious refuge either for Arriaga on his retreat from Zacapoaxtla on 20 November, or for Molina, as it had done in June 1868. As it happened, the jefe político chose instead to fall back on Cantero's bailiwick at Atagpan, while the rebel leader retreated to Apulco.

Of course, political expediency allied with tactical necessity may explain Molina's suspicions of Xochiapulco and choice of Atagpan. In the recent elections, *mendecista* agents had been active in Xochiapulco and from there established ties with Francisco Agustín and other *mendecistas* in Cuetzalan. In this respect, Xochiapulco was an electoral rival to Zacapoaxtla. Yet there was nothing illegal in this. Molina's suspicions of Xochiapulco's motives grew when alcalde Luis Antonio declined an invitation to come to Zacapoaxtla, claiming he was unwell. Instead, he sent a commission of Xochiapulco's council adding that, if necessary, he would come as soon as he could.[39]

While Molina had cause for distrusting Xochiapulco's alcalde, Luis Antonio possessed far stronger reasons for alarm. From his sick bed, he wrote to Molina that news was circulating that troops were preparing to occupy his town.[40] Xochiapulco's suspicions would have been heightened when, two days later, an order was received for the return of twelve rifles "necessary for arming the national guard of this cabecera," which Molina claimed had been only lent to them.[41] Xochiapulco's fears were confirmed on the night of 3 December when the Sixth Battalion of Light Infantry entered the municipality. The Federal commander, Robles Linares, reported that the purpose was to lay siege to the cabecera in a "pacific manner" (how troops laid siege peacefully to a population remained unclear).[42]

General Alatorre sent the Sixth Battalion to its unfortunate fate in Xochiapulco using emergency powers conferred on him by the state governor. On 24 November, Alatorre had received all the powers of the jefe político as well as the right "to apprehend dissidents who had raised the standard of rebellion even in the midst of pacific populations."[43] This order was signed by Pablo Mariano Urrutia, the Secretary of Government and Militias, ex-jefe político of Zacapoaxtla. Once more, it seems, Conservative Zacapoaxtecos were pulling the federal and state puppet strings in order to pursue their local feud against upstart Xochiapulco.

"Peaceful encirclement" spelled extinction to the Xochiapulquenses, who reacted in the way they had always done to hostile, invading forces. First they retreated, then they ambushed columns and blocked off paths of retreat. Lieutenant José María Vázquez, at the head of 400 Federal infantry, entered Xochiapulco on 3 December to find the town deserted. He decided to camp for the night. But at 2 A.M., an estimated 600 to 800 Xochiapulquenses attacked the Federal force. The trails which were later found suggested that the approach was made by men crawling on their stomachs and that a "savage war cry" signaled the start of battle. Some men of the Sixth Battalion fled to Zacapoaxtla. Others held on for forty hours, until the arrival of a relief column of the Fourth Battalion of Light Infantry, some artillery, and a section of the Zacapoaxtla National Guard. These reinforcements temporarily secured Xochiapulco. The government reported losses of 41 dead and 72 wounded. The Xochiapulquenses lost at least 14 dead and an unknown number of wounded. Between 3 and 5 December, the Federals fired 18,210 shots.

Alatorre immediately transferred his headquarters to Xochiapulco. His officers occupied the house of General Lucas. Alatorre then placed the entire district under a state of siege.[44] Apart from the inhabitants of the barrio of Las Lomas, who had cooperated with the Federal force (confirming our suspicion of local complicity in the conception of the invasion of Xochiapulco), the rest of the population of the municipality of Xochiapulco withdrew to settlements across the district boundary in Tetela.[45]

Was the dispatch of the Sixth Battalion to Xochiapulco on 2 December 1869 merely an innocent peace-keeping patrol, intended to protect the rights and guarantees of the Xochiapulquenses, as Alatorre had indicated? If so, why was it necessary to send a full battalion of four hundred men to a municipality whose disarmament Alatorre had personally supervised after the rebellion in 1868? Perhaps he had more devious motives, as proposed by Florencia Mallon: "Alatorre ordered the invasion of Xochiapulco precisely to force a reaction, which would then allow him to step up repression."[46] Unfortunately, this explanation does not fit comfortably with Alatorre's reputation as a conciliator, borne out in the Sierra in 1868. Clearly, in the heat of the moment, after losing forty-one of his men, Alatorre did not mince his words about the baseness of his enemies. But the emergency powers necessary for the suppression of a rebellion had already been granted, eight days before the Xochiapulco foray. Moreover, the rebels had just been easily routed on four occasions. Hence, Alatorre had no logical motive to "force a reaction," particularly from men who had not yet declared themselves in revolt and whose martial qualities he had experienced (and whom, later in his memoirs, he unreservedly praised).[47] Nor was there any tactical or strategic need to "step up repression." The iron fist had just been effectively applied, and by early December the moment had come for the velvet glove. That the Xochiapulquenses were unable to recognize this, and saw the Federal sortie as an invasion, should not lead us to impute deliberate provocation as Alatorre's objective.

A more likely, less Machiavellian motive can be proposed. Alatorre, having just dispersed the principal rebel concentration at Apulco on 30 November but having failed so far to meet with Lucas (who, like Luis Antonio Díaz, claimed to be sick at his Taxcantla ranch), chose to ensure the safety of his own forces and to complete the pacification of the district by occupying and temporarily isolating Xochiapulco from the wider theater of operations. From reports he had received in Zacapoaxtla (admittedly from sources hostile to Xochiapulco), Alatorre had good reason to believe that the Xochiapulquenses, even if disarmed, still had access to a cache of weapons kept by Lucas at Taxcantla. Alatorre perhaps calculated that a show of Federal strength would serve to deter the Xochiapulquenses from crossing the Apulco River to collect their arms from Taxcantla. Unfortunately, this is precisely what they must have done upon learning of the Federal advance upon their town and villages on 1–2 December.

Xochiapulco Joins the Arriaga Revolt

With the occupation of Xochiapulco by Federal troops, Arriaga and the few remaining rebels moved southwest to the sanctuary of mountainous Ixtacamaxtitlán. Here he replenished the gaps in rebel ranks left by the desertion of the Indian soldiers from Xochitlán and Cuetzalan, following the defeat at Apulco, by recruiting the fleeing Xochiapulquenses and men from villages such as Cuahuigtic that had supported Lucas during the European Intervention. Evidence of rebel recovery came on 19 December when Francisco Javier Arriaga, now joined by his brothers Mariano and Miguel, led four hundred infantry and sixty cavalry in a daring attack on Libres. They sacked businesses, commandeered clothing and money (including 600 pesos belonging to the Libres National Guard tax), and stole fifty horses and the seal of the district of San Juan de los Llanos.[48] Four days later, concealed by dense mist, rebels attempted unsuccessfully to recapture Xochiapulco. After two hours of battle, they retreated, taking their dead "as was the custom with them."[49]

The Arriaga brothers were now joined by companions at arms, and some enemies, from earlier struggles: Antonio and Paulino Noriega from the Sierra de Tulancingo, José de Jesús Domínguez from Chignahuapan, Luis León from Tlaxcala, and the Herrera brothers from Ixtacamaxtitlán. Described officially as "a horde of plundering bandits," these leaders nevertheless had developed strong ties with villages in their localities over many years, most of them as Conservatives and collaborators with the French and the Austrians.

Hence, Lucas and the Xochiapulquenses found themselves allied with a motley band of former Conservative caciques and squeezed between resurgent Conservatives in Zacapoaxtla, who were grasping the opportunity of a return to the "status quo before Xochiapulco," and a Federal force that was acting more ruthlessly than the conciliatory Second Division, which they had faced in 1868. The abandonment of Xochiapulco, the removal of its municipal autonomy, and its reincorporation to Zacapoaxtla signaled the end of the political aspirations not only of Xochiapulco but also of the Montaña.[50] Yet the clock could not be so simply turned back. The occupation of Xochiapulco by the Federal army, the scattering of much of its population, the placing of the entire district under a state of siege, and Alatorre's decision to replace Molina, a conciliator, with Remigio Varela, the heavy-handed alcalde of Zacapoaxtla, marked a further deterioration in the public order of the district. The rebel movement, which had been on the point of collapse in late November, had grown in size by late December and would successfully match government forces for a further six months.

Support for the Arriaga rebellion, which until mid-December had scarcely extended beyond short-term alliances of convenience between disappointed office seekers and *comunero* Indians in Cuetzalan and Xochitlán, now spread. General Lucas, a more popular and effective military leader than Arriaga, took over command of the rebellion. He soon succeeded in knitting together a formidable front stretching north from Ixtacamaxtitlán through Zautla, Xochiapulco, Xochitlán, and Cuetzalan to the *tierra caliente*, which provided the supplies.

The Reorganization of Zacapoaxtla's National Guard

The Federal occupation of Xochiapulco presented the first opportunity since the European Intervention for Conservatives in Zacapoaxtla to reestablish their control over the district, as well as for families who had lost out as a result of the Liberal reform to recoup their positions and settle old scores. Here, potentially, was the Federal military cantonment which Conservative Zacapoaxtecos had called for since 1859. Agustín Roldán and Francisco Balderrábamo, who had organized resistance to the *indios cuatecomacos* during the Three Years' War, once more returned to head the military affairs of the district. Cenobio Cantero and Valeriano Cabrera promptly put themselves at the service of General Alatorre, mobilizing the Indian barrios to the southwest, east, and north of Zacapoaxtla. Even José Miguel Salgado, who still claimed ownership of the hacienda of Xochiapulco and Manzanilla, entered the fray, along with twenty-seven other citizens of Tlatlauqui who voluntarily assembled a company to "repress and punish the rebels of Xochiapulco."[51]

Zacapoaxtla received no help in this task from its neighbor, Tetela. Although Pedro Contreras, Tetela's jefe político, at no point came out openly in favor of the rebellion, his district harbored many sympathizers, including General Méndez. Tetela also provided sanctuary for ever-increasing numbers of refugees, deserters, and rebels while continuing its traditional role as a source of arms, ammunition, and food supplies for rebel Xochiapulco.

In contrast to the sympathy of Tetelenses for the rebellion, Tlatlauqui's leaders feared that the rebellion might spread across the district boundary as it had done in 1868. Mariano Saborido, the jefe político, was alarmed that Alatorre's use of Cantero to help suppress the rebellion would encourage unruliness among Tlatlauqui's villages. So suspicious was he of the loyalty of his district's National Guard that early in December 1869 he offered Alatorre all thirty Guardsmen "because if some movement should occur, they are sure to be the first to pronounce."[52] But

Saborido retracted the offer on the following day, convinced that these thirty men would surely rebel if sent to Zacapoaxtla, and that it would be wiser to keep them under his control.[53] Later in the month, Saborido once more offered support against the Xochiapulco rebels, but this time not with the National Guard (which he had disbanded) but with an ad hoc force under his own command.[54]

Sandwiched between an openly hostile Tetela and an ambivalent Tlatlauqui, Zacapoaxtla's newly appointed jefe político, Remigio Varela, began the daunting task of reorganizing its National Guard. As a result of the rebellion, hatched in large part from within the National Guard, the military administration of the district was in chaos. The rebels had commandeered National Guard censuses from many villages, hampering both recruitment and the raising of revenue to finance the campaign. Some compensation came in mid-December when Varela received assurances that all the costs incurred by the National Guard would be paid by the Federation.[55] But his was a vain promise. In early December, Alatorre and the district authorities expected a swift end to the rebellion, such as had been possible in 1868. No one anticipated how long the rebellion would last (it finally ended in June 1870) or what formidable resistance the rebels would mount.

In his reorganization of Zacapoaxtla's National Guard, Varela hoped to build up forces in Xochitlán, Nauzontla, and Cuetzalan in the north of the district, now that Xochiapulco had been largely depopulated. Organizing new companies in these municipalities proved problematic. Members of the *gente de razón* of each municipality had backed the initial rebel movement and many of them were still at large.[56] Moreover, the *gente de razón* remained reluctant to arm an Indian population already driven to the verge of rebellion by the implementation of the *desamortización*. For its part, the Indian population abhorred military service and routinely melted into the forest at the sound of the bugle.[57]

In spite of these difficulties, Varela reported to the state government in mid-December that many people were fleeing rebel villages in search of protection and that the National Guard of the district was approaching full strength. But he desperately needed weapons to arm these recruits as well as federal funds to pay them.[58] Upon the renewal of the rebel offensive on 24 December, Varela insisted that funds were inadequate even for paying the force of fifty auxiliaries needed for defending Zacapoaxtla.[59]

Compounding these difficulties with recruitment were divisions between the Federal and local commanders. Alatorre had grown to rely upon the Indian National Guard commanders of the villages of Las Lomas and Atagpan, Valeriano Cabrera and Cenobio Cantero. They had provided invaluable services throughout December because of their knowledge of Xochiapulco's terrain and their traditional rivalry with, even hatred of, Lucas's followers.[60] Varela, however, saw these forces as "guerrilla auxiliaries," independent of his authority and potentially disturbers of the peace of the district. In his opinion, Zacapoaxtla's peace and prosperity required a strong, disciplined National Guard unit in each municipal cabecera, composed only of *gente de razón*. Alatorre's policy of harnessing local Indian fighters to the Federal cause risked intensifying local rivalries and rancors, thus complicating the task of pacification.

The Renewal of the Federal Offensive

By late December, Alatorre and Varela judged the Federal and district forces in southern Zacapoaxtla to be strong enough for a renewed offensive against the rebels in Xochiapulco.[61] The rebels had reoccupied Xochiapulco as the Federal force had withdrawn. Alatorre adopted the strategy that he had used successfully against Xochiapulco in 1868. He ordered a two-pronged movement against the rebel stronghold. Lieutenant Colonel Topete with twelve hundred men would move northward from the plateau through Zautla into the Sierra. Lieutenant Colonel José María Ramírez would lead with five hundred men southwest from Zacapoaxtla, through Las Lomas, Xochiapulco, and across the Tetcla boundary into the rebel mountain redoubts between Tetela de Ocampo and Ixtacamaxtitlán. Here, the two government forces would meet, having obliterated the rebels somewhere in between. Three successive victories over the rebels in a week indicated the success of this strategy. Although heavy rains prevented government troops from pursuing the scattered rebel forces, Ramírez declared the Sierra rebellion to be over.[62]

Yet each successive Federal assault increased the sense of injustice and will to resist of the Xochiapulquenses. After all, they had not rebelled against the Federation on 19–20 November 1869. Rather, they had been subjected to an unprovoked Federal invasion, without warning or any formal opening of hostilities. Moreover, Xochiapulco had become, in the minds of many hundreds of National Guard veterans from communities far beyond its municipal boundaries, the symbol of their patriotic sacrifices and the guarantee of their constitutional freedoms.

Pacification and the Prolongation of the Rebellion

After these setbacks and recognizing the superiority of Federal forces, Lucas sued for peace, offering the submission of his forces in return for guarantees. Rafael Cravioto, acting as mediator, doubted whether Lucas's conditions would be acceptable to Alatorre since Xochiapulco had failed to comply (so Cravioto asserted) with the previous act of submission in 1868, particularly on the matter of the handing in of arms.[63]

However, it was Alatorre's terms that were to prove unacceptable. Federal thirst for vengeance overcame the desire for peace. Whereas in August 1868, Alatorre had been prepared to allow the leaders of the rebellion to go free, in January 1870 a federal pardon was offered only to soldiers and, emphatically, not to "sergeants, officers, and chiefs." This exclusion, combined with the recent re-introduction of the death penalty for bandits and rebels, greatly reduced the incentive to surrender, thereby prolonging the campaign.[64]

In former rebel areas, now controlled by government forces, many soldiers did take advantage of the pardon offered to rebels who handed in their arms:[65]

Table 9–1.   **Arms Handed In from Xochiapulco and Huahuaxtla Soldiers, January 1870**

Village	Number of men handing in arms
Huahuaxtla	23
Eloxochitlan (Xochiapulco)	22
Yautetelco (Xochiapulco)	22
Atzalan (Xochiapulco)	10
Cuahutamanin (Xochiapulco)	7
Cuacualaxtin (Xochiapulco)	1
Total	*85*

Judging from the absence of surnames, it appears that all eighty-five soldiers who had surrendered their arms by 15 January 1870 were Nahuas. However, most of the population of Xochiapulco remained in rebellion, falling back with their families to the scattered *rancherías* of Tetela, Ixtacamaxtitlán, and Zacatlán that had harbored them during earlier struggles. Disturbances reported in the barrios of Ometepec and Taxco in mid-January may have resulted from this migration to these already poor and land-hungry communities.[66] Immigration would also partially account for why Tetela's highland population grew so rapidly during the late 1860s and early 1870s.

From the beginning of the campaign, rebels had been persuaded to lay down their arms on the offer of using absent rebels' land.[67] At first, peaceful Xochiapulquenses ignored the invitation to harvest the milpas belonging to the rebels. Only the inhabitants of Las Lomas and Jilotepec risked antagonizing their fellow Xochiapulquenses by allowing their sheep and goats to graze on unharvested maize fields. In mid-January, Alatorre prohibited this practice since he had other purposes for Xochiapulco's maize crop.[68] A month after normal harvest time (November–December), the ripened maize fields in Xochiapulco stood unharvested. This offered a tempting booty for the rebels. On 11 January, two hundred rebels led by Colonel Luis Antonio Díaz assembled on the Cerros de Tepehixhil and Cuatecomaco, where they briefly exchanged fire with troops commanded by Cantero.

By gathering at Cuatecomaco, these rebels did not intend to renew their attacks. They merely wanted to deter maize farmers who might answer Alatorre's invitation to harvest Xochiapulco's maize crop. The Federal commander had recently extended the invitation, originally addressed exclusively to inhabitants of Xochiapulco, to the entire district.[69] The alcaldes of Xochitlán and Cuetzalan were each instructed to send one hundred men from their jurisdictions to help with the harvesting of Xochiapulco's maize.[70] The Xochitecos responded with enthusiasm and the alcalde had no difficulty in recruiting men. The alcalde of Cuetzalan, on the other hand, reported great difficulty in mobilizing such a large number.[71] The greater responsiveness of the Xochitecos to the request for reapers can be explained by their proximity to Xochiapulco and a long-established custom of planting maize in the Xochiapulco area.[72] The alcalde of Cuetzalan put the reticence of his villagers down to the stubborn "disobedience" of the Indians under his charge, alluding to the refusal of the followers of Francisco Agustín to heed this or any other order from their cabecera.[73]

The Xochiapulco crop was finally harvested with the help of labor from Xochitlán and Cuetzalan. Alatorre ordered all the maize still stored in Xochiapulco to be brought to Zacapoaxtla.[74] By late January, Varela reported that cultivators from other parts of Xochiapulco were asking permission to plant maize on the milpas of absent rebels.[75] He expressed some reservations about this policy and inquired of the Secretary of Government whether it should be continued.[76] General Rafael Cravioto, who in January took command of the campaign against the rebels, suggested to Varela that those Xochiapulquenses who had submitted to the government at the beginning of the campaign should be allowed to return to their houses and to cultivate their land, but those still in rebellion should not be allowed back and should be apprehended. The state government affirmed this policy, which made any prompt pacification unlikely.[77]

Alatorre and Cravioto, in a practical military fashion, hoped to restore the security and pacify the area by denying the rebels a subsistence base and by populating Xochiapulco with grateful maize farmers. However, with as many as six hundred rebels still in the field (mostly enjoying the sanctuary of the district of Tetela), it soon became obvious to Varela and the Zacapoaxtla authorities that denying rebels the possibility of resettlement would prolong the uprising.

Varela now became openly critical of Alatorre's resettlement policy in Xochiapulco and especially his use of Indian auxiliaries from the barrio of Las Lomas and elsewhere to fight the rebels. The jefe político proposed, instead, a more radical policy of removing Xochiapulco's municipal autonomy and reincorporating it to its former cabecera. He also renewed the petition, dear to the hearts of all Conservative Zacapoaxtecos, for an *acantonamiento* (federal military settlement) to be established at Zacapoaxtla, which would act as a bulwark for sustaining the government's authority throughout the Puebla Sierra.[78] The state government foresaw constitutional complications with this proposal, which never achieved congressional support. Yet this threat to Xochiapulco's political integrity gave the rebels another cause for resistance and complicated the task of pacification.

Also counterproductive was a passport requirement for all inhabitants of the district desiring to travel beyond their villages. Anyone away from his village who was found without this document would forthwith be considered a rebel. Alcaldes were instructed to remind those leaving their villages that they might forfeit their claims to common land (a warning hardly likely to calm anxiety about the division of common lands), that they should pay all their taxes, rents, and debts before leaving, and, finally, that they should present a certificate to the authorities of the villages in which they chose to reside.[79] Alcaldes throughout the district soon complained that people were leaving their villages without permission or passports. Many relocated to villages in Tetela, where the passport decree was not applied. Others were stranded on their maize milpas in Papantla without passports, fearful of being arrested on the return journey to their villages.[80] These absences further diminished taxes and hampered the raising of contingents necessary for prosecuting the campaign. The policy also clashed with the attempts to mobilize the population for labor services: harvesting Xochiapulco's maize crop, strengthening Zacapoaxtla's fortifications, and providing services and porterage for the Federal army and National Guard.[81]

The Renewal of the Rebel Offensive

The clumsiness of these pacification measures contributed to the continuation of the rebellion for another six months. The government offensive of late December and early January had pushed the rebels across the district boundary into Tetela and Zacatlán, where rebel activity had increased.[82] Yet, in spite of frequent sallies by the National Guard battalions of Chalchicomula and Zacapoaxtla, based in Zautla and Xochiapulco, and the Fourth and Sixth Light Infantry based in Zacapoaxtla, the rebels still managed to regroup and mount formidable attacks against government forces.[83]

At the end of January, a force of fifty infantry and fifty cavalry, shouting "¡Viva Juan Francisco Lucas!," entered Cuyoaco. They sacked the house of General Rodríguez Bocardo, who had been assisting Alatorre with the suppression of the rebellion.[84] On 4 February, Cantero surprised a reunion of rebels at Las Lomas and captured ninety men.[85] Skirmishes and pitched battles continued throughout February. The determination of the rebels to assert their claim upon Xochiapulco's best maize land was behind the increased activity in this area. The barrio of Las Lomas became the most disputed part of the municipality, divided between those who wanted Xochiapulco as their cabecera and supported the rebels, and those who sought reintegration with Zacapoaxtla. Cantero, in cooperation with the Lomas commander, Valeriano Cabrera, promoted the aspirations of the latter group.[86]

By early February, the rebels had reoccupied much of Xochiapulco, only to be dislodged again by Cantero's forces backed by Federal artillery.[87] Ten days later, a more serious skirmish took place at Olocoxco, a high ridge on the district boundary with Tetela. The rebels had fallen back to positions just inside the district of Tetela (Ometepec, Tecuicuilco, Sacaloma, and Taxcantla). On the night of 18 February, under cover of dense fog, around two hundred rebels commanded by Lucas, Arriaga, and "Domínguez" (probably Colonel José de Jesús Domínguez of Chignahuapan) met the advance guard of government forces on the road to Iztactenango (Zautla).[88] An energetic hand-to-hand combat ensued, since the fog prevented the use of firearms. Two hours of close fighting left the field scattered with dismembered fingers, but there were only a few dead.[89] In spite of victory claims in the *Publicación Oficial*, General Cravioto's forces came off worse in this combat. The rebels swiftly regrouped and switched their strategy to harassing the eastern Sierra of Teziutlán.

Here, on 28 February, Lucas and the Arriaga brothers, leading four hundred men, mounted a daring attack on the district capital of Teziutlán. They occupied the town and obliged the jefe político to retreat to Chignautla. Lucas issued a proclamation in which he condemned the government for trampling upon "the sacrosanct and inalienable rights of good Mexicans." The rebels cut the telegraph line, demanded the keys of the *jefatura* from the secretary, removed all the funds from the district treasury, appropriated from the retail trade all of the available ammunition, gunpowder, lead, and arms of different calibers, and borrowed several horses belonging to private citizens. Before evacuating the plaza, the rebels imposed a loan of 5,000 pesos and fifty pieces of cotton cloth. Reinforcements arriving from Zacapoaxtla later in the day engaged the rebels in a brief skirmish but failed to inflict significant losses. The rebels left Teziutlán in the evening.[90]

Encouraged and materially strengthened by the successful raid upon Teziutlán, the rebels kept a low profile in the Sierra during March. Action shifted instead to the plateau. Throughout the district of Libres, "bandit" leaders—Luis León, Miguel Melgarejo, Angel Santa Anna, Miguel Arriaga, and Miguel Herrera—committed numerous robberies.[91] Even more alarming to the government was a *pronunciamiento* in Libres at the end of March against the Federation behind the Ixtacamaxtitlán leader, Miguel Herrera.[92] Villages in this area had become resentful of the abuses of Federal troops.

The state government succeeded in restoring order on the plateau fairly swiftly with the support of Rodríguez Bocardo and other cavalry commanders. Government forces gained a significant victory on 1 April over a force commanded by Angel Santa Anna and Francisco Javier Arriaga at

Zinacanapa, near Perote. They took thirty-six prisoners, including the two leaders, who all faced execution under the law of 13 April 1869 (only approved by the congress on 7 April 1870) that had suspended individual guarantees for highwaymen.[93] As a result of energetic petitioning, the executions were commuted to two years of forced labor.[94]

The Rebels Return to Xochiapulco and Renew Their Offensive

The rebellion did not end with the imprisonment of its leader, Francisco Javier Arriaga. Effective command had long since passed to Lucas. On the plateau, during March and April, daring raids struck the newly opened railway and telegraph communications. These attacks diverted attention from a more decisive development within the Sierra: the return of the rebels to their homes in Xochiapulco. They returned quietly, without confronting forces based in Las Lomas under the command of Cabrera or those at the redoubt at Apulco. The successful resettlement of Xochiapulco by the rebels would have a major impact upon the outcome of the rebellion and on the course of state politics over the two subsequent decades.

Active rebel resistance resumed in the Sierra late in March and continued throughout April. On 31 March, two hundred rebels commanded by Luis Antonio Díaz invaded Xochitlán. They raised a forced loan of 800 pesos, stole 211 pesos in cash, and apprehended four "honorable citizens," including alcalde Manuel Castañeda, as hostages.[95] This raid was a valuable coup for the rebels. Confined since early January to the arid pine forests of southern Tetela and Ixtacamaxtitlán, the capture of Xochitlán (a municipal cabecera and a vital transit point between the *tierra fría* and the *tierra caliente*) gave the rebels access to the more abundant resources of the lowlands. Luis Antonio Díaz, using the authority of the "General Command of the Northern Line of the State of Puebla," began to formalize contacts with subject authorities. He requested the alcalde of Nauzontla to furnish two hundred daily rations of tortillas and a loan of 300 pesos as well as to hand over the entire National Guard fund.[96]

After reestablishing this north-south axis, which cut off Zacapoaxtla from Tetela, the rebels initiated daring assaults east of Zacapoaxtla. In Tlatlauqui, raiders disarmed the prison guard and released the prisoners. The assailants fled with ten rifles, a bugle, and ammunition.[97] Varela expressed his alarm at the mounting rebel strength. Rebels now occupied strong positions on ridges surrounding Zacapoaxtla to the north, west, and south and exercised effective authority in Xochitlán, Cuetzalan, and the *tierra caliente* as well as across the district boundary in Tetela's municipalities of Huitzilan and Zapotitlán. The jefe político feared that the villages under his charge were now "the rebels' playthings."[98] Arguing against lifting the state of siege, Varela painted an alarming picture of the low morale of the forces under his command.

These warnings increasingly fell on deaf ears in the federal capital. After January 1870 the federal strategy for pacifying the Puebla Sierra changed radically. The original formula had involved a strong Federal force (the Second Division), backed by the district National Guard (for which the federal paymaster accepted financial responsibility), operating within a district under a state of siege. Officials now admitted this strategy had been a factor in the continuation of the rebellion as much as a solution to it. The federal government's response to the stalemate was to draw back from the conflict with the hope that the district authorities would devise a more effective means of pacification. Federal distancing from the rebellion can also be explained by a coordinated rash of uprisings in Michoacán, Jalisco, Zacatecas, and San Luis Potosí. These were considered more threatening than the "localist" events in the Sierra de Puebla. By early 1870, Juárez judged the challenge from General Trinidad García de la Cadena of Zacatecas to be more threatening than that of Méndez in the southeast, whom he considered to be a spent force. As a result, no Federal force was offered to support Varela's pacification measures after mid-January 1870.[99]

As the federal authorities became more aloof, the state government became more eager to find a way of pacifying the area. With the 1871 presidential election now in sight, Romero Vargas was determined to present a comfortable presidential vote for Sebastian Lerdo de Tejada from the state of Puebla. The prolongation of the rebellion and mounting pressure on his governorship, resulting from extraordinary war taxes, threatened to reinforce *porfirista* proclivities of the state. But the state government possessed more than one voice. While Romero Vargas preferred the velvet glove and a conciliatory approach, Pablo Urrutia, ex-jefe político of Zacapoaxtla and now state secretary, regarded the rebellion as an opportunity for destroying Xochiapulco for good. In early April the voice of Romero Vargas prevailed. Federal and state forces made a tactical withdrawal, leaving pacification to the trusted local National Guard commanders, Rafael Cravioto and Antonio Rodríguez Bocardo. As for the troubled district of Zacapoaxtla, from 5 April (the date of the suspension of the state of siege) full responsibility for pacification devolved upon Remigio Varela and the village authorities under his charge.

Varela was not at all happy with being left to cope with the rebellion on his own. The Federal garrison at Zautla, on Xochiapulco's southern flank, had been withdrawn in late March. On 4 April, in compliance with instructions from the Minister of War, Cabrera's garrison at Las Lomas and the force occupying the redoubt at Apulco also withdrew. Varela doubted whether villages in the Sierra possessed the stamina to continue resisting the rebellion, especially after recent rebel gains. He predicted that without properly equipped garrisons at Huahuaxtla, Las Lomas, and Apulco, backed by a reserve force in Zacapoaxtla, the district would soon be lost to the rebels.[100]

The Renewal of the State Government's Pacification of the Sierra

Although federal concern with the Puebla conflict continued to decline, the state government, probably on Urrutia's advice, took Varela's warnings seriously. On 9 April, State Secretary Urrutia instructed the old Conservative war-horse, General Roldán, to organize a force of 350 men in Zacapoaxtla on full pay. Within five days, Roldán reported the successful recruitment of five companies of infantry, numbering 400 men. Varela ordered the district exchequer to pay them punctually.[101] Urrutia also instructed that back pay be given to Indian commanders Cabrera and Cantero, whose contribution to the defense of the district had been crucial but whose loyalty had recently been suspected as wavering.[102]

The state government also made a renewed effort to generate financial support for these increased military costs. The well-to-do of Zacapoaxtla were invited to support the district's forces with loans. Officials drew up a list of notable citizens who between them were instructed to contribute a sum over 2,000 pesos. The individual assessments ranged from 5 to 200 pesos.[103] Teziutlán's commerce contributed substantial amounts to Zacapoaxtla's defense costs during April and May.[104] Toward the end of April, the financial position of the district was further strengthened when the state congress voted funds for the suppression of the rebellion.[105]

Improved finances paled next to the sheer scale of the task of pacification. In mid-April, Varela received detailed intelligence on the condition of rebel forces, which confirmed his fears that Zacapoaxtla was in imminent danger. A captured rebel soldier informed Cabrera in Las Lomas that 300 rebels, half of them with rifles, the other half unarmed, were operating in Quichaque, Xocoxintla, and Ixtacamaxtitlán. Moreover, a further 600 armed rebels had now settled in Xochiapulco. Lucas was expected to coordinate and lead the rebels to victory over Zacapoaxtla. Another female informer confirmed that Lucas "has the idea of spending Palm Sunday in Zacapoaxtla."[106]

In desperation, on 11 April, Varela urged the state government to send reinforcements for defending the Cerro de Apulco and the barrio of Las Lomas, two points that he considered vital for the security of the district.[107]

But to no avail. The next day, the jefe político reported to the alcalde of Cuetzalan that a force of 400–500 rebels had surrounded the redoubt at Apulco. Reinforcements and food supplies were desperately needed.[108] Rather than await the inevitable attack, Varela ordered 120 men into action against the rebel position at Apulco, driving the rebels back to Huahuaxtla, where they took refuge in the cemetery. Lack of ammunition obliged Varela's Guards to retreat.[109]

Palm Sunday passed without the feared assault by Lucas. Varela must have felt encouraged by the spirited performance of his Guards against a superior rebel force and pleased by the news of divisions within the rebel camp.[110] Nevertheless, the rebels swiftly regrouped, receiving reinforcements from Xochitlán and Nauzontla organized by Luis Antonio Díaz. Within two days they had returned to Apulco. They then mounted an unsuccessful attack upon the government position at Xochitonal, overlooking Zacapoaxtla. Varela observed ruefully that the rebels now occupied a line from Huahuaxtla to Zautla and were making daily raids on the villages of Jilotepec, Huahuaxtla, and Xochitlán, principally to extort food and money. Las Lomas was a favorite target (perhaps because this barrio reputedly had betrayed Xochiapulco in December 1869). In addition, houses belonging to Captain Cabrera were sacked and burned.[111]

Just before withdrawing on 23 April, Lucas drew up a list of his forces garrisoned at Huahuaxtla, on active service and on full pay:

Table 9–2. Daily Pay of Rebels Commanded by Lucas, Huahuaxtla, 17 April 1870

No. of Places	Section	Daily Pay
10	High Command	5.0 pesos
12	Mixed Party	6.0
8	Band	4.0
228	1st Xochiapulco Company	24.50
	2d Xochiapulco Company	31.50
	Eloxochitlan Company	21.00
	Chilapa Company	21.50
	Lomas Company	15.50
33	Huahuaxtla Company	16.50
129	1st Cuahuictic Company	16.00
	2d Cuahuictic Company	15.50
	3d Cuahuictic Company	19.00
	Huizcolotla Company	14.00
18	Tlamanca Company	9.00
162	Ometepec Company	44.50
	Taxco Company	12.00
	Cujanilco Company	12.50
	Moyoapa Company	12.00
10	Porters	5.00
610		*305.00 pesos*[112]

From this payroll, it is evident that Lucas was commanding forces from villages within municipalities that had provided the core of his following during the last two years of the European Intervention: Xochiapulco, Zautla, Tetela de Ocampo, and Ixtacamaxtitlán. This had become, and would long remain, the core of the Lucas *cacicazgo*.

In response to Roldán's strengthening of state government forces in the district, Lucas's 600–700 rebels abandoned Huahuaxtla on 23 April.[113] Some returned to Xochiapulco, where an estimated 800 rebels had settled by 25 April.[114] Others moved down to the *tierra caliente* in Xochitlán, Tuzamapa, and Jonotla.[115] Here they met Nahua rebels from Cuetzalan under Francisco Agustín.[116]

At Jonotla (in the heart of the *tierra caliente* of Tetela), three other important leaders awaited the Xochiapulco forces: Juan Nepomuceno Méndez, Juan Crisóstomo Bonilla, and Ireneo Reyes. They hoped to establish supply links with Papantla, but a shortage of ammunition prevented any immediate armed challenge to Varela.[117] Still others withdrew to Tetela where, on 26 April, Pedro Contreras reported that rebels had begun occupying villages in the south of the district and imposing forced loans.[118] Meanwhile, Luis León, the rebel cavalry commander from Tlaxco, Tlaxcala, was active in the Sierra de Tetela and planned raids upon Libres, Tetela de Ocampo, and Aquixtla.[119] By the end of the month, Varela reported that 800–950 rebels had returned from the northern Sierra with ammunition and money acquired from Tenampulco and La Casonera (near Papantla). They had settled in Xochiapulco and Xochitonal where they were cultivating and sowing.[120] Evidently, Roldán's reinforcement of the district's forces earlier in the month had come to nothing.

Both Roldán and Varela faced the perennial problem experienced by authorities confronting a fairly generalized insurrection. The cost of maintaining a fully equipped National Guard battalion numbering more than 450 men, on full alert and full pay, was prohibitive. With the help of financial backing from the state and a forced loan, pressure on the rebels might be sustained for a few weeks. But National Guardsmen were not professional soldiers. They had to attend to their businesses, especially planting maize before the rains became too heavy. Within three weeks, Roldán's rejuvenated Zacapoaxtla National Guard had atrophied.[121]

Throughout early May, the rebels operated within the Zacapoaxtla district and into surrounding areas with mounting impunity.[122] Andrés Juan complained from Xochitlán of the drunkenness and insulting behavior of the Xochiapulco rebels, reporting that "they banged on the doors of the houses of Señoras Doña María Hilaria Castañeda, Doña Juana González, and Doña Manuela Castañeda, and made offensive remarks about their husbands."[123] On 2 May, Mariano Saborido reported from Tlatlauqui that the rebels had attacked the district capital for the third time since the start of the rebellion.[124] Meanwhile, Francisco Agustín's movement resumed in

Cuetzalan.[125] Complaints also came from Nauzontla about the Xochiapulco commander, Miguel Español, and his Xochitlán counterpart, Miguel Mora, who together were extorting arms by force and threats.[126]

Varela received further bad news on 7 May. Part of the company commanded by Valeriano Cabrera at Las Lomas, along with the entire National Guard company of the same barrio, had defected to the rebels in Xochiapulco (probably because they had not been paid recently). Cabrera, along with Cantero, had been the cornerstone of the defense of the district capital since the start of the rebellion. Barrio authorities and citizens, totaling about 100 people, accompanied the estimated 120 defectors. The few remaining loyal members of Cabrera's company, and a handful of loyal villagers with their captain and officials, took refuge in Zacapoaxtla, which left their village unprotected. The rebels then returned to their village, backed now by troops from Xochiapulco, to prepare for the anticipated counterattack from Zacapoaxtla. A similar defection of National Guard conscripts occurred in Xochitlán on the same day, suggesting central coordination. This picket of thirty-three deserters, led by José Santiago and Miguel Francisco, headed for Huahuaxtla and Xochiapulco, where they hoped to be able to air their grievances before a commission due in Xochiapulco from the "Supreme Government."[127]

These defections, which left the state's pacification policy in the Sierra in tatters, deeply worried the authorities. On 11 May the state government assured Varela that all available forces would be dispatched immediately to confront the rebellion.[128] Rodríguez Bocardo was ordered into the Sierra in pursuit of León and Lucas (now described as a bandit), but predictably the cavalry proved useless in the Sierra.[129] A week later, Varela reported that Xochiapulco remained in rebellion, but no move had been made upon Zacapoaxtla or Apulco.[130]

Varela's guarded confidence was not shared by his National Guard commander. On the following day, Varela received a report from Colonel José de la Luz Molina that the rebels planned to attack on the morrow. Molina feared that the forces defending Zacapoaxtla were inadequate since the men lacked sufficient ammunition. Some soldiers, he reported, held their positions without a single cartridge. Consequently, he doubted that his forces would be able to defend the town. Nevertheless, he believed that the Guard under his command lacked only ammunition, not bravery.[131]

Fortunately for Zacapoaxtla, the National Guard of the district would not have to face the forces of Xochiapulco. On 3 May representatives of the state government, mandated by a resolution of the congress, had established direct contact with the rebels in Xochiapulco.[132] Although the overture resulted in a truce, it did nothing to halt the buildup of rebel forces. With no further progress by the end of May, Romero Vargas traveled to the Sierra in desperation.

On 1 June, from Zacapoaxtla, the governor sent an ultimatum to Lucas. Recognizing the "sublime efforts" which the villages in this area had made toward the defeat of the European Intervention, the rebels were offered a complete pardon in exchange for handing in all their arms and ammunition. Lucas had three days in which to reply or else accept the "fatal consequences." He convened a junta of his chiefs and soldiers which met on 3 June to consider the governor's proposal. The junta agreed upon an "act of submission" in which:

1) the rebels would submit to the national and state governments, handing in their arms and equipment;
2) the rebels and their leaders would receive amnesty from any punishment and would be permitted to return to their families to live in peace and in enjoyment of their full constitutional guarantees;
3) the junta requested the state government, in order to avoid future conflict, to remove Xochiapulco from the jurisdiction of Zacapoaxtla and place it under that of Tetela;
4) Lucas renounced any responsibility for the revenues or supplies he had received from villages for the support of his forces;
5) the rebels requested the release of Francisco Javier Arriaga and all the other prisoners of war;
6) Lucas asked for the suspension of the order that Méndez be arrested, in recognition of his service to previous patriotic struggles; and
7) Lucas requested safe conducts for the rebels who were not from Xochiapulco so that they could return to Libres, Teziutlán, Tlatlauqui, and Tetela.[133]

The state government accepted the rebel's terms on 4 June after some hesitation resulting from their request to have Luis León (Tlaxco) and Hermenegildo Carrillo (Chalchicomula) included in the pardon, a request that Romero Vargas refused to concede (unwisely, as it turned out, since Carrillo became the leading Sierra rebel during the Revolt of La Noria in the following year). The act of submission was signed by twelve chiefs, thirty captains, ten lieutenants, and twenty-six sub-lieutenants. The armaments submitted to the government—479 rifles and 5,820 cartridges—certainly fell short of the number of rebels (totaling just over 800 in June 1870). On 8 June, Ignacio Mejía, Minister of War, informed Romero Vargas that the Federation had approved all of Lucas's terms. On the following day, Puebla's official newspaper declared that "public tranquility has been completely restored."[134]

Secure in the amnesty and the restoration of constitutional guarantees, rebel leaders began to return to the district. The first to return were Miguel and Mariano Arriaga and Luis Antonio Díaz, followed by twenty others who had taken sanctuary in Tetela: nine from Zacapoaxtla, eight from

Xochitlán, two from Cuetzalan (Francisco Agustín and Octaviano Carpintero), and one from Nauzontla (Francisco Ruiz).[135]

Lasting peace in the Sierra was so important to Romero Vargas that he remained in Zacapoaxtla until early July attending to the details of pacification. The boundaries of Xochiapulco had to be resolved as well as the compensation to the Salgado family for the hacienda of Xochiapulco and Manzanilla. The state government confirmed the original expropriation decree of 1864 and took over responsibility for paying Salgado for the unmortgaged part of the estates and for the repayment of mortgages to Church bodies. The Xochiapulquenses accepted responsibility for the repayment of privately raised loans. The state also made 15,000 pesos available to ease the handing in of arms.[136]

With his Sierra business completed, Romero Vargas returned on 11 July to the state capital to general jubilation. A further sign of a new era of peace and conciliation came in late July with the inauguration of the newspaper, *El Eco de la Sierra*, which was to represent and promote the interests of the Sierra under the ensign of "peace, conciliation, order, liberty, and progress."[137] Romero Vargas's policy of conciliation and pacification continued throughout the rest of the year. His policy included financial help for Sierra municipalities for the completion of public works and schools, some initiated as early as the 1850s but delayed by civil and foreign wars. Municipalities were also promised help in equipping their bands with musical instruments.[138] Romero Vargas also proposed an ingenious boundary reform. Following the example of troublesome Xochiapulco's secession from Zacapoaxtla, he suggested the creation of an entirely new political district composed of three Sierra municipalities that had been engaged in long-standing conflicts with their district cabeceras. The new district, named after Miguel Cástulo Alatriste, the state's martyred Liberal leader of the Reform Wars, would comprise the municipalities of Chignahuapan (ex-district of Zacatlán), Aquixtla (ex-district of Tetela), and San Francisco Ixtacamaxtitlán (ex-district of Libres), with Chignahuapan as the district capital.

Leaving to one side the substantial discomfort felt by Liberal Ixtacamaxtitlán, finding itself now alongside Conservative Aquixtla and subject to Conservative Chignahuapan, the creation of the new district of Alatriste was an inspired move. It removed the basis of three ancient local rivalries that frequently aggravated the broader conflicts arising between the Sierra and the state and federal governments. It also provided the state government with a loyal wedge (the new district ran horizontally, east-west along the southern Sierra, in contrast to the other five Sierra districts that extended northward from the plateau to the lowland) that could act as a buffer and serve as a cordon sanitaire around the troublesome Sierra. Indeed, Alatriste's intended function was similar to the wall that had once traversed the principality of Ixtacamaxtitlán, separating the Olmec-Tlaxcalteco Sierra from Totonacapan.[139]

The state government made further gestures of conciliation. It intervened on behalf of eighty-five men impressed by the Federal army in Zautla and reappointed Juan Crisóstomo Bonilla as jefe político of Tetela. This move made Lucas's close friend and compadre responsible for settling Xochiapulco into its new district.[140]

Conclusion

The Arriaga rebellion had two distinct phases, characterized by quite separate, even opposing objectives. The phases were separated by the battle between the Sixth Federal Infantry Battalion and the Xochiapulquenses on 2–3 December 1869. The initial conspiracies and village revolts were shown to have been Conservative in inspiration and confined to the district of Zacapoaxtla. No evidence of involvement by Lucas, Xochiapulco, or leaders of the Montaña party was uncovered. Indeed, the Arriaga brothers were already identified before the rebellion as the principal contenders with the Montaña for the control of the central Sierra. This rivalry intensified after the peace accords.

Francisco Javier Arriaga envisaged a prosperous Sierra linked to the outside world by roads and canalized rivers. But as a patrician, he favored a traditional social order, with the Indians in their place, undisturbed by Liberal innovations such as the *desamortización*, and with the Church endowing an aura of stability and legitimacy. Xochiapulco—liberal, anticlerical, egalitarian, and assertively autonomous—offended this view of the world (one that Arriaga shared with many other patrician Zacapoaxtecos).

The second phase of the Arriaga rebellion, from when the Xochiapulquenses decided to resist the Federal foray into their territory on 2 December until peace was signed in June 1870, was essentially a movement of villages loyal to Lucas, in defense of their land, their harvests, and their municipal autonomy. The June peace accords, in certain respects, can be considered a rebel victory. Former rebels soon occupied district *jefaturas* and state and federal deputyships. Apart from the generosity of the terms, the condition that represented the major concession for the rebels— the handing over of arms—could not be effectively enforced, now that Xochiapulco was subject to the *mendecista* stronghold of Tetela. The continuing military strength of Xochiapulco was soon demonstrated in the revolt of La Noria, when Porfirio Díaz chose the Sierra de Puebla as the principal front for challenging Benito Juárez in the southeast. With the reemergence of Díaz on the national scene, Méndez, after almost two years of silence, resurfaced as the main Sierra leader.

10

The Fruits of Rebellion in Xochiapulco

In 1870, Xochiapulco was still little more than an informal alliance of barrios whose jurisdiction was fiercely contested by its neighbors and whose best maize lands were claimed by absentee landlords. The cabecera's unfinished ayuntamiento (which doubled as a school building) had housed enemy garrisons almost as often as it had the council. However, in June 1870 the Xochiapulquenses were in a stronger position than ever before to push through the gains in land and political autonomy promised by successive state governments and reaffirmed in the peace accord. After two years of fruitless struggle to reincorporate Xochiapulco to its former cabecera, Zacapoaxtla had at last abandoned the idea of a return to pre-Ayutla days. From June 1870, Xochiapulco no longer deferred to nearby Zacapoaxtla as its *jefatura* but to Tetela de Ocampo.

Population and Social Structure

The success of the Xochiapulquenses in establishing their autonomy from Zacapoaxtla owed much to the forested mountain terrain that provided cover during periods of occupation. Moreover, Xochiapulco's overall population was substantial and, as the authorities had found in 1869–70, not easily dispersed among the already crowded barrios of neighboring, less well-endowed jurisdictions. In 1868, Xochiapulco's cabecera and five subject barrios (Las Lomas, Yautetelco, Jilotepec, Atzala, Eloxochitlan) contained 638 families with an overall population of 2,504 (1,270 men and 1,234 women).[1] In 1869, between the two rebellions, the population of the expanded municipality (having annexed Chilapa from Zautla) had increased to 2,555 persons. Three years later, with the loss of Las Lomas (the largest barrio after the cabecera), the population had fallen to 2,011 (even with the new barrio of Ixehuaco formed by exiles from Las Lomas). Xochiapulco's population had recovered by 1873 to 2,425 (1,238 men and 1,187 women) within 524 families, settled on small scattered ranchos of which 599 were counted in 1869.[2]

Table 10–1. Population of Xochiapulco in 1869 and 1872 [3]

Barrio	Population		No. of Pueblos		No. of Ranchos
	1869	1872	1869	1872	1869
Cabecera	886	886	6	6	200
Chilapa	247	300	1	1	74
Jilotepec	193	200	1	1	38
Las Lomas	753	–	1	–	184
Ixehuaco	–	200	–	1	–
Yautetelco	191	100	1	1	40
Cuaximaloyan	196	216	1	1	47
Atzalan	89	109	1	1	16
Total	2,555	2,011	12	12	599

General Ortega's original decree, issued in Zacapoaxtla on 9 December 1864, anticipated a mild social hierarchy in Xochiapulco, reflected in the allocation of plots, graduated according to military rank, to those Xochiapulquenses who had participated in the battle of 5 May 1862. Ordinary soldiers would receive just one *almud de labor* (1 *almud* = 0.73 acres); corporals, two *almudes*; first and second sergeants, three *almudes*; sub-lieutenants, four *almudes*; lieutenants, five *almudes*; captains, six *almudes*; battalion commanders, seven *almudes*; and lieutenant colonels, eight *almudes*. Colonels would receive the princely amount of one *fanega* (1 *fanega* = 12 *almudes* = 8.81 acres). In fact, all but seven of those Xochiapulquenses present at the battle of 5 May 1862 had served as soldiers or non-commissioned officers (Luis Antonio Atahuit, Mariano de los Santos, Francisco Rivera, Miguel Jiménez, José Gabriel Valencia, and Juan Francisco Lucas served as captains, and Valeriano Cabrera served as a lieutenant). However, the decree extended the offer of Xochiapulco's land "to all those soldiers from the same mountains who have sustained the saintly cause of Independence with such brilliance."[4]

The census of 1873 conveys little sense of hierarchy, listing all but seven adult males as *jornaleros* (day laborers). Only Juan José Español, Luis Antonio Díaz, Juan Antonio, and Miguel Antonio were listed as *labradores* (owners of more substantial rural properties). There were also two bricklayers, one carpenter (a migrant from Tlaxcala), and one tailor. These artisans listed surnames, which was still a rare practice in Xochiapulco. Only seven men in the *municipio* were listed as literate. The record identified sixty-one adult men as "invalids" (presumably war veterans), exempt from military service and taxation. Lucas's family was honored as the first enumerated in the *padrón* (although he now resided in Tetela with his second wife, María Asunción Pérez).[5]

Political Status, Public and Ceremonial Life

A junta drawn from the entire jurisdiction of Xochiapulco reached a unanimous decision on 7 June 1870 to separate from the district of Zacapoaxtla and join the district of Tetela.[6] By early September, Xochiapulco voters had elected a constitutional council. Xochiapulco followed the letter of the constitution against reelection of council officials. Records of elections for 1874–1936 show no incidence of consecutive election and few examples of men serving more than once, which suggests widespread popular participation.[7] However, not everything was conducted in accord with constitutional propriety. In 1873, Tetela's jefe político

Table 10–2. Ayuntamiento of Xochiapulco, 5 September 1870 [9]

Title	Name	Duties
1st Alcalde	Juan Francisco Dinorín	Administration of justice
2nd Alcalde	Juan Martín	Primary and secondary education, geography and statistics
1st Alderman	Juan Miguel	Municipal properties, national fiestas, public entertainment
2nd Alderman	Juan Antonio Tecolco	Material improvements, urban policing, public hygiene
3rd Alderman	José Manuel Santos	Food supplies, inspection and collection of taxes
4th Alderman	Mariano Bríjido	Conservation of woods, granary, and Inspector of Weights and Measures
Syndic	Juan Francisco Naranja	Patron of fiestas

learned that, due to fire damage to the council building, Xochiapulco possessed no municipal jail. Instead, officials used General Lucas's house on the main square for the incarceration of prisoners.[8]

Schools took precedence over jails and chapels.[10] Less than five months after the end of the rebellion, in November 1870, the boys' school in the cabecera, built entirely with voluntary labor and contributions, neared completion. Juan Martín, the second alcalde, requested permission to purchase two bells: one to summon the children to school, and the other to call people to church. However, the church was never completed.[11] In the same month, jefe político Juan Crisóstomo Bonilla allowed voluntary workers to begin the construction of a small chapel to house Xochiapulco's saints that "due to the war, enemies of the village had carried off to the barrio of Las Lomas, where they lie abandoned, without the cult of their owners."[12] But Xochiapulco's authorities did not welcome the Catholic clergy, with whom relations had been tense since well before the revolution of Ayutla. In 1927 a Catholic church had still not been built.[13] Instead, Xochiapulco was one of the first places in the Sierra not to collect the *Dominica* tax for funding clergy. This policy provided an additional incentive for many to settle in the new municipality.[14] Moreover, in 1886

Xochiapulco became one of the first municipalities in Puebla to welcome a
Methodist mission.[15] Alongside Methodism, Freemasonry and secular education flourished there during this time. By the turn of the century, Manuel
Pozos, Xochiapulco's school director for twenty-seven years, reported that
the municipality enjoyed a 44 percent male and 13 percent female literacy
rate, the highest in the state outside the capital city.[16]

Jurisdictional Conflicts

Political secession from Zacapoaxtla and annexation to the district of Tetela
did not occur painlessly. The factionalism in Yautetelco, Las Lomas, and
Chilapa that was evident during the 1869–70 rebellion continued into peacetime. Since the peace accord of 5 June 1870, Zacapoaxtla's jefe político had
pressed the state government to approve a district boundary with Tetela along

a line south from the barrio of Atzalan to Jilotepec following the Manzanilla and Papaloateno tributaries. This would effectively incorporate the barrios of Atzala, Yautetelco, Las Lomas, and Jilotepec under the jurisdiction of Zacapoaxtla as well as secure the mountain ridge between Xochiapulco and Zacapoaxtla for the district capital. This would give Zacapoaxtla a marked strategic advantage over its newly emancipated neighbor.[17]

Conflict over this boundary rumbled for the next twenty years. The chief discord between Xochiapulco and its former cabecera centered on the barrio of Las Lomas, which was strategically located on the main route between Xochiapulco and Zacapoaxtla. Las Lomas, like Xochiapulco, had been in recent memory a private estate belonging to the Molina family of Zacapoaxtla.[18] In July 1865 the barrio's houses and crops were razed by Colonel Kodolitch, on orders of Count Thun, to punish the population for the execution and dismemberment of a Mexican soldier serving in the Austrian garrison in Zacapoaxtla.[19] Las Lomas was then resettled by the families of Imperial soldiers brought from Tlatlauqui. These soldiers, followers of Cenobio Cantero, were seen by Xochiapulquenses as traitors and intruders.

In the interlude between the fall of the Empire and the rebellion of 1869–70, practically all adult males in Xochiapulco were inscribed in the National Guard. Nevertheless, Las Lomas had the largest number of men in the jurisdiction who were paying taxes to avoid military service (Las Lomas had sixty-one out of sixty-eight *rebajado* payers in the entire jurisdiction). Lomeños kept peace with their municipal cabecera by regularly paying their *rebajado* tax.[20] Yet relations between the municipal government and the barrio authorities remained tense. Several Lomeños refused in 1868 and 1869 to denounce common land through the *desamortización* by claiming prior ownership of the land which Xochiapulco regarded as municipal commons.[21]

During the 1869–70 rebellion, Captain Valeriano Cabrera recruited Lomeños who served directly under the Federal commander, Ignacio Alatorre, rather than in the Zacapoaxtla National Guard, which would have been the normal practice. This arrangement, which allowed Las Lomas to serve as a buffer between warring Xochiapulco and Zacapoaxtla, broke down with the peace negotiations. In June 1870, when the Lomas company was disbanded, its captain, Lucas Martín, was assassinated and several Lomeños were captured on their return to the barrio (reportedly by other Lomeños who had joined the rebels) and taken to Xochiapulco. Even though the culprits were eventually arrested and sent to the new cabecera in Tetela for trial, the murder of Martín was the first of a rash of sinister political assassinations throughout the southern Sierra, which became even more common after the revolt of La Noria.[22]

In August 1870 several Lomeños, including Cabrera and Juan Martín (Lucas Martín's brother), bought the estate of Xopeyaco and Albaradoyas from the Molina Alcantara family of Zacapoaxtla, for the sum of 3,500 pesos. The land was leased at an annual rent of 12.5 percent per annum to one hundred *vecinos* of the barrio.[23] The distribution of hitherto privately owned land greatly strengthened the hold of Cabrera and the pro-Zacapoaxtla group in the barrio. Violence toward those *vecinos* still loyal to Xochiapulco increased, and the barrio's officials openly disregarded the authority of the cabecera.

Early in October 1870, Lomeños who had fled this violence to form the new barrio of Ixehuaco complained that their houses, crops, and fruit trees in Las Lomas were being stolen and destroyed.[24] They also reported that they were being fired upon at night and asked Tetela's jefe político whether it might not be wiser for them to accept Zacapoaxtla, rather than Xochiapulco, as their cabecera.[25] The tension mounted in November when Lomeño exiles, who were returning to harvest their milpas, found their land already occupied and their crops harvested.[26]

Each side disclaimed responsibility for the violence and factionalism, and accused the other of deliberately stirring up trouble in pursuit of its wider strategic objectives. Late in January 1871 the state government finally resolved that Jilotepec and Atzalan (and, by implication, Yautetelco) should acknowledge Xochiapulco as their cabecera. However, the ayuntamiento of Zacapoaxtla continued to send circulars to these barrios as late as September 1873, which irritated Luis Antonio Díaz and the jefe político of Tetela.[27] In November 1871, just before the revolt of La Noria broke out in the Sierra, Las Lomas was formally detached from Xochiapulco and placed under the jurisdiction of Zacapoaxtla. In return, Xochiapulco gained another new barrio, La Manzanilla, which was established on the old hacienda of that name.[28] The revolt made the conflicts in Las Lomas more acute as the Xochiapulco authorities (who supported the revolt) attempted to form a council in the barrio independent of Zacapoaxtla. The dispute smoldered, then flared up again in 1879, when Valeriano Cabrera was again found to be intimidating Lomas *vecinos* into leaving and inviting others to settle there.[29]

Xochiapulco also had tense relations with its southern neighbor, Zautla. Zautla's barrio of Chilapa had provided José Manuel Lucas and the Cuatecomacos with a company of soldiers as early as 1857. In that year, José Manuel died in an ambush in Chilapa along with two local captains, José de la Caridad and José Eugenio.[30] As soon as Xochiapulco acquired its municipal status in 1861, Chilapa petitioned to join the new municipality. Chilapa again petitioned the military governor of the state in 1863 to be allowed to recognize Xochiapulco as its cabecera, due to its geographical proximity and common patriotic struggle. The request was repeated in 1866 and 1868. Finally in 1869 the state legislature and both municipalities approved the secession (although the decree was not issued because of the rebellion). Only with the peace settlement in 1870 did Chilapa's association with Xochiapulco receive recognition by the state government.[31] However, relations between Xochiapulco and Zautla remained tense throughout the 1870s and 1880s when Lucas's clientele in Zautla extended beyond Chilapa to include other barrios, in particular, Tenampulco. From this barrio, a Nahua National Guard captain called José Máximo succeeded in attaining the municipal presidency of Zautla after the revolution of Tuxtepec.

The Division of the Commons and the Hacienda

Two months after the victory over the French in May 1862, the alcalde of Xochiapulco requested information on how to divide the commons of the new municipality. The jefe político in Zacapoaxtla replied that he should convene a junta that included himself, a sindic, an alderman, and a citizen. He reminded the alcalde that land should be offered first to those in need.[32] It was six years before adjudication of Xochiapulco's commons began in earnest. But once started, it was completed in fifteen months ending in October 1869, just before the outbreak of the rebellion.

Dividing Xochiapulco's commons presented only minor difficulties. Some discord developed over whether claimants should be expected to pay interest (with Luis Antonio Díaz in favor and Juan Antonio against) and uncertainty existed about the precise extent of the commons. Zacapoaxtla's barrio of Comaltepec accused the Xochiapulquenses of encroaching on its lands. But a junta of *vecinos* from both barrios met on the mountain between the two jurisdictions and resolved the conflict.[33] Bickering also arose in Las Lomas between old families, who regarded the commons as theirs since "time immemorial," and new immigrants who sought individual plots. In one incident, a Las Lomas resident, "the querulous José Francisco," representing an extended family living there for generations, complained that *vecinos* from Comaltepec were settling on land claimed by his sister. Luis Antonio Díaz dismissed José Francisco's complaint as invalid by claiming (wrongly) that a woman could not legally denounce or inherit land.[34] By 1 October 1870 only a few unclaimed parcels remained of Xochiapulco's commons.[35]

Of much greater importance than the division of common land for the future of Xochiapulco was the distribution of the private lands of several haciendas in the municipality. In December 1868 residents of Jilotepec paid 300 pesos to Miguel Salgado of Tlatlauqui for the Rancho de Horta. Most of the twenty-one beneficiaries had surnames. Perhaps this accounted for the antagonism between this mestizo barrio and the Nahua authorities in Xochiapulco that culminated eventually in secession.[36] In August 1870 residents of Las Lomas bought the hacienda of Xopeyaco and Avaradoya to distribute among over one hundred tenants. The largest estate awaiting subdivision was the hacienda of Xochiapulco and Manzanilla that General Ortega had promised to Xochiapulco's patriotic soldiers in the decree of 5 December 1864, a promise still unfulfilled in June 1870.[37]

Soon after peace was signed in June 1870, Romero Vargas promised that the hacienda would be distributed in accord with the original 1864 decree but added that the Xochiapulquenses would be expected to compensate the owner. A *junta popular* placed responsibility for the distribution of the land and for the compensation of the Salgado family in Lucas's hands.[38] Romero Vargas then did nothing for six months. After continual pressure from the Xochiapulco authorities, culminating in a prolonged legislative debate, the matter was finally resolved.[39] On 24 December 1870, Bonilla, jefe político of Tetela, instructed Francisco Dinorín, alcalde of Xochiapulco, to begin dividing up the lands of the hacienda among the *vecinos*. A general junta met in Xochiapulco on 30 January 1871 to discuss how to accomplish this. The junta agreed that recipients of the plots would have to pay for the costs of the commission charged with dividing the hacienda, but no mention was made of compensation.[40]

The final distribution was delayed again by a writ of *amparo* issued in 1875 by Lic. Pascual Bonilla, who represented the Salgado family. He claimed that the family had not yet been compensated. Only after the revolution of Tuxtepec was the hacienda firmly secured for the Xochiapulquenses. On 30 July 1878 the state congress reaffirmed the 1864 decree and voted full compensation for José Miguel Salgado.[41] At last, the division of the hacienda could proceed without impediment. Between 17 November 1874 and 11 March 1890, 1,183 titles to plots were issued, which benefited hundreds of National Guard veterans and widows.[42]

The hesitancy that marked Xochiapulco's passage from an uncertain status as squatter barrios to becoming a municipality of small property holders was a consequence of recurrent violent conflicts. These conflicts re-surfaced as the presidential election of 1872 approached.

11

The Revolt of La Noria

The Montaña's armed strategy, following the amnesty of June 1870 and the disarming of the rebels commanded by Lucas, surely now would be replaced by more peaceful means for the attainment of power. Méndez had succeeded in avoiding any official involvement in the Arriaga revolt. Freed from his Federal army commission, Méndez could now stand for election, certain that his reputation and popularity, if not enhanced, at least had not been seriously damaged during the unpopular governorships of Rafael García and Ignacio Romero Vargas. Once more, however, national political strategy took precedence in the state of Puebla. Squabbles between rival *juarista, lerdista,* and *porfirista* factions in the federal congress interrupted the process of conciliation initiated in the June amnesty. By the autumn of 1871, Méndez had taken up arms once again, this time against both the federal and the state governments, in support of Porfirio Díaz's Plan de la Noria.

Puebla in National Congressional Politics

Congressional factionalism increased as the federal elections scheduled for July 1871 approached. The prospect of another four years under the autocratic Benito Juárez, President since 1858, provoked a potentially formidable congressional alliance against his deputies. In January 1871, Sebastian Lerdo de Tejada resigned from the cabinet and began organizing his supporters in the congress and in the states (notably several governors, among them, Puebla's Ignacio Romero Vargas). Lerdo's congressional party formed a tactical alliance with deputies loyal to Porfirio Díaz.

The national chamber of deputies remained constitutionally supreme. Juárez had still not been able to introduce the constitutional reforms that would strengthen the executive power which he had signaled in the *convocatoria* of September 1867. Failure to secure these constitutional reforms had obliged Juárez, on several occasions, to assume emergency powers. Against this novel *lerdista-porfirista* alliance, Juárez was effectively powerless, with only presidential patronage and congressional obstructionism to counter-balance "the parliamentary dictatorship."[1]

The agreement between *lerdista* and *porfirista* deputies—called the "Liga"—presented obvious complications in the state of Puebla. Here *porfirista* rebels until recently had been locked in armed combat with the *lerdista* state governor, Romero Vargas. Puebla's *porfiristas,* led by Méndez and the Montaña party, wanted Romero Vargas out and a *serrano* in the governor-ship. This rift between the Liga's federal congressional strategy and party strategies on the state level eventually caused the national *lerdista-porfirista* accord to collapse. Indeed, Puebla's Llanura-Montaña rivalry brought down the Liga. As the elections approached, Porfirio Díaz's principal political agent, Justo Benítez, forged a temporary alliance in Puebla between *porfiristas* and *juaristas* against Romero Vargas.

The supporters of the national Liga warned that Benítez was ruining an agreement by which eight to ten *porfirista* congressmen would be elected from Puebla (presumably with the consent and cooperation of Romero Vargas), with other *porfirista* congressmen elected from Morelos and San Luis Potosí.[2] As we have seen, Romero Vargas was prepared to conciliate the Montaña opposition. For his political survival, he might well have co-operated with the Liga's plan. But he reversed his conciliation of the Montaña when attacks in the national congress culminated in an attempt to impeach him in May 1871. Romero Vargas survived by a narrow margin because of a division within *porfirista* ranks. The issue split the Liga and ended the congressional influence of the *porfirista* delegates.[3]

Whatever the impact of Benítez's anti-*romerista* campaign in the national congress, his intervention in Puebla state politics provoked the third major Sierra insurrection since the restoration of the Republic in June 1867. Had Benítez not chosen to use local Puebla grievances to advance his national strategy, Romero Vargas likely would have succeeded in conciliating Sierra grievances and co-opting leaders such as Bonilla, Arriaga, Márquez Galindo, and even, perhaps, Méndez into his administration. After all, they belonged to the same Liberal family. But Puebla politics had never escaped wider political rivalries; the state's proximity to the federal capital made it peculiarly susceptible to external meddling.

Hence, the *lerdista-porfirista* alliance against Juárez's executive centralism foundered on indiscipline within Díaz's ranks. The disagreement lay more in differences of overall political strategy than in congressional tactics. Benítez targeted *lerdista* governors, hoping to provoke Lerdo, incensed by attacks upon his governors, into revolt. This would leave Díaz in a powerful position, given his influence within the armed forces, especially the state National Guards, to dominate the ensuing conflict. Yet Benítez misjudged *lerdismo,* an essentially civilian movement unlikely to take to arms.[4] His underlying assumption was that, ultimately, an armed challenge to the national government would be necessary. In the federal congress, *porfiristas* divided between the Zamacona group, who favored the legal path to victory through the Liga, and the Benítez group, who believed that insurrection likely provided the only route to power. Thus, Mexico edged ever closer to insurrection, despite agreement among most politicians that civil war must be avoided at all costs. The yearning for peace and order after decades of conflict was still not matched by the confidence that Juárez could prevent the country from slipping back into war.[5]

The failure of the Liga in May 1871 brought the reemergence of the dominant *lerdista-juarista* bloc in the national congress. Confronted by 160 *lerdistas* and *juaristas,* the 52 *porfiristas* faced extinction. The armed strategy, considered seriously since December 1870 and actively prepared for since February 1871, now seemed to be the only option for Díaz.

The Onset of the Revolt of La Noria in the Puebla Sierra

The Puebla Sierra occupied a crucial place in Díaz's military and strategic thinking. He recognized the region's geographical centrality and appreciated its legendary impregnability. In the Montaña, Díaz could count on a loyal, militarily seasoned, well-disciplined circle of leaders with similar cultural backgrounds and Liberal-patriotic pedigrees similar to those of his own men in Oaxaca. Indeed, no region of Oaxaca would prove so loyal during the revolt of La Noria, when Porfirio and his brother, Félix Díaz, Oaxaca's state governor, came under attack from the Hernández and Meijueiro *cacicazgos* of the Sierra de Ixtlán and from Juchitán in the isthmus. Armed opposition from its peripheries effectively undermined Oaxaca's utility as a springboard for a national rebellion. These *cacicazgos* also furnished Alatorre's Federal Second Division with local allies who greatly aided the pacification of the state. Denied a home base, Porfirio Díaz had no choice but to adopt a peripatetic insurrectionary strategy, and to depend upon his alliances in the north (principally Gerónimo Treviño of Nuevo León), in the northwest center (principally Trinidad García de la Cadena in Zacatecas, Donato Guerra in Durango, and, in desperation, Manuel Lozada in Tepic), and in the Puebla Sierra, which would serve as the vital strategic reserve in the southeast.[6]

The maneuvering of parties and the stirrings of insurrection on the national level inevitably affected Puebla's state and local politics. In spite of a formal truce and amnesty in June 1870, the Puebla Sierra had remained a troubled place, principally due to conflicts arising from the sale of village lands. The Indian movement in Cuetzalan continued throughout 1870–71 as Francisco Agustín became an increasingly prominent rebel leader in the *tierra caliente* of Zacapoaxtla and Tetela.[7] Armed and seditious movements occurred in Xochitlán (Zacapoaxtla) and Tzinacantepec (Tlatlauqui) in December 1870, and in Hueyapan (Teziutlán) in February

1871.[8] Serious conflicts accompanied the subdivision of Jonotla's (Tetela) ejido in April 1871.[9]

Political factionalism spread from the village to the district level in February 1871 with the call for the election of the state governor, deputies, senators, and supreme court judges.[10] Romero Vargas had greatly strengthened his powers as governor after reforming the state constitution in December 1870, in line with Juárez's 1867 *convocatoria* (which called for the centralization of executive power, but had still not been introduced nationally). The reforms restricted the powers of the state legislature and increased those of a new upper chamber and of the governor. By increasing the number of deputies and by requiring that two-thirds of all deputies or senators be present for a quorum, it was hoped that "accidental majorities" (majorities orchestrated by a small number of deputies in a poorly attended session) would be avoided. Also, impeachment of the governor now required a vote of two-thirds of all deputies. The reforms also included a new territorial division of the state and abolished the popular election of jefes políticos, henceforth to be nominated by the governor. The jefes políticos, in turn, could nominate candidates for municipal elections. Political centralization and Montaña anxiety were further increased by the centralization of the *rebajado* tax by the state treasury, formerly the prerogative of the jefes políticos. A chorus of opposition to these constitutional reforms immediately ensued. Opposition in Puebla was further encouraged by a constant campaign of vilification against Romero Vargas in the columns of the national newspaper, *El Monitor Republicano* (culminating after the revolt of La Noria in an unsuccessful attempt to impeach him).[11]

The renewal of organized opposition in Puebla was coordinated with Porfirio Díaz's national strategy.[12] On 28 February 1871, Francisco Javier Arriaga (leader of the November 1869 rebellion) organized 127 citizens in Libres to protest both against the anticipated reelection of Romero Vargas as governor and his constitutional reforms.[13] Further protests against these reforms came from the state capital, Acatlán, San Martín Texmelucan, Zacapoaxtla, and Teziutlán.[14] However, the jefes políticos of Zacapoaxtla and Huauchinango pledged their support for the governor.[15]

Díaz's role in the upsurge of activity is illustrated by a letter Lucas received in May 1871 from the Gran Comisión Electoral in Veracruz. This letter proposed the principle of no reelection and gave support for the nomination of Luis Mier y Terán for the Veracruz governorship, General Fernando Corona for the supreme court, and Díaz for the presidency.[16] Méndez's correspondence with Lucas resumed at this time, along with the dispatch of large amounts of salt and *chilpotle* pepper to Lucas's ranch at Taxcantla (for the supply of troops), and an expression of gratitude for a charge Lucas had carried out in Tlatlauqui.[17] Lucas's political correspondence intensified, confirming his role in the elections in the central Sierra.[18]

The election results for federal deputyships were published in mid-July 1871. Zacapoaxtla chose Francisco Arriaga and Tetela picked Ramón Márquez Galindo, with Díaz's supporters also doing well elsewhere in the state: Manuel Zamacona and Manuel Romero Rubio in the capital, Ignacio Mont in Tehuacán, Antonio Gamboa in Tepeji, and Carlos Pacheco in Cholula.[19] Perhaps these *porfirista* successes account for the relative tranquility of the northern Sierra compared with the south of the state, where banditry escalated into insurrection during August and September 1871. The widespread unrest in Oaxaca and Guerrero during the second half of 1871 was linked with the breakdown of order in southern Puebla.[20]

The Onset of the Revolt of La Noria

Díaz belatedly issued the Plan de la Noria on 13 November 1871. It was long on criticism of the regime but short on precise suggestions for what might replace Juárez's liberal centralism. Díaz made no apology for his lack of a clear program. In his view, the constitution of 1857 contained everything necessary for guiding the political life of the nation. His plan called for the principle of no reelection to public office and charged Juárez with "the regimentation of a congressional majority," curtailment of the independence of the judiciary, the use of the army for political repression and electoral fraud, the imposition of state governors, and the failure to abolish the *alcabala.* It called for a return to the early principles of the Reform enshrined in Alvarez's Plan de Ayutla. He urged the people to rise up with the words, "the Constitution of 1857 and electoral freedom will be our banner, less government and more liberty our program."[21]

Throughout the summer of 1871, from his headquarters at his hacienda of La Noria in Oaxaca, Díaz energetically assembled his forces. He also developed lines of supply with the United States through his old companion at arms, Gerónimo Treviño, governor of Nuevo León. Local opposition to a mass levy of forces in Oaxaca, especially from the hitherto dependable Sierra de Ixtlán, caused the long-anticipated national revolt against Juárez to begin in the north. In September 1871, Juárez was returned to the presidency with an anticipated working majority in the congress that permitted him to proceed with his constitutional reforms, which had been projected now for over five years. For the *porfirista* opposition, only armed revolt remained. Late in September 1871, Generals Treviño, Pedro Martínez, and Manuel Márquez rebelled in Monterey (Nuevo León), Galeana (Durango), and Mazatlán (Sinaloa), respectively. On 1 October the garrison in Mexico City's Ciudadela rose up behind disgruntled senior officers (Generals Aureliano Rivera and Miguel Negrete being the best known). Forces loyal to Juárez, commanded by General Sostenes Rocha, ruthlessly suppressed this barracks revolt.

The initiative at this point passed to Díaz in the southeast. The state of Oaxaca declared rebellion on 23 October, although Díaz did not formally take over its leadership until 18 November. From his headquarters at Huajuapan de León, Díaz appealed to his old companions at arms in the Federal army to defect, presenting the insurrection as a continuation of the Liberal struggle. In Puebla, Díaz's invitation at first met with little response. At the headquarters of the Second Division in Tecamachalco, General Pedro Galván (who had commanded the state during the last months of the Reform Wars) went over to Díaz with the entire Fifteenth Regiment of Cavalry. The National Guard of Atlixco also pledged support for him, rebelling under the jefe político, Márquez Galindo (the key leader of the Montaña after Méndez).[22] Yet the strategically critical Tehuacán garrison remained loyal, providing General Alatorre with a springboard for entering and pacifying the increasingly divided state of Oaxaca. The Puebla Sierra only came out openly in rebellion in late November and early December.

The Puebla Sierra Joins the Revolt

Following the bloody suppression of the Ciudadela uprising, few pronouncements and uprisings for Díaz came from the center and south of the country, in contrast to the more generalized armed opposition to Juárez in the north. Hesitation in Puebla to joining the rebellion reflected the heavy concentration of Federal forces in the state. Méndez had shown his willingness to back any *porfirista* movement from the moment that congressional *juaristas* and *lerdistas* had allied in August 1871. But this was met, immediately, by the dispatch of a brigade of Federal troops to the Sierra under General Ceballos.[23] Moreover, the presence of the Federal Second Division at Tecamachalco, which guarded the two routes to Oaxaca, precluded support from the southeast. Finally, many district authorities in the Sierra faced problems closer to home with the violent conflicts and factionalism accompanying the division of common land.

The most acute of these conflicts occurred in Tetela's lowland territory of Jonotla where, on several occasions between February and December 1871, factions fought violently for control of the ayuntamiento (and hence over the authority to divide the municipality's commons). The principal contenders were armed highland corn farmers from Huahuaxtla and Xochitlán led by a Nahua Indian, Santiago Cientos, who, backed by forces from Xochiapulco, fought to retain access to Jonotla's extensive commons for their annual corn planting. They opposed the designs of mestizo cattle farmers, led by Joaquín López, who sought to denounce the commons as private property. The disturbances in Jonotla, along with those in Cuetzalan, were of great concern to district authorities in Tetela and

Zacapoaxtla, who took opposing positions. Tetela favored leaving Jonotla's commons intact, while Zacapoaxtla favored their sale. The revolt of La Noria offered these authorities the prospect of tightening their grip over unruly territories.[24] However, in the last count, external influences would prove more decisive in propelling district authorities from obedience to rebellion.

Since late September 1871, General Miguel Negrete had been encouraging the resurgence of local insurrectionary movements throughout the Sierra de Tulancingo and the Huasteca region of Hidalgo.[25] He also sought to resurrect old allegiances in the Puebla Sierra. In mid-October, General Hermenegildo Carrillo, jefe político of Zacapoaxtla, found evidence that a revolt was about to break out in the central Sierra under Lucas and Francisco Javier Arriaga. To preempt this, Romero Vargas permitted Carrillo to deploy two hundred men in Zacapoaxtla.[26]

Of more immediate concern than the Sierra to the state government was the menace of banditry in the south of the state (in Chiautla, Chietla, Acatlan, and Matamoros) and its suspected coordination by Negrete.[27] Romero Vargas's doubts concerning the loyalty of southern Puebla were confirmed in early November when the Atlixco garrison of National Guard disavowed the Juárez government.[28] The rebels swiftly moved south and gathered support in Matamoros. The Federal army responded quickly. By 20 November, over two thousand troops took up stations in Acatlán, Tepeji, and Chiautla to create a cordon sanitaire between Puebla's rebels and Díaz's forces in Oaxaca. Following skirmishes with Federal forces, the rebels slipped away into the vastness of the Mixteca.

By mid-November, the rumors of a general uprising in the Sierra were amply confirmed. Romero Vargas bolstered state forces in the north by a further 1,850 infantry and 125 cavalry. Half this force would be placed in Tetela de Ocampo from where two columns of 500 men would "seek out the rebels." The other half went to garrison Zacapoaxtla, where two companies of National Guard had defected behind Francisco Javier Arriaga.[29] Recognizing the seriousness of the threat from the north, Romero Vargas chose personally to lead his forces into the Sierra. He appointed Rafael Cravioto to command the Second Division of state forces and charged him with suppressing the rebellion.[30]

General Méndez finally proclaimed against the national government on 1 December 1871 from Xochiapulco. He called upon *serranos* to rise up again in defense of their rights and their *patria*.[31] On the same day, General Hermenegildo Carrillo joined two hundred other citizens of the Villa de Libres in disavowing the Juárez government. They subscribed to the Monterey plan and chose Díaz as their leader.[32] Carrillo's defection came as a great shock to Romero Vargas, who had counted on his influence on the plateau between Perote and San Andres Chalchicomula to contain any rebellion in the Sierra. Both the Sierra and the plains of Atzompa were now in full rebellion, which prompted the state executive to assume extraordinary powers.[33]

Federal and state forces in Puebla now had to wage war on two fronts. In the south, General Rocha and the Federal army continued their pursuit of the Atlixco rebels who, a month after the outbreak of the rebellion, numbered an estimated sixteen hundred cavalry and one hundred infantry.[34] Although the federal government covered the cost of the southern campaign, the state government had to meet the cost of mobilizing four thousand men for the suppression of the insurrection in the Sierra. Romero Vargas pleaded for federal financial support, claiming that more than one-half of state forces was now in rebellion, with one-half of state revenues (from the *rebajado* tax) directly entering rebel coffers.[35] He also resorted to extraordinary measures such as forced loans and the arming of prisoners and vagabonds released from Puebla's penitentiary and workhouse.[36]

The first move in any Sierra rebellion was always to attempt to take Teziutlán. On 7 December 1871 the small garrison of only fifty men fell to a superior rebel force, numbering almost four hundred, commanded by Arriaga and Carrillo. Juan Crisóstomo Bonilla, still officially jefe político of Tetela, also assisted in the taking of Teziutlán. His plea for clemency saved Teziutlán's defending force from the firing squad.[37]

A letter from a "citizen of Teziutlán" to Romero Vargas provides a taxonomy of the rebel leadership of the Sierra at this early stage of the insurrection. Leading the rebellion was General Méndez, supported by an *estado mayor* of Lucas, Bonilla, Francisco Javier Arriaga, Carrillo, Miguel Melgarejo (cacique of Altotonga), and Luis León (from Tlaxco). Next in seniority were Miguel and Mariano Arriaga from Zacapoaxtla, Luis Antonio Díaz, Anatolio and Ireneo Reyes from Xochiapulco, Francisco Agustín from Cuetzalan, Francisco Herrera from Ixtacamaxtitlán, Dionisio Leal from Cuahuigtic, and Sabino Ramos and Víctor Méndez from Tetela. Attached to this core of seasoned *serrano* infantry commanders, many of whom had fought together during the Three Years' War and the European Intervention (and in certain cases, against each other as well), was an assortment of cavalry commanders, several of whom had been "tried as bandits in earlier times."[38]

Alarmed at the loss of the strategically important and prosperous town of Teziutlán and seeking to prevent any collusion between the Sierra rebels and *porfiristas* in Veracruz, Romero Vargas ordered Rafael Cravioto to mount a massive counterattack upon the rebels. On 15 December, Cravioto arrived at the hacienda of Mazapa, just south of Xochiapulco, with a force of 985 men (510 recruited from the Sierra and the rest from the state capital). They were reinforced by a small detachment of Federal regulars commanded by General Guillermo Carbó. The rebels were estimated to have 1,500 men positioned along a line between Zacapoaxtla and Mazapa.[39] After three skirmishes in which little resistance was offered, the rebels were dislodged from their positions on the peaks around Zacapoaxtla (to which they had been laying siege) and forced to retreat to fortified positions on the heights of Apulco.[40] On the same day, General Carbó retook Teziutlán.

While Cravioto and Carbó pressed home the attack on the rebels of the central and southern Sierra, Romero Vargas ordered the arrest of senior members of the Márquez clan in Zacatlán in an attempt to preempt an insurrection, which was timed to coincide with the arrival in the southern Sierra of Porfirio Díaz and a large force of cavalry on 20–21 December.[41] Whether Díaz intended to establish a stronghold in the Puebla Sierra or merely wanted to draw General Alatorre away from his home state is unclear. In any case, the spectacular defeat of the principal rebel force in Oaxaca at San Mateo Xindihui on 22 December obliged Díaz to beat a hasty retreat. However, he arrived too late to save his brother's governorship from collapse. The Federal army occupied Oaxaca in late December, forcing Félix Díaz to take flight to the isthmus where, late in January 1872, Juchitán rebels killed and dismembered him in retribution for an earlier act of iconoclasm.[42]

The collapse of Oaxaca reduced the likelihood of any successful challenge to Juárez coming from the southeast.[43] From now on, the thrust of the insurrection came from the north. The rebellion in the Puebla Sierra became primarily defensive; the rebels served as a decoy to the Federal army and the mountains as a sanctuary for rebels from elsewhere.[44]

The Sierra Revolt

As in previous insurrections, rebel mobilization in the Sierra had a dual motive. On one hand, the rebels supported Díaz's call to arms against the illegal reelection of Juárez and defended Méndez's *cacicazgo* in the Puebla Sierra from a renewed onslaught by Federal and state forces. On the other hand, rebel leaders were determined to maintain control over their unruly and fractious districts in this period of momentous change in land ownership that accompanied the privatization of village commons. The tactics would be the same as during previous struggles. As Bonilla expressed to Méndez in March 1872, "I believe that our plan must be, as Juan (Lucas) knows, that of the time of the Empire: to await the enemy and then to come down on any one of their columns with all of our forces."[45]

In mid-December, just as the revolt in Oaxaca collapsed, the insurrection in the Puebla Sierra spread from the southern margins at Ixtacamaxtitlán to Zacatlán in the west and Papantla in the north. Papantla's National Guard battalion rebelled under the leadership of Manuel Pérez and was seconded by Méndez, Lucas, Bonilla, and Eufemio Rojas.[46] As with previous insurrections, rebels attempted to hold two axes. To the west, rebels in Zacatlán and Chignahuapan co-ordinated their campaign with allies in the Sierra de Tulancingo. In the south of the Sierra, the National

Guards of Tetela, Xochiapulco, and Cuahuigtic provided the bulk of the rebel force. As with previous insurrections, the western Sierra proved more vulnerable to external attack than the physically more impregnable southern Sierra. Zacatlán finally pronounced in late December behind Colonel Vicente Márquez.[47] Cravioto's brigade promptly engaged and dispersed Márquez's force on 31 December and pushed the rebels back to positions along the boundary with Tetela. Throughout the revolt, this western front continually faced challenges: in the south from the loyal *juarista* towns of Chignahuapan and Aquixtla; in the core of the district of Zacatlán from the rival clan to Márquez, which was led by Colonel Eraclio Sosa of Ahuacatlán; and in the north from the *juarista* stronghold of Huauchinango, which was controlled by Cravioto.

Following Márquez's coup in Zacatlán, Bonilla declared the district of Tetela to be in open rebellion on 30 December.[48] Faced with the broadening of the rebel front in the Sierra and fearing an imminent offensive on the plateau, General Carbó evacuated the Sierra. He left only small Federal garrisons at Zacatlán, Zacapoaxtla, and Teziutlán, which were backed by local National Guard. Meanwhile, Cravioto moved south to northern Tlaxcala to block a rebel advance upon the plateau. This first serious Sierra offensive since the fall of the Empire, led by Francisco Javier Arriaga and Miguel Negrete, proved to be ephemeral and resembled more a series of bandit raids upon *llanura* district capitals than a coherent plan to take the plateau. Following three defeats at Huamantla, Chalchicomula, and in the Sierra de Zongolica (where Díaz was leading the rebel force), Méndez indefinitely postponed plans for a major offensive.[49]

Méndez's refusal to join the offensive in January can probably be explained by the difficulties he was experiencing with recruitment. January, the time for tilling fields in preparation for sowing in April, usually proved to be a bad month for leading men out of the Sierra. On 22 January 1872, Tetela troops stationed on the heights of Apulco demanded two weeks' leave for just this purpose.[50] Holding large numbers of men in readiness for an offensive presented other problems. The commanders of Tetela's barrios of San Esteban and Tonalapa complained that many of the younger men were leaving their positions after having observed that men from other barrios (they mentioned Totutla, San Cristobal, and San Pedro) did not have to serve.[51]

General Rocha withdrew to Mexico City in late January so his command could be deployed to confront the northern rebel army. This took some pressure off the southern Sierra throughout February, but Cravioto and his Aquixtla ally, José María Bonilla, remained active in the area, occupying Méndez, Bonilla, and Márquez Galindo. This prevented Méndez from answering calls for help from the isolated and beleaguered rebel force at Papantla.[52] In spite of these reverses and virtual encirclement, hope for national success remained high at this time, with General Bonilla receiving regular news of Federal defeats and the southward advance of the rebel armies.[53] This encouraged a further offensive on the tableland in late February by the same commanders—Negrete, Arriaga, Betanzos, and León—as a month earlier, but this time they had reinforcements commanded by Márquez Galindo and Carrillo. This offensive foundered when the rebels failed to take the strategic town of Huamantla, which was defended by a Federal garrison under Colonel Rafael Tarbe.[54]

On 5 March 1872, General Rocha won a spectacular victory over the northern rebels at La Bufa. Alatorre then moved from Oaxaca to assume the military command of Puebla. Both actions made the rebel position in the Sierra seem precarious. Following their defeat at Huamantla in late February, Negrete and Carrillo fell back to a defensive position at Cuahuigtic, where Carrillo successfully resisted a Federal assault on 12 March.[55] Ten days later, rebel garrisons at Papantla and San Pablo fell, which dissolved the rebellion in the northern Sierra.[56] Alatorre returned to Zacapoaxtla at the end of March to supervise personally the suppression of the rebellion.[57] At the same time, Aquixtla's commander, José María Bonilla, broke through the rebel defensive line between Tonalapa, Xaltatempa, and Otlatlán and opened the way for an assault upon the rebel stronghold and headquarters at Tetela de Ocampo.

After severe fighting around the fortified rebel barrio of Otlatlán, enemy forces occupied Tetela de Ocampo.[58] However, holding Tetela offered only risks to the government, given the rebel strength at Taxcantla and the rebel sympathies of most of Tetela's subject barrios. Therefore, with news that Negrete had moved his force of eight hundred men toward Huauchinango, the government force abandoned Tetela. Cravioto went in pursuit of Negrete and soundly defeated him on 9 April.[59]

The southern Sierra front also came under intense pressure in early April when a Federal force under General Carbó pushed back the Xochiapulquenses, commanded by Francisco Dinorín, to Huahuaxtla. This was the only occasion during the revolt that Lucas was reported as acting as a rebel commander. Although, throughout the revolt, Lucas lent energetic support to the supply of rebel lines, there is no other evidence that he actually engaged in any fighting. He was not included in Lerdo's October amnesty, thereby surviving with his military rank intact.[60]

Buoyed by these successes, government forces advanced in mid-April via Tlamanca, San Pedro, and Aquixtla into the western Sierra and attacked the Márquez stronghold at Otlatlán on 21 April.[61] On 22 April, Estevan Márquez and Lauro Luna fell back to Taxcantla, where Juan Crisóstomo Bonilla concentrated forces in anticipation of a further rebel offensive.[62] The Federal commanders, Carbó and Santibañez, with their Sierra allies, Cravioto and Bonilla of Aquixtla, chose not to press their advantage, which allowed the rebels to reoccupy their positions. This hesitation reflected the renewal of the government offensive in the north against rebels in Nuevo León and Tamaulipas.[63] The suspected presence of Díaz in Tepic in April and the possibility of an alliance with Manuel Lozada also increased the government's anxiety and wariness about getting bogged down in the Puebla Sierra.[64]

Following the recall of Carbó and Santibañez to Mexico City and their replacement by General Cabañas in early May, the Federal offensive in the southern Sierra was renewed. As during previous conflicts, Federal commanders had for some time been attempting to transfer responsibility for the maintenance of security to the local population. Once again, Cenobio Cantero was instructed by the Minister of War to organize one hundred thirty men from the barrio of Atagpan, "to be independent of the Zacapoaxtla National Guard," whose commanders' rebel sympathies were well known.[65] Another veteran of earlier conflicts, Captain Valeriano Cabrera of Las Lomas, was to be found defending Zacapoaxtla with forty men against a rebel assault on 23 May.[66]

The rebels intensified mobilization of Indian communities in the districts of Zacapoaxtla and Tetela. Francisco Agustín, the Nahua commander from Cuetzalan, was reported to be forcibly recruiting soldiers in the *tierra caliente* of Tetela.[67] The lowland, largely Totonac jurisdictions of Tuzamapa, Jonotla, and Tenampulco also came under pressure for recruitment and supplies from the Papantla rebel leader, Manuel Pérez. In late May, government forces razed Tenampulco.[68]

The political consequences of this renewed mobilization of Indian communities resounded throughout the 1870s in the form of escalating inter- and intra-community conflicts and assassinations. In the short term, government efforts to build bases of local support in Zacapoaxtla probably did more to hamper than to aid the pacification of the Puebla Sierra. General Cabañas's Federal garrison in Zacapoaxtla and forward post at Apulco came under attack on at least three occasions in late May with rebels seizing officials and extorting funds from merchants resident in Xochitlán and Nauzontla.[69] This tense state of affairs in Zacapoaxtla convinced state and Federal commanders to direct their next offensive upon the southwestern flank of the Sierra through Ixtacamaxtitlán, seen as the Achilles' heel of the rebel headquarters at Taxcantla. At this time, Juan Crisóstomo Bonilla, with Lucas's help, was active in mobilizing the *tierra caliente* to ensure a steady flow of *totopo* (maize tortillas), *chilpotle, panela,* and coffee for the garrisons at Taxcantla and Cuahuigtic.[70] The most serious fighting of the Sierra rebellion was about to begin.

The first encounter between government and rebel forces on the southwestern front occurred on 25 May 1872. Carrillo, the rebel commander, reported a "splendid victory." His cavalry, reinforced by another company commanded by the future state governor, Colonel Rosendo Márquez (a *porfirista* from Jalisco), and eighty Cuahuigtic infantry under Colonel Dionisio Leal, defeated and put to flight a force of some five hundred men under the command of José María Bonilla of Aquixtla. The enemy suffered forty dead and nineteen wounded.[71] Bonilla fell back to Aquixtla to regroup and returned on 30 May greatly strengthened by the arrival of General Carbó's Federal forces. Carbó's fifteen hundred infantry and one hundred fifty cavalry scattered the eight hundred infantry that Carrillo had entrenched at Cuahuigtic. José María Bonilla was killed in the fighting, and both sides experienced heavy losses. The Federals dispersed the rebels, most of whom retreated to Taxcantla except for the five officers and over one hundred infantry who were taken prisoner.[72]

Yet again, General Carbó and the Federal force, perhaps feeling exposed in the wilderness of the southern Sierra, chose not to press home the attack. They allowed Carrillo to regain his positions at Cuahuigtic and Otlatlán within days of the defeat.[73] Juan Crisóstomo Bonilla suspected that the enemy was considering taking Taxcantla and Tetela from the east, via Huahuaxtla. He ordered this barrio to be held at all costs. Losing Huahuaxtla would leave the *tierra cálida* and the *tierra caliente* exposed to enemy extortions and would cut off the headquarters at Taxcantla from its region of supply.[74]

Fierce fighting throughout June and early July indicated the priority Juárez now gave to pacifying the Puebla Sierra.[75] On 9 June the enemy returned to Ixtacamaxtitlán with five hundred infantry, two hundred cavalry, and three pieces of artillery. Another force of equal numbers, which was intent upon displacing Carrillo from his Cuahuigtic stronghold, approached from Timixtla.[76] Fighting erupted in Zautla in mid-June. The National Guard company formed by Lucas during the previous rebellion unsuccessfully engaged Carbó's force.[77] To distract the renewed government offensive on the southwestern flank, Méndez mounted a rebel offensive in the eastern Sierra that had been at peace since the federal attempts at local recruitment in April. On 11 June a rebel force of seven hundred men (under Colonels Pérez, Martínez, Francisco Balderrábamo, and Mauricio Ruiz) succeeded in briefly taking Teziutlán only to evacuate the plaza once government cavalry reinforcements arrived.[78]

Dogged rebel strength in the eastern Sierra (at least in numbers) resulted from Méndez's efforts to counter federal recruitment by building up Nahua militia in the Tlatlauqui villages of Chignautla and Tzinacantepec.[79] This mobilization allowed these National Guard *cacicazgos* in Tzlatlauqui to remain a law unto themselves long after the formal pacification of the Sierra in August. In early July, General Carbó inflicted several defeats upon rebels in the districts of Teziutlán and Tlatlauqui. He pushed the forces commanded by Mauricio Ruiz and Miguel Melgarejo back into Veracruz.[80] At this point, Carbó considered the task of pacification completed and returned to Mexico City.

Meanwhile, General Cravioto reoccupied Aquixtla, threatening Carrillo's position at Cuahuigtic. The rebel commander held Cuahuigtic well into July and prevented a government assault on his headquarters at Taxcantla.[81] The rebels' success in holding their line in the southwest

Sierra resulted from a combination of factors. First, government forces could not match the strong defensive positions of rebel forces at Taxcantla, Cuahuigtic, and Otlatlán, which, even after successive defeats, were easily reoccupied. From these positions, the Márquez brothers (Manuel and Vicente), Carrillo, and Leal could periodically mount daring tax-gathering raids upon headtowns such as Ahuacatlán and Aquixtla. Government troops held these towns but never consolidated support in the barrios. Second, the rebel garrisons at Cuahuigtic and Taxcantla had an intricate network of supply and reinforcement stretching back into the district of Tetela. Bonilla and Lucas orchestrated this network from Taxcantla and ensured that troops had ample provisons and arms furnished by municipal cabeceras and barrios from the remotest corners of the district.[82] Bonilla even maintained a field hospital in Totutla (Huitzilan).[83]

The last major rebel movement occurred on 10 July 1872 when eight hundred infantry from Otlatlán, Tetela, and Cuahuigtic, commanded by Carrillo, León, Leal, and Manuel Márquez, attempted to retake Aquixtla. The attack failed; and, on the following day, government troops (mainly recruited from Tlaxcala) broke up the rebel force.[84] This time, the rebels did not regroup. The men returned home when they learned an amnesty had been declared on 19 July in the wake of Juárez's death.

Other rebels continued to fight. Throughout August, Sierra jefes políticos reported rebel activity: in Huauchinango, among villages bordering on Zacatlán and Papantla; in Zacapoaxtla, where Francisco Agustín still dominated Cuetzalan; in Zacatlán, where Vicente Márquez still held San Miguel Tenango (renowned since the Three Years' War for its arms foundry) and was able briefly to storm and hold Zacatlán on 22 August; in Libres, where the *municipios* of Zautla and Tepeyahualco remained in disobedience; and in Tlatlauqui, where rebels occupied a stronghold on the Cerro de Guadalupe overlooking the road to Yaonahuac.[85] The Márquez brothers of Otlatlán were among the last to accept the amnesty.

As late as 16 September 1872, Ixtacamaxtitlán and Otlatlán still had not submitted to the authority of the state government.[86] Nothing had changed five weeks later.[87] No reports were received from the district of Tetela throughout the entire period of the rebellion. Díaz finally submitted in late October when his Tetela supporters also ended their rebellion. Only late in October did Negrete, the éminence grise behind the rebellion in the Sierra, pledge support to Juárez's successor, Sebastián Lerdo de Tejada.[88]

Bonilla and the Administration of a District in Revolt

Because Lucas had decided to adhere officially to the terms of the 1870 amnesty (that required him to retire to private life), Juan Crisóstomo Bonilla, the jefe político of Puebla at the time of the outbreak of the revolt, was the military commander most responsible for coordinating the revolt of La Noria in the Puebla Sierra. A bundle of correspondence concerning the day-to-day administration of Tetela during the revolt, between Bonilla's headquarters at Taxcantla and Manuel Vázquez in Tetela de Ocampo, charged with the civil government of the district, offers clues for why this territory proved so effective in sustaining the revolts over such a prolonged period.[89] From the instructions received from Bonilla at Taxcantla and the communications that Vázquez received from subaltern military commanders and village authorities, it is possible to piece together how the war effort was sustained and the district's political order preserved and reinforced over the ten months of insurrection.

Many factors demonstrate how firmly established were personal and political relationships from before the outbreak of the revolt: the familiarity of much of the correspondence; the use of Christian names and terms of endearment; the evidence of a widespread network of co-parenthood and godparenthood; the exchange of gifts, especially aguardiente and cane syrup; and the skill in dealing with Nahua village leaders.[90] To Bonilla and Vázquez was sent correspondence from military commanders and village authorities throughout the Puebla Sierra, from rebel leaders in the neighboring sierras of Veracruz and Oaxaca, and from leaders as far afield as Jalisco, Durango, and Nuevo León. This steady flow of military intelligence from an archipelago of military colonies protecting the southern and eastern flanks of the district, from a more distant circle of allies in neighboring districts, and from an outer ring of allies in Hidalgo, Veracruz, and Tlaxcala, accounts for the longevity of the revolt in the Puebla Sierra.

The ties linking the front in the southern part of Tetela with village authorities in the center and the north of the district were also quite as intense and intimate. Without material support from these allies, the revolt would have collapsed within weeks. Military recruitment was confined to the barrios in the center and along the southern margins of the district. In exchange for exemption from military service and gifts, such as musical instruments for newly formed *cuerpos filarmónicos*, the Nahua and Totonac communities of the north (in the municipalities of San Esteban Cuautempan, Huitzilan, Zapotitlán, Jonotla, Tuzamapa, and Tenampulco) were expected to provide porters, taxes, maintenance of a field hospital, and prodigious amounts of *totopo*, *panela*, coffee, *chilpotle*, and aguardiente.

How did the district command at Tetela and Taxcantla succeed in securing this surplus? A few of the mechanisms are illustrative. The revolt of La Noria broke out in the Sierra just as the hiatus accompanying the application of the *desamortización* was reaching its height. After a series of violent upheavals late in 1871, the municipalities of Jonotla and Tuzamapa were granted the right to prevent their common lands and recently granted ejidos from being claimed by nonresidents or by people from beyond the district.[91] This concession was intended to block a potentially large-scale transfer of common land into private ownership that would have benefited coffee planters and merchants from Cuetzalan and Zacapoaxtla. Had this occurred, the secession of these municipalities to join the district of Zacapoaxtla (to compensate for Xochiapulco's annexation by Tetela in 1870) would almost certainly have resulted.[92] Without the revenues and, above all, food supplies from Jonotla and Tuzamapa, Tetela's capacity to sustain the insurrection would have been severely curtailed. Hence, authorities in Jonotla and Tuzamapa traded obedience and hefty tributes for Tetela's respect for their autonomy and protection against the challenge from Zacapoaxtla.

Jonotla and Tuzamapa's circumspection toward the *desamortización* contrasts with the comparatively unrestrained privatization of common land in the sugar-rich municipalities of San Esteban, Zapotitlán, and Huitzilan. This had benefited not only the Tetelenses, who controlled the commerce in *panela* and aguardiente, but also many local families, who had become the beneficiaries of common land privatization in their jurisdictions. These local non-Indians and "rich Indians" were available to serve as military commanders, village secretaries, and schoolmasters, which reinforced ties of patronage between the district capital and municipal cabeceras.[93] In exchange for their obedience and material support during military campaigns and elections, these local clientele of the Tetelenses expected the *jefatura* to recognize and defend their gains and to guarantee exemption from any military service that might disrupt their businesses. Such guarantees also helped local military commanders in these municipalities to retain some credit among heavily taxed and commercially exploited villagers.

Throughout the rebellion, Bonilla carefully balanced the power of non-Indian entrepreneurs and village secretaries with the traditional network of Indian village officeholders. He was particularly fastidious in the appointment of prominent Indians as the local military commanders. Only when the external pressures upon villages threatened to become too great, as in the case of the Totonac community of Totutla (a subject barrio of Nahua Huitzilan), did Bonilla advise that the village be placed under a non-Indian political authority. In this case, the object of replacing the Indian commander by a *comandante de razón* was to preempt an anticipated uprising from villagers enraged by their excessive tax burden.[94] Usually, such a drastic measure was unnecessary. In most other Indian communities throughout the district, military command was exercised by local Indian *principales*.

If in his appointment of Indians to village military commands Bonilla was sensitive to their traditions of self-government, he was also responsive to the desire for material self-improvement which these *caciquillos* were acquiring during this period of commercial expansion. In April 1872, Miguel Cipriano, the Nahua military commander of Huitzilan, wrote to Bonilla's treasurer, Gregorio Zamítez, emphasizing that he would need the full support of the *jefatura* to be able to resist the blandishments of "the enemy" (merchants from Zacapoaxtla). He requested Zamítez to send a tiler from Tetela to help with the improvement of his house on the main square. This request was handled promptly.[95] Throughout the rebellion, the flow of taxes, supplies, and loyalty to the district authorities was encouraged by regular tours of visitation, even to the remotest of barrios, by Generals Méndez and Lucas. Discipline and obedience were further reinforced by regular patriotic musters of local units of the Ejército Restaurador de la Libertad in the municipal cabeceras and by the equipping of municipal bands with sheet music and modern wind instruments.

Conclusion

If Díaz's principal objective in the revolt of La Noria was to avoid major confrontations with the Federal army and to debilitate and demoralize the regime by organizing multiple points of resistance, then the performance of Puebla's *serranos* accorded well with his strategy. No other region of Mexico absorbed so many Federal and state forces over such a protracted period. Lacking support in his own state, Díaz was left with the option of opening a broader front from a steadfastly loyal and militarily effective territory in the Mexican southeast. He was able to capitalize on this option in 1876.

What did the Sierra's leaders achieve from ten months of rebellion? When they laid down their arms between August and October 1872, the rebels held stronger positions throughout the southern Sierra than they had when the rebellion began in December 1871 (as had also been the case after the previous amnesty in June 1870). In particular, the Márquez brothers of Otlatlán, in close collaboration with Méndez and Bonilla, had created a *cacicazgo* in the western Sierra that endured until shortly after the death of Venustiano Carranza in 1920. Likewise, Bonilla and Lucas's meticulous organization of the district of Tetela, the center of the rebellion, further reinforced the importance of the territorial heartland of the Montaña, which enabled Tetela to serve as the springboard for the revolt in 1876.

In spite of the difficulties with recruitment, desertions, and barrio disobedience, participation in the rebellion of La Noria enabled the Montaña to increase its control over even the remotest part of the district of Tetela, and beyond. The success of this enterprise was based on Lucas's construction of an impregnable archipelago of militarized villages around Tetela's southern boundaries, which stretched from Xaltatempa, in the west, through Cuahuigtic, Taxcantla, northern Zautla, and Xochiapulco to Huahuaxtla in the east. From this core, Bonilla and Méndez consolidated alliances across the district boundaries, in particular with Vicente Márquez of Zacatlán, Francisco Agustín of Cuetzalan, and with their former enemies, the village National Guard *cabecillas* of southern Zacapoaxtla,

Tlatlauqui, and Teziutlán. Tetela's alliances even extended across state boundaries to Veracruz, reaching the Pérez *cacicazgo* of Papantla and Miguel Melgarejo's bailiwick in Altotonga.

Apart from extending these political and military friendships, the rebellion also served to quell serious unrest in the *tierra caliente* of Tetela, which resulted from the division of village commons and the penetration of Jonotla, Tuzamapa, and Tenampulco by rival groups of migrant commercial farmers and corn planters from the district of Zacapoaxtla. Indeed, the revolt provided a means for Tetela's leadership to restore and strengthen the political and territorial integrity of the district, which had been on the verge of disintegration in the autumn of 1871.

12

Conciliation and Violence, 1872–1875

The harsh terms of the amnesty of 27 July 1872 stripped rebels of their rank, decorations, weapons, and all credits upon the treasury. It specified that the rebels could not return to their posts and ordered them to report to their local jefes políticos for their names to be passed on to the Ministry of War.[1] The *porfiristas* also lost ground on the national level as former *juaristas* moved into the *lerdista* camp. The remaining Díaz supporters in the congress were now completely out in the political cold, with no possibility of resurrecting the alliances that had given them appreciable congressional strength before the revolt of La Noria. Díaz's followers in the Puebla Sierra must have wondered whether they had made the wrong political choice. They now confronted a governor more firmly installed than ever, whose patron occupied the National Palace. This realization helped Romero Vargas in his renewed efforts to conciliate the Montaña.

Díaz's surrender to Generals Florentino Carrillo and Ignacio Mejía in Durango in October 1872 ended a rebellion that had lasted over a year. The Republic was again superficially at peace.[2] Yet, in the Puebla Sierra, the interlude between the revolt of La Noria and Díaz's revolution of Tuxtepec in 1876 was anything but tranquil. Village rebellions, political assassinations, and National Guard mobilizations occurred frequently, particularly in the heartland of Lucas's influence, the barrios along the southern edge of the Sierra within the districts of Alatriste, Tetela, Zacapoaxtla, Tlatlauqui, and Teziutlán.

During the previous two decades, fighting in the Sierra was confined, in large part, to organized military campaigns. During the Lerdo presidency, violence assumed an altogether more sinister pattern characterized by village factionalism, intimidation, and assassinations. In part, this pattern came as a consequence of the changing context of state and federal politics resulting from Juárez's death and Díaz's ignominious forced retirement from politics. In the absence of these two protagonists, Puebla's two parties—the Llanura and the Montaña—fragmented as factions competed for patronage from Romero Vargas, who was now more strongly entrenched than any Puebla executive since the revolution of Ayutla.

Conciliation, Elections, and the Renewal of Conflict

The Lerdo regime in the state of Puebla began peacefully. The presidential elections of October 1872, which coincided with Lerdo's amnesty, passed quietly.[3] This was helped by the moderate application of the draconian terms of the amnesty in the Puebla Sierra. Leading rebel commanders retained their ranks and even their commands, and many received high civilian posts. Romero Vargas made every effort to conciliate the opposition. In a speech on 6 August 1872, he called for peace and reconciliation among the "great Liberal family." His desire to conciliate his enemies, particularly the Montaña, can be seen in his choice of jefes políticos for the Sierra districts. Tetela went to Alberto de Santa Fé, a radical Liberal from the state capital, who nevertheless had been a staunch *mendecista* during the revolt of La Noria. Zacapoaxtla went to Hermenegildo Carrillo, who, after Méndez, was the most important rebel commander during the La Noria insurrection.[4] Later, in November 1873, Zacapoaxtla was transferred to Francisco Javier Arriaga, a rebel leader on three occasions since the restoration of the Republic in 1867.[5] The crucial district of Teziutlán went to Romero Vargas's nephew, Beníto Marín, a decision soon to have fatal consequences.[6]

Romero Vargas's determination to conciliate his enemies and to restore confidence in his leadership can also be seen in the decrees governing the conduct of municipal elections and returning the control of the National Guard tax to local councils.[7] The governor intended both provisions to curtail the power of the jefes políticos, especially their control over the district National Guard battalions, and to strengthen municipal autonomy. The elections for ayuntamientos in September and for state deputies and senators in December–January 1872–73 passed quietly.[8] Again, the governor's desire for conciliation appeared evident in the bipartisan results. Antonio Méndez, brother of General Méndez, won the election in Tetela. Manuel Márquez, brother of Vicente Márquez (both prominent Noria rebels and members of the Montaña), was elected deputy for Zacatlán. Loyal *romeristas* won seats in Huauchinango (Simón Cravioto), Zacapoaxtla (Tirso Cordova, state secretary and editor of the *Periódico Oficial*), Teziutlán (Luciano Cabañas), and Tlatlauqui (Manuel Vargas).[9]

Just as Romero Vargas appeared to be succeeding in placating Montaña-Llanura rivalries through the judicious use of electoral patronage, the political order on the local level once more became strained. The elections marked the beginning of a cycle of political violence that would continue until Díaz's call to arms in 1876. Order in the villages of the Puebla Sierra depended upon effective management by jefes políticos and caciques (such as Lucas) of the hierarchy of authority and obedience between barrios, *pueblos sujetos,* municipal cabeceras, and the district capital. General Bonilla's success in holding out for eight months during the revolt of

La Noria rested upon his efficient management of the district of Tetela. But rebel success in Tetela came at the price of a deterioration of political order in the neighboring districts of Zacapoaxtla and, especially, Tlatlauqui.

Since the revolution of Ayutla, Tlatlauqui, more than any other Sierra district, had proved peculiarly vulnerable to external influences. In part, this resulted from unresolved boundary conflicts with its economically more dynamic neighbors, Zacapoaxtla and Teziutlán. In addition, leaders from beyond the Sierra frequently sought to gain a foothold in the southern Sierra by organizing forces in Tlatlauqui's villages to confront rebels in Zacapoaxtla and Tetela or to defend Teziutlán. These efforts undermined Tlatlauqui's political stability.

During the rebellion of La Noria, this trend was further accentuated by the decision of General Carrillo and Miguel Melgarejo, who for a decade had organized Tlatlauqui's villages on behalf of the state and central governments, to join the revolt. From serving the constituted authorities as mercenaries for short periods, Tlatlauqui's villages now became rebel colonies, subject to the whims of National Guard captains appointed by the rebel headquarters at Taxcantla. This not only undermined the authority of Tlatlauqui's district capital over its villages but also marginalized Cenobio Cantero, the leader who for almost two decades had exercised the greatest influence upon the villages in this area. During the revolt of La Noria, this external intervention reached an extreme when Tetcla's rebels imprisoned the entire district leadership: Tlatlauqui's jefe político (Justo Saborido), municipal syndic, and vice president remained in Xochiapulco's jail for several months.[10]

On 31 December 1872, election day for National Guard commanders, Cenobio Cantero was brutally murdered. As captain of Atagpan's National Guard company, Cantero had served the Conservatives during the Three Years' War, recruited forces in support of the Europeans during the Intervention, and helped the state government with the suppression of insurrections in the Sierra since 1867. He was valued for his ability to mobilize and deploy Indians from the communities to the east and north of Zacapoaxtla and neighboring Tlatlauqui as a counterpoise to the Méndez-Lucas *cacicazgo* in Xochiapulco and Tetela. His death marked the beginning of a process of political decomposition within Zacapoaxtla, Tlatlauqui, and Teziutlán that continued well into the 1880s, a testimony to Cantero's importance in disciplining this area.

Cantero was killed by six shots and twenty-eight bayonet lunges "by six men dressed in the style of Indians from Tzinacantepec," a barrio within the jurisdiction of Tlatlauqui.[11] General Carrillo's's report on the crime confirmed that the six assassins came from Tzinacantepec led by one Juan Tamariz, from Atagpan, Cantero's own barrio.[12] Cantero's supporters believed that Méndez and Lucas (and by association Carrillo) were behind the assassination. In their judgment, Cantero had died because he had remained "faithful to the orders of the Government, for many years, rebuffing the invitations, promises, and threats employed by the revolutionary band to attract him to their side." Cantero's secretary, Anatolio Flores, warned that "one of the principal obstacles to the revolution has been removed."[13]

The Escalation of Violence in the Southern Sierra

Cantero's murder ushered in a wave of assassinations of local leaders. The recrudescence of political violence in the Sierra coincided with Díaz's return from exile to reside at the Rancho de la Candelaria, near Tlacotalpan. (He arrived during the festival of La Candelaria when cotton growers and merchants flocked to Tlacotalpan from the entire Costa de Sotavento as well as the highlands of Puebla and Oaxaca.) Díaz could not have chosen a better location for gathering information and maintaining links with his friends throughout the southeast. Although formally announcing his retirement from politics, Díaz immediately began reestablishing contacts that would serve him three years hence in the revolution of Tuxtepec. He wrote to Lucas inviting him to visit him on his sugarcane ranch.[14]

The disturbances to public order in the southern Sierra continued. Late in March, Indians from the barrios of Chignautla (Teziutlán) and Tzinacantepec (Tlatlauqui) rose up and surrounded the district capital in response to the arrest of four Indians accused of Cantero's assassination. Bonilla and Lucas persuaded the rebels to return to their homes. However, there was little prospect for peace since the Chignautla rebels had returned home carrying their weapons.[15]

Two months later, Captain Antonio Conde and Nahua National Guards from Chignautla, numbering between one and two hundred, attacked Teziutlán. They captured and wounded the *romerista* jefe político, Benito Marín, who later died from his wounds.[16] This time, the assassins fled with all the arms and ammunition they could carry to Xochiapulco, from where Romero Vargas and Alberto de Santa Fé, using Lucas's influence, unsuccessfully sought to have them removed.[17] The governor then placed Teziutlán under Colonel Manuel Camacho, a local man (unlike Marín), who proved to be a ruthless leader of the district until he was toppled during the revolution of Tuxtepec.[18]

The electoral calendar continued throughout June and July 1873. Results for the federal legislature and the state governorship included: Hermenegildo Carrillo for Zacapoaxtla, Emilio Velasco for Tetela (where Bonilla acted as president of the electoral college), Ramón Márquez Galindo for Zacatlán, Rafael Cravioto for Huauchinango, and Rafael Martínez de la Torre for Teziutlán. The bipartisan selection from the Sierra offered further evidence that Romero Vargas was continuing to conciliate the Montaña.[19] However, national political priorities were soon to complicate the governor's efforts to deal with his *serrano* opponents.

Seemingly oblivious to national sensibilities, President Lerdo determined to elevate the Reform Laws to constitutional provisions, thereby reopening conflicts that had remained dormant since the end of the Reform Wars. Particularly offensive were the laws that pertained to matters of conscience and limited the public role of the Church: religious toleration, compulsory secular primary education, restrictions on religious festivals and processions, limitations upon bell-ringing, the prohibition on wearing clerical dress in public, the civil register of births, deaths, and marriages, and the proscription of religious vows and suppression of religious orders. Hitherto, these laws had been honored largely in the breach, particularly in Tlatlauqui, the ancient center of the Franciscan evangelization of the Puebla Sierra, where religious festivals continued to be celebrated with considerable exuberance and, often, disorder.

Rigorous application of the religious clauses of the Reform Laws could not have come at a worse time to the southern Sierra. District authorities already confronted widespread disobedience from subject barrios where National Guard companies had become a law unto themselves. Tlatlauqui's correspondent for *El Monitor Republicano* reported on the response of the barrio of Teteles (near Tlatlauqui) to the arrival by post of the decrees ordering the enforcement of the anti-clerical laws. On receiving the laws, the ayuntamiento and other public employees met publicly to pledge to obey the constitution. On the next day, when the excommunications arrived, the same officials retracted their oaths. They paraded the act of disavowal in a procession, accompanied by music, rockets, and bell-ringing. In the main square, the laws were then burned to the shouts of "Death to the heretics! Death to the Masons!"

The *Monitor* correspondent catalogued an upsurge of religious sentiment throughout the district, as priests and *beatos* led pilgrimages and processions, which were backed by hundreds of women.[20] He was convinced that the state governor secretly was arming and encouraging local National Guard commanders opposed to the Reform Laws, such as Miguel Justo of Tzinacantepec and Manuel Amador of Yaonahuac, against the *mendecista* commanders, such as Antonio Conde of Chignautla (Marín's assassin). These village militias daily increased their arms and recently had acquired lead and gunpowder from Papantla. In Yaonahuac, where the correspondent suspected the preparations for the rebellion to be centered, two municipal officials had recently been assassinated. Apart from arming and promoting village National Guard captains, the *Monitor* correspondent reported how Romero Vargas was also encouraging religious devotion, by "giving the rebels processional candlesticks, lamps, crosses, and musical instruments" as a means of combating Tetela and Xochiapulco's secularizing influences.[21]

Apart from pandering to anti-Liberal fanaticism, Romero Vargas continued to explore the potential of conciliation and patronage as a means for undermining the hold of the Montaña over the southern Sierra. In November

1873 he appointed Francisco Javier Arriaga, longtime rebel and *mendecista*, to the district of Zacapoaxtla.[22] Arriaga's project (mentioned at the outbreak of the rebellion in November 1869) of uniting the plateau with the river Tecolutla by an elaborate and costly system of roads, bridges, and canals also received support from Romero Vargas.[23] To finance this ambitious program of public works, Arriaga introduced a head tax with prison sentences for non-payment.

In exchange for state government backing, Arriaga was expected to disarm and demobilize Zacapoaxtla's National Guard, a task he carried out with relish. This developmentalist visionary believed that what the district now needed were work gangs of Indians to build roads, not troublesome Guardsmen. Resentment among the Indian population about the unconstitutional taxation and labor demands (compulsory labor services had been abolished in the 1857 constitution) contributed to their support for the Plan de Tuxtepec in the district, particularly among the followers of Francisco Agustín in Cuetzalan.[24]

Romero Vargas's opportunism in the Sierra incurred certain risks. Giving the Guardsmen a free hand in Tlatlauqui meant exposing the constitutional civil authorities to intimidation, forced removal, and even assassination. The governor's decision to grant jefes políticos the power to impose municipal officers was intended to respond to this. In November 1873 the principle of untrammeled municipal democracy was abandoned in favor of a system in which jefes políticos would be entitled to replace ineffectual or disobedient municipal authorities with persons of confidence. Tlatlauqui and Zacapoaxtla received mention as two districts in which such measures might well be necessary.[25]

Although Romero Vargas's dispensation of patronage and involvement in local factional disputes succeeded in certain villages in neutralizing the influence of the Montaña in the southeastern Sierra, matters could easily get out of hand, as events in Tzinacantepec in January 1874 revealed. To undermine the influence of the Xochiapulquenses in the municipality, the state government donated 2,000 pesos of *rebajado* tax to help the Indians rebuild their chapel that had been burned during the revolt of La Noria. Upon completion of the work, "the jefe político, the ayuntamientos of all the municipalities, a large number of employees, and many private citizens" were invited to Tzinacantepec to celebrate with a fiesta on 22 December. The festival included processions, music, dances, fireworks, and bell-ringing followed by religious ceremonies until late in the evening, when the majority of the Indians had become intoxicated by *chiringuito* and *tepache* (rural alcoholic beverages).

Notwithstanding this merriment, and apart from a few insults directed at the *gente de razón*, whom the Indians called *coyotes*, the day passed without disorder. However, after nightfall the National Guard commander sent patrols throughout the barrios, where they committed a "series of scandals and abuses" and forced many families to flee. Personal enemies of the National Guard commander were disturbed in their homes, and some were severely beaten. One man, Jacinto Roque, died from his wounds. The witness reported that these conflicts resulted from "the profound hatred which all Indians profess toward white people." The events in Tzinacantepec were repeated throughout the district, with the greatest intensity in the barrios of Chignautla, Atempan, Yaonahuac, and much of the *tierra caliente*.[26]

Local disorders continued into 1874 throughout the Sierra. The priest of Aquixtla (Alatriste), Luis Bonilla, was accused of gathering an armed following against the civil authority. The local National Guard broke up this movement.[27] A more serious conflict arose at Atempan, a municipality disputed by Teziutlán and Tlatlauqui. Captain José María Díaz, the *jefe de armas* (a new term which came to be associated with Gabriel Barrios's rule during the 1920s) of Atempan, had requested help from the jefe político of Tlatlauqui to confront a force of National Guard under Captain Conde from Chignautla (Teziutlán), who "had sought to disarm the Atempan garrison." The jefe político of Tlatlauqui sent Captain Andrés Mirón with fifty men to confront Conde's force. In the ensuing skirmish three officers were killed, fifteen soldiers were wounded, and thirty-seven were taken prisoner and sent to Teziutlán.[28] The opposition press held Manuel Camacho, jefe político of Teziutlán, responsible for the bloodshed. It was on his orders that Conde had marched to disarm the Atempan Guards and prevent the village from seceding to join Tlatlauqui.[29]

The Atempan incident became a cause célèbre in the national press. Mexico City's *El Monitor Republicano* and *El Eco de Ambos Mundos* and Puebla's *El Constitucional* claimed that over fifty Indians had lost their lives as a consequence of a concerted campaign by the jefes políticos of Zacapoaxtla, Tlatlauqui, and Teziutlán to stamp out the National Guard *cacicazgos*. Prominent *porfirista* congressman José Francisco de Zamacona argued that the decision of the Teziutlán authorities to disarm these men and to detain their commanders, on the mere rumor of a conspiracy, was as provocative as it was unconstitutional. He reminded everyone that Mexican citizens had the right to bear arms and belong to the National Guard. José María Díaz of Atempan and other village commanders had therefore been justified in resisting arrest and disarmament.[30]

Violence continued over the second half of 1874 during the gubernatorial elections, in which Romero Vargas won a resounding victory (with 101,426 votes against a combined total of 8,000 votes for twenty-one rival candidates). Méndez received a mere 885 votes, which demonstrated how the Montaña had dissolved as an electoral force. Romero Vargas's strategy of buying off former enemies with *jefaturas*, military commands, state and federal deputyships, and municipal presidencies, and of disarming the village militias that had served as the Montaña electoral machine, appeared to have been a resounding success, whatever the costs in local violence.[31]

Bloody local conflicts continued in the southern Sierra into 1875, often involving armed Indians from Tzinacantepec, which was considered the "Xochiapulco" of the 1870s. News of these disorders regularly appeared in national newspapers where they were presented as part of a renewed Montaña challenge to the Romero Vargas governorship.[32] It fell to Alberto de Santa Fé, jefe político of Tetela, to attempt to convince Lucas to use his influence to curb these disorders and to persuade villages to accept Romero Vargas's new order in the Sierra. Santa Fé warned Lucas that these "little provocations" (*escandalitos*) might serve as an excuse for a Federal force to intervene in the Sierra, intimating that Xochiapulco might become the target. He urged Lucas to persuade villagers to chose their electors and to help make Tetela a viable electoral district. Particularly, he encouraged Lucas to establish direct correspondence with President Lerdo, who, Santa Fé assured Lucas, held the Nahua cacique in great respect.[33]

Evidently, Lucas remained active in the electoral politics of the district, although, to the jefe político, Lucas was not active enough. Romero Vargas's constitutional reforms, especially those limiting municipal autonomy and permitting jefes políticos to impose municipal authorities, had removed any basis for a competitive electoral system. Moreover, throughout the Lerdo regime, Tetela's electoral status was kept deliberately uncertain. The district's electors were obliged to travel to electoral colleges at Aquixtla or Zacapoaxtla, and electoral results from Tetela on several occasions were annulled.[34] In the elections for federal deputies in July 1875, a lawyer from Puebla, Joaquin Alcalde (a friend of Santa Fé and a *lerdista*) was elected to the district of Tetela. Civilian radicals from the state capital had now displaced the Montaña in their own territory. Also worrying to the Montaña was Zacapoaxtla's choice of Pablo Urrutia as jefe político, an old enemy of the Montaña and Xochiapulco. Under these unfavorable circumstances, all the Montaña could do was to await the next opportunity to mount a rebellion.[35]

Romero Vargas's constitutional reforms culminated in May 1875 in a law that created new, highly centralized state "public security" forces to replace the democratic and decentralized National Guard envisaged by the law of 1861. The new law replaced the election of captains by their companies with the appointment of officers by the governor. It also established a central inspector of state forces, named by the governor, with powers to remove officers at will.[36] The days of the autonomous village National Guard company had ended.

Conclusion

During the Lerdo regime, Romero Vargas attempted various strategies to undermine the National Guard network that formed the basis of Montaña power in the Sierra and that threatened his control of the state. Yet, in the end, he failed to make significant inroads into a factionalized political terrain. At first, the governor used his powers of nomination of jefes políticos to conciliate his opponents through patronage. He hoped to detach them from their allegiance to the Montaña high command (Méndez, Bonilla, and Lucas). This strategy succeeded only in the short term, by eliminating electoral opposition to his reelection in 1874. But in the longer term, conciliation failed. In 1876 most of his appointees—Hermenegildo Carrillo, Alberto de Santa Fé, Ramón Márquez Galindo, the Márquez brothers of Otlatlán, Rafael Cravioto—joined the Tuxtepec revolt against Lerdo, fresh from the command of their districts.

At first, Romero Vargas combined this patronage at the district level with an attempt to remove an important element in the jefe político's authority: his control of the National Guard. Instead, ayuntamientos were given control of National Guard companies and of the *rebajado* tax and were made directly answerable to the governor. Romero Vargas also involved himself in a risky strategy that encouraged the revival of the Catholic cult as a means of undercutting the secularizing influence of the Montaña's network of schoolteachers. The governor's support for church building and religious festivals coincided with the national application of the anti-clerical clauses of the Reform Wars. This policy of restoring an "old order" of communal political and ceremonial autonomy on the local level backfired. Local National Guard *cabecillas* proved impossible to control while popular religiosity, after so many decades of neglect, soon got completely out of hand. Moreover, the removal of the jefe político's moderating influence upon village politics and religious expression intensified local factional violence and threatened to upset the political order in much of the southern Sierra.

Romero Vargas's response to the breakdown of order in the southern Sierra was to tighten the jefes políticos' control over municipalities, giving them the power to nominate local government officers. Then, early in 1874, he ordered the jefes políticos of Zacapoaxtla, Tlatlauqui, and Teziutlán to demobilize and disarm those village National Guard companies that still retained a degree of autonomy. However, these policies of concentrating the authority of jefes políticos, disarming the villages he suspected of sympathizing with the Montaña, and buying the favor of the Montaña's former allies greatly exacerbated local factionalism and increased the level of violence. They also left the villages once more defenseless in the face of Liberal reforms and increased their propensity to answer Díaz's call to revolt in 1876.

13

The Revolution of Tuxtepec and the Montaña in Power, 1876–1880

The anticipated reelection in 1876 of Sebastian Lerdo de Tejada as President of the Republic provoked a rash of uprisings, much as the reelection of Juárez had done in 1871. This time, the presidential incumbent confronted not only *porfiristas* but also the clergy and Catholics, who were enraged by the enforcement of the religious laws, and Conservatives, who were frustrated by a decade of political exclusion. Lerdo also faced disloyalty in his own camp when José María Iglesias, the president of the supreme court, became a rival candidate.[1] Discontent was also rife in the Federal army, where many officers had been unhappy about being ordered to suppress the Lozada uprising and then the Cristero rebellions in Jalisco and Michoacán.[2] Porfirio Díaz neither authorized nor orchestrated this discontent. Rather, his genius was to choose the right moment to take the initiative and assume leadership of numerous disparate local uprisings.

Díaz left Veracruz late in December 1875, accompanied by General Manuel González, aboard the British Atlantic packet, *La Córsica*. The ship was bound for Europe, but Díaz disembarked at Brownsville, Texas. Two months later, accompanied by four hundred poorly armed men, Díaz crossed into Mexico, attacking the port of Matamoros.[3] By the time the city fell in early May, several rebel movements in southern Mexico were already well under way, in accord with Díaz's strategy of encouraging multiple centers of revolt.

The Tuxtepec Revolution in Puebla

The opportunistic and ideologically eclectic character of the opposition to Lerdo was reflected in the rebel movements that surfaced in the Puebla Sierra from December 1875. Unrest and rumors of uprisings in the Sierra had persisted throughout Lerdo's presidency. In 1875 the Catholic press had predicted that local uprisings of enraged Catholics would coalesce into a general revolt. The first warning of insurrection came on 15 September, when forces from Xochiapulco attempted, unsuccessfully, to capture the Apulco aguardiente factory, strategically situated at the bridge dividing Zacapoaxtla's *tierra fría* from the *tierra caliente*.[4] General Hermenegildo Carrillo, whom Díaz had chosen to lead the revolt in the Sierra, denied involvement in this movement, but he must already have been preparing for the revolt he would lead in January 1876.

Díaz chose the Puebla Sierra as the cradle for the revolt in the southeast because of its proven strategic value and the common belief, trumpeted for years by *El Monitor Republicano*, that the *serranos* were always poised for revolt against Romero Vargas, whom they regarded as a tyrannical governor. In his memoirs, General Ireneo Paz recalls being sent by Díaz to Puebla to prepare the ground for the uprising.[5] His task was to convince the wealthy Poblano lawyer and landowner, Joaquín Ruiz, to persuade his fellow landowners to provide financial support for the rebellion. With widespread discontent in the city of Puebla and the hacienda districts of the central plateau caused by excessive taxation, Díaz and Paz felt that their chances for success were good.[6]

Choosing to ignore Carrillo's pronouncement against the regime in January, the *Periódico Oficial* attempted to play down the disturbances in the Sierra while the governor made desperate attempts to retain Lucas's loyalty. However, when Fidencio Hernández rebelled in Oaxaca in early February, provoking the declaration of a national state of emergency, Romero Vargas decided personally to lead a force of eight hundred cavalry into the Sierra in a preemptive move.[7]

Juan Nepomuceno Méndez, whom Díaz had appointed as general in chief of the Ejército Popular Constitucionalista, Linea del Oriente, had already established a headquarters at Taxcantla equipped with a printing press, munitions factory, and foundry. By late February the rebels had seized several important Sierra towns, which drove Romero Vargas to take desperate measures. He levied a tax on all fixed and mobile capital and called up the five battalions of the "old National Guard" that he had demobilized over the previous four years.[8] As a Montaña creation, calling up the National Guard had its risks. But the governor had little choice, in the face of an uprising of disgruntled landowners in the central valley of Puebla under General José María Coutolenc. Starting with a mere seventy-five peons from his own estate at Tecamachalco, Coutolenc's insurrection quickly attracted other landowners and local leaders. Moreover, the entry of the cavalry commander, Antonio Rodríguez Bocardo, caudillo of the Llanos de Atzompa, gave the rebels access to this vital stepping stone for any Sierra offensive on the plateau.[9]

Romero Vargas's offensive strike into the Sierra prevented the two rebel forces from meeting. Coutolenc and Rodríguez Bocardo moved southeast to meet up with forces from Oaxaca at Tehuacán, where, on 31 March, they were defeated by General Loaeza.[10] Coutolenc turned west to seek sanctuary and forage on the haciendas of eastern Morelos while Rodríguez Bocardo went north to offer his services to the Sierra rebels.

With the revolt on the plateau temporarily crushed, the initiative passed back to the Sierra. During April and May, the Sierra rebels mounted daring raids on the Mexico-to-Veracruz railway.[11] *Serrano* infantry operated on the plateau at a considerable disadvantage in the face of the more mobile and better armed Federal cavalry, as revealed in two bloody defeats in April and May at Libres.[12] Carrillo fell back to the relative safety of the Sierra between Zacapoaxtla and Altotonga, from where he continued to organize a force of thirteen to fifteen hundred men until he returned to the plateau for the battle of Tecoac in November 1876.[13]

As with previous wars and insurrections in the Puebla region, differences marked the nature of forces and strategy between the infantry of the Sierra and the cavalry of the plateau. The infantry remained reluctant to abandon the security of the mountains and the cavalry needed to keep on the move, both to satisfy the horses' voracious appetite for forage and to escape the equally mobile government forces. Coordinating these two forces proved difficult, compounded by rivalries between chieftains.[14]

With Carrillo's advance upon the plateau blocked, fighting continued in the western Sierra along the Tlaxco-Chignahuapan-Zacatlán axis. In late March, General Ramón Márquez Galindo took Zacatlán, where he was joined by Rafael Cravioto. In spite of commanding fourteen hundred men, these former enemies failed to meet up on the plateau with Miguel Negrete, who was leading forces from the Sierra de Tulancingo. Márquez Galindo and Cravioto endured a series of crippling defeats, one resulting in the death of Rodríguez Bocardo. Coupled with Carrillo's defeat at Libres, any hope of a successful *serrano* offensive on the plateau was now dashed in the short term.[15]

With the insurrection seemingly defeated in the western and southern Sierra, the initiative passed to the central valley and south of the state, where General Coutolenc regrouped forces numbering some two thousand cavalry and infantry, mainly recruited from the state capital. This unit was reinforced by Luis Mier y Terán with men from Veracruz. Fidencio Hernández controlled much of Oaxaca, but would not move out of the state. Hence, the rebels on the Puebla plateau now looked to be the most likely force to tip the military balance in southeastern Mexico in Díaz's favor.[16]

Rebel forces from Puebla, Veracruz, and Oaxaca gathered throughout May 1876 behind Coutolenc, Mier, and Hernández in preparation for the long-awaited offensive. On 28 May, four days after Lerdo had announced the presidential elections, just over four thousand rebels attacked Ignacio Alatorre's Federal force of a similar size at San Juan Epatlán, near Izucar de Matamoros.[17] During a cloudburst of epic proportions, the two armies battled. Neither side achieved supremacy, and when both armies eventually withdrew, they left the battleground mulched with the highest casualties of the Tuxtepec revolt. Without winning a clear victory, Alatorre succeeded in breaking up Coutolenc's army and in delaying a rebel advance on the strategically critical Puebla plains until the battle of Tecoac in November 1876.[18]

Rebel spirits were further dashed by news of the defeat of Díaz and his northern allies—Gerónimo Treviño, Francisco Naranjo, and Hipólito Charles—at Icamole on 20 May 1876 (the victory that prompted Lerdo to call the presidential election).[19] By mid-May, the rebellion in Durango, Zacatecas, and Jalisco, under Pedro Galván, Donato Guerra, and Rosendo Márquez, upon which Díaz was pinning his hopes for a pincer movement upon the national capital, had been crushed.[20] By the end of the month, Coutolenc's rebel army on the Puebla plateau had also been dispersed.

With rebels all over the Republic reeling in disarray from a succession of defeats, this was no time for mounting an offensive. Inexplicably, the warhorse from Tetela, Juan N. Méndez, chose early June to move his forces against Tulancingo. Perhaps the perils of waiting any longer in the face of demoralization setting in among his men outweighed the uncertain prospects of victory. In addition, Méndez, whom Díaz had placed in charge of the entire Ejército Regenerador, Linea del Oriente in January, had yet to establish his authority over the patchwork of autonomous chieftains in the southeast.[21]

Seven months after declaring for the rebellion, Méndez still had not seen any action. Díaz's other division commanders—Negrete, Mier y Terán, Hernández, Coutolenc, Cravioto, Carreón, and Carrillo—had done all the fighting. Méndez had remained at Taxcantla, working with Lucas and Bonilla to consolidate supply lines from a wide range of Sierra communities.[22] Perhaps Méndez approached Tulancingo only to test the terrain, particularly the traditional areas of sympathy in the Sierra de Tulancingo, where Méndez and Cravioto had coordinated rebellions since the 1850s.

In mid-June, Méndez, accompanied by fourteen generals, led more than four thousand men onto the cereal-producing plains of Tulancingo to confront a four-hundred-man garrison of National Guard commanded by Justino Fernández, governor of the state of Hidalgo. After a light skirmish followed by negotiations, the rebels retreated to their own regions. Méndez's decision to withdraw came at a time of great uncertainty about Díaz's location, with rumors that he had lost his life after the battle of Icamole.[23]

The Tulancingo fiasco also resulted from disunity within the rebel camp. Negrete refused to obey Méndez, who had been his subordinate throughout much of the French Intervention. No love was lost between the Tetela caudillo and Rafael Cravioto, commander of the Third Division, who, as a loyal *juarista,* had been the hammer of the rebel Méndez, since 1867. After the Tulancingo episode, Cravioto retreated north in disgust and prepared for opening a campaign against the port of Tuxpan, in anticipation of Díaz's southward campaign from Matamoros and Tampico.[24] Coutolenc, who commanded the Second Division and represented the rival Llanura party, also refused to accept the authority of Méndez.

After the failure at Tulancingo, Coutolenc and Hernández moved their troops, bypassing Méndez's headquarters at Taxcantla, to Chalchicomula where Coutolenc deposited his arms and equipment. Hernández and the First Division continued into Veracruz where they suffered a crushing defeat, retreating in disarray to the Sierra de Ixtlán. Hernández was captured and imprisoned at El Fortín.

Following the Tulancingo debacle, Romero Vargas stepped up the pressure on the rebels. He instructed each rancho and hacienda to provide two armed horsemen for a *guardia movíl* (mounted guard) to pursue the "bandits."[25] Rebel districts throughout the state were restored to government control, so that by mid-July, only Zacapoaxtla, Tetela, and Huauchinango still remained in rebel hands.[26] Only Coutolenc's forces in his bailiwick at Tecamachalco remained active on the plateau.[27] Then, on 12 August, Colonel Joaquín Berastegui defeated Coutolenc's rump of three hundred rebels at Molcajac near Tepeji.[28] The Tuxtepec revolution in Puebla and the southeast seemed close to extinction.

The Revival of the Southern Rebellion

Díaz returned to Oaxaca in early July with the southeastern rebellion at its lowest ebb and its leaders in disarray: Hernández was a captive, Méndez had failed to reassert his authority after his retreat from Tulancingo, Cravioto and Negrete both preferred to operate independently, and Coutolenc had retired from the campaign.[29] Díaz's only comfort lay in the fact that the Federal forces in the southeast, commanded by General Ignacio Alatorre, were no better off than the Tuxtepecanos.

After having failed to retake Oaxaca at a considerable cost of arms and men, General Alatorre based the Second Division at Tehuacán, the southern gateway to the Puebla tableland. However, keeping a full division in one place was a costly operation. By September, the Second Division's needs of 80,000 pesos per month could not be met from the mere 2,000 pesos remaining in the quartermaster's chest. The penury of the Second Division was matched by the bankruptcy of the federal treasury. Adding to the financial problem was Alatorre's deteriorating relationship with President Lerdo, which began with the general's opposition to the reinstatement of emergency powers. After Iglesias's defection, Lerdo suspected Alatorre's loyalty. Alatorre and the Second Division were seen as awaiting the appropriate moment for abandoning the regime.[30] The inactivity at Tehuacán of this normally energetic general seemed to confirm this view.

Díaz took advantage of Alatorre's inertia to reorganize the rebel command in the southeast, keeping Lucas regularly informed of developments.[31] A month after his return to Oaxaca, Díaz ordered Méndez at Xochiapulco and Rafael Cravioto at Huauchinango to initiate a general offensive upon the central tableland.[32] However, the campaign was delayed by the sensational departure of Iglesias from the Lerdo government.

At the end of July, Manuel González arrived in the Huasteca at the head of a ragged but appreciable force from northern Mexico. His presence galvanized resistance throughout the Huasteca, much as Negrete had done in 1866 against the Austrians. By September, rebels from the Huejutla and from the sierras of Huauchinango and Tulancingo were ready to embark upon an offensive. On 22 September a force of two thousand rebels attacked and narrowly failed to take the mining city of Pachuca, gateway to the Valley of Mexico.[33] The rebellions in the Hidalgo and Puebla sierras enabled Díaz to break out of his encirclement in Oaxaca.

At the beginning of October, Díaz, who was tired of waiting for Alatorre to invade Oaxaca, informed his allies that he was now marching to meet the enemy.[34] "In order to economize on Mexican blood," he urged Lucas and Méndez to lead Puebla's *serranos* into battle immediately, promising to reimburse Lucas for all war costs.[35] For Lucas and Méndez, this order came just in time. After eight months of preparations, with a large rebel force having to be kept constantly on a war footing, desertions and defections from rebel ranks were causing concern. Troop indiscipline on the front combined with mounting political disorders in the Sierra villages, which for eight months had chafed under military authorities and had become weary of onerous demands for supplies and recruits.[36]

However demoralized, the rebels in the Puebla Sierra were still perceived by Alatorre as a formidable enemy. After all, the Federal commander had fought with or against them on many previous occasions.[37] His plan was to prevent, at all costs, rebels from northern and southern Puebla from joining forces. This strategy accounts for his fatal decision to abandon Puebla on 13 November.[38] Delayed by having to await reinforcements under General Carbó, Alatorre arrived at Huamantla too late to prevent Díaz from moving north to join the forces from the Puebla Sierra led by Méndez, Lucas, and Bonilla.[39]

With González's force half a day's march away at Tlaxco, Alatorre decided on 15 November to engage Díaz's forces of around four thousand men near Huamantla, close to the hacienda of Tecoac. Federal forces soon gained the upper hand, but just as the *serrano* line started to break, Manuel González arrived with reinforcements, snatching victory from the jaws of defeat.[40] Alatorre ordered a retreat to Mexico City where his bedraggled force arrived on 19 November. The following day, President Lerdo and his ministers abandoned the national capital, which Díaz entered on the afternoon of 23 November, arriving at the railway station of Buenavista.[41]

Despite the narrowness of the rebel victory at Tecoac, and the fragility of the Sierra rebellion at this moment, Puebla's principal Tuxtepecano leaders did well from the division of spoils. As Díaz marched north on 19 November 1876, he conferred the interim presidency on Méndez, the governorship of the Federal District on Bonilla, and the governorship of the state of Puebla on Coutolenc.[42] Meanwhile, to the initial horror of Mexico City's *gente decente*, Nahua troops from the Puebla Sierra performed a vital role in policing the capital. Their presence contributed to Díaz's successful bid for power against Iglesias and to the initial consolidation of his regime.[43] Troops from the Puebla Sierra remained in Mexico City until March 1877, when they returned to their homes.

The Aftermath of the Revolution of Tuxtepec in Puebla

Governor Coutolenc, in one of his first acts, decreed that all public employees of the Lerdo regime would be divested of their posts. Districts were placed temporarily under the authority of the municipal presidents who had functioned before 1870 (before the constitutional reforms).[44] He then derogated the unpopular constitutional reforms of December 1871 and declared the constitution of 1861 to be fully in force, restoring direct municipal and district elections. This action also restored the right of mayors of district cabeceras to petition for or against constitutional and legislative changes (their only recourse against arbitrary power throughout much of the Restored Republic). These decrees reveal how Puebla's Tuxtepec rebels had been motivated by local issues and resistance to the centralization of power.

Further evidence of a *municipio libre* impulse behind the Tuxtepec Revolution can be found in the decree of 30 November 1876 that forbade municipalities from selling their public lands. Instead the decree instructed them to dedicate the revenues generated from their remaining properties to public education and other works of public benefit.[45] Petitions from rebel soldiers and municipalities in the district of Zacapoaxtla presented to Méndez at the National Palace display a widespread desire for the enforcement of the Reform Laws which had abolished compulsory services to Church and state and for the cessation of the sale of communal lands.[46]

Shortly before renouncing the governorship, Coutolenc responded to these grievances by visiting Zacapoaxtla, where he received a deputation of representatives of the ayuntamientos of the district, who went away "very satisfied."[47] Less welcome, however, was Coutolenc's decree that all firearms and ammunition were to be handed in to the jefes políticos. Moreover, Tetela was enraged by the decision to retain the district of Alatriste—the cordon sanitaire designed by Romero Vargas to keep the Sierra in check—which initially had been abolished shortly after the victory at Tecoac.[48] As a patrician landowner of recent French immigrant descent, Coutolenc was socially and culturally distant from Díaz and the leaders from the Puebla Sierra. And lacking a national patron, his governorship looked increasingly precarious.[49]

On 3 January 1877, Coutolenc renounced the Puebla state governorship, in preparation for standing as the Llanura candidate in the forthcoming elections. He acted without instructions from Díaz, in order to gain a head start in the contest while his rival, Méndez, remained occupied as interim president. This imprudent move by Coutolenc obliged Díaz to make up his mind, perhaps sooner than he would have liked, about whom to back for the Puebla governorship. Coutolenc's military eclipse was already evident in early December when the Minister of War, on orders from Méndez, established a new unit, the Division of National Guard of the East, under the command of General Juan Crisóstomo Bonilla. This new force comprised the five brigades from the states of Puebla, Tlaxcala, Guerrero, and Oaxaca that had participated in the last stages of the Tuxtepec campaign. Generals Sarmiento and Luis Figueroa served as commanders along with two Puebla *serranos*, Vicente Márquez Galindo (Zacatlán) and José María Isunza (Tetela). Próspero Cahuantzi, in charge of a brigade of three companies of Tlaxcala National Guard, was the only officer from the plateau.[50]

The prospect of the Llanura matching this Montaña-dominated army seemed slim. Bonilla promptly put the National Guard to work. In mid-January, he ordered the officers and men of his division to return to their homes in the Sierra to prepare for the forthcoming elections. Deprived of any leverage with the National Guard, Coutolenc also lost control of local officials when jefes políticos were returned to direct election.[51] The few hundred factory workers whom Coutolenc could mobilize in street demonstrations in the state capital could hardly compete with the thousands of men still at arms, controlled by the Montaña.[52]

Díaz returned to Mexico City to assume executive authority on 15 February. He rewarded Méndez with the presidency of the federal senate, a rather paltry prize since the Plan de Tuxtepec had sworn to abolish this chamber. However, Díaz demonstrated his commitment to the Montaña when he gave his official backing to Bonilla as the candidate for the governorship in Puebla. For his part, Coutolenc received compensation with a seat in the federal legislature. Méndez's continued absence from the state as federal senator represented some recompense for the Llanura.[53] This began Díaz's long process of conciliation of Puebla's acute regional party differences.[54]

The results of state governorship elections, reported on 20 April, showed Bonilla with a clear majority, winning 53 percent (65,348) of the vote. Predictable charges of fraud appeared.[55] However, the electoral returns indicated far greater electoral competition than with Romero Vargas's reelection in 1874 (when the incumbent had gained almost 90 percent of the votes cast). Nevertheless, the results revealed an improbable level of unanimity within the Montaña and Llanura heartlands, presaging future electoral conflicts and abstentionism.[56] Illness prevented Bonilla from taking office immediately, but by early May he was well enough to take over from interim governor Carlos Pacheco, who left for Cuernavaca to assume the governorship of Morelos.[57]

Montaña Policies

While in opposition, Montaña leaders, particularly those from Zacatlán and Tetela, had consistently trumpeted a radical brand of Liberalism, which placed great emphasis on the unfettered exercise of popular sovereignty and respect for individual rights and guarantees. The federal constitution of 1857 and the state constitution of 1861 already enshrined municipal freedoms, direct elections, the principle of no reelection, strong controls by state and federal legislatures over the executive power, an independent judiciary, a locally accountable National Guard, compulsory, free, and lay education, a criminal code reform (abolition of imprisonment for debt, corporal punishment and the death penalty), strictly enforced laws separating Church and state, and restrictions on public aspects of the religious cult such as dress, bell-ringing, and religious processions, and the abolition of compulsory services and parish fees.

Between April and September 1867, when Méndez served briefly as governor, the state of Puebla experienced a foretaste of the combination of realpolitik and radicalism that would mark Montaña policy. Méndez reintroduced the 1861 state constitution in its entirety, which reaffirmed the principle of direct elections for municipal councils and jefes políticos. He increased the power of the state governor by reducing the number of ministries from four to one. He revamped the state's National Guard regulations forbidding any other armed forces (*guardias rurales, guardias moviles, contra-guerrillas*) in the state and set fines for anyone who addressed the National Guard by any other name. All arms belonging to those who had collaborated with or fought for the Empire were to be submitted to local National Guard units.

Scrupulous attention to military organization was combined with an evangelical determination to transform Puebla de los Angeles into Puebla de Zaragoza, a capital fit for patriotic heroes. Streets were renamed after Liberal-patriotic generals. The 5th of May was declared a perpetual holiday, the decree outlining in meticulous detail the liturgy for the celebration. A permanent patriotic committee would organize the ceremonies in the state capital, whose festivities were to serve as a model for every town and village in the state. The National Guard and military bands played at every stage.

Religious festivals, by contrast, encountered hostility. Processions, dances, and *mayordomías* were to be confined to the atrium or, better, the interior of a church. Bell-ringing should not exceed ten minutes for Masses, religious functions, and funerals. These limits did not apply to secular festivals when government officials would determine the appropriate interval for bell-ringing. The governor further penalized the Church for its complicity with the Empire with a graduated tax on the clergy based on seniority. Priests had to pay between 100 and 400 pesos, canons 500 pesos, and the bishop 1,000 pesos. Méndez's pro-Indian sympathies were evident in a decree that forbade landowners from having jails on their estates and from whipping their workers. Both issues had been on the Liberal agenda since the days of Intendant Manuel Flón in the 1790s.[58]

This radical legislative agenda was soon interrupted by Juárez's imposition of Rafael García as governor. Over the decade of the Restored Republic, neither the beleaguered García nor his Conservative successor, Romero Vargas, chose to resume the radical reforms initiated by Méndez. By contrast, Bonilla, as president of the federal chamber of deputies early in 1877, showed every sign that he intended his tenure of the Puebla governorship to be remembered as the dawning of a new age of liberty and equality which would be protected by constitutional guarantees and new enlightened institutions.[59] In his first speech to the federal congress, Bonilla paid tribute to the villages and towns that had upheld the constitution against its enemies and supported the Army of Regeneration in 1876. He praised "the sovereign will of the people in their struggle against the

General Juan Crisóstomo Bonilla, Governor of the State of Puebla, 1877–1880

oligarchy and their determination to destroy the shackles imposed by the absurd municipal laws."[60] His statements expressed the natural political instincts of someone from a small town, in a remote under-represented district, who had worked for fourteen years as a primary schoolteacher in even smaller communities, and whose long political career had so far been confined to persuading villages to petition, pronounce, support, and fight military campaigns against state, federal, and foreign governments.[61]

On returning to take up the Puebla governorship, Bonilla immediately restored the 1861 constitution in its entirety, annulling Romero Vargas's constitutional reforms of 1871. Municipal governments and jefes políticos once more were to be elected directly, and ayuntamientos resumed the right to petition collectively and to initiate legislation in the state congress. Bonilla even proposed that the municipalities should become a "fourth power," although this suggestion never came to a vote.[62] This *municipio libre* idealism quickly faded as the state governor learned to appreciate the advantages of concentrating rather than decentralizing power. Within two years of taking office, Bonilla was proposing constitutional reforms that would empower the state governor to appoint jefes políticos and grant them increased powers to intervene in municipal politics. These proposals were vigorously attacked by León Guzmán, president of the state supreme court.[63] The hope that Puebla would become a model of Rousseauian democracy quickly faded.

Bonilla had nurtured other programs during the long period in opposition.[64] Highest on the list stood education. Bonilla's conviction that the school would become the guarantee of popular sovereignty reflected his personal experience. Like Lucas, he began his career as a village schoolmaster, having taken charge of a primary school in Tetela in 1849 at the age of fourteen. He moved on to become the district's first director of public schools at the age of twenty, and later established (with Lucas) Xochiapulco's first public school. He believed passionately that basic education (literacy, numeracy, and *historia patria*), to be provided free in municipal schools and removed from the surveillance of the clergy, was essential for sustaining the new Liberal order.[65]

Bonilla received widespread praise for having established Mexico's first Normal School for training teachers.[66] With so many other calls upon public funds, establishing this college (which even boasted a Professor of Nahuatl among its original staff) was a remarkable achievement. Puebla's Normal School, under the direction of Rafael Ramírez (who had recently been prevented by Conservatives from establishing a Normal School in Mexico City), provided free training for schoolteachers from Puebla and the Mexican southeast during the Porfiriato. Without being provocatively anti-Catholic, Bonilla and his successor, Méndez, encouraged the diffusion of Protestant schools and congregations throughout the state. The founding of a Methodist secondary school in 1877, with a teachers' training college added in 1882, further confirmed Puebla as the center of Liberal pedadogy in southeastern Mexico.[67]

Besides establishing the Normal School, the governor greatly expanded the system of primary education. The Primary Education Law of 2 March 1878 ordered every population center to establish a primary school for boys and girls within a month. It also directed each municipal cabecera to create a night school for teaching adult literacy and a special school for deaf-mutes, to be opened within six months. Primary education would be financed and administered by municipalities, under a strict system of public inspection.[68] Bonilla tried to reform higher education as well. He issued new regulations for the state college and established a state medical and pharmaceutical school.[69]

In the years through to the mid-1890s, the educational program resulted in a rapid increase in the number of schools, pupil enrollment, and literacy.[70] Because primary schooling depended almost entirely upon municipal funding, with little or no subsidy from the state or Federation, the decline in municipal finances toward the end of the century brought a concomitant decline in school enrollment and literacy.[71] The district of Tetela experienced a particularly impressive growth of literacy, and the municipality of Xochiapulco attained 44 percent male literacy by 1900, the same level as the state capital. Between 1870 and 1879, school enrollment in Xochiapulco increased from 70 to 229, with 25 girls. In the district, over the same period, the number of schools increased from 39 to 42, the number of boy students from 1,312 to 1,994, and girls, from 140 to 423. The greatest increases in students came in schools of the economically dynamic coffee- and sugar-producing *tierra cálida* and *tierra caliente* (San Estevan Cuautempan, Totutla, Zapotitlán, Huitzilan, Tuzamapa, and Jonotla). In the *tierra fría*, apart from Xochiapulco and Ometepec, school enrollment remained static or slightly declined between 1870 and 1879. Indeed, two schools closed in the declining Indian barrios of Xochititán and Xilitetitla, near the district capital.[72]

To pay for education and public improvements such as new buildings, bridges, and roads, Bonilla's congress on frequent occasions allowed municipalities to raise ad hoc taxes or to hold fairs. Nevertheless, the basis of municipal finance was the *contribución personal*, decreed on 18 June 1877, which resembled, in some respects, the old *capitación*, except that it was now to be paid by everyone rather than just by Indians.

Social reform did not extend to agrarian matters. The governor showed little sympathy for the peasant rebels of San Martín Texmelucan and Huejotzingo who, inspired by Alberto de Santa Fé's agrarian Ley del Pueblo, demanded land and freedom from clerical dues.[73] Without any apparent hesitation, Bonilla in January 1879 called upon Federal forces to suppress the movement that he described as "a Communist uprising."[74] Bonilla's unwillingness or inability to respond to this dispute except with repression suggests that he and other *serranos* felt out of their depth in the more socially divided and conflictual terrain of the Puebla plateau. After all, Santa Fé belonged to the same Masonic lodge as Bonilla and Méndez, had been jefe político of Tetela, and was an old companion at arms. Moreover, the conflict in San Martín was similar to Cuatecomaco's struggle with the owners of the hacienda of Xochiapulco and the authorities in Zacapoaxtla, where Bonilla had been directly instrumental in gaining land and municipal autonomy for armed Xochiapulquenses.[75] In the central valley, where commercial estate agriculture was responding dynamically to the construction of a railway network and widening access to markets, such Liberal agrarianism risked confronting powerful landed interests. In the case of the valley of San Martín Texmelucan, for example, the Irish Gillow family already had begun to build a palatial hacienda and to transform agricultural production.[76]

The social and cultural gulf between the rustic and relatively humble Liberal leaders of the Sierra and the landed elites of the plateau contributed to their political isolation once they took power in Puebla.[77] Holding state power also necessarily distanced Montaña leaders from radical Liberal circles in Puebla with whom, in any other circumstances, they would have had much in common. Moreover, Bonilla endured two long bouts of illness, at the beginning and end of his governorship, that required convalescence in Tetela. Under the circumstances, it is doubtful if Bonilla could have overcome his political isolation during his three years as governor.

Bonilla completed the legislative agenda of the first Montaña administration when he abolished bullfighting and the death penalty and finally suppressed the *alcabala*.[78] José Manso's modern state penitentiary, begun before the American War, was also finally completed. He also supported a plethora of tax exemptions and inducements to encourage settlers willing to move into the insalubrious *tierra caliente* to plant coffee and grow sugarcane.[79] Tetela became a judicial as well as a political district, recovering its jurisdiction over the troublesome Aquixtla, and the district of Alatriste was once more abolished. The governor had General Méndez declared *benemérito del estado* (most honored citizen of the state). He also rewarded the patriotic National Guard villages in the southern Sierra, Ometepec and Taxco in Tetela and San Miguel Tenextlatiloyan in Zautla, by upgrading them to municipalities.[80]

Local and Federal Elections in 1877 and 1878

The wisdom of returning to the system of direct elections for jefes políticos was put to the test in May 1877. In the Sierra, the results reveal a high level of electoral competition with only Francisco Cravioto in Huauchinango and Vicente Márquez Galindo in Zacatlán garnering comfortable majorities. In Tetela, on the other hand, Bonilla's preferred candidate, Lauro Luna, defeated José Daniel Posadas by a margin of only 144 votes (2,238 to 2,094). In

Tlatlauqui, Bonilla's close friend and fellow Tetelense, Manuel Vázquez, only won against Joaquín Díaz Ortega (who had won a plurality of votes) with the help of the committee of electoral scrutiny in the state congress. By the same process, Xochiapulco's National Guard veteran, Colonel Luis Antonio Díaz, narrowly lost Zacapoaxtla to Justo Martínez (both Díaz and Martínez were friends of the Montaña). Teziutlán, Alatriste, and Libres experienced similarly closely fought elections. Reports of electoral irregularities came from across the state, revealing the fragility of the Montaña's hold on power and the risks of direct elections based on universal male suffrage.[81]

In the July 1878 elections for the federal congress, the Llanura decided it could not risk electoral extinction. Its leaders adopted a strategy of organizing separate elections from the official ones in eight districts: the Llanura strongholds of Cholula, Tecamachalco, Atlixco, Izucar de Matamoros, Huejotzingo, and Tepeaca as well as the Sierra districts of Zacatlán and San Juan de los Llanos.[82] The Llanura accused Bonilla of sanctioning armed force to protect official candidates and to secure electoral victories.[83] The citizens voted peacefully with the exception of a violent bout of local factionalism, aggravated by racial conflict, in Atzala (Chiautla), which resulted in twenty-six deaths.[84]

The Challenge to the Montaña in the Sierra

In November 1879 the National Guard company of Atagpan (Cenobio Cantero's old bailiwick), accompanied by several prominent Zacapoaxtecos, stormed Zacapoaxtla, stealing available arms and ammunition and breaking down the doors of the jail to release the prisoners. Xochiapulco's forces promptly captured and disarmed the rebels, allowing them to return peacefully to their barrios. Chastened by this first armed challenge on the Montaña's home turf, Bonilla suppressed news of the raid for a month.

The Atagpan uprising began a cycle of violence in the Sierra which would last for over a year. Armed encounters accompanied the elections for the jefes políticos, in which Lucas was standing for Tetela; for the governorship, in which Méndez expected to succeed Bonilla; and for the federal presidency, in which Díaz, forbidden from succeeding himself, sought to ease into power his trusted companion, Manuel González. The choice of Lucas as jefe político in Tetela, nerve center of the Montaña, demonstrates the importance that Bonilla and Méndez gave to his influence in the southern Sierra. The disorders accompanying and following the election illustrate some of the benefits and the hazards of this choice.

In June 1879 the second direct elections for jefes políticos of the Tuxtepec era were held. Given the jefes políticos' responsibility for organizing the elections, these positions were bound to be hotly disputed.[85] As in 1877, it was in the Llanura core districts of Chalchicomula, Tepeaca, Tecamachalco, Matamoros, and in the Montaña "marginals" of Libres, Alatriste (an electoral, but no longer a political, district), and in Teziutlán that the elections were the most disputed and subject to complaints of fraud. Across Puebla, Montaña National Guard commanders remained in office as jefes políticos. In many districts, the Guard participated actively in the electoral process by organizing the transport of ballots from remote locations to be counted, intimidating voters by their presence at the urns, and stuffing ballot boxes.[86] Indeed, voting results show a correlation between a strong National Guard presence and large electoral majorities. For example, Cravioto won 5,736 of the 5,871 votes returned in Huauchinango; Márquez Galindo won 4,800 of the 6,600 votes returned in Zacatlán; and General Lucas won Tetela comfortably with 3,202 of the 4,372 votes cast. Montaña leaders saw National Guard involvement as a necessary counterweight to the custom of peon bloc voting for the hacendado's candidate on the central plateau, a practice, they argued, that favored the Llanura.[87]

Juan Francisco Lucas, age 45, as Jefe Político of the District of Tetela in 1879

Lucas's campaign for the leadership of the district of Tetela illustrates the processes involved in the popular election of jefes políticos. The campaign started in April when Lucas was appointed to serve as president of the Comisión de Hacienda de la Junta Popular de Tetela de Ocampo, which was charged with organizing the celebration of the battle of 5 May throughout the municipality.[88] This enabled the candidate to become directly involved in organizing a ceremony that included a series of military maneuvers, cannonades, and mock battles in the only part of the district where the Montaña faced opposition.[89] After distributing five thousand voting papers in May among the district's nine municipalities, jefe político Lauro Luna then handed command over the district to Tetela's mayor, Vicente Bonilla y Hernández, an aguardiente distiller from Huitzilan, who enjoyed close business and personal ties with Méndez and Bonilla.[90] In the election in May, Lucas achieved a clear majority. The breakdown of results by barrio demonstrates, however, that he encountered fierce opposition from the rival candidates, Bonilla y Hernández and José Daniel Posadas, in the barrios of the municipality of Tetela, especially San Nicolas, Tonalapa, and Xaltatempa bordering with Aquixtla. However, in the rest of the district, villagers voted almost unanimously for Lucas.[91]

Lucas took command of the district on 28 June. He issued a typically self-effacing message "to the sons of the district," thanking them for their support and placing himself at their service. He announced that there would be "no pompous program"; "my theme will be the law, with which I shall impart the guarantees which are given to you as a right." This determination to govern the district by the letter of the law soon provoked such violent opposition that Lucas resigned within a year of being elected.

The Zautla Riot

The turbulent events in Zautla late in 1879 provide an example of the clash between energetic district government, in the spirit of enlightened Liberalism, and government through local custom. Lucas's involvement in Zautla began as early as 1857 when, at the start of the Three Years' War, his father, José Manuel, was killed and he was seriously wounded in an ambush laid by a certain Luis Arrellano, under instructions from Zautla's parish priest.[92] Lucas's determination to control Zautla can be explained by this first unfortunate encounter and by his appreciation of Zautla's strategic location on the vulnerable southern edge of the Sierra, close to the altiplano. His immediate response to the murder of his father had been to organize National Guard companies in the subject barrios on the other side of the Apulco River to Zautla's cabecera.

During the Restored Republic, the strategic value of Zautla to the Montaña was appreciated in the state capital. As a result, the municipality

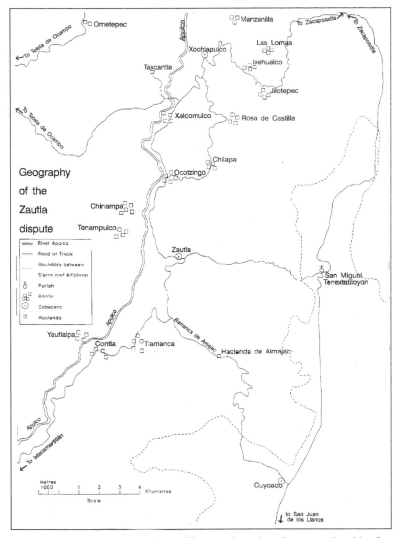

Geography of the Zautla dispute

split into two irreconcilable halves. The northern barrios organized by Lucas, more often than not, were in open rebellion against the state government. The cabecera and southern part were controlled by the state government through the wealthiest local family, the Bernal. Colonel José de Jesús Bernal owned the hacienda of Almajac, located along the narrow valley stretching south toward Cuyoaco. During the Lerdo regime, Bernal organized a force of rural guards in Zautla and was military commander of the district of San Juan de los Llanos when the revolution of Tuxtepec broke out.

With Díaz's ascent to power nationally, and with the Montaña in the Puebla governorship, the balance of power in Zautla shifted to its northern Nahua barrios. In 1879, José Máximo, a National Guard captain from the barrio of Tenampulco and a close companion of Lucas, was elected to the municipal presidency of Zautla. Among his first acts was the enforcement of the Reform Laws on excessive bell-ringing, the use of the civil register and public cemetery, and the prohibition of religious processions beyond the church precincts. Another National Guard commander, Colonel Indalecio Sánchez, a Freemason and close friend of both Lucas and Governor Bonilla (a fellow Mason), from neighboring Xochiapulco, was appointed director of Zautla's public schools. Colonel Sánchez proceeded to apply the Law of Public Instruction to the letter. In accord with the constitution, he removed the religious catechism of Ripalda from use in the municipality's schools and forbade the parish priest from any involvement in the education of children.

What was quite acceptable in Xochiapulco proved anathema to many Zautlecos. In hindsight, given the known aversion of Zautlecos in the cabecera to the Montaña, Sánchez was unwise to select Zautla for a crash program in applied liberalism. Before Lucas had held office for a month, people in Zautla had organized a riot against the municipal authorities. His report on the suppression of this disturbance reveals much about the practical limits of popular liberalism.[93]

The demonstration was the culmination of several weeks of mounting tension between the parish priest and the municipal authorities. In October the priest had refused to preside over the reburial in the municipal cemetery of the corpse of a child that had been left in an open grave at a calvary on the edge of the town. Indeed, to add insult to injury, the priest had insisted that the corpse was that of a dog. On Sunday, 2 November, during the festival of the Day of the Dead, José Máximo had prohibited the ringing of church bells, whereupon the priest had convoked a meeting of "the most prestigious residents, among whom could be found Citizens José de Jesús Bernal, Juan de Dios Aguilar, Juan José Contreras, Juan López, and various others" who, in turn, attracted a crowd of more than ninety. They gathered in front of the council building and demanded freedom to organize public religious acts. The following day, an even larger crowd assembled and demanded the doubling of the allotted time for bell-ringing and the suspension of Indalecio Sánchez as schoolmaster. The crowd grew larger with the arrival of a multitude of women who insisted that the priest and religious processions be allowed to accompany litters on the way to the cemetery. The women demanded that prayers and the catechism of Ripalda be reintroduced to the school. They also wanted children over the age of eleven to be exempted from school and sought the removal of Sánchez, whom they held responsible for the enforcement of "these ridiculous laws."

The council yielded on the schoolmaster and the catechism but not on processions. Unsatisfied with this response, the crowd invaded the council building and then pelted Sánchez's house with stones, obliging the schoolmaster to flee to Xochiapulco and José Máximo and his councillors to take refuge across the Apulco. From the safety of the barrio of Tenampulco, José Máximo wrote to Lucas describing the events, adding that he and his fellow councillors had been prevented by a group of *vecinos* from the cabecera from organizing the recent election in several sections of the municipality.[94]

It was probably this electoral consideration that convinced Governor Bonilla to instruct Lucas to restore order in Zautla. Lucas first passed through Xochiapulco where he mustered the National Guard, and arrived in Zautla at six A.M. on 23 November. Numerous arrests were then made. After interrogation, most villagers were released, although some were sent to Libres under an escort of twenty-five Guards. Lucas then disarmed the population of the cabecera and handed over the weapons to the Tetela National Guard.[95]

With the municipality restored to the constitutional order, José Máximo and the aldermen returned to the council building. Lucas found the accounts and records for the three-month period since José Máximo had taken office to be in perfect order. But noting that treasury accounts did not exist for earlier years, Lucas concluded that non-Indians in Zautla simply had never paid taxes, an obligation locally associated exclusively with the Indian population. In his view, the underlying cause of the disorders was not the question of religious freedom, but Máximo's determination to tax the entire population. The offending schoolmaster had, after all, already stepped down and the Ripalda catechism had been returned to the desks of local schools.

Lucas judged that Zautla's *gente de razón* had rebelled when José Máximo had attempted properly (and constitutionally) to administer a municipality accustomed for decades to neglect and lawlessness. As he stated in his report to Bonilla: "The real cause of the unrest here is that the major part of the neighborhood has been accustomed to living in eternal orgy, flagrantly gambling and quarreling, in continuous drunkenness, and every kind of scandal that stems from the idleness and immorality which this Ayuntamiento has made its aim to eradicate, desiring to shake the neighborhood out of its old ways and to ensure that the rule of law shines for the first time in this place."

What Lucas may not have realized in November 1879 was that the violent attempt to remove José Máximo from the municipal presidency of Zautla was part of a wider strategy, orchestrated by Colonel Carlos Pacheco, now Díaz's Minister of War, aimed at ending Montaña control of the state. Although Pacheco did not formally declare his candidacy for the Puebla governorship until shortly before the elections in July 1880, rumors began late in 1879 that Ignacio Romero Vargas was canvassing for him.[96] In the Sierra, Pacheco's agents found support in towns and villages where the Montaña had traditionally faced opposition or where entrenched local conflicts offered an opportunity to widen political rivalries. The uprising in Zautla in 1879 was just one of a growing number of incidents in which Montaña officials came under pressure.

Ometepec's Abortive Easter Uprising

Early in 1880, Tetela, the heart of the Montaña *cacicazgo*, came under attack. In January, Francisco Vidal led a raid on Lucas's ranch at Taxcantla and made off with six bulls. Lucas sent a force of National Guards after them; they retrieved five of the bulls in Amazoc, where the sixth already was hanging with half of its meat removed.[97] Shortly afterward twenty-nine prisoners broke out of the Tetela jail. In pursuit, officials killed three prisoners, recaptured two, and wounded two others (who were presumed dead), but twenty-two got away.[98] Although the two incidents were probably unconnected, Lucas found his authority as jefe político under challenge. Throughout the first six months of 1880, although Tetela was officially reported to be "in complete tranquility," he faced constant pressure. To the opposition, Lucas personified all the qualities of the new order they most objected to: anticlericalism, enthusiasm for secular education, frequent use of the National Guard for electoral purposes, and a reversal in the traditional hierarchy of ethnic power.

In Tetela the challenge to Lucas came principally from the cabecera and from its outlying barrio of Ometepec. Since the Three Years' War, Ometepec had been Tetela's most patriotic, yet most troublesome, barrio. Strategically situated on the principal route between Tetela and Zacapoaxtla, the Ometepecanos faced arduous military demands, which they provided grudgingly and conditionally. Second only to Tonalapa, Ometepec had sacrificed more of its sons in patriotic struggles during the Reform Wars and French Intervention than any other Tetela barrio.[99] These two barrios had seen their homes twice reduced to ashes by the enemy. The southern boundaries of the barrio abutted upon Lucas's estate at Taxcantla. In recognition of its sacrifices, Ometepec and its neighboring barrio, Tececuilco (close to Huahuaxtla), were granted full municipal status by the state congress on 20 October 1877. Appropriately, the new municipality took the name "Quautimoctzin," after the last heroic Aztec emperor.[100]

Villagers formally inaugurated Ometepec de Quautimoctzin on 1 January 1878 in an elaborate ceremony held in the schoolhouse. Officials present included Lauro Luna, the jefe político, and the full councils of Tetela de Ocampo, Ometepec, and Tececuilco. During the proceedings, General Lucas acted as interpreter in the "Mexican language."[101] The rousing speech by Luna drew parallels between the heroic struggles of the two barrios and the life of "one of the most loved persons of our history, the immortal Cuautemoc." The national anthem, fireworks, and fusillades followed as the presidency of the new council was presented to Isidro Segura, Ometepec's renowned National Guard veteran.

This recognition of Ometepec's patriotic sacrifices did not guarantee the barrio's loyalty to the Montaña. On 24 March 1880, Valentín Sánchez, commander of Ometepec's National Guard, reported that a certain José de la Luz Domínguez had been inciting residents to take part in an assault on Tetela, "against people opposed to the ministers of the Catholic religion." With the uprising timed to break out on Easter Sunday, leaders were expected to receive support from prominent citizens in the cabecera and from the barrios of San Nicolas and Tonalapa (villages which had opposed Lucas as jefe político in the elections of the previous year) as well as from certain Zacapoaxtecos (rumors mentioned Miguel Arriaga).

Lucas later learned that the conspiracy resulted in part because he had recently expelled the parish priest from Tetela. The priest had been supporting those in Ometepec opposed to the construction of a new secular school to be built on land taken from the Church. Lucas was directly involved because he had backed this school by donating a plot of his own land as a contribution toward the teacher's salary. Isidro Segura, a longtime companion in arms of Lucas, joined the conspiracy.[102]

The principal issues at the heart of the Ometepec conspiracy—religious freedom, secular schools, the role of the parish priest in public affairs—were also those at the root of the Zautla episode. Lucas knew Ometepec's religious sensibilities as he was long accustomed to hearing grievances from its Guardsmen against their officers. He knew that alongside Ometepec's record of patriotic service ran a parallel history of a village that took its religion particularly seriously and consequently was often in disagreement, if not rebellion, against its cabecera, the secularizing Tetela. Ometepec's complaint over an incense burner, contracted from a Puebla silversmith in 1854 but still not delivered in 1861, and the barrios's request for permission in 1876 to hold a full Corpus Christi procession, show that villagers sought respect for religious freedom and for local custom in return for their patriotic services.[103] There were therefore abundant local precedents for Ometepec's opposition to its cabecera. However, the complicity of several residents of the cabecera in the Ometepec plot, and the rumor that Miguel Arriaga, commander of the Zacapoaxtla National Guard, was behind everything, convinced Lucas that outsiders were instrumental in hatching the conspiracy. This prompted his request to Lauro Luna, now jefe político of Zacapoaxtla, to arrest Arriaga and send him to Tetela for trial.

Since the restoration of the Republic in 1867, the Arriaga brothers had vied with Tetela's National Guard veterans—Méndez, Bonilla, Lucas, Luna, and Rivera—for control of the central Sierra. For brief periods, such as during the 1869–70 rebellion, the Arriaga and the Montaña had combined forces against the state government. But after the revolt of La Noria, the Arriaga had cast their lot with Romero Vargas and benefited from his gubernatorial patronage, at Tetela's expense. After Tuxtepec, with the Tetelenses in power, the position was reversed and patronage from the state government dried up. Miguel Arriaga had inherited the leadership of Zacapoaxtla's National Guard after the violent death of his brother,

Francisco Javier (leader of the 1869–70 revolt), in local feuding that preceded the revolution of Tuxtepec. He was the obvious candidate for Carlos
Pacheco to select as his principal agent in the Puebla Sierra.

Miguel Arriaga and his friends in Zacapoaxtla expected something in return for their support for Pacheco. Counting on his benign influence from the
Ministry of War, in April 1880, Arriaga and sixty-seven others from
Zacapoaxtla's most prominent families (including the Molina, Betancurt,
Macip, Tirado, Mora, Sayago, Becies, Limon, Sosa) petitioned the Minister
of the Interior to station a Federal garrison in the town. They extolled the
economic benefits that the spending power of a Federal garrison would bring
to a district that had sacrificed so much in the Tuxtepec revolution, a sacrifice
that so far had gone unrewarded. Arriaga also calculated that a Federal cantonment would restore Zacapoaxtla to its proper place as the political center
of the Puebla Sierra, a position usurped since 1876 by Tetela. In mid-April,
the federal government turned down the petition just as the conspiracy in
Ometepec, Tonalapa, and San Nicolas was discovered.[104]

Nipping in the bud the "Easter uprising" of Tetela's barrios made
Lucas's task of unearthing the wide conspiracy much harder. The Indian
conspirators whom he interrogated pleaded drunkenness as the excuse for
their involvement and for their inability to recall who else was implicated.[105] However, the failure of the uprising prompted Lucas's enemies to
take more desperate measures. On 17 May 1880 a single rifle shot jarred
the quiet of the Tetela morning. The bullet knocked off Lucas's straw hat as
he crossed the patio of his home. (The bullet was later found on the kitchen
floor.) Witnesses saw José María Rodríguez, married to General Méndez's
sister, Policarpa, shooting from the roof of the church. The jefe político
promptly arrested the culprit, who had an Austrian carbine in his possession. Lucas had him immediately imprisoned and, after a brief investiga-
tion, ordered the arrest of several prominent Tetela citizens—Gregorio
Zamítez, Vicente Antonio Bonilla, Antonio Herrera, Juan Rodríguez,
Pascual Hernández, Claudio Segura, and Francisco de Paula Bonilla—
believed to be implicated in a conspiracy to assassinate him. Lucas also
suspected various friends of the parish priest, José de Jesús Sánchez, who
had left Tetela shortly before the attempted uprising at Easter.[106]

Undeterred, Lucas's opponents kept up their pressure through direct action and, later, through *juicios de amparo* (court injunctions). According to the
constitution, suspects of a crime could only be detained for a maximum of
three days. Francisco de Paula Bonilla, as a member of the Tetela cabildo, had
immunity and was released immediately. Gregorio Zamítez was also allowed
to return home due to poor health, on the condition that he report to Lucas
daily. Those remaining in prison had their hopes raised by demonstrations
hostile to Lucas and by an attack upon the prison. To keep order, Lucas summoned a force of National Guard from Xochiapulco and doubled the patrol at
the prison. After four days of mounting disorder, he decided to remove the

prisoners, under armed guard, to his estate at Taxcantla. He charged the hefty cost of maintaining the guards to the families of the prisoners and others suspected of involvement in the conspiracy.

For the next month the prisoners remained at Taxcantla, and Xochiapulquense and Zautleco troops patrolled the streets of Tetela. News of this state of affairs soon spread to the state capital and the national press, which caused the Puebla government considerable embarrassment. General Méndez's sister, Policarpa, became especially vocal in drawing attention to Lucas's unconstitutional judicial practices. She filed a *juicio de amparo* calling for the prisoners' release. In response, Lucas insisted that they had been held in conditions of comfort, safety, and hygiene in a new house he had recently built at Taxcantla. Nevertheless, he ordered the prisoners to be returned to Tetela.[107]

Pachequismo and the Perception of Montaña Power

The failed Easter uprising and the attempt upon Lucas's life in May 1880 were part of a wider strategy deployed by Carlos Pacheco to divide the Sierra and promote his candidature for the governorship. Pacheco publicly launched his candidature on 25 May and, like Coutolenc, he appealed for the support of the state's nascent working class, a constituency ignored by the Montaña. In the Sierra, where no such class existed, Pacheco looked for support from anyone discontented with the Montaña.

Pachequismo gained force in the Sierra during the first half of June with a vigorous newspaper campaign vilifying the *cacicazgos* of the Montaña.[108] Pacheco promoted *La Tribuna*, the most virulently anti-Montaña newspaper, to sway opinion in Mexico City. It portrayed Tetela as a constitutional desert where dissenters faced imprisonment in "the caves of Xochapulco [*sic*]." In Tlatlauqui, soldiers whipped a man for reading a newspaper critical of Méndez. In Zacapoaxtla, an assassin in the pay of Lauro Luna, the Montaña jefe político, made an attempt on the life of Miguel Arriaga.[109] In Zacatlán, similar "scandals" had been witnessed. *La Tribuna* maintained a commentary on the iniquities of the Montaña throughout July and early August, accusing Bonilla of failing to register voters or to distribute voting slips as well as of intimidation, violence, and arbitrary imprisonment. Generals Carrillo and Pacheco confirmed such practices in correspondence from Tehuacán.[110]

These criticisms were not entirely unfounded. Holding on to power in Tetela, and protecting his own life, obliged Lucas to keep the National Guard on an active footing. Unable to trust the Tetela ayuntamiento, which was staffed in large part by political enemies who were intent upon physically eliminating the Nahua cacique, Lucas now ruled the district from Taxcantla through trusted National Guard commanders.[111] Yet no state of emergency had been declared and these troops had no constitutional authority over the civil power. In the long run, the authority of the jefe político, as the agent of the governor, could only be effective if he could count upon the compliance of ayuntamientos and *juntas municipales* in carrying out state government decrees. With the ayuntamiento of Tetela de Ocampo in a virtual state of rebellion, Lucas could do little other than rely on his control of the National Guard and his possession of a tactical retreat in his fortified ranch at Taxcantla.

The problems of maintaining authority in unruly districts pushed Montaña deputies in the state congress in 1879 to enact constitutional changes that allowed jefes políticos to supervise municipalities more directly. A powerful objection to these new laws, as an unconstitutional increase in the power of the executive at the expense of the municipality, was expressed by León Guzmán, president of Puebla's supreme tribunal of justice. Guzmán objected to the assumption of autonomous executive power by elected jefes políticos of districts who, initially, were intended as mere agents of the state governor. Now the congress wanted to treat the district as a "natural community" and the jefe político as the individual embodiment of district sovereignty—both absurd and dangerous notions in Guzmán's opinion. The only political body that he considered "natural" was the municipality. By upgrading the district and the office of jefe político, the Montaña threatened the autonomy of the municipality. Moreover, unlike the state governor, the jefe político lacked any legislative check on his powers.

An example of the jefe político's intrusion into what was properly the province of Tetela's ayuntamiento can be observed in early June 1880. The ayuntamiento's committee of electoral scrutiny (two members of which had been implicated in the conspiracy against Lucas) uncovered "irregularities" during the primary elections for the federal congress. Just before the voting began, Lucas had sent out a patrol to arrest Francisco and Gregorio Zamítez (the president and first secretary of the "casilla electoral de la sección 2a" and plotters in May), with the consequence that the outcome of the election favored the primary electors for the Montaña candidate, Miguel Méndez, son of the general.[112] Nevertheless, ultimate authority in Mexico came from the national executive. The ability of the Montaña to stave off mounting pressure from *pachequismo* on its home ground ultimately rested upon the attitude toward Puebla's contending factions expressed by President Díaz.

Federal Elections in Puebla, January to July 1880

The importance that Díaz placed on Puebla can be seen in the high caliber of the two agents—Guillermo Prieto and Agustín Pradillo—whom he sent to the Puebla de Zaragoza in the summer of 1880 to deal with the political crisis there.[113] In Bonilla, Méndez, and Lucas, Díaz could count on long, firmly established friendships and deep loyalties. Moreover, the Montaña possessed the military capacity not only to maintain themselves in power but also to be available in the case of Díaz facing difficulties with his reelection in 1884. However, there were problems with the Montaña *cacicazgo*. The strong-armed means used to assert its authority had provoked increasingly vocal opposition in Puebla as well as criticism in the national press, which provided useful ammunition to the opposition. In backing Méndez for the Puebla governorship in 1880, Díaz showed that he was willing to risk this criticism in exchange for the Montaña's ability to deliver the appropriate votes for the federal congress and the presidency. These votes would be vital for ensuring Díaz's reelection in 1884. His continuing support for Méndez and the Montaña also reflected his assessment of the weakness and disarray of the Llanura, particularly the lack of resolve of its leader, Coutolenc. Moreover, Díaz and his advisers recognized the danger that the Conservatives or a clerical party might steal a march in Puebla if the federal government withdrew its backing from the Montaña before ensuring an acceptable successor.[114]

Elections for various national offices—the presidency, senate, supreme court, and chamber of deputies—were held on 11 July. Díaz achieved his objectives in Puebla. Manuel González received a resounding majority and the state elected dependable federal deputies. Puebla's importance to Díaz is reflected in the number of prestigious non-Poblanos elected from Puebla constituencies: Manuel Payno in Huauchinango, Guillermo Prieto in Puebla, José María Vigil as his substitute, Agustín Pradillo in Tecali, Albino Zertuche in Tepeaca, Mucío Martínez (future state governor) as the substitute in Tepeji.[115] Díaz, through his agents Prieto and Pradillo, secured a distribution of patronage in Puebla that achieved national rather than local objectives. Handling the elections for the state governorship proved much more difficult.

Lucas and *Pachequismo* in the Sierra: Zacapoaxtla

Carlos Pacheco, on Díaz's orders, renounced his candidacy for governor of Puebla on 22 June 1880. This did not end the opposition to the Montaña and to the candidature of Juan N. Méndez. Indeed, political violence continued until well after the elections for the state governorship.[116] Under Lucas, the district of Tetela was held virtually in a state of siege. Hence, the focus of opposition shifted east to Zacapoaxtla. In June an unsuccessful attempt was made on the life of Colonel Luis Antonio Díaz in Xochiapulco. Lucas suspected Miguel Arriaga, who had recently escaped assassination himself, as the principal instigator behind this outrage. He arrested Arriaga and detained him in Tetela. This action provoked an uprising.

Late in June, the National Guard company of Zacapoaxtla's barrio of Atagpan (which had rebelled in December 1878 against jefe político Lauro Luna and again in November 1879 against Justo Martínez) took up arms behind Captain Santos Ventura Sánchez against Zacapoaxtla. Again, rumors blamed Arriaga as the instigator whose aim was to wrest the district of Zacapoaxtla from the control of the Montaña. The conspiracy spanned much of the district, was coordinated with the opposition in Tetela, and enjoyed support from former candidate Pacheco. Lucas also suspected the involvement of Pablo Mariano Urrutia, Arriaga's father-in-law and Lucas's sparring partner during the Intervention, Santos Ventura, and Carlos Cantero, Cenobio's son.[117] Zacapoaxtla's battle lines, drawn up originally during the Three Years' War, had returned.

This time the Montaña defended the state government rather than attacked it. Zacapoaxtla's leading families confirmed their complicity in the Atagpan uprising on 2 July 1880 when a deputation of prominent citizens, including Urrutia, Carlos Betancurt, José de la Luz Molina, and Braulio Alcántara, accompanied by fourteen Atagpanecos, called on Luna to urge him not to engage the rebels who, one week later, still threatened Zacapoaxtla. The trouble had also spread to other barrios. Luna feared the complicity of Miguel Negrete, who had recently been seen in Zacapoaxtla with the rebels, in some statewide scheme.[118]

At the same time, disaffected National Guards in the pay of Carlos Pacheco conspired to topple the district authorities in Tlatlauqui and Tetela. Pacheco suborned Colonel Andrés Mirón, for years a loyal *mendecista*, who organized the rebel movement in Tlatlauqui. Mirón visited Pacheco in Mexico City on two occasions between February and August 1880. Pacheco gave him money, arms (including a pistol as a personal gift), and ammunition. Anticipating an uprising, Lucas instructed forty National Guards from Tlatlauqui's barrio of Tatauzoquico to arrest Mirón. Instead, in the presence of his wife, Yrene Rodríguez de Mirón, the Guards executed him on the road to Zacapoaxtla on 12 August 1880.[119] This mother of eight orphaned children wrote to Díaz requesting justice for the murder of her husband, on the instructions of authorities in Tlatlauqui who were still in place and determined to cover up the crime. Díaz granted the widow a pension of 30 pesos per month.

Two days after Mirón's murder, Ometepecanos once more began massing on the peak overlooking Tetela, poised to take the town.[120] The rebel strategy to coordinate pressure upon all three district capitals aimed to overstretch Lucas's capacity to police the southern Sierra. Responding to these threats, on 12 July, Lauro Luna convoked an emergency meeting of eighteen prominent Zacapoaxtla citizens to advise him on a prudent course of action.[121] They agreed on the need to use force, citing the precedent that National Guards from lowland Jonotla had just suppressed the uprising in Ometepec and Tececuilco. Luna ordered Lucas to engage the Atagpan rebels who had been surrounding Zacapoaxtla since the beginning of the month. Lucas reluctantly led six hundred men to expel the rebels from their positions on the peaks above Zacapoaxtla.[122]

Rebels also attempted to overthrow the *mendecista* Cuetzalan authorities under the municipal presidency of Francisco Agustín Dieguillo, the Nahua National Guard commander who had served Méndez and Lucas since 1861. Throughout June and July, Francisco Agustín reported clandestine meetings and electoral irregularities in Cuetzalan and Tzinacapan. The reports at one point warranted the dispatch of one hundred National Guardsmen from Zacapoaxtla. Francisco Agustín succeeded in defeating the *pachequista* challenge; and, throughout July, he proved effective at catching rebels from Atagpan and Ometepec who had taken refuge in the *tierra caliente*.[123]

Lucas's defeat of the Atagpan rebellion ended the most serious challenge to the authority of the Montaña to date, securing peace during the gubernatorial elections in early August. No one was more relentless and effective in the pursuit of rebel suspects than Lucas during his last weeks as jefe político. He tracked the Ometepec and Atagpan rebels remorselessly throughout July and August. A few found sanctuary on the Molina Alcántara hacienda at Mazapa, but many were caught and detained until well after the elections.[124]

Puebla's gubernatorial elections, held on 8 August 1880, took place peacefully. Guillermo Prieto, with characteristic flourish, reported complete peace in the state capital: "The troops remain in their barracks, the people are going about their devotions and promenades, the theaters are full, and the governor is happy playing cards in the Lonja [a café]."[125] Again, the Llanura, as in 1878, organized double elections in as many districts as possible in the vain hope that they could form a separate, officially approved legislature. Thus, there was little potential for violent clashes over single electoral slates. However, Díaz stoutly opposed double legislatures in principle. The rival chamber of the Llanura party, which Guillermo Prieto (Díaz's agent in Puebla) called the Cofradía de los Despamparados (Confraternity of the Hopeless), had no prospect of official support.[126]

Méndez won an overwhelming majority, with 83 percent (92,499) of the vote. His closest rival, Pacheco, polled only 9 percent (10,315). The scale of the victory was a reflection of the opposition's strategy of organizing a double election. Moreover, the mobilization of the National Guard throughout the Sierra created an intimidating environment. Critics charged Bonilla with failing to register voters and distribute voting slips and accused him of using violence and arbitrary imprisonment to intimidate potential voters.[127]

Even in its own regions of Tepeaca, Tecamachalco, and Huejotzingo, the Llanura made little showing. The party did garner some support in the southern districts of Chiautla and Matamoros, perhaps a result of Pacheco's recent governorship of neighboring Morelos. In the Sierra, official opposition was almost nonexistent: only four citizens in Tetela, fifty-four in Zacapoaxtla, seventeen in Teziutlán, and nineteen in Tlatlauqui dared to vote for Pacheco. In Zacatlán, where the opposition press described an election conducted much like a military exercise, the twenty-two votes not going to Méndez went to Bonilla, the incumbent governor and ineligible for reelection.[128]

Méndez received a much less decisive majority than the official figures suggest. Even in his base of Tetela, Zacapoaxtla, and Tlatlauqui, he faced a mounting armed challenge dating from the abortive Easter uprising of Tetela's barrios. But Lucas had contained this challenge to his compadre's candidature energetically and effectively. On 7 September 1880 the state congress confirmed Méndez as governor.

The Aftermath of *Pachequismo* in Tetela

Lucas's effectiveness as district policeman derived from a combination of qualities. He knew the villages of the southern Sierra intimately, having organized them militarily for a quarter of a century. Village officials also knew and trusted him, often acknowledging his authority over that of their formal superiors. Apart from enjoying an unrivaled network of information spanning several districts, from the plateau to the *tierra caliente*, Lucas possessed the means to defend the *cacicazgo* through his control of the National Guard. In practical terms, this meant that Lucas could arrest, escort, detain, and guard prisoners in Tetela's jail or at his Taxcantla ranch. The National Guard could prevent violent attempts to disrupt elections and was also effective at intimidating opposition and drilling voter conformity with official Montaña candidates on election day.

Lucas's frequent use of the National Guard gave a martial appearance to his term as jefe político and inevitably made him a target of criticism. Much of this came from Doña Policarpa Méndez, whom Lucas had kept under house arrest in Tetela's vicarage, which he had commandeered after the departure of the priest. From confinement, Policarpa waged a newspaper war against what she described as the Jacobin reign of terror in Tetela. Typical of her charges, she wrote: "What is happening in Tetela is terrible: old people and children murdered, properties confiscated at the whim of the despot, and, the height of infamy, respectable women of the town are suffering every kind of vexation, and lastly, even members of the cacique's family (Méndez) suffer persecution, banishment, and even insults."[129]

Are these accusations fair that Lucas singled out the *gente decente* and *gente de razón* of Tetela for persecution? Patrician and non-Indian families were conspicuous among Lucas's prisoners, but several Indians (at least persons without surnames), involved in the conspiracies and uprisings, were also jailed alongside the *gente de razón*. Moreover, the *gente decente* were frequently permitted to leave their cells on bail while Policarpa Méndez was ordered to reside in Lucas's own house, when an injunction ended her detention in the vicarage.[130] Indian political prisoners, meanwhile, languished in Tetela's leaky jail.

In September 1880 the electoral anguish that had gripped the Sierra for over a year at last abated. Méndez was firmly installed as Puebla governor and Manuel González as president. Late in August, Lucas resigned as jefe político of Tetela and returned to private life.[131] In one of his last official acts, he informed the alcalde of Ometepec that the state congress had stripped the village of municipal autonomy as a penalty for its disloyalty, demoting Ometepec to the status of barrio, subject to the cabecera of Tetela de Ocampo. The deputies made only one concession. In recognition of their patriotic services, they allowed Ometepec and Tececuilco to retain the names of the two great Nahua warriors, Cuautimoctzín and Xicotencatl.[132]

In Lucas's place, the more conciliatory Guanajuato miner, Isidro Grimaldo, son-in law of Governor Méndez, took charge of the district. He would remain in office throughout much of the Porfiriato. As one of his first acts, he returned Miguel Arriaga and four other Zacapoaxteco prisoners held in Tetela's jail for trial in Zacapoaxtla, where they were released upon arrival. This conciliatory gesture in the still-heated political environment of the southern Sierra brought only a brief respite. Within six months, opposition forces were reported to be gathering in the district of Alatriste. Within two years, Miguel Arriaga had again put himself at the head of an armed movement drawing support from Cuahuigtic and Ometepec, villages that once had formed the heartland of Lucas's support. Seven hundred men from Tetela, Xochiapulco, and Zacatlán, commanded by Lucas and Indalecio Sánchez, were needed to put down the revolt.[133] With such extensive grass-roots opposition in the heart of the Montaña's *cacicazgo*, combined with mounting opposition elsewhere in the state, and a perceptible cooling of Díaz's support for Méndez, it became apparent that the days of Montaña party rule in Puebla were numbered.

Conclusion

Early in 1880, Bonilla was fit enough to return from convalescence in Tetela to the cold state capital to attend the inauguration of his crowning achievement, Mexico's first secular teachers' training college.[134] The electoral violence of his last year as governor, and the increasingly martial character of Montaña power, had tended to obscure Bonilla's impressive legislative achievements.

In 1880, perhaps more out of considerations of realpolitik than of loyalty to old and faithful companions at arms, Díaz allowed the chieftains of the Puebla Sierra to demonstrate their electoral strength and hold on to the state. After all, it might well be necessary to call on Méndez's services for the reelection in 1884. Díaz also knew that Méndez, as a regional caudillo without national ambitions, would never pose a threat to his candidacy. Yet, supporting Méndez as candidate for the gubernatorial succession in Puebla incurred certain risks.

Although unswervingly loyal to Díaz over two decades, Méndez nevertheless had a mind of his own. He maintained close relations with his regional base of support in the Sierra, where he liked to manage directly his extensive farming, agricultural, and mining interests in Tetela. These small-town *serrano* roots made Méndez a natural federalist. By 1880 he saw himself as the senior Tuxtepecano and the national spokesman for a Jacobin Liberalism that he shared with other leading Tuxtepecanos, such as José María Vigil, Vicente Riva Palacios, and Trinidad García de la Cadena.[135] In December 1878, Méndez had convoked a national meeting of state governors to discuss the presidential succession. He had also vigorously opposed the candidature of Díaz's long-term friend and confidant, Justo Benítez. These pretensions, from a caudillo so close to the capital, would ultimately have to be disabused. For the moment, however, Díaz was happy to see Méndez at last take command of the state which he initially had been promised in 1858, but which had eluded him for twenty-two years.

14

The Resurgence of Central Power, 1880–1888

Governor Juan Nepomuceno Méndez followed policies similar to those of his *paisano*, Juan Crisóstomo Bonilla. He expanded secular education, increased popular awareness of constitutional rights by translating the state constitution of 1861 into Nahuatl, enhanced the fiscal (albeit not the political) autonomy of the municipality, maintained the National Guard as the guardian of these rights, reduced indirect taxes while maintaining the system of direct taxation (chiefly the "personal contribution"), removed obstacles to economic activity, and encouraged enterprise with incentives and investment in transport and infrastructure, particularly railways.[1] In his inaugural address to the state congress, Méndez praised his predecessor's modesty, honesty, humility, and concern for education. He vowed to uphold these virtues during his governorship. His empathy with the poor was demonstrated each year during the fiesta of 5 May with the distribution of clothing to needy families. Yet, in spite of its pious intentions, the Méndez governorship was plagued from the start by problems of public order suggesting widespread discontent with the Montaña regime.

The Montaña Machine and Its Critics

In one of the first acts of his governorship, Méndez abandoned direct popular elections of local officials and returned to the two-tier elections for ayuntamientos and to the appointment of jefes políticos by the state governor. During Bonilla's governorship, constitutionally untrammeled popular sovereignty, combined with single-party patronage, had proved too potent a concoction for the system to withstand. In the Sierra, the election of Nahua Indians to the municipal presidencies of Cuetzalan and Zautla, already fraught with ethnic tensions, had provoked serious dissent among the *gente de razón*. The direct elections of ayuntamientos increased rather than diminished the tendency of jefes políticos to exceed their supervisory role and become directly involved in nominations and electoral intimidation. The popular and direct election for jefes políticos had created a new sovereign territoriality—the district—that was never intended to exist. The direct election of Juan Francisco Lucas and Lauro Luna, old patriotic warriors, to Tetela and Zacapoaxtla, however popular, nevertheless rendered these two districts ungovernable and threatened the core of Montaña power.

The return to jefes políticos appointed by the governor and to two-tier municipal elections reduced the electoral calendar and took some of the heat out of local and district politics. Nonetheless, violence accompanied the elections for the state legislature in April 1882, requiring the dispatch of one hundred infantry to the district of Zacatlán, where local opponents of the Márquez Galindo clan had attacked Ahuacatlán. In October 1882, Tetela once more came under siege from the south and east, with Miguel Arriaga coordinating rebels from Ometepec and Cuahuigtic. Serious disturbances in Chiautla, in the south of the state, also required the dispatch of Federal troops.

Juan Nepomuceno Méndez, Governor of the State of Puebla, 1880–1885

In his 1883 message to the state congress, Méndez reported that the seriousness of these disorders had required the mobilization of the National Guard. One hundred infantry from Zacatlán had been deployed in the state capital (as a palace guard), and were relieved soon afterward by one hundred Xochiapulquenses.[2] Significantly, Méndez's message to the congress did not mention the most serious challenge to the public order of the state: the *pronunciamiento* of Colonel Cristóbal Palacios in Tepeji (although this already had come to the attention of Porfirio Díaz). Palacios explained to Díaz in Oaxaca that his actions had been provoked by Méndez's arbitrary style of government. Palacios was behind the wave of banditry that gripped the southern district of Acatlán throughout 1882, which required the state cavalry and the Batallón Zaragoza to be constantly on active duty. Bands of outlaws still plagued Acatlán and Tepeji as late as September 1884, when the state went to the polls for the election of the governor.[3] These problems of political order were compounded by fiscal problems as local councils found some difficulty in raising the personal tax, still the basis of state revenues.[4] Palacios's control of Tepeji and influence in Tehuacán and Acatlán would be an important factor in the fall from power of the Montaña in 1885.[5]

Yet more threatening to Méndez's control of the state was the mounting opposition on the Montaña's home ground in the Sierra. Since 1880 the opposition had chosen the Montaña *cacicazgo* in Zacatlán as its favorite target. With the principal Montaña leaders away from Tetela (Méndez in the state capital and Bonilla posted away from the state), the Zacatlán National Guard became the bulwark of the Montaña's armed power in the Sierra.

In spite of Méndez's frequent reiteration of the importance of municipal autonomy, it was precisely through the control of municipal elections that the Montaña had achieved an iron grip over the district of Zacatlán. In February 1884, commenting on the recent municipal elections, *El Progreso de Zacatlán* referred to the newly elected council as:

> the legitimate offspring of the Montaña party. . . . It is well known that the ayuntamiento elections, like all others, are made by determined individuals, whose names are so firmly lodged in the memory that they can be recited at any time. The places where the tables are to be installed are known long before, as are those who set them up to enact the electoral comedy, pretending that they are receiving polling cards from voting citizens, when really all they are doing is helping those already in authority to keep their electoral files in order. The same electors always appear in the electoral college, whose president, secretaries, and returning officers are the same people who have occupied these offices for years. The *jefatura política*, fiscal administration, municipal offices, the secretaries, and even elected offices are linked to determined people who occupy them in perpetuity, at least for their lifetimes, and with the right to pass them on to their descendants after their deaths.[6]

Similar criticism had been expressed by José María Maldonado of the Conservative *camarilla* that dominated Tlatlauqui and Teziutlán and aspired to control Zacapoaxtla in 1862, although a notable difference was evident in the Montaña emphasis upon bureaucracy and electoral machinery. Márquez Galindo controlled an expanded public arena, with patronage reaching down to the village schoolteacher, who often doubled as the secretary, and to the National Guard captain in the remotest hamlet. The Conservative *camarillas* described by Maldonado sought to circumscribe the public arena by exercising direct private control through dominant landed families and the parish clergy. The Montaña's critics complained of too much government, rather than too little, and of the control of this expanded state by men whose Masonic ties were stronger even than those of blood. They insisted that the frantic legislative activity of the Montaña, throughout its eight years in office, was directed more at maintaining power than benefiting the citizens whom it claimed to be serving.[7] The editor of *El Progreso de Zacatlán* listed recent incidents of electoral violence and intimidation, which ranged from arbitrary arrests to assassinations, all perpetrated by the Montaña's agents.[8]

The Federal Imposition of Rosendo Márquez

Méndez would have entered the election year of 1884 with a sense of foreboding. His governorship had been a troubled one, characterized by a noticeable coolness in his relations with President Manuel González, who, only under duress, had provided the minimum federal support for the suppression of dissent in the south of the state.[9] To make matters worse, Bonilla's death on 30 January removed Méndez's right-hand man and preferred successor. Having honored Bonilla with a huge secular funeral in the state capital, which included speeches from the directors of the various educational institutions he had founded and which closed with long Masonic orations, Méndez took temporary leave from the governorship in order to direct personally the electoral preparations.[10]

After Bonilla, the only two possible Montaña candidates for the governorship were Lucas, who would certainly have declined the offer, and the governor's son, Miguel. The younger Méndez had served in the state legislature between 1879 and 1880, and as federal deputy for Tetela since 1880. Rather than a flagrant case of nepotism, the choice of Miguel demonstrated the extreme personalism (and smallness) of the Montaña party. The death of Ramón Márquez Galindo in February 1877—throughout the French Intervention and the Restored Republic the *tres Juanes*' closest companion at arms—had removed the option of the Montaña succession passing to Zacatlán. Thereafter, the Montaña, in essence, meant the *tres Juanes*, now reduced to two, within a territory comprising the district of Tetela and satellite communities within the southern Sierra. Any shift in the Montaña's axis, from its heartland in Tetela, say, to Zacatlán, or to Huauchinango, was now inconceivable.[11] That the two other main candidates for the governorship, Rafael Cravioto and Hermenegildo Carrillo, also drew their support from the Sierra demonstrated the narrowness of the Montaña's territorial and personal base.

Before the election for governor came the elections for the federal presidency and supreme court. To guarantee a secure return to the presidency, Díaz needed to be able to count on the state of Puebla. He had no reservations about Méndez's personal loyalty but questioned his ability to conciliate his enemies and pacify the state. The danger for Díaz was that the weak or unpopular Montaña regime in Puebla might threaten the stability of the entire Mexican southeast. He also had begun to question Méndez's political judgment, first in the convocation, for a second time, of a *junta de gobernadores*, composed of loyal Tuxtepecano generals, to deliberate upon the presidential succession; and second, on the choice of Méndez's own son for the Puebla governorship.

In April 1884, Díaz sent his trusted colleague, General Rosendo Márquez, to Puebla with instructions to offer Méndez a permanent commission as Brigadier General in the regular army as well as the presidency of the supreme court of military justice, in exchange for withdrawing his son's candidacy for governor.[12] At first, Méndez resisted these blandishments. But he was forced to accept the arrangement when Díaz dispatched six thousand Federal troops to Puebla, ostensibly to ensure stability during the elections. Provocatively, Hermenegildo Carrillo, rival for the governorship, was given command of these forces. He stationed three thousand in Zacapoaxtla, effectively encircling Xochiapulco, and distributed the rest throughout the state. The Seventeenth Infantry Brigade took positions at Libres, with cavalry squads dispatched to guard the railway and telegraph lines. No clearer demonstration could have been made of the federal government's determination to prevent the Montaña from influencing the electoral process. This time, the Montaña could not dispatch National Guards to "protect" the polling booths.

Ostensibly, Federal troops were sent to Puebla to ensure that federal nominees were elected to the presidency, supreme court, and legislature. But this was recognized as a transparent justification since the Montaña had always been, and remained, loyal to Díaz and would willingly have fallen in with his national strategy. The main purpose for sending the Federal force to Puebla was to prevent the Montaña from mobilizing guards to influence the forthcoming gubernatorial elections. However, managing state elections proved a much harder task than Díaz and his advisers had ever envisaged.

In the primary elections for governor in November, the Montaña won an impressive victory. Rafael Cravioto received only three votes for the electoral college; Miguel Méndez gained a clear majority.[13] He should have gone on to win the governorship, but Díaz had already decided that Puebla politics was too dangerous to be left to the Poblanos and that the governorship should go to Rosendo Márquez. Díaz put forward this candidacy very late, leaving Governor Méndez no time to organize opposition or to find an alternative.[14] Now the task for Díaz was how to persuade Méndez and Lucas to accept his choice without provoking the Montaña into rebellion.

Díaz made an inspired selection in Rosendo Márquez for the Puebla governorship. He was well known, not only to Méndez and Lucas but also to Carrillo. They had all fought together in the Sierra during the revolt of La Noria and shared a degree of mutual respect and trust. Like Díaz and the leaders of the Montaña, Márquez had emerged from humble origins, working in a Tepic textile mill during his twenties before earning promotions in the Liberal army in Jalisco.

Rosendo Márquez realized that his candidature would get nowhere in the southern Sierra without Lucas's cooperation. After several unanswered letters, Márquez decided to visit Tetela personally in early July, accompanied by the Ninth Federal Brigade, in an effort to break Lucas's silence. On 1 July, from the district capital, Márquez wrote again to Lucas, placing himself at the cacique's orders, expressing the desire for a meeting with the old friend whom he had not seen for over ten years. To his polite and deferential tone, Márquez hinted at the possible deployment of force with the news that he had stationed Federal troops at Huahuaxtla, thus effectively cutting off Xochiapulco from the *tierra caliente*, its source of supply during any rebellion.[15]

Effectively encircled, Lucas must have realized that continued silence would only lead to a tightening of the federal vice.[16] Moreover, just as Márquez entered the Sierra, Miguel Arriaga and Isidro Segura (of Ometepec) ordered one and one-half leagues of telegraph lines across the plains of Xicalhuata to be destroyed, hoping to put the blame on Lucas and thus sow distrust between Márquez and the cacique. Márquez did not fall for this ruse and ordered both Arriaga and Segura arrested.[17] Nevertheless, their action was a preview of the complex, often violent, local repercussions to the dismantling of the Montaña's control of state government.

Later in July, with the primary elections for the presidency and federal legislature completed, Márquez left the Sierra. Although he had succeeded in establishing communication with Lucas, Márquez had still failed to meet him personally.[18] Lucas's reticence to meet Márquez was perhaps due to genuine concern for his own security, as the last Montaña leader still resident in the Sierra. Lucas also wanted firm guarantees from Díaz before agreeing to abandon his long-standing alliance with the Tetelenses, and to swear allegiance to Márquez.

Hence, Lucas pressured Díaz to confirm his rank as Brigadier General and his post as inspector of the state's forces. Although Díaz delayed the promotion until 17 February 1885 (after Méndez's removal from the state), he offered effusive flattery to Lucas, insisting that nothing would be done in the forthcoming gubernatorial elections without his consent and that of Méndez.[19] Rosendo Márquez finally announced his candidature on 1 December 1884.[20] Lucas assured him that all Sierra districts had voted for him on Méndez's instructions, and promised to cooperate with his administration while expressing the hope that Márquez would continue the traditions of patriotism and liberty laid down by his two predecessors.[21]

In spite of the close contacts between Márquez and Lucas since June and the tacit accord between Díaz and Méndez, neither the Montaña's electoral machinery nor Méndez's enemies, who were keen now to take advantage of his imminent removal, could easily be restrained. Montaña jefes políticos throughout the state, backed by troops sent from the Sierra (those who succeeded in slipping past the Federal cantonments), were poised to ensure that the election went in the Montaña's favor. Llanura politicians such as Coutolenc, who were eager to redress the political imbalance, succeeded in persuading Díaz to place the Fourth Corps of Rural Guard at Libres under the command of José de Jesús Bernal, the Montaña's mortal enemy. This action neutralized Montaña electoral influence in the politically strategic southern margins of the Sierra.[22]

Díaz and Méndez finally agreed upon Puebla's gubernatorial succession at a meeting in Mexico City in early December only days before the secondary elections. Even after this meeting, Méndez fought a rearguard action pointing out the difficulty of backing Márquez rather than Carrillo (now the preferred Montaña candidate) as most electors and jefes políticos had committed themselves and were bound by ballots. Díaz warned Méndez to proceed with extreme caution and sent Federal troops throughout the state to prevent disorders.[23]

Because a constitutional reform of 1883 had fixed gubernatorial terms to exactly four years, Méndez did not have to hand over his office until the end of January 1885.[24] During his last month in office, the Tetela caudillo fortified the governor's palace with artillery while rumors of an imminent Sierra uprising abounded.[25] Márquez found Méndez to be cold and aloof. Indeed, he so distrusted the outgoing governor that he placed garrisons at all the railway stations between Puebla and Mexico City to ensure that Méndez did not disembark for the Sierra.[26] Finally, at the end of January, Méndez traveled to Mexico City to accept the presidency of the supreme military tribunal, a post he retained until his death. He was never allowed to return to the Sierra and his native Tetela.

Márquez swore the oath as governor on 1 February 1885. The following substitutes were named: Lauro Luna and Miguel Remedios Méndez (both part of the Montaña inner circle from Tetela), Coutolenc (leader of what remained of the Llanura party), and Mucío Martínez (federal military commander of the southern part of the state and future governor).[27] The mixture of parties and regional influences reflected Díaz's insistence (in spite of Márquez's privately expressed advice to the contrary) that the state government should contain elements from both the Montaña and the Llanura. In one of his first actions, Márquez confirmed Lucas's rank as Brigadier General and named him the inspector of state forces. This act made Lucas the client of the federally imposed general from Jalisco and confirmed that the days of the Montaña as an autonomous regional political force had ended.[28]

The Consolidation of the Márquez Regime in the Sierra

Throughout the spring and summer of 1885, Márquez kept to his word concerning the inviolability of the Montaña jefes políticos and regularly sought Lucas's advice on nominations in the Sierra.[29] But at the same time, the governor began constructing a counterpoise to the Montaña, both by reorganizing and centralizing the state's armed forces and by imposing his own nominees on the strategic districts of Libres, Chiautla, Tepeji, and Tehuacán.[30] This process proved to be a perilous one. The clumsy substitution in Tehuacán of the incumbent Enrique Mont, by Cristóbal Palacios, cacique of Tepeji, nearly sparked a rebellion.[31] The bandit-infested south of the state, along an arc running from Tehuacán to Chiautla and Acatlán, confronted Márquez (much as it had his predecessor) with a perennial problem of maintaining order and shoring up unpopular jefes políticos. But Márquez feared disorder in the northern Sierra far more, and realized that good relations with Lucas were the key to the overall political stability of the state.

At first, Márquez kept his side of the bargain concerning Montaña appointments in the Puebla Sierra by allowing Lucas to retain carte blanche with civil appointments in the districts of Tetela, Alatriste, and northern Libres (in the *municipio* of Zautla).[32] To maintain security in correspondence with Lucas, he decided to adopt a code (a policy he was soon to follow with most Sierra district authorities and informants).[33] Lucas's continued favor with the governor infuriated powerful local interests in the Sierra who had expected to move into the vacuum left by Méndez's departure.[34] In an effort to discredit Lucas, Miguel Arriaga, Isidro Segura, José María Leal (of Cuahuigtic), and José de Jesús Bernal mounted a coordinated campaign of rumors, political assassination, and sabotage.

In Bernal's view, allowing Lucas to supervise elections in the southern Sierra was like "placing the Church in the hands of Luther."[35] Late in 1885, to disguise a campaign of electoral violence of their own, Bernal, Arriaga, and Leal insisted that Lucas and Braulio Alcántara of Zacapoaxtla were planning a rebellion timed for the December local elections.[36] Márquez, now well informed about affairs in the Sierra and convinced that Lucas had been won over, dismissed these rumors.[37] Yet, notwithstanding his trust in Lucas, Márquez found the violence and factionalism in the Sierra disturbing.

Lucas strove to take full advantage of his standing with the governor. Throughout late 1885 and 1886 he frequently informed Márquez of cases of intimidation and personal violence perpetrated by Bernal, jefe político of Libres. Complaints ranged from intimidation during municipal elections, confiscation of land of those unable or unwilling to pay rents or the personal tax, arrest of villagers unable or unwilling to pay hefty contributions for the equipping of municipal brass bands, and violence against Nahuas who refused to remove their hats or to dismount from their horses in the presence of the jefe político or his sons. Ethnic tension suffused many of these conflicts. Bernal seemed determined to reverse the gains achieved by Nahua villagers in return for their patriotic services against the European Intervention and their participation in the revolt of La Noria and the revolution of Tuxtepec.[38] Lucas and Porfirio Díaz finally convinced Márquez in August 1886 to reassign Bernal to a district distant from the Sierra after he had sent a squadron of cavalry to Xochiapulco to apprehend fugitive *peones* from his hacienda who had sought sanctuary there.[39] But within a few weeks, Bernal was back in Libres to resume his campaign to extinguish the *cacicazgo* of the Tetelenses.

Electoral violence in the southern Sierra paled next to the mounting challenge in the western Sierra from the ambitious Cravioto family. The Craviotos had served the Liberal, and especially the federal, cause since the Three Years' War and now expected their rewards. Throughout 1885 and 1886 brothers Rafael, Francisco, and Simón Cravioto of Huauchinango, who had alternated as governors of the adjoining state of Hidalgo since their participation in the Tuxtepec revolt in 1876, came under attack for abuse of power in the influential Mexico City newspaper *El Partido Liberal*, which was owned by Díaz's father-in-law, Manuel Romero Rubio.[40] Díaz had to prepare for the possibility that the Craviotos might be driven out of Hidalgo and forced to return to the core of their *cacicazgo* in Huauchinango. The presence of another ambitious caudillo in the Puebla Sierra filled Díaz with apprehension, particularly the prospect of a combination between Lucas and the Cravioto brothers to challenge the state government, as they had done in 1867 and again in 1876.

To preempt this threat, Díaz and Márquez selected the Montaña stronghold of the Márquez Galindo family at Zacatlán. Ramón Márquez Galindo (son) had been playing on Márquez's fear of the Craviotos' resurgence since the summer of 1885, when he first reported the arming of villages throughout Huauchinango.[41] In a coded letter of 29 May 1886, Márquez Galindo outlined to the state governor the suspected strategy that the Craviotos would adopt and the means that he would use to prevent any rebel combination in the western Sierra. The Zacatlán cacique recommended close vigilance along the routes from Huauchinango to Tetela where a deposit of rebel arms had been hidden. He had visited San Miguel Tenango and Otlatlán, villages bordering with Tetela, personally dictating security measures. He believed an agreement between Lucas and Rafael Cravioto, who were long-standing enemies, to be most unlikely. In addition, Cravioto had all the arms he needed, having recently distributed more than two thousand rifles throughout the district of Huauchinango.[42]

The cordon sanitaire established by Márquez Galindo to deter the Craviotos' reentry to Puebla politics succeeded. By the summer of 1888, Governor Márquez felt sufficiently confident of his control of the northwestern Sierra to allow General Francisco Cravioto, governor of Hidalgo, to make an official visit to his hometown, where he was fêted by wind bands and floral tributes.[43]

Zautla and the Waning of Popular Liberalism

The stability secured by Márquez Galindo in Zacatlán and Huauchinango proved harder to achieve in the southern Sierra. Here, the surviving popular bases of the Montaña, particularly the influence of Lucas among the Nahua population, clashed with Márquez's desire for greater central control. Throughout 1886 and 1887, Díaz and Márquez received reports of the violent efforts of Arriaga, Bernal, and others to intimidate municipal presidents and village leaders elected under the Bonilla and Méndez regimes. Francisco Agustín was finally toppled from the presidency of Cuetzalan early in 1887, but he continued to fight a rearguard action against the new cacique, Jesús Flores, throughout the subsequent seven years.[44] Xochitlán seethed with similar conflicts. Nahua barrio dwellers, who had been promised interest-free land titles and exemption from the personal tax by a previous Montaña jefe político, Vicente Ortuño, clashed with the new, more oppressive ayuntamiento backed by jefe político Carlos María Betancurt Molina of Zacapoaxtla.[45] But it was the villages on the edge of the southern Sierra, along the boundary between the districts of Zacapoaxtla, Tetela, Alatriste, and Libres, which were the most frequent flashpoints over such issues as taxation, electoral autonomy, the immunities of National Guards, control over land privatization, compulsory services, and forced contributions to the costs of forming municipal brass bands.

The most disputed and divided municipality in this zone was Zautla, whose sensitive location between Lucas's strongholds at Taxcantla and Xochiapulco and Bernal's lair at the hacienda of Almajac and base at Libres gave local events an immediate resonance in the state and federal capitals. The onset of the campaigns for the 1888 presidential and gubernatorial elections, in which both Díaz and Márquez would seek reelection, projected Zautla and Xochiapulco once more into the national limelight.

In December 1887, Díaz received an alarming report from the Minister of War, General Bibiano Davalos, of an insurrection brewing both in the Sierra Norte and in Chiautla (in the south of the state) against Díaz's projected reelection. The insurrection would start with protests against the revision of Articles 78 and 108 of the federal constitution that permitted the consecutive reelection of the President. A plan would be issued on 4 February 1888. To preempt such an event, Davalos dispatched 150 infantry to Zacapoaxtla under Lt. Col. Florencio Díaz and a further 100 backed by 113 cavalry to Chiautla under General Mucío Martínez.[46]

Mucío Martínez, who had been organizing both irregular and regular forces in southern Puebla since the early 1880s, felt confident that he could keep the peace in the south of the state.[47] The Puebla Sierra presented more of a problem. True to form, faced with the approach of Federal troops, Xochiapulco mobilized its own National Guard battalion. This prompted

Florencio Díaz to station his infantry in Xochiapulco and the barrio of Ixehuaco until after Porfirio Díaz's reelection.[48]

Díaz inquired of Márquez whether Lucas had ordered the mobilization of the Xochiapulco battalion, or whether it had occurred "spontaneously, with a revolutionary character." Márquez assured Díaz that the cacique had not been involved, and that he remained "a person of absolute confidence." The Xochiapulco battalion had been mobilized, the governor explained, only upon receiving rumors, spread by Miguel Arriaga, that state and Federal troops were moving to disarm them. At that point, men from Xochiapulco's barrios had marched to their cabecera to oppose any attempt at disarmament.[49] In a lengthy explanation of the events to Díaz, Lucas confirmed Márquez's conviction that there had been no conspiracy in Xochiapulco. The conspiracy, Lucas insisted, had been hatched by certain oppressive jefes políticos who, by presenting him as a troublemaker, sought to attract Federal troops to back them in the suppression and disarmament of National Guard veterans in the villages.[50] Lucas urged Díaz to convince Márquez to appoint "honorable and suitable" jefes políticos who would protect the rights and guarantees of the villagers. He reminded Díaz that these villagers had taken up arms in defense of the nation and of the constitution, without expecting anything in return. He assured the President that he would do all in his power to keep the peace. But to achieve this end, he needed Díaz's help in persuading Márquez to rein in abusive jefes políticos such as Bernal of Libres.[51]

Two months later, during the elections for the federal congress in June 1888, the abuses suffered by villages in the southern Sierra were still occupying Porfirio Díaz in frantic correspondence with Lucas.[52] Luis Antonio Díaz reported to Lucas that men from the Zautla barrios of Ocotzingo, Xalcomulco, Chilapa, and Chinampa, complaining that the authorities in Zautla were persecuting them, had come to Xochiapulco to hand in their arms. Luis Antonio Díaz asked Lucas whether he should take in their weapons or send the fugitives back to Zautla armed. They also informed Luis Antonio Díaz that their representative, Manuel Calixto, had been murdered on Bernal's orders (later, it was revealed that Calixto had only been kidnapped and then released).[53] Lucas instructed Luis Antonio Díaz to give 25 to 30 pesos to each man, to be drawn from municipal funds. When Manuel Crisolís, Xochiapulco's mayor, reported that such large sums could only be lent with interest to the men, Lucas suggested that they should be put to work at Cuauximaloya, Crisolís's estate, or sent to Taxcantla where, as it was sowing time, he would be able to provide them with maize for planting.[54]

Lucas wrote to the President again in mid-June, spelling out the reason for the unrest in the southern Sierra. He expressed concern for the men who had served in the National Guard and had earned exemption from taxation, but who now were being ordered to pay the personal tax. The state of Puebla's National Guard law was being ignored now that the deputies, who formerly had upheld these immunities, were no longer effectively doing so. Lucas insisted that the tax exemption for veterans represented the very least the nation could offer in exchange for the sacrifices these men had made during the Three Years' War, the French Intervention, and later revolutions. He conceded that soldiers' immunities would inevitably be curtailed in peacetime; nevertheless, he pleaded for veterans and orphans. He feared that the violent application of the decree would destroy "our work" of pacifying the country and singled out Bernal as culpable of maltreating former Guardsmen.[55]

Lucas's correspondence reveals that he was playing two tunes. In his dealings with the President and the governor, he stressed compliance with the law, but urged flexibility and magnanimity with veterans while warning of dangers to public order if the district authorities persisted with the humiliation of their Nahua subjects. In his dealings with the municipal authorities of Xochiapulco and the barrios of Zautla, Lucas urged resistance. Thus, rather than return fugitive Guardsmen to Zautla to suffer Bernal's arbitrary administration, Lucas ordered Colonel Juan Dinorín, commander of Xochiapulco's National Guard, to take in their arms in exchange for receipts and cash. Of the 128 men who handed in their weapons, some chose to go to Taxcantla and others to remain in Xochiapulco. Many, attracted by offers of free pasture for the first two months and then reasonable rents thereafter, brought their sheep and cattle. Others were allowed to plant corn or other crops, with equal shares between worker and landowner. All were permitted to cut as much wood as they needed for their own use but not for sale.[56]

Officially these men were to be disarmed and given receipts and a prize for handing in their weapons. In practice, those who chose not to return to Zautla kept their weapons. Rather than pass on the weapons that were handed in, either to Bernal or the governor, Dinorín divided them among the residents of Xochiapulco's cabecera and the barrio of Cuahuaximaloyan. In the hands of veterans, these arms were safe from official attempts at disarmament, but only as long as the state recognized the privileges and immunities of veteran Guardsmen.[57] This accounts for why Lucas was so emphatic about the rights of veterans conferred by Puebla's National Guard law. Ensuring the continued arming of Xochiapulco's National Guard was hardly an insurrectionary strategy. Lucas kept Porfirio Díaz regularly informed of the state of affairs. The President saw it as a local problem and urged Márquez to exercise the utmost fairness and attention to the sensibilities of loyal and patriotic subjects.[58]

Lucas doubted Márquez's assurances that the privileges and immunities of veterans would be respected, and he insisted to Díaz that there was more to the Zautla problem than tax evasion and unruly veteran Guardsmen. He accused Bernal of stirring up trouble in the municipality. José Máximo, National Guard captain and justice of the peace for the barrio of Tenampulco (and Zautla's municipal president between 1878 and 1885) recently had narrowly escaped death in a beating administered by Bernal's sons. Bernal had then invited several people of this barrio to his hacienda where they had been ordered to withhold their taxes, disobey the authorities, and go to the cabecera (Zautla) to "simulate" their grievances.[59] Apart from intimidating and undermining the authority of public officials in Zautla's barrios, Bernal planned to end the practice of Tetela providing sanctuary for fugitive estate workers and day laborers from Zautla. The jefe político used the harsh collection of the personal tax as a means of drafting labor onto his estates, and he regularly sent forces across district boundaries to arrest these hapless *peones,* many of whom had fled as far afield as the Veracruz cantons of Papantla and Jalacingo.[60]

Márquez agreed that much of the turmoil stemmed from misunderstandings about the grounds for exemption from the personal tax and from the fact that this tax was now being collected in villages which, since the abolition of the *capitación* (Indian tribute) in 1855, had become accustomed to exemption from all taxation in exchange for military service. The vague wording of the exemption clauses was partly to blame. The original personal tax law of 21 June 1877 exempted the physically disabled, college students, schoolteachers, mayors, and alderman, and soldiers on active service, on leave, or called to duty. The law of 25 December 1886 had added "those retired or mutilated in campaign fighting to defend national independence or institutions." This last clause had invited a multitude of claims of tax exemption on the basis of past service in the National Guard— claims which Márquez considered to be without foundation since "the National Guard (is) an institution which has not been regulated and one for which there is no longer any need." Yet the National Guard regulations remained on both the federal and state statute books. Indeed, obligatory membership in the National Guard was written into the constitution. However, in 1875, Governor Romero Vargas had decreed a Ley Orgánica de las Fuerzas de Seguridad Pública del Estado (Organic Law of State Public Security Forces) that had centralized, reduced, and professionalized the armed forces of the state. After Díaz had taken power, rather than reconstitute Puebla's state force on the basis of the National Guard, Bonilla and Méndez had used the same regulations. Thus, in 1888, the National Guard had been in abeyance for twelve years.[61]

Admitting to Díaz that there were widespread misconceptions about tax exemption, Márquez was nevertheless convinced that a political motive lay behind the disobedience of so many barrios in the southern Sierra to the district authorities. Tax evasion occurred especially in the districts of Tetela, Tlatlauqui, and certain municipalities of San Juan de los Llanos, "where those influenced by Juan Francisco abound . . . (men who) are constantly interrupting the good working of the public administration." Márquez had tried conciliation in March by increasing the number of exemptions from thirteen to twenty, among whom "are chiefs, officers, and troops of the Federal Army, individuals serving actively in the armed forces of the state, prison guards and those mutilated in the campaign in defense of National Institutions and Independence." Former Guardsmen in Zautla's Nahua barrios rejected these exemptions. In 1875, Governor Romero Vargas, using Bernal, had strengthened the state "security force" in the cabecera, and these men stood to benefit now from the tax exemption. Thus, Márquez's amendment threatened to reverse the political gains made by National Guard commanders such as José Máximo on behalf of their Nahua barrios and to shift the political equilibrium back in favor of the *gente de razón* of the cabecera, who manned Bernal's "rural defense force."

Apart from his pique at the disobedience of Zautla's Nahua barrios, Márquez was also deeply concerned about the implication of National Guard immunities for Puebla's public finances, which remained in a parlous state.[62] The governor warned that if those who claimed to have belonged to the National Guard were also exempted from the tax along with all the other categories claiming exemption—"those who hold local public offices, those who work as jurors, tax inspectors, those who in any way help in the progress of public education, the section inspectors, the members of philharmonic corps, the fathers of families with three or more tax-paying sons, the notoriously poor"—then district finances would wither entirely. Districts in Sierra received virtually nothing from the taxes on manufacturing and commerce, or from plots adjudicated from village commons through the laws of *desamortización*. Hence, the personal tax "was the only one in these localities which can satisfy the needs of local administration."[63]

Bonilla and Méndez had overcome the fiscal deficit that resulted from exempting so many *serranos* from the personal tax by licensing local councils to raise ad hoc taxes for specific projects, such as road and school building. Such levies tended to discriminate against the better-off, with ready cash available. The personal contribution, by contrast, although graduated according to income, was a less progressive tax and harder to evade. Márquez defended himself against the accusation that he was punishing good patriots with claims that he continually responded to their demands: "Juan Francisco is paid a salary as Inspector of State Forces; Luis Antonio (Díaz) has received diverse subsidies, and a multitude of ordinary soldiers have been helped as well, and always when they have demonstrated some need." He had even agreed that the committee to determine tax exemptions would be made up of people recommended by Lucas, assuring that justice would be done.[64]

In responding to the crisis, Porfirio Díaz had to weigh the risk of undermining Márquez's authority in a critical reelection year against the danger of allowing his jefes políticos to provoke unrest in the southern Sierra. The governor was also coming under pressure elsewhere in the state. As a former National Guard commander, Díaz understood and sympathized with Lucas's campaign in favor of his veteran Guardsmen. If Márquez could rein in the predatory district authorities of the southern Sierra, particularly Bernal in Libres, the conflict could surely be managed. But Márquez possessed very little leverage on the authorities of districts in which the *gente de razón* relished the best opportunity in three decades for reasserting their control over the majority Indian population.[65]

Lucas, now without a patron on the state level, understood how the balance of power in the southern Sierra had changed since Méndez's removal to Mexico City in 1885. It was clear to him that the residents of Zautla's barrios were migrating to Tetela, not so much because of the existence of the personal tax but because of the violent and discriminatory way in which the law was being enforced. People had fled from Zautla's northern barrios because there was no other option. Only forceful action by the state governor could remedy this situation. Guarantees must be provided, Lucas advised Márquez, before the men would return home.[66]

Lucas's role in moderating rather than in exacerbating conflicts between villages and district authorities received further confirmation in July 1888 when he secured the secession of Xochiapulco's barrios of Las Lomas and Jilotepec to rejoin their former cabecera, Zacapoaxtla. He accomplished this despite external meddling in Xochiapulco by the Zacapoaxtla district authorities.[67] People in Zacapoaxtla had persuaded some residents of Las Lomas and Jilotepec to petition for secession, against the will of the majority of inhabitants of these barrios. Lucas confided to Díaz that, as the solution to the long-standing problem of Las Lomas and Jilotepec, secession was unlikely to succeed because most people in these villages still wanted to belong to Xochiapulco.[68] As a return gesture, Márquez admitted that Zautla authorities had acted clumsily and asked Lucas for any suggestions about who might serve in Zautla's ayuntamiento in the following year.[69] By late July, relations between Lucas and Márquez had improved, helped by an unspecified donation from Márquez to the Tetela cacique.[70]

In July and August 1888, Márquez needed every friend he could find as his campaign for reelection as governor faced opposition from every quarter. Representatives of all of the city of Puebla's barrios signed a petition supporting the candidacy of Apolinar Castillo, recently governor of Veracruz and close friend of Luis Mier y Terán. Márquez's unpopularity in the state capital was confirmed by a petition opposing his reelection, signed by the city's artisans and shopkeepers. Another anonymous petition from the capital accused Márquez of drunkenness, gambling, and debauchery on top of nepotism and peculation of state funds. Moreover, he had also shamefully neglected the educational improvements introduced by his two predecessors. Even José María Juárez, Díaz's electoral agent in Puebla, was unhappy about Márquez's candidature.[71] Despite these circumstances, Díaz was reluctant to hand the governorship back to a native son of the state who might revive the now almost extinct Montaña-Llanura rivalry. Moreover, notwithstanding his unpopularity, Márquez was sufficiently entrenched politically to manage his own reelection. His effort was simplified because popular support did not collect around an opposition candidate. Instead, twenty-one candidates, including Hermenegildo Carrillo and Apolinar Castillo, divided and confused the challenge to the incumbent.[72]

Díaz's backing for Márquez removed any remaining chance that Méndez might return to Puebla to stage an electoral comeback. Besides, the heartland of the Montaña, in the districts of Zacatlán and Tetela, was now split following Márquez Galindo's alliance with the state governor. Like Lucas, Méndez was learning that the best chance to influence politics in Puebla was through Díaz and Márquez. This received confirmation in late July when Díaz agreed to recommend the Tetela caudillo's brother, Víctor Méndez, for a senior post in Puebla after the forthcoming elections.[73] Márquez, however unpopular in Puebla, made a useful ally for Díaz: he was scrupulously loyal, lacked the distractions and partiality of a local appointment, governed with the Pavlovian obedience of a military man, and possessed some political skill. In addition, Márquez had first proposed the constitutional reform that would permit presidential reelection. The least that Díaz could offer in return was support for his compadre's reelection in Puebla.[74]

Following the temporary truce accompanying Márquez's reelection, the tax conflict reemerged in Zautla. Lucas reported arbitrary imprisonments, beatings, and expulsions of stubborn barrio authorities who resisted taxation by invoking their immunities.[75] One eloquent case occurred on the night of 10 September 1888 in Zautla. Nine armed *gente de razón*, acting on orders from the municipal president, Antonio Parra, went to the barrio of Santa Cruz, where they forced Manuel Francisco Bonifacio, the former municipal president, out of bed and jailed him for failure to pay his head tax. The vigilantes stole his savings of 6 pesos. Bonifacio soon escaped custody and fled to sanctuary in Xochiapulco.

Bonifacio's account of the events following his flight to Tetela revealed that the governor still favored Bernal and Zautla's authorities over the inhabitants of the barrios in spite of his promise to Lucas that he would accept his advice on candidates for the next municipal election. Parra had traveled to Puebla to meet Márquez to discuss the flight of residents from Xalcomulco and Chinampa barrios to Xochiapulco. The governor gave Parra carte blanche to arrest and tax these men if they returned. In his parting remarks to Parra, Márquez revealed his contempt for the Montaña and made clear that the time had ended when the "Tetela Boys" governed Puebla. He added that they would either have to get into line or get killed.[76] The governor concluded the meeting with Parra by giving assurances that he would support his bid to retain the presidency of the Zautla council during the next year. In contrast to the indulgent way with which Parra had been received, the governor rebuffed Bonifacio's request for a hearing by claiming that the ill health of his wife prevented a meeting—clearly an excuse.

Unable to voice their grievances directly to the governor, the persecuted Zautlecos turned again to Lucas. In September 1888 the cacique claimed that, during the previous year, more than eight hundred men, women, and children had fled Zautla and its barrios to Tetela. Racial antipathies suffused the conflict.[77] Zautla's *gente de razón*, backed by the governor and jefe político, now controlled the council and wanted to assert their authority over previous Indian officeholders and National Guardsmen by forcing them all to pay the personal tax.

The racial issue in Zautla receives further confirmation in the muster list of the Chinampan barrio's company of security forces in July 1888. This force of sixty-one men was commanded by Francisco and Miguel Arriaga, from Zacapoaxtla (not Zautla) and stout opponents of Lucas since 1876. Other officers were Francisco Martín and Juan de la Cruz, who had organized the secession of Las Lomas barrio from Xochiapulco; Juan and Manuel Dinorín, of a Xochiapulco family once close to Lucas but enemies since Tuxtepec; and Antonio and Gregorio Parra, the current municipal president of Zautla and his brother. Not one soldier in the company lacked a surname, implying a force of *gente de razón*. Operating on the boundary of Zautla, Xochiapulco, and Zacapoaxtla at the height of the conflict over the personal tax and the approach to the gubernatorial elections, this mounted company was behind much of the intimidation that motivated so many Zautlecos from the barrios to seek sanctuary in Tetela.[78] Among the hundreds of men who took refuge in Tetela could be found many former members of Zautla's First Company mustered by José Máximo eight years earlier, who were divested now of their National Guard ranks and immunities.

A powerful sense of the loss of Liberal freedoms and guarantees and the return to an age of more arbitrary and coercive relations between Indians and *gente de razón* is conveyed in a letter from Lucas to Márquez, written in December 1888, as the governor embarked upon a second term in office. Over the second half of December, numerous inhabitants of Zautla's barrios had traveled to Tetela to complain to Lucas about a range of abuses committed by the municipal authorities. Men of between twelve and seventy years of age were being forced to pay quotas of between 1 and 2.5 pesos toward the cost of forming a *cuerpo filarmónico*. If unable to pay, the tax collectors confiscated property, animals, and even essential agricultural implements, which were not returned if the tax remained unpaid within a fortnight. Other barrio dwellers complained that land that had been adjudicated to them under José Máximo's presidency was being confiscated because they had not paid *censos* (interest), from which they claimed exemption on grounds that their plots were valued at less than 200 pesos. The municipal president and his secretary, who daily toured the municipality collecting *censos* and confiscating the plots, tools, and property of those

unable to pay, informed citizens that land confiscated would not be returned since it was not common land but belonged to the saints and to the
Church, and was therefore needed for supporting the cult. However, several
witnesses observed that confiscated plots were being worked by the president and secretary of the ayuntamiento for their own benefit. Lucas insisted
that what aggrieved the inhabitants of Zautla's barrios was "not so much
having to pay but the extremely insulting way in which the president and
his secretary mistreated them on their rounds." The timing of this aggressive tax farming, on the eve of the municipal elections on 31 December,
was also significant. Citizens who were disarmed, intimidated, indebted,
landless, and deprived of the tools necessary for ensuring their subsistence
were unlikely to be assertive voters. Indeed, the tax campaign seems to
have been intended to hasten the emigration of Zautla's barrio dwellers and
to ensure that the municipality would never again be governed by Nahua
Indians. Evidently, the preference of Zautla's *gente de razón* was for more
Verdi and less popular Liberalism.[79]

Conclusion

The Zautla problem proved to be the most intractable of Márquez's governorship. Although the governor presented Lucas's part in the conflict as in-
flammatory and seditious, the cacique performed an important cushioning,
mediating, and conciliating role in a struggle that might well have grown
into a major Sierra rebellion of the kind that had challenged the governments of the Restored Republic. Although Lucas never threatened revolt,
he did predict unrest, the prospect of which, in the crucial reelection year
of 1888, constituted a risk that neither Díaz nor Márquez could afford.
Lucas's ability to ensure a safe haven for the fugitive Guardsmen in
Xochiapulco by offering them sharecropping agreements on his ranch at
Taxcantla provided a political and physical space that helped to defuse the
tension. Additionally, Lucas's willingness to support the secession of the
troublesome Jilotepec and Las Lomas left the Zacapoaxtecos feeling less
directly menaced by their Jacobin neighbors.

   Lucas succeeded in defusing potential unrest, but he could not prevent
the continued erosion of individual rights and guarantees, the protection of
which had always formed the basis of his authority. The events in Zautla,
between Bernal's initial uprising in 1879 and the terror he sowed in 1888,
illustrate the limits of radical Liberalism in rural Mexico during the late
nineteenth century. A certain brand of egalitarian Liberalism, emphasizing
self-government and constitutional guarantees against arbitrary government, exercised a strong appeal among the Nahua population of the southern Sierra, especially within barrios subject to cabeceras controlled
traditionally by non-Indians. The locally controlled National Guard and

popular elections for municipal councils offered an opportunity for barrios to enhance their autonomy from their cabeceras. The fiscal exemption accompanying Guard service further reinforced this autonomy. Popular elections even opened a possibility for the barrios, where most people lived, to propel one of their own into the municipal presidency, as had occurred in Zautla in 1878 and 1884 with the election of José Máximo and Manuel Francisco Bonifacio.

All this rocked the traditional hierarchy of ethnic power in the Sierra. Once the National Guard, the guarantor of the new freedoms, came under pressure to disband, the pendulum swung back in favor of the old order. The ethnic enmities underlying the conflict in Zautla were starkly illustrated in attitudes toward taxation. The personal tax, introduced by Governor Bonilla in 1877, was merely the old National Guard *rebajado*, raised since 1855, under a new name. However, while the old tax was remarkably successful in providing for local civil and military expenditures, the new tax provoked dissension from the start.

The success of the *rebajado* came in part as a consequence of the troubled times. Warfare provided an incentive to pay the tax for those who wanted to avoid military service and a reward in tax exemption to those who chose to serve. In the southern Sierra, non-Indians often mustered out while Indians in certain villages tended to serve, confident that acceptable terms of military service would be guaranteed by Lucas. The personal tax resembled the *rebajado* in that it applied, with a few exceptions, to everybody. But from the start, perceptions of the personal tax varied significantly between the two ethnic groups. Indians such as José Máximo and Lucas viewed the personal tax as similar to the *rebajado*. They saw it as a tax to be raised from all citizens, regardless of caste or class, signifying their equality as citizens. The proceeds of the taxes would fund secular education and other municipal expenses. Bernal's uprising in 1879 was a reaction by the non-Indian population against this assumption of equality and shared secular administrative goals. Once non-Indians regained control of Zautla after 1885, they proceeded to raise this tax in a punitive way, targeting Indian barrios, particularly those which hitherto had enjoyed tax immunity in return for National Guard service. No longer a charter of citizenship, the tax now became a reminder of former oppression.

The conflicts in Zautla also reveal several other themes: the importance of Masonry among the Indian population; the role of the director of primary schools and the parish priest in exacerbating conflicts within the municipality; the emergence of centrally controlled and largely non-Indian security forces, acting after 1875 as a counterpoise to the National Guard; and, not least, Porfirio Díaz's sensitivity to local issues. The President's desire to defend those who had brought him to power in 1876 clashed with increasingly arbitrary and oppressive district and state authorities, which put the interest of large landowners over the constitutional rights of ordinary citizens.

Above all, the Zautla case illustrates the obstacles facing the long-term diffusion of popular liberalism, once the Reform had passed through its military phase. The conflicts between Bernal and José Máximo and Manuel Francisco Bonifacio demonstrate how the collective power of the National Guard, and the citizens' possession of arms, were essential prerequisites for the enjoyment of certain Liberal guarantees. They also show that the same martial face of Mexican Liberalism compromised its legitimacy in the minds of those less willing to be convinced of the merits of "ideas of the century."

The conflicts that so divided the municipality of Zautla between 1879 and Márquez's reelection in the summer of 1888 were part of a more general process of neutralization of the social and political bases of the Montaña *cacicazgo,* once the Tetelenses had lost their hold upon power in the state. Méndez and Bonilla of Tetela, Lucas, Indalecio Sánchez and Luis Antonio Díaz of Xochiapulco, José Máximo and Manuel Francisco Bonifacio of Zautla, and Francisco Agustín of Cuetzalan had achieved power through the effective combination of three factors: local military organization, Liberal reform (especially the separation of Church and state, secular education, individual guarantees against arbitrary power, direct elections, and municipal autonomy), and community control over the process of common land distribution. The Montaña's failure lay in its inability, during the eight years in control of the state government, to shift from a military to civilian basis for the exercise of political power and the enjoyment of constitutional rights.

The extent of this failure was demonstrated in the southern Sierra in 1888 when the violent disarming and demobilization of veteran National Guardsmen removed the last obstacle preventing the restoration of arbitrary district government. However effective Lucas may have been in securing the peace and cushioning the impact of these measures by providing sanctuary to fugitive Guardsmen, the events of 1888 revealed his inability to guarantee respect for individual rights beyond the jurisdiction of Xochiapulco.

15

Public and Private Life, 1889–1910

By the early 1890s the Sierra was at peace, at least on the surface. The constitutional reform permitting reelection to public office had taken much of the heat out of politics. Electoral competition, with its attendant disorder, dwindled with the likelihood that incumbents would seek reelection or impose their own nominees. Only those who failed to pacify their jurisdictions, or intervened in the affairs of their neighbors, or developed unwarranted political ambitions were likely to be eased out by Porfirio Díaz.

The era of relatively free suffrage, decentralization, and no reelection (promised with the Tuxtepecano victory in 1876) proved to be short-lived. The trend of executive centralism, inaugurated by Benito Juárez with his *convocatoria* in 1867, was reaffirmed under Manuel González and Díaz. The system of two- and three-tier elections ensured that voting did not get out of hand. The direct election of jefes políticos (revived in 1876) was replaced in 1880 with jefes políticos nominated by the state governor. Direct municipal elections likewise reverted to indirect elections in 1880, under the close vigilance of appointed jefes políticos.[1]

Díaz's persistence in the presidential office after 1884 was matched in Puebla by two outsiders, who were both military men close to Díaz: General Rosendo Márquez from Jalisco (1885–1892), and General Mucío Martínez from Nuevo León (1892–1911). At the district level, many jefes políticos stayed in office for decades. For much of the Porfiriato, the wealthy Guanajuato miner, Isidro Grimaldo, son-in-law of Juan N. Méndez, governed the district of Tetela. Sons of Méndez, Bonilla, and Lucas, or close companions at arms, represented Tetela in the state congress throughout the Porfiriato and the Revolution.[2] On the municipal level, the habit of no-reelection occasionally survived. In Xochiapulco not a single case of reelection occurred during the Porfiriato.[3] But La Villa del Cinco de Mayo was a democratic relic in the increasingly oligarchical milieu of the later Porfiriato.

Brigadier General Lucas

For all his frequent declarations of retirement into private life, Lucas remained a full Brigadier General on the active list throughout the Porfiriato.[4] In this capacity, he dutifully wrote a monthly letter to the Minister of War, adopting precisely the same format, each month, for twenty-three years from October 1891 until January 1914:

> Tetela de Ocampo
>> In compliance with No. 2625 of the General Ordinance of the Army, I have the honor to report to you that I have established my residence in this town, State of Puebla, where I await orders that the supreme government dictates through you.
>> With great honor, my general, I give you my subordination and respect.
>> Liberty and Constitution.
>> Juan Francisco Lucas.[5]

The salary of a Brigadier General, fixed in 1885, was 375 pesos per month, which he continued to be paid throughout the Porfiriato and first years of the Revolution.[6] Political exigency sometimes made payment of his salary irregular. In July 1888, at the height of the Zautla conflict when Márquez was seeking reelection, Lucas received a note promising him full pay.[7] In October 1890 the governor had to apologize for not having paid Lucas's salary since January, which serves as evidence of how peaceful the Sierra had become a mere two years after the troubled year of 1888.[8]

Lucas maintained a regular, albeit increasingly formal, correspondence with Díaz concerned mainly with birthday greetings, funeral condolences, and the commemoration of great patriotic events such as the battles of 5 May 1862 and 2 April 1867. Over the space of twelve months, between August 1889 and July 1890 (a quiet mid-term year), Lucas had the following communications with higher authorities:

> 21/8/89 to Díaz with birthday greetings and news of peace in the Sierra;
> 4/11/89 to Díaz with greetings and news of peace in the Sierra;
> 8/11/89 to Díaz on "the inalterable tranquility of the villages of the Sierra";
> 20/1/90 to General Hermenegildo Carrillo congratulating him on his birthday;
> 25/2/90 from Díaz thanking Lucas for information on the "tranquility" of the Sierra;
> 2/4/90 from Díaz on the anniversary of the battle of 2 April 1867;
> 2/4/90 to General Carlos Pacheco thanking him for his good wishes;
> 2/4/90 to Díaz in commemoration of the battle of 2 April 1867;
> 2/4/90 from Rafael Cravioto, governor of the state of Hidalgo, congratulating Lucas, to which Lucas replies with effusive thanks;
> 17/4/90 from Romero Rubio, Minister of the Interior, introducing José Lames, agent of the Companía Nacional Constructora, who is searching for labor for the construction of the Jalapa-Veracruz railway;

7/5/90 from Díaz introducing Señor Sullivan of the Companía
Constructora Mexicana who pays well, every Saturday, in special tokens,
the value of which Sullivan will guarantee;
16/6/90 from Díaz congratulating Lucas on his birthday (24 June);
24/6/90 to Díaz reporting peace in the Sierra.[9]

By the mid-1890s these communications had become routinized and
depersonalized. Díaz had taken increasingly to sending printed and unsigned messages. By 1904, a presidential election year, all Lucas received
was a single, standardized New Year's card with a stamped signature—no
longer any congratulations for 5 May, 2 April, or on his birthday.

Yet there remained a rapport between the two men. On the president's
side, Díaz continued to appreciate the strategic value of the Sierra where
Lucas's personal influence appeared to be holding up. The dictator's desperate pleading for Lucas to come to Mexico City during the last months of the
regime is evidence enough of the importance that Díaz placed upon his
friendship with the Tetela cacique. On Lucas's side, friendship with Díaz
gave him prestige as well as tactical room to maneuver in his dealings with
higher authorities. These relationships once again became problematic during the summer of 1889.

Conflict Management

On 8 April 1889, Lucas received a letter from Luis Antonio Díaz in
Xochiapulco describing an incident in Zautla, which was reminiscent of
the conflict over the personal tax in 1888. Two Xochiapulquenses, José
Isidro and Juan Francisco, returning from Matlehuacala with maize, had
been attacked near the hacienda of Almajac by mastiffs belonging to one
of José de Jesús Bernal's sons. In self-defense, they killed one of the dogs
with a machete. After attempting, unsuccessfully, to disarm the men,
young Bernal returned to Almajac to inform his father that the
Xochiapulquenses had attempted to kill him. José de Jesús, with characteristic impetuosity, sent out a party to capture, disarm, and imprison the
men in the Libres jail. The Xochiapulco authorities asked Lucas what he
could do to correct this injustice.[10]

Lucas protested immediately both to Díaz and Márquez. The governor
promptly ordered the release of the two men, and informed Lucas that he
would order Colonel Bernal to reprimand his son and instruct him to avoid
such incidents in the future.[11] Díaz also assured Lucas that he had instructed Márquez to reprimand Bernal strongly for allowing an incident
which so endangered "relations with friends in the Sierra." Díaz's fear of
the rupture this incident threatened to cause between Lucas and Bernal led
him to urge Márquez to visit Zautla, if only for a few hours, to resolve the
conflict. It is not known how Márquez responded to this suggestion.[12]

The conflict in Xochiapulco's seceded barrio of Las Lomas also re-surfaced on Easter Saturday of 1890 when violence broke out between two factions. In what appears to have been retribution for the arrest of eight Lomeños two years earlier by the Xochiapulco authorities, eight Xochi-apulquenses were arrested and three Zacapoaxtla judges were called to handle the situation.[13] Márquez urged Lucas to assist with the problem. In the governor's view, the incident had resulted because armed men from Xochiapulco, several of them *faltistas* (non-payers of the personal tax) "who roam freely through Ixtacamaxtitlán, Zautla, and Xochiapulco," had invaded the barrio. They had attacked the justice of the peace and other no-table citizens of Las Lomas with a plan to re-create the divisions within the barrio.[14] Lucas responded that he no longer enjoyed any influence or au-thority in the barrio now that Las Lomas was subject to Zacapoaxtla.[15] Five months later, two of the Xochiapulquenses arrested in Las Lomas in April still languished in the Zacapoaxtla jail with their cases unheard.

Luis Antonio Díaz, Xochiapulco's alcalde, gave Márquez quite a dif-ferent account of the events of Easter Saturday. Far from being invaded by men from Xochiapulco, the Lomeños had invited residents of Xochia-pulco's barrio of Ixehuaco to a dance (Ixehuaco, it will be recalled, was the barrio established by families exiled from Las Lomas during the French Intervention and the rebellion of 1869–70). The dance was a trap. Close to the house where it was being held, more than thirty club-wielding Lomeños lay in wait. In defending themselves, the Xochiapulquenses wounded five of their assailants, before being captured themselves. Four were sent to Zacapoaxtla for trial of whom two escaped; the two remaining still awaited trial in mid-August. Luis Antonio doubted whether they would receive a fair hearing since the only witnesses willing to travel to Zacapoaxtla were Lomeños: "Our Ixehuaquenses are being submitted to revenge more than punishment . . . The conflict should be resolved administratively for, rather than a criminal matter, this is more a political wrangle between those who today are inhabitants of Las Lomas, and those who were once but now be-long to Ixehuaco in our municipality."[16] Unfortunately for the hapless pris-oners, the Zacapoaxtla authorities had no incentive to resolve a conflict that offered them a lever against old enemies in Xochiapulco. Besides, Lucas no longer possessed the means, in the National Guard, to achieve the kind of direct justice for which he was renowned in the past (during the 1850s and 1860s, a daring jail break would have been sufficient).

After this incident, Lucas's correspondence over conflicts deemed to be threatening to public order decreased markedly. During the last two decades of the Porfiriato, the Sierra became a more peaceful and prosper-ous place. Inter- and intra-village conflicts diminished with the completion of the division of common lands in most parts of the Sierra by the early 1890s. Ancient inter-communal enmities, such as that between Atempan and Chignautla in Teziutlán, were more easily contained once party rivalry gave way to *continuismo*.[17] Prudent jefes políticos, such as Emilio Betancurt in Teziutlán, preferred to ensure against further agrarian conflict by denying access to the infamous surveying companies.[18] A new order emerged and matured in many cabeceras with wealthier non-Indian and some Indian families, who had adjudicated generous swaths of community land, feeling much more sure of their control over formerly troublesome barrios. For example, Cuetzalan, divided between warring factions throughout much of the 1860s and 1870s, became by the 1890s and 1900s a monument to Porfirian stability and prosperity, and even acquired the suffix "del Progreso." Francisco Agustín, the Nahua leader who had allied with Méndez and Lucas to order to oppose the sub-division of commons, and who had occupied the municipal presidency of Cuetzalan for ten years after Tuxtepec, was finally arrested in 1894 for leading a fruitless uprising against the *gente de razón* who now, in league with a resurgent clergy, firmly controlled this commercially dynamic coffee town.[19] Throughout the Sierra, many other cabeceras shared in Cuetzalan's experience.[20]

The Sierra had ceased being a factor of instability in state politics. Indeed, with the growth of labor and agrarian activism in the center of the state, the Sierra became a more reliable political anchor for Mucío Martínez. Although the governor acquired most of his estates in southern Puebla, he clearly considered it prudent to assemble a sizeable estate in the Sierra, located strategically at the intersection of the boundaries of the districts of Tetela, Zacapoaxtla, and Zacatlán, at the heart of the Montaña *cacicazgo*, adjoining land belonging to the Márquez of Otlatlán and Lucas families. From here, he was able not only to store cattle for the moment when prices in the Puebla abattoir (which he also owned) were high but also to keep an eye on the principal leaders of a traditionally rebellious zone. An additional advantage gained from the possession of this estate was the more direct access it gave to raising military recruits from the beleaguered villages of the Sierra de Zacatlán.[21]

Apart from these private interests, Martínez could count on a military reserve in Xochiapulco, where National Guard companies, now technically "auxiliaries" of the Federal army, acted as a palace guard for him during the last decades of the Porfiriato.[22] The tense relations between the National Guard of the southern Sierra and district authorities, which were so evident during Márquez's first term, were overcome. Xochiapulco's veteran Guardsmen now journeyed to Puebla to beg for pensions, rather than resort to armed struggle in order to secure their constitutional rights, as they had done in the past.[23] With this more direct government control and patronage in the Sierra, Lucas was no longer so much in demand as an intermediary.

Yet Lucas's public life during the 1890s and 1900s was not confined exclusively to drafting condolences and birthday greetings, and celebrating patriotic holidays. Because of the Sierra's natural electoral strength, due to its demographic preponderance in the state, politics there still required close monitoring, for the region's physical inaccessibility always left open the possibility of the resurgence of opposition. Lucas remained the leading figure in the Sierra to whom Díaz and the state governor could turn during those short interludes of rumor and instability that still accompanied state and federal elections.

One such flutter was in 1892 when, at the peak of Rosendo Márquez's unpopularity (culminating in his resignation in September), rumors began to circulate that the Montaña might stage a comeback.[24] Díaz instructed Lucas to ensure support in the Sierra for Martínez's candidacy for the governorship.[25] However, with the death of Juan N. Méndez in 1894, the Montaña also passed away for, as Díaz well knew, Lucas possessed no political ambitions beyond the Sierra.

The electoral period 1895–96 also caused Díaz concern. Within two years of his election to the governorship, Martínez had succeeded in antagonizing Puebla's upper class, who, tired of being governed by outsiders, revived the candidacy of the old Llanura leader, José María Coutolenc, in the summer of 1895. Opposition to Martínez greatly increased in July 1895 when he was implicated in the murder of the director of the influential Puebla Catholic newspaper, *El Amigo de la Verdad*. Fearing that opposition might spread beyond Puebla and complicate his own bid for reelection, Díaz had no option but to provide Martínez with full support for his reelection.[26]

Díaz was also concerned by reports of opposition clubs in Tetela where there was mounting resentment of the shameless self-enrichment of the jefe político, Isidro Grimaldo.[27] During the summer of 1895, an opposition candidate for the governorship was named, and Lucas furnished Díaz with a list of Martínez's opponents.[28] One of these, José María Quintero, was president of San Esteban Cuautempan, the municipality in which Grimaldo was accumulating most of his land (Quintero's son, Tranquilino, later became Lucas's closest confidant during the Revolution). In September 1895, Díaz instructed Martínez to proceed against these men and advised Lucas to discourage the formation of political clubs in the district. This was the last "political crisis" of Porfirian Puebla, until Aquiles Serdán rose up on the eve of the Revolution.

During the last fifteen years of the Porfiriato, Lucas's skills as mediator and political informer were only rarely called upon. The decline in his political role was confirmed during the 1890s when, for several years, the authorities saw no need to repair the broken telegraph line that linked Tetela de Ocampo with the outside world. As military men, Díaz and Martínez perhaps felt secure in the knowledge that each month, with clockwork regularity, Lucas reported for service to the Secretaría de Guerra y Marina, in exchange for his substantial wages. The Xochiapulco militia was occasionally called upon to provide guard duty in the state capital. Such patronage must have been welcome in a municipality which long had appreciated that the provision of military service earned official respect for local autonomy.[29]

The final recorded public incident of the Porfiriato involving Lucas occurred in May 1903, during festivities commemorating the battle of 5 May. The precise cause of the conflict between the jefe político and the priest in 1903 is not clear, but the incident recalled a similar affair in Tetela in 1867, also involving the Cinco de Mayo festivities, when the priest had refused to lend a red carpet kept in the church to the *junta patriótica* of Tetela. This lack of patriotism resulted in scuffles and the temporary expulsion of the priest from the town. In 1903 the jefe político ordered Jacinto Méndez, the parish priest, to be arrested for contravening the Reform Laws. While Méndez was being escorted to jail, "women from the barrios on their way to the market, animated by alcohol, attempted to snatch the priest away from the police. Various citizens intervened to prevent this and a scandal ensued during which several people were punched. But order was quickly restored and the priest remained under arrest."[30] In jail, the priest briefly endured a hunger strike on 5 and 6 May. What is noteworthy from this otherwise rather insignificant incident is the way that Lucas entered so directly both in the policing of Tetela during the May festivities and in the custody of the priest. The last incident of which there is direct evidence of Lucas assuming such duties occurred in 1879–80, when he served as the popularly elected jefe político of Tetela.

Here, then, is more than a suggestion that Lucas retained an effective coercive power in Tetela. Moreover, such an exercise of arbitrary power (albeit to uphold the constitution) was considered as quite legitimate by the state and federal authorities, to whom he had reported the incident. This residual military power, and the official appreciation of it, receives further confirmation by the visit paid to Lucas in April 1903 by two Federal army officers. Miguel Arriaga, Lucas's erstwhile enemy and cacique of Zacapoaxtla, organized the visit. On 24 April he wrote Lucas introducing Colonel Wenceslao González, commander of the Fourteenth Regiment of Cavalry, and Antonio Flores Ramírez, who had expressed a desire "to know the military potential of the Sierra." Arriaga suggested that Lucas take the two officers hunting at his ranch at Taxcantla.[31] In reply, Lucas, reporting that conditions at Taxcantla were too dry for successful hunting, proposed that Gónzalez and Flores be directed to the *tierra caliente*. Nevertheless, he invited the officers to inspect his ranches.[32]

Lucas appears as a willing client of the regime, still in possession of military authority recognized as a valuable strategic asset both by the federal military and by the state government. In all appearances he had become a paragon of the Porfirian regime. No wonder Díaz turned to his old friend as the regime began to founder in January 1911.

Private Life

Only a porous line separates the private and public lives of any cacique. One biographical source places Lucas's retirement into private life as early as 1867, another with the amnesty in June 1870, and another in 1877, following the Tuxtepec victory.[33] Even Lucas, in his short autobiography, omits almost two decades of active military life, claiming that he dedicated himself exclusively to his private pursuits between 1867 and 1885, when Márquez offered him the inspectorship of state forces.[34] During the later Porfiriato, Lucas continued to receive a salary from the Ministry of War. He was consulted over public appointments and received individual and collective representations from the villages.

When, in October 1868, Lucas left his home in Xochiapulco to reside at Taxcantla with his new wife, he left behind a family whose direct descendants, still resident in Xochiapulco, numbered almost one hundred in 1985.[35] The source of this large surviving cohort of descendants can be observed in the 1873 census, with the Lucas family as the first household listed:

Table 15–1.   The Lucas Household in Xochiapulco, 1873[36]

Name	Age	Occupation
María Josefa	40	Spinster
Juan Francisco Lucas	17	Laborer (Literate)
María del Carmen Lucas	15	
María Ascención Lucas	13	
José Antonio Lucas	13	
Joaquín Lucas	12	
Aurelio Lucas	4	

María Josefa had agreed to look after Lucas's four children after the death of his first wife, María Felipa. Lucas began this family in 1855, shortly after returning from Altotonga. From the gap of eight years between the births of Joaquin and Aurelio, it seems likely that María Felipa died in 1859. Aurelio would have been conceived (with María Josefa?) shortly before Lucas married María Asunción Pérez, a mestiza from Zautla, in a civil ceremony on 31 March 1868.[37]

After his move to Tetela and marriage into the mestizo caste, Lucas continued to provide for his Xochiapulco family. Indeed, María Josefa may well have been Lucas's common-law wife as she bore at least three more of his children. Lucas ensured that "the widow Doña María Josefa" received a small plot of one *almud*, valued at 10 pesos in 1874, at the start of the adjudication. Other gifts of land followed. In 1877 he gave her an additional plot valued at 400 pesos, close to the center of the cabecera, and in 1885 he gave her land in Xochiapulco.[38]

Compared with the army of Lucas's descendants that still populates Xochiapulco, Lucas's descendants are much fewer in Tetela. In 1991, Juan

Juan Francisco Lucas and María Asunción Pérez, c. 1900

Lucas, the postmaster, and his family were the only direct descendants of Lucas still resident in Tetela.[39] The Tetela censuses reveal a large household, especially in 1881, the year after Lucas's term as jefe político, when twenty-one people lived under his roof. By 1887, however, his household had shrunk to the immediate family, without even a servant. By 1902, Dolores, Lucas's daughter, had died but four youths and two young children, Miguel Méndez and Juan Nepomuceno (probably the orphaned grandchildren of General Méndez), had joined the household.[40]

A Sierra biographer wrote of Lucas:

Enemy of idleness, he would very rarely assemble his troops in one place; if they were not on active service, they would always be at home working. He never employed a personal guard, and his friends and even enemies asked to see him at all hours of the day or night. At the height of war he gave equal attention to the care of cattle, sheep, goats, hens, cats, dogs or to work in the fields, which is what made him most happy in life, on

> any one of the small estates which he liked to move between with fre-
> quency. He would rather not be alive than not be able to build houses,
> roads, corrals, or sow crops. . . . This idiosyncracy lasted until the last
> moments of his life. You never saw him with his hands or mind unoccu-
> pied, even if only at some work of little significance.[41]

This description of Lucas's work habits clarifies why he reported such diverse occupations to the census taker—*labrador* in 1873, *comerciante* in
1881, *militar* in 1887, and *agricultor* in 1902. The description also pin-
points the integral relationship between his agricultural skills and his management of men on campaign, whether it involved raising war supplies,
obtaining provisions of corn and land for fugitive Guardsmen seeking sanctuary, or negotiating for their resettlement.

Despite the temptation to see Lucas as the embodiment of an egalitarian
"peasant" ethos, he formed part of a small incipient bourgeoisie, distinguish-
able from its fellow Xochiapulquenses by virtue of its literacy, possession of
more land, and the use, by some, of surnames. His position came in part
from his father's status as the administrator of the hacienda of Xochiapulco.
Later, the act of foundation of Xochiapulco presupposed substantial differences in landholding between officers, non-commissioned officers, and men.
By the end of the European Intervention, Lucas had even outgrown this small
group of Xochiapulco *gente decente*, helped by his marriage to María
Asunción Pérez, whose father had obtained title to two estates—Taxcantla
and Xaltatempa—formerly municipal *propios* of Tetela.

Lucas's father-in-law, Francisco Pérez, successfully acquired a patchwork of ranches specializing in maize, barley, beans, and pork that
stretched from the boundaries of Xochiapulco with Zacapoaxtla in the east
to Xaltatempa to the west of the district of Tetela, bordering with Zacatlán.
Many Tetela and Zacapoaxtla families preferred to acquire titles of common and municipal land in the *tierra caliente* that were suitable for sugarcane, coffee, and other cash crops. By contrast, Pérez's properties were
located within the *tierra fria*, where he grew maize, produced wool and
goat hides, fattened pigs, and extracted tallow, all of which he marketed
from a store on the corner of the plaza in Tetela de Ocampo.[42]

Pérez's largest estate was the Taxcantla ranch. Lucas moved there with
his wife in October 1868, after his father-in-law's death. Pérez had
obtained Taxcantla by auction for 4,166 pesos in December 1866, when the
municipality of Tetela had been forced to sell its properties to defray
the costs of renewed Republican resistance. Its value more than doubled by
the time of his death in 1868.[43] In the last months of Pérez's life, Lucas became the administrator of the estate, assuming outstanding liabilities as
well as credits.

Taxcantla encompassed arable fields, pasturage, a forge that could be
converted into an arsenal, and a large pine forest renowned for its game. Its
location gave the estate an incomparable and unassailable strategic posi-

tion, guarding the southern and eastern boundaries of the district of Tetela.[44] Taxcantla also had political status as a *ranchería*, with a justice of the peace and, by the 1880s, a small primary school.

Taxcantla's distance from its cabecera at Tetela de Ocampo permitted a certain autonomy, even lawlessness. In May 1855, Captain López, police superintendent of Tetela, expressed concern about the fandangos, dances, and drinking of untaxed aguardiente on the estate.[45] The reputation of the Taxcantlecos for rustic manners and good living had become sufficiently well established by 1890 for Governor Rosendo Márquez to joke about them in a letter to Lucas, in which he expressed his pleasure at having met Lucas's son, Miguel, who was attending the Colegio del Estado in Puebla. Márquez found Miguelito to be "very charming, with good manners and a gentlemanly demeanor, without the famous fat belly of Taxcantla."[46] Having been stationed at Taxcantla during the revolution of La Noria and attended hunting parties on Lucas's estate, Márquez and Lucas could share quips about the locals. The point remained that Taxcantla was a bountiful ranch that supported a paunchy resident labor force.

Pérez's other main property was the Xaltatempa ranch, also acquired by him through the land division in 1855. Xaltatempa (now called Xaltatempa de Lucas) occupies a sandy bluff in Tetela's barrio de San Nicolas, overlooking a tributary of the Zempoala, and, like Taxcantla, in an excellent strategic position, on the boundary with Zacatlán and overlooking the principal route between Tetela de Ocampo and the *tierra caliente*.[47] Pérez also owned several smaller properties close to Tetela de Ocampo, a store, and a substantial house on the plaza. His estate at his death in October 1868 was valued at 16,742 pesos, an exceptionally large sum in the Sierra.[48]

Pérez died intestate. As the administrator, Lucas became the executor of the estate that was divided between the daughter, María Asunción, and the son, Luis Antonio. Lucas immediately liquidated part of the estate.[49] The sale of several ranches coincided with periods of intense warfare in the southern Sierra, when all available funds were being directed toward the war effort. Yet, as a result of his fortunate marriage, Lucas became one of the wealthiest men in the district of Tetela.[50] Eight months of resistance during the revolt of La Noria would have been impossible without Taxcantla's strategic advantages and Lucas's private wealth. During the revolt, Bonilla's letters from Taxcantla to Manuel Vázquez in Tetela were punctuated with advice from Lucas on when beef and pork fattened at Taxcantla should be sold in the market of the cabecera, and for how much.[51]

During the late 1870s, Lucas faced problems of liquidity, having in 1878 to cede the possession of the Rancho de Xaltatempa, which he had acquired from his brother-in-law in 1874, to General Méndez, Lauro Luna, and Isidro Grimaldo because he was unable to pay the interest of 6 percent on the estate's value of 5,753 pesos.[52] In spite of this failure, which he put down to the poor harvest of 1877, Lucas could rely upon the continuing commercial viability of his principal possession, the Rancho de Taxcantla.

During the 1880s, as his public responsibilities diminished, Lucas's personal fortune as an agriculturalist improved. The notarial records for Tetela show him to have been an assiduous moneylender and acquirer of land during this decade. Improved economic circumstances allowed Lucas to send both his sons for their secondary education to the Colegio del Estado during the 1880s, helped by a grant from Governor Méndez and renewed by Márquez on Méndez's request in 1886.[53] A secondary education set Miguel and Abraham apart both from the previous generation, for whom even a completed primary education was exceptional, and from most of their fellow Tetelenses, for whom the costs and practical difficulty of secondary education in the state capital remained prohibitive. Lucas's two educated sons could now compete with the Zamítez, the Méndez, and the Bonilla families for federal and state deputyships and the most desirable local offices.

Notarial records reveal the variety of Lucas's business dealings, ranging from the purchase and sale of properties, loans, powers of attorney, sureties, bills of exchange, and donations:

Property Purchases and Sales   Apart from two plots of land in Totutla (Huitzilan), Lucas bought very little land during his life. As we know, he inherited his Tetela properties from his father-in-law. The Xochiapulco council donated his properties there, while he confined purchases in Tetela to plots adjoining his wife's house where, by 1890, Lucas possessed the entire block on the eastern side of the square. He also consolidated a small estate between Tetela and the barrio of La Cañada, next to that of General Méndez, on Tetela's ejido. He used this property for grazing livestock brought from Taxcantla and farther afield and for growing corn.[54] Lucas's prime interest in temperate agriculture moved him in 1883 to sell two plots planted with fruit and coffee trees in remote tropical Jonotla, which had been adjudicated in his favor.[55] Otherwise, he chose to donate rather than to sell his properties.

Loans   Lucas regularly lent money at rates of interest of between 4 and 6 percent per annum to smallholders, many of whom, when unable to repay their loans, lost their property to him. Some of these defaulted on loans that he had inherited from his father-in-law. Several embargoed properties belonged to widows who were unable to work them. Seven defaults brought Lucas two houses and eight small ranches, most of which, within a few years, had been passed on to his children or given to the municipality of Xochiapulco for funding the school.[56]

Powers of Attorney and Sureties   Lucas traveled little beyond the Sierra. Needing someone of trust to act on his behalf in Mexico City, he conferred powers of attorney upon both General Méndez and his son Miguel. In turn, Lucas accepted powers of attorney in the district capital which he exercised on behalf of wealthy sugar-producing families in Zapotitlán.[57] His solvency enabled him to provide guarantees for tax collection. He also offered cash for resolving long-standing disputes between former tenants adjudicating plots and their former landlords.[58]

The Financial Crisis of 1889–90   This crisis uncovered an important business practice in the Sierra: the promissory note. The letter of exchange had become a major medium during the 1880s. In 1889 the sudden evaporation of liquidity prompted numerous *protestaciones de pagares* (demands for payment). Seven of these cited Lucas, three as payer and four as payee. The three letters that Lucas was ordered to pay were issued by silver miners Sacramento Cruz and Isidro Grimaldo of La Cañada valued at 172 pesos.[59] Lucas was ordered to be paid four letters, valued at 160 pesos, by José Daniel Posadas and Benigno Cortes, both of Tetela, and Ramón Francisco of Las Lomas and José Valeriano of Xochiapulco.[60] The letters of exchange from the two miners included no interest charge, in contrast to Lucas's letters, all of which specified a 6 percent rate of appreciation. These payment problems demonstrate the importance of Tetela as a mining center and the chain of credit that this created in the surrounding areas.

Lucas increased his rural holdings as a result of the financial crisis by more than one-third. In 1890 he was taxed on rural estates valued at 6,446 pesos. In 1891 they were valued at 9,046 pesos. However, he received no income in 1890 from his three urban properties due to an illness preventing their completion. His agricultural activities were also "not leaving any profit," a general complaint in the district where "no one can make agriculture pay." In April 1891, Lucas wrote to the governor requesting exemption from taxation on his urban properties, a reduction of 400 pesos from the tax assessment on his rural properties, and a dispensation from the 2 percent tax on transfers of ownership.[61] Márquez acceded to all three requests.

Miscellaneous   Many miscellaneous notarized activities have survived. At four P.M. on 3 December 1881, Lucas registered his will, persuaded to do so perhaps by the attempt upon his life in June 1879 while serving as jefe político.[62] In April 1883, Lucas, on Antonio Armenta's behalf, signed a contract of sale on a house in Aquixtla because "he could not write."[63]

Donations   The 1890–91 crisis marked a watershed in Lucas's business life. After 1890, he acquired few new properties. Instead, he began disposing of much of his estate. By 1891, his three legitimate children had now grown up; Miguel was twenty-three years old, Abraham was twenty, and Dolores was seventeen. Between 1891 and 1894, Lucas donated five small properties to Miguel, five to Dolores, and eight (mainly urban) to Abraham. All eighteen properties had been acquired through loan defaults and individually were valued at between 80 and 700 pesos.[64]

The gifts to his children demonstrate that he entertained no illusions of consolidating a great estate in the southern Sierra. In the context of generalized land ownership and small farming units, Lucas's financial and commercial skills, not his ownership of land, were more valuable assets. Nevertheless, the process of land accumulation by the second generation continued during the 1890s and 1900s. Miguel and Abraham acquired numerous small rural and urban properties around Tetela, Tececuilco, Xaltatempa, Taxcantla, and Cuahuigtic, several at the cost of indebted former allies of their father, such as Juan Rivera and Ignacio Leal of Cuahuigtic.[65]

No inventory was found for Lucas's estate at his death in 1917. But in 1921, Abraham took over three urban properties in Tetela and the estate of Taxcantla, paying his mother 7,566 pesos, which was only a few pesos less than the estate which Lucas had received as his share at his father-in-law's death in 1868. It is doubtful whether Lucas owned much more than this at his death in 1917.[66]

Lucas's generosity toward Xochiapulco continued during the 1890s. He donated three ranches in Caxhuacan (just across Tetela's boundary in Zacatlán, close to Xaltatempa) to help fund schools in the cabecera of Xochiapulco and two of its barrios of Cuauximaloyan and Ixehuaco.[67] He also donated a large public clock to La Villa del Cinco de Mayo that still stands, encased in an unbecoming concrete shell, above the town hall. Delivering this clock resembled a military operation requiring fifty-eight porters with numerous pack animals to be sent to collect the machine from Puebla, with Lucas's expenses running into thousands of pesos.[68]

Farmer-Merchant   In spite of divesting himself of most of his rural property during the early 1890s, Lucas remained very much a farmer. His correspondence with his son Miguel, who resided in Xochiapulco during the 1890s and 1900s (where he commanded the force of auxiliary infantry), reveals that he remained intimately involved with the routines of the agricultural calendar, the opportunities of the marketplace, and the public affairs of Xochiapulco.[69] Lucas spent much of the Revolution in the relative safety of his estate at Taxcantla, from where he continued to conduct business as well as organize, with the help of his son Abraham, the Brigada Serrana, while Miguel moved to the Rancho de Acatlán on the western boundary of Tetela at Xaltatempa. This estate figures prominently in Lucas's correspondence with Miguel during the early part of the Revolution when the cacique was too stiff to make the journey there on horseback.[70]

This correspondence portrays the range and dexterity of Lucas's farming and commercial activities and confirms that he still directly managed the estates that he had donated to his children twenty years earlier. Apart from a wide range of temperate agriculture, especially maize, Lucas bred and fattened beef cattle, grazed sheep and goats, traded in wool (his father's main line of business), reared and fattened pigs, and manufactured lard and tallow. He dealt in *tequesquite* (quicklime), essential for tanning and soap making.[71] He also traded in sugar, asking Miguel in June 1914 to inform him of the weight of *panela* sent from Zapotitlán.[72]

Lucas's correspondence with Miguel exhibits a seasonal rhythm. In March his letters to Miguel concerned maize planting, with meticulous instructions about the preparation of the soil, the soaking of the seed, wage rates, and what the field hands should be fed and how they should be treated. A passage from one letter illustrates this concern: "I am sending you one hundred pesos with the boy for the wages of the workers from Ometepec who earn two and a half pesos, thirty-one centavos a day, their lunch and supper. Make sure you give them coffee and that they lack nothing. This is democracy ('Ese es la democracia')." Juan Francisco also sent Miguel detailed instructions on the intricacies and hazards of maize and bean planting. Peppered with Nahua terms, his instructions told his son not to leave the plough and tools outside lest they rust, to store the maize sacks carefully so that they could be re-used, and to ensure that the plot was well fenced and the cattle enclosed. He specified the details of sharecropping contracts with the farmers settled on the estate. One is reminded that Lucas, in his eightieth year, was first and foremost a highland corn farmer.[73]

In June, Juan Francisco instructed Miguel to plant yellow and black beans on the Acatlán estate, and in July to sow barley (used for animal feed) between rows of maguey cacti higher up the hill where the field met the pine forest. Even at this late stage of his life, Lucas introduced improvements to Taxcantla. A new house was built in 1914 with a road leading to it bordered by maguey plants.[74] During the Revolution, Lucas continued to benefit from the labor of fugitive soldiers from throughout the Sierra and beyond, to whom he would offer protection and subsistence. In June 1914 he instructed Miguel to send him "the tall Federal soldier who is from Torreón" (presumably a deserter) to help with the construction of the new house at Taxcantla.[75]

The Revolution and Fragmentation of Estates

The Revolution brought to an end the cycle of land concentration that had originated with the law of *desamortización* in 1856. After 1917, several of Tetela's larger temperate and sub-tropical ranches were sold to their tenants. Their owners may have had little choice. As with the Liberal and patriotic struggles of the 1850s and 1860s, soldiers who were recruited from or settled upon these estates expected some reward once peace returned. Apart from raising agrarian expectations among these soldier-tenants, the Revolution provided the opportunity for more ambitious individuals, working through municipalities and the military, to challenge the position of the generation that had spearheaded the Liberal Reform and consolidated itself economically during the Porfiriato. Both these trends are evident in the way many of the estates belonging to Tetela's great Liberal families—Lucas, Méndez, Grimaldo—were sold and divided between 1917 and 1920.

Between March and June 1919, Abraham Lucas sold the Rancho del Paraiso in Xaltatempa in lots valued at between 50 and 100 pesos to eighty-three tenants, mostly born on the estate, others from the nearby barrios of Cuacuila, Omitlán, Atlamajac, Xilitetitla, and Ixtolco, and others from farther afield such as Chignahuapan and Tlaxcala. The value of the estate to Abraham had evidently lain in rent paid by these tenants.[76] Most of them possessed surnames which fifty years earlier would have distinguished them as *gente de razón*. But two generations of primary schooling had convinced many Indians to adopt last names, and these tenants probably still used Nahua as their first language. Nahua is still spoken throughout Xaltatempa. All the tenants receiving plots were listed as *jornaleros* except for three brothers: Bardomiano, Gabriel, and Demetrio Barrios, from the Zacatlán barrio of Cuacuila, who were listed as merchants.[77]

During the Revolution, Major Gabriel Barrios served Lucas as the commander of the Batallón Juan N. Méndez of the Brigada Serrana (commanding in May 1916 some 20 officers, 560 infantry, and 20 cavalry) based at Cuacuila. After Lucas's death, Gabriel Barrios swiftly rose to become the main force in the Puebla Sierra. As Lucas had discovered fifty years earlier, military command in the Sierra brought economic rewards. Bardomiano purchased properties in Tlamanca and Xilitetitla in 1918–19, Gabriel purchased a large house in Tetela in 1919, and Demetrio bought a shop in Tetela in the same year.[78]

Sub-division and liquidation also affected the estates of Tetela's other leading Liberal families. In 1919–20 two large ranches consolidated by Juan N. Méndez's energetic female offspring—Josefa, Juana, and Margarita (jefe político Grimaldo's widow)—were divided among their tenants. In Cuautempan, seventy tenants of the Santa Elena ranch paid an average of 30 pesos for their plots.[79] In Huitzilan, La Estrella ranch, situated on land long contested by the municipality, was divided among its residents, leaving only a small estate still in the possession of the Méndez family.[80]

Standing to benefit from the liquidation of the Méndez properties around Cuautempan was the Quintero family. In 1895, José María Quintero, municipal president of Cuautempan, had organized opposition to jefe político Isidro Grimaldo (Méndez's nephew), who, during the 1890s, consolidated two large ranches specializing in coffee and citrus fruit on the former commons of Cuautempan and Huitzilan. José María also acquired his own private holdings in Cuautempan during the 1890s.[81] During the Revolution, José María's son Tranquilino became the political confidant and close friend of Lucas. In May 1916, Lt. Col. Tranquilino Quintero, stationed in Chignahuapan, commanded 22 officers, 369 infantry, and 24 cavalry of the Batallón Tetela de Ocampo of the Brigada Serrana.[82] Lucas's granddaughter Aurora, who lived with her grandfather during the Revolution, recalled Tranquilino as a constant member of the household and an intimate companion of Lucas in his last years.

As with Gabriel Barrios, friendship with Lucas and military success brought economic rewards, once peace returned. In 1917, after organizing Lucas's splendid funeral, Tranquilino bought several plots of land from Miguel Lucas in Tececuilco and San Nicolas, and a house in Tetela from Sergio Bonilla (nephew of Juan Crisóstomo).[83] In 1919 he bought another house as well as a citrus and coffee orchard in Huitzilan from Ignacio Betancurt.[84] In 1920, Tranquilino's brothers, Jacinto and Pablo, on behalf of the municipal council of Cuautempan, completed the "redemption" of Méndez's Santa Elena ranch, paying Miguel Méndez 350 pesos.[85] The honor of his father had been satisfied, and the Quinteros were now the undisputed masters of San Esteban Cuautempan.

Death, Memory, and Survival

From the mid-1880s, starting with the death of Juan Crisóstomo Bonilla in January 1884, Lucas's circle of friends, compadres, and old companions at arms grew smaller. Writing to his son Miguel with news of Bonilla's death, he gave a hint of his religious faith: "We feel this very much but it conforms with the will of the Supreme Being."[86] Another close companion at arms, Lauro Luna, died in the following year.[87] Three years later, General Méndez's son, Miguel, was buried in an elaborate Masonic ceremony in Xochiapulco, presided over by Byron Hyde, the town's Methodist minister. Then, in 1894, Méndez died, leaving Lucas as the sole survivor of the Sierra troika. Their close associate and fellow patriot, General Miguel Negrete, died on 1 January 1897. Lucas answered a request for funds for the construction of a more imposing tomb for Negrete with a donation of 10 pesos. Lucas could not attend the memorial service held in Mexico City in September 1897, when Negrete was honored by the poet Miguel Portillo y Rojas and accompanied to his grave to the strains of Jaime Nunó's National Anthem, Rossini's *William Tell*, and Verdi's *Il Trovatore*.[88]

Old companion at arms Miguel Melgarejo, cacique of Altotonga, congratulated Lucas upon his sixty-third birthday in 1897 and reminded him that "little by little the companions of another epoch are disappearing and very few of those who defended the cause of the great Caudillo in the plans of La Noria and Tuxtepec still remain. If we look around for the old and distinguished generals who guided us in former times in defense of the cause of the People, we see with sadness that General Bonilla, General Méndez, Generals González, Terán, Carrillo, Luis León, Pedro Galván, as well as a great number of our comrades and friends, have disappeared, as we too will disappear soon."[89] Expressing his delight and surprise that Melgarejo was still alive, and apologizing for his delay in replying due to the aches and pains of old age, Lucas lamented the loss of "such meritorious chiefs and companions" and expressed the hope that soon "they all would be together in Eternity."[90]

Lucas was invited on several occasions to participate in the writing of biographies of the illustrious Liberals who were now passing away. But he always declined, with self-effacing apologies for his lack of the necessary literary abilities. However, Lucas helped with the circulation of commemorative publications such as the pamphlet "5 de Mayo" issued by José Carrasco, editor of *Publicaciones Ilustradas*, in 1897. Of the twenty copies he received, Lucas was able to distribute only eleven and returned the remaining nine.[91]

Unfortunately, Lucas never wrote his memoirs for he had a fine memory, read widely in history, agriculture, and practical medicine, and enjoyed a uniquely long and varied political and military career.[92] Unlike his comparably long-lived contemporary, Higinio Aguilar, Lucas possessed a clear set of political principles and exhibited a constancy toward those whom he represented.[93] These qualities were put to the test early in 1911 when Mexico, once more, slipped back into revolution and Lucas assumed the military command of the Puebla Sierra.

16

Lucas and the Mexican Revolution, 1910–1917

From the outset of the revolution in 1910 to his death in 1917, Lucas demonstrated that his stewardship of the Sierra was no aberration. He deftly and successfully managed to make the transition from one of Díaz's principal allies to a supporter of the governments of Francisco I. Madero (1911–1913), Victoriano Huerta (1913–1914), and Venustiano Carranza (1915–1920). Unlike so many of his contemporaries who failed at this deadly game, Lucas proved to be not just a survivor but also a skillful politician who knew when and how to make the next move.

Greatly aiding Lucas in his endeavors was the backing of the large number of *serranos* with whom he shared ethnic and cultural affinities, including the Nahua language, and who saw in him mythical powers and even mystical qualities. He represented to the *serranos* a keen sense of independence of spirit and distrust of distant government that had always characterized the region. Federal and state authorities understood the strength of Lucas's appeal and recognized him, albeit sometimes reluctantly, as the key to controlling the region.[1]

The Last Tuxtepecano

In spite of fifteen years of fighting side by side and a further quarter century of political friendship, Lucas's relationship with Díaz was not always a smooth one. Díaz respected Lucas, but the cacique's autonomy alarmed him. He feared rumors that Lucas might use his hold on the Sierra, consolidated over half a century, to create a new political entity out of the Sierra region that would encompass parts of Puebla, Tlaxcala, and Veracruz. He repeatedly invited Lucas to come to Mexico City, but Lucas always refused. On one occasion, when Díaz wanted to see him, Lucas tartly replied that "the distance from here [Tetela] to Mexico City is the same as from Mexico City to here."[2]

Moreover, Lucas's Indian followers increasingly chafed at the deteriorating working conditions, changing markets caused by the coming of the railroad, the loss of land to large owners, the increasing numbers of mestizos in the region, the takeover of forests by lumber companies, inroads on local political autonomy, forced recruitment into the army, and onerous taxes. These changes left many *serranos* perplexed and intimidated and reinforced the region's traditional suspicion of and resistance to outsiders. Many Indians fled farther into the interior of the Sierra. One sign of the growing discontent was the increasing role of the Protestant Church, principally Methodist, in parts of the Sierra. Methodist ministers' appeal to constitutional liberties and civil rights struck a positive chord among many longtime Liberals, including the Lucas family.[3]

Formal challenge to the regime began as early as 1901 in the Sierra when individuals formed clubs, drawing on the long tradition of Liberalism going back to the wars of Independence, in the towns of Chignahuapan, Tetela, and Zacatlán. This movement would form the basis for the more radical Partido Liberal Mexicano (PLM), established in 1905 and led by Ricardo Flores Magón from Tepeaca. Although little evidence exists to indicate the degree of Flores Magón's influence in the region in the years after 1906, he must have helped pave the way for later, more moderate political efforts. As the *magonistas* concentrated on organizing the more populated and industrialized areas of the state, the *reyistas* and then the *maderistas* became active in the Sierra after 1909.[4]

Initially, Lucas resisted the appeals of the opposition. Despite his dislike for the unpopular state governor, Mucio P. Martínez, Lucas's loyalty to the regime prompted him to send units from Xochiapulco to Puebla City in November 1910 to bolster the capital's defenses in the wake of the ill-fated Aquiles Serdán uprising.[5] But the changing political climate soon forced Lucas to reevaluate his relationship with Díaz.

The pressure on Lucas to withdraw his support from Díaz increased dramatically over the next three months. In November 1910, Lucas's old rival from neighboring Zacapoaxtla, Colonel Miguel Arriaga, along with three of his sons, pronounced in favor of Madero. On 1 December, with the support of a cross-section of the district including some functionaries, merchants, and landowners, they took over the municipal and district government of Zacapoaxtla.[6] Then, only days later, some two hundred villagers from Xochiapulco and Zapotitlán in Lucas's own district pronounced in favor of Madero. The Manzano and Rivera clans headed this campaign. Martín Rivera, the Xochiapulquense leader (like so many revolutionary leaders, a schoolteacher) was Lucas's nephew.[7]

A month later, in January 1911, the five Márquez brothers, whose family had had political ties to Lucas since the 1860s, joined the *maderista* cause and occupied Chignahuapan. Relatively well-off ranchers and merchants from Otlatlán, they were led by Esteban, the intellectual of the group, and Emilio, the best soldier. They gained the backing of persons representing diverse socio-economic groups, including several high officials in the district of

Alatriste and its capital, Chignahuapan. The Márquez clan paid their followers by transporting a machine to the Sierra that minted coins. Chignahuapan's longtime rivalry with neighboring Zacatlán, which was strongly *porfirista*, played a role in the rebellion just as had Tetela's relationship with Zacapoaxtla. Most of these revolutionary groups exhibited more courage than military hardware; some men wielded no weapons, and others had only old rifles or shotguns.[8] Lucas could not ignore the mounting anti-government mood and sensed the danger to his regional leadership if rival caciques switched sides leaving him isolated and supporting a bankrupt regime.

It must have been hard for Lucas to abandon his longtime ally. Indeed, his first reaction was to evade making such an unpalatable choice by retiring completely into private life, but his prominent role in the affairs of the region prevented this option. Some evidence exists that he may have committed himself to lead the Manzano and Rivera group in Xochiapulco soon after its pronouncement in December 1910, but not until February 1911 did he fully compromise himself. With anti-government uprisings occurring daily, Lucas arranged a deal with the *maderistas*: he assured them of his neutrality and allowed their agents to operate freely in the Sierra.[9]

Aware of his subordinate's wavering support, Díaz urgently requested that the cacique travel to Mexico City for consultation. Lucas declined the invitation claiming that the aches and pains of old age (Lucas was seventy-seven years old at the time, Díaz was eighty), his tendency to become nauseous when traveling by car or on horseback, and his fear of the railroad, on which he had never ridden, prevented him from journeying such a distance. Díaz then ordered the jefe político of Tetela, Pomposo M. Bonilla (son of Juan Crisóstomo), to keep an eye on Lucas.[10] A month later, Lucas was still making excuses to Díaz for his inability to travel to Mexico City. As a precaution and a clear indication that he was playing both sides, he did send in his stead his son, Abraham, to see the president. Even as late as mid-April, Lucas was writing to Díaz to report on political events in Tetela.[11]

As a result of Lucas's political drift, the *maderistas* quickly made significant military gains in the region. In March, the Márquez brothers overran the district capitals of Chignahuapan, Tetela, and Zacatlán. Other rebels captured Xicotepec near Huauchinango and threatened the Necaxa hydroelectric works, which supplied power to much of central Mexico including Mexico City, Pachuca, Puebla City, and the El Oro mines in the state of México. During April, most of the far northwest of the state came under the control of Chignahuapan insurgent Gabriel Hernández, while dissident ranchero Manuel F. Méndez recruited an army around Tetela. In May the remaining major towns of the Sierra fell to the rebels. Díaz made some attempt to check the rising tide of opposition by changing jefes políticos and reducing taxes, but ultimately he could do little but write off the strategic Puebla Sierra whose inhabitants had served him so loyally since 1862.[12]

President Madero

The fall of Díaz in May 1911 ushered in a period of reformist government under Francisco Madero, leader of the November 1910 insurrection, from the state of Coahuila, who formally took up the office of president in November 1911. Despite the optimism generated by the overthrow of the dictatorship, Madero's government proved to be unstable. Elements both from the old regime and from among those who wanted faster implementation of political and especially socio-economic change challenged the new regime. Madero himself made a series of political and tactical blunders, including keeping intact the Porfirian army while dismantling the revolutionary forces that had brought him to power.

Lucas proved to be a loyal *maderista*, doing what he could to aid the embattled national leader. He accepted Madero's choice of the conservative Francisco León de la Barra as interim president, even though de la Barra's interim governor in Puebla, Rafael Cañete, tried to stop Lucas's son Abraham from being named jefe político to Tetela, nearly causing a revolt among local residents. He also backed the creation by Madero of a new political party, the Partido Constitucional Progresista (PCP), to replace the maligned Partido Antireeleccionista. Indeed, Lucas's active participation in organizing the PCP in the Sierra effectively blunted its Anti-Reelectionist opposition that argued that Madero had betrayed his movement. The local PCP clubs elected Lucas to serve as their delegate to the national convention held in Mexico City in late August 1911, but he failed to attend, again claiming ill health.[13]

In the spring of 1912, Lucas put his prestige and resources on the line for the president. Madero faced a serious rebellion in the Sierra nominally headed by Emilio Vázquez Gómez, a former leading *maderista* who had become disillusioned with the regime. The movement in Puebla had the support of adherents of the old Anti-Reelectionist Party who were angered by what they saw as Madero's imposition of Nicolás Meléndez as governor in December 1911. Others, headed by army officers and the opportunistic cacique, Miguel Arriaga, wanted more sweeping reforms. Within a matter of days in February 1912, the rebels captured several district capitals including Teziutlán, Tetela, and Zacapoaxtla as well as smaller towns and much of the hinterland.[14]

In response to this challenge, which increased the following month when the *vazquistas* joined forces with the even larger anti-government insurgency of Pascual Orozco in the north of the country, Madero persuaded Lucas to come out of retirement. As in earlier wars, federal authorities needed Lucas to convince *serranos* to enlist in the army. Villagers in the Sierra feared that joining the Federal military would mean an indefinite commitment which countered their traditional fifteen- to thirty-day stints under arms before returning to their fields. Lucas agreed to create and lead a special force in the Sierra of some 700 local men plus 350 additional troops assigned to him by the Minister of War. The federal government promised to equip and pay the unit, and Madero ordered a member of his personal military staff, Bruno M. Trejo, to act as his personal liaison with Lucas.[15]

After several weeks of fighting, Lucas's force, along with federal *rurales* and volunteers from liberal political clubs in the state, managed to disperse the rebels. Madero then gave Lucas the task of maintaining permanent garrisons in those towns wrested from the *vazquistas*. Although this arrangement helped pacify the region, it also threatened to upset the political balance in the Sierra by providing Lucas with an opportunity to enhance his local political control and thereby increase his autonomy vis-à-vis the central authorities.

Lucas took advantage of Madero's weakness to do more than perform mere guard duty in the towns that he patrolled (which included Tetela, Teziutlán, Zacapoaxtla, Zapotitlán, Zautla, and Zoquiapan). He requested more troops and interfered in local politics by closing down town governments, replacing municipal and district officials as well as jefes políticos, protecting authorities charged with rebellion, ordering villages and individuals not to pay taxes, and releasing prisoners, all without the authorization of the state. Madero, concerned about Lucas's unchecked power, ordered the cacique to send more *serrano* troops to fight outside Puebla, but Lucas ignored the president. A furious Governor Meléndez protested to Madero and accused the president's staff of aiding and abetting Lucas. The chief state executive threatened to wage war with the Sierra leader if Madero did not intervene.[16]

Madero and his aides finally persuaded Lucas to dissolve his force, but in return Lucas demanded one hundred carbines. Madero, expressing his mistrust of the Indian, gave him fifty. Their relationship would never again be quite the same. For example, in October 1912, Madero provided federal monies to Lucas to combat Félix Díaz's rebellion, but the aid came nowhere near matching what Lucas had received in the spring.[17]

Recognition of Lucas's importance in the region came once again in early February 1913 when, following a hotly disputed gubernatorial election, three candidates claimed the position. Upon the inauguration of the Madero-backed aspirant, Juan Carrasco, one of the losers, Agustín del Pozo, supported by more conservative elements including the army, formed his own state government in Tetela de Ocampo. Del Pozo had been currying Lucas's support for months, and it is clear that the former Rural Guard commander could not have based himself in Tetela without at least the tacit cooperation of Lucas.[18]

Madero insisted to Lucas that Del Pozo's claim to the governorship would never be recognized and urged the Sierra leader to combat this newest insurgency. So concerned was Madero with maintaining Lucas's loyalty that, even before the rebellion, he had urged Carrasco to quash the state legislature's attempt to deny a seat to Lucas's son Abraham, who had been recently elected to that body. The congress claimed that the younger Lucas's credentials were invalid, but most likely the lawmakers knew of his father's connection to Del Pozo. Abraham briefly joined the legislature, but then took an indefinite leave for alleged health reasons in late January. Not coincidentally, perhaps, on that same day the legislature voted to exempt residents of the cabecera of Tetela from paying city taxes for 1910 and 1911. Officially, Lucas remained neutral on the Del Pozo affair, waiting to see which way the political winds would blow. In the end, his move away from Madero proved to be the correct one. Only a few days later a rebellion erupted in Mexico City led by army officers Félix Díaz and Bernardo Reyes. At the same time, the Federal military head in Puebla City, Colonel Luis G. Pradillo, seconded the Mexico City uprising. The Puebla revolt soon fizzled out, but not the one in the national capital. In Mexico City, Federal army commander Victoriano Huerta joined the insurgents, over-throwing and killing Madero. Circumstantial evidence indicates that Del Pozo had ties to the right-wing conspirators in both Mexico City and Puebla; if so, Lucas, too, was aware of the impending coup.[19]

President Huerta

Lucas's next dilemma became how to come to an accommodation with the illegitimate Huerta regime, in order to protect the interests of the Sierra and his political base, yet not be branded a reactionary and traitor to the memory of Madero and the ideals of the Revolution. His position was made increasingly difficult when, during the spring of 1913, anti-Huerta rebels, operating under the auspices of Venustiano Carranza's Constitutionalist movement based in northern Mexico, began to battle the Federal army in the Puebla Sierra. In late April, Carranza appointed General Gilberto Camacho to organize the resistance and name officers to the Constitutionalist army in the region. The Federal army's brutal efforts to stem the rising insurgency drove more and more *serranos* into the arms of the *carrancistas* and endangered Lucas's position. Huerta's troops attacked and even razed whole villages and arbitrarily executed suspects, replaced local officials, and forcefully recruited additional men to fight locally as well as outside the state.[20]

Both sides wanted Lucas's support and pressured him to make an open commitment. Huerta wanted to secure peace in the Sierra so as more freely to pursue his campaign against the *carrancistas* in the north of the country. He also came under pressure from Puebla City merchants who feared disruption of their profitable economic links with the Sierra. Huerta ordered his Minister of War to urge Lucas to help form a two- to three-thousand-man army in the Sierra to be used in Puebla and neighboring states. In return, Abraham would be named one of its commanders. Lucas deftly declined the overture by claiming that his followers had their homes to look after and their land to till and therefore had no interest in joining the army, particularly when it meant fighting away from the Sierra. He added that if the government thought the matter important enough, then it should send a fully accredited agent (and thereby formally recognize Lucas's position of authority in the region) to negotiate with him about the formation of a contingent for the defense of the Sierra only.[21]

Lucas had to balance the advantages of coming to terms with Huerta against the danger to his authority posed by the increasing number of groups opposed to Huerta. Some insurgents, as in earlier conflicts, even undertook action in Lucas's name, responsibility for which he consistently denied. Especially serious was the May 1913 decision of the Márquez brothers, Lucas's associates, to revolt against Huerta even as Lucas recommended that their leader, Esteban, be named head of government forces in Chignahuapan. The Márquez were joined by a number of individuals from important Sierra families including the Cabrera of Zacatlán and, even closer to home, the Barrios of Cuacuila. Then in June, longtime colleagues in Xochiapulco, led by his nephews Manuel and Martín Rivera, also declared for Carranza. The rebels set up their headquarters in Tetela, condemning Huerta and his ties to the Catholic Church. These events, which Lucas seemed incapable of controlling, along with Abraham's prolonged absence from the state legislature, reportedly to participate in the insurrection, only increased the government's suspicion of Lucas and undermined its faith in him.[22]

In Xochiapulco, where anti-Huerta sentiment had been running high since Madero's assassination, serious fighting broke out in late June. Some one hundred thirty villagers, supported by the Rivera clan and led by Federico Dinorín and Antonio Muñoz, rebelled in Lucas's name when Governor Joaquín Maass ordered state troops into the town to disarm and conscript into the army those residents who refused to cooperate with the authorities. The Xochiapulquenses already were angry at the state's replacement of the jefe político with an unknown outsider who many feared would step up the government's military recruiting effort. The rifles in question were ones that Lucas himself had received from federal authorities to be distributed among his followers in order to help pacify the area. The rebels replaced the municipal officials and revived the title given to the community in 1864: La Villa del Cinco de Mayo.[23]

In the wake of the revolt, Lieutenant Ricardo Vigueras, commander of the state forces in the area, arrested Lucas's sons, Abraham and Miguel, for being rebel collaborators. He threatened to shoot them along with several others if the insurgents attacked Tetela. Abraham managed to escape from the Tetela municipal building where they were being held. Ignoring Vigueras, rebels led by Gaspar Márquez then attacked Tetela and captured the lieutenant. In the end, Vigueras put up so little resistance that the government moved to court-martial him for treason, but he was executed by the insurgents beforehand.[24]

Meanwhile, during July 1913, Carranza's commanding officer in the state, General Gilberto Camacho, undertook the task of forging a coherent military force out of disparate insurgents. Their numbers totaled approximately twelve hundred. From his headquarters, now based in Lucas's hometown of Tetela, Camacho called for a general uprising against Huerta. This appeal was soon followed by the announcement of the creation of the Constitutionalist army. Esteban Márquez, to be promoted to general, would command its forces in the Sierra while Camacho would have jurisdiction over the remainder of the state (once captured from the Federal army). Unfamiliar with the principles of the *carrancista* movement and the methods of a professional military, Camacho distributed Carranza's Plan de Agua Prieta, drilled the *serranos* into a semblance of a professional army, selected local officers, and forwarded their names to Carranza for approval. Nevertheless, *carrancista*-style professionalism did not alter the established practice of electing local officers, as witnessed when a junta of citizens voted Martín Rivera captain of Xochiapulco's company in early August.[25]

During the summer months of 1913, Camacho and Márquez, along with other important *carrancistas*, including the Riveras and Antonio Medina, ranged the length of the Sierra. They captured Cuetzalan and Zacapoaxtla, Tetela's traditional rival and the immediate origin of federal attacks on Tetela. They also seriously threatened several other major towns as well as the Canadian-controlled Necaxa hydroelectric works near Huauchinango and the U.S.-owned Teziutlán Copper Company. In addition, they developed contacts with other anti-Huerta groups in the state including the Junta Revolucionaria Constitucionalista in Puebla City, of which Carmen Serdán, the sister of martyred Aquiles Serdán, was an important spokesperson.[26]

Meanwhile, Lucas continued to play both sides. While he was concerned with maintaining contact with Huerta and therefore kept a low profile, evidence exists that he and his sons did help to plan and carry out attacks on Cuetzalan, Tlatlauqui, and Zacapoaxtla, exercises that were familiar to Lucas from earlier struggles. State and company officials, receiving reports of increased rebel activity, demanded that Lucas keep his forces (referred to as "Indians") in check.[27]

Desperate to prevent full-scale warfare in the Sierra, which would provide the excuse for wholesale penetration of the region by outside forces, Lucas attempted to arrange a truce by offering to mediate between the two sides. To Huerta he offered neutrality and the pacification of the region if the central and state governments would guarantee local political autonomy, the withdrawal of all Federal troops, and the end of forced recruitment into the army. Having convinced the insurgents to allow him to represent them, and despite *carrancista* objections, Lucas entered negotiations with the Huerta regime in late July 1913.

Miguel Lucas traveled to the state capital to represent his father, carrying demands from the Márquez brothers of guarantees of appointment to federal deputy and jefe político posts if they ended hostilities. The federal government, represented by Sergio Bonilla, went so far as to agree to allow changes in local officials and offered the jefe político position of Tetela to the elder Lucas. However, Governor Maass, Huerta's brother-in-law, refused to agree to the withdrawal of government troops from the region. He was angered at the rebels' continued activity while negotiations took place and resented federal intervention in what he considered a state affair.[28]

With negotiations at a standstill, the rebels tried to break the impasse by intensifying their offensive, starting in late August. In early September, with Tetela, Zacapoaxtla, and Tlatlauqui plus several other smaller towns in their control, the rebels turned their attention to Teziutlán, the Sierra's largest and most important town. Heavy fighting took place in the surrounding area, culminating in a ten-day siege in mid-September. Eighteen hundred rebels, using a variety of artillery pieces, some of which Lucas's troops had employed during the French Intervention, forced Teziutlán to the verge of surrender. However, heavy rains, lack of ammunition, and the arrival of Federal reinforcements stalled the insurgents' offensive. Lucas then halted the siege, leaving behind one hundred fifty Federal and fourteen Constitutionalist soldiers dead.[29]

With both sides momentarily at a stalemate, Lucas seized the opportunity to pursue a political solution. The negative impact of the fighting was being felt throughout the Sierra. Schoolchildren as young as nine years old followed their teachers onto the battlefield. Rebels, branded Masons and Liberals by the Catholic press, had begun to attack priests, especially ones from outside the Sierra. As in earlier conflicts, the Federal army targeted communities along the southern margin of the Sierra for recruitment. Finally, it was the foreigners at Necaxa and Teziutlán who provided the catalyst for a deal.[30]

During the first three weeks of October 1913, Lucas and Esteban Márquez met with *huertista* representatives (among them, one of Márquez's brothers, who apparently had arranged an earlier truce with Huerta's government, as well as General Mariano Ruiz, a personal friend of Lucas). The agents brought letters from high *huertista* officials including Jacinto Treviño, Aureliano Blanquet, and Huerta himself, plus offers of money, if the *serranos* would make a deal. As a result, Lucas obtained cash and arms to bolster Tetela and, with the aid of the North American general manager of the Teziutlán Copper Company, G. H. Carnahan, arranged a cease-fire in the region.[31]

Finally, after additional talks, including ones with Agustín del Pozo, who represented the state government, Lucas arrived at a far-reaching settlement referred to as the Sierra Pact. In a truly unusual yet beneficial arrangement for the region's autonomy, as well as for the cacique personally,

Lucas, Márquez, and *huertista* General Ruiz, with the blessing of the Canadian and U.S. business interests in the region, signed an agreement on 28 October 1913. It called for the withdrawal of the Federal army from the Sierra and the creation of a federally financed two-thousand-man force under the command of Lucas and Márquez. These troops would replace the Federal soldiers and maintain a neutral peace in the area. The Federal army agreed to end all recruiting in the north of the state and to allow Indians forcibly inducted to transfer to the Brigada Serrana. Elections for new local officials were to take place under the contingent's supervision. Free primary education was to be offered to all beginning in early 1914. As its part of the agreement, the copper company, with its nearly two thousand employees, promised to remain in business and make new investments. To seal the pact, Abraham Lucas and Esteban Márquez journeyed to the state capital to meet with Governor Maass.

The pact fulfilled Lucas's desire to reestablish peace, gain full control over the Brigada Serrana, prompt the departure of outsiders, and reassert jurisdiction over the Sierra. It also went a long way toward the realization of a long-held ideal among many in the Sierra, the creation of a separate state or federal territory, referred to as the "República de la Sierra."[32]

Despite the Huerta government's optimistic pronouncements that peace in the region had been restored, the accord began to unravel even as the ink dried. Before its signing, Gilberto Camacho had denounced Lucas and Márquez for prematurely withdrawing from the siege of Teziutlán in order to deal with the Huerta government. With Carranza's blessing, he tried to block the agreement and denounced it once consummated. Moreover, pro-*carrancista* revolutionary juntas in Mexico City and Puebla, which saw no advantage in a deal with Huerta, backed Camacho. Antonio Medina, another prominent Constitutionalist officer, declared against the compromise in late November when Lucas and Márquez, acceding to General Ruiz's and Teziutlán residents' demands, blocked Medina from occupying the city. The Sierra army (including contingents in the neighboring states of Hidalgo, Tlaxcala, and Veracruz) of thirty-five hundred men now split. Constitutionalist forces clashed with troops under Lucas and Márquez, and each side competed for the loyalty of uncommitted Indian groups.[33]

Condemnation of the Sierra Pact also came from other quarters. The *zapatistas*, as anti-*huertistas*, criticized Lucas and Márquez for dealing with a treacherous impostor. Even some *huertistas* disliked the agreement charging that Lucas's army was made up of ex-bandits, undesirables, and *zapatistas*. However, General Ruiz defended the move and disputed the charges against the men commanded by Lucas and Márquez.[34]

The federal government made Lucas's and Márquez's jobs even more difficult by removing its forces slowly from the Sierra, especially the key population centers such as Teziutlán, Tetela, and Zacatlán. Not only did the army reluctantly turn over such strategic positions, but also many townspeople preferred a Federal garrison as the lesser evil compared to armed Indians under their increasingly radicalized commanders, many of whom were not even *serranos*. Indeed, resistance by Teziutlán to the replacement of Federal troops by insurgents from Chignautla, under the command of Antonio Medina, forced Lucas and Márquez to compromise and send a Xochiapulco contingent headed by the Rivera brothers, Sierra natives. Moreover, the issue of who would control the appointment of new local and district officials compounded the uncertainty of people in these towns.[35]

Such delays undermined the position of Lucas and Márquez. By the time the Brigada Serrana officially entered Teziutlán during the second week of December 1913, after nearly a month's wait, its leaders had come under severe criticism for their cooperation with the regime. Soldiers wrote to Lucas implying that Márquez and other officers had pocketed government funds. Their forces had so little clothing and food that they had to go barefoot and survive on handouts from the local population. Márquez, they claimed, lived on a hacienda in Teziutlán provided by General Ruiz, who, they feared, might turn them over to the Federal army. Lucas dismissed these complaints, ordered the men to obey their officers, and, considering the opportunistic nature of Márquez, naively declared that Márquez would not betray them. Meanwhile, disillusioned *serranos* joined the anti-Huerta insurgents, some operating in the name of Lucas. Even such traditional Lucas strongholds as Zapotitlán experienced desertions, and his commander in Teziutlán, Manuel Rivera, captured armed men from the town of Xiutetelco who claimed they had infiltrated the city on Lucas's orders.[36]

Lucas's efforts to hold the October agreement intact received another severe blow in mid-December. Gaspar Márquez, ordered by his brother Esteban to help reinforce Zacatlán as retreating government soldiers left the important western Sierra town, instead entered the community before Huerta's troops had evacuated it. Gaspar's arrival provoked a clash in which he disarmed the Federal force, captured a large quantity of matériel including arms and horses, imposed forced loans on the citizenry, and allegedly pronounced in favor of the *carrancistas*. His principal motive for the attack may have been to pay and provision his troops, a task the federal government had promised to undertake in the Sierra Pact but had done little to fulfill. Whatever the case, Gaspar, joined by the district's jefe político, Benjamín Méndez, maintained a defiant stance for several days. Finally, Gaspar returned to the fold. When faced with General Ruiz's threat to send a Federal column after him,[37] he acceded to Lucas and his brothers' petitions, on the promise that Emilio Márquez would become jefe político of Zacatlán (which was adamantly opposed by most residents of the city who did not trust the Márquez clan from rival Chignahuapan).

The Zacatlán affair weakened the already uneasy working relationship between Lucas and Esteban Márquez, the two men responsible for keeping the accord with the Huerta government intact, and also increased the government's doubts about the effectiveness of Lucas's authority beyond the core of his *cacicazgo* in Tetela.[38] Noting the mounting tension between Lucas and Márquez, Huerta proposed that the Sierra be divided up between the two leaders, allowing them to operate separately in their respective regions of influence. Márquez would control the western districts of Alatriste, Huauchinango, and Zacatlán; and Lucas, along with his nephews, the Rivera brothers of Xochiapulco, would exercise jurisdiction over Tetela, Teziutlán, Tlatlauqui, and Zacapoaxtla. Although Huerta's design was never formally implemented, when Lucas and Márquez became adversaries in 1914, their control of the region followed his outline.[39]

While Lucas professed neutrality in the conflict and a dedication to making the October accord work, his son Abraham hedged the family's bets by aiding the rebels and setting up a shop in his home where he manufactured ammunition at his own expense for the insurgents. In addition, he used his personal funds to feed soldiers in the Tetela hospital and also established a similar institution for wounded soldiers in nearby Taxcantla, his father's ranch. General Antonio Medina held out the rank of Colonel to Abraham if he would openly join the *carrancistas*; however, Abraham remained cautious, well instructed by his father in the art of political circumspection, and rejected the overture.[40]

Meanwhile, Huerta felt increasingly unsure of the Lucas family's commitment to uphold the government's interests. He tried to promote closer ties to the clan by reiterating his regime's intention to respect its authority in the Sierra and by, in effect, bribing Abraham. General Ruiz offered Abraham the post of inspector of military forces in the region, an offer he turned down, claiming the position would compromise him in the eyes of the people of the Sierra. Not satisfied, Ruiz then offered Abraham the jefe político post of Tetela, which he also declined.[41]

In late 1913 and early 1914, as the Huerta government's hold on power weakened in Puebla and throughout the nation, and as Lucas and Márquez came under increasing criticism for their cooperation with the regime, the two men began to recognize the possibility that they would be dealt with as traitors in the case of a Constitutionalist victory. To forestall such a fate, Lucas asked the U.S. consul in Veracruz to contact the revolutionaries and explain to them that he and his *serrano* allies were not hostile to the *carrancista* cause. Lucas's petition got lost, it seems, in the depths of the State Department.[42]

Then, in early January 1914, Esteban Márquez made a much more serious effort to open negotiations with the Constitutionalists, again through the auspices of the U.S. government. He commissioned Carnahan, already party to the Sierra Pact, to negotiate with Carranza through Woodrow Wilson's special agent to Mexico, John Lind. Márquez urged Carnahan to reach an agreement with Carranza in which the Constitutionalists would recognize the *serrano* accord with the Huerta government. Márquez claimed that Lind promised to bring up the subject personally with President Wilson.

Moreover, Márquez added that Washington would be favorable toward the *serranos* because they did not condone banditry like Pancho Villa's movement. In the end, however, nothing came of the initiative. No record exists of the Lucases' role in this second attempt to negotiate with Carranza. Esteban Márquez invited Abraham to a meeting in Zacapoaxtla to discuss the effort, but the evidence does not indicate whether or not he attended.[43]

Shortly thereafter, Lucas called for a campaign against Antonio Medina, who had been operating in the Teziutlán area virtually unmolested. Instead of heeding Lucas, Márquez and his brothers hosted a conclave of some ten Sierra leaders to which Lucas was not invited. They denounced the Sierra Pact and declared for the Constitutionalists in their battle against the Huerta government. Márquez minimized the October accord, claiming it was merely a truce; he justified breaking it because of the crooked October 1913 presidential election and Huerta's killing of opposition Chiapaneco Senator Belisario Domínguez. When Lucas's nephew, Colonel Manuel Rivera, objected to this betrayal, Márquez arrested Rivera. Always an opportunist, Márquez most likely submitted to the growing pressure of his more restless followers, including his brothers, who had never liked the deal with the government and now convinced Esteban that Huerta would surely fall from power. Enticements from the *carrancistas* also contributed to his decision.[44]

Lucas and his allies opposed Márquez's defection to the Constitutionalists and attempted to distance themselves from this faction. None of the family signed Márquez's publicly distributed broadside announcing his break with the Huerta regime, nor a second edict in which Márquez promised protection only for those people who remained neutral or actively helped the Constitutionalist cause. Lucas sent peace feelers to Huerta at least through March. Press reports from as late as June 1914 claim that Lucas denied the rebels access to his Taxcantla ranch and that he told the Huerta government that he was not collaborating with them nor planning to help them to attack Puebla City. Moreover, Abraham and Miguel took no part in the fighting. Abraham remained constantly at his father's side as an advisor and spokesman; Miguel ran a business in Tetela and was often incapacitated by alcoholism. Likewise, Lucas's longtime cohorts, the Barrios at Cuacuila and the Riveras at Xochiapulco, stood guard over Tetela's western and eastern flanks and took no active part in the fighting.

Nevertheless, over the longer run, the cacique had little choice but cautiously to accede to Márquez and tacitly support the anti-Huerta rebels. Reports filtered out of the Sierra that Lucas was ill and confined to Taxcantla, which was surrounded by rebel troops—in effect, he was Márquez's prisoner. Furthermore, Márquez, now enjoying the support of most Sierra leaders, expressed his intention to persecute Lucas loyalists. The tide of battle favored the insurgents.[45]

Meanwhile, Márquez assumed general command of all pro-Constitutionalist forces in the Sierra, although he was not formally recognized as an officer in the Constitutionalist army until June 1914. With the aid of arms and money sent by the *carrancistas* via the Veracruz coast, he set about securing the region. In an attempt to strengthen his popular support, he abolished taxes and replaced local officials, especially jefes políticos.[46]

Lucas's efforts to isolate the Sierra from all-out warfare had failed. Heavy fighting now spread throughout the entire region, with nearly all major towns coming under attack. Fighting destroyed the mines and equipment of the Teziutlán Copper Company, and its North American personnel fled the state. Trains, haciendas, commercial establishments, and tax offices became favorite targets while attacks on the Catholic clergy were reported in some rebel-held areas. Another indication of the increasingly radical nature of the fighting can be detected in the persecution of the middle and upper classes by Indians who deliberately destroyed their homes and businesses. The government retaliated by forcefully removing the population, by razing villages, and by establishing free-fire zones in the vacated areas. Captives were summarily shot. In addition, food shortages and disease, including diphtheria and smallpox, ravaged civilians and soldiers alike.[47]

Despite their leaders' uneasy relationship, by April 1914 the Sierra rebels had made significant gains on the battlefield. They controlled the districts of Tetela, Tlatlauqui, and Zacapoaxtla and parts of Chignahuapan, Huauchinango, San Juan de los Llanos, Teziutlán, and Zacatlán. Esteban Márquez operated principally on his home ground in the western Sierra while Antonio Medina, with Lucas's tacit consent, led the *carrancistas* in the eastern sector. The total number of insurgents approximated five thousand, although not all were well armed despite the output of an arsenal at Zacapoaxtla. Lucas reportedly had some one thousand men under his command in Tetela. Government forces of less than three thousand were able to slow but not stop the enemy's advances.[48]

To reverse his losses, Huerta contemplated declaring a state of siege in the Sierra, thereby halting communications with the area and embargoing the entrance of all basic goods. However, the U.S. capture of Veracruz in April 1914 provided the president with an alternative strategy to defeat his internal opponents. He attempted to rally Mexicans of all political persuasions behind him in a nationalistic crusade to oust the invaders and bolster his sagging government. Huerta appealed to the famed Liberal patriotic traditions of the *serranos*, announcing a fifteen-day amnesty to give the rebels time to take up his offer. If they refused to cooperate, Huerta threatened to charge them with treason and persecute them without mercy.[49]

Rebel leaders found themselves in the difficult position of not wanting to be perceived as anti-Mexican yet unwilling to cooperate in any way with Huerta against the North American invaders. After some wavering, they first rejected the government's appeal, condemning the Huerta regime as corrupt and arguing that only the *carrancistas* could put into effect the 1878 Ley del Pueblo, which called for far-reaching agrarian reform. They also appealed for support by referring to the martyred Belisario Domínguez and Aquiles Serdán, whose father helped write the Ley del Pueblo, but whose principal author was Alberto de Santa Fé, former jefe político of Tetela. They then attempted to persuade the local population that it was not the North Americans who had invaded Veracruz but Mexican naval forces who had revolted against Huerta. When this ruse failed, they called on their followers to join the Constitutionalist army, not the Federal one, in order to chastise the Yankee aggressors. Finally, the Lucas-Márquez-Medina groups managed to sidestep the issue by unilaterally declaring a temporary cease-fire in order to defend, they claimed, the nation against the invader. In this manner they avoided any direct cooperation with or recognition of the Huerta regime. This policy of no contact with the Huerta government (at least publicly) followed that of the underground pro-*carrancista* Revolutionary Junta in Puebla City, with whom the Sierra rebels maintained regular contact.[50]

In the longer run, the nationalistic ire provoked by the U.S. invasion, and the cease-fire by the *serranos,* did little to help Huerta's increasingly desperate situation. The withdrawal of Federal troops from the Sierra to the Gulf Coast to confront the foreign enemy, and the loss of the port of Veracruz with its customs receipts and arms imports, soon placed the government in dire straits. The Constitutionalists quickly took advantage of the situation and by late May 1914 were in a position to make their final push to topple the regime. They instructed the *serranos* to be prepared for the upcoming offensive and sent them additional war matériel through the Gulf port of Tuxpan.[51]

In June, *carrancista* General Cándido Aguilar arrived from northern Mexico to lead the offensive. To keep the muted yet potentially serious rivalry among the principal Constitutionalist commanders in the Sierra in check, Carranza sought help from the Revolutionary Junta in Puebla City. He also promoted the two principal protagonists, Márquez and Medina, to Brigadier General with co-jurisdiction in the region and named a civilian to handle finances and reestablish public services in the Sierra. Now, Sierra forces stood at some six to eight thousand men. By 15 July, when Huerta fled Mexico City for Europe, all of northern Puebla, except Teziutlán, Huauchinango, San Juan de los Llanos, and Zacatlán, was held by the rebels. Teziutlán fell five days later, and Huauchinango and Llanos followed suit in early August. Zacatlán, not as crucial in terms of the drive to capture the state capital, remained in federal hands until late August.[52]

President Carranza

The Constitutionalist military authorities met with mixed responses in the Sierra. Most citizens yearned to resume their daily lives and, given their insular tradition, resented any action by outsiders that smacked of interference in local affairs. Some merchants, including Miguel Lucas, for example, at first refused to accept Constitutionalist-issued currency and in turn were threatened with fines. Other people resisted paying taxes to the new government, and complaints about high tax burdens (apparently collected on a per capita basis) in a period of insecurity and economic downturn were common. Restrictions on sales of alcohol, and rising prices, hardly cultivated adherents either.[53]

The Lucas clan soon adjusted itself to the new situation, however, with Juan Francisco Lucas playing the role of mediator. He encouraged local officials to turn taxes over to the regime with the claim that it needed the revenues. He consulted with Constitutionalist agents over nominations for government posts and the distribution of forces in the area. His close confidant, Tranquilino Quintero, was named commander of the district of Tetela. Lucas urged him to maintain the district's good name and not to fall to the temptations of intrigue, praise, or liquor. Abraham, too, cooperated with the new government by serving as the *carrancista*-appointed municipal president of Tetela.

Nevertheless, Lucas proved less cooperative with the Constitutionalists when it came to sending his troops outside the region to fight. As the drive on the state capital and pacification of the remainder of Puebla continued and pressure mounted on him to commit soldiers to the campaign, Lucas firmly but diplomatically let it be known that his men would be available beyond the Sierra only when their presence directly contributed to the defense of the region.[54]

In early September 1914 the Constitutionalists officially established a new state government in Puebla de Zaragoza. They named General Francisco Coss governor, undercutting Medina's and Márquez's aspirations for the office. Medina was placed in overall charge of military operations in the Sierra. Esteban Márquez, accompanied by his brother Emilio, had the same charge in the south. Each received wide authority to name officials in his respective jurisdiction.[55]

Márquez had served barely a month in his new post when he joined revolutionary leaders from throughout the country at the Convention of Aguascalientes, convoked to form a new national government and army. On his return, Márquez declared his adherence to the newly created Conventionist faction led by Pancho Villa and Emiliano Zapata. His opportunism went beyond the mere fact that the Conventionists enjoyed military superiority at the time. During 1913 and 1914, while operating in the Sierra, he had had to share authority with General Medina, an outsider from northern Mexico. Now, Medina, his principal rival, had been named commander of the Sierra while he, Márquez, a native of the region, had been sent to the south of the state, an unfamiliar area where he had few connections and no political base. Late in 1914 the Conventionists seemed to offer Márquez a securer route to the state governorship than waiting his turn as a middle-ranking Constitutionalist.[56]

Not satisfied with their successful recruitment of Márquez (who soon was joined by his brothers and several other important Sierra figures), the Conventionists also placed heavy pressure on Lucas to change sides. Emilio Márquez personally visited him to persuade him to defect. Lucas refused, but then in a gesture of *serrano* solidarity, he also prevented Antonio Medina from arresting the Márquez siblings.[57] Emiliano Zapata even offered Lucas the rank of Brigadier General in the Conventionist army with the right to operate in the Sierra, and invited Lucas to attend a meeting of revolutionary officers who had adhered to his Plan de Ayala. Zapata's letter to Lucas contained twenty-one silver pesos, perhaps to convince him of his sincerity and the *zapatistas'* relative wealth (they minted their own coins) contrasting with the poverty of the *carrancistas.* Lucas neither accepted the proposition, citing his advanced age, nor did he send a representative. Zapata tried once again in January 1915 to get Lucas's support, on this occasion to help defend *zapatista*-held Puebla City from a Constitutionalist counterattack. By this time, Lucas was fully committed to Carranza and did not even bother to respond to Zapata.[58]

Medina, too, was sorely tempted to switch sides. He noted the overwhelming support for the Conventionists among most military men, and he, too, had political ambitions. Understanding the potential dividends of treating recently surrendered *huertista* officers and soldiers with some degree of leniency, he also resented Governor Coss's threats against those Constitutionalist officers who refused to sign formal pro-Carranza declarations. Medina reserved the final decision about whom to support until returning to the Sierra from Aguascalientes, accompanied by Carmen Serdán. Following talks with Lucas and Serdán (who represented the Revolutionary Junta in Puebla), Medina remained in the Constitutionalists' ranks.[59]

In hindsight, Lucas probably made a mistake in neither attending the Aguascalientes convention nor sending a personal representative as General Medina and others had suggested. Perhaps he did not perceive fully how the Revolution, by exposing the Sierra more directly to external forces and by providing local opportunists like the Márquez brothers with the chance to challenge the status quo, had already partially undermined his traditional role as "patriarch." Of course, even by going to Aguascalientes, Lucas may not have been able to prevent the defection of Márquez to the Conventionists, but other officers might have been persuaded to stay with him and the Constitutionalists. Lucas still enjoyed a great deal of respect in the region. When he did have direct contact with people, as, for example, with Gabriel Barrios and his brothers (who did not go to the convention), he managed to convince them to remain in the *carrancista* camp. Lucas's inability to hold the *serrano* leadership together would mean another full year of devastating warfare resulting in the continued erosion of the Sierra's autonomy and his own control over the region.[60]

Juan Francisco Lucas, age c. 81,
Commander in Chief of the Brigada Serrana, c. 1915

The new Conventionist president, Eulalio Gutiérrez, rewarded
Márquez for abandoning Carranza by naming him provisional governor
and military commander of Puebla. Nevertheless, Márquez was barely established in the new state capital, Huauchinango, when a meeting of
zapatista-dominated Conventionist officers in recently captured Puebla
City vetoed Gutiérrez's decision. Disliking Gutiérrez's close ties to
Pancho Villa, they claimed that he had acted illegally in naming Márquez
and voted to replace him with *zapatista* Colonel Francisco Salgado, a
more trustworthy and long-standing adherent to the cause.[61]

Rebuffed by the Conventionists over the governorship, Márquez contacted Alvaro Obregón, Carranza's principal general. He offered to suspend
hostilities and join the Constitutionalist forces in the attack on
Conventionist-held Mexico City. Obregón rejected the overture.[62] In response, Márquez maintained his claim to the governorship and, as a relatively autonomous actor, continued to fight for dominance of the Sierra in
the name of the Conventionists against Lucas, Medina, and the *carrancis-*

tas. With his three thousand followers, he carried on the war requisitioning matériel for his troops, persecuting people, minting coins, growing crops on seized haciendas, and imposing officials. Receiving arms via the Gulf port of Nautla, Márquez controlled large parts of the western Sierra including at times its principal towns, Chignahuapan, Huauchinango, and Zacatlán. In April 1915 his forces even managed to seize the strategic Necaxa hydroelectric works. On occasion he operated in a loose alliance with Eulalio Gutiérrez in Hidalgo, Domingo Arenas in Tlaxcala, and Manuel Peláez in Veracruz.[63]

General Antonio Medina now headed the Constitutionalist effort in the Sierra. Lucas took no active role in the fighting, but he was in nominal charge of the defense of Tetela, commanding eight hundred men. In this effort he relied on several longtime confidants including his two sons and a grandson, Luis Moreno, the Rivera brothers, and Gabriel Barrios and his siblings. Above all, he continued to serve as an important symbol in the *carrancista* effort to keep the loyalty of as many Sierra villages as possible. For example, Medina named Lucas chief of the Third Brigade upon Carranza's explicit order—not for his fighting ability, which was almost nil given his advanced age, but because of the respect so many people in the region and beyond had for the cacique. In Cuetzalan and surrounding towns such as San Miguel Tzinacapan and Xaltipan, Lucas's influence greatly aided Barrios's efforts against Márquez. Even Obregón, a stranger to the Sierra, asked for a photo of the cacique. Furthermore, Lucas's home in Tetela served as the unofficial Constitutionalist headquarters. Dozens of military and political officials passed through his doorway, many spending the night and eating at his table, all at his expense.[64]

Real political control of the region, however, increasingly lay in the hands of the *carrancistas*. This fact became especially apparent during the winter and spring of 1915 as Lucas, desperate to end the destructive fighting in the Sierra, attempted to make peace with Márquez. The latter offered to fight for the Constitutionalists in the north of the country if the *carrancistas* would guarantee that Medina, too, abandon the Sierra. Obregón urged a wary Carranza to accept Márquez's proposal, as it would offer the opportunity to get rid of troublesome regional chiefs. Then Eulalio Gutiérrez quit the presidency and fled Mexico City, thereby removing Márquez's last remaining link to the Conventionists. In response, Márquez offered to resign as Conventionist governor, thus creating another opportunity for an accommodation with the *carrancistas*.

These overtures provided Lucas with an opportunity to reunite the Sierra and bring about peace. However, Medina, with Carranza's concurrence, blocked the reconciliation. Neither man trusted Márquez, and they felt he could be defeated on the battlefield. Moreover, neither wanted an agreement that would compromise the Constitutionalists' hard-won presence and latitude in the strategic northern area of the state.[65]

Spurned, Márquez reaffirmed his connection to the Convention and its new president, Roque González Garza, as well as his claim to the governorship. With over two thousand troops under his command, he continued the war during the spring and summer months of 1915. Using dynamite obtained at Necaxa, he manufactured bombs in Zacatlán. He focused on disrupting the railroad link between Veracruz and Mexico City and preventing *carrancista* forces and supplies from entering the Sierra from the west through Tulancingo, from the south through Tlaxco, and from the east through Libres. Most fighting took place within a roughly vee-shaped area in the central Sierra that ran from Villa Juárez and Jonotla in the north to Ixtacamaxtitlán in the south. Between these axes, which divided Conventionist-held territory to the west from *carrancista*-occupied territory to the east, lay Tetela, Lucas's home base and the key to control of the region.[66]

The Constitutionalist presence in the region not only undermined Lucas's traditional influence but also introduced a disturbing level of ineptitude, abuse, and corruption among military and civilian leaders, including native *serranos*. Conflicting orders from the federal and state governments, for example, only exacerbated a situation in which Sierra officials worked at cross purposes, fought among each other, failed to fight to their full ability, arbitrarily replaced local authorities, and exploited the populace for personal enrichment. Villagers commonly protested their treatment by *carrancista* officers and soldiers. Many citizens also resented the fact that the area's Constitutionalist leadership tolerated and even cooperated with former *huertistas*.[67]

Serranos also chafed under the Constitutionalist government's refusal to recognize any special political status for the region. Carranza's military governors, none of whom was from Puebla, suspended all state and local political institutions and appointed all local officials. Moreover, whenever the issue of the selection of a new governor arose, *serranos* and others strongly urged Carranza to name one of their own. Among those most often suggested was Colonel Eulogio Hernández, who reportedly enjoyed support in other areas of Puebla as well and was a committed Constitutionalist, having served as general inspector of police in Mexico City. Carranza ignored these appeals. This situation underlined the further weakening of the Sierra's traditional autonomy and prompted renewed pressure for the creation of a separate state.[68]

Lucas kept abreast of these grievances. At one point he asked then-Minister of War Alvaro Obregón to remove outside troops from the Sierra and especially to rid the region of officers Jorge N. Sánchez, Federico Dinorín, and Delfino F. Cruz, because of their abuses against the local population. Lucas also noted the pernicious actions of the priest of Cuetzalan, who was agitating his parishioners against the government. Lucas's complaints, in the end, had little long-lasting effect.[69]

Nor could either Medina or Lucas, the two principal leaders of the Constitutionalist forces in the Sierra, escape charges of condoning if not directly participating in such abuses. The land reform they undertook, for example, had more to do with the desire to check the Márquez-Zapatista influence than with a genuine concern for the propertyless villagers.[70] The two men were charged with needlessly (in the case of Medina, perhaps even purposefully) prolonging the war. Medina and the Márquez brothers were accused of pursuing each other only halfheartedly, with the two sides cooperating by exchanging prisoners within days of capture. A *carrancista* agent sent to the region to bring about a peace accord claimed that Medina and others wanted the fighting to go on because they benefited politically and financially from it. The officers, including Abraham Lucas, sent to battle Márquez were novices who fought poorly and impeded pacification. Moreover, they commanded forced recruits who were underarmed and irregularly paid. Soldiers who complained about such conditions received death threats. The agent characterized Juan Francisco Lucas as especially uncooperative. The old cacique would only take orders directly from Carranza, kept his soldiers concentrated in Tetela and Teziutlán, and refused to allow them to fight outside the region.[71]

In addition to tolerating corruption and incompetence among their followers, Medina and Lucas used their positions and the wartime conditions in the Sierra to enrich themselves and their relatives. For example, Camilo Cruz, a hacendado, mine owner, and Abraham's father-in-law, attempted to get a special concession from Carranza. He asked for a permit to create a mining company consisting of himself, Abraham, and Medina that would include tax breaks and the right, presently held by Juan Francisco Lucas, to mint coins.[72]

In the face of severe food shortages and rising prices, exacerbated by the influx of war refugees into urban areas, *carrancista* policy called for the regulation of the sale and transport of basic commodities in order to help ensure more equitable distribution and lower costs. The city of Teziutlán, for example, placed sharp restrictions on the marketing of foodstuffs, authorized local officials to inspect vendors' stocks to combat hoarding, and solicited monies from the upper classes to buy goods to sell at subsidized prices to the poor.[73] Yet Lucas, who owned three ranches, argued against such restrictions, claiming that they would only harm farmers and merchants and lead to even greater shortages in the longer run. Whatever the merits of this argument, they do suggest that he himself had been using the free market to his advantage. The price of corn in Tetela in May 1915, for example, was approximately five pesos per decaliter, while in Ayotla and Huauchinango it was only seventy-five centavos. At that time, Lucas reportedly held large quantities of corn in his personal possession for speculative purposes.[74]

Medina, too, was financially well off, having an interest in a Teziutlán bank. He allegedly trafficked in confiscated properties, returned haciendas to their original owners for a price, speculated in scarce goods, issued financial paper with no backing, and claimed fictitious soldiers under his

command in order to pocket the additional salaries. He also reportedly permitted his brother, Federico, to use the Constitutionalist general's influence
to enhance his financial operations in the region and to protect his friends.
This group profited from the war and the disorder by conducting business
with the Márquez brothers and dealing in counterfeit money.[75]

During the summer and early autumn of 1915, the Márquez faction
began to observe the tide of the Revolution turning in Carranza's favor. As
Constitutionalist pressure mounted and the Conventionist government disintegrated, Márquez's forces began to suffer a lack of arms and funds, desertions, and internal division. In July, Márquez abandoned Huauchinango
for more secure headquarters at Chignahuapan. In August, General Pablo
González ordered a concerted effort to wrest the important Necaxa hydroelectric works from Márquez. Control of the installation changed hands at
least twice with the Constitutionalists ultimately prevailing. Meanwhile, in
the south, Márquez lost Tlaxco and was then forced to abandon Chignahuapan and Zacatlán.[76] Then, in November, following U.S. recognition of
the Carranza government, Márquez sued for peace and submitted to
González. The surrender called for the disarming of Márquez and his followers and the return to their homes.[77]

Márquez and many of his adherents, rather than accept these humiliating terms, crossed into Veracruz where they bided their time waiting for an
opportunity to return to the Sierra. After Obregón's rejection of his bid to
join the Constitutionalist army, Márquez reentered the area in November
1916 in an effort to revive his insurgency. He justified the renewal of his rebellion by claiming that Carranza had failed to restore democracy to the nation and had permitted foreigners to invade the country (referring to the
Pershing Expedition in pursuit of Pancho Villa). The movement gained
some initial support, such as in Zacapoaxtla, but few people outside
Márquez's hometown of Otlatlán demonstrated any firm commitment to his
cause. Most villagers now backed Lucas. Fighting sputtered on for a couple
of months before the Constitutionalists, including Lucas and Barrios, with
reinforcements from the state and federal capitals, suppressed the revolt.
By early 1917 the bulk of the rebels had returned to Veracruz from where
they continued sporadic and at times disruptive, but not regime-threatening,
forays into the Sierra.[78]

Yet Márquez's defeat, due in large part to the villagers' loyalty to
Lucas, did little to enhance the autonomy of the Sierra. Indeed, it helped
pave the way for the renewal of the central government's control of the region. With the threat from Márquez virtually ended, Lucas attempted to rebuild his traditional sphere of influence in the western Sierra. In the spring
of 1916, General Medina agreed that Lucas's soldiers would be paid punctually, not have to serve guard duty, and, except in an emergency, would
serve only in Tetela, Chignahuapan, and Zacatlán.[79] Fearing the creation of
an autonomous zone so close to Mexico City, Carranza ignored the agree-

ment and moved to restructure the military command in the Sierra. He had received reports of the willingness of Lucas and Medina to incorporate former *huertistas* into their ranks and of their unwarranted distribution of land to towns in the region. Whatever the merit of these reports, they provided the excuse sought by Carranza to isolate and separate the two men. In early May, the First Chief removed Lucas's brigade from the Third Division of the Army of the East and put it under the jurisdiction of the Federal commander in Puebla City.[80]

With this move, Carranza undermined Lucas's independence in two important ways. First, Puebla, as the state capital, always guarded its influence in the north much more jealously than the more distant Mexico City, which often worked at cross-purposes to the state because of its broader policy objectives. Also, by removing Lucas from the Third Division, the opportunity for another Lucas-Medina alliance, combining the power and influence of a division commander and regional cacique, was diminished.

Carranza postponed the immediate plan to remove Medina from the Sierra because of the continued rebel threat there, in spite of rumors that Medina, using Lucas and the Sierra as a power base, was planning to stand for the state governorship and maybe even try to dislodge the First Chief from power. However, the residency requirement of the state constitution prohibited Medina from running in the June 1917 election. He therefore backed a business associate, Ignacio Hermoso, an hacendado and native of San Juan de los Llanos. Barred from power in Puebla, Medina appealed to *serrano* sentiment for the creation of a separate state. He used a heavy hand against his opponents, including followers of Lucas, whose recent death gave Medina an opportunity to consolidate even more power in his own hands. People forced to flee Tetela because of Medina included city councilmen, Lucas's grandson, and his personal secretary, Ricardo Márquez Galindo. Nevertheless, Hermoso lost. The winner, Alfonso Cabrera (brother of Carranza's adviser, Luis Cabrera), was also a native of the Sierra (Zacatlán), but he enjoyed the president's full backing and represented no autonomous tendencies that might threaten the regime's control over the region. By the end of the summer, Medina and his troops were being removed from the Sierra and repositioned in southern Puebla.[81]

While these conflicts over leadership of the state raged, Lucas's frail physical condition prevented him from making any serious effort to recover the political initiative. His reduced influence was evident shortly before his death, when, reminiscent of the ebbing of his power during the 1880s, he advised *serranos* to keep the peace and, if harassed by the state government or the military, to seek redress directly from Mexico City.[82]

Over the last months, Lucas more and more referred to his aches and pains in letters to friends and continued to depend, as he had for several years, on medicine brought from Mexico City. In November 1916 he caught a cold and, in the following weeks, rapidly declined. He died of an intestinal inflammation at 2:45 in the afternoon of 1 February 1917, at the age of eighty-three, in Xochiapulco. Abraham remained at his side until the end. In a final testimony to his Liberal, anti-Catholic beliefs, a Methodist minister presided over the funeral service. He was buried in the municipal cemetery in Tetela in an impressive ceremony attended by thousands of his loyal followers. The old cacique, who first fought in March 1856 during the siege of Puebla, had seen his last battle.[83]

Conclusion

The fall of Díaz, and his puppet in Puebla, Mucío Martínez, reinstated at one stroke the strategic attractiveness which the Sierra had represented to state and national leaders throughout the third quarter of the nineteenth century. The onset of the Revolution also revived the autonomist aspirations of *serrano* leaders, who, had they been permitted to press home the temporary advantage they were offered by the collapse of central power, would probably have favored an arrangement resembling the "state sovereignty" solution achieved in Oaxaca.[84] In essence, this was what the short-lived Sierra Pact, brokered by Lucas in October 1913 but a dead letter after Márquez's defection in January 1914, had amounted to. However, not only was there no return to the autonomy enjoyed by *serranos* for much of the nineteenth century, but external pressures also increased to unprecedented levels.

The strategic value of the Sierra, with its perceived abundance of revenues, supplies, and recruits, drew successive regimes and their opponents to attempt to control the region. The Sierra's Indian communities, organized within traditional *cacicazgos,* presented state and federal political leaders with fewer political uncertainties than did the labor and agrarian conflicts, class divisions, and ideological polarization of the state capital and the plateau. Under these new circumstances, the most that *serrano* leaders could hope for was some freedom to select the most promising external ally, in the hope of gaining an advantage over their local rivals.

In this game of brinkmanship, Lucas possessed three advantages over local rivals such as the Márquez brothers of Otlatlán, and outsiders such as General Antonio Medina: an already established reputation as the "Patriarch of the Sierra," the trust of the Indian population, and, not least, his intimate and long-standing ties with Xochiapulco, particularly with the municipality's auxiliary forces, commanded by his own kin. This last advantage, the availability of a core of seasoned militiamen in Xochiapulco (the only municipality in the Sierra not to have been disarmed during the Porfiriato), proved to be the critical factor in the revival of Lucas's leadership, first under Madero's sponsorship, then with Huerta's Sierra Pact, and finally under the Constitutionalists. Each of Lucas's important moves was prompted by initiatives from Xochiapulco. The *pronunciamientos* there against Díaz in December 1910 and against Huerta in June 1913, and the distancing of the Rivera clan of Xochiapulco from the Sierra Pact from January 1914, convinced Lucas to follow the same routes at an appropriate moment (usually the last), shortly afterward.

If Xochiapulco, its surrounding villages, and its zone of refuge in the district of Tetela still served as Lucas's "natural" territory and source of recruitment, the municipality also continued to exemplify the kind of preemptive, martial Liberalism that had characterized Lucas's style during the third quarter of the nineteenth century. Between 1910 and 1917, as in earlier times, Lucas's appeal and his authority rested upon his effective organization of military units in strategically located villages around the edge of the district of Tetela—Xochiapulco, Cuacuila, Xaltatempan, Cuautempan—in defense against arbitrary and unconstitutional external demands. The terms of military service that Lucas demanded from Madero, Huerta, and Carranza embodied recognition of the same code of citizens' rights and duties that he had elicited from regional, state, and federal leaders during the nineteenth century: voluntary recruitment, locally elected commanders, short terms of service beyond the region, and subordination of military to civil authorities. Lucas's political strategy was also the same as before: options ranging from intimation of rebellion in the villages to outright insurrection were combined with an openness to negotiations with those external authorities most likely to be in a position to provide effective guarantees.

In spite of this pragmatism in the selection of external alliances, Lucas and the Xochiapulquenses were by nature Constitutionalists, concerned above all with reestablishing an equilibrium between free municipalities, well-managed districts, and legitimate state and national authorities. Hence, their struggle between 1910 and 1917 was much more a continuation of the revolution of Tuxtepec—a revolution to restore respect for the constitution of 1857—than a twentieth-century social revolution concerned with achieving structural changes. The emphasis upon invoking existing legitimacies accounts for why overtures from the *zapatistas* were rejected and the Conventionists kept at a distance. Land reform was not an important issue in the Sierra. Mutually beneficial ties with the center of power were always preferred to risky alliances with other regional movements, such as *villismo* and *zapatismo*.

The costs and the benefits of this pact with the federal government were graphically demonstrated during the 1920s, when Gabriel Barrios, Lucas's successor, held sway throughout the Sierra. Barrios quickly achieved peace and security. He even secured the regional autonomy and political unity to which Lucas had aspired during the Revolution, while also attracting federal subsidies for telephones, road improvements, and soldiers' pay. But these benefits came at a price. Barrios sacrificed some of the central constitutional ideals that Lucas and the Xochiapulquenses had always struggled to uphold throughout the second half of the nineteenth century: freedom from compulsory services and the draft, municipal autonomy, and equality of citizenship. The Sierra had to wait until the 1930s before the progressive ideals of the federal constitution, such as universal secular education and the political emancipation of the Indian population, were again reasserted vigorously, once more with Xochiapulco at the vanguard.

Epilogue

Of the numerous letters of condolence received by the Lucas family, one from Sergio Bonilla was among the most perceptive. Juan Francisco's death would be felt not only by friends and family but also "by this whole region and the many people for whom he was a mentor and guide. As for our countrymen, especially the Indians, let us hope that someone can be found who can advise them with the affection and prudence that your deceased father always showed."[1] The letter revealed the uncertainty felt by a Tetelense who had realized that neither of Lucas's sons possessed the necessary influence for succeeding his father as "Patriarch of the Sierra," and that the time when Tetela de Ocampo was the nerve center of Sierra politics had long since passed.

Lucas's death provided an opportunity for the central government further to increase its influence in the Puebla Sierra. President Carranza bypassed the heir apparent, Abraham Lucas, and, seemingly on Juan Francisco's advice, reached outside the immediate family to name Major Gabriel Barrios as head of the Brigada Serrana.[2] Barrios, a little-known but close aide to the late cacique, also was rumored to have been Lucas's offspring (presumably illegitimate). He came from the village of Cuacuila in the district of Zacatlán, first joining Lucas in 1913 and fighting with him during the Revolution. Abraham, a colonel, objected to the naming of Barrios, arguing that he outranked him. To placate Abraham, Carranza ordered that the brigade be divided into two, with Barrios and Lucas each heading a corps, but under the overall command of General Cesáreo Castro. Nevertheless, it soon became clear that Mexico City favored Barrios. In 1918, Carranza appointed him general and head of military operations in the Sierra, a post he held for over a decade. Abraham Lucas would continue to play a political role in the region, serving as municipal president of Tetela and state and federal deputy from the district in later years, but his impact on the Sierra would never match that of his father or of Barrios. While the Lucas siblings distrusted Barrios, they proved unable to stop their father's legacy, the Sierra *cacicazgo,* now in the hands of Barrios, from coming under much greater central government control.[3]

Barrios not only enjoyed less latitude than Lucas, but he also proved to be more ruthless and cynical. In the summer of 1917, in the midst of negotiations with Esteban Márquez and his surviving brothers, Barrios's men attacked and massacred them in their home in Otlatlán. In return for his loyalty to and protection of the government against its opponents, Barrios received full backing from both Governor Alfonso Cabrera and the president. Cabrera and Carranza provided Barrios with generous amounts of arms and monies for his troops. In May 1920, as the regime collapsed around them, both Cabrera and Carranza headed toward Barrios's stronghold in Tetela. Following the precedent set by his master, Barrios switched his support to the opposition *obregonistas* at the last minute. Cabrera fled toward Central America, and Carranza ended up in Tlaxcalantongo in the Sierra de Huauchinango, where, denied his promised bodyguard, he was murdered in a trap.[4]

Barrios differed from Lucas in other important ways. Rather than basing his authority on a loose network of mutual loyalty and respect, Barrios was more authoritarian and employed more coercive methods of control than Lucas. He appointed officials (*jefes de armas* and *secretarios*) to administer and keep close tabs on each town. He used forced labor to build schools, roads, and a sophisticated telephone system. The network of loyal *jefes de armas* and his monopolization of the phone network (Barrios seldom allowed private individuals and never the general public to use it) served especially well to enhance his control over the region and greatly to extend the geographical range of the *cacicaczgo*.

Whereas Lucas's zone of direct political control, even at its height during the European Intervention, extended only along the southern margins of the Sierra, with reserve forces and supplies drawn from farther north in the districts of Tetela and Zacapoaxtla, Barrios's *cacicazgo* extended well beyond the Sierra de Puebla into neighboring Hidalgo and Veracruz. Its territorial extent and the intrusiveness of the village authorities who formed the basis of his *cacicazgo* were measures of the increasing external economic and political pressures upon the Sierra, due to improvements in transport and communications, and the production or development of coffee, cattle, aguardiente, minerals, and hydroelectric power (the economic progress that had eluded the Sierra's leaders of the Reform generation).

Like Lucas, Barrios enjoyed his position because of the weakness of the state government and the backing of federal officials. However, Barrios's *cacicazgo,* although having the potential for causing trouble, no longer posed a serious threat to the central authorities of the kind presented by Lucas at the peak of his authority during the 1860–1870s. For over a decade, as long as Barrios remained loyal and maintained relative stability in the region, the government left him to his own devices.[5]

In 1929, when the Partido Nacional Revolucionario (PNR) was being formed, the federal government moved to strip Barrios of his *cacicazgo.* The former President and then Minister of War, Plutarco Elías Calles, ordered Barrios to Mexico City, where his battalion was reorganized. Meanwhile, newly elected Governor Leonides Andrew Almazán withdrew recognition of those municipal authorities whom Barrios had imposed. Eventually, Barrios was transferred, with many of his Nahua soldiers, to a more distant command in Chiapas, in an act reminiscent of Aztec military expansion in this Maya zone before the Conquest.[6]

Barrios's services as an intermediary between the outside world and the Sierra peasantry were no longer needed. His presence now only hindered the increasingly powerful federal and state governments in their efforts to deal more directly with formerly isolated regions such as the Puebla Sierra. Since the Carranza period, federal and state authorities slowly but surely had been penetrating the area, making their own contacts, recruiting politically ambitious local people into the system, and building up a political base. Now, after more than a decade of consolidation of central power, Barrios could be eliminated and the Sierra incorporated into more direct bureaucratic control.

The Memory of Lucas and Barrios

Throughout Mexico, the memory of dead leaders and past patriotic struggles is perennially refreshed, not only in school textbooks and public celebrations but also in a fertile tradition of storytelling. In towns and villages throughout the Puebla Sierra, the daring deeds of Juan Francisco Lucas are continually retold. The first substantial attempt by local people to record these oral traditions was published in 1994, based upon stories recorded between 1973 and 1986 from among the Nahua population of San Miguel Tzinacapan, a village close to Cuetzalan in the northern part of the former district of Zacapoaxtla.[7] These narratives are organized chronologically and present the history of the village in five stages: foundation; conquest by Spain and religious conversion; independence from Spain; the struggle against the *analtekos* (the French and Austrians or, literally, "those who come from the other side"); and the Revolution. Identified very prominently and positively with the last two stages are Juan Francisco Lucas and Gabriel Barrios.

Although Lucas survived the armed phase of the Revolution, dying in 1917, he is associated in San Miguel Tzinacapan exclusively with the struggle against the European Intervention and the Empire.[8] Even his sons, Miguel and Abraham (who participated more actively than their father in the Revolution), are found fighting the French at the bridge of Apulco in 1863, before they were actually born, and they do not reappear in stories during the Revolution.[9] In Tzinacapan the Revolution is remembered chiefly through tales of famine, disease, and atrocities committed by foraging forces from beyond the region, and for the intense local factional

*Xochiapulco Veteran, c. 1930, inscribed "Soldado Ramón Mora, Estuvo en la Batalla
del 5 de Mayo de 1862"*

conflict between the Flores family of Cuetzalan, caciques during the Porfiriato,
and the followers of Salvador Vega Bernal, *villistas*, and allies of the Márquez
brothers. Gabriel Barrios is gratefully acknowledged as the *carrancista* general
who came down from Cuacuila (Zacatlán) to "calm things" in Cuetzalan: "It
took a long time for things to calm down here. It was Gabriel Barrios and his
carrancistas who calmed things. From then on until today we have lived in
peace. For this we cannot praise only ourselves. General Barrios helped us and
fought with us . . . Like this we won the war."[10]

However, this gratitude to Barrios is tempered by unhappy memories
of Agustín Cruz, whom he appointed as *jefe de armas*, charged with organizing defense forces throughout the municipality. A *maseual* (Indian com-
moner) from Cuetzalan, Cruz represents a direct link between the last two
stages of Tzinacapaneco time—between two kinds of caciquismo represented by Generals Lucas and Barrios, and between Mexico's two great
Liberal revolutions.

Agustín Cruz was related to Francisco Agustín Dieguillo (called variously "Pala Agustín" and "Pancho Agustín" in these accounts), whom

Tzinacapanecos recall as having sheltered Lucas during the European occupation of Cuetzalan in 1863. Hidden in the Rancho de la Providencia, Francisco Agustín's wife fed Lucas on worms from a jonote tree while her husband organized the *maseualmej* (Indians) of Cuetzalan for resistance against the *analtekos* (foreigners).[11] Afterward, Lucas, the other two *Juanes,* and Francisco Agustín armed the *maseualmej* of Tetela, Zacapoaxtla, and Tlatlauqui. They defended the honor of the women of the area, drove out the *analtekos,* and defeated the Franco-Austrian army almost singlehandedly in street-to-street fighting at Puebla, in an imaginative blending of the victories over the French on 5 May 1862 and over the Austrians on 2 April 1867.

The stories relating to the European Intervention possess little of the detail or the political complexity of those referring to the Revolution. The *analtekos* and *koyomej* (non-Indians) are merged into a common enemy whom the *maseualmej*, under Lucas and Dieguillo's guidance, effectively neutralize. As in other oral accounts of this period, anecdotes abound: General Lucas's mastery of disguise; his suspected immortality (revived by a mysterious washerwoman who attended to his wounds after a battle against the French at Teziutlán); his penchant for the democratic gesture (pretending to be a beggar on Tetela's main square whom two federal officers visiting the General asked to look after their horses); his tactical use of the ambush and of networks of tunnels (under the city of Puebla on 5 May 1862). All accounts point not only to a leader with mystical powers but also to a man of the people, the embodiment of the egalitarian and democratic ideals of the time: "General Lucas, a *maseual* of Xochiapulco . . . is remembered in the region not only because he was a good general, but because until the end of his life he was seen as a *maseual* who helped his people."[12] The European Intervention, then, not the Revolution, is remembered as Tzinacapan's moment of entry into the modern Mexican nation-state, with Lucas freeing the *maseualmej* from the *analtekos,* leading them in their patriotic sacrifices, and guaranteeing their rights of citizenship.

In contrast to this positive view of Lucas, Tzinacapaneco accounts of General Barrios reveal an ambivalence. On the one hand, Barrios, like Lucas, was someone whom the *maseualmej* could turn to when faced with persecution by forces from beyond the Sierra. One account records how a group of Tzinacapanecos planting corn in Zoquiapan, in the lowlands of Tetela, were forcibly recruited by *villistas* under Vega Bernal. They later escaped with their weapons and made their way to Cuacuila, where Barrios offered them more acceptable terms of service.[13] This, surely, was the kind of injustice that had driven Cuetzalan's *maseualmej* into Lucas's service since the beginning of the Reform Wars. But other stories reveal a much less favorable side to Barrios's rule.

Tzinacapanecos remember how, at the end of the Revolution, Barrios came down to Cuetzalan from Tetela, armed the local *maseualmej*, and succeeded in driving away the rapacious *villistas* led by Vega Bernal. Although

Barrios restored order throughout the region, the *jefes de armas* whom
Barrios put in the place of Vega Bernal's men, especially Agustín Cruz, are
remembered less fondly. From the Totonac pyramid complex at
Yohualichan near Cuetzalan, Agustín Cruz orchestrated a campaign of intimidation throughout the region designed to ensure sufficient revenue and
labor for the construction of roads and schools. The whip, imprisonment,
and even death faced the village idler or the disobedient. Under the cover
of an anti-witchcraft campaign, Agustín Cruz persecuted village elders, further reducing the protection of villagers against his arbitrary demands.
Although he was eventually removed and imprisoned in Puebla in 1926,
Tzinacapanecos still remember the heavy price they had to pay Agustín
Cruz for restoring peace.[14]

The case of Agustín Cruz highlights an important difference between
pre- and post-revolutionary caciquismo in the Puebla Sierra. Both Lucas
and Barrios extended their clientele into the Cuetzalan area through supporting and arming local indigenous leaders. But whereas Lucas developed
his alliance with Francisco Agustín as often as not in the face of opposition
from the state and federal governments, the extension of Barrios's *cacicazgo* into Cuetzalan through Agustín Cruz contributed directly to the
Sonorenses' concentration of power nationally (albeit in the face of opposition from Zacapoaxtla backed by the state government during the mid-
1920s).[15] Moreover, after receiving help from Francisco Agustín in the
struggle first against the Europeans and later against Juárez and Lerdo,
Lucas left the Cuetzalan leader to his own devices. By contrast, Barrios
used Agustín Cruz (as he used other *jefes de armas* and village authorities
throughout the Sierra) to mobilize local resources for development projects
approved from Cuacuila and backed by the federal government. Both leaders sought Nahua clientele and favored indigenous self-government, but
Barrios encroached far more upon the autonomy of indigenous communities of the Sierra, and over a much wider area, than had Lucas.

The Passing of Tetela as a City-State

On 1 March 1917, one month after Lucas's death, on the initiative of the
"Honorable and Free Municipality of Zautla," Ricardo Márquez Galindo,
his personal secretary, organized a memorial tribute to the leader in Tetela
de Ocampo's council chamber on behalf of the officers and men of the
Brigada Serrana. The program began with a symphonic melody, especially
composed by Delfino Cruz, followed by the funeral oration given by
Professor Efraín Bonilla. The school choir then sang "Our Offering," also
composed by Cruz, to words by Daniel Pérez y Pérez who, after a speech
by Modesto Herrera, read from the "Biographical Details of Citizen
General Juan Francisco Lucas" written by the long-serving Xochiapulco

schoolmaster, Manuel Pozos. This was followed by a piano recital by María Luisa Méndez, a schoolgirl and General Méndez's granddaughter, entitled "The Dream of an Angel," which echoed the choice of the sculpture of an angel to guard Lucas's tomb. Schoolboy Leopoldo Sánchez then declaimed a poem, "To the Humble Hero, General Juan Francisco Lucas," followed by another speech by a pupil of the Liberty School. Finally, Zautla's band (against whose formation Lucas and the Zautlecos had so protested to Governor Márquez in 1888 because of the forced contribution) played the "General Juan Francisco Lucas" funeral march, also composed for the occasion by Cruz. A procession then left the council building to lay wreaths at Lucas's tomb in the municipal cemetery.[16]

This memorial service combined elements central to understanding Lucas's success and longevity as a regional leader: an armed citizenry within assertive and politically autonomous municipalities such as Zautla and Tetela; a network of closely related families—Pérez, Bonilla, Méndez, Márquez Galindo, Cruz—occupying the public arena; the ritual centrality of schoolteachers and schoolchildren; the importance of band music and oratory; the replacement of Roman Catholicism by a secular cult of the patriotic hero and egalitarian citizenship; and, not least, deference to an idealized Nahua leader who had helped the Indian population of the Sierra to accommodate itself to Liberalism, saved its Creoles and mestizos from a caste war, and provided them with a source of regional identity.

Lucas, who had been prepared on so many occasions to take up arms, and was capable of mobilizing villagers who would follow no other leader, personified this secular, Liberal-patriotic universe centered on Tetela de Ocampo and its precocious, non-conformist satellite, Xochiapulco. However, long before the fall of Díaz, the district of Tetela, whose nineteenth-century leaders had embraced the ideas of the century with such single-minded enthusiasm, was beset by economic decline and administrative atrophy. In spite of a short-lived revival of the district's strategic importance during the Revolution, Tetela's economic and fiscal decline continued unabated, which accounts for why Tetelense visions of an independent state (to be called variously "La República de la Sierra Madre," or "El Estado Libre y Soberano de Zempoala") came to nothing. After the Revolution, the advantages from which the district's nineteenth-century greatness had been constructed— remoteness from the centers of secular and clerical power, defendability, far-flung administrative and fiscal ties with rich *tierra caliente* municipalities, its own mines, mint, and arsenal, the determination of Tetelenses to produce their own home-grown version of modernity through universal schooling— now became liabilities and anachronisms. Following the abolition of the jefes políticos and political districts in 1916, the administrative and educational ideals that had animated Tetela's leaders during the nineteenth century became fiscally unsustainable or simply were absorbed into the state and federal administrations.

Visiting Tetela de Ocampo in 1927, Moisés Saenz, sub-secretary of public education, observed that little, apart from the massive and imposing town hall, remained of the city's glorious Liberal past. Indeed, Saenz was peeved to find resistance from this former avatar of secular public education to his plans for a federal co-educational school: "Tetela, a city of Liberal traditions; once the cradle of the three great '*Juanes* of the Sierra,' Juan Crisóstomo Bonilla, Juan Nepomuceno Méndez, and Juan Francisco Lucas; Tetela, a city fallen on hard times, with houses enough for three thousand people but inhabited today by only seven hundred, offering a sad spectacle of stagnation and ineffectiveness."[17]

However, Saenz received more encouragement from the next town he visited, La Villa del Cinco de Mayo. Xochiapulco had recently welcomed a new federal school, presaging the pioneering role its teachers and *internado indígena* (Indian boarding school) would play during the 1930s. Indeed, Xochiapulco took over from Tetela as the vanguard of educational and social reform initiatives in the Sierra. This reforming mission ensured that the conflicts with its Conservative neighbor, Zacapoaxtla (with which this study began and which gave it its subject), would continue far into the twentieth century.[18]

Notes

Abbreviations Used in Notes

AAA	Archivo de Amado Aguirre, Universidad Nacional Autónoma de México, Mexico City
ACE/A	Archivo del Congreso del Estado, Libros de Actas, Puebla
ADN	Archivo de la Defensa Nacional, Mexico City
AE	*American Ethnologist*
AEZ	Archivo de Emiliano Zapata, Archivo General de la Nación, Mexico City
AFM	Archivo de Francisco Madero, Mexico City
AGE/J2D/A	Archivo General de Estado, Juzgado Segundo de Distrito, Sección de Amparos, Puebla
AGN	Archivo General de la Nación, Mexico City
AGNP	Archivo General de Notarias de Puebla
AHDN/C	Archivo Histórico de la Secretaria de la Defensa Nacional, El Colegio de México
AI	*América Indígena*
AJA	Archivo de Jenaro Amezcua, CONDUMEX, Mexico City
AJB	Archivo de Juan Barragán, Universidad Nacional Autónoma de México, Mexico City
AJT	Archivo de Jacinto Treviño, Universidad Nacional Autónoma de México, Mexico City
AM	*The Americas*
AMCh	Archivo Municipal de Chignahuapan
AMG	Archivo de Manuel W. González, CONDUMEX, Mexico City
AMTdeO	Archivo Municipal de Tetela de Ocampo
AMZ	Archivo Municipal de Zacapoaxtla
AOC	Archivo Obregón-Calles, Archivo General de la Nación, Mexico City
APD	Archivo de Porfirio Díaz, Universidad Iberoamericana, Mexico City
APG	Archivo de Pablo González, University of Texas at Austin

APJFL	Archivo Particular de Juan Francisco Lucas, Puebla
AVC	Archivo de Venustiano Carranza, CONDUMEX, Mexico City
BECM	*Boletín Editorial de El Colegio de México*
BLAR	*Bulletin of Latin American Research*
BN-ABJ	Biblioteca Nacional - Archivo Benito Juárez, Mexico City
BSMGE	*Boletín de la Sociedad Mexicana de Geografía e Estadística*
BSMG	*Boletín de la Sociedad Mexicana de Geografía*
CIHS/UAP	Centro de Investigaciones Históricas y Sociales, Universidad Autónoma de Puebla
CLDELSP	Colección de Leyes y Decretos del Estado Libre y Soberano de Puebla, Puebla
CMHLB	*Cahiers du Monde Hispanique et Luso-Brésilien*
CR	Convención Revolucionaria, Archivo General de la Nación, Mexico City
CT	CONDUMEX, telegrams, Mexico City
FOC	Fondo Alvaro Obregón-Plutarco Elías Calles, Ramo de Presidentes, Archivo General de la Nación, Mexico City
HAHR	*Hispanic American Historical Review*
HM	*Historia Mexicana*
HMMPVPI	*Historia Moderna de México. El Porfiriato. La Vida Política Interior*
HMMRRVP	*Historia Moderna de México. La República Restaurada. La Vida Política*
INAH	Instituto Nacional de Antropología e Historia, Mexico City
INAH-AJP	Instituto Nacional de Antropología e Historia - Archivo Judicial de Puebla, Mexico City
INEHRM	Instituto Nacional de Estudios Históricos de la Revolución Mexicana, Archivo General de la Nación, Mexico City
JLAS	*Journal of Latin American Studies*
LARR	*Latin American Research Review*
MIR	U.S. Military Intelligence Reports, 1919–1941, National Archives, Washington, DC
MS/EM	*Mexican Studies/Estudios Mexicanos*
RDS	Records of the Department of State Relating to the Internal Affairs of Mexico, 1910–1929, Record Group 59, Microfilm, Washington, DC
RG	Ramo de Gobernación, Periódico Revolucionario, Archivo General de la Nación, Mexico City
SEP	Secretaria de Educación Pública, Mexico City
TTOSACEPEC	Taller de Tradición Oral de la Sociedad Agropecuaria de CEPEC

| UNESCO | United Nations Educational, Scientific, and Cultural Organization |
| UTA-LAC | University of Texas at Austin, Latin American Center |

Notes

Introduction, xi–xviii

1. G. Marcos Barrios Bonilla, *El café en Cuetzalan* (Cuetzalan, 1991).

2. Lawrence Stone, "The Revival of the Narrative: Reflections on a New Old History," *Past and Present* 85 (1979): 3-24; Jesús Ferrer Gamboa, *Los tres Juanes de la Sierra de Puebla* (Mexico, 1967); TTOSACEPEC, *Les oíamos contar a nuestros abuelos: Etnohistoria de San Miguel Tzinacapan* (Mexico, 1994).

3. Sierra Nahuat, the dialect of Nahuatl spoken in the central and southern Puebla Sierra (Tetela, Zacapoaxtla, Tlatlauqui, and Teziutlán), is substantially different from that of the eastern Sierra (Zacatlán and Huauchinango) and the valleys of Puebla, Tlaxcala, and Mexico. The Sierra Nahuat are descended from the Olmeca-Xicalancas group, ousted from Cacaxtla (Tlaxcala) by the Chichimec Mexica and pushed north into the Sierra during the tenth and eleventh centuries. In 1971 this dialect was spoken by an estimated sixty thousand persons within the Cuetzalan-Teziutlán-Chignahuapan triangle. For an extended discussion, see James Mownsey Taggart, "The Factors Affecting the Developmental Cycle of Domestic Groups in a Nahuat-Speaking Community in Mexico" (Ph.D. diss., University of Pittsburgh, 1971); D. F. Robinson, *Sierra Nahuat Word-Structure* (Santa Ana, 1961); and Bernardo García Martínez, *Los pueblos de la Sierra. El poder y el espacio entre los indios del norte de Puebla hasta 1700* (Mexico, 1987), 42-43. Even these linguistic boundaries break down at the microlevel. In the municipality of Cuetzalan, several different dialects of Nahuatl are spoken, locals attributing these differences to diversity of origin on the altiplano before the pre-Conquest migration of Nahuat speakers into the Sierra. See TTOSACEPEC, *Les oíamos contar a nuestros abuelos*.

4. Guy P. C. Thomson, "Agrarian Conflict in the Municipality of Cuetzalán (Sierra de Puebla): The Rise and Fall of 'Pala' Agustín Dieguillo, 1861-1894," *Hispanic American Historical Review* 71 (1991): 205-58 (hereafter cited as *HAHR*).

5. For comparisons between Mexico and Colombia, see David Bushnell and Neill Macaulay, *The Emergence of Latin America in the Nineteenth Century* (Oxford, England, 1988), 193-220.

6. D. A. Brading, "Liberal Patriotism and the Mexican Reforma," *Journal of Latin American Studies* 20 (1987): 41 (hereafter cited as *JLAS*); idem, *The Origins of Mexican Nationalism* (Cambridge, England, 1985), 101; idem, *The First America: The Spanish Monarchy, Creole Patriots and the Liberal State, 1492-1867* (Cambridge, England, 1991), 648-74.

7. Charles A. Hale, *Mexican Liberalism in the Age of Mora, 1821-1853* (New Haven, CT, 1968); Richard N. Sinkin, *The Mexican Reform, 1855-1876: A Study in Liberal Nation-Building* (Austin, TX, 1979), 177; Walter Scholes, *Mexican Politics During the Juárez Regime, 1855-1872* (Columbia, MO, 1957); Jacqueline Covo, *Las ideas de la Reforma en México, 1855-1861* (Mexico, 1983).

8. François-Xavier Guerra, *Le Mexique: De l'ancien régime à la révolution*, 2 vols. (Paris, 1985), 2:305-19; Daniel Cosío Villegas, *La constitución de 1857 y sus críticos* (Mexico, 1957); Jean-Pierre Bastian, "El paradigma de 1789: Sociedades de ideas y revolución mexicana," *Historia Mexicana* 38 (1988): 79-110 (hereafter cited as *HM*); idem, "Jacobinismo y ruptura revolucionaria durante el porfiriato," *Mexican Studies/Estudios Mexicanos* 8 (1991): 29-46 (hereafter cited as *MS/EM*); idem, "Itinerario de un intelectual popular protestante, liberal y francmasón en México: José Rumbia Guzmán," *Cristianismo y Sociedad* 25 (1987): 91-108; idem, *Los disidentes, sociedades protestantes y revolución en México, 1872-1911* (Mexico, 1989).

9. Laurens Ballard Perry, *Juárez and Díaz Machine Politics in Mexico* (DeKalb, IL, 1978); Daniel Cosío Villegas, *Historia Moderna de México. La República Restaurada. La vida Política* (Mexico, 1955) (hereafter cited as *HMMRRVP*); idem, *Historia Moderna de México. El Porfiriato. La Vida Política Interior*, pt. 1 (Mexico, 1970), pt. 2 (Mexico, 1972) (hereafter cited as *HMMPVPI*); Charles A. Hale, "The Liberal Impulse: Daniel Cosío Villegas and the *Historia moderna de México*," *HAHR* 54 (1974): 479-98.

10. Brian Hamnett, *Juárez* (London, England, 1994).

11. Charles A. Hale, *The Transformation of Liberalism in Late Nineteenth-Century Mexico* (Princeton, NJ, 1989); Alan Knight, "El liberalismo mexicano desde la Reforma hasta la revolución (una interpretación)," *HM* 35 (1985): 59-85.

12. Hale, *Mexican Liberalism*; Jesús Reyes Heroles, *El liberalismo mexicano*, 3 vols. (Mexico, 1961).

13. Guerra, *Le Mexique*, 1:38-45; Marcello Carmagnani, "Territorialidad y federalismo en la formación del estado mexicano," in *Problemas de la formación del estado y de la nación en hispanoamérica*, ed. Inge Buisson et al. (Vienna, 1984), 289-304; Jaime Rodríguez, "La constitución de 1824 y la formación del estado mexicano," *HM* 40 (1991): 507-35; Nettie Lee Benson, *La diputación provincial y el federalismo mexicano* (Mexico, 1955); idem, ed., *Mexico and the Spanish Cortes, 1810-1822* (Austin, TX, 1966); idem, "The Plan of Casa Mata," *HAHR* 25 (1945): 45-56; Brian R. Hamnett, "Factores regionales en la desintegración del régimen colonial en la Nueva España: El federalismo de 1823-24," in *Problemas de la formación del estado y de la nación en hispanoamérica*, ed. Inge Buisson et al. (Vienna, 1984), 305-18; J. Lloyd Mecham, "The Origins of Federalism in Mexico," *HAHR* 18 (1939): 164-82.

14. Alicia Hernández Chávez, *La tradición republicana del buen gobierno* (Mexico, 1993); François-Xavier Guerra, "The Spanish-American Tradition of

Representation and Its European Roots," *JLAS* 26 (1994): 1-35; Marie Danielle Demélas-Bohy and François-Xavier Guerra, "Un processus révolutionnaire méconnu: L'adoption des formes représentatives modernes en Espagne et en Amérique (1808-1810)," *Cahiers du Monde Hispanique et Luso-Brésilien* 60 (1993): 5-57 (hereafter cited as *CMHLB*); Antonio Annino, "Otras naciones: Sincretismo político en el México decimonónico," in *Imaginar la nación*, ed. F. X. Guerra and Monica Quijada (Hamburg, 1994), 215-55; Peter Guardino, *Peasants, Politics, and the Formation of Mexico's National State: Guerrero, 1800-1857* (Stanford, CA, 1996).

15. Peter Guardino, "Barbarism or Republican Law: Guerrero's Peasants and National Politics, 1820-1846," *HAHR* 75 (1995): 185-214; Jorge Flores, *La revolución de Olarte en Papantla (1836-1838)* (Mexico, 1938); Angel M. Cabrera, *Apuntes relativo a la historia de Zacatlán* (Mexico, 1889), 13-17; Leticia Reina, *Las rebeliones campesinas en México (1819-1906)* (Mexico, 1986), 325-40; John M. Hart, "The 1840s Southwestern Mexico Peasants' War: Conflict in a Transitional Society," in *Riot, Rebellion, and Revolution: Rural Social Conflict in Mexico*, ed. Friedrich Katz (Princeton, 1988), 249-68; Juan Ortiz Escamilla, "El pronunciamiento federalista de Gordiano Guzmán, 1837-1842," *HM* 38 (1988): 241-83; Jaime Olveda, *Gordiano Guzmán: Un cacique del siglo XIX* (Mexico, 1980); Fernando Díaz y Díaz, *Caudillos y caciques: Antonio López de Santa Anna y Juan Alvarez* (Mexico, 1972); Guy P. C. Thomson, "Popular Aspects of Liberalism in Mexico, 1848-1888," *Bulletin of Latin American Research* 10 (1991): 121-52 (hereafter cited as *BLAR*).

16. Sinkin, *The Mexican Reform*, 185-89.

17. Guy P. C. Thomson, "Federalism and Cantonalism in Mexico, 1824-1892: Sovereignty and Territoriality," in *Wars, Parties and Nationalism: Essays on the Politics and Society of Nineteenth-Century Latin America*, ed. Eduardo Posada Carbó (London, 1995), 27-54.

18. Hernández, *La tradición republicana*, 72-81.

19. Charles A. Weeks, *The Juárez Myth in Mexico* (Tuscaloosa, AL, 1987).

20. Hernández, *La tradición republicana*, 86-87.

21. D. A. Brading, "Heroes republicanos y tiranos populares," *Cuadernos Americanos* 5 (1989): 21; Raymond Buve, "Political Patronage and Politics at the Village Level in Central Mexico: Continuity and Change in Patterns from the Late Colonial Period to the End of the French Intervention (1867)," *BLAR* 11 (1992): 1-28; idem, "Transformación y patronazgo político en el México rural: Continuidad y cambio entre 1867 y 1920," in *El liberalismo en México*, ed. Antonio Annino and Raymond Buve (Hamburg, 1993), 143-76.

22. Florencia Mallon, *Peasant and Nation: The Making of Post-colonial Mexico and Peru* (Berkeley, CA, 1995).

23. Ibid., 97.

24. Jan Bazant, "Puebla: La historia y sus instrumentos," *HM* 29 (1970): 432-37.

25. Apart from Gamboa's *Los tres Juanes*, there is no substantial published account of Lucas's life. Short hagiographical accounts include Ernesto Bello Martínez, *El patriarca de la Sierra* (Teziutlán, Puebla, 1947); Vicente Lombardo Toledano, "Hombres célebres de la Sierra Norte del estado de Puebla," *Conferencias Históricas*, no. 7 (Mexico, 1943); Secretaria de Educación Pública, Dirección General de Internados de Enseñanza Primaria, *Homenaje al heroe Nacional Gral. Juan Francisco Lucas patriarca de la Sierra* (Zacapoaxtla, 1956); and Octavio Manzanio Díaz, *El indígena de la Sierra Norte de Puebla y sus luchas por la libertad* (Mexico, 1987). Lucas receives frequent mention in Mallon, *Peasant and Nation*; Donna Rivera, *Xochiapulco: Una gloria olvidada* (Puebla, 1991); Manuel Pozos, "Lijeros apuntes históricos del municipio de Xochiapulco y especialmente de su cabecera: Villa del Cinco de Mayo," in *La batalla del 5 de mayo*, ed. Miguel A. Sánchez Lamego et al. (Mexico, 1963), 147-51; Antonio Carrión, *Historia de la ciudad de Puebla de los Angeles*, vol. 2 (1897; reprint ed., Puebla, 1970); Miguel Galindo y Galindo, *La gran década nacional o relación histórica de la Guerra de Reforma: Intervención extranjera y gobierno del archiduque Maximiliano, 1857-1867* (Mexico, 1906); and Sánchez Flores, *Zacapoaxtla*, 150-90.

Chapter 1, Regional Leader, 1–23

1. Lourdes Arizpe, *Parentesco y economía en una sociedad Nahua: Nican Pehua Zacatipan* (Mexico, 1973), 63-64.

2. Carlos Bravo Marentes, *Relatos revolucionarios* (Huauchinango, Puebla, 1986), 56-69; Donna Rivera, *Xochiapulco: Una gloria olvidada* (Puebla, 1991), 277-79.

3. Alan Knight, *The Mexican Revolution* (Cambridge, England, 1986), 2:56.

4. Enrique Márquez, "Gonzalo N. Santos o la naturaleza del 'tanteómetro político,'" in *Estadístas: Caciques y caudillos*, ed. Carlos Martínez Assad (Mexico, 1988), 381.

5. For Lucas's official service record, see ADN, *Cancelados*, C-64 S/111/2/425, 2 vols.

6. Other Liberal leaders with comparable regional influence include: Porfirio Díaz (Oaxaca), Diego Alvarez (Guerrero), Manuel Lozada (Tepic), Mariano Escobedo, Gerónimo Treviño, Francisco Naranjo, and Santiago Vidaurri (Coahuila and Nuevo León), Trinidad García de la Cadena (Zacatecas), Servando Canales (Tamaulipas), Luis Terrazas (Chihuahua), Juan N. Cortina and Ignacio Pesqueira (Sonora); Richard Sinkin, *The Mexican Reform, 1855-1876* (Austin, TX, 1979), 37-39, 181-84.

7. Elio Masferrer Kan, "Religión y política en la Sierra Norte de Puebla," *México Indígena* 46 (1986): 331-44 (hereafter cited as *MI*); Serge Gruzinski, *Man-Gods in the Mexican Highlands: Indian Power and Colonial Society, 1520-1800* (Stanford, CA, 1989).

8. Florencia Mallon, "Reflections on the Ruins: Everyday Forms of State Formation in Nineteenth-Century Mexico," in *Everyday Forms of State*

Formation: Revolution and the Negotiation of Rule in Modern Mexico, ed. Gilbert M. Joseph and Daniel Nugent (Durham, NC, 1994), 89-99.

9. Carlos Bravo Marentes, "Hombres-mito y heroes civilizadores: Juan Francisco Lucas, El patriarca de la Sierra Norte de Puebla" (paper presented to the Second Colloquium of the History of Meso-American Religion, UNAM, 1986), 1-13; idem, *Relatos revolucionarios*; Antonio Rimada Oviedo, "Caracterización de los aspectos nagualísticos del General Juan Francisco Lucas en la comunidad de la Sierra Norte de Puebla" (paper presented to the twenty-first roundtable of the Sociedad Mexicana de Antropología, Mérida, October 1989), 1-11; Alfredo López Austin, *Cuerpo humano e ideología: La concepción de los antiguos nahuas* (Mexico, 1980); George Foster, "Nagualism in Mexico and Guatemala," *Acta Americana* (Sociedad Interamericana de Antropología y Geografía) 2 (1944): 85-103; Gonzalo Aguirre Beltrán, *Medicina y magia: El proceso de aculturación en la estructura colonial* (Mexico, 1963), 98-114.

10. For example, see María Dolores Posada Olayo, *Voz peregrinante (Poesía laureada)* (Mexico, 1980); idem, *Joyel de estrellas* (Mexico, 1980).

11. Lauro Luna, *Batallón de la Guardia Nacional de Tetela de Ocampo, 1862-1867: (Memorias)* (Puebla, 1995), 7.

12. For General Alatorre's praise for the patriotism and bravery of *serrano* forces, see José López Portillo y Rojas, *Elevación y caida de Porfirio Díaz* (Mexico, 1975), 139-40.

13. For Díaz's attempt to resolve these contradictory pressures in San Luis Potosí, see Donald Fithian Stevens, "Agrarian Policy and Instability in Porfirian Mexico," *The Americas* 29 (1982): 153-66 (hereafter cited as *AM*).

14. Carlos Martínez Assad, ed., *Estadístas, caciques y caudillos* (Mexico, 1988); Nicole Girón, *Heraclio Bernal: ¿Bandolero, cacique o precursor de la revolución?* (Mexico, 1976); Jaime Olveda, *Gordiano Guzmán: Un cacique del siglo XIX* (Mexico, 1980); Moisés González Navarro, "La venganza del sur," *HM* 21 (1972): 677-92; and Fernando Díaz y Díaz, *Caudillos y caciques: Antonio López de Santa Anna y Juan Alvarez* (Mexico, 1972).

15. For a discussion of twentieth-century caciquismo in the Puebla Sierra, see Keith Brewster, "Caciquismo in Rural Mexico During the 1920s: The Case of Gabriel Barrios," *JLAS* 28 (1996): 105-28; Luisa Paré, "Caciquismo y estructura de poder en la Sierra Norte de Puebla," in *Caciquismo y poder político en el México rural,* ed. Roger Barta (Mexico, 1975), 31-36; idem, "Inter-ethnic and Class Relations (Sierra Norte Region, State of Puebla)," in *Race and Class in Post-Colonial Society*, ed. United Nations Educational, Scientific, and Cultural Organization (UNESCO) (Paris, 1977), 377-420. For caciquismo elsewhere in the Mexican center and southeast, see Paul Friedrich, *Agrarian Revolt in a Mexican Village* (Englewood Cliffs, NJ, 1970); idem, *The Princes of Naranja: An Essay in Anthropological Method* (Austin, TX, 1986); Gonzalo N. Santos, *Memorias* (Mexico, 1984); Gilbert Joseph, "Caciquismo and the Revolution: Carrillo Puerto in Yucatán," in *Caudillo and Peasant in the Mexican Revolution*, ed. D. A. Brading (Cambridge, England, 1980),

193-221; Victor Goldkind, "Class Conflict and Cacique," *Southwestern Journal of Anthropology* 22 (1966): 325-45; idem, "Social Stratification in the Peasant Community: Chan Kom Revisited," *American Anthropologist* 67 (1965): 863-84; Hennings Silverts, "The 'Cacique' of K'ankujk," *Estudios de Cultura Maya* 5 (1965): 339-60; and Jan Rus, "The 'Comunidad Revolucionaria Institucional': The Subversion of Native Government in Highland Chiapas, 1936-1968," in *Everyday Forms of State Formation: Revolution and the Negotiation of Rule in Modern Mexico*, ed. Gilbert M. Joseph and Daniel Nugent (Durham, NC, 1994), 265-300.

16. Elio Masferrer Kan, "Religión y política en la Sierra Norte de Puebla," *América Indígena* 46 (1986): 531-44.

17. For an example of such caciques, see Chapter 3, p. 58, this volume.

18. Victor Nunes Leal, *Coronelismo: The Municipality and Representative Government in Brazil* (Cambridge, England, 1977); Luis Roniger, "Caciquismo and Coronelismo: Contextual Dimensions of Patron Brokerage in Mexico and Brazil," *Latin American Research Review* 32 (1987): 1-99 (hereafter cited as *LARR*).

19. Renowned village caciques include: Isidro Segura of Ometepec, Dionisio Leal of Cuahuigtic, Luis Antonio Díaz of Xochiapulco, Valeriano Cabrera of Las Lomas, José Máximo and José Bonifacio of Zautla, Santiago Cientos of Xochitlán, Cenobio Cantero of Atagpan, Francisco Agustín of Cuetzalan, Antonio Conde of Chignautla, Miguel Justo of Tzinacantepec, and Manuel Amador of Yaonahuac.

20. Prominent municipal caciques include: Octaviano Bonilla of San Esteban Cuautempan, Vicente Bonilla y Hernández of Huitzilan, Apolinar Martínez of Hueytlapan, the Diego and Nieto families of Zapotitlán, the Reyes of Tuzamapa, the González and Castañeda families of Xochitlán, the Arriaga of Nauzontla, and the Mora and Flores families of Cuetzalan.

21. Lloyd J. Mecham, "The Jefe Político in México," *Southwestern Social Science Quarterly* 13 (1933): 333-52; Lázaro Pavia, *Ligeros apuntes biográficos de los jefes políticos de los partidos* (Mexico, 1891); Francisco Téllez Guerrero, "La organización administrativa del Estado de Puebla, 1824-1910," in CIHS, *Puebla en el siglo XIX: Contribución al estudio de su historia* (Puebla, 1983), 63-64.

22. For the decline of native *cacicazgos* and the appropriation of supra-local levels of government by the Spanish, see Bernardo García Martínez, *Los pueblos de la Sierra: El poder y el espacio entre los indios del norte de Puebla hasta 1700* (Mexico, 1987), 63-114.

23. Apart from the *tres Juanes* of Tetela (Lucas, Bonilla, and Méndez), other notable district-level cacique clans were the Márquez Galindo (Zacatlán), the Sosa (Ahuacatlán) and the Márquez (Otlatlán) of Zacatlán, the Cravioto and Andrade Parraga of Huauchinango, the Arriaga (Nauzontla) of Zacapoaxtla, the Bernal (Zautla) of Libres, the Vargas of Tlatlauqui, the Avila and Camacho of Teziutlán, and the Melgarejo of Altotonga (in neighboring Veracruz).

24. Lucas confided once to his nephew that his refusal to accept repeated invitations from Díaz to travel to Mexico was due to his belief that Díaz had ordered the poisoning of both Bonilla and Méndez in 1884 and 1894. His circumspection toward the outside world was generally disguised in his correspondence by an air of self-effacing modesty; see Martin Rivera Torres, "General Juan Francisco Lucas," in Rivera, *Xochiapulco*, 165-66.

25. Charles Hale, *Mexican Liberalism in the Age of Mora, 1821-1853* (New Haven, 1968), 215-47; idem, "Political and Social Ideas in Latin America, 1870-1930," in *Cambridge History of Latin America*, ed. Leslie Bethell (Cambridge, 1989), 4:368; George Foster, *Tzintzuntzan Mexican Peasants in a Changing World* (Boston, 1967); James Gregory, "Image of Limited Good or Expectation of Reciprocity," *Current Anthropology* 16 (1975): 73-79; Teodor Shanin, *Peasants and Peasant Societies* (London, England, 1988), 357-77.

26. D. A. Brading, *The First America: The Spanish Monarchy, Creole Patriots and the Liberal State, 1492-1867* (Cambridge, England, 1991), 661-74; Brian Hamnett, *Juárez* (London, England, 1993), 49-70.

27. Jean-François Lecaillon, "Los indígenas y la intervención francesa," *México Indígena* 16 (May-June 1987): 19-21; J. A. Dabbs, *The French Army in Mexico* (The Hague, 1963); Mario Alfonso Aldana Rendón, *Rebelión agraria de Manuel Lozada: 1873* (Mexico, 1983); Jean Meyer, *Esperando Lozada* (Zamora, Michoacán, 1984); María del Carmen Vázquez Mantecón, "Espacio social y crisis política: La Sierra Gorda, 1850-1855," *MS/EM* 9 (1993): 47-70.

28. Francisco Javier Arriaga, *Expediente geográfico-estadístico por . . . el distrito de Zacapoaxtla* (Mexico, 1873), 29-30; Hugo G. Nutini and Barry L. Isaac, *Los pueblos de habla nahuatl de Tlaxcala y Puebla* (Mexico, 1974), 166-71.

29. T. G. Powell, "Priests and Peasants in Central Mexico: Social Conflict during the Reforma," *HAHR* 57 (1977): 298-301.

30. William Taylor, *Drinking, Homicide, and Rebellion in Colonial Mexican Villages* (Stanford, CA, 1979); idem, "Conflict and Balance in District Politics: Tecali and the Sierra Norte de Puebla in the Eighteenth Century," in *The Indian Community in New Spain*, ed. Arij Ouweneel and Simon Miller (Amsterdam, 1990), 270-94; Guy P. C. Thomson, "Agrarian Conflict in the Municipality of Cuetzalan (Sierra de Puebla): The Rise and Fall of 'Pala' Agustín Dieguillo," *HAHR* 71 (1991): 209-13.

31. ADN, Histórico, XI/481.3/8657, f. 131.

32. Guy P. C. Thomson, "Bulwarks of Patriotic Liberalism: The National Guard, Philharmonic Corps, and Patriotic Juntas in Mexico, 1847-88," *Journal of Latin American Studies* 22 (1990): 31-68; Anne Staples, "El estado y la iglesia en la República Restaurada," in *El Dominio de la Minorías*, ed. Anne Staples et al. (Mexico, 1989), 15-53; Mary Kay Vaughan, "Primary Education and Literacy in Nineteenth-Century Mexico: Research Trends, 1968-1988," *LARR* 24 (1989): 31-66.

33. Thomson, "Bulwarks of Patriotic Liberalism," 61-67.

34. See Chapter 13, this volume.

35 AMTdeO, Gobierno, Box 6, Exp. 6, 15 August 1855, Junta Municipal; AMTdeO, Gobierno, Box 7, Exp. 9, "Borrador de Oficios de 1856," 22 August 1856; AMTdeO, Gobierno, Box 8, Exp. 2, 31 May 1858; AGNP, *Zacapoaxtla* VII, f.16.

36. Moisés González Navarro, "El trabajo forzoso en México, 1821-1914," *HM* 27 (1977-78): 588-615; Sinkin, *The Mexican Reform*, 186.

37. AMZ, "Correspondencia del Jefe Político, 1868-1869," 28 November 1868, Governor Ibarra, Puebla, to Jefe Político; AMZ, 23 May 1868, Joaquín Martínez, Puebla, to Jefe Político; AMZ, 18 December 1868, Joaquín Martínez, Puebla, to Jefe Político; AMZ, 21 June 1869, Carlos Báez, Puebla, to Jefe Político.

38. *Periódico Oficial* VIII, 37, 4 April 1877.

39. AMZ, "Borrador de Oficios de la Gefatura Política del Distrito de Zacapoaxtla, 1862-63," 11 July 1862, Jefe Político to Alcalde of Xochiapulco; AMZ, "1862, Correspondencia del Jefe Político," 1 July 1862, José Palomino, Yautetelco, to Jefe Político.

40. AMZ, "1862, Correspondencia del Jefe Político," 24 February 1862, Ramón Herrera to Jefe Político.

41. AMZ, "Correspondencia del Jefe Político, 1868-1869," 10 March 1869, Ignacio Arrieta, Cuetzalan, to Jefe Político.

42. AMZ, "Correspondencia del Jefe Político, 1868-1869," 21 June 1869, Carlos Báez, Puebla, to Jefe Político.

43. AMZ, "Correspondencia del Jefe Político, 1868-1869," 10 November 1869, N. Estévez, Xochitlán, to Jefe Político, Zacapoaxtla.

44. Thomson, "Agrarian Conflict," 216-56.

45. AMZ, "1862, Correspondencia del Jefe Político," 14 April 1862, Cipriano García, Xochitlán, to Jefe Político, and AMZ, 31 March 1862, Manuel Jaime, Xocoyolo, to Jefe Político.

46. See Chapters 13 and 14, this volume.

47. AMTdeO, Gobierno, Box 10, 1867-69, Exp. 2, 23 March and 14 April 1867, Manuel Luis, Zapotitlán, to Jefe Político.

48. *Publicación Oficial* I:114, 27 August 1870. A further bridge crossing the Zempoala at Totomoxtla near Cuatempan, christened "Juan N. Méndez," was opened in 1882. See *Periódico Oficial* IX: 25 September 1882.

49. AMTdeO, Gobierno, Box 37, "Criminales," 21 October 1876, Miguel Bonilla to Lauro Luna, Comandante del Distrito.

50. Thomson, "Agrarian Conflict," 245-46; AMZ, February 1877, Exp. 49, "Expediente relativo a un ocurso presentado ante el ejecutivo de la unión por el ciudadano Francisco Agustín Dieguillo y otros vecinos de Cuetzalan pidiéndole les devuelvan los terrenos que algunos C.C. se han adjudicado"; AMZ, January 1877, Exp. 27, "Espediente relativo a un ocurso que algunos guardias nacionales de este distrito presentaron ante el presidente interino de

la república quejándose de ciertos abusos que dicen se cometen con la clase indígena por estas autoridades."

51. AMZ, 1877, Exp. 116, "Expediente sobre la escitativa hecha por el C. General Juan Francisco Lucas al pueblo de Xochitlán para que le auxile en los trabajos del puente que se este construyendo en Falcosama," 29 July and 15 August 1877, Ignacio Castañeda, Xochitlán, to Jefe Político.

52. Guy P. C. Thomson, "Cabecillas indigénas de la Guardia Nacional en la Sierra de Puebla, 1854-1889," in *La indianización de América, siglo XIX*, ed. Leticia Reina (Mexico, 1997), 121-36.

53. Guy P. C. Thomson, "Bulwarks of Patriotic Liberalism," 31-68; idem, "Los indios y el servicio militar en el México decimonónico: ¿Leva o ciudadania?," in *Indio, nación y comunidad en el México del siglo XIX*, ed. Antonio Escobar (Mexico, 1993), 207-52; Alicia Hernández Chávez, "Origen y ocaso del ejército porfiriano," *HM* 39 (1989): 257-96; idem, "La guardia nacional y movilización política de los pueblos," in *Patterns of Contention in Mexican History*, ed. Jaime E. Rodríguez O. (Wilmington, DE, 1992), 207-26.

54. Ross Hassig, *Aztec Warfare, Imperial Expansion, and Political Control* (Norman, OK, 1988), 55-72.

55. In 1855 the municipality of Tetela owned ten small ranches, together earning an annual rent of 761 pesos, ranging from 1 peso for La Carbonera to 250 pesos for the Rancho de Taxcantla; AMTdeO, Gobierno, Box 6, Exp. 6, 16 August 1855, Juan N. Méndez, Tetela, to Ramón Márquez, Zacatlán. The three most valuable of these properties, the income from which had been "exclusively destined for developing primary education," were auctioned on 22 January 1867, raising 11,749 pesos "which has been taken and invested in the expenses of the war"; AMTdeO, Actas de Cabildo, 7 November 1866-27 June 1871, Session of 29 December 1866.

56. AMTdeO, Gobierno, Box 7, Exp. 9, "Borrador de Oficios," 23 October 1856, sale of the "rancho de Rodríguez" belonging to "Archicofradía del Santísimo de esta Parroquia" to Juan Crisóstomo Bonilla. Juan N. Méndez purchased the Rancho de Calapa, from the Cofradía de Nuestro Padre de Jesús, on 21 December 1862; AMTdeO, Gobierno, 1862, Box 8, Exp. 8

57. AMTdeO, Gobierno, Box 8, Exp. 11, 9 August 1864, Juan Luján, Jonotla, to "General en Jefe"; AMTdeO, 3 August 1864, Fabian Lucas, Tuxtla, to "General en Jefe"; AMTdeO, 2 August 1864, Gabriel Peralta, Nanacatlán, to "General en Jefe."

58. Thomson, "Bulwarks of Patriotic Liberalism," 61-67.

59. For resistance from the landowner to the jefe político's adjudication of the hacienda of Caldera and the Rancho de Tepehucalco for the benefit of the landless *vecinos* of certain barrios of San Francisco Ixtacamaxtitlán, see *Alegato del Lic. Prisciliano María Díaz González como apoderado sustituto de Doña María de la Luz González . . . contra los procedimientos del jefe político de Alatriste* (Mexico, 1883).

60. The creation of Xochiapulco is examined in Chapter 10, this volume. Comparable agrarian trouble spots, rewarded for their patriotic services and support for the Montaña after the revolution of Tuxtepec, were the barrios of Ometepec, Tecuicuilco, and Taxco (Tetela), adjoining the hacienda of Taxcantla, which became "Ometepec de Quautimoctzin" in October 1877; the barrios Coayuca, Atecchoco, Chaucingo, and La Lagunilla, adjoining the hacienda of Coayuca (Alatriste), which became "Coayuca de la Unión" in July 1879, and several barrios in Zautla (Libres) were upgraded to become San Miguel Tenextlatiloyan in July 1878; *Periódico Oficial* 8, no. 95: 24 October 1877; *Colección de leyes y decretos del estado libre y soberano de Puebla* (Puebla, 1878), 71, 107-8, 112, 156; *Colección de leyes y decretos del estado libre y soberano de Puebla* (Puebla, 1879), 97-98. The Tlaxcalteco Liberal leader, Miguel Lira y Ortega, showed comparable gratitude to the *vecinos* of the barrio of Alzayanca near Tlaxco, upgrading it to a municipality in June 1871 and endowing it generously with land embargoed from neighboring estates. See Andrés Angulo, *Herencia política del C. Coronel Miguel Lira y Ortega* (Mexico, 1956), 85.

61. Guy P. C. Thomson, "Order through Insurrection: The Rise of the District of Tetela during Mexico's Liberal Revolution, 1854-1876," in *In Search of a New Order: Essays on the Politics and Society of Nineteenth-Century Latin America*, ed. Eduardo Posado-Carbó (London, 1998), 84-105.

62. Article 3 of the constitution of 1857 established free primary education. Josefina Vázquez de Knauth, *Nacionalismo y educación en México* (Mexico, 1970), 44-59; Sinkin, *The Mexican Reform*, 174.

63. José María Esteva, *Cartas a Fausto escritas desde un pueblo de la Sierra de Norte de Puebla por el cura de aquel lugar* (Mexico, 1871); Michéle Misser, "Literatura y mundo rural en Puebla: Siglo XIX," in *Puebla en el siglo XIX*, ed. CIHS (Puebla, 1983), 225-48.

64. AMTdeO, Gobierno, Box 7, Exp. 1, 19 May 1855, Juan Crisóstomo Bonilla, Tetela, to Fernando López.

65. AMTdeO, Gobierno, Box 7, Exp. 4, 1 March, 2 April, 14 May, 1 June 1855, Comisario, Tuzamapa and Tenampulco, to Sub-Prefect, Tetela.

66. Mary Kay Vaughan, "Women School Teachers in the Mexican Revolution: The Story of Reyna's Braids," *Journal of Women's History* 2 (1990): 143-68; idem, "Economic Growth and Literacy in Late Nineteenth-Century Mexico: The Case of Puebla," in *Education and Economic Development since the Industrial Revolution*, ed. Gabriel Tortella (Valencia, 1990), 89-112; Mallon, "Reflections on the Ruins," 81-89.

67. Mary Kay Vaughan, "The Educational Project of the Mexican Revolution: The Response of Local Societies (1934-1940)," in *Molding the Hearts and Minds: Education, Communications, and Social Change in Latin America*, ed. John A. Britton (Wilmington, DE, 1993), 119.

68. Archivo Municipal de Chignahuapan (hereafter cited as AMCh), Box 2, "Expediente relativo a que los terrenos de Coayuca que hoy esten agregados a Aquixtla vuelven a pertenecer a Istacamastitlán," 5 January 1871.

69. AMCh, Box 1, Exp. 10, 3 December 1870, Angel Cabrera, Ixtacamaxtitlán, to Jefe Político.

70. Sánchez Flores, *Zacapoaxtla*, 133; Rivera, *Xochiapulco*, 164-65.

71. Juan C. Bonilla, *Ley de instrucción pública para el estado de Puebla* (Puebla, 15 December 1878).

72. Jean Pierre Bastian, *Los disidentes: Sociedades protestantes y revolución en México, 1872-1911* (Mexico, 1989), 105-45; Vaughan, "The Educational Project," 118-20.

73. AMTdeO, Box 14 (1888) Bis, "Correspondencia Xochiapulco: Crónica de las honras fúnebres que el Ayuntamiento de Xochiapulco hizo el día dos de mayo de 1888 al finado Diputado C. Miguel Méndez."

74. Vaughan, "The Educational Project," 118-20; idem, "Economic Growth and Literacy," 37.

75. "Manifestación para solemnizar la fiesta a Juárez en Xochiapulco, Puebla," *Diario del Hogar*, 16 March 1901, cited in Bastian, *Los disidentes*, 73-85, 225.

76. For complaints from fathers who preferred to allow their children to help their mothers to bring food to the fields, or to gather charcoal, than to send them to school, see AMTdeO, Gobierno, Box 7, Exp. 4, 20 March 1855, Comisario, Tuzamapa, to Sub-Prefect. For complaints from poor women and widows in Zapotitlán's subject barrios that alcaldes were ordering their sons to school when they were old enough to earn a salary to care for their "poor mothers," see AMTdeO, Gobierno, Box 10, 1867-69, Exp. 1, 31 May 1867, Manuel Luiz, Zapotitlán, to Jefe Político. For complaints of the drunkenness, gaming, and disturbing the public order of Joaquín Fuentes, schoolmaster of Tetetilla, and request for his replacement by the sober Ramón Carcamo, see AMTdeO, Gobierno, Box 9, Exp. 4, 9 January 1867, Tiburcio Reyes, Tuzamapa, to Jefe Político. For complaints about the drunkenness of Víctor Manzano, schoolmaster and aguardiente distiller, and of the use of the school locale for aguardiente sale and consumption, see AMTdeO, Gobierno, Box 7, Exp. 3, 21 May 1855, Ramón Nieto, Zapotitlán, to Sub-Prefect. For a description of the threatening reception for a schoolteacher from *vecinos* of Ahuacatlán calling "que biba la religión y mueran los puros federales," see AMZ, "1862, Correspondencia del Jefe Político," 12 February 1862, Martin Antonio, Ahuacatlán, to Jefe Político. For a report on the attempt by a Totonac parent to encourage non-attendance at Tuzamapa's public school, see AMTdeO, Gobierno, Box 13 Bis, Exp. 1, 11 May 1870, José Galbán to Jefe Político. For several examples of conflict between parents, schoolteachers, and municipal officials, see Mallon, *Peasant and Nation*, 286-94.

77. AMTdeO, Miscellaneous Box, 29 December 1868 and 4 January 1869, Francisco Toral et al., Jonotla, Zoquiapa, and Ecatlan, to Jefe Político.

78. Moisés Saenz, *Escuelas federales en la Sierra de Puebla* (Mexico, 1927).

Chapter 2, Tetela in the Puebla Sierra, 25–40

1. Donna Rivera Moreno, *Xochiapulco: Una gloria olvidada* (Puebla, 1991), 164.

2. Manuel Flón, "Noticias Estadísticas de la Intendencia de Puebla (1804)," in *Descripciones económicas regionales de Nueva España, Provincias del Centro, Sureste y Sur, 1766-1827*, ed. Enrique Florescano and Isabel Gil Sánchez (Mexico, 1976), 158-81; *Periódico Oficial* 10:84, 18 October 1879; Vicente Lombardo Toledano, *Geografía de las lenguas de la Sierra de Puebla con algunas observaciones sobre sus antiguos y sus actuales pobladores* (Mexico, 1931).

3. Flón, "Noticias Estadísticas"; AMTdeO, Censos de la municipalidad de Tetela de Oro (1849 y 1860); *Boletín de la Sociedad Mexicana de Geografía* (hereafter cited as *BSMG)* 2:306; AMTdeO, Box 14 Bis, 1871, "Correspondencia varias autoridades," 19 May 1871, Tetela; *Periódico Oficial* 10:84, 18 October 1879; Toledano, *Geografía de las lenguas.*

4. Flón, "Noticias Estadísticas."

5. Ramón Márquez, "Departamento de Zacatlán, Noticias estadísticas del Estado de Puebla," *BSMGE* (1849): 257-58.

6. Toledano, *Geografía de las lenguas*; Flón, "Noticias Estadísticas."

7. Enrique Palacios, *Puebla: Su territorio y sus habitantes* (Mexico, 1917), 44-45, 154; François Estragnat, "La Sierra del Estado de Puebla. Apuntes geognósticos, mineralógicos y metalurgicos," *El Minero Mexicano* 2, 1874-75.

8. Palacios, *Puebla: Su territorio*, 98.

9. Bernardo García Martínez, *Los pueblos de la Sierra* (Mexico, 1987), 41-71.

10. For a political genealogy of Ixtacamaxtitlán, see AMCh, Box 2, "Expediente relativo a que los terrenos de Cuayuca que hoy están agregados a Aquiztla vuelvan a pertenecer a Istacamastitlán"; and Brian Hamnett, *Roots of Insurgency: Mexican Regions, 1750-1824* (Cambridge, England, 1986), 139-42.

11. García Martínez, *Los pueblos de la Sierra*, 160-61, 185.

12. Guy P. C. Thomson, "La 'Bocasierra,' ¿cuna del liberalismo? Los casos de Zautla, Xochiapulco y Cuetzalan, 1857-1891," in *La responsabilidad del historiador*, ed. Shulamit Goldsmit and Guillermo Zermeño (Mexico, 1992), 185-200.

13. García Martínez charts the development of Huauchinango as a transport center from the early seventeenth century, *Los pueblos de la Sierra*, 135-49; Palacios, *Puebla: Su territorio*, 303-04.

14. Antonio García Cubas, "Una excursión a la tierra caliente: De Teziutlán a Nautla," *Publicación Oficial*: 42-48, May-June 1874; Luis Audirac, *Teziutlán: Apuntes geográficos e históricos* (Mexico, 1959); Sandalio Mejía Castelán, *Huauchinango histórico* (Puebla, 1965); Ricardo Vaquier, *Breves datos históricos y político-sociales del distrito de Huauchinango, estado de Puebla* (Puebla, 1953); Canuto Amaya and Vicente Andrade, *Estudio sobre la ciudad de Huauchinango* (Mexico, 1912).

15. Ramón Sánchez Flores, *Zacapoaxtla: Relación histórica* (Zacapoaxtla, 1984); Francisco Javier Arriaga, *Expediente geográfico-estadístico . . . por el distrito de Zacapoaxtla* (Mexico, 1873); Ciro Molina, *Reseña histórica de la ciudad de Zacapoaxtla* (Puebla, 1952).

16. Manuel M. Vargas, *Proyecto de una via de comunicación de la Mesa Central a la costa de Papantla pasando por el distrito de Tlatlauqui promovido ante la H. Asamblea del Estado por el diputado de la misma C. Manuel M. Vargas, y llevado al Hon. Congreso de la Unión* (Puebla, 1874).

17. In 1841 the sub-prefect declared that the municipality of Tetela contained no cattle pens (*potreros*); AMTdeO, Box 5, Exp. 6,"Agricultura," July 1841.

18. García Martínez, *Los pueblos de la Sierra*, 42-43.

19. Peter Gerhard, *A Guide to the Historical Geography of New Spain* (Cambridge, England, 1972), 388-90.

20. For conflicts along the Nahua-Totonac boundary in Jonotla during the eighteenth century, see AGN, Tierras, 583, Exp. 1 (San Miguel Zozocolco against San Juan Jonotla and San Martín Tuzamapa, 1738-41); AGN, Tierras, 971, Exp. 4 (Santa María Tenampulco against San José del Espinal, 1773-74). For evidence of the continuation of ethnic conflict in this region well into the republican period, when, during the Olarte rebellion of 1836, Nahua troops were recruited in the highlands to fight lowland Totonac rebels, see ADN, Histórico, XI/481.3/1188, ff. 67, 90-91, 11 November 1836; García Martínez, *Los pueblos de la Sierra*, 243.

21. Flón, "Noticias Estadísticas."

22. AGN, Tierras, 885, Exp. 1, for Tetela's claim over the Rancho de Coayuca in 1757-1768.

23. García Martínez, *Los pueblos de la Sierra*, 239.

24. Bernardo García, "Pueblos de indios, Pueblos de castas: New Settlements and Traditional Corporate Organization in Eighteenth-Century New Spain," in *The Indian Community of Colonial Mexico*, ed. Arij Ouweneel and Simon Miller (Amsterdam, 1990), 109-11.

25. García Martínez, *Los pueblos de la Sierra*, 281, 286-87, 300-309.

26. Liudmila Borisovna de León and Francisco Téllez Guerrero, "La división territorial del estado de Puebla, 1824-1910," in *Puebla en el siglo XIX*, ed. CIHS (Puebla, 1983), 7-18.

27. AGNP, Zacapoaxtla, Vol. 7 1849, 20 March 1849, Pascual Angeles Lobato. Mallon incorrectly sees this incident as a consequence of Tetelense expansionism, rather than an ingenious attempt by commercial interests in Zacapoaxtla to wrest these lowland dependencies from Tetela's "time immemorial" control. However, the point she makes about the efforts of Zacapoaxtla's Creoles to develop alliances with Indian village authorities, within and beyond the district, is an important one; see Florencia Mallon, *Peasant and Nation: The Making of Post-Colonial Mexico and Peru* (Berkeley, CA, 1995), 29.

28. AMZ, June 1870, "Espediente relativo a la manifestación que hacen las autoridades y vecinos del distrito solicitando del Supremo Gobierno del Estado la anexión de la municipalidad de Jonotla para indemnizarle la de Xochiapulco que fué agregada por disposición superior de Tetela."

29. AMTdeO, Gobierno, Box 6, Exp. 5, 13 August 1855, Fernando López, "representante del común de Tetela," to Juan N. Méndez.

30. *La Razón* (Puebla) 1:2, 9 October 1855.

31. *Constitución política del estado libre y soberano de Puebla* (Puebla, 1861), 17.

32. *Periódico Oficial* 1:67, 17 February 1868; AMTdeO, "Correspondencia: Diversas Autoridades," Law of 25 December 1867; AMTdeO, Gobierno, Box 10, Exp. 4, Decree of 14 March 1868.

33. AMTdeO, Gobierno, Box 4 Bis, 1871, "Correspondencia del Gobierno del Estado," 16 June 1871.

34. Francisco Téllez Guerrero, "La organización administrativa del estado de Puebla, 1824-1910," in *Puebla en el siglo XIX*, ed. CIHS (Puebla, 1983), 63-64.

35. Guy P. C. Thomson, "Federalism and Cantonalism in Mexico, 1824-1892: Sovereignty and Territoriality," in *Wars, Parties and Nationalism,* ed. Eduardo Posada-Carbó (London, 1995), 27-54.

36. Alberto de Santa Fe, *Reformas y adiciones a la constitución de 1857* (Puebla, 1875), 26-33; AMTdeO, 1869, "Noticia que manifiesta el movimiento de la Guardia Nacional," 28 December 1869; *Periódico Oficial* 11:26, 31 March 1880.

37. For the continued influence of Tetelense *panela* and aguardiente dealers during the 1960s, see James Taggart, *The Factors Affecting the Developmental Cycle of Domestic Groups in a Nahuat-Speaking Community in Mexico* (Ph.D. diss., University of Pittsburgh, 1971), 31.

38. AMTdeO, Gobierno, Box 439, Exp. 4, 6 April 1872, Andrés Velázquez, Huitzilan, to Gregorio Zamítez.

39. Lourdes Arizpe, *Parentesco y economía en una sociedad Nahua: Nican Pehua Zacatipan* (Mexico, 1973), 125.

40. AMTdeO, "Jefe Político, Borrador de Oficios de 1866," 28 March 1866, list of liquor merchants and distillers; AMTdeO, Gobierno, Box 36, 1876, "Borrador de Oficios de 1876," List of owners of aguardiente factories.

41. Juan de Carrión, *Descripción del Pueblo de Gueytlalpan* (Xalapa, 1965), 28.

42. For such challenges, see Chapters 4 and 11, this volume.

43. AGNP, Tetela, 1890-1894 (1891 Apéndice al protocolo), ff. 29-37 (Will of Mariano Santos Bonilla, Huitzilan); AGNP, Tetela, Comprobantes del protocolo de 1878, 11 November 1877, ff. 1-2 (Will of Ramón Nieto, Zapotitlán); AGNP, Tetela, Apéndice a los protocolos de 1883, 15 March 1883, f. 12 (Will of Lorenzo Diego, Zapotitlán).

44. Pierra Durand, *Nanacatlán: Sociedad campesina y lucha de clases en México* (Mexico, 1986), 213-32. For the economic bases for the Nieto dynasty in "Zapotitlán de Méndez," Nanacatlán, and Zongozotla, see AGNP, Tetela (Comprobantes), 1880, ff. 4, 12; AGNP, Tetela (Comprobantes), 1881, ff. 25, 27, 28, 30, 33, 36; AGNP, Tetela, 1882, 10-15, 17, 75-76; AGNP, Tetela, 1920-21, ff. 74, 104-05, 108-9.

45. Moisés Saenz, *Escuelas federales en la Sierra de Puebla: Informe sobre la visita a las escuelas federales en la Sierra de Puebla* (Mexico, 1927), 82.

46. James Taggart, *Nahuat Myth and Social Structure* (Austin, TX, 1983), 33-34.

47. Frank Schenk, "La desamortización de las tierras comunales en el estado de México (1856-1911). El caso del distrito de Sultepec," *HM* 45 (1995-96): 3-37.

48. For examples of this rhetoric, see AMTdeO, Gobierno 1864, Box 8, Exp. 11, 9 August 1864, Juan Luján to "Sr. General en Jefe del Distrito de Tetela"; Box 9, Exp. 4, 10 March 1867, Tiburcio Reyes, Tuzamapa, to Jefe Político.

49. Mallon, *Peasant and Nation*, 67-68, 75-76.

50. Arizpe, *Parentesco y economía*; James Taggart, "The Fissiparous Process in Domestic Groups of a Nahuat-Speaking Community," *Ethnology* 1 (1972): 132-49; idem, *Nahuat Myth and Social Structure*; Enzo Segre, *Metamorfosis de lo sagrado y de lo profano. Narrativa náhuat de la Sierra Norte de Puebla* (Mexico, 1990); María Elena Aramoni, *Talokan Tata, talokan nana: Nuestras raíces* (Mexico, 1990); *TTOSCEPEC, Les oíamos contar a nuestros abuelos: Etnohistoria de San Miguel Tzinacapan* (Mexico, 1994).

51. *El Libre Pensador* III, 29, 28 October 1869.

52. Taggart, *Nahuat Myth and Social Structure*; Aramoni, *Talokan tata, talokan nana*; Segre, *Metamorfosis de lo sagrado*.

53. García Martínez, "Pueblos de indios, Pueblos de castas," 103-16.

Chapter 3, Rebellion and Revolution, 41–53

1. Juan Francisco, son of José Manuel and María Josefa, was baptized on 26 June 1834 by Cura Luis Valiente. See Ramón Sánchez Flores, *Zacapoaxtla: Relación histórica* (Zacapoaxtla, 1984), 133-35.

2. Interview with descendant, Natalia Molina, Zacapoaxtla, June 1984.

3. Flores, *Zacapoaxtla*, 133.

4. María Dolores Posada Olayo, "En la historia, La verdad como Norma," in *La Batalla del 5 de Mayo*, ed. Miguel A. Sánchez Lamego (Puebla, 1963), 171.

5. APJFL, Juan Francisco Lucas, "Autobiographical fragment, 1908."

6. Enrique Cordero y Torres, "El Partido Liberal en la Sierra Poblana," in *La Batalla del 5 de Mayo*, 111-13; Felipe Franco, *Indonomía geográfica del Estado de Puebla* (Puebla, 1976), 303.

7. Octavio Manzano Díaz, *El indígena de la Sierra Norte* (Mexico, 1987), 11-13.

8. AGN, Tierras 802, Exp. 4, ff. 3-56, cited in Sánchez Flores, *Zacapoaxtla*, 77-78.

9. Ana Maria Huerta, "La descomposición y formación de grupos sociales en Zacapoaxtla (a propósito de la sublevación 1868-1870): Los Salgado y los Molina," in *Puebla en el siglo XIX*, ed. CIHS (Puebla, 1983), 249-88.

10. John Tutino, *From Insurrection to Revolution in Mexico: Social Bases of Agrarian Violence, 1750-1940* (Princeton, 1986), 215-76.

11. I found no evidence for this. Indeed, sugarcane is not grown commercially at this high altitude. Florencia Mallon, *Peasant and Nation: The Making of Post-Colonial Mexico and Peru* (Berkeley, CA, 1995), 26-27.

12. Instituto Nacional de Antropología e Historia, Microfilm Collection, Archivo Judicial de Puebla (hereafter cited as INAH-AJP), Roll 37, 55.

13. INAH-AJP, Roll 37, "Auto promovido por el Pueblo de San Miguel Huahuaztla contra el de San Esteban de Tetela sobre propiedad de unos terrenos." For another agrarian confict in this area, see Moisés González Navarro, *Anatomia del poder en México, 1848-1853* (Mexico, 1977), 167. The prosperous ranches established by *gente de razón* from Tetela on land bought from San Esteban's Indian communities were valued by Tetela's council in 1856 for their revenue; AMTdeO, Gobierno, Box 7, Exp. 9, "Borrador de Oficios de 1856."

14. INAH-AJP, Roll 37, "Auto promovido por el Pueblo de San Miguel Huahuaztla contra el de San Esteban de Tetela"; AMTdeO, Padrón del Distrito (1873); AMZ, "Borrador de Oficios del Jefe Político, 1862," 5 August 1862, Jefe Político to Lucas.

15. Leticia Reina, *Las rebeliones campesinas en México (1819-1906)* (Mexico, 1986), 17-20, 61-63, 117-28, 157-68, 240-42, 291-304, 341-55, 366-416, 425; Tutino, *From Insurrection to Revolution*, 249-25; Mallon, *Peasant and Nation*, 152-62; Peter Guardino, *Peasants, Politics, and the Formation of Mexico's National State: Guerrero, 1800-1857* (Stanford, 1996), 168-210.

16. Antonio Carrión, *Historia de la Ciudad de Puebla* (Puebla, 1970), 2:307-39.

17. Sánchez Flores, *Zacapoaxtla*, 128-29, 267-70.

18. Ibid., 132-33.

19. See chapters by María Cristina Torales Pacheco, Stephanie Wood, and Bernardo García Martínez in *The Indian Community of Colonial Mexico*, ed. Arij Ouweneel and Simon Miller (Amsterdam, 1990), 87-129; Bernard García Martínez, *Los pueblos de la Sierra* (Mexico, 1986), 221-24, 259-304.

20. Huerta, "La descomposición," 253.

21. Manuel Pozos claimed that the barrios on the Cuatecomaco ridge saw their houses burnt to the ground eleven times and their leaders

imprisoned on frequent occasions between 1852 and 1860; Manzano Díaz, *El indígena de la Sierra Norte*, 12-15.

22. Jan Bazant, *Cinco haciendas mexicanas, tres siglos de vida rural en San Luis Potosí (1600-1910)* (Mexico, 1975), 119; Francisco de Paula Arrangoíz, *México desde 1808 hasta 1867* (Mexico, 1968), 421-22; Carmen Vázquez Mantecón, *Santa Anna en la encrucijada del estado: La dictadura (1853-1855)* (Mexico, 1986), 111.

23. Peter Guardino, "Barbarism or Republican Law: Guerrero's Peasants and National Politics, 1820-1846," *HAHR* 75 (1995): 185-214.

24. Francisco Pérez, *Decreto sobre arreglo de la capitación* (Puebla, 1853); APJFL, Letter, n.d., from Cura Ladrón de Guevara, Gobierno Eclesiástico de Puebla, to "El ocurso de los barrios de Comaltepec, Atacpan y Cuacalaxtla."

25. Guy P. C. Thomson, "Movilización conservadora, insurrección liberal y rebeliones indígenas en la Sierra Norte de Puebla, 1854-1876," in *America Latina: Dallo stato coloniale allo stato nazione*, ed. Antonio Annino (Turin, 1987), 2:592-614.

26. Richard A. Johnson, *The Mexican Revolution of Ayutla, 1854-1855* (Rock Island, IL, 1939); Anselmo de la Portilla, *Historia de la revolución de México contra la dictadura del general Santa Anna, 1853-1855* (Mexico, 1856).

27. AMTdeO, Gobierno, Box 6, Exps. 5 and 6, for the adhesion of Tetela de Oro and Zapotitlán to the Plan de Ayutla, on 15 and 23 August 1855, respectively.

28. On 14 November 1855, Zacapoaxtla's council finally embraced the Plan de Ayutla although the sub-prefect made no attempt to convene a junta of the municipalities of the district to discuss it; *La Razón*, Puebla, 21, 22 November 1855.

29. AMTdeO, Gobierno, Box 6, Exp. 5, 5 October 1855, Miguel González, Zacapoaxtla, to Sub-Prefect.

30. APJFL, Sergio Bonilla, "Datos Biográficos del Señor General Don Juan Francisco Lucas."

31. José Estevan, Juan José Español, José Manuel Lucas, José Jiménez, José de la Cruz, and Pedro Cipriano went on to become National Guard captains. Among the prisoners were also several of the first recipients of land parcels in the Villa del Cinco de Mayo in 1864: Captain José de la Cruz, José Manuel, Juan Antonio, and José Silverio. AMTdeO, Gobierno, Box 7, Exp. 4, 5 October 1855, Camilo Tirado, Zacapoaxtla, to Sub-Prefect; Donna Rivera Moreno, *Xochiapulco: Una gloria olvidada* (Puebla, 1990), 224-26.

32. AMTdeO, Gobierno, Box 6, Exp. 5, 10 September, 6 October 1855, Ramón Márquez, Zacatlán, to Sub-Prefect.

33. AMTdeO, Gobierno, Box 7, Exp. 3, 14 May 1855, Ramón Nieto, Zapotitlán, to Sub-Prefect; Exp. 4, 20 November, 3, 7, 10 December 1855, Juan Nieto, Zapotitlán, to Sub-Prefect; 8 December, Ramón Márquez, Zacatlán, to Sub-Prefect; AMTdeO, Gobierno, Box 7, Exp. 3, 1 October 1855, Ramón Nieto, Zapotitlán, to Sub-Prefect.

34. José Diego was reported to have risen up against the authorities on several previous occasions. Like José Manuel Lucas, José Diego was clearly a "rich Indian" with considerable influence locally: "como rico se lleva la voz del pueblo para sus depravados intentos"; AMTdeO, Gobierno, Box 7, Exp. 4, 20 November 1855, Juan Nieto, Zapotitlán, to Sub-Prefect.

35. AMZ, 1861, Correspondencia del Jefe Político, Exp. 176, "Noticia de las Municipalidades, Cabeceras, Pueblos, Haciendas, Rancherías, Ranchos, Molinos y Predios rústicos comprendidos en el Distrito de Zacapoastla."

36. AGNP, Zacapoaxtla, 7, f. 87.

37. For the repartition of Molina Alcántara's lands among tenants during the 1860s and 1870s, see AGNP, Zacapoaxtla, 7, ff. 52-54, 17-118; Tetela, 2, ff. 15, 24-26, 28-29; and Huerta, "La descomposición," 249-88.

38. APJFL, Manuel Pozos, "Lijeros apuntes históricos del municipio de Xochiapulco y especialmente de su cabecera: Villa del Cinco de Mayo."

39. Ibid.

40. Ramón Márquez, prefect of Zacatlan, regarded Indians as children, and whatever misconduct, as "disobediencia" or "insolencia." The younger generation of Liberals, represented in Zacatlán by Ramón Márquez Galindo (no relation to the prefect of Zacatlán), discovered that there was more political mileage to be had from treating Indians as citizens; AMTdeO, Gobierno, Box 7, Exp. 4, 8 December 1855, Ramón Márquez, Zacatlán, to Sub-Prefect.

41. AMTdeO, Gobierno, Box 7, Exp. 4, 4 December 1855, Ramón Márquez, Zacatlán, to Sub-Prefect.

42. Manzano Díaz, *El indígena de la Sierra Norte*, 14-15.

43. AMTdeO, Gobierno, Box 7, Exp. 4, 1, 4 and 6 December 1855, Ramón Márquez, Zacatlán, to Sub-Prefect.

44. AMTdeO, Gobierno, Box 7, Exp. 4, 7 December 1855, Juan Nieto, Zapotitlán, to Sub-Prefect.

45. AMTdeO, Gobierno, Box 7, Exp. 9, "Borrador de Oficios, 1856."

46. AMTdeO, Gobierno, Box 7, Exp. 4, 19 and 26 December 1855, Ramón Márquez, Zacatlán, to Sub-Prefect.

47. Anselmo de la Portilla, *Méjico en 1856 y 1857: Gobierno del General Comonfort* (New York, 1858); idem, *Episodio histórico del gobierno dictatorial del Señor Don Igno. Comonfort en la República Mexicana, años de 1856 y 1857* (Mexico, 1861).

48. Francisco de Paula Ortega y García had developed a close relationship with the monarchist conspirator, Francisco Javier Miranda, while attached to the Cathedral of Puebla. See Sánchez Flores, *Zacapoaxtla*, 275.

49. The Plan de Zacapoaxtla disavowed the Plan de Ayutla and called for the re-adoption of the "Bases Orgánicas," the centralist Conservative constitution of 1837. Jan Bazant, *Antonio Haro y Tamariz y sus aventuras políticas, 1811-1869* (Mexico, 1985), 105-6; AMTdeO, Box 7, Exp. 9, 12 December 1855, "Plan de Zacapoastla."

50. Bazant, *Antonio Haro y Tamariz,* 114-15.

51. Mallon, *Peasant and Nation,* 157.

52. Antonio Carrión, *Historia de la Ciudad de Puebla de los Angeles* (Puebla, 1970), 2:322-39.

53. Only one account states specifically that Lucas served with the Conservative rebel force in 1856; Octavio Guzmán, "Aclaraciones indispensables sobre el mito de las zacapoaxtlas en las conmemoraciones anuales de la batalla del 5 de Mayo de 1862," in *La Batalla del 5 de Mayo,* ed. Miguel A. Sánchez Lamego (Mexico, 1962), 99.

54. Jan Bazant, *Alienation of Church Wealth in Mexico: Social and Economic Aspects of the Liberal Revolution, 1856-1875* (Cambridge, England, 1971), 47.

55. Carrión, *Historia,* 2:340-45.

56. *La Razón: Periódico del Gobierno de Puebla,* 2a época, 87, 9 October 1856.

57. ADN, Histórico, XI/481 3/8157, f. 228, "Proyecto sobre la formación de un escuadrón de los gefes y oficiales reaccionarios que se hallaban en la plaza de Puebla."

58. ADN, Histórico, XI/481 3/8162, ff. 93-107.

59. ADN, Histórico, XI/481 3/8157, ff. 249-254.

60. APJFL, Manuel Pozos, "Lijeros apuntes históricos."

61. AMTdeO, Gobierno, Box 7, Exp. 4, 11 December 1855, Manuel Arroyo, Zacapoaxtla, to Sub-Prefect.

62. For Francisco Pérez's will, see AGNP, Tetela 2, ff. 16-18; his plot facing Tetela's main square later became Lucas's principal residence. AMTdeO, Gobierno, Box 7, Exp. 9, "Borrador de Oficios," June 1856; AMTdeO, Gobierno, Box 5, Exp. 3, 2 October 1856.

63. AGNP, Zacapoaxtla, 1854, f. 7; AGNP, Zacapoaxtla, 1855, f. 2

64. AGNP, Zacapoaxtla, 1854, f. 48; AMTdeO, Gobierno, Box 7, Exp. 1.

65. AMTdeO, Gobierno, Box 7, Exp. 4 and Box 6, Exp. 5, Case of Miguel Sánchez, 26 December 1855.

66. AMTdeO, Gobierno, Box 7, Exp. 9, 3 January 1856, Juan N. Méndez, Tetela.

67. For Gutiérrez's rebellion, see ADN, Histórico, XI/481, 3/5321.

68. ADN, Histórico, XI/481, 3/5435, f. 1, 29 August 1856, Ramón Iglesias, Veracruz, to Minister of War; ADN, Histórico, XI/481, 3/5321, f. 18, 14 November 1856, Roldán to Gutiérrez.

69. ADN, Histórico, XI/481, 3/5321, ff. 11, 73-16, 19 and 29 November 1856, Soto, Zacatlán, to Minister of War.

70. ADN, Histórico, XI/481 3/4167, ff. 1-10, 23 June 1857, Portilla, Zacapoaxtla, to Minister of War.

71. Manzano Díaz, *El indígena de la Sierra Norte,* 72.

Chapter 4, The Three Years' War, 55–71

1. Brian Hamnett, *Roots of Insurgency, Mexican Regions, 1750-1824* (Cambridge, England, 1986), 139-42.

2. AGN, Gobernación, Seguridad Pública, 1a 1858(1)(2), Exp. 7.

3. ADN, Histórico, XI/481 3/6392, f. 11, 27 March 1858, Ulloa, Tulancingo, to Minister of War; XI/481 3/06433, f. 1, 14 April 1858, Noriega to Minister of War; XI/481 3/6439, ff. 1-3, 21 May 1858, Noriega to Minister of War.

4. Antonio Carrión, *Historia de la Ciudad de Puebla* (Puebla, 1970), 2:390; ADN, Histórico, XI/481 3/6439, f. 1.

5. Miguel Galindo y Galindo, *La gran década nacional, 1857-1867* (Mexico, 1904), 1:141.

6. APJFL, "Datos biográficos."

7. ADN, Cancelados, C-64 D/111/2.425, vol. 1, ff. 1-4.

8. Galindo y Galindo, *La gran década,* 1:139-40.

9. The Cuatecomacos received one hundred percussion rifles, thirty-five carbines, thirty-five flintlock rifles, six short carbines, five shotguns, twenty-six mattocks (*marrazos*), fifty-eight bayonets, eighty gun belts, ten swords, twenty-one lances, thirteen horses, and eight mules; ADN, Histórico, XI/481 3/6467, ff. 1-6, 28 July 1856, Alatriste to Minister of War.

10. Galindo y Galindo, *La gran década,* 1:142.

11. ADN, Histórico, XI/481 3/6829, ff. 5-6.

12. ADN, Histórico, XI/481 3/5321, ff. 6, 22-37; Ramón Sánchez Flores, *Zacapoaxtla: Relación histórica* (Zacapoaxtla, 1984), 133, 151-53.

13. AMZ, Correspondence of Jefatura Política, Exp. 71, 14 February 1861.

14. AMTdeO, Gobierno, Box 7, Exp. 8, 28 September 1858, Pilar Rivera, Tetela, to Prefecture, Zacatlán.

15. ADN, Histórico, XI/481 3/5876, 21 July 1858, Roldán, Zacapoaxtla, to Manuel Noriega, Puebla.

16. Was José María Ascensión perhaps not aware that Alvarez had left the presidency almost three years earlier? ADN, Histórico, XI/481 3/6829, f. 1, 30 July 1858, Roldán, Zacapoaxtla, to Noriega, Puebla.

17. ADN, Histórico, XI/481 3/5882, f. 1, 30 July 1858, Roldán, Zacapoaxtla, to Noriega.

18. Galindo y Galindo, *La gran década,* 1:145-56.

19. AMTdeO, Gobierno, Box 8, Exp. 4, 3 September 1858, Juan N. Méndez, Zacatlán, to Pilar Rivera.

20. ADN, Histórico, XI/481 3/5794, f. 1, 17 September 1858, Roldán, Zacapoaxtla, to Noriega, Puebla; Galindo y Galindo, *La gran década,* 1:157-59.

21. Carrión, *Historia,* 2:390-91.

22. ADN, Histórico, XI/481 3/7111, f. 10, 23 January 1859, Pérez, Puebla, to Minister of War.

23. Ibid., f. 1, 10 February 1859, Pérez to Minister of War.

24. Ibid., f. 4, 10 February 1859, Pérez to Minister of War.

25. ADN, Histórico, XI/481 3/6443, f. 1, 18 February 1859, Alatriste, Teziutlán, to Minister of War; ADN, Histórico, XI/481 3/7116, f. 1, 22 February 1859, Pérez, Puebla, to Minister of War.

26. Galindo y Galindo, *La gran década*, 1:246.

27. ADN, Histórico, XI/481 3/7111, f. 10, 23 January 1859, Pérez, Puebla, to Minister of War.

28. ADN, Histórico, XI/481 3/6443, f. 1, 18 February 1859, Alatriste to Minister of War, Veracruz.

29. Hugo Leicht, *Las Calles de Puebla* (Puebla, 1967), 6; Angel W. Cabrera, "Biografía del Licenciado Dn. Miguel Cástulo de Alatriste," in *Liberales ilustres mexicanos de la Reforma y la Intervención,* ed. Enrique M. de los Ríos (Mexico, 1890), 132-36.

30. "In moments of rest he would discourse with this priest, in literary conversations full of 'esprit,' in scientific discussions about mathematics and Mexican antiquities, matters in which the priest Cabrera was well versed." Cabrera, "Biografía," 134.

31. ADN, Histórico, XI/481 3/70124, f. 25, 7 October 1859, Melchor Ocampo, Veracruz, to Márquez Galindo, Zacatlán.

32. 1,012 rifles, 40 boxes of ammunition (containing 1,000 cartridges each), and 36 sheets of lead; ADN, Histórico, XI/481 3/7433 2, 5 May 1859, Ocampo, Veracruz, to Alatriste, Zacapoaxtla; ADN, Histórico, XI/481 3/6958, ff. 1-3, 30 July 1859, Méndez, Zacatlán, to Ocampo, Veracruz.

33. The distribution of the 1,012 rifles sent to Méndez by Ocampo in April 1859 is as follows: Batallón de Zacatlán, 375 (Méndez); Batallón de Huauchinango, 125 (Cravioto); Batallón de Tetela, 212 (Pilar Rivera); Batallón de Tlaxcala, 200 (Antonio Carbajal); Compañía de Aquixtla, 41; and Compañía de Cuatecomaco, 59. Ibid., 13, 14 May 1859, Méndez, Zacapoaxtla, to Ocampo, Veracruz.

34. ADN, Histórico, XI/481 3/7433, ff. 21-2, 8 October 1859, Cravioto to Ocampo, Veracruz.

35. Ibid., ff. 35-6, 15 April 1859, Rafael Avila, Teziutlán, to Ocampo, Veracruz, and 9 May 1859, Ocampo, Veracruz, to Avila, Teziutlán.

36. Galindo y Galindo, *La gran década*, 1:272-74; ADN, Histórico, XI/481 3/7474, ff. 32-46, 25 July 1859, Manuel Díaz de la Vega to Minister of War.

37. ADN, Histórico, XI/481 3/7433, ff. 18, 57-8, 18 July 1859 and 5 August 1859, Alatriste, Zacapoaxtla, to Ocampo, Veracruz; Galindo y Galindo, *La gran década*, 1:328-29.

38. Carrión, *Historia,* 2:396-97.

39. ADN, Histórico, XI/481 3/7433, f. 9, 31 August 1859, Méndez to Ocampo, Veracruz; Carrión, *Historia,* 2:397.

40. ADN, Histórico, XI/481 3/7024, ff. 22, 29, 31-4; ADN, Histórico, XI/481 3/7014, f. 5; Crisanto Cuellar Abaroa, *Antonio Carbajal: Caudillo Tlaxcalteco* (Mexico, 1962); ADN, Histórico, XI/481 3/7458, 7711, 8031.

41. ADN, Histórico, XI/481 3/7024, ff. 25-7, 7 and 17 October 1859, Ocampo, Veracruz, to Márquez Galindo and Méndez, Zacatlán.

42. Ibid., ff. 12-13.

43. Ibid., f. 9; Galindo y Galindo, *La gran década*, 1:337.

44. Galindo y Galindo, *La gran década*, 2:335; ADN, Histórico, XI/481 3/7014, f. 5; ADN, Histórico, XI/481 3/7024, ff. 21, 25-7, 49-50, 12 October 1859, Méndez, Zacatlán, to Minister of War, Veracruz; 7 and 17 October 1859, Ocampo, Veracruz, to Márquez Galindo and Méndez, Zacatlán; 21 October 1859, Méndez, Zacatlán, to Ocampo, Veracruz.

45. Ibid., ff. 36-9, 45, 46, 47-8.

46. ADN, Histórico, XI/481 3/7748, f. 1, 20 December 1859, Ramón Márquez Galindo, Zacapoaxtla, to Rafael Cravioto, Huauchinango; ADN, Cancelados, Box 67/111/2/442, f. 13, 24 March 1860, Alatriste, Tlaxcala, to Minister of War, Veracruz.

47. ADN, Histórico, XI/481 3/8025, f. 19, 13 April 1860, Márquez Galindo, Zacapoaxtla, to Minister of War, Veracruz.

48. Ibid., ff. 21-2, 26.

49. Galindo y Galindo, *La gran década*, 1:410; ADN, Histórico, XI/481 3/8057, f. 16, 3 May 1860, Alatriste, Teziutlán, to Minister of Interior; ADN, Histórico, XI/481 3/8057, ff. 11-12, 3 and 8 May 1860, Méndez, Tetela, to Minister of Interior, Teziutlán; ADN, Histórico, XI/481 3/8057, f. 13, 7 May 1860, Márquez Galindo, Zacapoaxtla, to Minister of Interior, Teziutlán, and ff. 62-3, 15 May 1860, Ignacio Sosa, Ahuacatlán, to Minister of Interior, Teziutlán.

50. ADN, Histórico, XI/481 3/8077, ff. 5-6, 1 May 1860, Pedro Ampudía, Veracruz, to Minister of War, Veracruz.

51. Ibid., ff. 24-25, 38. For a biographical portrait of Ignacio Romero Vargas, see Galindo y Galindo, *La gran década*, 1:330-31.

52. ADN, Histórico, XI/481 3/8057, f. 181, "Contribución de rebajados de servicio de la Guardia Nacional."

53. Ibid., ff. 133-34.

54. Ibid., f. 134.

55. Ibid., f. 79; ADN, Cancelados, C-64 D/111/2/425, I, f. 70.

56. ADN, Histórico, XI/481 3/6056, 92, 6 August 1860, Joaquín Telles, Zacapoaxtla, to Minister of War.

57. Galindo y Galindo, *La gran década*, 1:445.

58. Carrión, *Historia*, 2:400-402.

59. Ramón Kuri Camacho, *Micro historia de Chignahuapan*, 3 vols. (Chignahuapan, Puebla, 1985), 2:29-34.

60. Florencia Mallon, *Peasant and Nation: The Making of Post-Colonial Mexico and Peru* (Berkeley, CA, 1995), 32-43. In her explanation of the rivalry between Méndez and Alatriste, Mallon makes much of the differences between their social bases and in their racial attitudes. Méndez favored a more "communitarian" Liberalism while Alatriste was disposed to a more "elitist" variant of the doctrine. However, I see political rivalry between leaders, local political antagonisms, and political contingency as the prime factors that explain the divisions within Puebla's Liberal Party.

Chapter 5, From Reform to Patriotic Resistance, 73–88

1. AMZ, "Comunicaciones de la Comandancia," No. 75, 2 January 1861, Méndez, Tetela, to Comandancia Militar; Antonio Carrión, *Historia de la Ciudad de Puebla* (Puebla, 1970), 2:404-5.

2. Jesús Ferrer Gamboa, *Los tres Juanes de la Sierra de Puebla* (Mexico, 1967), 66.

3. Urrutía grew rich during the Reform Wars from dealing in contraband, when he established close links with Alatriste's peripatetic government. He left Papantla to reside in Zacapoaxtla in September 1857; *Periódico Oficial* 2:91, 21 November 1871.

4. AMZ, "Espediente promovido por el C. Jefe Político de Tetela de Ocampo en lo que pide que conforme a las reformas constitucionales se agreguen a aquel Distrito los pueblos que forman la municipalidad de Xochiapulco con escepción del barrio de las Lomas"; AMTdeO, Gobierno, Box 14, "Correspondencia de varios authoridades . . . Xochiapulco," 13 November 1871, Lucas and Dinorin, Xochiapulco, to Jefe Político, Tetela.

5. APJFL, 2 March 1861, Urrutia, Zacapoaxtla, to Lucas, Xochiapulco.

6. Accounts of Xochiapulco's military expenditures sent by Lucas to Urrutia between August and December 1861 show a steady reduction: 368.5 pesos in August, 190 pesos in October, 100 pesos in December; AMZ, (1861) "Correspondencia del jefe político," Exp. 50.

7. Alatriste's departure left the capital vulnerable to the enemy, who briefly occupied Puebla on the night of 1 September 1861; see Hugo Leicht, *Las Calles de Puebla* (Puebla, 1967), 7.

8. By the 1880s most *cabeceras* and many *pueblos sujetos* possessed a *cuerpo filarmónico*; see Guy P. C. Thomson, "The Ceremonial and Political Role of Village Bands, 1846-1974," in *Rituals of Rule, Rituals of Resistance: Public Celebrations and Popular Culture in Mexico*, ed. William H. Beezley (Wilmington, DE, 1994), 307-42.

9. Ramón Sánchez Flores, *Zacapoaxtla: Relación histórica* (Puebla, 1984), 151.

10. Gamboa, *Los tres Juanes*, 65.

11. Carrión, *Historia*, 2:407-9; Miguel Angel Granados Chapa, *Alfonso Cravioto: Un liberal Hidalguense* (Mexico, 1984), 9-14.

12. Lauro Luna, *Batallón de la Guardia Nacional de Tetela de Ocampo, 1862-1867 (Memorias)* (Puebla, 1995), 6.

13. Carrión, *Historia*, 2:410; ADN, Histórico, XI/481 3/8396, f. 50, 12 November 1861, Francisco Ibarra, Puebla, to Minister of War, Mexico; Leicht, *Las Calles*, 7.

14. On 26 December 1861, 20 January, 26 March, 1 May, and 12 June 1862 the state government sent circulars to Urrutia urging greater effort in raising men for the district's *contingente de sangre*. See AMZ, (1862) "Correspondencia distintas autoridades," No. 26; AMZ, (1862) "Correspondencia del jefe político y comandante militar," January-December

1862; AMZ, (1862) "Borrador de oficios de la gefatura política del Distrito de Zacapoastla."

15. Guy P. C. Thomson, "Los indios y el servicio militar en el México decimonónico: ¿Leva o ciudadanía?," in *Indio, nación y comunidad en el México del siglo XIX*, ed. Antonio Escobar (Mexico, 1993), 207-52.

16. Sánchez Flores, *Zacapoaxtla*, 167-68.

17. APJFL, 15 April 1862, Urrutia, Zacapoaxtla, to Lucas, Xochiapulco; AMZ, (1861) "Correspondencia del jefatura politica," No. 75, 2 January 1861, Méndez, Tetela, to Jefe Político; Sánchez Flores, *Zacapoaxtla*, 194.

18. APJFL, 16 April 1862, Lucas, Xochiapulco, to Urrutia.

19. AMZ, (1862) "Correspondencia de la jefatura política," 12 April 1862, Naranja, Xochiapulco, to Urrutia; AMZ, (1862) "Noticia que la gefatura política de Zacapoastla produce al Superior Gobierno del Estado, de los ausilios que este Distrito ha proporcionado para la campaña contra los extrangeros y traidores con espresión del dinero que se ha colectado, número de caballos, totopo, Guardias Nacionales y reemplazos para el Ejército, por el contingente que se le asignó."

20. The Liberal army lost over two hundred dead and wounded and three hundred imprisoned at the battle of Atlixco; ADN, Histórico, XI/481 3/8704, ff. 32-6, 11 April 1862, Mendoza, Puebla, to Minister of War.

21. AMZ, (1862) "Noticia que la gefatura política de Zacapoastla produce . . . de los ausilios que este Distrito ha proporcionado para la campaña contra los extrangeros y traidores."

22. Luna, *Batallón*, 6-7.

23. Donna Rivera Moreno, *Xochiapulco: Una gloria olvidada* (Puebla, 1991), 86.

24. In spite of his rivalry with Méndez, José María Maldonado gives the Sixth Battalion almost all of the credit for the Mexican victory; Sánchez Flores, *Zacapoaxtla*, 152.

25. Ibid., 139-49.

26. ADN, Histórico, XI/481 3/8853, 127. The unit on 5 May included: Commanders Méndez, Rivera, Contreras, Luna, and Esperón; Captains Rivera, Urias, Arroyo, Valencia, Lucas, and Bonilla; Lieutenants Ramón Gómez, Miguel Luna, Tomás Segura, Tiburcio Fernández, and Valeriano Cabrera; Sub-lieutenants José María Sosa, Vicente Bonilla, Vicente Anselmo Bonilla, Miguel Mancilla, and Miguel Hernández. There were also 126 NCOs, soldiers, and bandsmen (of whom 41 are presumed to have been Indian since they were listed without surnames).

27. Ignacio Zaragoza, *Cartas al General Ignacio Mejía* (Mexico, 1962), 172-73, 175.

28. AMZ, (1862) "Correspondencia del jefe político," 6 July 1862, Ochoa to Urrutia.

29. AMZ, (1862) "Correspondencia del jefe político," 3 March, 5 April, 30 June 1862, Santín to Urrutia.

30. The arms included 31 percussion rifles, 18 flintlocks, and a large amount of ammunition; see AMZ, (1862) "Correspondencia del jefe político," 11 July 1862, Santín to Urrutia.

31. AMZ, (1862) "Borrador de oficios de la jefatura política," 11 July 1862, Urrutia to Secretario de Gobierno, Puebla; Sánchez Flores, *Zacapoaxtla*, 153; Carrión, *Historia*, 2:459.

32. AMZ, (1862) "Correspondencia del jefe político," 12 July 1862, Urrutia to "Todos los alcaldes de los barrios y jueces."

33. Carrión claims, mistakenly, that Urrutia returned to Puebla. Maldonado, upon whose memoir Carrión based his account of Sierra politics during the Intervention, states that it was Santín who returned to give his version of events to Governor Mejía; see Carrión, *Historia*, 2:459; Sánchez Flores, *Zacapoaxtla*, 154.

34. AMZ, (1862) "Correspondencia del jefe político," 11 July 1862, Zamítez, Tetela, to Urrutia.

35. Sánchez Flores, *Zacapoaxtla*, 159.

36. AMZ, (1862) "Correspondencia del jefe político," 17 July 1862, Relvas, Zacapoaxtla, to Urrutia; 17 July 1862, Zamítez, Tetela, to Urrutia; AMZ, (1862) "Borrador de oficios de la jefatura política," No. 878, 18 July 1862, Urrutia to Lucas; APJFL, 18 July 1862, Santín, Puebla, to Lucas, Xochiapulco.

37. On 5 August 1862 exaggerated reports of the landing of 200,000 French troops at Veracruz and the approach of 12,000 Conservative troops under Leonardo Márquez reached Jesús Bazán, the military commander of the remote municipal cabecera of Cuetzalan; see AMZ, "Correspondencia del jefe político," 5 August 1862, Bazán, Cuetzalan, to Jefe Político.

38. AMZ, "Borrador de oficios de la jefatura política," No. 948, 29 July 1862, Urrutia to Captains of the National Guard of Xochiapulco, Cuetzalan, Xochitlán, and Nauzontla.

39. This report was a deliberate deception on Urrutia's part. Although in early July, Lucas had returned forty of the fifty rifles requested by Urrutia, by as late as 17 August he had still failed to send the sixty men Urrutia had requested; AMZ, "Borrador de oficios de la jefatura política," No. 1069, 17 August 1862, Jefe Político to Márquez Galindo; 11 August 1862, Manuel Jaimes, Xocoyolo, to Jefe Político; 8 August 1860, Jefe Político to Captain of First Company of Sixth Battalion; 11 August 1862, Jefe Político to Presidente del Ayuntamiento, Zacapoaxtla.

40. AMZ, "Correspondencia del jefe político," 31 July 1862, Bonilla, Nauzontla, to Jefe Político; 30 July 1862, Castañeda, Xochitlán, to Jefe Político; 31 July 1862, Pérez, Cuetzalan, to Jefe Político.

41. AMZ, "Borrador de oficios de la jefatura política," 11 August 1862, Jefe Político to Officers of the National Guard.

42. AMZ, "Borrador de oficios de la jefatura política," 20 August 1862, Jefe Político to Márquez Galindo; 30 August 1862, Jefe Político to Alcalde de Cuetzalan; 30 August 1862, Jefe Político to Jefe Político, Zacatlán.

43. AMZ, "Borrador de oficios de la jefatura política," 17 August 1862, Jefe Político to Márquez Galindo.

44. This was the number of National Guards that Urrutia had allowed Lucas to keep at arms when he had demobilized the Cuatecomacos in March 1861. Lucas thus paid respect to the legalities of Xochiapulco's relationship with its cabecera while ensuring that the new circumstances of the patriotic struggle did not contribute to any significant shift of power back to Zacapoaxtla; see APJFL, 2 March 1861, Jefe Político to Lucas, Xochiapulco; AMZ, "Correspondencia de la jefatura politica," 19 August 1862, Lucas, Xochiapulco, to Jefe Político.

45. Sánchez Flores, *Zacapoaxtla*, 161-62.

46. ADN, Cancelados, LIVa221-42 (Cenobio Cantero, Capitán de Infantería).

47. Sánchez Flores, *Zacapoaxtla*, 161.

48. Luna, *Batallón*, 7.

49. Márquez Galindo had used the same method to recruit in the *tierra caliente* of Teziutlán and Tetela in 1860. He offered arms to Indians in Tenampulco and El Chacal and urged them to invade the land of Rafael Avila, cacique and jefe político of Teziutlán; see ADN, Cancelados, 67/111/2/442, f. 13, 24 March 1860, Alatriste, Tlaxcala, to Minister of War, Veracruz; ff. 14-19, 12, 15, 18 and 21 March 1860, Rafael Avila, Teziutlán, to Cástulo Alatriste.

50. AMZ, "Borrador de oficios de la jefatura política," 20 August 1862, Jefe Político to Márquez Galindo.

51. Carríon, *Historia*, 2:460.

52. For Maldonado's record of service, see ADN, Cancelados, 100, 111-3-1021.

53. Sánchez Flores, *Zacapoaxtla*, 170.

54. Ibid., 462-63.

55. Ibid., 166-67, 173.

56. UTA/LAC, Ms. G504.

57. APJFL, 2 October 1862, State Government to Lucas.

58. Sánchez Flores, *Zacapoaxtla*, 169.

59. APJFL, 5 October 1862, Miguel Perdomo, Jalacingo, to Lucas; Sánchez Flores, *Zacapoaxtla*, 176.

60. AMZ, "Correspondencia de la jefatura política," 12 November 1862, to Military Governor, Puebla.

61. Sánchez Flores, *Zacapoaxtla*, 176-77.

62. ADN, Histórico, XI/481 3/8759, f. 9, 20 December 1862, General González Ortega, Puebla, to Minister of War.

63. ADN, Histórico, XI/481 3/8759, f. 11, 29 December 1862, Angel Parrodi, Mexico, to Minister of War.

64. ADN, Histórico, XI/481 3/8758, f. 27, 24 December 1862, González Ortega, Puebla, to Minister of War; Carríon, *Historia*, 2:464.

65. Sánchez Flores, *Zacapoaxtla*, 178-79.

66. Luna, *Batallón*, 9; AMZ, "Correspondencia de la jefatura política," 27 December 1862, Zamítez, Tetela, to Maldonado; AMZ, "Borrador de oficios," 29 January 1863, Maldonado, Zacapoaxtla, to State Governor.

67. AMZ, (1863) "Borrador de oficios del jefe político."

68. UTA/LAC, Ms. G504.

69. On his arrival in Zacapoaxtla, Osorio was shocked to find French money in licit circulation, observing how, quite openly, "many bad Mexicans are trafficking with the enemy"; AMZ, "Correspondencia de la jefatura política," 1 January 1863, Antonio Osorio, Zacapoaxtla, to Maldonado; UTA/LAC, Ms. G504.

70. AMZ, "Borrador de oficios de la jefatura política," 12 January 1863, Maldonado to Lucas.

71. APJFL, 13 January 1863, Lucas, Xochiapulco, to Rivera, Libres.

72. ADN, Histórico, XI/481 3/9043, ff. 36-37, 17 January 1863, Julio González, Teziutlán, to González Ortega, Puebla, and Eduardo Santín, Zacapoaxtla, to González Ortega.

73. AMZ, "Borrador de oficios de la jefatura política," 18 January 1863, Maldonado, Zacapoaxtla, to Antonio Osorio, Zacapoaxtla.

74. Ibid., 25 January 1863, Jefe Político, Zacapoaxtla, to General en Jefe del Ejército del Oriente.

75. Carrión, *Historia*, 2:465.

76. AMZ, "Borrador de oficios de la jefatura política," 10 and 12 February 1863, Maldonado to Comandante de Tlatlauqui; 12 February 1863, Maldonado to Juez Suplente de Ehuiloco.

77. Jack Autrey Dabbs, *The French Army in Mexico: A Study in Military Government* (The Hague, 1963), 42-49.

78. Ibid., 59.

79. Carrión, *Historia*, 2:498.

Chapter 6, The Battle for the Sierra, 89–111

1. Antonio Carrión, *Historia de la Ciudad de Puebla* (Puebla, 1970), 2:492; Lauro Luna, *Batallón de la Guardia Nacional de Tetela de Ocampo, 1862-1867 (Memorias)* (Puebla, 1995), 10.

2. ADN, Histórico, XI/481 3/9058, f. 71, 29 June 1865, Minister of War to Negrete.

3. ADN, Histórico, XI/481 3/9058, f. 71, 10 June 1865, Negrete, Huauchinango, to "los habitantes de los estados de Puebla y Tlaxcala."

4. APJFL, Certificate of promotion, 10 June 1863, Negrete, Huauchinango, to Lucas.

5. The pro-Intervention enthusiasm of Tlatlauqueños at this time is illustrated in Nochebuena's service record, ADN, Cancelados, 111-8/18278, f. 1.

6. Carrión, *Historia*, 2:465.

7. APJFL, Certificate of promotion, 30 July 1863, Negrete to Lucas.

8. Carrión, *Historia*, 2:495-96.

9. APJFL, 17 August 1865, Quevedo, Teziutlán, to Lucas.

10. Luna, *Batallón*, 10.

11. Carrión, *Historia*, 2:496-97.

12. Bernardo García Martínez, *Los pueblos de la Sierra* (Mexico, 1987), 160-62.

13. Luna, *Batallón*, 14.

14. Aymard drew support from General Canorgue, the French commander in Tlaxcala, and the Mexican "traitor," General Liceaga, active on the Llanos de Apam; see AMTdeO, Gobierno, Box 8, Exp. 9, 28 August 1865, Negrete, Huauchinango, to Francisco Zamítez.

15. Carrión, *Historia*, 2:498-99.

16. Ibid., 2:500; UTA/LAC Ms. G504.

17. Carrión, *Historia*, 2:502.

18. Ibid., 2:504-5.

19. Ibid., 2:506.

20. García Martínez, *Los pueblos de la Sierra*, 45-54.

21. Carrión, *Historia*, 2:506-7; ADN, Histórico, XI/481 3/9052, f. 14, 5 October 1865, Maldonado, Huahuaxtla, to Cravioto.

22. Ibid., f. 1, 4 October 1865, Lucas, Huahuaxtla, to Cravioto.

23. Lucas requested two hundred infantry from Cravioto, who was unable to oblige due to more pressing military needs closer to home (the recapture of Zacatlán from the French); ADN, Histórico, XI/481 3/9032, f. 11, 9 October 1865, Cravioto, Huauchinango, to Minister of War.

24. Guy P. C. Thomson, "Bulwarks of Patriotic Liberalism: The National Guard, Philharmonic Corps, and Patriotic Juntas in Mexico, 1847-88," *JLAS* 22 (1990): 40-44.

25. ADN, Histórico, XI/481 3/9109, ff. 261-62, 30 October 1865, Pavón, Tulancingo, to Minister of War.

26. ADN, Histórico, XI/481 3/9109, f. 306, 20 November 1865, Pavón, Tulancingo, to Minister of War.

27. Carrión, *Historia*, 2:509-10; AGN, Leyva, 45, 19 October 1863, Ayala, Tlatlauqui, to Maldonado, Zacapoaxtla.

28. AGN, Leyva, 45, 20 October 1863, Lucas, Cuetzalan, to Maldonado.

29. Carrión, *Historia*, 2:511-12, 514.

30. Ibid., 2:515-16.

31. Miguel Galindo y Galindo, *La gran década nacional, 1857-1867* (Mexico, 1904), 2:79; Carrión, *Historia*, 2:519-21, 524, 538-41.

32. Carrión, *Historia*, 2:516, 520-21.

33. Ibid., 2:520-23.

34. *El Eco Patriótico* (Teziutlán), No. 11, 24 July 1864, 2-3 (Located in ADN, Histórico, XI/481 3/9587, folder of Sierra republican newspapers).

35. John Tutino observed this pattern in Chalco; *From Insurrection to Revolution in Mexico* (Princeton, NJ, 1986), 143-48.

36. *El Eco Patriótico*, No. 11, 24 July 1864.

37. ADN, Histórico, XI/481 3/9583, 218, 4 June 1864, Lastiri, Chigna-huapan, to Pérez, Tulancingo; Galindo y Galindo, *La gran década*, 2:85-92.

38. ADN, Histórico, XI/481 3/9519, ff. 15, 55, 15 August 1864, Arroyo, Chignahuapan, to Pavón, Tulancingo, and 9 October 1864, Pavón, Tulancingo, to Minister of War.

39. Carrión, *Historia*, 2:538.

40. ADN, Histórico, XI/481 3/10043, f. 45, 4 December 1864, Pavón, Tulancingo, to Minister of War.

41. Galindo y Galindo, *La gran década*, 2:109-15; ADN, Histórico, XI/481 3/9583, f. 221, 15 December 1864, Pavón, Tulancingo, to Minister of War.

42. Carrión, *Historia*, 2:538.

43. ADN, Histórico, XI/481 3/10044, f. 149, 7 February 1865, Carrillo, Teziutlán, to Juan Calderón, Jalapa; ADN, Histórico, XI/481 3/10043, 14 February 1865, Pavón, Tulancingo, to Minister of War; Ernst Pitner, *Maximilian's Lieutenant: A Personal History of the Mexican Campaign, 1864-67* (Albuquerque, NM, 1993), 49.

44. Carrión, *Historia*, 2:538-40; Galindo y Galindo, *La gran década*, 2:162-64.

45. ADN, Histórico, XI/481 3/10042, f. 35, 13 February 1865, Ormachea, Tlaxcala, to Minister of War; ADN, Histórico, XI/481 10044, ff. 86-88, 20 January 1865, Aguilar, Chignahuapan, to Pavón, Tulancingo.

46. Luna, *Batallón*, 12-15.

47. ADN, Histórico, XI/481 3/10043, f. 57, 24 February 1865, Ormachea, Tlaxcala, to Minister of War; Galindo y Galindo, *La gran década*, 3:161-73; Carrión, *Historia*, 2:541-42.

48. Carrión, *Historia*, 2:540-41.

49. APJFL, 14 February 1865, Ortega, Zacapoaxtla, to Lucas. On 12 February 1865, Ortega appointed Lucas commander of the district of Zacapoaxtla, with extraordinary powers over all branches of the administration; see APJFL, 12 February 1865, Ortega, Ciudad del 25 de Abril (Zacapoaxtla), to Lucas.

50. Carrión, *Historia*, 2:541.

51. Ibid., 2:543; ADN, Cancelados, 100 111-3-1021, f. 44, 7 March 1865, Lucas, Xochiapulco, to Minister of War.

52. Carrión, *Historia*, 2:542.

53. ADN, Histórico, XI/481 3/10047, f. 170, 9 March 1865, José María Esteva, Puebla, to Minister of War; ADN, Cancelados, Leg. 22, XI/111 3-248, f. 14, 31 July 1882, Lucas, Tetela de Ocampo, to Minister of War.

54. Galindo y Galindo, *La gran década*, 3:174; Carrión, *Historia*, 2:542-43.

55. Galindo y Galindo, *La gran década*, 3:174-75.

56. ADN, Histórico, XI/481 3/10046, ff. 205-06, 16 and 17 March 1865, Actas de Adhesión de Ahuastepec y Naupan.

57. Letter of 13 April 1865 from Thun to Lucas in Galindo y Galindo, *La gran década*, 3:234-35.

58. Letter of 15 April 1865 from Lucas to Thun in Galindo y Galindo, *La gran década*, 3:236-37.

59. AGN, Gobernación, Sec. 1a 860, 61, 62, 63, 64, 65 (1) (11), 29 March 1865, Esteva, Puebla, to Minister of Interior.

60. AGN, Gobernación, Sec. 1a 860, 61, 62, 63, 64, 65 (1) (11), 5 April 1865, Castillo Urizar, Zacapoaxtla, to Minister of Interior.

61. For the "continual attacks" by Agustín Roldán and the Arriaga brothers (Francisco Javier, Miguel, and Mariano) on Xochiapulco throughout 1864, see Luna, *Batallón*, 14; ADN, Histórico, XI/481 3/10005, ff. 596-97, 12 April 1865, Minister of Interior to Minister of War.

62. ADN, Histórico, XI/481 3/10005, f. 565, 20 April 1865, Polack, Puebla, to Minister of War.

63. ADN, Histórico, XI/481 3/10110, f. 17, 6 April 1865, Thun, Puebla, to Minister of War.

64. ADN, Histórico, XI/481 3/10005, f. 632, 25 April 1865, Minister of Interior to Minister of War.

65. ADN, Histórico, XI/481 3/10005, f. 633, 17 April 1865, Lucas, Huahuaxtla, to Military Commander of Cuetzalan.

66. ADN, Histórico, XI/481 3/10009, ff. 131-41.

67. APJFL, Act of 6 June 1865, Fernando María Ortega et al., Xochitlán, to "los habitantes del distrito"; Galindo y Galindo, *La gran década*, 3:237-42.

68. Letter of 13 July 1865 from Lucas, Cuartel General in Xochiapulco, to "los habitantes del Distrito de Zacapoastla," in Galindo y Galindo, *La gran década,* 3:248-49.

69. Luna, *Batallón*, 18-20.

70. Galindo y Galindo, *La gran década*, 3:247-75.

71. ADN, Histórico, XI/481 3/10084, f. 70, 28 July 1865, Prefect, Libres, to A. Ricoy, Tulancingo.

72. ADN, Cancelados, C-64 S/111/2/425, Leg. 1, 23 December 1887, Lucas, Tetela, to Minister of War.

73. Galindo y Galindo, *La gran década*, 3:276.

74. ADN, Histórico, XI/481 3/9999, f. 206, 16 August 1865, "Sobre indemnización a los vecinos de Zacapoastla por haber sido arrasadas algunas siembras."

75. Carrión, *Historia*, 2:548.

76. Galindo y Galindo, *La gran década,* 3:323-24.

77. Ibid., 3:325; ADN, Histórico, XI/481 3/10115, f. 1, 17 September 1865, Sub-Prefect of San Juan de los Llanos to Minister of War.

78. ADN, Histórico, XI/481 3/9968, f. 101, 11 October 1865, Carillo, Chilchotla, to Thun, Puebla.

79. For a detailed account of this meeting, see Luna, *Batallón*, 33-34.

80. Galindo y Galindo, *La gran década*, 3:325-26.

81. Luna, *Batallón*, 35-36.

82. Galindo y Galindo, *La gran década*, 3:328-29; ADN, Histórico, XI/481 3/10066, f. 20, 3 November 1865, Ormachea, Tlaxcala, to Minister of War.

83. ADN, Histórico, XI/481 3/10086, 17 November 1865, Ormachea, Tlaxcala, to Minister of War.

84. Galindo y Galindo, *La gran década*, 3:330-32.

85. The Austrians lost twenty-six dead (including two officers) and had fifty soldiers wounded. The Republicans lost twenty-eight dead and had more than eighty wounded with all but two hundred (a company from Maloapa) of their force dispersed. ADN, Histórico, XI/481 3/10086, f. 185, 29 November 1865, Thun, Puebla, to Minister of War.

86. Galindo y Galindo, *La gran década*, 3:334.

87. Ibid., 3:379; Ignacio Alatorre blamed Méndez and the "imperfect organization of his National Guards"; see ADN, Histórico, XI/481 3/10143, f. 2, 17 January 1866, Alatorre, Misantla, to Minister of War.

88. Ibid., f. 1, 14 January 1866, Schonowsky, Papantla, to Minister of War.

89. AMTdeO, (1866) "Borrador de oficios del jefe político."

90. AGN, Tranquilidad Pública, 3a. 866 (1) (1), Exps. 4, 5, 7, 8.

91. By early March, Lucas had drawn up a meticulously calculated account of these credits; see APJFL, "Distribución que el que suscribe ha dado a ocho mil pesos que, para cubrir los créditos que bajo su responsibilidad personal contrajo para el sostenimiento de las fuerzas republicanas de su mando, le fueron entregados por el gobierno imperial al someterse dichas fuerzas." The terms of the capitulation are reproduced in Octavio Manzano Díaz, *El indígena de la Sierra Norte de Puebla y sus luchas por la libertad* (Mexico, 1987), 30-31.

92. AGN, Tranquilidad Pública, 3a 866 (1) (I) Exp. 8, 21 February 1866, Galicia y Arostegui, Zacapoaxtla, to Esteva, Puebla.

93. AMTdeO, "Borrador de oficios del sub-prefecto," 27 July 1866, Sub-Prefect, Tetela, to Thun, Puebla.

Chapter 7, The Defeat of the Empire, 113–25

1. Egon Caesar Count Corti, *Maximilian and Charlotte in Mexico* (1928; reprint, New York, 1968), 613-17.

2. Ibid., 627; for Austrian demoralization, see Ernst Pitner, *Maximilian's Lieutenant: A Personal History of the Mexican Campaign, 1864-67* (Albuquerque, NM, 1993), 99-169.

3. Corti, *Maximilian and Charlotte*, 656. Colonel Kodolitch replaced Thun in command of Austrian forces in October; see Jack Autrey Dabbs, *The French Army in Mexico: A Study in Military Government* (The Hague, 1963), 189.

4. Miguel Angel Granados Chapa, *Alfonso Cravioto: Un liberal Hidalguense* (Mexico, 1984), 15-16; Ramón Sánchez Flores, *Zacapoaxtla: Relación histórica* (Puebla, 1984), 215-16.

5. AGN, Segundo Imperio, 16, 1866, 2 July 1866, Vicente Ricoy to "Señores Editores de *La Sociedad*."

6. AGN, Gobernación, 3a. 866 (4) (1) 1866, Exp. 272, 17 August 1866, A. M. León to Minister of Interior.

7. ADN, Cancelados, C-64 D/111/2/425, f. 4; Miguel Galindo y Galindo, *La gran década nacional, 1857-1867* (Mexico, 1904), 3:427.

8. AMTdeO, 1866 Box, 21 August 1866, Lucas, Teziutlán, to "Soldados Libres de la Sección Pérez, Soldados Libres de la Sección Montoya, Soldados Libres de la Brigada de Zacapoastla."

9. Ibid., "¡Viva la República Libre! Acta levantada el dia 12 Agosto del año del mil ochocientos sesenta y seis."

10. Galindo y Galindo, *La gran década*, 3:423; Lauro Luna, *Batallón de la Guardia Nacional de Tetela de Ocampo* (Puebla, 1995), 25-26; AMTdeO, 1866 Box, 10 August 1866, Nicolás Damian, Rafael Santos, Juan de los Santos, and 26 other signatures (mostly without surnames), Huitzilan; Act of Tuzamapa, 19 August 1866; Act of Jonotla, 24 August 1866; Act of Zapotitlán, 3 September 1866.

11. AMTdeO, 1866 Box, 24 August 1866, Lucas, Zacapoaxtla, to Posadas, Tetela.

12. Ibid., 26 August 1866, Díaz, Tehuizingo (Acatlán), to Méndez.

13. AGN, Gobernación, 3a. 866 (4) (1) 1866 Exp. 272, 17 August 1866, A. M. León to Minister of Interior.

14. Ibid., 5 September 1866, Méndez, Zacapoaxtla, to Posadas, Tetela; Luna, *Batallón*, 43.

15. Galindo y Galindo, *La gran década*, 3:440-44; Laurens Ballard Perry, *Juárez and Díaz Machine Politics in Mexico* (DeKalb, IL, 1978), 55; Florencia Mallon, *Peasant and Nation: The Making of Post-Colonial Mexico and Peru* (Berkeley, CA, 1995), 107.

16. AMTdeO, 1866 Box, Decrees of Governor Rafael García, 7 September 1866-21 December 1866. For the affairs of García's first governorship, see the official state newspaper, *La Idea Liberal* (Zacapoaxtla), September-December 1866, full run in AMZ.

17. Ibid., 9 September 1866, Márquez, Zacatlán, to Posadas, Tetela.

18. APJFL, 16 September 1866, Méndez, Zacapoaxtla, to Lucas, Xochiapulco.

19. AMTdeO, 1866 Box, 18 September 1866, Márquez Galindo, Otlatlán, to Lucas, Xochiapulco; ibid., 22 September 1866, Macario González, Zacatlán, to Jesús Gutiérrez, Zacapoaxtla.

20. Ibid., 19 and 19 September 1866, José María Bonilla to Lucas; 19 September 1866, Méndez to Pilar Rivera; 22 September 1866, Rafael Herrera, Ixtacamaxtitlán, to Lucas. For the full "actas de desconocimiento," see *La Idea Liberal* 2-3, 13 and 20 October 1866.

21. AMTdeO, 1866 Box, 29 September 1866, Jefe Político, Huauchinango, to Jesús Gutiérrez.

22. *La Idea Liberal* 2, 13 October 1866.

23. AMTdeO, 1866 Box, 28 September 1866, Méndez, Libres, to Jefe Político, Tetela; 28 September 1866, Méndez, Libres, to Rafael García, Zacapoaxtla. Dupin was far too occupied in covering the retreat and evacuation of the French Army from Veracruz to be able to risk confronting Republican forces in northern Puebla; see *La Idea Liberal* 4, 24 October 1866.

24. BN-ABJ, 11-1562, f. 3, October 1866, García, Zacapoaxtla, to Juárez, Saltillo.

25. AMTdeO, 1866 Box, 18 September 1866, Vicente Bonilla, Tlatlauqui, to Lucas, Xochiapulco; AMTdeO, Box 9, Exp. 6, "1867 Borrador de Oficios"; AMTdeO, 1866 Box, 7 October 1866, Joaquín Caesarin, circular to districts of Zacapoaxtla, Tetela, Tlatlauqui, and Teziutlán.

26. AMTdeO, 1866 Box, 5 October 1866, Pilar Rivera to Jefe Político, Tetela.

27. Ibid., 15 October 1866, Méndez, Libres, to Lucas, Xochiapulco.

28. Ibid., 15 October 1866, Bonilla, Libres, to Lucas, Xochiapulco.

29. Ibid., 16 October 1866, Cravioto, Huauchinango, to Márquez Galindo, Zacatlán.

30. Dabbs, *The French Army,* 175-76; ADN, Cancelados, 26-D/111/31307, f. 107.

31. *La Idea Liberal* 2-11, October-November 1866.

32. Sánchez Flores, *Zacapoaxtla,* 216-17.

33. *La Idea Liberal* 12, 21 November 1866.

34. Troops from the Sierra were acknowledged by Alatorre to have fought with particular bravery, receiving much of the credit for victory; see *La Idea Liberal* 10, 14 November 1866.

35. The Sierra infantry received special mention; see *La Idea Liberal* 9, 19 November 1866.

36. AMTdeO, 1866 Box, 6 December 1866, Méndez, Huamantla, to Bonilla, Zacapoaxtla.

37. Ibid., 5 December 1866, Méndez, Huamantla, to Bonilla, Zacapoaxtla.

38. Ibid., 8, 11, and 14 December 1866, Méndez, Huamantla, to Jefe Político, Tetela.

39. *La Idea Liberal* 5, 27 October 1866; Sánchez Flores, *Zacapoaxtla,* 217.

40. ADN, Cancelados, C-64 D/111/2/425, ff. 1-4; AMTdeO, "Borrador de oficios de la jefatura política 1866," Communications of 22 October, 22 November, and 10-13 December 1866.

41. AMTdeO, 1866 Box, 5 December 1866, Méndez, Huamantla, to Bonilla, Zacapoaxtla.

42. AGN, Gobernación, 3a. 866 (4) (1), Exp. 272, 21 December 1866.

43. See Chapter 13, this volume.

44. AMTdeO, Box 1866, 17 and 31 December 1866, Pilar Rivera, Tlaxco, to Jefe Político, Tetela.

45. APJFL, 11 January 1867, Segura, Ometepec, to Lucas.

46. Ibid., 16 January 1867, Segura, Ometepec, to Lucas.

47. Ibid., 17 January 1867, Segura, Ometepec, to Lucas.

48. Ibid., 20 January 1867, Luis Ramón Sánchez, Ometepec, to Lucas, and 20 January 1867, José Eleuterio and José Dionisio, Ometepec, to Lucas, Xochiapulco.

49. Visiting Bonilla at Libres, Méndez approved this arrangement; see ibid., 18 January 1867, Bonilla, Libres, to Lucas, Xochiapulco, and 25 January 1867, Méndez, Libres, to Lucas, Xochiapulco.

50. AMTdeO, Box 9, Exp. 10, 5 May 1867, Luis Antonio Díaz, Puebla, to Alcalde de Ometepec.

51. AMTdeO, "Cabildo 1867-71," Sessions of 22 January and 9 March 1867.

52. APJFL, 28 December 1866 and 23 January 1867, Martínez, Tlatlauqui, to Lucas, Xochiapulco.

53. Corti, *Maximilian and Charlotte*, 772-73.

54. Díaz had confirmed Méndez in the command of the Second Division of the Army of the East (made up of three Brigades under Márquez Galindo, Lucas, and Cravioto) on 27 February 1867; see AMTdeO, Box 9, Exp. 10, 27 February 1867, Bonilla, Libres.

55. Ibid., 28 February 1867, Méndez, Huamantla, to Rivera, Tetela.

56. In February 1867, Guerrero was temporarily detained in Tenango (Zacatlán) on the charge of the rape of Nicolasa Flores; AMTdeO, Box 9, Exp. 6, 19 and 28 February, 26 March 1867, Pilar Rivera, Tetela, to Gefe de la Guardia de Tenampulco.

57. Corti, *Maximilian and Charlotte*, 776.

58. Luna, *Batallón*, 43-46.

59. APJFL, 25 April 1867, Díaz, Guadalupe Hidalgo, to Lucas.

60. Perry, *Juárez and Díaz*, 55.

61. AMTdeO, 1867, Exp. 55, "Relación de los C. C. muertos y heridos."

62. Guy P. C. Thomson, "La Contra-Reforma en Puebla, 1854-1886," in *El conservadurismo mexicano del siglo XIX*, ed. Will Fowler and Humberto Morales (Puebla, 1998), forthcoming.

Chapter 8, The First Montaña Rebellion, 127–45

1. José Fuentes Mares, "La Convocatoria de 1867," *HM* 14 (1964): 423-44; Laurens Ballard Perry, *Juárez and Díaz Machine Politics in Mexico* (DeKalb, IL, 1978), 38-43; Walter V. Scholes, *Mexican Politics During the Juárez Regime, 1855-1872* (Columbia, 1957), 118-23; Daniel Cosío Villegas, *Historia Moderna de México. La República Restaurada. La Vida Política* (Mexico, 1955), 168-72.

2. Perry, *Juárez and Díaz*, 41.

3. Cosío Villegas, *República Restaurada*, 168.

4. Jorge L. Tamayo, *Benito Juárez: Documentos, discursos y correspondencia* (Mexico, 1964-72), 12: 451-52, 17 September 1867, García, Puebla, to Juárez.

5. ADN, Cancelados, XI/111/1-31, I, ff. 20, 218-19, 23 September and 14 October 1867, Méndez, Puebla and Huamantla, to Mejía; BN-ABJ, 18-2964, 30 September 1867, García, Puebla, to Juárez.

6. BN-ABJ, 21-2503, 25 September 1867, José de Jesús Islas, Tepeji de Rodríguez, to Méndez; Perry, *Juárez and Díaz*, 75.

7. Méndez's National Guard maneuvers, designed to instill alarm in the state capital, are described in his correspondence with Díaz; see Albert María Carreño, *Archivo del General Porfirio Díaz: Memorias y documentos* (Mexico, 1947-61), 5:83, 26 September 1867.

8. On 23 August 1867, Méndez had requested freedom from the customs duty on twenty-five hundred rifles brought from New York, by José Ferrer, merchant of Teziutlán, and paid for from the state's *rebajados* fund; see BN-ABJ, 21-3495, 23 August 1867, Méndez to Juárez. On 26 September 1867, the day after stepping down, Méndez ordered sixteen hundred rifles to be sent from Teziutlán to Tetela, with two hundred of these to be left in Tlatlauqui and four hundred in Xochiapulco; see AMTdeO, Box 9, Exp. 10, "Borrador del jefe político," 26 September 1867.

9. Carreño, *Archivo*, 5:82-83, 26 September 1867, Méndez, Huamantla, to Díaz, Tehuacán.

10. María Dolores Posada Olayo, "La historia: La verdad como Norma," in *La Batalla del 5 de Mayo*, ed. Miguel A. Sánchez Lamego (Mexico, 1963), 171-74.

11. The Xochiapulco battalion of National Guard in April 1867 included two lieutenant colonels, one battalion commander, two adjutants, two sub-adjutants, seven captains, seven lieutenants, six first sergeants, twenty-five second sergeants, six bandsmen, fifty corporals, two hundred eighty soldiers; see APJFL, "Ejército del Oriente, Segunda División, Segunda Brigada, Segunda Batallón de Guardia Nacional de Xochiapulco," Puebla, April 1867. The presence of Xochiapulco forces at the siege of Querétaro seems likely. Bonilla wrote to Lucas on the day of the fall of Querétaro (16 May 1867) and implies the Xochiapulquense presence at the siege; see APJFL, 16 May 1867, Bonilla, "Linea avanzada al norte de México," to Lucas.

12. BN-ABJ, 15-2390, 3 October 1867, Carbajal to Juárez.

13. BN-ABJ, 8-2965, 3 October 1867, García to Juárez; 18-2987, 3 October 1867, Juárez to García; APJFL, 5 October 1867, Juárez to Lucas; BN-ABJ, 20-3375, 10 October 1867, Lucas to Juárez.

14. BN-ABJ, 18-2972, 12 October 1867, García to Juárez.

15. BN-ABJ, 18-2966, 6 October 1867, García to Juárez.

16. BN-ABJ, 20-3376, 12 October 1867, Juárez to Lucas (this letter is reproduced in Jorge Tamayo, *Epistolario de Benito Juárez* [Mexico, 1957], 416); BN-ABJ, 18-2971, 14 October 1867, García to Juárez.

17. APJFL, Juárez to Lucas, 14 October 1867; BN-ABJ, 18-2976, 14 October 1867, García to Juárez.

18. Perry, *Juárez and Díaz*, 83-84.

19. BN-ABJ, 16-2595, 28 October 1867, Cravioto to Juárez.

20. BN-ABJ, 20-3396, 26 October 1867, Maldonado to Juárez; and ADN, Cancelados, Box 100, 111-3-1021, 22; BN-ABJ, 20-3393, 3394, 5, 13, 18, and 20 October 1867, Maldonado to Juárez; Perry, *Juárez and Díaz*, 81.

21. Guy P. C. Thomson, "Montaña and Llanura in the Politics of Central Mexico: The Case of Puebla, 1820-1920," in *Region, State and Capitalism in Mexico: Nineteenth and Twentieth Centuries*, ed. Wil Pansters and Arij Ouweneel (Amsterdam, 1989), 59-78, 82.

22. BN-ABJ, 20-3377, 23 October 1867, Lucas to Juárez. For a damning description of *juarista* intimidation of Indian voters, see Carreño, *Archivo*, 5:64, Reply to letter of 1 December 1867, Méndez to Díaz.

23. By late October 1867, the Xochiapulco battalion had 600 places, 232 more than in April. Xochiapulquense officers (Luis Antonio Díaz and Pedro Real) traveled on several occasions to Mexico City to collect credits from the federal treasury; see BN-ABJ, 16-2595, 21 and 28 October 1867, Cravioto, Huauchinango, to Juárez; BN-ABJ, 20-3378, 31 October 1867, Lucas to Juárez; 14 November 1867, Juárez to Lucas.

24. BN-ABJ, 24-3969, 16 November 1867, Ruiz to Juárez; 23 November 1867, Juárez to Ruiz.

25. It seems that Méndez indeed retained his commission in the army, at least until his visit to Mexico City in December 1867, and possibly as late as January 1868; see ADN, Cancelados, XI/III/I-31, Vol. I, 22 and 23 November 1867, Palafox, Puebla, to Mejía; BN-ABJ, 23-3924, 29 November 1867, Romero Vargas to Juárez.

26. BN-ABJ, 23-3924, 29 November 1867, Romero Vargas to Juárez.

27. Even after the January 1868 elections, doubt still remained about Méndez's eligibility to stand for the governorship since his enemies claimed that he had not yet resigned his army commission. However, in early February, Juárez insisted to Lucas that the federal government "has remained neutral in the electoral campaign of Puebla, and conceded the leave from the army that Sr. Méndez requested in order that he could figure as a candidate in the elections"; see Perry, *Juárez and Díaz*, 84-88.

28. Méndez was judged to have won an outright majority after a revised calculation based upon the annulment of results from two electoral districts where irregularities had been reported.

29. The state constitution required the ratification of an election by the state congress, if no candidate possessed a clear majority; see *Boletín de las Leyes y Disposiciones del Gobierno del Estado Libre Soberano de Puebla, Año de 1867* (Puebla, 1868), 1:123.

30. Immediately after García's removal, the followers of Romero Vargas in the congress had broken with Méndez's supporters and assembled a *romerista-rafaelista* alliance to combat the Montaña; see BN-ABJ, 20-3399, 2 December 1867, Maldonado to Juárez.

31. *El Monitor Republicano*, no. 4820, 26 February 1868, reporting on the session of the Puebla state congress of 19 February 1868; Ana Maria

Huerta Jaramillo, *Insurrecciones rurales en el Estado de Puebla, 1868-1870* (Puebla, 1985), 30.

32. For a fuller discussion of the wider implications of congressional maneuvers during this electoral period, see Florencia Mallon, *Peasant and Nation: The Making of Post-Colonial Mexico and Peru* (Berkeley, CA, 1994), 104-9, 248-55.

33. *El Monitor Republicano*, nos. 4892, 4900, 11, 18 March 1868, Actas from Puebla de Zaragoza (27 February 1868), Libres (25 February 1868), Zapotitlán (27 February 1868), Huitzilan (27 February 1868), Xochiapulco (6 March 1868).

34. Huerta Jaramillo, *Insurrecciones rurales*, 32-33; Perry, *Juárez and Díaz*, 84-85.

35. ADN, Histórico, XI/481 3/9786, f. 95, Telegram of 2 January 1868, Benito Marín, Teziutlán, to Minister of War; AMZ (1868), Exp. 8, "Expediente relativo a la ley de desamortización en el pueblo de Cuetzalan incluyendo los hechos sediciosos de los indígenas por esta causa," 21 January 1868, Ignacio Arrieta, Cuetzalan, to Jefe Político, Zacapoaxtla; Guy P. C. Thomson, "Agrarian Conflict in the Municipality of Cuetzalan (Sierra de Puebla): The Rise and Fall of 'Pala' Agustín Dieguillo, 1861-1894," *HAHR* 71 (1991): 205-58.

36. Perry, *Juárez and Díaz*, 85; ADN, Histórico, XI/481 3/9892, 27 February 1868, Kampfner, Apam, to Mejía, Mexico, and 28 February 1868, García, Puebla, to Mejía, Mexico.

37. Ibid., ff. 26-27, 26 March 1868, García to Minister of War.

38. Carreño, *Archivo*, 6:154-55, 27 February 1868, Díaz to Méndez.

39. ADN, Histórico, XI/481 3/9786, f. 107, 28 February 1868, José Rojo, Tulancingo, to Minister of War; 9892, ff. 4, 11, 20, 27 February 1868, Kampfner, Apam, to Minister of War; 2 and 5 March 1868, General Toro, Huamantla and Zacatlán, to Minister of War.

40. John M. Hart, "Miguel Negrete: La epopeya de un revolucionario," *HM* 24 (1974): 79-83; BN-ABJ, 4904, 21 January 1868, Cravioto to Juárez; BN-ABJ, 4906, 3 February 1868, Cravioto to Juárez; Carreño, *Archivo*, 6:87, 5 February 1868, Díaz to Romero.

41. Perry, *Juárez and Díaz*, 85.

42. García was dumbfounded at the naiveté of the Federal commander. He pointed out that Vicente Márquez had merely withdrawn to Ahuacatlán "en las escabrosidades de la Sierra," where an arsenal had been established. Cravioto confirmed the seriousness of the Zacatlán movement, reporting that the arms buildup, the mobilization of the National Guard, and the amassing of *rebajado* revenues had commenced well before the events of 25 February; see ADN, Histórico, XI/481 3/9892, f. 23, 9 March 1868, García to Minister of War.

43. Ibid., f. 29, 26 March 1868, García to Minister of War.

44. Ibid., ff. 32-34, 29 March 1868, García to Minister of War.

45. BN-ABJ, 5298, 23 April 1868, Lucas, Xochiapulco, to García.

46. BN-ABJ, 5298, 24 April 1868, García to Juárez; BN-ABJ, 5299, 25 April 1868, García to Juárez.

47. BN-ABJ, 5304, 30 April 1868, García to Juárez.

48. Mallon, *Peasant and Nation*, 110-11.

49. BN-ABJ, 5312, 11 May 1868, Arriaga to García.

50. BN-ABJ, 5302, 28 April 1868, García to Juárez; BN-ABJ, 5306, 2 May 1868, García to Juárez; ADN, Histórico, XI/481 3/9902, f. 3, 26 April 1868, Saborido to Minister of War.

51. BN-ABJ, 5307, 3 May 1868, García to Juárez; AMTdeO, 1868 Box, "Correspondencia Diversas Autoridades," 6 May 1868, Martínez to Méndez.

52. BN-ABJ, 5113, 12 May 1868, García to Juárez; BN-ABJ, 4912, 15 May 1868, Cravioto to Juárez; BN-ABJ, 5316, 20 May 1868, Méndez to Cravioto; BN-ABJ, 5318, 22 May 1868, García to Juárez; ADN, Histórico, XI/481 3/9892, 38, 2 June 1868, García to Minister of War; Huerta Jaramillo, *Insurrecciones rurales*, 48, 67-68; ADN, Histórico, XI/481 3/9895, ff. 1-55, "Sublevación de Chiautla."

53. ADN, Histórico, XI/481 3/9890, f. 2, 28 May 1868, Galván, Huamantla, to Minister of War; ibid., f. 3, 28 May 1868, Murrieta, Teziutlán, to Pomposo Campillo, Perote.

54. BN-ABJ, 5319, 27 May 1868, García to Juárez; AMTdeO, 1868 Box, "Correspondencia diversas autoridades"; AMZ, "Expediente relativo a los movimientos militares habidos por motivo el desconocimiento de . . . Rafael J. García," ff. 10-13, 30-33, 5 June 1868, Junta de Zacapoaxtla; ADN, Histórico, XI/481 3/9894, f. 11, 8 June 1868, Eraclio Sosa, Topala, to Minister of War.

55. AMZ, 1868, "Expediente relativo a los movimientos militares," f. 29, 10 June 1868, Lucas.

56. ADN, Histórico, XI/481 3/9892, f. 38, 2 June 1868, García to Minister of War; ibid., 9894, ff. 7-8, 8 June 1868, Cravioto, Huauchinango, to García.

57. AMZ, "Expediente relativo a los movimientos militares," ff. 34-37, 15 June 1868, Juárez to Lucas.

58. AMZ, 1868, "Expediente relativo a las operaciones del cuartel general de la 2a División por motivo de la sublevación," ff. 1-2, 17 and 22 June 1868, Martínez, Tlatlauqui, to Jefe Político. On 26 June, Lucas convoked a further general junta of rebel leaders from Zacatlán (José María Ricaño), Tetela (José Daniel Posadas, Francisco de Paula Zamítez, Pilar Rivera, and Miguel Castillo), Zacapoaxtla (Juan Francisco Lucas and Juan Francisco Molina Alcántara), Tlatlauqui (Antonio and Mario Martínez), and Teziutlán (Ramón Bandala); see AMTdeO, 1868 Box, "1868 Correspondencia diversas autoridades," 21 June 1868, Lucas, Xochiapulco, to Jefe Político; AMZ, 1868, "Expediente relativo a los movimientos militares," f. 44; BN-ABJ, 5321, 1 July 1868, Juárez to García.

59. AMTdeO, 1868 Box, "1868 Correspondencia diversas autoridades," 22 June 1868, Márquez to Jefe Político, Tetela; BN-ABJ, 4916, 2 July 1868,

Cravioto to Juárez; ADN, Histórico, XI/481 3/9894, f. 16, 1 July 1868, Cravioto to García.

60. BN-ABJ, 4917, 11 and 13 July 1868, Cravioto to Juárez.

61. BN-ABJ, 5321, 29 June 1868, García to Juárez.

62. Huerta Jaramillo, *Insurrecciones rurales*, 33.

63. In May 1868 the federal government authorized García to purchase 4,000 rifles and ammunition, conceding the state government the necessary credits upon the Veracruz customhouse; BN-ABJ, 5309, 7 May 1868, García to Juárez; ibid., 5310, 8 May 1868, García to Juárez; ibid., 5113, 12 May 1868, García to Juárez; ibid., 5328, 13 July 1868, García to Juárez.

64. AMZ, 1868, "Expediente relativo a los movimientos militares," 7 July 1868, Sala Capitular, Zacapoaxtla.

65. ADN, Histórico, XI/481 3/9893, f. 45, 9 July 1868, Alatorre, Tlatlauqui, to Lucas, Xochiapulco.

66. ADN, Histórico, XI/481 3/9893, f. 47, 10 July 1868, Lucas to General Alatorre; Huerta Jaramillo, *Insurrecciones rurales*, 50-51.

67. AMTdeO, 1868 Box, "Correspondencia diversas autoridades," 10 July 1868, Lucas, Xochiapulco, to Jefe Político; 12 July 1868, Jefe Político to Lucas, Xochiapulco; ADN, Histórico, XI/481 3/9893, f. 46, 12 July 1868, Lucas to Negrete.

68. ADN, Histórico, XI/481 3/9893, f. 50, 17 July 1868, Alatorre, Zacapoaxtla, to Minister of War; BL-ABJ, 5332, 18 and 19 July 1868, García to Juárez.

69. AMTdeO, 1868 Box, "Correspondencia diversas autoridades," 21 July 1868, Lucas to Jefe Político.

70. AMTdeO, 1868 Box, "Correspondencia diversas autoridades," 22 July 1868, Colonel Pilar Rivera to Lauro Luna.

71. Molina annotated a letter from Lucas concerning disarmament with the sentence: "Tell him that once he has agreed to handing in arms, this force will then agree to do the same"; see AMZ, 1868, "Expediente relativo a las operaciones del cuartel general," f. 5, 21 July 1868, Lucas, Xochiapulco, to Jefe Político, Apulco.

72. Ibid., 25 July 1868, Rivera to Lucas.

73. ADN, Histórico, XI/481 3/9893, f. 66, 25 July 1868, Molina, Apulco, to Alatorre.

74. AMTdeO, 1868 Box, "Correspondencia diversas autoridades," 25 July 1868, Rivera, Tolcasama, to Jefe Político.

75. Ibid., 25 July 1868, Lucas, Xochiapulco, to Jefe Político.

76. Ibid., 25 July 1868, Lucas, Xochiapulco, to Rivera.

77. ADN, Histórico, XI/481 3/9893, f. 64, 26 July 1868, Lucas, Xochiapulco, to Alatorre, Zacapoaxtla.

78. AMZ, 1868, "Expediente relativo a las operaciones del cuartel general," f. 19, 26 July 1868, Alatorre, Zacapoaxtla, to Castillo, Zacapoaxtla.

79. AMTdeO, 1868 Box, "Correspondencia diversas autoridades," 28 July 1868, Pilar Rivera, Apulco, to Jefe Político.

80. ADN, Histórico, XI/481 3/9893, f. 114, 1 August 1868, Alatorre to Minister of War.

81. Ibid., f. 138, 16 August 1868, Alatorre to Minister of War.

82. ADN, Histórico, XI/481 3/9831 and 9796, for the insurrection in the Sierra de Tulancingo.

83. AMZ, 1868, "Expediente relativo a las operaciones del cuartel general," f. 5, 18 August 1868, Andrés Antonio, Yancuitlalpan, to Jefe Político.

84. The Federal army was assisted at this time by the completion of a railway, which linked the plains of Huamantla, Apizaco, and Apam with the capital and permitted the swift movement of troops and supplies to the Sierra front; see ADN, Histórico, XI/481 3/9786, f. 149.

85. The infantry "Batallón de Libres de México" and the "Tiradores de México" (artillery) under General Equílez.

86. ADN, Histórico, XI/481 3/9893, ff. 157-58, 23 August 1868, Alatorre, Zacapoaxtla, to Minister of War; ibid., f. 179, 20 August 1868, Cortina, Tetela de Oro [*sic*], to Minister of War.

87. Ibid., f. 151, 23 August 1868, Alatorre, Zacapoaxtla, to Minister of War.

88. ADN, Histórico, XI/481 3/9786, f. 154, 24 August 1868; AMZ, 1868, "Expediente relativo a las operaciones del cuartel general," ff. 63-64, 26 August 1858, Alatorre, Zacapoaxtla, to Comandante Militar del Distrito.

89. ADN, Histórico, XI/481 3/9873, 26 August 1868, Alatorre, Zacapoaxtla, to Minister of War.

90. Ibid., f. 173, 24 August 1868, Alatorre to Minister of War.

91. AMZ, 1868, "Expediente relativo a las operaciones del cuartel general," f. 31, 3 August 1868, Alatorre to Molina.

92. On 26 August 1868, Alatorre informed the Minister of War that "the first signs of disturbances among the indigenous class" in Cuetzalan had been observed, almost nine months after the first reports of trouble in the municipality; see ADN, Histórico, XI/481 3/9893, f. 189, 26 August 1868, Alatorre, Zacapoaxtla, to Minister of War.

93. AMZ, 1868, "Expediente relativo a la ley de desamortización," 24 August 1868, Ignacio Arrieta, Cuetzalan, to Comandante de Zacapoaxtla; ADN, Histórico, XI/481 3/9893, f. 92, 7 August 1868, Rafael García, Puebla, to Minister of War.

94. Arrieta stressed that two hundred well-equipped men were urgently needed to defeat Pala Agustín; see AMZ, 1868, "Expediente relativo a la ley de desamortización," 25 August 1868, Ignacio Arrieta, Cuetzalan, to Comandante Militar, Zacapoaxtla.

95. AMZ, 1868, "Expediente relativo a la ley de desamortización," 27 and 28 August 1868, Guerrero, Limontitan (Teziutlán), to Molina, Zacapoaxtla.

96. ADN, Histórico, XI/481 3/9873, f. 204, 6 September 1868, Alatorre, Zacapoaxtla, to Minister of War.

97. BN-ABJ, 5348, 9 October 1868, García to Juárez.

98. BN-ABJ, 5347, 10 October 1868, García to Juárez.

99. Tamayo, *Epistolario*, 476, 19 December 1868, Juárez to Alatorre.

100. ADN, Histórico, XI/481 3/9893, f. 252, 28 December 1868, Alatorre to Minister of War.

101. AMZ, 1868, "Expediente relativo a la ley de desamortización," 2 and 9 November 1868, Mora, Cuetzalan, to Jefe Político.

102. AMZ, 1869, "Espediente relativo al decreto del C. Fernando M. Ortega que por el Gobierno del Estado sean pagados los terrenos de Xochiapulco y Manzanilla," 8 January 1869, Juan Antonio, Xochiapulco, to Jefe Político.

103. This marriage also tied Lucas, through his mother-in-law, to the influential Contreras family of Zautla. Pedro Contreras, a friend of Lucas since the Three Years' War, was a leading Liberal and Méndez supporter who was elected as jefe político of Tetela in 1869, of Acatlán in 1871, and of San Juan de los Llanos in 1872; see ADN, Histórico, XI/481 3/9893, f. 215, 4 October 1868, Lucas, Taxcantla, to Juárez; ibid., f. 221, 19 October 1868, García, Puebla, to Minister of War.

104. AMZ, 1869, "Espediente relativo al decreto del C. Fernando M. Ortega que por el Gobierno del Estado sean pagados los terrenos de Xochiapulco y Manzanilla," 4 March 1869, Juan Antonio, Xochiapulco, to Jefe Político.

Chapter 9, The Arriaga Rebellion and the Xochiapulco Revolt, 147–74

1. BN-ABJ, 5347, 9 October 1868, García to Juárez; Ana María Huerta Jaramillo, *Insurrecciones rurales en el Estado de Puebla, 1868-1870* (Puebla, 1984), 54.

2. AGN, Gobernación, Tranquilidad Pública, 4a, 372 (1) (3), 1 January 1869, García, Chietla, to Minister of Interior.

3. Brian Hamnett, *Juárez* (London, England, 1984), 210.

4. For the Negrete movement, see AGN, Gobernación, Tranquilidad Publica, 4a, 369 (1) (6), Exps. 25 and 81.

5. BN-ABJ, 5447, 9 October 1868, García to Juárez.

6. Huerta Jaramillo, *Insurrecciones rurales*, 54.

7. Juan Carlos Garavaglia and Juan Carlos Grosso, "El entorno agrario de Tepeaca. Propiedad, crédito y desamortización en las haciendas mexicanas (1700-1870)," *Siglo XIX Revista de Historia* 5 (1990): 58.

8. ADN, Cancelados, D/111/3/1247, f. 3.

9. *El Libre Pensador* 3:7, 7 September 1869. For a good, albeit unsympathetic, sketch of the career of Romero Vargas, see Miguel Galindo y Galindo, *La gran década nacional, 1857-1867* (Mexico, 1904), 1:330-31.

10. For Article 30 of the state constitution, see *El Libre Pensador* 3:8, 9 September 1869.

11. *El Libre Pensador* 3:5, 2 September 1869.

12. Francisco Téllez Guerrero, "La organización administrativa del Estado de Puebla, 1824-1910," in *Puebla en el Siglo XIX*, ed. CIHS/UAP (Puebla, 1983), 63.

13. *El Libre Pensador* 3:10, 14 September 1869.

14. *El Libre Pensador* 3:9, 11 September 1869.

15. *El Libre Pensador* 3:23 and 25, 14 and 19 October 1869.

16. *El Libre Pensador* 3:29, 28 October 1869.

17. *El Libre Pensador* 3:33, 6 November 1869.

18. *El Libre Pensador* 3:34, 9 November 1869.

19. AMZ, 1869, "Espediente formado por la sublevación verificada en el distrito," 19 November 1869, Marín, Teziutlán, to Jefe Político.

20. Ibid., 18 November 1869, Saborido, Tlatlauqui, to Jefe Político.

21. "In none of the reports that I have gathered is there evidence that Xochiapulco has taken part in the uprising, except for the rebels' boasts"; AMZ, 1869, "Sumario en averiguación del movimiento sedicioso, efectuado en la plaza de Zacapoastla la madrugada del dia 20 del presente mes," 1 December 1869, Manuel Castañeda, Xochitlán, to José María Castro.

22. Ibid., 20 November 1869, Andrés Antonio, Xochitlán, to Arriaga.

23. Francisco Javier Arriaga, *Expediente geográfico-estadístico por el Ciudadano Francisco Javier Arriaga Diputado al 60 Congreso General por el Distrito de Zacapoaxtla en el estado de Puebla* (Mexico, 1873); for information on the Arriaga brothers, see Huerta Jaramillo, *Insurrecciones rurales*, 124-30.

24. AMZ, 1869, "Sumario en averiguación del movimiento sedicioso," 10 December 1869, Vázquez, Cuetzalan, to Jefe Político.

25. In January 1869, Juan Sayago's brother, Vicente, was involved in a "seditious movement" in Teziutlán, opposed to the sale of common land. Apart from inviting Xochiapulco forces to join them, Vicente Sayago attempted to rally the village of Chignautla with appeals to "religión y fueros," calling for the return of Antonio López de Santa Anna; see AGN, Gobernación, Tranquilidad Pública, 4a, 872 (1) (3), 1 January 1869, García, Puebla, to Minister of War.

26. My analysis of the events in Xochitlán, Cuetzalan, and Zacapoaxtla between 18 November and the end of the month is based upon the records of the military inquiry carried out under the instructions of General Alatorre, following the events of 20 November 1869; see AMZ, 1869, "Sumario en averiguación del movimiento sedicioso."

27. Huerta Jaramillo, *Insurrecciones rurales*, 96-97.

28. AMTdeO, Box 10, Exp. 9, "Correspondencia de Jonotla," 27 November 1869, Francisco Arriaga to Pedro Juárez, Jonotla. For the complete plan, see Huerta Jaramillo, *Insurrecciones rurales*, 155.

29. *Publicación Oficial* 1:1, 4 December 1869; AMTdeO, Box 10, Exp. 9, "Correspondencia de Jonotla," 25, 27, 28 November 1869, Juárez, Jonotla, to Contreras, and Colonel in Chief, Apulco, and 27, 28, 29 November 1869, Arriaga, Apulco, to Juárez, Jonotla.

30. AMTdeO, Box 10, Exp. 9, "Correspondencia de Jonotla," 30 November 1869, Pedro Juárez, Jonotla, to Jefe Político.

31. AMZ, 1869, Exp. 69, "Espediente relativo a la sublevación de los indígenas de la municipalidad de Cuetzalan," 22 November 1869, Miguel Mora, Xocoyolo, to José María Mora, Cuetzalan, and 29 November 1869, Juan Francisco, Yancuitlalpan, to Proveedor General, Apulco.

32. Before advancing to meet the enemy at Apulco, jefe político Molina first established his base at Cantero's bailiwick in the village of Atagpan; see AMZ, 1869, "Espediente formado por la sublevación," 19 November 1869, José María Ramos and Vicente Ruiz, Ahuacatlán, to Jefe Político, and 25 November 1869, José María Trinidad, Taictic, to Jefe Político.

33. Ibid., 24 November 1869, 3 and 5 December, Calderón, Cuetzalan, to Jefe Político.

34. AMZ, 1869, "Espediente formado por la sublevación," 25 November 1869, Rodríguez, Cuyoaco, to Molina, Tlatlauqui.

35. Ibid., Molina, Zacapoaxtla, to Gobernación, Puebla, and to Jefes Políticos of Tlatlauqui, Teziutlán, and Libres.

36. Ibid., 30 November 1869, Molina, Apulco, to General en Jefe.

37. AMZ, 1869, "Sumario en averiguación del movimiento sedicioso," 18 November 1869, Díaz, Xochiapulco, to Molina, and 9 November 1869, Cantero, Atagpan, to Díaz, Xochiapulco.

38. Ibid., 20 November 1869, Díaz, Xochiapulco, to Molina, Zacapoaxtla.

39. Ibid., 29 November 1869, Díaz, Xochiapulco, to Molina.

40. Ibid.

41. AMZ, 1869, "Espediente formado por la sublevación," 1 December 1869, Jefe Político to Alcalde, Xochiapulco.

42. *Publicación Oficial* 1:1, 4 December 1869.

43. AMZ, 1869, "Espediente formado por la sublevación," 24 November 1869, Urrutia, Puebla, to Jefe Político.

44. *Publicación Oficial* 1:3, 9 December 1869.

45. *Publicación Oficial* 1:1, 3, 7, 11; 4, 7, 9, 11, 18, 28 December 1869. For a fuller description of these events, see Florencia Mallon, *Peasant and Nation: The Making of Post-Colonial Mexico and Peru* (Berkeley, CA, 1995).

46. Ibid., 126.

47. José López Portillo y Rojas, *Elevación y caída de Porfirio Díaz* (Mexico, 1975), 139-40.

48. *Publicación Oficial* 1:10, 25 December 1869; Huerta Jaramillo, *Insurrecciones rurales,* 57.

49. *Publicación Oficial* 1:13, 1 January 1870.

50. AMZ, 1870, "Espediente relativo a la consulta que se hizo a la superioridad a respecto de la anexación de los barrios de Xochiapulco a esta cabecera," 28 January 1870, Jefe Político to Gobernación, Puebla.

51. *Publicación Oficial* 1:10, 25 December 1869.

52. AMZ, 1869, "Espediente formado por la sublevación," 4 December 1869, Saborido, Tlatlauqui, to Molina.

53. Ibid., 5 December 1869, Saborido, Tlatlauqui, to Molina.

54. Among the twenty-seven Tlatlauqueños offering their services to Alatorre on 17 December was José Miguel Salgado (owner of the expropriated but still uncompensated hacienda of Xochiapulco and Manzanilla); see *Publicación Oficial* 1:10, 25 December 1869.

55. AMZ, 1869, "Expediente; Asuntos Militares," 13 December 1869, Nieto, Puebla, to Jefe Político.

56. AMZ, 1869, "Espediente formado por los hechos sediciosos en la municipalidad de Xochitlán"; AMZ, 1869, "Espediente formado por la sublevación," 30 November 1869, Castañeda, Xochitlán, to Jefe Político.

57. For examples of recruitment problems in Xochitlán, Nauzontla, and Xochitlan, see AMZ, 1869, "Espediente formado por la sublevación," and "Espediente formado por motivo de las disposiciones militares emanadas de la Gefatura política y militar del distrito."

58. AMZ, 1869, "Espediente formado por la sublevación," 19 December 1869, Jefe Político to Gobernación, Puebla.

59. AMZ, 1869, "Espediente: Asuntos militares," 31 December 1869, Jefe Político to Administrador de Rentas del Distrito.

60. *Publicación Oficial* 1:17, 11 January 1870.

61. *Publicación Oficial* 1:15, 6 January 1870.

62. *Publicación Oficial* 1:17, 19; 11 and 15 January 1870.

63. *Publicación Oficial* 1:14, 4 January 1870.

64. *Publicación Oficial* 1:18, 13 January 1870.

65. AMZ, 1870, "Espediente relativo al indulto que el Cuartel General concede a los sublevados del Distrito que se presenten deponiendo sus armas."

66. *Publicación Oficial* 1:19, 15 January 1870.

67. AMZ, 1870, "Espediente relativo al indulto que el Cuartel General concede a los sublevados," 26 January 1870, Varela, Zacapoaxtla, to Cravioto, Tetela.

68. Ibid., 18 January 1870, Varela to Alcaldes of Jicotepec and Las Lomas.

69. Ibid., 11 January 1870, Varela, Zacapoaxtla, to Alatorre, Zautla, and 11 January 1870, Alatorre, Zautla, to Varela.

70. AMZ, 1869, "Espediente formado por la sublevación," 13 January 1870, Varela to Alcalde, Cuetzalan, and 12 January 1870, Castañeda, Xochitlán, to Varela.

71. As a penalty, Varela ordered the thirty-two Cuetzaltecos who were sent up to Xochiapulco to be kept there until they had carried out the work of one hundred men; see ibid., 13 January 1870, Vázquez, Cuetzalan, to Varela, and 12 January 1870, Castañeda, Xochitlán, to Varela.

72. AMZ, 1866, "Borrador de Oficios, No. 392," Jefe Político to Alcalde, Huahuaxtla.

73. The rebellious barrio of San Andrés Tzicuilan sent only thirteen men of the twenty-five requested; see AMZ, 1869, "Espediente formado por la sub-

levación," 4 January 1870, Vázquez, Cuetzalan, to Varela, and 13 January 1870, Juan Martín, Tzicuilan, to Varela.

74. Ibid., 25 January 1870, Medrano, Zacapoaxtla, to Varela.

75. AMZ, 1870, "Espediente relativo al indulto que el Cuartel General concede a los sublevados," 26 January 1870, Varela to Cravioto.

76. Ibid., 28 January 1870, Varela to Gobernación.

77. Ibid., 29 January 1870, Cravioto to Varela, and 30 January 1870, Nieto, Puebla, to Varela.

78. AMZ, 1870, "Espediente relativo a la consulta que hizo a la superioridad a respecto de la anexación de los barrios de Xochiapulco a esta cabecera," 28 January 1870, Varela to Gobernación.

79. AMZ, 1869, "Espediente formado por la sublevación," 24 January 1870, Varela to Alcaldes of Nauzontla, Xochitlán, and Cuetzalan.

80. Ibid., 22 January 1870, Camilo Bonilla, Nauzontla, to Varela.

81. AMZ, 1869, "Espediente formado por la sublevación," 24 January 1870, Varela to Gobernación.

82. *Publicación Oficial* 1:18, 25; 13 and 29 January 1870.

83. *Publicación Oficial* 1:25, 29 January 1870; AMZ, 1869, "Espediente formado por la sublevación," 11 January 1870, Varela to Alatorre.

84. *Publicación Oficial* 1:29, 8 February 1870; AMZ, 1870, "Espediente relativo a los partes de tranquilidad pública que deben rendirse a la Sria. del Gobierno," 31 January 1870, Varela to Gobernación.

85. *Publicación Oficial* 1:29, 8 February 1870.

86. AMZ, 1870, "Espediente promovido por el Jefe Político de Tetela de Ocampo en que pide que conforme a las reformas constitucionales se agreguen a aquel Distrito los pueblos que forman la municipalidad de Xochiapulco con excepción del barrio de las Lomas."

87. AMZ, 1870, "Espediente relativa a los partes," 8 February 1870, Varela to Gobernación.

88. ADN, Cancelados, C-115, D111/4/1813 (Colonel Antonio Domínguez).

89. The rebels lost three dead (including Antonio Domínguez) and thirty-two prisoners. Government forces lost five dead and seventy-eight wounded; see *Publicación Oficial* 1:39, 47, 3 and 22 March 1870.

90. *Publicación Oficial* 1:40, 41, 5 and 8 March 1870; AMZ, 1870, "Espediente relativo a los partes," 28 February 1870, Varela to Gobernación; ADN, Historico, XI/481 3/789, f. 21, 11 January 1870, Alatorre, Jalapa, to Minister of War.

91. *Publicación Oficial* 1:48, 24 March 1870.

92. *Publicación Oficial* 1:51, 31 March 1870.

93. Daniel Cosío Villegas, *Historia Moderna de México. La República Restaurada. La Vida Política* (Mexico, 1955), 268-69.

94. *Publicación Oficial* 1:56, 12 April 1870.

95. AMZ, 1870, "Espediente relativo a los partes," 1 April 1870, Varela to Gobernación.

96. AMZ, 1870, "Espediente relativo a los movimientos," 30 March 1870, Díaz, Xochitlán, to Alcalde, Nauzontla.

97. This raid may well have come from Cuetzalan rather than Xochiapulco; see ibid., 2 April 1870, Saborido, Tlatlauqui, to Varela, and 5 April 1870, Castañeda, Cuetzalan, to Varela.

98. Ibid., 3 April 1870, Varela to Representante del Supremo Gobierno.

99. Cosío Villegas, *República Restaurada*, 261-68.

100. AMZ, 1870, "Espediente relativo a los movimientos," 3 April 1870, Jefe Político to Representante del Supremo Gobierno.

101. Ibid., 13 April 1870, Varela to Administrador de Rentas.

102. Ibid., 16 April 1870, Urrutia, Puebla, to Jefe Político.

103. Ibid., "Lista de los Ciudadanos y Establecimientos a quienes se impone un préstamo para las atenciones de la campaña."

104. Ibid., 26 April and 1 May 1870, Marín, Teziutlán, to Jefe Político.

105. Ibid., 27 April 1870, Nieto, Puebla, to Jefe Político.

106. Ibid., 9 April 1870, Cabrera, Lomas, to Jefe Político. On 17 April, Lucas estimated that he had 610 men at arms in Huahuaxtla; see APJFL, 17 April 1870, Lucas to Luis Antonio Díaz. Palm Sunday was the most important festival in Zacapoaxtla's religious calendar. Traditionally, the image of the Señor del Triunfo was taken down from the sanctuary in the barrio of Tatoxcac on the hill above Zacapoaxtla and carried in procession to the main church, accompanied by the Indians (but not the *gente de razón*) of the municipality. During the wars of Independence, this image acquired a special significance. A force of insurgents, commanded by José Francisco Osorno, had been on the point of attacking Zacapoaxtla. Deterred by the multitude in the procession and frightened by the flashes from the mirrors of the dancers, they took flight. From then on, it became normal practice to place religious images at the head of columns in military encounters; see Ramón Sánchez Flores, *Zacapoaxtla: Relación histórica* (Puebla, 1984), 111.

107. AMZ, 1870, "Espediente relativo a los movimientos," 11 April 1870, Jefe Político to Gobernación, Puebla.

108. Ibid., 12 April 1870, Jefe Político to Alcalde, Cuetzalan.

109. *Publicación Oficial* 1:62, 28 April 1870.

110. Following the skirmish on 12 April, a company of rebels at Huahuaxtla pronounced in favor of the government. Their sergeant was executed on Lucas's orders. The corporal and soldiers were imprisoned, but one soldier escaped to the redoubt at Apulco to tell the tale; see AMZ, 1870, "Espediente relativo a los movimientos," 22 April 1870, Cabrera, Las Lomas, to Jefe Político.

111. AMZ, 1870, "Espediente relativo a los partes," 20 April 1870, Varela to Gobernación, Puebla.

112. APJFL, "Estado de fuerzas," April 1870.

113. AMZ, 1870, "Espediente relativo a los movimientos," 23 April 1870, Jefe Político to Gobernación, Puebla.

114. Ibid., 25 April 1870, Cabrera, Las Lomas, to Jefe Político.

115. On 23 April, Xochitlán was taken by fifty rebels from Xochiapulco, who mustered eleven porters to help them with their planting in Tuzamapa; see ibid., 25 April 1870, Andrés Juan, Xochitlán, to Jefe Político.

116. Ibid., 24 April 1870, Vázquez, Cuetzalan, to Jefe Político.

117. Ibid., 23 April 1870, Jefe Político to Gobernación, Puebla.

118. *Publicación Oficial* 1:66, 7 May 1870.

119. AMZ, 1870, "Espediente relativo a los movimientos," 23 April 1870, Jefe Político to Gobernación, Puebla.

120. Ibid., 29 April 1870, Jefe Político to Gobernación, Puebla.

121. Ibid., 30 April 1870, Jefe Político to Gobernación.

122. Manuel Ayala, Jefe Político of Libres, reported that although the plateau was at peace, the municipalities of Zautla and Ixtacamaxtitlán "continuamente son invadidas por los bandidos que acaudillan Luis León y Juan Francisco Lucas"; see *Publicación Oficial* 1:68, 12 May 1870.

123. AMZ, 1870, "Espediente relativa a los partes," 1 May 1870, Andrés Juan, Xochitlán, to Jefe Político, Zacapoaxtla.

124. *Publicación Oficial* 1:73, 24 May 1870; AMZ, 1870, "Espediente relativo a los movimientos," 2 May 1870, Varela to Saborido.

125. Ibid., 2 May 1870, Varela to Gobernación.

126. Ibid., 9 May 1870, Gutiérrez, Nauzontla, to Jefe Político.

127. Ibid., 7 May 1870, Rivera, Xochitlán, to Jefe Político.

128. Ibid., 11 May 1870, Nieto, Puebla, to Jefe Político.

129. *Publicación Oficial* 1:69, 14 May 1870.

130. AMZ, 1870, "Espediente relativa a los partes," 17 May 1870, Jefe Político, Zacapoaxtla, to Gobernación, Puebla.

131. Ibid., 18 May 1870, Molina, Zacapoaxtla, to Gobernación.

132. Huerta Jaramillo, *Insurrecciones rurales*, 62.

133. *Publicación Oficial* 1:82, 14 June 1870.

134. *Publicación Oficial* 1:86, 23 June 1870; Huerta Jaramillo, *Insurrecciones rurales*, 101.

135. AMZ, 1870, "Espediente relativo a la capitulación de las fuerzas que se hallan sublevadas en Xochiapulco," 11 June 1870, Jefe Político to Gobernación, Puebla.

136. Huerta Jaramillo, *Insurrecciones rurales*, 101; *Publicación Oficial* 1:94, 101, 12 and 28 July 1870.

137. *Publicación Oficial* 1:101, 28 July 1870.

138. Mallon, *Peasant and Nation*, 128.

139. Bernardo García Martínez, *Los pueblos de la Sierra* (Mexico, 1989), 62-63; Huerta Jaramillo, *Insurrecciones rurales*, 104; *Publicación Oficial* 2:11, 26 January 1871.

140. *Publicación Oficial* 1:124, 20 November 1870.

Chapter 10, The Fruits of Rebellion in Xochiapulco, 175–82

1. AMZ, "Padrón de la municipalidad de Xochiapulco, 30 June 1868."

2. AMTdeO, "Padrón General que manifiesta el número de habitantes . . . Xochiapulco (1873)."

3. AMZ, 1869, "Espediente formado de la noticia estadística de censo y establecimientos industriales, agricultura y minería"; AMTdeO, Gobierno, 1872, Box 15, Exp. 9, "Correspondencia de Xochiapulco," 18 December 1872, Dinorín to Jefe Político. It was pointed out in the *padrón* that these ranchos were much smaller than the normal ranchos of the plateau.

4. Donna Rivera Moreno, *Xochiapulco: Una gloria olvidada* (Puebla, 1991), 86-87; *Periódico Oficial* 4:65, 14 August 1878.

5. AMTdeO, "Padrón General que manifiesta el número de habitantes . . . Xochiapulco (1873)."

6. AMTdeO, Exp. 113, "Correspondencia oficial de Xochiapulco," 7 June 1870, Díaz, Xochiapulco, to Jefe Político.

7. Rivera, *Xochiapulco*, 39.

8. AMTdeO, 1873, "Correspondencia oficial de Xochiapulco," 4 January 1873, Dinorín, Xochiapulco, to Jefe Político.

9. Ibid., 5 September 1870, Díaz, Xochiapulco, to Jefe Político.

10. For the insistence of Xochiapulco's *juez municipal* that the construction of a school in Cuauximaloyan should take precedence over finishing the barrio's chapel, see Florencia Mallon, *Peasant and Nation: The Making of Post-Colonial Mexico and Peru* (Berkeley, CA, 1995), 291-92.

11. On 15 November, Juan Martín announced the completion of the boys' primary school; see AMTdeO, Exp. 113, "Correspondencia oficial de Xochiapulco," 9 and 15 November 1870, Juan Martín, Xochiapulco, to Jefe Político.

12. AMZ, 1868, Exp. 59, "Espediente relativo a las licencias que del Superior Gobierno solicitan los pueblos del Distrito para edificar capillas."

13. Moisés Saenz, *Escuelas federales en la Sierra Norte de Puebla* (Mexico, 1927), 68-69.

14. Avoidance of payment of the *Dominica* was a factor in the secession of the barrio of Chilapa from neighboring Zautla to join Xochiapulco; see AMTdeO, 1873, "Correspondencia oficial de Xochiapulco," 12 March 1873, Juan María de la Cruz, Xochiapulco, to Jefe Político.

15. AGNP, Tetela II, (1886), ff. 1-2, 51-52.

16. Mary Kay Vaughan, "The Educational Project of the Mexican Revolution: The Response of Local Societies (1934-1940)," in *Molding the Hearts and Minds: Education, Communications, and Social Change in Latin America*, ed. John Britton (Wilmington, DE, 1993), 119.

17. Zacapoaxtla's position was based upon a resolution of the state congress of 4 May 1870 that the boundary between Xochiapulco and Zacapoaxtla should follow a line north from Jilotepec to Atzala; see AMTdeO, Gobierno, 1872, Box 14, "Correspondencia Diversa."

18. Rafael Molina had bought the Rancho de las Lomas from Agu⟨⟩ Salgado in December 1841; see AGNP, Tetela II, ff. 24-25.

19. ADN, Histórico, XI/481 3/10084, f. 70, 28 July 1865, Rico⟩ Tulancingo, to Gral. Comandante de la División Territorial, Mexico.

20. AMZ, 1869, "Copia de los rebajados del servicio de guardia nacional. Municipalidad de Xochiapulco," 15 February 1869, Juan Antonio, Juan José Español, and Luis Antonio Díaz, Xochiapulco, to Jefe Político. An interesting feature of the list of names of the Las Lomas *rebajados* was the number of Nahua toponymic surnames. Toponymic surnames were rare in the municipality, and why they were so common in Las Lomas is uncertain. The list includes several members of the following families: Tepáncal, Tácomol, Téta, Ahuacatlán, Cuatetamánis, Tepetzintan, Capoltitan, Ocotítan, Ocatálen, Xicuapango, Talquexpan, Atahuit, Tzontecomaco, Chauta, Xocotítan, Tepexteno, Contan, Capillero, Teoloco, and Ylit. For a discussion of Nahua toponymic surnames, see Lourdes Arizpe, *Parentezco y economía en una sociedad Nahua* (Mexico, 1973), 191.

21. AMZ, 1868, No. 112, 30 March 1868, 24 April and 12 October 1869, Ramón Francisco, Juan Antonio, and Díaz, Xochiapulco, to Jefe Político; ibid., 24 April 1869, Juan José Agustín, Las Lomas, to Alcalde, Xochiapulco.

22. AMZ, 1870, No. 93, "Espediente relativo al asesinato perpetrado en la persona del capitán Lucas Martín en el barrio de las Lomas."

23. AGNP, Tetela II (1887-88), ff. 17, 24-25, 28-29. This fiscal obligation was finally abolished as few tenants possessed land worth more than 100 pesos.

24. For the creation of the barrio of Yautetelco, see AMTdeO, 1870, Exp. 113, "Correspondencia Oficial con Xochiapulco," 23 September, 2, 3, and 10 October 1870, Dinorín, Xochiapulco, to Jefe Político, and 11 October 1870, Bonilla, Tetela, to Dinorín, Xochiapulco.

25. Ibid., 24 and 26 October 1879, Dinorín to Jefe Político.

26. Bonilla put the problem down to the bad influence of Valeriano Cabrera, "from the moment this bad *vecino* settled in Las Lomas, discords between one and another began"; see AMZ, 1870, "Espediente relativo a las quejas puestas por los vecinos del barrio de las Lomas que pasaron a avecindarse a Xochiapulco, contra los que han permanecido en la jurisdicción del mencionado barrio," 3 October 1870, Bonilla, Tetela, to Jefe Político, Zacapoaxtla. Conflicts similar to those in Las Lomas also divided the barrio of Yautetelco; see AMZ, 1870, "Espediente relativo al informe que previno la superioridad se le rindiese respeto a la pretensión de algunos vecinos de los barrios de las Lomas y Yautetelco para segregarse de esta municipalidad y anexarse a la de Xochiapulco del Distrito de Tetela," 12 August 1870, Jefe Político to Gobernación.

27. AMTdeO, Box 14 Bis 1871, "Correspondencia de varias autoridades," and Box 18 (1872-73), "Correspondencia de Xochiapulco," 27 September 1873, Díaz, Xochiapulco, to Jefe Político.

28. AMTdeO, Box 14 Bis 1871, "Correspondencia de varias autoridades."

29. See Chapter 13, this volume.

30. Octaviano Manzano, *El indígena de la Sierra de Puebla* (Mexico, 1987), 72.

31. Lucas's principal agent in Chilapa throughout the Reform Wars and European Intervention was Captain Mariano de la Cruz, alcalde of the barrio in 1869; see AMZ, 1868-69, No. 77, "Espediente relativo a la agregación del barrio de Chilapa a la municipalidad de Xochiapulco," 20 January 1869, Juan Antonio, Xochiapulco, to Jefe Político; and AMTdeO, Box 18 Bis 1871, "Correspondencia de Xochiapulco," 12 March 1875, Juan María de la Cruz, Villa del Cinco de Mayo, to Jefe Político.

32. AMZ, No. 879, "Borrador de oficios del Jefe Político," August 1862.

33. AMZ, 1868, "Espediente relativo a una queja interpuesta por el ayuntamiento de Xochiapulco en motivo de los abusos que cometen los vecinos de Comaltepec," 26 September 1868, Juan Antonio, Xochiapulco, to Juez del Barrio de Comaltepec.

34. See AMZ, 1868, Exp. 112, for a lengthy correspondence between Xochiapulco and Zacapoaxtla on the distribution of Xochiapulco's common land. See also AMZ, 1869, Exp. 125, "Escrituras y denuncias de Tierras, Xochiapulco, marzo-junio de 1869."

35. AMTdeO, 1870, "Correspondencia con Xochiapulco," 7 October 1870, Juan Martín to Jefe Político.

36. AGNP, Zacapoaxtla, 1868, ff. 117-18.

37. For correspondence between the alcalde of Xochiapulco, the President of the Republic, and the state government concerning the fulfillment of the decree, see AMZ, 1869, Exp. 5, "Espediente relativo al decreto del C. Fernando María Ortega para que por el Gobierno del Estado sean pagados los terrenos de Xochiapulco y Manzanilla," 8 January 1869, Juan Antonio, Xochiapulco, to Jefe Político; for Lucas's negotiations with the Salgado family, who claimed to be living in poverty in Tlatlauqui as a consequence of the expropriation, see APJFL, 31 January 1867, Salgado, Tlatlauqui, to Lucas, Xochiapulco.

38. AMTdeO, 1870 Gobierno, Box 15, "Correspondencia de Xochiapulco."

39. AMTdeO, 1870, Exp. 124, "Solicitudes para el repartimiento de terrenos hechas por la autoridad de Xochiapulco."

40. Ibid., 1 February 1871, Jose Miguel Ataguit, Xochiapulco, to Jefe Político.

41. *Publicación Oficial* 6:63, 25 September 1875; ibid., 9:65, 14 August 1878.

42. Rivera, *Xochiapulco*, 220-26.

Chapter 11, The Revolt of La Noria, 183–200

1. Laurens Ballard Perry, *Juárez and Díaz Machine Politics in Mexico* (DeKalb, IL, 1978), 154-55.

2. The scale of the Puebla congressional bloc of twenty was exceeded only by Jalisco with twenty-one of the 227 deputyships in the federal congress. Other large delegations included Guanajuato with eighteen, Mexico and Oaxaca with sixteen, Michoacán with fifteen, and San Luis Potosí with twelve.

3. Perry, *Juárez and Díaz*, 162.

4. Ibid., 163.

5. The national mood in this period is brilliantly evoked by Daniel Cosío Villegas, *Porfirio Díaz en la Revuelta de la Noria* (Mexico, 1953).

6. Ibid., 64-66, 167.

7. Guy P. C. Thomson, "Agrarian Conflict in the Municipality of Cuetzalan (Sierra de Puebla): The Rise and Fall of 'Pala' Agustín Dieguillo, 1861-1894," *HAHR* 71 (1991): 243-44.

8. *Publicación Oficial* 1:162, 17 December 1870; 2:18, 11 February 1871.

9. AMTdeO, Gobierno, 1871, Box 14, Exp. 1

10. *Publicación Oficial* 2:21, 18 February 1871.

11. *Publicación Oficial* 1:153, 161; ibid., 2:21, 22, 27, 35. For the impeachment crisis, see Osvaldo A. Tamaín, "El Porfirismo en Puebla, 1867-1910," in *Puebla: Una historia compartida,* ed. Carlos Contreras Cruz (Puebla, 1993), 312.

12. Cosío Villegas, *Porfirio Díaz*, 19-20.

13. Further grievances expressed by Arriaga were the removal of Ixtacamaxtitlán from its ancient cabecera, Libres, to join the new district, Alatriste (the cordon sanitaire through which Romero Vargas hoped to contain the troublesome Sierra). Also, Arriaga and "the citizens of Libres" objected to the humiliating requirement that electors from Libres travel to San Andrés Chalchicomula for the electoral college and those from Zautla, "since time immemorial" subject to Libres, to Zacapoaxtla; AMTdeO, (Leyes y Decretos) Gobierno, 1871, Box 13 Bis, "Protesta de los Ciudadanos del Distrito de Libres," 28 February 1871.

14. *El Comercio Periódico Semanal de la Lonja Mercantíl* (Puebla) 1:3, 4 March 1871; *Publicación Oficial* 2:27, 34, 4 and 21 March 1871.

15. *Publicación Oficial* 2:32, 14 March 1871.

16. APJFL, 30 May 1871, Gran Comisión Electoral, Veracruz, to Lucas, Tetela de Ocampo.

17. APJFL, 30 May 1871, Méndez, Tetela, to Lucas, Taxcantla.

18. APJFL, 4 June 1871, Bonilla, Tetela, to Lucas, Taxcantla; 16 June 1871, Bonilla, Tetela, to Lucas, Taxcantla; 17 June 1871, Arriaga, Zacapoaxtla, to Lucas, Taxcantla.

19. *El Siglo XIX* 53:9690, 20 July 1871.

20. *Publicación Oficial* 1:157, 6 December 1870; *Periódico Oficial* 2:40, 41, 26 and 29 April 1871; 2:50, 24 June 1871; 2:58, 30 August 1871; 2:67, 26 September 1871; 2:69, 3 October 1871.

21. *Publicación Oficial* 2:89, 16 November 1871.

22. Cosío Villegas, *Porfirio Díaz*, 118-19, 164.

23. Alberto María Carreño, ed., *Archivo del General Porfirio Díaz: Memorias y documentos* (Mexico, 1947-61), 9:264.

24. AMTdeO, Box 18, 1871, 24 February 1871, Vicente García, Xonotla, to Jefe Político; Box 14 Bis 1871, "Correspondencia de varias autoridades," 25 September 1871, Juan Francisco Molina to Juan Crisóstomo Bonilla; AMZ, December 1871, Exp. 221, "Expediente relativa a la sublevación del indígena Santiago Cientos, vecino de Xochitlán, en companía de otros vecinos del mismo pueblo y Huahuaxtla."

25. ADN, Histórico, XI/481 3/9787, f. 54, 27 September 1871, Antonio Tagle, Tulancingo, to Minister of War.

26. The *Periódico Oficial* questioned the validity of these reports and doubted the potential of local movements to become a general insurrection; see ADN, Histórico, XI/481 3/9787, f. 6, 12 October 1871, H. Carrillo, Perote, to Minister of War; *Periódico Oficial* 2:79, 24 October 1871.

27. *Periódico Oficial* 11:78, 79, and 81; 21, 24, and 28 October 1871.

28. Over six hundred signatures appear on the Plan de Atlixco; see *Periódico Oficial* 2:87, 88, 11 and 14 November 1871.

29. ADN, Histórico, XI/481 3/787, f. 100, 25 November 1871, Romero Vargas, Teziutlán, to Minister of War.

30. ADN, Histórico, XI/481 3/9799, f. 137, 20 November 1871, Romero Vargas to Minister of War; AMTdeO, Box 14 Bis 1871, 21 November 1871, Luis Flores, Puebla, to Jefe Político.

31. *El Monitor Republicano* 21:302, 20 December 1871.

32. *Periódico Oficial* 2:101, 14 December 1871.

33. *Periódico Oficial* 2:98, 7 December 1871.

34. *Periódico Oficial* 2:104, 21 December 1871.

35. ADN, Histórico, XI/481 3/99, f. 138, 18 November 1871, Colonel Robles Linares, Puebla, to Minister of War.

36. *Periódico Oficial* 2:96, 2 December 1871.

37. *Periódico Oficial* 2:103, 19 December 1871; 2:102, 16 December 1871.

38. *Periódico Oficial* 2:103, 19 December 1871.

39. *Periódico Oficial* 2:105, 23 December 1871.

40. AMTdeO, File of Intercepted Mail, December 1871, 18 December 1871, Antonio Rivera, Zacapoaxtla, to Ignacio Rivera, Puebla.

41. Ibid., 18 December, Romero Vargas, Puebla, to Colonel Domínguez, Chignahuapan, and M. Llenero, Jefe Político of Zacatlán; *Periódico Oficial* 2:105, 23 December 1871; José María Domínguez Castilla, *Ensayo crítico-histórico sobre la revolución de La Noria* (Mexico, 1934), 271-72.

42. Charles Berry, *The Reform in Oaxaca, 1856-76: A Microhistory of the Liberal Revolution* (Lincoln, 1981), 120-27.

43. *Periódico Oficial* 3:1, 2, 2 and 4 January 1872; 3:10, 12, 23 and 27 January 1872.

44. Daniel Cosío Villegas, *Historia Moderna de México. La República Restaurada. La Vida Política* (Mexico, 1955), 716-17.

45. AMTdeO, Gobierno, Box 439, Exp. 4, 30 March 1872, Bonilla, Xochiapulco, to "Compadrito" (Méndez).

46. *Periódico Oficial* 2:108, 31 December 1871; 3:7, 16 January 1872, "Acta de Sublevación de Papantla, 17 December 1871." For pronouncements in Zacatlán and Hueytlalpan on the same day (17 December 1871), see *Periódico Oficial* 11:105, 23 December 1871.

47. AMTdeO, Gobierno, Box 16, 1872, Exp. 14, "Correspondencia del Cuartel General," Márquez, Zacatlán, to Bonilla, Tetela.

48. *Periódico Oficial* 3:2 and 3, 4 and 6 January 1872; AMTdeO, Gobierno, Box 12 Bis 1871, Exp. 1, 30 December 1871, Bonilla to Presidente Municipal.

49. AMTdeO, Gobierno, Box 439, Exp. 4, 23 January 1872, Méndez, Taxcantla, to Bonilla; *Periódico Oficial* 3:9, 20 January 1872; ibid. 3:8, 10, and 12, 18, 23, and 27 January 1872; ibid. 4:13, 30 January 1872.

50. AMTdeO, Gobierno, Box 15, 1872, Exp. 211, 22 January 1872, Juan López y Hernández, Apulco, to Gral. en Jefe.

51. Ibid., 29 January 1872, José Montero, San Esteban, to Bonilla, and 10 February 1872, Dolores López, Tonalapa, to Bonilla.

52. AMTdeO, Gobierno, Box 439, Exp. 4, 5 and 6 February 1872, Méndez, Taxcantla, to Bonilla.

53. AMTdeO, Gobierno, Box 439, Exp. 4, 15 January 1872, Méndez, Xochiapulco, to Bonilla, Tetela; AMTdeO, Gobierno, Box 12 Bis 1871, Exp. 1 (file of intercepted mail), 8 February 1872, B. Just, Zacatecas, to Gral. Bonilla.

54. *Periódico Oficial* 3:26, 29 February 1872.

55. AMTdeO, Gobierno, Box 439, Exp. 4, 12 March 1872, Miguel Negrete, Cuahuigtic, to Méndez, Taxcantla.

56. *El Regenerador* 1:4, 26 March 1872.

57. AMTdeO, Gobierno, Box 439, Exp. 4, 30 March 1872, Bonilla, Xochiapulco, to "Compadrito."

58. Ibid., 30 March 1872, Méndez to Manuel Vázquez, Tetela; 8 April 1872, Bonilla, Taxcantla, to Manuel Vázquez, Tetela; 10 April 1872, Bonilla, Taxcantla, to Gregorio Zamítez.

59. Ibid., 10, 12, 13, 15, 16, 26 April 1872, Bonilla, Taxcantla, to Manuel Vázquez, Tetela; 11 April 1872, Bonilla to Gregorio Zamítez; *El Regenerador* 1:9 and 12, 13 and 26 April 1872.

60. AMTdeO, Gobierno, Box 439, Exp. 4, 12 April 1872, Bonilla, Taxcantla, to Manuel Vázquez, Tetela; *El Regenerador* 1:10, 16 April 1872.

61. AMTdeO, Gobierno, Box 439, Exp. 4, 18 April 1872, José Márquez, Otlatlán, to Manuel Vázquez, Tetela; 21 April 1872, Bonilla, Taxcantla, to Vázquez, Tetela.

62. AMTdeO, Gobierno, Box 439, Exp. 4, 22 and 23 April 1872, Bonilla to Vázquez.

63. Cosío Villegas, *Historia Moderna*, 709-11.

64. Ibid., 722-30.

65. In October 1871, in anticipation of the Sierra uprising, Cantero was given the rank of Captain of Infantry in the regular army. His influence in the Indian barrios of Tlatlauqui was reported, at this time, to have diminished to insignificance. Like many other caciques in this period, Cantero was actively extending his landholdings through the *desamortización*, denouncing several plots in the barrio of Atagpan between 1868 and 1870; see AMZ, 1870, "Espediente relativo a la organización militar del Distrito," 12 May 1872, Cenobio Cantero, Tlatlauqui, to Jefe Político of Zacapoaxtla; *El Monitor Republicano* 21:284, 29 November 1871; AGN, Cancelados, LIV a 221-42 (Cenobio Cantero); AMZ, April 1871, "Espediente relativo a las adjudicaciones de terrenos del común en las municipalidades de Cuetzalan y Xochitlán."

66. *El Regenerador* 1:23, 4 July 1872.

67. AMTdeO, Box 15, Gobierno, "Correspondencia Militar, Tuzamapa," 9 May 1872, José Vázquez, Tuzamapa, to Cuartel General, Taxcantla.

68. AMTdeO, Gobierno, Box 439, Exp. 4, 28 May 1872, Bonilla, Taxcantla, to Vázquez, Tetela.

69. *El Regenerador* 1:24 and 26, 7 and 14 June 1872.

70. AMTdeO, Gobierno, Box 439, Exp. 4, 21 and 22 May 1872, Bonilla, Taxcantla, to Zamítez and Vázquez, Tetela.

71. Ibid., 25 May 1872, Carrillo to Méndez, Taxcantla.

72. Ibid., 30 May and 7 June 1872, Bonilla, Taxcantla, to Vázquez, Tetela. Carbó's account of the battle of Cuahuigtic to General Alatorre estimated that there were one thousand rebel infantry and more than two hundred cavalry facing two Federal army battalions (the Eighteenth and Nineteenth), two hundred men of the National Guard of Chignahuapan, and cavalry commanded by General Agustín Roldán; see *El Regenerador* 1:3, 4 June 1872; and ADN, Histórico, XI/481 3/9787, 221, 302, 308-11.

73. *El Regenerador* 1:26, 14 June 1872.

74. AMTdeO, Gobierno, Box 439, Exp. 4, 7 June 1872, Bonilla, Taxcantla, to Vázquez, Tetela.

75. *El Regenerador* 1:32, 5 July 1872.

76. AMTdeO, Gobierno, Box 439, Exp. 4, 9 June 1872, Méndez, Taxcantla, to Vázquez, Tetela.

77. *El Regenerador* 1:27, 16 June 1872.

78. AMTdeO, Gobierno, Box 439, Exp. 4, 12 and 14 June 1872, Bonilla, Taxcantla, to Vázquez, Tetela; *El Regenerador* 1:26, 14 June 1872, 11 June 1878, Telegram from Gabriel Rodríguez, Teziutlán, to General Alatorre; *El Regenerador* 1:27 and 29, 18 and 25 June 1872.

79. Méndez removed the municipal officials of the barrios of Hueyapan and Yaonahuac in Tlatlauqui and replaced them with *mendecista* National Guard commanders; see AMTdeO, Gobierno, Box 439, Exp. 4, 14 June 1872, Méndez, Taxcantla, to Vázquez, Tetela; *El Regenerador* 1:32, 5 July 1872.

80. *El Regenerador* 1:34, 12 July 1872.

81. AMTdeO, Gobierno, Box 439, Exp. 4, 26 July 1872, Carrillo, Cuahuigtic, to Vázquez, Tetela.

82. AMTdeO, Gobierno, Box 439, Exp. 4, general correspondence of Juan Crisóstomo Bonilla, military commander of the district, Manuel Vázquez, civil authority, with subject authorities throughout the district; *El Regenerador* 1:32, 5 July 1872.

83. AMTdeO, Gobierno, Box 439, Exp. 4, 16 and 25 July 1872, Miguel de León, Totutla, to Manuel Vázquez, Tetela.

84. Ibid., 8 July 1872, Bonilla, Tetela, to Méndez; *El Regenerador* 1:36, 19 July 1872.

85. *Periódico Oficial* 3:34, 35, 36, 27 August and 3 September 1872.

86. *Periódico Oficial* 3:44, 1 October 1872.

87. *Periódico Oficial* 3:50, 22 October 1872.

88. *Periódico Oficial* 3:53, 1 November 1872.

89. AMTdeO, Gobierno, Box 439, Exp. 4, "Correspondencia Taxcantla-Tetela, noviembre de 1871-agosto de 1872."

90. The *tres Juanes* acted as a troika in organizing the revolt. Méndez supervised the overall military command, while Bonilla was more concerned with the political administration of the district and the defense of the headquarters of the revolt at Taxcantla. Lucas was concerned, above all, with supply matters, recruitment, and dealing with problems such as desertion and conflicts within villages. Méndez, Bonilla, and Lucas referred to each other in correspondence using the codes "uno," "dos," and "tres." The impersonality of these codes often was softened by the addition of terms of endearment and ritual kinship: "Queridos dos y tres," "de tu querido compadre tres," and on one occasion "Querido Juanito dos." See AMTdeO, Gobierno, Box 439, Exp. 4.

91. For an examination of the conflicts in Tetela's lowland dependencies for control over the process of land privatization in 1869-70, see Florencia Mallon, *Peasant and Nation: The Making of Post-Colonial Mexico and Peru* (Berkeley, CA, 1995), 120-25.

92. AMTdeO, 1871, Gobierno, Box 14, Exp. 1, "Queja contra Joaquín López"; ibid., Box 18, 1871-73, "Correspondencia Jonotla."

93. The village secretary of Huitzilan's intimacy with the Tetela leadership is revealed when Andrés Velázquez, Huitzilan's most prominent producer of aguardiente, ends his letter by giving his "finos recuerdos" to "Mi maestro Don Juanito (Bonilla) y demás amigos," sending two bottles of *melado* (syrup) as a gift; see AMTdeO, Gobierno, Box 439, Exp. 4, 23 February 1872, Velázquez, Huitzilan, to Zamítez.

94. Ibid., 21 April 1872, Bonilla, Taxcantla, to Manuel Vázquez, Tetela.

95. AMTdeO, Gobierno, Box 439, Exp. 4, 5 April 1872, Miguel Cipriano, Huitzilan, to Gregorio Zamítez, Tetela.

Chapter 12, Conciliation and Violence, 201-9

1. Laurens Ballard Perry, *Juárez and Díaz Machine Politics in Mexico* (DeKalb, IL, 1978), 179-80.

2. *Periódico Oficial* 3:53, 1 November 1872.

3. *Periódico Oficial* 3:53, 1 November 1872; for the harshness of the terms of the amnesty, which Perry sees as a significant factor in keeping alive the spirit of revolution, see *Juárez and Díaz*, 179-80; *Periódico Oficial* 3:29, 9 August 1872.

4. Apart from the *jefatura política* of Zacapoaxtla, Romero Vargas also gave Carrillo, contrary to all the conditions of the amnesty, the command of the Northern Line of Puebla's National Guard; see ADN, Cancelados, C-41 XI/ 111/1-41.

5. *Periódico Oficial* 4:95, 29 November 1873.

6. *El Monitor Republicano* 23:295, 10 December 1873.

7. *Periódico Oficial* 3:35 and 65, 30 August and 13 December 1872.

8. *Periódico Oficial* 4:3, 11 January 1873.

9. *Periódico Oficial* 4:16, 26 February 1873.

10. They were released in mid-July upon payment of large fines and securities and conditional upon their not returning to the district capital; see *Periódico Oficial* 3:30, 13 August 1872.

11. For the activities of Tzinacantepeceños during earlier conflicts, see Ramón Sánchez Flores, *Zacapoaxtla: Relación histórica* (Puebla, 1984), 168; ADN, Cancelados, XI/111/3-248, ff. 1-5; and Guy P. C. Thomson, "Agrarian Conflict in the Municipality of Cuetzalan (Sierra de Puebla): The Rise and Fall of 'Pala' Agustín Dieguillo, 1861-1894," *HAHR* 71 (1991): 231.

12. Carrillo's testimony should be treated with some caution. As a Méndez supporter, he had an interest in presenting the crime as a symptom of intra-Atagpan factionalism rather than as an act directed from Xochiapulco; see *Periódico Oficial* 4:25, 29 March 1873.

13. ADN, Cancelados, XI/111/3-248.

14. APJFL, 4 March 1874, Díaz, Hacienda de Tepetates, to Lucas, Ixtacuistla; *Periódico Oficial* 4:22, 19 March 1873; Carmen Blázquez Domínguez, "San Cristobal de Tlacotalpan: Postrimerías Coloniales en una Región Sotaventina (1760-1800)," *Anuario* (Jalapa) 6:7-38.

15. *Periódico Oficial* 4:24, 26 March 1873; ibid., 4:28, 9 April 1873.

16. *Periódico Oficial* 4:47, 14 June 1873.

17. AMTdeO, Box 18 (1872-73), Exp. 8, 14 June 1873, Santa Fe to Secretaría del Gobierno y Milicias, Puebla.

18. *Periódico Oficial* 4:51, 28 June 1873; Camacho resigned the *jefatura* on 23 September 1874; see *Periódico Oficial* 5:81, 21 October 1874.

19. *Periódico Oficial* 4:55, 12 July 1873; ibid., 68, 27 August 1873.

20. *El Monitor Republicano* 23:269, 6 and 9 November 1873; ibid., 24:18, 21 January 1874; ibid., 24:23, 27 January 1874; ibid., 23:282, 25 November 1873.

21. *El Monitor Republicano* 23:282, 25 November 1873; *Periódico Oficial* 4:103, 27 December 1873.

22. *Periódico Oficial* 4:95, 29 November 1873.

23. *Periódico Oficial* 4:29, 12 April 1873.

24. Thomson, "Agrarian Conflict," 244-45.

25. *El Monitor Republicano* 23:272, 13 November 1873.

26. *El Monitor Republicano* 24:6, 7 January 1874.

27. *Periódico Oficial* 5:6, 21 January 1874; ibid., 5:8, 28 January 1874; ibid., 5:9, 31 January 1874.

28. *Periódico Oficial* 5:16, 28 February 1874.

29. For conflicting versions of the events at Atempan, see *El Siglo XIX* 56: 10,651, 8 March 1874; *Periódico Oficial* 5:18, 7 March 1874; ibid., 5:25, 8 April 1874; ibid., 5:27, 10 April 1874.

30. *Periódico Oficial* 5:48, 20 June 1874.

31. In mid-August, Captain Dionisio Leal, renowned National Guard commander of Cuahuigtic and former ally of Lucas, was assassinated in his house by a force of 30 men. The jefe político of Alatriste suspected the crime to be the work of the rival Cuahuigteco commander, José Palestina, backed by Lucas and the authorities of Xochiapulco and Libres, who had been attempting to bring Leal to trial; see *Periódico Oficial* 5:69, 5 September 1874.

32. *Periódico Oficial* 6:46, 24 July 1875; ibid., 6:47, 31 July 1875.

33. APJFL, 18 July 1875, Santa Fe, Tetela, to Lucas, Taxcantla.

34. The state deputy elections of February 1875 in Tetela were annulled and held again in March. These elections were accompanied by disorders in the districts of Matamoros, Chiautla, Atlixco, Tecamachalco, Tepeji, and Chalchicomula; see *Periódico Oficial* 6:8, 10 February 1875.

35. *Periódico Oficial* 6:10, 20 February 1875.

36. *Periódico Oficial* 6:27, 12 May 1875.

Chapter 13, The Revolution of Tuxtepec and the Montaña in Power, 211–40

1. Laurens Ballard Perry, *Juárez and Díaz Machine Politics in Mexico* (DeKalb, IL, 1978), 187; Robert Case, "El Resurgimiento de los Conservadores en México, 1876-77," *HM* 25 (1975): 204-31.

2. Daniel Cosío Villegas, *Historia Moderna de México. La República Restaurada, La Vida Política* (Mexico, 1955), 776-93.

3. *Periódico Oficial* 7:32, 6 May 1876.

4. Cosío Villegas, *República Restaurada,* 809-10.

5. Ibid.

6. Galindo y Galindo confirms Romero Vargas's unpopularity with landowners and the commercial classes due to high taxation. The rebels were also attracted by the obvious military potential of two prolific sulphur springs and saltpeter works owned by Joaquín Ruiz; see Ireneo Paz, *Algunas campañas memorias escritas de Ireneo Paz* (Mexico, 1885), 3:351-55; Cosío Villegas, *República Restaurada,* 839-40; Miguel Galindo y Galindo, *La gran década nacional* (Mexico, 1904), 1:330-31; Hugo Leicht, *Las Calles de Puebla* (Puebla, 1967), 210, 386, 447.

7. *Periódico Oficial* 7:7, 9, and 11, 29 January, 5 and 12 February 1876.

8. AMTdeO, Gobierno, Box 37, Cuartel General y Comandancia Militar 1876; Cosío Villegas, *República Restaurada*, 796; ADN, Cancelados, C-41 X1/III/1-401, ff. 221-23; *Periódico Oficial* 7:12, 13, 15, 16, and 18; 12, 16, 24, and 26 February and 8 March 1876.

9. *Periódico Oficial* 7:19, 11 March 1876.

10. *Periódico Oficial* 7:24 and 25, 25 March and 5 April 1876.

11. *Periódico Oficial* 7:25, 26, and 35, 5 and 8 April, 17 May 1876.

12. AMTdeO, Gobierno, Box 37, 13 April 1876, Comandante Militar, Tetela, to Méndez, Taxcantla; *Periódico Oficial* 7:27, 36, 37, 15 April, 20 and 27 May 1876.

13. ADN, Cancelados, C-41 XI/III/1-40, f. 23.

14. For a description of this problem in Oaxaca, see *Periódico Oficial* 7:26, 8 April 1876.

15. AMTdeO, Gobierno, Box 37, 22 March 1876, Márquez Galindo, Zacatlán, to Méndez, Taxcantla; *Periódico Oficial* 7:10, 19 April 1876; AMTdeO, Gobierno, Box 37, 30 April 1876, Miguel Negrete, Actopan, to Méndez, Taxcantla; Cosío Villegas, *República Restaurada*, 847.

16. *Periódico Oficial* 7:30, 37, 26 April and 27 May 1876.

17. *Periódico Oficial* 7:37, 38, 27 and 31 May 1876.

18. *Periódico Oficial* 7:38, 31 May 1876.

19. Díaz's strategy in the North was to avoid major encounters and to draw Federal forces away from the center and southeast where, in spite of a string of defeats, the strength of the revolution lay. Icamole, hailed as a great Federal victory, was in fact little more than a skirmish; see Perry, *Juárez and Díaz*, 234.

20. Ibid., 255-57.

21. ADN, Cancelados, XI/III 1-31, I, f. 83, 1 November 1876, Porfirio Díaz to Minister of War. During the revolt of La Noria, Díaz had first named Méndez "Jefe de los Estados de Puebla, Tlaxcala, Veracruz y Comandante del Cuerpo de Ejército." He then promoted Méndez to Second in Command of the Army of the East.

22. AMTdeO, Gobierno, Box 36, "Correspondencia con autoridades subalternas," contains accounts and correspondence between the headquarters at Taxcantla and village authorities throughout Tetela and neighboring districts concerning recruitment, desertions, supply, and taxation.

23. Perry, *Juárez and Díaz*, 245-46.

24. Cosío Villegas, *República Restaurada*, 843-46.

25. *Periódico Oficial*, Loose leaf, August 1876.

26. *Periódico Oficial* 7:53, 22 July 1876.

27. *Periódico Oficial* 7:59, 12 August 1876.

28. *Periódico Oficial* 7:61, 19 August 1876.

29. Cosío Villegas, *República Restaurada*, 391.

30. Ibid., 886-93.

31. APJFL, 8 July and 23 August 1876, Díaz, Oaxaca, to Lucas, Xochiapulco.

32. APD, 1876, Legajo 1-00001-A.

33. Cosío Villegas, *República Restaurada*, 901.

34. Cosío Villegas, *República Restaurada*, 903.

35. APJFL, 3 October 1876, Díaz, Nochustlán, to Lucas, Xochiapulco.

36. AMTdeO, Box 36, "Correspondencia con autoridades subalternas"; *Periódico Oficial* 7:77, 14 October 1876; ibid., 7:81, 25 October 1876; ibid., 7:81, 28 October 1876; ibid., 7:84, 8 November 1876.

37. José López-Portillo y Rojas, *Elevación y caída de Porfirio Díaz* (Mexico, 1975), 140.

38. Cosío Villegas, *República Restaurada*, 898-99, 904.

39. Had Carbó reached Puebla earlier, the Lerdo regime might have been saved, given the weakness of rebels in the Puebla Sierra and the fragile state of Díaz's Oaxaqueño forces, which had dwindled from 4,000 to 2,147 from desertions; see *Periódico Oficial* 7:84, 8 November 1876.

40. Cosío Villegas, *República Restaurada*, 910-11; the defection at Tlaxco on 18 November 1876 of General Jesús Alonso, who had been posted to block González's entry onto the Mexican tableland, contributed critically to the rebel victory; see Perry, *Juárez and Díaz*, 315.

41. Perry, *Juárez and Díaz*, 320-21.

42. On 6 December 1876, Díaz appointed Méndez as Second in Command of the Army, provisionally in charge of the Supreme Executive Power of the Nation; see *Periódico Oficial* 8:6, 13 December 1876.

43. Pedro Ogazón, *Memoria presentada al Congreso de la Unión por el Secretario del Estado y del Despacho de Guerra y Marina de la República Mexicana* (Mexico, 1878), 125; for Federico Gamboa's vivid childhood recollections of the arrival and presence in the capital of troops from the Puebla Sierra, see José Emilio Pacheco, ed., *Diario de Federico Gamboa (1892-1939)* (Mexico, 1977), 86-89. I am grateful to D. A. Brading for this reference.

44. *Periódico Oficial* 8:2, 29 November 1876.

45. *Periódico Oficial* 8:7, 16 December 1876.

46. AMZ, 1877, "Espediente relativo a un ocurso ante el Ejecutivo de la Unión por el Ciudadano Francisco Agustín Dieguillo y otros vecinos de Cuetzalan pidiéndole les devuelvan los terrenos que algunos C.C. se han adjudicado"; AMZ, 1877, "Espediente relativo a un ocurso que algunos guardias nacionales de este distrito presentaron ante el Presidente interino de la república quejándo de ciertos abusos que dicen se cometen con la clase indígena por estas autoridades."

47. *Periódico Oficial* 8:7, 16 December 1876; 8:17, 18 January 1877.

48. *Periódico Oficial* 8:16, 18 January 1877.

49. Daniel Cosío Villegas, *Historia Moderna de México. El Porfiriato. La Vida Política Interior*, 1:311-14; *Periódico Oficial* 8:1, 25 November 1876; 8:15, 13 January 1877.

50. APD, 1876, Legajo 1 000 265.

51. *Periódico Oficial* 8:17, 18 January 1877.

52. *Periódico Oficial* 8:15, 13 January 1877; 8:17, 18 January 1877.

53. *Periódico Oficial* 8:75, 15 August 1877.

54. Cosío Villegas, *El Porfiriato*, 314.

55. *Periódico Oficial* 8:43, 25 April 1877.

56. Ibid.

57. *Periódico Oficial* 8:45, 2 May 1877.

58. *Boletín de las leyes y disposiciones del Gobierno del Estado Libre y Soberano de Puebla* (Puebla, 1868), 3, 4, 10, 11, 33-35, 43-57. "Tlalixqueras, castigos injustificables, azotes" were still reported on haciendas near Chignahuapan in 1890; UTA-LAC, Rosendo Márquez Correspondence, 13 July 1890, Miguel Muñoz, Chignahuapan, to Márquez.

59. ADN, Cancelados (Juan Crisóstomo Bonilla) C# 22 I/III/3-248; Miguel Galindo y Galindo, *Apuntes para la biografía del General Don Juan Crisóstomo Bonilla* (Puebla, 1984; 1st edition appeared as a *Corona Funebre*, published in Mexico in 1884); Valeria Carroll, *La vida fascinante de Juan Crisóstomo Bonilla* (Mexico, 1966); Jesús Ferrer Gamboa, *Los tres Juanes de la Sierra de Puebla* (Mexico, 1967), 31-62.

60. *Periódico Oficial* 8:38, 7 April 1877.

61. Cosío Villegas, *El Porfiriato*, 314.

62. *Periódico Oficial* 8:61, 27 July 1877.

63. As governor of Guanajuato, Guzmán had joined Méndez as the most vociferous opponents of Juárez's centralizing *convocatoria* of 1867; see León A. Guzmán, *Algunas observaciones en contra del monstruoso proyecto de reformas a la Constitución del Estado* (Puebla, 1879).

64. In 1870, General Lucas had been appointed as the correspondent of the Companía Lancasteriana de México in Tetela de Ocampo; APJFL, 6 December 1870, "Cia. Lancasteriana de México" to Lucas.

65. 5 August 1879, Guillermo Prieto, Mexico, to Bonilla, Puebla, in *Documentos relativos al establecimiento de las escuelas normales de profesores de instrucción primaria y secondaria del Estado de Puebla* (Puebla, 1879), 6. The fact that many schoolmasters also doubled as village secretaries led the more cynical critics of the Montaña to see its school-building program as primarily motivated to tighten its hold on power; see *El Progreso de Zacatlán* 2:23, 1 February 1884; Gamboa, *Los tres Juanes*, 31-60.

66. Mary Kay Vaughan, "Economic Growth and Literacy in Nineteenth-Century Mexico: The Case of Puebla," in *Education and Economic Development Since the Industrial Revolution*, ed. Gabriel Tortolla (Valencia, 1990).

67. Jean Pierre Bastian, *Los disidentes: Sociedades protestantes y revolución en México, 1872-1911* (Mexico, 1989), 105-6, 145, 150.

68. *Colección de leyes y decretos del Estado Libre y Soberano de Puebla* (Puebla, 1879), 15-25; Juan Crisóstomo Bonilla, *Ley de Instrucción Pública para el Estado de Puebla* (Puebla, 15 December 1878); Lic. Luis Malanco, *Proyecto de reforma de la instrucción primaria en las escuelas municipales de México* (Puebla, 1875), upon which the Puebla law was partly based.

69. *Colección de leyes, decretos y circulares relativas a la pensión de herencias a favor del Colegio del Estado* (Puebla, 1885); *Colección de leyes y decretos del Estado Libre y Soberano de Puebla* (Puebla, 1879), 3.

70. In 1849 there were 600 municipal primary schools in the state, increasing to 762 in 1880 and 1,161 in 1894; see Mary Kay Vaughan, "Economic Growth and Literacy in Nineteenth-Century Mexico," 106.

71. Ibid.

72. *Publicación Oficial* 1:154, 29 November 1870; *Periódico Oficial* 11:26, 31 March 1880.

73. Bastian, *Los disidentes*, 68.

74. *Informe que remite a la VI Legislatura el C. General Juan Crisóstomo Bonilla, Gobernador Constitucional del Estado Libre y Soberano de Puebla, sobre el estado que guarda la administración publica desde el dia 2 de mayo de 1877 hasta el 16 de setiembre de 1880* (Mexico, 1880), quoted in Gastón García Cantú, *El Socialismo en México: Siglo XIX* (Mexico, 1969), 220-22, 480-81; idem, *El Pensamiento de la Reacción Mexicana (1860-1926)* (Mexico, 1987), 2:161.

75. Only six months earlier (on 30 July 1878) the state congress finally approved the expropriation of the hacienda of Xochiapulco and Manzanilla from Miguel Salgado and brothers, to be paid 5,000 pesos annually by the state until its full value was paid off; *Periódico Oficial* 9:65, 14 August 1878.

76. Antonio Serafín Sodi, *"Tu ya no soplas" : Monografías de San Martín Texmelucan y Hacienda de Chautla* (Puebla, 1978).

77. A description of the regime soon after Bonilla took power suggests his social isolation and points at the cultural gulf that separated the political class of the plateau from the new leaders from the Sierra; *El Siglo XIX* 72:11,673, 2 July 1877. For a reply to this criticism, see *Periódico Oficial* 8:66, 14 July 1877.

78. The decree abolishing the death penalty was issued in time to save a bandit whose sentence, on 30 May 1877, was commuted to five years imprisonment; *Periódico Oficial* 8:54, 2 June 1877; *Colección de leyes y decretos del Estado Libre y Soberano de Puebla* (Puebla, 1878), 157.

79. *Colección de leyes y decretos del Estado Libre y Soberano de Puebla* (Puebla, 1878), 172, 174, 179, 184, 186, 216; *Colección de leyes y decretos del Estado Libre y Soberano de Puebla* (Puebla, 1879), 105, 186, 188.

80. *Colección de leyes y decretos del Estado Libre y Soberano de Puebla* (Puebla, 1878), 71, 107-8, 121, 156.

81. *Periódico Oficial* 8:53, 30 May 1877.

82. APD, Legajo 3/1 00249.

83. *Periódico Oficial* 9:58, 20 July 1878.

84. *Periódico Oficial* 9:79, 80, 101, 2 and 5 October 1878 and 18 December 1878.

85. *Periódico Oficial* 10:53, 2 July 1879.

86. *Periódico Oficial* 10:54, 5 July 1879.

87. Guzmán, *Algunas observaciones*, 34.

88. AMTdeO, 1879 Box, 1 April 1879, Lucas to Alcalde, Ometepec.

89. For the program for the 5th of May festivities in Tetela in 1879, see *Periódico Oficial* 10:37, 7 May 1879.

90. AMTdeO, 1879 Box, Exp. 34, "Circulares de la Secretaría de Gobernación."

91. AMTdeO, 1879 Box, "Cuadro sinóptico o escrutinio general de los votos emitidos para Jefe Político . . . Mayo de 1879."

92. Manzano Díaz, *El indígena de la Sierra*, 72.

93. AMTdeO, Gobierno, 1879, Box 49; AMTdeO, Gobierno, 1880, Box 54.

94. AMTdeO, Gobierno, 1880, Box 54, 26 November 1879, Lucas, Zautla, to Sec. de Gobernación y Milicias.

95. *Periódico Oficial* 10:99, 10 December 1879.

96. Pacheco had gained experience in managing elections in Puebla when, as interim governor, he had secured Bonilla's election in 1877; see Cosío Villegas, *El Porfiriato*, 1:313.

97. AMTdeO, 1880 Box, Exp. 10, "Tranquilidad y seguridad pública en el Distrito."

98. AMTdeO, 1880 Box, Exp. 88, "Espediente relativo a la fuga de los prisioneros de la carcel de esta Villa."

99. AMTdeO, 1867 Box, Exp. 55, "Relación de Muertos y Heridos."

100. *Periódico Oficial* 8:95 and 107, 24 October 1877 and 5 December 1877.

101. AMTdeO, Gobierno, 1880, Box 51, Exp. 3.

102. AMTdeO, 1880 Box, Exp. 72, "Averiguación contra José de la Luz Domínguez acusado de rebelión," 24 March 1880, Valentín Sánchez to Jefe Político.

103. AMTdeO, Gobierno, Box 8, Exp. 6, 8 December 1861, Miguel Sánchez to Alcalde, Tetela; AMTdeO, Gobierno, Box 37, 1876, Isidro Segura and twenty-two "vecinos de Ometepec" to Comandante Militar.

104. AGN, Gobernación Seguridad Pública 2a. 880 (15) (8), 18 April 1880, Miguel Arriaga et al., Zacapoaxtla, to Gobernación.

105. AMTdeO, 1880 Box, Exp. 72, "Averiguación contra José de la Luz Domínguez acusado de rebelión," 24 March 1880, Sánchez to Jefe Político.

106. AMTdeO, Box 1879, "Borrador del jefe político," No. 617; AMTdeO, Gobierno, 1880, Exp. 107, "Expediente sobre el atentado de homicidio cometida por José María Rodríguez y socios en la persona del Gral. C. Juan Francisco Lucas Jefe Político de este Distrito," 17 May 1880, Lucas to Juez Sustituto del 1a Instancia.

107. Ibid.

108. Accompanying this year of elections, Puebla experienced a remarkable flurry of political newspapers in 1880, few of which survived the year: *Periódico Oficial, La Revista Eclesiástica, La Cruz, La Lealtad, La Palabra Libre, La Bandera Blanca, El Estado, La Revista del*

Foro, El Amigo de la Verdad, La Unión Liberal, La Escuela, La Libertad, La Emulación, El Hijo del Trabajo, El Radical, La Voz de la Justicia, La Voz del Pueblo, El Perrito, La Página Teatral, El Angel de la Guarda, La Pagina Roja, El Sol, El Mexicano, La Voz de la Sierra; see Osvaldo Tamaín, "Puebla y las elecciones de 1880," in *Espacios y perfiles: Historia regional mexicana del siglo XIX*, ed. Carlos Contreras Cruz (Puebla, 1989), 1:245.

109. Puebla's *Periódico Oficial* insisted that Arriaga had been wounded in a drunken brawl with Vicente Sayago. For a reproduction of the article, see *La Tribuna* 2:21, 2 June 1880.

110. *La Tribuna* 2:267, 269, 11 and 13 August 1880; APD, 5/3/1365/66, 5 August 1880, Carrillo and Pacheco to Díaz.

111. For the National Guard companies kept on active service in Tetela, see APJFL, "Papeles de 1880."

112. Guzmán, *Algunas observaciones*; AMTdeO, Gobierno, 1880, Box 54, "Espediente relativo a elecciones primarias de poderes generales."

113. Casío Villegas, *El Porfiriato*, 1:466, 523-25, 531-32; Osvaldo Tamaín, "Puebla y las elecciones de 1880," 246.

114. Hermenegildo Carrillo received considerable support from the Catholic Church, which ensured respectable numbers of votes in Chalchicomula, Atlixco, Puebla, and Tecamachalco; *Periódico Oficial* 11:71, 11 September 1880.

115. *Periódico Oficial* 11:62, 4 August 1880.

116. *La Tribuna* 2:230, 26 June 1880.

117. AMZ, 1880, "Espediente relativo a la sublevación del barrio de Atagpan," 30 June and 8 July 1880, Lucas, Tetela, to Luna, Zacapoaxtla; 2 July 1880, Luna, Zacapoaxtla, to Sec. de Gobernación y Milicias del Estado; AGN, Gobernación, 2a, 880 (15) (3), 13 July 1880, Bonilla, Puebla, to Gobernación.

118. AGN, Gobernación, 2a Relaciones con los Estados, Tranquilidad Pública, 880 (15) (3), 13 July 1880, Bonilla, Puebla, to Gobernación.

119. ADN, Cancelados, 609 D/1111.4/7363. 1-14; APD, L. S/4 001649, 12 August 1880, Yrene Rodríguez de Mirón to Díaz.

120. AMTdeO, Gobierno, 1880, Box 54, "Expediente relativo a los sublevados del pueblo de Ometepeque comprensión de este Distrito"; AGN, Gobernación, 2a, Relaciones con los Estados, Tranquilidad Pública, 880 (15) (3), 13 July 1880, Bonilla, Puebla, to Gobernación.

121. AMZ, 1880, "Espediente relativo a la sublevación del barrio de Atagpan," 8 July 1880, Luna, Zacapoaxtla, to Sec. de Gobernación y Milicias del Estado, Puebla.

122. Ibid., 13 July 1880, Luna, Zacapoaxtla, to Sec. de Gobernación y Milicias del Estado, Puebla.

123. Ibid., 12 July 1880, Miguel Calderón, Cuetzalan, to Jefe Politico; 13 July 1880, Luna, Zacapoaxtla, to Dieguillo, Cuetzalan; 18, 20, 27 and 27 July 1880, Dieguillo, Cuetzalan, to Jefe Político, Zacapoaxtla.

124. AMTdeO, Gobierno, 1880, Exp. 125, "Contra Miguel Arriaga y socios, acusados de sublevación y conato de homicidio en las personas del Gral. C. Juan Francisco Lucas y Coronel C. Luis Antonio Díaz"; Exp. 155, "Expediente relativo a los sublevados del pueblo de Ometepec . . . de este Distrito."

125. APD, 5/3/001369, 8 August 1880, Prieto to Díaz.

126. APD, 5/3 0001380, 11 August 1880, Díaz to Prieto.

127. *Periódico Oficial* 11:51, 26 June 1880. These practices were also confirmed by Generals Carrillo and Pacheco from Tehuacán; see *La Tribuna* 2:267, 269, 12 and 13 August 1880; APD, 5/3 1365-66, 3 August 1880, Carrillo and Pacheco to Díaz.

128. APD, 5/3 001 381-82, 9 August 1880, Prieto to Díaz.

129. APD, 5/3 001 404, 23 July 1880, Encarnación Méndez to Juan Nepomuceno Méndez; *La Tribuna* 2:259, 1 August 1880.

130. APD, 5/3 001 381-82, 9 August 1880, Prieto to Díaz.

131. AMZ, 1880, "Espediente relativo a la sublevación del barrio de Atagpan de esta municipalidad."

132. AMTdeO, 1880, Exp. 128, "Derogación del decreto que erigió en pueblo a los barrios de Ometepec y Tececuilco," 27 August 1880, Lucas to President of the Ayuntamiento de Ometepec; *Periódico Oficial* 11:63, 7 August 1880.

133. *Periódico Oficial* 13:3, 10 April 1881.

134. *Periódico Oficial* 8:45, 2 May 1877; 11:1, 3 January 1880; Gamboa, *Los tres Juanes*, 60.

135. Cosío Villegas, *El Porfiriato* 1:523-25, 531-32.

Chapter 14, The Resurgence of Central Power, 241–60

1. *Periódico Oficial* 13:3, 17 February 1881; for railway projects in Puebla during the Méndez governorship, see Georgette José Valenzuela, *Los ferrocarriles y el General Manuel Gónzalez* (Mexico, 1994), 195-250.

2. Daniel Cosío Villegas, *Historia Moderna de México. El Porfiriato. La Vida Política Interior*, 1: 623-24; *Mensaje que el gobernador del estado remitió el dia 2 de julio a la Legislatura* (Puebla, 1883), 8-9.

3. *Mensaje que el gobernador del estado remitió el dia 2 de enero a la Legislatura* (Puebla, 1885), 12.

4. *Mensaje que el gobernador del estado remitió el dia 10 de julio a la Legislatura* (Puebla, 1884), 7-12.

5. APD, 7/2 000411, 29 April 1882, Manuel Dublán, Mexico, to Díaz, Oaxaca; 000425, 27 April 1882, Palacios, Tepeji, to Díaz, Oaxaca; *Mensaje que el gobernador del estado remitió el dia 2 de julio a la Legislatura* (Puebla, 1883), 9.

6. *El Progreso de Zacatlán* 2:23, 1 February 1884.

7. *El Progreso de Zacatlán* 2:22, 15 January 1884.

8. *El Progreso de Zacatlán* 2:23, 1 February 1884.

9. Cosío Villegas, *El Porfiriato* 1:624.

10. Miguel Galindo y Galindo, *Corona Funebre Apuntes para la biografía de General Juan Crisóstomo Bonilla* (Puebla, 1884); Cosío Villegas, *El Porfiriato,* 1:625; "Elecciones en el Estado de Puebla (1884)," in *Catalogo de documentos y cartas de la Colección Porfirio Díaz noviembre-diciembre 1884,* ed. María del Carmen Ruiz de la Garza (Mexico, 1987), xxx.

11. Ramón Márquez Galindo died on 24 February 1877; see *Publicación Oficial* 8:24, February 1877.

12. Cosío Villegas, *El Porfiriato* 1:626, 827.

13. Ibid., 626.

14. Ibid., 623.

15. APJFL, 1 July 1884, Márquez, Tetela, to Lucas, Xochiapulco.

16. APJFL, 2 June [*sic*] 1884, Lucas, Xochiapulco, to Márquez, Tetela; 7 July 1884, Márquez, Tetela, to Lucas, Xochiapulco.

17. APJFL, 6 July 1884, Lauro Luna, Tetela, to Lucas, Xochiapulco; 7 July 1884, M. Galindo, Tetela, to Lucas, Xochiapulco.

18. APJFL, 22 July 1884, Márquez, Puebla, to Lucas, Xochiapulco.

19. APJFL, 3 and 17 November 1884, 17 February 1885, Lucas, Xochiapulco, to Díaz, Mexico; 9 November, 1 December 1884, Díaz, Mexico, to Lucas, Xochiapulco.

20. APJFL, 1 December 1884, Márquez to Lucas, Xochiapulco.

21. APJFL, 1 December 1884, Lucas, Xochiapulco, to Márquez.

22. Ruiz de la Garza, "Elecciones," 34.

23. Ibid., 40-46.

24. UTA-LAC, Rosendo Márquez Papers, Roll 159; for the Report on constitutional terms for the governorship, see 31 January 1885.

25. APJFL, 20 and 22 December 1884, Vázquez, Teziutlán, to Lucas.

26. Ruiz de la Garza, "Elecciones," 45.

27. Ibid., 46-47.

28. APJFL, 1, 14, and 16 February 1885, Márquez, Puebla, to Lucas, Xochiapulco; 13 February 1885, Lucas to Márquez.

29. APD, 10/C/4 001707, 001730, 10/6/002853, 10/6/002666.

30. APD, 10/6 002849, 16 March 1885, Márquez to Díaz.

31. APD 10/16 002787, 28 February 1885, Enrique Mont, Tehuacán, to Díaz; 10/6 002804 and 002805, 2 and 6 March 1885, Márquez to Díaz.

32. For Lucas's recommendations for the ayuntamiento of Zautla, see UTA-LAC, Rosendo Márquez Papers, Roll 159, 19 October 1885, Lucas, Tetela, to Márquez.

33. APJFL, 12 December 1885, Márquez to Lucas.

34. APJFL, 8 September 1885, Márquez to Lucas; 6 September 1885, Márquez to Lucas; 18 September 1885, Lucas to Márquez; 2 November 1885, Lucas to Márquez; 9 November 1885, Márquez to Lucas.

35. UTA-LAC, Rosendo Márquez Papers, Roll 159, 30 November 1885, Bernal, Libres, to Márquez.

36. APD, 10/24 11744; AMTdeO, Gobierno, 36, "Correspondencia Huitzilan," Apolinar Martínez, Comandante Militar, February-November 1876; APD, Letter Books, 40-5, 7 December 1885, Díaz to Márquez; APD, 10/23 011, 1867, December 1885, Márquez to Díaz; 10/23/011225, 6 December 1885, Arriaga to Bernal; 10/24 011/44, 5 December 1885, Galván to Díaz; 10/23 011224, 11 December 1885, Márquez to Díaz; UTA-LAC, Rosendo Márquez Papers, Roll 159, 30 November 1883, Bernal, Libres, to Márquez.

37. UTA-LAC, Rosendo Márquez Papers, Roll 159, 3 December 1885, José de Jesús Bernal, Libres, to Márquez, and reply to Bernal from Márquez.

38. UTA-LAC, Rosendo Márquez Papers, Roll 159, 7 July 1885, Bernal to Márquez; 20 July 1885, Bernal to Márquez; 30 November 1885, Bernal to Márquez; 1 December 1885, Bernal to Márquez; Roll 160, 8 February 1886, Díaz to Márquez; 24 February 1886, Márquez to Díaz; 24 February 1886, Lucas to Márquez; 3 March 1886, Lucas to Márquez; 28 March 1886, Vecinos del Barrio de la Cañada, Libres, to Márquez; 14 December 1886, Márquez Escobedo, Chignahuapan, to Bernal; 24 February 1887, Antonio Parra, Zautla, to Márquez.

39. APJFL, 16 December 1885, Lucas to Márquez; APD, 11/19 09169, 30 August 1886, Díaz to Márquez; 11/20 009813, 6 December 1886, Márquez to Díaz.

40. Cosío Villegas, *El Porfiriato*, 2:75-79; Miguel Angel Granados Chapa, *Alfonso Cravioto: Un liberal Hidalguense* (Mexico, 1984), 21-22.

41. UTA-LAC, Rosendo Márquez Papers, Roll 159, 11 June 1885, Márquez Galindo, Zacatlán, to Márquez.

42. APD, 11/13 006131-2, 5 June 1886, Márquez to Díaz.

43. For a description of these festivities in Huauchinango, see UTA-LAC, Rosendo Márquez Papers, Roll 161, 21 May 1888, Emilio Betancurt to Márquez.

44. Pablo Valderrama Rouy and Carolina Ramírez Suárez, "Resistencia étnica y defensa del territorio en el Totonacapan serrano: Cuetzalan en el siglo XIX," in *Indio, nación y comunidad en el México del siglo XIX*, ed. Antonio Escobar (Mexico, 1993), 202; UTA-LAC, Rosendo Márquez Papers, Roll 160, 27 November 1887, Betancurt Molina, Zacapoaxtla, to Márquez; Roll 161, 7 February 1888, Betancurt Molina, Zacapoaxtla, to Márquez.

45. UTA-LAC, Rosendo Márquez Papers, Roll 160, 21 December 1886, Betancurt Molina, Zacapoaxtla, to Márquez; 10 February 1887, Betancurt Molina, Zacapoaxtla, to Márquez.

46. APD, 12/25 12199, 10 December 1887, Márquez to Díaz; 12028, 10 December 1887, Davalos to Díaz.

47. Mucio Martínez formed his corps of *rurales* from the remnants of a force of bandits "from the *tierra caliente*"; see APD, 10/15 007460, 9 July 1885, Márquez to Díaz; ADN, Cancelados, XI/481 3/3758; APD 12/25 012212.

48. APD, 12/25 012030, 16 December 1887, Davalos to Díaz.

49. Márquez added that the rumors of troop mobilization in the Sierra had gained additional credence because of the habit of timing the election of National Guard commanders to coincide with municipal elections in December and January; see APD, 12/25 012206, 13 December 1887, Díaz to Márquez; 12/25 012206, 20 December 1887, Márquez to Díaz.

50. ADN, Cancelados, C-64 D/I11/2/425 II, f. 83, 19 December 1887, Davalos to Lucas; f. 84, 22 December 1887, Lucas to Davalos; f. 85, 23 December 1887, Lucas to General en Gefe de la 9a Zona Militar.

51. APJFL, 6 and 13 January, 15 February and 16 April 1888, Lucas to Díaz.

52. UTA-LAC, Rosendo Márquez Papers, Roll 161, 12 June 1888, *Convocatoria* for federal congressional deputies.

53. APJFL, 17 June 1888, Luis Antonio Díaz to Lucas; UTA-LAC, Rosendo Márquez Papers, Roll 161, 15 June 1888, Bernal, Libres, to Márquez; 16 June 1888, Lucas, Teteia, to Márquez; 21 June 1888, Bernal, Libres, to Márquez.

54. APJFL, 18 June 1888, Manuel Crisolís to Lucas; 18 June 1888, Lucas to Crisolís.

55. APJFL, 18 June 1888, Lucas to Díaz.

56. APJFL, 20 June 1888, Lucas to Dinorín.

57. APJFL, 19 June 1888, Juan Dinorín to Lucas.

58. APD, 13/12 005839 18, 27 June 1888, Lucas to Díaz; APJFL, 27 June 1888, Díaz to Lucas; APD, 13/12 005895, 22 June 1888, Díaz to Márquez.

59. APJFL, 23 and 25 June 1888, Márquez to Lucas; UTA-LAC, Rosendo Márquez Papers, Roll 161, 15 June 1888, Bernal, Libres, to Márquez; 24 June 1888, Márquez to Lucas.

60. APJFL, n.d., Lucas to Márquez; 25 June 1888, Lucas to Márquez; 27 June 1888, Lucas to Díaz; APD, 005838, 27 June 1888, Lucas to Díaz.

61. Articles 31, 35, and 36 of the federal constitution all allude to the National Guard. Article 36 states that it is the "obligation of every citizen of the Republic . . . to enlist in the National Guard"; see *Constitución de los Estados Unidos Mexicanos expedido por el congreso primera Constituyente el dia 5 de febrero de 1857 con sus adiciones y reformas* (Mexico, 1905), 16-18, quoted in Robert Alexius, "The Army and Politics in Porfirian Mexico" (Ph.D. diss., University of Texas, 1976), 115-17.

62. For an examination of the fiscal problems that plagued the Márquez governorship, see Osvaldo A. Tamaín, "El Porfirismo en Puebla, 1867-1910," in *Puebla: Una historia compartida* (Mexico, 1993), 325-35.

63. For the full personal tax law of 21 June 1877, see APD, 13/14 006998, 31 March 1888. Railway workers were also exempted, and many *serranos* were away working on railways at this time.

64. APD, 13/14 006978, 27 June 1888, Márquez to Díaz.

65. APD, 13/14 006981, 2 July 1888, Díaz to Márquez; 13/14 006983, 3 July 1888, Díaz to Márquez; 13/14 006992, 7 July 1888, Márquez to Díaz.

66. APJFL, 2 July 1888, Lucas to Márquez.

67. UTA-LAC, Rosendo Márquez Papers, Roll 161, 24 June 1888, Betancurt Molina, Zacapoaxtla, to Márquez; 25 and 29 June 1888, Isidro Grimaldo, Tetela, to Márquez; 28 June 1888, Márquez to Grimaldo.

68. APJFL, 5 July 1888, Márquez to Lucas; 10 July 1888, Lucas to Márquez; 10 July 1888, Márquez to Lucas.

69. APJFL, 11 July 1888, Márquez to Lucas.

70. APJFL, 19 July 1888, Lucas to Márquez.

71. APD, 13/15 007127, July 1888, Luis Olivares et al. to Díaz; 1 July 1888, José María Juárez to Díaz.

72. APD, 13/12, 29 July 1888, Juárez to Díaz.

73. APD, 13/15, 007001, 30 July 1888, Díaz to Márquez.

74. Cosío Villegas, *El Porfiriato*, 2:96-99.

75. APJFL, 3 September 1888, Lucas to Márquez.

76. Márquez's own words were: "Que se vayan a Xochiapulco a hacer la revolución; ya se acabó el tiempo que los niños de Tetela mandaban el Estado, hoy cabrestran o se mueren"; see APJFL, 25 September 1888, Manuel Francisco Bonifacio to Lucas.

77. APJFL, 3 September 1888, Lucas to Márquez; UTA-LAC, Rosendo Márquez Papers, Roll 161, 2 July 1888, Lucas, Tetela, to Márquez.

78. APJFL, "Batallón de Guardia Nacional de Zautla, Primero Companía," 2 July 1888; ibid., "Segundo Companía de Fuerzas de Seguridad, Chinampan," 10 July 1888.

79. UTA-LAC, Rosendo Márquez Papers, Roll 162, 31 December 1888, Lucas, Tetela, to Márquez.

Chapter 15, Public and Private Life, 261–78

1. *Constitución Política del Estado Libre y Soberano de Puebla reformada conforme a los decretos expedidos por el congreso constitucional del mismo estado en 5 de julio de 1880 y en 30 de septiembre de 1883* (Mexico, 1883).

2. The local Aquixtla historian, José María Domínguez, claims that Díaz was careful to ensure that Tetela was free from tyrannical jefes políticos and that the "hijos del distrito" were well represented in the state and national congresses; see *Ensayo crítico-histórico sobre la revolución de la Noria* (Mexico, 1934), 166. Antonio Méndez served as state deputy for Tetela in 1877-78, Miguel Méndez in 1879-80, Lauro Luna in 1885-86, Pomposo Bonilla in 1887-94 and 1897-1904, Juan Crisóstomo Bonilla in 1895-96 and 1905-12, Abraham Lucas in 1913-16 and 1921-23, and Ricardo Márquez Galindo in 1917-19; see Archivo del Congreso del Estado, Puebla.

3. Donna Rivera Moreno, *Xochiapulco: Una gloria olvidada* (Puebla, 1991), 37-40.

4. Lucas's salary was paid by the state governor until 1891 when the Ministry of War took over its payment. In the following year, Lucas declined Mucío Martínez's offer of the post of inspector of state forces.

5. ADN, Cancelados, C-64 D/111/2/425, II, f. 94.

6. APJFL, 3 February 1885, Díaz to Lucas; ADN, Cancelados, C-64 D/111/2/425, 1, f. 30. In 1899, Lucas was listed as one of the five surviving "Generales de Brigada Auxiliares en disponibilidad" along with Lazaro Garza Ayala (1863), Pedro C. Brito (1867), Hipólito Charles (1877), and Francisco Estrada (1879); see *Memoria que el Secretario del Estado y del Despacho de Guerra y Marina, General de División Felipe B. Berriozabal presente al Congreso de la unión y comprende de 19 de marzo de 1896 a 30 de junio de 1899* (Mexico, 1899), Anexos, 11; ADN, Cancelados, C-64 D/111/2/425, I, f. 86; II, ff. 94, 258.

7. ADN, Cancelados, C-64 D/111/2/425, I, f. 86, 23 July 1888, Lucas to Minister of War.

8. APJFL, 28 October 1890, Márquez to Lucas.

9. APJFL, Folders 1889, 1890.

10. APJFL, 8 April 1890, Luis Antonio Díaz to Lucas.

11. APJFL, 25 May 1890, Márquez to Lucas.

12. APJFL, 27 May 1890, Díaz to Lucas; APD, Letter Books, 41/15 and 17, 11 and 17 May, Díaz to Márquez.

13. UTA-LAC, Rosendo Márquez Correspondence, Roll 161, 24 June 1888, Betancurt Molina, Zacapoaxtla, to Márquez; 25 and 29 June 1888, Isidro Grimaldo, Tetela, to Márquez; 28 June 1888, Márquez to Grimaldo; APJFL, 19 April 1890, Lic. Lobato, Vicente Luna, and Venancio Lobato.

14. APJFL, 26 April 1890, Márquez to Lucas.

15. Lucas seemed anxious to play down the significance of the conflict; APJFL, 5 May 1890, Lucas to Márquez; 11 May 1890, Lucas to Díaz.

16. UTA-LAC, Rosendo Márquez Correspondence, Roll 163, 15 August 1888, Luis Antonio Díaz to Márquez.

17. Ibid., 13 July 1888, Emilio Betancurt, Teziutlán, to Márquez.

18. Ibid., 2 July 1888, Emilio Betancurt, Teziutlán, to Márquez.

19. Guy P. C. Thomson, "Francisco Agustín Dieguillo: Un liberal cuetzalteco decimonónico (1861-1894)," in Jane-Dale Lloyd and Laura Pérez Rosales, eds., *Paisajes rebeldes: Una larga noche de rebelión indígena* (Mexico, 1995), 132-37.

20. Ramón Sánchez Flores, *Zacapoaxtla: Relación histórica* (Mexico, 1984), 223-41.

21. *El Hijo de Ahuizote*, 4 April 1897, 223, quoted in Robert Alexius, "The Army and Politics in Porfirian Mexico" (Ph.D. diss., University of Texas, 1976), 36.

22. David LaFrance, *The Mexican Revolution in Puebla, 1908-1913: The Maderista Movement and the Failure of Liberal Reform* (Wilmington, DE, 1989), xxxiii.

23. UTA-LAC, Rosendo Márquez Correspondence, Roll 163, 3 August 1890, Luis Antonio Díaz, Xochiapulco, to Márquez.

24. Osvaldo A. Tamaín, "El porfirismo en Puebla, 1867-1910," in *Puebla: Una historia compartida* (Puebla, 1993), 332.

25. APJFL, 18 March, 7 April, 4 May, 4 June, 4 July, 15 August 1892, Díaz to Lucas; 23 March, 2 April, 1 June, 28 June, Lucas to Díaz.

26. Daniel Cosío Villegas, *Historia Moderna de México. El Porfiriato, La Vida Política Interior* 2:448-49; Tamaín, "El porfirismo," 336-37.

27. For Isidro Grimaldo's business interests in San Esteban Cuautempan and Huitzilan, see AGNP, Tetela, 1881, ff. 1-2; Tetela, 1880, ff. 2, 18; Tetela, 1918-19, ff. 4-29; Tetela, 1920-21, ff. 114-25.

28. Unfortunately, the name of this alternative candidate is not mentioned; see APJFL, 20 September 1895, Díaz to Lucas; 24 October 1895, Díaz to Lucas.

29. LaFrance, *The Mexican Revolution*, xvii-30.

30. Punctuation has been altered in the quotation; see APJFL, 3 May 1901, Lucas to Díaz and Lucas to Martínez; 4 and 6 May 1901, Lucas to Méndez.

31. APJFL, 24 April 1903, Miguel Arriaga, Zacapoaxtla, to Lucas.

32. APJFL, 27 April 1903, Lucas to Miguel Arriaga.

33. Octaviano Manzano Díaz, *El indígena de la Sierra Norte de Puebla y sus luchas por la libertad* (Mexico, 1987), 73; Enrique Cardenas de la Peña, *Mil personajes en el México del Siglo XIX, 1840-1870* (Mexico, 1979), 2:397; Rivera, *Xochiapulco*, 163.

34. APJFL, Autobiographical fragment.

35. Rivera, *Xochiapulco*, 277-79.

36. AMTdeO, Padrón Familiar de Xochiapulco, 1873.

37. AMZ, Registro Civil, 1868.

38. Sánchez Flores, *Zacapoaxtla*, 133-54; APJFL, Escrituras, 5 December 1874, Juan Francisco Ramírez, Miguel Español, and Indalecio Sánchez to María Josefa, and 22 August 1877, Juan Francisco Dinorín, Miguel Español, and Arcadio Romero to María Josefa; AGNP, Tetela, 1885, ff. 8-9.

39. Doña Dolores Manzano, Lucas's granddaughter (Miguel's daughter), has recently sold her property in Tetela.

40. AMTdeO, Padrones de 1873, 1881, 1887, and 1902.

41. APJFL, "Juan Francisco Lucas por 'Un Serrano,'" 1920.

42. AGNP, Tetela, 1890, ff. 16-18.

43. ADN, Histórico, 9893, f. 215, 4 October 1868, Lucas to Ciudadano Presidente de la República.

44. Its actual extension was a subject of dispute. In 1861, Pérez successfully resisted the claims of two *vecinos* of Zautla, backed by their alcalde, that some of the best arable land of the estate belonged to the "común de Zautla"; see AMTdeO, "Libros de Actas del Ilustre Ayuntamiento de Tetela de Oro, ano de 1861 . . . sesión de cabildo 25 mayo 1861."

45. AMTdeO, Gobierno, Box 7, Exp. 1, 2 May 1855, López to Sub-Prefect.

46. APJFL, 28 October 1890, Márquez to Lucas.

47. AGNP, Tetela, 1855, ff. 11-12.

48. AGNP, Tetela, 1868, ff. 7-8

49. AGNP, Tetela, 1868, ff. 24, 50-51; AMTdeO, Gobierno, 1872, Box 439, Exp. 4.

50. This was evident in 1871 when Lucas put up 1,000 pesos for Bonilla, jefe político, as security for collection of the district's National Guard tax; see AGNP, Tetela, 1871, ff. 22-23.

51. AMTdeO, Box 439, Exp. 4, Bonilla-Vázquez correspondence, December 1871-August 1872.

52. Méndez, Luna, and Grimaldo, who took over management of the estate for a period of ten years, had all recently invested in silver-mining ventures in Tetela and were interested in the estate's reserves of timber as well as the rents from over forty smallholders; see AGNP, Tetela, 1878, ff. 16-19, 31-32.

53. UTA-LAC, Rosendo Márquez Correspondence, Roll 160, 30 January 1886, Méndez, Mexico, to Márquez.

54. AGNP, Tetela, 1881, ff. 10-11; Tetela, 1884, f. 33; Tetela, 1885, ff. 23-24; Tetela, 1886, 17 August 1886; Tetela, 1887-88, ff. 45-46; Tetela, 1890, ff. 16-18.

55. AGNP, Tetela, 1883, ff. 65-66.

56. AGNP, Tetela, 1882, ff. 51-52; Tetela, 1882, ff. 97-99; Tetela, 1882, ff. 105-13, 138-39; Tetela, 1883, ff. 46-47; Tetela, 1884, ff. 38-39; Tetela, 1886, ff. 1-3, 36-37, 64; Tetela, 1890, f. 3.

57. AGNP, Tetela, 1877, ff. 34-35; Tetela, 1886, ff. 13-14; Tetela, 1886, ff. 14-16; Tetela, 1887-88, ff. 47.

58. AGNP, Tetela, 1871, ff. 22-23; Tetela, 1887-88, ff. 15-17, 23-29.

59. AGNP, Tetela, 1889, ff. 24-25, 54, 56.

60. AGNP, Tetela, 1889, ff. 70-71, 89, 58, 61.

61. UTA-LAC, Rosendo Márquez Correspondence, Roll 163, 1 April 1891, Lucas, Tetela, to Márquez.

62. AGNP, Tetela, 1881, f. 33.

63. AGNP, Tetela, 1883, ff. 19-20.

64. AGNP, Tetela, 1891, ff. 1, 2, 9, 10, 14-15, 16, 46, 47.

65: AGNP, Tetela, 1891, f. 18; Tetela, 1892, ff. 30-31, 106; Tetela, 1893, f. 55; Tetela, 1894, ff. 65, 181; APJFL, Titles of "Tetel-Xalatajco," "Xicalahuata," and "Elotepec," 9 January 1902; AGNP, Tetela, 1920-22, ff. 10-12.

66. AGNP, Tetela, 1920-22, ff. 77-78,

67. Rivera, *Xochiapulco*, 103.

68. An initial gift of a clock for Xochiapulco came from Luis Mier y Terán, governor of Veracruz in 1877. It is uncertain whether this was the same clock that Lucas delivered in 1900; see APJFL, 27 November 1877, Luis Mier y Terán, Jalapa, to Lucas, Taxcantla; APJFL, "Reloj para la Villa del Cinco de Mayo," 5 July 1900, Martín Xalteno and Juan Manuel Santos to Lucas.

69. APJFL, 3 June 1900, Juan Francisco to Miguel Lucas, Xochiapulco.

70. Lucas's granddaughter Aurora recalled that he preferred the Rancho de Acatlán in the barrio of Xaltatempa; interview with Aurora Lucas, Puebla, April 1984.

71. At the Tetela Sunday market of 13 January 1900, Lucas could sell only eight *arrobas* of pork, sending the meat that remained to Miguel to sell in Xochiapulco. He kept behind the four *arrobas* of tallow, the most valuable part of the animal, which he marketed beyond the region; see APJFL, 13 January 1900, Juan Francisco, Tetela, to Miguel, Xochiapulco.

72. APJFL, 11 June 1914, Juan Francisco, Tetela, to Miguel, Acatlán.

73. APJFL, 9 March 1914, Juan Francisco, Tetela, to Miguel, Acatlán.

74. APJFL, 14 July 1914, Juan Francisco, Taxcantla, to Miguel, Acatlán.

75. APJFL, 11 June 1914, Juan Francisco, Tetela, to Miguel, Acatlán.

76. AGNP, Tetela, 1918-19, ff. 61, 73-90.

77. AGNP, Tetela, 1918-19, ff. 98-99; ADN, Cancelados, C-64 D/111/2/425, II, f. 370, 9 February 1917.

78. AGNP, Tetela, 1918-19, ff. 41-42, 44-45, 53-54, 119-22.

79. AGNP, Tetela, 1920-21, ff. 1-2, 114-25, 126-32.

80. AGNP, Tetela, 1918-19, ff. 4-29.

81. AGNP, Tetela, 1894, ff. 257-58.

82. ADN, Cancelados, C-64 D/111/2/425, II, 24 May 1916, Lucas, Tetela, to General Alvaro Obregón.

83. AGNP, Tetela, 1917, ff. 6, 90-91.

84. AGNP, Tetela, 1918-19, ff. 70-71.

85. AGNP, Tetela, 1920-21, ff. 1-2.

86. APJFL, 17 February 1884, Juan Francisco, Tetela, to Miguel.

87. In 1995, upon the centenary of his death, Lauro Luna's unpublished memoirs were handed over to the state government by Marina Fuentes Sánchez of Tetela de Ocampo, descendant of Miguel Sánchez, friend of Luna and fellow veteran of the battle of 5 May 1862; see Lauro Luna, *Batallón de la Guardia Nacional de Tetela de Ocampo, 1862-1867 (memorias)* (Puebla, 1995).

88. APJFL, 29 July 1897, José Carrasco, Mexico, to Lucas.

89. APJFL, 15 June 1897, Colonel Miguel Melgarejo, Perote, to Lucas.

90. APJFL, 20 June 1897, Lucas to Melgarejo.

91. APJFL, 10 August 1897, Lucas to José Carrasco. Five copies were retained by Lucas and six sold to José de Segura (son of Ometepec National Guard Captain Isidro Segura), Víctor Méndez (brother of Juan N. Méndez), Isidro Grimaldo (jefe político), Miguel Cruz (Ometepec), Manuel Gómez, and Vicente Bonilla (son of Juan C. Bonilla).

92. APJFL, "Juan Francisco Lucas" by "Un Serrano," 1920.

93. Javier Garciadiego, "Higinio Aguilar: Milicia, rebelión y corrupción como modus vivendi," *HM* 41 (1992): 437-88.

Chapter 16, Lucas and the Mexican Revolution, 279–304

1. AMTdeO, 5 April 1913, 418, Aureliano Lucas to Jefe Político; interview with Aurora Lucas, Puebla, April 1984; Carlos Bravo Marentes, ed., *Relatos revolucionarios* (Puebla, 1986), 8, 56, 66-69; Donna Rivera Moreno,

Xochiapulco: Una gloria olvidada (Puebla, 1991), 164; Alan Knight, *The Mexican Revolution* (Cambridge, 1986), 2:232; Moisés Saenz, *México integro* (Mexico, 1982), 144-45.

2. Enrique Cordero y Torres, *Crónicas de mi ciudad* (Puebla, 1955), 79-80; Rivera, *Xochiapulco*, 164.

3. APD, 281:5063, 7 March 1911, Citizens of Tetela to Díaz; 282:6264, 6 April 1911, Bonilla to Díaz; Bravo Marentes, *Relatos*, 67; Saenz, *México integro*, 144-45; Lourdes Arizpe, *Parentesco y economía en una sociedad nahua: Nican Pehua Zacatipan* (Mexico, 1973), 32-34; Ramón Sánchez Flores, *Zacapoaxtla: Relación histórica* (Puebla, 1984), 245-46; Jean-Pierre Bastian, *Los disidentes sociedades protestantes y revolución en México, 1872-1911* (Mexico, 1989), 69-128.

4. APD, 262:12823, 16 August 1909, M. Martínez to Díaz; David LaFrance, *The Mexican Revolution in Puebla, 1908-1913* (Wilmington, DE, 1989), 1-21.

5. Interview with Aurora Lucas; *Mexican Herald*, 20 November 1910.

6. Sánchez Flores, *Zacapoaxtla*, 246-47.

7. Rivera, *Xochiapulco*, 194, 287.

8. APD, 281:4683, 8 March 1911, Cahuantzi to Díaz; Ramón Kuri Camacho, *La realidad en el mito: Microhistoria de Chignahuapan* (Puebla, 1985), 2:62-63; Bravo Marentes, *Relatos*, 37; Luisa Paré, "Caciquismo y poder político en el México rural," in *Caciquismo y poder político en el México rural*, ed. Roger Bartra et al. (Mexico, 1975), 44; Rivera, *Xochiapulco*, 194. One source claims that the Márquez brothers were nephews of Lucas, but this fact has not been confirmed; see *Mexican Herald*, 15 May 1915. Federal troops arrested and searched the home of Chignahuapan's municipal president, Trinidad Rivera, whose brother's father-in-law was Esteban Márquez. Nothing incriminating was found. However, the Riveras of Chignahuapan had fought alongside the Márquez of Otlatlán since the European Intervention; see APD, 281:5141, 9 March 1911, Luis Valle to Díaz.

9. AGN, RG, 4a, 1910(2), 4, 11 February 1911, Tapia to Madero; APJFL, 18 May 1911, A. Lucas to Miguel Arriaga; interview with Aurora Lucas; Rivera, *Xochiapulco*, 194.

10. APD, 279:2630, 20 February 1911, Lucas to Díaz; ADN, Cancelados, C-64 D/111/2/425, I, ff. 24-27, 23-24 February 1911, Lucas to Díaz, 24 February 1911, Díaz to Lucas, 27 February 1911, Díaz to Pomposo Bonilla; Jesús Ferrer Gamboa, *Los tres Juanes de la Sierra de Puebla* (Mexico, 1967), 23-25.

11. LaFrance, *The Mexican Revolution*, 69-70, 73, 75, 80.

12. APD, 281:5851, 31 March 1911, Lucas to Díaz; 282:6858, 12 April 1911, Lucas to Díaz.

13. APJFL, 20 June 1911, Aurelio M. Bravo to A. Lucas, 11 August 1911, J. F. Lucas to Madero, 14 August 1911, A. Lucas to Manuel Amieva, 16 August 1911, Amieva to J. F. Lucas, 19 August 1911, A. Lucas to Pres. del Club

Reforma, 28 October 1911, Rafael Cañete to A. Lucas; AGN, RG, 1a, 1911-12(1), 9, Tranquilino Quintero to Francisco Vázquez Gómez, 24 July 1911.

14. LaFrance, *The Mexican Revolution*, 179-80.

15. AGN, AFM, 57:1:391, 26 February 1912, Madero to J. F. Lucas; 57:1:416, 6 March 1912, Madero to J. F. Lucas; 52:1487, 15 March 1912, Bruno M. Trejo to Madero; 22:562-2, 7 April 1912, J. F. Lucas to Madero.

16. AGN, AFM, 22:562-2, 7 April 1912, J. F. Lucas to Madero; 3:77:2246-47, 27 June 1912, Meléndez to Juan Sánchez Azcona; 3:77:2258-59, 3 July 1912, Meléndez to Madero.

17. AGN, AFM, 52:1487, 21 July 1912, Trejo to Madero; 52:1487, 26 July 1912, Madero to Trejo; APJFL, 6 August 1912, Trejo to J. F. Lucas; 21 October 1912, Madero to J. F. Lucas; 26 October 1912, J. F. Lucas to Director General de Correos Interino.

18. INAH (microfilm), 12:291, 30 August 1912, Madero to J. F. Lucas; LaFrance, *The Mexican Revolution*, 199-228; *El País*, 3 February 1913.

19. INAH (Microfilm), 11:394, 24 January 1913, Madero to Carrasco; 12:439, 1 February 1913; 22:3939, 1 February 1913, Madero to Trejo; ACE/A, Legislature debate, 28 January 1913; LaFrance, *The Mexican Revolution*, 226-28.

20. AJB, 1:8:75-76, 20 October 1913, Camacho to Carranza.

21. APJFL, 2 May 1913, Manuel Mondragón (Sec. de Guerra) to J. F. Lucas; 12 May 1913, J. F. Lucas to Maass; *El País*, 5 November 1913.

22. APJFL, 30 May 1913, J. F. Lucas to Mondragón; Rivera, *Xochiapulco*, 181-82; Kuri Camacho, *Microhistoria*, 2:67-68; *El País*, 9 August, 10 November 1913.

23. APJFL, 25 June 1913, A. Lucas to J. F. Lucas; 1 July 1913, J. F. Lucas to Aureliano Blanquet; 2 July 1913, M. Lucas to Sergio Bonilla; Rivera, *Xochiapulco*, 196, 220.

24. APJFL, 18 July 1913, Eulalio Díaz Párraga to J. F. Lucas; 2 August 1913, A. Lucas, memorandum; *Mexican Herald*, 26 July, 1 August 1913; *El País*, 25 July 1913; *El Imparcial*, 20, 23, 24 July 1913.

25. AJB, 1:8:83, 6 July 1913, Camacho et al., manifesto; 1:8:66, 22 July 1913, Camacho to Carranza; Rivera, *Xochiapulco*, 183, 251.

26. AMTdeO, 414, 27 May 1913, José B. Posadas and Amador T. Muñoz to Enrique Contreras; AJB, 1:8:64, 26 June 1913, Camacho to Carranza; 1:8:65, 7 July 1913, Camacho to Carranza; 1:8:67, 4 August 1913, Camacho to Carranza; RDS, 812.00/8162, 27:556-57, 8 July 1913, A. C. Davenport to William W. Canada; INEHRM, 1:6/2:6, 29 May 1913, Marco Serrato [pseud. for Carmen Serdán] to Modesto González Galindo; APJFL, 30 July 1913, G. Camacho to Esteban Márquez; Francisco Vela González, *Diario de la Revolución: Año de 1913* (Monterey, 1971), 262, 276, 287; Luis Audriac, *Teziutlán: Apuntes geográficos e históricos* (Mexico, 1959), 64.

27. APJFL, no date, Maass to J. F. Lucas; RDS, 812.00/8162, 27:556-57, 8 July 1913, Davenport to Canada; Rivera, *Xochiapulco*, 196-97; Vela González, *Diario de la Revolución*, 276, 287, 298; *El País*, 3 August 1913.

28. AGN, AFM, 1, 12, 13 August 1913, 87, Aureliano Urrutia to Maass; APJFL, 30 July, 8 August 1913, J. F. Lucas to Urrutia; 9, 17 August 1913, Sergio Bonilla to J. F. Lucas; *Mexican Herald*, 9, 14 August 1913; *El Imparcial*, 2, 12, 16, 17 August 1913; *El País*, 3 August 1913.

29. RDS, 812.00/8530, 28:406, 23 August 1913, Canada to William Jennings Bryan; 812.00/8852, 29:6-7, 28 August 1913, Canada to Bryan; 812.00/9223, 29:1397-98, 18 September 1913, Canada to Bryan; APJFL, 27 August 1913, Juan Francisco Ramírez to Esteban Márquez; AJB, 1:8:68, 26 August 1913, Camacho to Carranza; 1:8:69, 2 September 1913, Camacho to Carranza; 1:8:70-71, 18 September 1913, Camacho to Carranza; Rivera, *Xochiapulco*, 191, 198, 252; *El Pueblo*, 21 August 1913; *El Imparcial*, 22, 24 August, 10, 18 September 1913.

30. Knight, *The Mexican Revolution*, 2:55-56; *El Amigo de la Verdad*, 6 August 1913; Audriac, *Teziutlán*, 63-66, says that eighteen of Teziutlán schoolteacher Efraín Pozos's third-grade students, all between the ages of nine and eleven, fought along with Pozos under General Antonio Medina against the Huerta government. In the subsequent fighting, in 1913-15, all but two of the pupils died.

31. APJFL, 2 September 1913, Enrique Arroyo to J. F. Lucas; 16 September 1913, J. F. Lucas to Arroyo; 22 September 1913, Victoriano Huerta to J. F. Lucas; 2 October 1913, J. F. Lucas to Esteban Márquez; AJB, 1:8:74, 20 October 1913, Camacho to Carranza; RDS, 812.00/9224, 29:1407-11, 17 September 1913, G. H. Carnahan to Canada; *El Imparcial*, 10 October 1913; *El País*, 3 August, 3 November 1913.

32. *El Imparcial*, 27 September 1913.

33. AMG, 6:772, 21 October 1913, Esteban Márquez to Camacho; RDS, 812.00/9970, 32:162-64, 20 November 1913, Canada to Bryan; APJFL, 27 November 1913, Esteban Márquez to J. F. Lucas; 19, 29 November 1913, Ruiz to J. F. Lucas; 9 December 1913, Feliciano Pérez et al., manifesto; AJB, 1:8:74-76, 20 October 1913, Camacho to Carranza; 1:8:81, 25 October 1913, Camacho to Carranza; Miguel A. Sánchez Lamego, *Historia militar de la revolución constitucionalista* (Mexico, 1956-60), 3:428; Vela González, *Diario de la Revolución*, 368, 397, 461; *El País*, 16 November 1913.

34. *El Imparcial*, 11 December 1913; INEHRM 1:6/5:14, 9 December 1913, Ignacio Maya to "Soldados del Ejército Revolucionario."

35. APJFL, 19, 28, 30 November 1913, Ruiz to J. F. Lucas; 22, 28 November 1913, Esteban Márquez to J. F. Lucas; 3 December 1913, Ruiz, proclamation; 9 December 1913, Feliciano Pérez et al., manifesto; *El Regional*, 10 December 1913; *El Imparcial*, 15 November 1913.

36. APJFL, 6 December 1913, Dolores Pineda, manifesto; 9 December 1913, Feliciano Pérez et al., manifesto; 22 November 1913, Rosendo Flores et al. to J. F. Lucas; 23 November 1913, J. F. Lucas to Flores Martínez et al.; 10 December 1913, Esteban Márquez to J. F. Lucas; 26 December 1913, Manuel Rivera to J. F. Lucas; Rivera, *Xochiapulco*, 207.

37. APJFL, 12 December 1913, J. F. Lucas to Esteban Márquez; 23 December 1913, J. F. Lucas to Ruiz; 25, 27 December 1913, Ruiz to J. F. Lucas; *El Amigo de la Verdad*, 18 December 1913, 3 January 1914; *El Regional*, 17 December 1913; *El País*, 14, 18, 19, 20 December 1913.

38. APJFL, 12 December 1913, J. F. Lucas to Esteban Márquez; 12 December 1913, J. F. Lucas to Félix Pérez; 12 December 1913, J. F. Lucas to Ruiz; 12, 20 December 1913, A. Lucas to Ruiz; ADN, Cancelados, C-64 D/111/2/425, II, f. 384, 22 January 1914, A. Mange, report; Rivera, *Xochiapulco*, 164.

39. *El Regional*, 14 January 1914, in Rivera, *Xochiapulco*, 247.

40. APJFL, Teodoro Escalona Cortés, statement, 26 April 1940.

41. ADN, Cancelados, C-64 D/111/2/425, II, f. 384, 22 January 1914, A. Mange, report; APJFL, 26 December 1913, A. Lucas to Ruiz; 27 December 1913, Ruiz to J. F. Lucas.

42. Knight, *The Mexican Revolution*, 2:56-57.

43. APJFL, 7 January 1914, Esteban Márquez to A. Lucas.

44. APJFL, January 1914, Esteban Márquez et al., manifesto; 14 January 1914, Emilio Márquez, report; RDS, 812.00/10976.5, 1, 25 February 1914, John Lind to Bryan; *El Amigo de la Verdad*, 21 January 1914; *El País*, 23 January 1914.

45. ADN, Cancelados, C-64 D/111/2/425, II, f. 384, 22 January 1914, A. Mange, report; AMTdeO, 422, 28 August 1914, Comandante Militar, circular; INEHRM, 1:6/5:15, 1 February 1914, Esteban Márquez et al. to José Veramendi; *El Amigo de la Verdad*, 22, 23, 24, 27, 30 January, 6, 13, 20 February, 2, 10, 16 March 1914; *El Imparcial*, 4, 23 June 1914; *El País*, 10 February, 20 March 1914.

46. APJFL, 22 February 1914, People receiving Constitutionalist arms and money in the Sierra; *Mexican Herald*, 29 January, 1 February 1914; *El Renovador*, 25 June 1914; *El País*, 17 March 1914.

47. RDS, 812.00/11742, 36:701, 12 April 1914, E. D. Turnbull to Canada; Kuri Camacho, *Microhistoria*, 2:75; *El Amigo de la Verdad*, 3, 15, 19 February, 6, 8 March, 2, 9 May 1914; *Mexican Herald*, 12 February, 4, 8, 20, 30 March, 9 April 1914; Armando Bartra, ed., *Regeneración, 1900-1918: La corriente más radical de la revolución de 1910 a través de su periódico de combate* (Mexico, 1972), 408; *La Patria*, 27 January 1914; *El Imparcial*, 1, 3, 11 March, 14 May 1914; *El País*, 29 January, 10, 20 March 1914.

48. RDS, 812.00/11154, 35:427, 5 March 1914, Canada to Bryan; *El Amigo de la Verdad*, 10 March 1914; *Mexican Herald*, 5 March 1914; *El País*, 28 January 1914.

49. APJFL, 18 April 1914, Esteban Márquez, manifesto; 20 April 1914, Pineda, manifesto; 22 April 1914, Zerafín de la Torre to Jefe Político of Chignahuapan; 22 April 1914, J. Jiménez Castro to Medina; 22 April 1914, Javier Rojas, manifesto; 5 May 1914, Rafael Luna Bonilla, manifesto; Rivera, *Xochiapulco*, 185; *El País*, 8 March 1914.

50. APJFL, 20 April 1914, Pineda, manifesto; 22 April 1914, Medina, manifesto; 25 April 1914, Esteban Márquez, manifesto; 27 April 1914, Gabriel Soto to Presidente Municipal, Tlapacoya; INEHRM, 1:6/2:14, 15 July 1914, Luis Bonafide to Carranza; LaFrance, *The Mexican Revolution*, 6. One generally pro-government source claims that Lucas accepted U.S. help against the Huerta government, but this cannot be confirmed; see *El Imparcial*, 18 May 1914.

51. AMG, 16:2390, 29 May 1914, Pablo González to Camacho; *El Amigo de la Verdad*, 2 May 1914.

52. APJFL, 23 June 1914, Esteban Márquez, manifesto; 20 July 1914, Medina to J. F. Lucas; 3 August 1914, Tranquilino Quintero to J. F. Lucas; 24 August 1914, A. Lucas to J. F. Lucas; CT, 16-29 June 1914:XXI, 28 June 1914, Carranza to Medina; RDS, 812.00/12438, 38:1049, 24 June 1914, Canada to Bryan; 812.00/12754, 34:1295, 27 July 1914, Canada to Bryan; IN-EHRM, 1:6/2:12, 12 May 1914, Sec. de Junta Revolucionaria to Medina; 1:6/2:13, 24 June 1914, Modesto González Galindo to Medina; 1:6/6:30, 29 June 1914, José María Pérez to Mariguita [María Gómez]; 1:6/2:20, 29 July 1914, Camacho to Junta Revolucionaria; *El Amigo de la Verdad*, 2 August 1914; *El Renovador*, 16 July 1914; *Mexican Herald*, 9 June 1914.

53. APJFL, 5 September 1914, Bartolomé Hernández to J. F. Lucas; AMTdeO, 422, 28 August 1914, Comandante Militar, circular; 421, 21 October 1914, Sacramento P. Mora to Presidente del Consejo de Administración Superior; ADN, Cancelados, C-64 D/111/2/425, II, f. 20, 17 July 1916, Citizens of Tzinacantepec (Tlatlauqui) to J. F. Lucas.

54. APJFL, 18, 29 July 1914, A. Lucas to Medina; 28 July 1914, Medina to A. Lucas; 6 September 1914, J. F. Lucas to Hernández; 11 September 1914, [J. F.] Lucas to Quintero; AVC, 92:10390, 13 August 1916, A. Lucas et al. to Carranza; *El Pueblo*, 11 October 1916; *Mexican Herald*, 12 August 1914.

55. APJFL, 2 September 1914, Medina to J. F. Lucas; INERHM, 1:6/2:18-19, 29 July 1914, Camacho to Guadalupe Narváez B.; 1:6/2:20, 29 July 1914, Camacho to Junta Revolucionaria.

56. APJFL, 6 August 1914, Federico Cabrera to A. Lucas; CR, 1:4:11, 13 October 1914, Esteban Márquez et al., report; 2:1:13, 19 November 1914, Permanent Commission; Kuri Camacho, *Microhistoria*, 2:75-76.

57. AJB, 2:15:51-53, 5 February 1915, Medina to Carranza.

58. AJA, 2:167, 3 October 1914, Zapata to C. G. Martínez; AEZ, 3:2:66, 2 January 1915, Aurelio Bonilla to Zapata; Ferrer Gamboa, *Los tres Juanes*, 26-27.

59. APJFL, 13 November 1914, J. F. Lucas, report; 17 November 1914, A. Lucas to J. F. Lucas; INEHRM, 1:4:2-3, 11 August 1914, "Acta levantada en Teziutlán."

60. APJFL, 4 November 1914, A. Lucas to J. F. Lucas; Kuri Camacho, *Microhistoria*, 2:75-76. In January 1915 one of the three principal *carrancista* officers in the Sierra, Gilberto Camacho, following differences with Governor

Coss, revolted and joined the *zapatistas*; see AVC, 25:2490, 20 January 1915, Antonio Ortiz to Carranza; 29:3069, 24 February 1915, Ramón Orosco to Carranza.

61. APJFL, 4 December 1914, Miguel Méndez Galicia, manifesto; AGM, 23:1:14, Typescript of the Conventionist newspaper, "La Convención," 31 December 1914; *Mexican Herald*, 30, 31 December 1914; *El Monitor*, 13, 26 December 1914.

62. AJB, 2:15:51-53, 5 February 1915, Medina to Carranza.

63. APJFL, 27 March 1915, Esteban Márquez, decree; AJB, 2:15:51-53, 5 February 1915, Medina to Carranza; APG, 1: , 27 May 1915, Medina to González; Kuri Camacho, *Microhistoria*, 2:76-80; *Mexican Herald*, 13 April, 16 May 1915.

64. APJFL, 25 October 1916, J. F. Lucas to Obregón; AJB, 2:15:51-53, 5 February 1915, Medina to Carranza; AVC, 38:4148, 5 May 1915, Medina to Carranza; interview with Aurora Lucas; Rivera, *Xochiapulco*, 261-62; Taller de Tradición Oral, *Les oíamos contar a nuestros abuelos: Etnohistoria de San Miguel Tzinacapan* (Mexico, 1994), 399-483. The governor and state military commander, General Cesáreo Castro, for example, stayed at Lucas's home; see *El Demócrata*, 14 November 1916.

65. AJB, 3:6: , 27 March 1915, Obregón to Carranza; 3:6: , 28 March 1915, Carranza to Obregón; 2:15:17, 15 May 1915, Esteban Márquez, manifesto; AVC, 38:4144, 5 May 1915, Eulogio Hernández to Castro; APG, 14: , 28 May 1915, E. Hernández to González; APJFL, 15 April 1915, Medina to J. F. Lucas; 15 May 1915, Esteban Márquez, manifesto.

66. APG, 16: , 28 May 1915, E. Hernández to P. González; ARGG, 19:198, 24 April [1915], Memorandum [Esteban Márquez to R. González Garza]; 18:157, 8 June 1915, R. González Garza to Convencíon; CR, 7:9:27-28, 8 June 1915, R. González Garza to Asamblea; AJB, 5:15:26, 20 July 1915, José M. Cabrera to Juan Barragán; 4:35:21, 11 July 1915, L. Vázquez Mellado to Tranquilino Quintero; 2:10:24, 15 July 1915, Alfonso Herrera to Carranza; 4:35:23, 1 July 1915, Alex Infanzón to Trinidad Quintero; 2:14:69, 28 July 1915, J. F. Lucas to Carranza; 1:17:20, 28 September [1915], Certucha to Carranza; *Mexican Herald*, 15-16 May 1915; *El Monitor*, 15-16 May 1915.

67. AVC, 32:3426, 23 March 1915, Guadalupe Baez to Carranza; ADN, Cancelados, C-64 D/111/2/425, II, ff. 21-22, 24 June 1916, Felipe Lorenzo to J. F. Lucas; APG, 22: , 8 March 1916, Teodoro Escalona to González; AGE/J2D/A, 11:158, 28 January 1916, David Vilchis et al., manifesto; Kuri Camacho, *Microhistoria*, 2:76-78; Bravo Marantes, *Relatos*, 52, 84. Complaints about Constitutionalist army abuses, and specifically about Medina, continued after Lucas's death; see AJB, 9:21:1-3, 12 June 1917, Carranza's secretary, memorandum; 6:25:4, 22 June 1917, Manuel L. Márquez to Juan Barragán; 6:25:6, 7 August 1917, M. L. Márquez to Barragán; 6:25:5, 14 July 1917, Barragán to M. L. Márquez.

68. APG, 16: , 24 October 1915, Dario Téllez et al. to González; 22: , 25 October 1915, González to Medina; 16: , 26 October 1915, Francisco Hernández et al. to González; 16: , 27 October 1915, Francisco Miranda et al. to González; 16: , 30 November 1915, F. Pachcan to González; AVC, 92:10402, 26 August 1916, Pedro Lópes et al. to Carranza; 95:10707, 13 September 1916, E. Lozano et al. to Carranza; 96:10897, 23 September 1916, Pascacio Mayorga et al. to Carranza. Town council elections were resumed in September 1916; see *El Demócrata*, 14 September 1916.

69. ADN, Cancelados, C-64 D/111/2/425, I, f. 18, [1916], J. F. Lucas to Obregón.

70. APJFL, 31 December 1914, Unsigned manifesto; AVC, 85:9524, 22 June 1916, Castro to Carranza; Isidro Fabela and Josefina E. de Fabela, eds., *Documentos históricos de la revolución mexicana* (Mexico, 1960-73), 21:168-82, 207-18, 220-26.

71. AVC, 38:4144, 5 May 1915, Eulogio Hernández to Castro; APG, 14: , 5 May 1915, Hernández to Carranza; 16: , 28 May 1915, Hernández to González; 5: , 30 May 1915, Un hijo del pueblo to González; Bravo Marentes, *Relatos*, 54.

72. AVC, 27:2870, 14 February 1915, Camilo Cruz to Carranza.

73. *El Pueblo*, 19 April, 18 May, 3, 19 August 1915; *El Demócrata*, 20 August 1915.

74. APJFL, 11 April 1915, J. F. Lucas to Medina; APG, 16: , 28 May 1915, Hernández to González; interview with Aurora Lucas.

75. RG, 157:79, 2 October 1915, Sec. de Gobernación to Governor; AVC, 98:11166, 7 October 1916, Macario Hernández to Carranza; APG, 3: , 28 May 1915, Un hijo del pueblo to González; 3: , 5 June 1915, Varios comerciantes to González; *El Universal*, 11 June 1917.

76. RDS, 812.00/16382, 49:214-15, September 1915, Carson to George McFall; 812.00/16276, 48:1329, 23 September 1915, Silliman to Lansing; 812.00/16315, 49:22, 27 September 1915, Silliman to Lansing; 812.00/16333, 49:77, 30 September 1915, Silliman to Lansing; *El Demócrata*, 28 September 1915; *Mexican Herald*, 8 August, 23, 29 September 1915; Kuri Camacho, *Microhistoria*, 2:78-85; Juan Barragán Rodríguez, *Historia del ejército y de la revolución constitucionalista* (Mexico, 1985-86), 3:42.

77. APG, 22: , 24 November 1915, González et al., surrender agreement; 34: , 24 November 1915, González, decree; RG, 154:95, 30 November 1915, Lauro González to Sec. de Gobernación; AJT, 4:16:1736-39, 18 November 1916, Esteban Márquez et al., manifesto; *El Demócrata,* 11 November 1915.

78. APJFL, 18 November 1916, A. Lucas to Miguel Huerta; 29 November 1916, A. Lucas, "Noticias"; 20 December 1916, T. Quintero to J. F. Lucas; AJT, 4:16:1736-39, 18 November 1916, Esteban Márquez et al., manifesto; AHDN/C, 7115/2, 6, 9 January 1917, Miguel Alemán to A. Millán; 16 April 1917, Cesáreo Castro to Sec. de Guerra; CT, 1915-1925:XXI-4, 31 January, 8 February 1916, Medina to Carranza; November-December 1916:XXI-4,

16 November 1916, Mario Méndez to Carranza; Kuri Camacho, *Microhistoria*, 2:80-85; Dudley Ankerson, *Agrarian Warlord: Saturnino Cedillo and the Mexican Revolution in San Luis Potosí* (DeKalb, IL, 1984), 81; Edwin Lieuwen, *The Political Rise and Fall of the Revolutionary Army, 1910-1940* (Albuquerque, 1968), 35.

79. APJFL, Medina, J. F. Lucas, and Gabriel Barrios, agreement, 20 April 1916.

80. APJFL, 19 July 1916, Feliciano Pérez to Delfino E. Cruz; 7 August 1916, J. F. Lucas, report; AVC, 67:7402, 11 February 1916, Heliodoro Guerrero et al. to Carranza; 77:8495, 12 May 1916, J. F. Lucas to Carranza; 85:9524, 22 June 1916, Castro to Carranza; RG, 154:95, 30 November 1915, L. González to Sec. de Gobernación; APG, 22: , 24 March 1916, González to Medina; APG, 22: , 28 March 1916, Medina to González.

81. AJB, 9:21:1-3, 12 June 1917, Carranza's secretary, memorandum; APG, 3: , 20 September 1916, Baraquiel M. Alatriste to González; AVC, 78:8602, 1 May 1916, Castro to Carranza; CT, November-December 1915: XXI-4, 9 November 1915, Carranza to Agustín Millán; November-December 1915:XXI-4, 25 November 1915, Medina to Carranza; 1915-1925:XXI-4, May 1916, Castro to Carranza; RDS, 812.00/18835, 55:156-57, 1 August 1916, Rogers to Lansing; *El Demócrata*, 23, 25 April 1917; *Excélsior*, 29 June 1917; *El Pueblo*, 7, 10, 14, 18, 26 June, 6 September 1917; *El Universal*, 17 February, 8, 10, 11, 13, 15, 17 June, 25 August 1917. Cabrera did, however, make the obligatory visit to Lucas's grave during the election campaign; see *El Pueblo*, 16, 17 May 1917.

82. *Excélsior*, 12 November 1917.

83. APJFL, 7 August 1916, J. F. Lucas, report; 25 October 1916, J. F. Lucas to Obregón; 1 February 1917, Juan C. Rivera, report; 21 February 1917, A. Lucas to Sobrina Elena.

84. Francisco José Ruiz Cervantes, *La Revolución en Oaxaca: El movimiento de la Soberanía, 1915-1920* (Mexico 1986).

Epilogue, 305–12

1. APJFL, 8 February 1919, Sergio Bonilla to Miguel Lucas.

2. Keith Brewster, "Caciquismo in Rural Mexico during the 1920s: The Case of Gabriel Barrios," *JLAS* 28 (1996): 125-26.

3. AJB, 4:19: , 9 February 1917, Obregón to Carranza; 4:20: , 14, 17 February 1917, Obregón to Carranza; ADN, Cancelados (Lucas), 2:370, 9 February 1917, Agustín Maciel to Depto. de Cuenta y Administración; AOC, 209-Q-7, n.d., M. Lucas to Obregón; MIR, 8:476, 23 May 1933, Robert E. Cummings to War Dept.; interview with Aurora Lucas, Puebla, April 1984; Baudelio Candanedo, *Zacatlán histórico* (Puebla, 1979), 9-10; Enrique Cordero y Torres, *Diccionario biográfico de Puebla* (Puebla, 1986), 1:79-80; Gustavo Abel Hernández Enríquez, *Historia moderna de Puebla, 1917-1926* (Puebla, 1986-88), 2:52, 3:109, 253; Carlos Bravo Marentes, ed., *Relatos revolucionarios* (Puebla, 1986), 8.

4. Manuel Kuri Camacho, *La realidad en el mito: Microhistoria de Chignahuapan* (Chignahuapan, 1985), 2:85-87; Almazán, in *El Universal*, 26 December 1957; Luisa Paré, "Caciquismo y estructura de poder en la Sierra Norte de Puebla," in *Caciquismo y poder político en el México rural*, ed. Roger Bartra et al. (Mexico, 1976), 44-45; Ramón Beteta, *Camino a Tlaxcalantongo* (Mexico, 1990), 64-126; Gustavo de la Torre, *Los trágicos sucesos del 21 de mayo de 1920 en Tlaxcalantongo* (Puebla, 1989), 35; Porfirio del Castillo, *Puebla y Tlaxcala en los días de la Revolución* (Mexico, 1953), 263-64, 278-80; AHDN/C, 7155/3, 12 August 1917, Pedro Morales to Carranza; AJA, 5:424, 26 May 1920, Elisa Acuña Rossete to Amezcua; *El Universal*, 14, 16, 17, 26, 30, 31 August 1917, 10, 16, 20 May 1920. Fernando Benítez, in his novel, *El viejo rey* (Mexico, 1959), 83-93, also deals with Barrios's betrayal of Carranza.

5. AAA, 2:5:50, 5 November 1919, Trinidad W. Flores to Roque Estrada; AGE/J2D/A, 13:95, 30 March 1920, Miguel Rosas et al. to Juez de Distrito; MIR, 6:403, 6 May 1930, Cummings to War Dept.; 8:476, 23 May 1933, Cummings to War Dept.; interview with Aurora Lucas; Moisés Saenz, *México íntegro* (Mexico, 1983), 149-52; Cordero y Torres, *Diccionario*, 179-80; Enrique Cordero y Torres, *Historia compendiada del estado de Puebla* (Puebla, 1986), 3:92; Carlos Garma Navarro, *Protestantismo en una comunidad totonaca de Puebla, México* (Mexico, 1987), 37-39; Hernández Enríquez, *Historia moderna*, 3:88-89; Kuri Camacho, *Microhistoria*, 3:5, 15; Manuel Luis Sosa, *Crónica* (n.p., 1938), 102, 108, 134-35; James Mouncey Taggart, *Estructura de los grupos domésticos de una comunidad de habla nahuatl de Puebla* (Mexico, 1975), 28; Hans Werner Tobler, *La Revolución Mexicana: Transformación social y cambio político, 1876-1940* (Mexico, 1994), 581; Gustavo Verduzco, *Campesinos itinerantes* (Zamora, 1982), 42-43; Carlos Bravo Marentes, ed., *Arrieros somos: El sistema de arriería de la Sierra Norte de Puebla* (Mexico, 1988), 7; Bravo Marentes, *Relatos*, 13, 20, 32, 38; Paré, "Caciquismo," 45-46; Del Castillo, *Puebla y Tlaxcala*, 262; *Excélsior*, 29, 30 December 1919; *El Universal*, 1 April 1920. See also AOC, 332:816-P-45, 1 May 1923, Juan Andrew Almazán, *informe*, who dismisses the many complaints against Barrios by residents of the Sierra.

6. MIR, 6:446, 1 July 1930, Gordon Johnston to War Dept.; 8:476, 23 May 1933, Cummings to War Dept.; interview with Aurora Lucas; Cordero y Torres, *Historia*, 3:92; Cordero y Torres, *Diccionario*, 1:79-80; Paré, "Caciquismo," 45-46.

7. Taller de Tradición Oral, *Les oíamos contar a nuestros abuelos: Etnohistoria de San Miguel Tzinacapan* (Mexico, 1994).

8. Even in Xochiapulco, the memory of Lucas's patriotic contributions obscure his participation in civil wars; see Donna Rivera Moreno, *Xochiapulco: Una gloria olvidada* (Puebla, 1991), 101-3, and for an explanation of this collective amnesia, see Florencia Mallon, *Peasant and Nation: The Making of Post-Colonial Mexico and Peru* (Berkeley, 1995), 276-309.

9. Taller de Tradición Oral, *Les oíamos contar*, 106.

10. Ibid., 483.

11. Ibid., 105, 472.

12. Ibid., 101.

13. Ibid., 446-51.

14. Ibid., 469-82.

15. Brewster, "Caciquismo in Rural Mexico," 105-28.

16. APJFL, "Programa, Tetela de Ocampo, 1 March 1917."

17. Tetela's decline, which predated the Revolution, had to do with a shift in the economic equilibrium of the Sierra away from the administrative capitals of the *tierra fria* (particularly such isolated ones as Tetela) to the coffee and sugar towns of the *tierra caliente* (especially Zapotitlán and Cuetzalan) and to commercial towns on the edge of the Sierra closer to railway connections (such as Huauchinango, Chignahuapan, and Zaragoza); see Moisés Saenz, *Escuelas federales en la Sierra de Puebla* (Mexico, 1927), 54; Pierre Durand, *Nanacatlán* (Mexico, 1986), 213-31.

18. Mary Kay Vaughan, *Cultural Politics in Revolution: Teachers, Peasants, and Schools in Mexico, 1930-1940* (Tucson, 1997), 102-36.

Index

Acatlán (district): 130, 133, 135, 186, 189, 243, 248
Acatzingo (Tepeaca): 66, 148
Acultzingo: battle (April 1862), 77
Agrarian conflict and reform: 41–43, 292, 299, 301–3. *See also* Cuetzalan; Xochiapulco
Aguardiente. *See* Sugar
Aguascalientes. *See* Convention of Aguascalientes
Aguilar, Cándido: 293
Agustín (Dieguillo), Francisco: battle of 5 May 1862, 77; and Lucas, 133, 308–10; mayor of Cuetzalan, 237, 250; military career and leadership of Cuetzalan revolt, 139–40, 150, 155–56, 163, 170, 173, 185, 190, 194, 196, 199, 206, 260, 265
Ahuacatlán (Zacatlán): 33, 56, 66, 69, 94, 104, 136, 137, 192, 196, 242
Alamán, Lucas: opposition to new municipalities, 45
Alatorre, Ignacio: opinion of *serranos*, 5; European Intervention, 68; Sierra revolts of 1868–70, 30, 137–63, 179; revolt of La Noria, 185, 188, 191, 193; Tuxtepec revolution, 213–16
Alatriste (district): 29, 52, 55–71, 73, 76, 173, 201, 217, 224–25, 239, 248, 281, 289
Alcabala. *See* Taxation
Alcántara, Braulio: complicity in Atagpan uprising, 236; alliance with Lucas, 248

Almajac. *See* Hacienda of Almajac
Almazán, Leonides Andrew: deposes Gabriel Barrios, 307
Altamirano, Ignacio: intolerance of Indian communities, 9
Altotonga (cabecera and canton): 25, 41, 84, 99, 103, 119, 190, 200, 213, 277
Alva, Miguel (priest of Zacapoaxtla): preaches seditious sermon, 120
Alvarado (Veracruz): 119
Alvarez, Juan: agrarianism, 44, 70; relations with Cuatecomacos, 59, 125. *See also* Revolts and revolutions
Amador, Manuel: 205
American War. *See* Mexican War
Ampudía, Pedro: 65
Analtekos: 307, 309. *See also* French; Austrians
Andrade Parraga, Miguel: campaign of *desamortización* in Huauchinango, 16–17
Apam (Hidalgo): 98, 118, 134
Apulco (Zacapoaxtla): strategic bridge, 60, 104, 212, 307; torrential river, 29, 31, 106, 158; precipitous gorge, 35, 106; redoubt on heights of, 92, 137, 139, 152, 168, 169, 191–92, 194; divides municipality of Zautla, 226, 229; battle (October 1863), 93–94
Aquixtla (Alatriste): 8, 29, 34–35, 53, 91, 94, 98, 100, 103, 117, 140–41, 170, 173, 192, 194, 196, 207, 223, 226
Arenas, Domingo: and Lucas, 3, 297

Latin American Silhouettes
Studies in History and Culture

William H. Beezley and
Judith Ewell
Editors

Volumes Published

Silvia Marina Arrom and Servando Ortoll, eds., *Riots in the Cities: Popular Politics and the Urban Poor in Latin America, 1765–1910* (1996). Cloth ISBN 0-8420-2580-4
Paper ISBN 0-8420-2581-2

Roderic Ai Camp, ed., *Polling for Democracy: Public Opinion and Political Liberalization in Mexico* (1996). ISBN 0-8420-2583-9

Brian Loveman and Thomas M. Davies, Jr., eds., *The Politics of Antipolitics: The Military in Latin America*, 3d ed., revised and updated (1996).
Cloth ISBN 0-8420-2609-6
Paper ISBN 0-8420-2611-8

Joseph S. Tulchin, Andrés Serbín, and Rafael Hernández, eds., *Cuba and the Caribbean: Regional Issues and Trends in the Post-Cold War Era* (1997).
ISBN 0-8420-2652-5

Thomas W. Walker, ed., *Nicaragua without Illusions: Regime Transition and Structural Adjustment in the 1990s* (1997). Cloth ISBN 0-8420-2578-2
Paper ISBN 0-8420-2579-0

Dianne Walta Hart, *Undocumented in L.A.: An Immigrant's Story* (1997).
Cloth ISBN 0-8420-2648-7
Paper ISBN 0-8420-2649-5

Jaime E. Rodríguez O. and Kathryn Vincent, eds., *Myths, Misdeeds, and Misunderstandings: The Roots of Conflict in U.S.-Mexican Relations* (1997). ISBN 0-8420-2662-2

Jaime E. Rodríguez O. and Kathryn Vincent, eds., *Common Border, Uncommon Paths: Race, Culture, and National Identity in U.S.-Mexican Relations* (1997). ISBN 0-8420-2673-8

William H. Beezley and Judith Ewell, eds., *The Human Tradition in Modern Latin America* (1997). Cloth ISBN 0-8420-2612-6   Paper ISBN 0-8420-2613-4

Donald F. Stevens, ed., *Based on a True Story: Latin American History at the Movies* (1997). Cloth ISBN 0-8420-2582-0   Paper ISBN 0-8420-2781-5

Jaime E. Rodríguez O., ed., *The Origins of Mexican National Politics, 1808–1847* (1997).   Paper ISBN 0-8420-2723-8

Che Guevara, *Guerrilla Warfare*, with revised and updated introduction and case studies by Brian Loveman and Thomas M. Davies, Jr., 3d ed. (1997).
Cloth ISBN 0-8420-2677-0
Paper ISBN 0-8420-2678-9

Adrian A. Bantjes, *As If Jesus Walked on Earth: Cardenismo, Sonora, and the Mexican Revolution* (1998).
ISBN 0-8420-2653-3

Henry A. Dietz and Gil Shidlo, eds., *Urban Elections in Democratic Latin America* (1998). Cloth ISBN 0-8420-2627-4 Paper ISBN 0-8420-2628-2

A. Kim Clark, *The Redemptive Work: Railway and Nation in Ecuador, 1895–1930* (1998). ISBN 0-8420-2674-6

Joseph S. Tulchin, ed., with Allison M. Garland, *Argentina: The Challenges of Modernization* (1998). ISBN 0-8420-2721-1

Louis A. Pérez, Jr., ed., *Impressions of Cuba in the Nineteenth Century: The Travel Diary of Joseph J. Dimock* (1998). Cloth ISBN 0-8420-2657-6 Paper ISBN 0-8420-2658-4

June E. Hahner, ed., *Women through Women's Eyes: Latin American Women in Nineteenth-Century Travel Accounts* (1998). Cloth ISBN 0-8420-2633-9 Paper ISBN 0-8420-2634-7

James P. Brennan, ed., *Peronism and Argentina* (1998). ISBN 0-8420-2706-8

John Mason Hart, ed., *Border Crossings: Mexican and Mexican-American Workers* (1998). Cloth ISBN 0-8420-2716-5 Paper ISBN 0-8420-2717-3

Brian Loveman, *For* la Patria: *Politics and the Armed Forces in Latin America* (1999). Cloth ISBN 0-8420-2772-6 Paper ISBN 0-8420-2773-4

Guy P. C. Thomson, with David G. LaFrance, *Patriotism, Politics, and Popular Liberalism in Nineteenth-Century Mexico: Juan Francisco Lucas and the Puebla Sierra* (1999). ISBN 0-8420-2683-5

K. Lynn Stoner, ed./comp., with Luis Hipólito Serrano Pérez, *Cuban and Cuban-American Women: An Annotated Bibliography* (1999). ISBN 0-8420-2643-6

Robert Woodmansee Herr, in collaboration with Richard Herr, *An American Family in the Mexican Revolution* (1999). ISBN 0-8420-2724-6

Juan Pedro Viqueira Albán, trans. Sonya Lipsett-Rivera and Sergio Rivera Ayala, *Propriety and Permissiveness in Bourbon Mexico* (1999). Cloth ISBN 0-8420-2466-2 Paper ISBN 0-8420-2467-0

David E. Lorey, *The U.S.-Mexican Border in the Twentieth Century* (1999). Cloth ISBN 0-8420-2755-6 Paper ISBN 0-8420-2756-4

Joanne Hershfield and David R. Maciel, eds., *Mexico's Cinema: A Century of Films and Filmmakers* (1999). Cloth ISBN 0-8420-2681-9 Paper ISBN 0-8420-2682-7

Stephen R. Niblo, *Mexico in the 1940s: Modernity, Politics, and Corruption* (1999). ISBN 0-8420-2794-7

Peter V. N. Henderson, *In the Absence of Don Porfirio: Francisco León de la Barra and the Mexican Revolution* (2000). ISBN 0-8420-2774-2

Mark T. Gilderhus, *The Second Century: U.S.-Latin American Relations since 1889* (2000). Cloth ISBN 0-8420-2413-1 Paper ISBN 0-8420-2414-X

Catherine Moses, *Real Life in Castro's Cuba* (2000). Cloth ISBN 0-8420-2836-6 Paper ISBN 0-8420-2837-4